I. Mary,
Virgin.

I. Title.

THE MOTHER OF JESUS
IN THE
NEW TESTAMENT

JOHN McHUGH

THE MOTHER OF JESUS
IN THE
NEW TESTAMENT

Doubleday & Company, Inc.
Garden City, New York
1975

ISBN: 0-385-04748-7
Library of Congress Catalog Card Number: 74-33652
© John McHugh, 1975
Printed in the United States of America

CONTENTS

PART I

MOTHER OF THE SAVIOUR

(*Luke 1–2*)

PART II

VIRGIN AND MOTHER

(*The Virginity of Mary in the New Testament*)

PART III

MOTHER OF THE WORD INCARNATE

(*Mary in the Theology of Saint John*)

PREFACE

Twelve years ago, in the spring and summer of 1962, as the Second Vatican Council was about to assemble, there was a measure of anxiety in many minds. For in 1961 a campaign had been launched against the way in which New Testament exegesis was taught at the Pontifical Biblical Institute in Rome. By the spring and summer of 1962, the allegations first voiced in Rome had been repeated throughout the world, and the Biblical Institute was no longer the only target: almost any Catholic who employed modern critical methods in the teaching of the New Testament was liable to be suspected of doctrinal unorthodoxy. A determined and well-concerted effort was being made to ensure that the Council, when it met, would put a stop to what was being denounced as a dangerous revival of Modernism. Thus on the eve of the Council there was apprehension and foreboding on two sides. There were those who feared that the Council, by condemning the use of literary and historical criticism, might so restrict freedom of investigation in biblical matters that movement would be virtually impossible; this, they felt, would be a disaster, for how could the Church then present the gospel in meaningful terms to men of the twentieth century? On the other side were many equally sincere men, oppressed by equally genuine anxiety, who were deeply disturbed by the findings of modern biblical research. They in their turn feared that if the Council did *not* condemn the use of historical criticism in biblical studies, all certainty in the most fundamental matters of faith would be destroyed.

Many pamphlets and articles were written at that time to explain how the employment of modern critical methods in exegesis, far from undermining the Christian faith, helps to set it firmly on more secure foundations. These writings, however, were of necessity produced in a hurry, to meet the urgent crisis of 1962, and to avert any condemnation of modern biblical scholars. As a result, most of them treated the matter in a rather theoretical fashion, stressing above all that Pius XII, in his encyclical *Divino Afflante Spiritu* (1943), had positively commanded all Catholic lecturers in Holy Scripture to follow the methods of literary and historical criticism. Where they did cite examples, they selected only secondary and rather simple illustrations of the principles (such as the temptations of Jesus in the desert). This was understandable in 1962. Time was simply not available for anyone to demonstrate the advantages of modern critical scholarship by a thorough examination of a major topic.

Since then, however, and especially since the close of the Council in 1965, other writers have not hesitated to tackle primary and central problems, such as the miracles of Jesus and his claim to be the Messiah or the son of God. This is wholly admirable, for these are the questions most discussed today, and which people really worry about. Unfortunately, some of these authors have embarked on the popularization of novel and rather radical theories which have caused considerable confusion and anxiety among ordinary Catholics. For instance, it is not hard to find examples of popular writing, by Catholics, where the historicity of the virginal conception of Jesus, or the fact of his bodily Resurrection, is called into question or openly denied. It is not surprising that many, especially priests and school-teachers, are asking whether such apparently outlandish views represent the consensus of modern Catholic biblical scholarship. They do not have access to the findings of the real scholars in the highly technical theological journals, and cannot be expected to be able to distinguish in popular writing between the wheat and the chaff. Hence when views like those just mentioned are put before the general public in the popular press, on the radio or on television, it is little wonder that many of the ordinary churchgoers are deeply distressed and would willingly say with St John Fisher, 'The fort is betrayed even of them that should have defended it!'

There has therefore been for some years, at least in Great

Britain, a genuine need for a fairly serious treatment of some New Testament problem of major importance, to show what happens in practice when modern critical methods are adopted and applied by a Roman Catholic who is not prepared to throw overboard the traditional teaching of his Church (and others besides Roman Catholics may be interested in the result). Hence the present book is offered in the first place as a specimen of the kind of course in New Testament exegesis that is nowadays taught in Catholic seminaries, and I do not think that any reader who studies these pages carefully will feel that the fundamental dogmas of Catholicism are being undermined. Perhaps some Catholics may feel that the book is rather Protestant; but I am sure no Protestant will make that mistake.

The subject, *The Mother of Jesus in the New Testament*, was indicated by a variety of reasons. First, if the work was to be done thoroughly and yet finished within a reasonable period of time, the subject chosen had to be one on which there were relatively few texts to examine. Secondly, it had to be a matter of primary importance, so that problems acutely felt could be discussed. The prominence of Marian doctrine in the Roman Catholic Church, and the widespread uneasiness felt there over attacks on the historical value of the Infancy Narratives, made the choice of subject, at this point, almost self-evident.

But there was a third factor also, pointing in the same direction. There is today within the Roman Catholic Church a real tension about the role of Mary, a tension already visible in the debates of the Second Vatican Council. When the Council Fathers were asked, on 29 October 1963, to vote whether their doctrine concerning the Blessed Virgin should be presented as the final chapter of the document on the Church, or as a separate document, they were very evenly divided. 1114 voted in favour of treating Marian doctrine as part of the doctrine concerning the Church; 1074 voted against, with 5 voting papers null and void. A majority of only 40 means that 21 votes altered could have given the opposite result. Nowhere was the Council so profoundly split, and that division among the bishops probably reflects very accurately the tension felt at large within the Roman Catholic Church today. Not surprisingly, this tension can sometimes lead to a dangerous polarization of opinions, when exaggeration on one side provokes an equally extreme reaction in the opposite direction. There are some who seem so to exalt Mary as to detract from the unique position of her Son, the one and only mediator with the Father; and there are others who, reacting against that view, appear to assign her a very ordinary place in the work of our redemption, and in the company of the saints. Admittedly, both these extremes are, at least in Great Britain, comparatively rare, but one does meet in this country Catholics who, in their determination to differentiate themselves from Protestants, overstress the role of Mary, and others who, in their enthusiasm for ecumenical activity, try to play down the importance of Marian doctrine and devotion. Both attitudes are contrary to ancient Catholic tradition. I have tried to show that they are equally at variance with the picture of the mother of Jesus given in the New Testament, and that only the ancient Catholic tradition does justice to the evidence presented in Scripture. These, then, were three motives of strictly Roman Catholic interest which led to the choice of subject.

But there were other reasons too which recommended this topic. There is probably no area in the whole field of doctrine or devotion where the Catholic and Orthodox tradition is more widely divided from the Reformed tradition than on the position to be assigned to the mother of Jesus. In an age when Christians from all the major Churches are earnestly seeking to repair the schisms of the past, it is simply tragic that they should quarrel concerning her whom all confess to be the mother of their Saviour. Some serious effort must be made to bridge this crevasse, or at least to talk to one another across the chasm about ways and means of bridging it. The bitter controversies and disputes of the past cannot be tolerated any longer by anyone who claims to be a follower of Jesus Christ: the only proper attitude to Mary is the one he had. Yet the reason that Protestants cannot share the Catholic attitude to Mary is most often that they believe it to be profoundly unbiblical, and indeed contrary to the teaching given in the New Testament. This subject is dealt with at length in the

Introduction, where I have tried to show that differences concerning Marian doctrine are to a large extent a consequence of much deeper differences concerning the relationship of Scripture and tradition. Once again, it seemed that a book about Mary in the New Testament might have real interest for those who wonder how a Roman Catholic can accept the modern methods of biblical criticism and still retain full confidence in the teaching of his Church, and in its· devotional practices, concerning the Blessed Virgin.

This rather lengthy preamble has been necessary in order to explain certain features of the book which might otherwise strike a number of readers (and certainly all reviewers) as somewhat bizarre. The first question any reviewer asks himself is, 'Who is this book written for?' The answer here is that it is addressed simultaneously to all the classes of people so far mentioned. It is addressed to the non-specialist, in particular to the Roman Catholic priest or candidate for ordination, who wants to know where the consensus of Catholic scholarship on Marian doctrine lies; but it is addressed also to scholars, in particular to those outside the Roman Communion who would be interested in the answers a Roman Catholic would give to the questions and objections they put to him. Hence certain footnotes (*e.g.* the one which describes what the Mishnah is) are meant to assist and guide the non-specialist, while others (including most of the Detached Notes at the end) are strictly for scholars who want to know the evidence on which certain statements are founded. It is addressed to Catholics who are worried about the orthodoxy of theologians today, and several pages which may seem irrelevant to the critic are meant to calm their fears; it is addressed also to Catholics who blame the more traditionally-minded theologians for lack of courage, and for not going far enough in the jettisoning of older views. It is addressed very earnestly to all members of the Reformed Churches who want to understand the Roman Catholic viewpoint on Mary the mother of Jesus. I have endeavoured to take every one of their questions extremely seriously, to see it from their point of view, and to give them a serious answer. As a result, not everything in the book is meant for everyone, but everything is addressed to someone. I trust that the reader who finds certain pages or footnotes irrelevant for him will be patient, and accept that they may be very important for another reader. It is a bit untidy, but it is the best that could be done.

In this endeavour to make the book intelligible to a wide and non-specialist public, I have in the text of the book (as distinct from the notes) always given quotations from foreign languages in an English translation, except on rare occasions. Occasionally, I have kept Latin in the text, where the expression seemed particularly graceful, and supplied a translation in the footnotes; one or two Latin tags, etc. and two verses of a Christmas hymn have been left untranslated. The footnotes are nearly all directed to scholars or students who might want further evidence for statements in the text, or have objections to raise which would hardly occur to the ordinary reader; and here I have felt free to quote, without translation, the original texts. A greater difficulty lay in deciding what to do about Greek (and, to a lesser extent, Hebrew). In order to keep down costs by a sparing use of Greek type-fount, and at the same time to help the reader who has no Greek, I have often used circumlocutions such as 'the Greek word for *Rejoice*': for in the end one cannot talk about the New Testament without reference to the Greek, any more than one can talk about Shakespeare without any reference to the fact that he wrote in Elizabethan English.

Two smaller facts should be mentioned for the guidance of readers. As a rule, the second-person singular is used in biblical quotations to avoid the tiresome task of explaining whether the text is addressed to one individual or several. Also, longer quotations are often indented in the paragraph, when they are given simply as quotations (*i.e.* when I wish to stand neutral in judgment on their content). But whenever a rather lengthy quotation is *not* indented (*e.g.* in the quotations from Père Congar in the Introduction, or in the citation from St Bede at the end of Part II), this quotation is part of the argument. Very occasionally, it may be an objection which is best recorded in the words of the man who made it; more often, as in the quotation from Bede, it means that there is no more felicitous expression of the argument.

It only remains to record my thanks to everyone who has helped in any way towards the making of this book. The following list of names is inevitably rather a litany, and the order of their meriting is strictly chronological, not hierarchical. In publishing this work, I think first of all of my former teachers: of those who trained me in classical languages, and of Dr A. Theissen, who gave me my first lessons in Hebrew and in Scripture, at Ushaw thirty years ago; of those who taught me theology at the Gregorian University in Rome, and especially of Fr Paul Galtier, S.J., who spared no pains in introducing me to the study of the Fathers; of the professors of the Biblical Institute in Rome, especially of Fr S. Lyonnet and Fr M. Zerwick, S.J.; and of the professors of the Ecole Biblique in Jerusalem, where in 1955–6 Fr P. Benoit lectured on the Infancy Gospels and Fr M.-E. Boismard introduced me to the study of St John. The staff and students at Ushaw deserve a special vote of thanks. The students have for more than a decade patiently endured the lectures out of which this book was shaped, and never complained. To Mgr P. M. Loftus, the President, particular thanks are due for arranging that I should be able to take six months' sabbatical leave in 1973 in order to complete the work; as also to the Revs. R. J. Taylor and P. M. Cookson, who undertook my lecturing and tutorial commitments while I was away. Most of the final version was written in the Rhineland and in the valley of the Rhône. This I owe to the generosity of the Pallottine Fathers at Vallendar, near Koblenz, to their then Rector, Fr Rathofer, and to Drs Heinrich M. Köster and Alfons Weiser; and to Fr Paul Bony, Rector of the Grand Seminaire of the Archdiocese of Lyons at Francheville (Rhône). Professor C. K. Barrett and the other members of the Department of Theology in Durham have always been ready to help. Working with them has been a real education in thinking ecumenically, and Professor Barrett, in spite of his many commitments, generously agreed to read the entire typescript before publication. Mr John M. Todd has waited many years for the delivery of the manuscript, and (though he must have been sorely tempted at times) has never once pressed me to sacrifice quality for speed. Finally, all readers owe their thanks to the Rev. Bernard Payne, M.A., Librarian at Ushaw. For forty-five years his meticulous indexing of the Ushaw Library has been slowly transforming a very valuable collection of books into a highly efficient instrument of research where one can now find any book or article without trouble. I personally would thank him for all the care he took thirty years ago to teach my own generation here how to write English prose. Now he has crowned a lifetime of service by correcting the proofs of this work. *Quorum omnium nomina scripta sint in libro vitae.*

Ushaw College, Durham   John McHugh
25 March 1974

ACKNOWLEDGEMENTS

THE author and the publishers wish to thank the following for permission to make use of copyright material:

A. and C. Black Ltd., for permission to quote passages from *The Revelation of Saint John the Divine* by Dr C. B. Caird (The New Testament Commentaries); M. Henri Cazelles and P. Lethielleux, Paris, for permission to summarize, in Detached Note II, an article published in the *Bulletin de la Société Française d'Etudes Mariales* 21 (1964); Dr H. M. Köster, for permission to reproduce, in Detached Note IX, his list of opinions held concerning the virginal conception.

ABBREVIATIONS

AAS   *Acta Apostolicae Sedis* (Rome, 1909 ff.)

BSFEM *Bulletin de la Société Française d'Etudes Mariales* (Paris, 1935–8 and 1947 ff.)

CBQ   *Catholic Biblical Quarterly* (Washington, D.C., 1939 ff.)

CC   *Corpus Christianorum: Series Latina* (Turnhout)

CT   *Concilium Tridentinum. Diariorum, actorum, epistularum, tractatuum nova collectio* (published for the Görresgesellschaft at Freiburg-im-Breisgau, 1901 ff.)

Danby   H. Danby, *The Mishnah* (Oxford, 1933)

DB   Denzinger-Bannwart. *Enchiridion Symbolorum*, first edited by H. Denzinger in 1854, and later revised by C. Bannwart and others. (DB = 10th edition, Freiburg-im-Breisgau, 1908, to 31st edition, Barcelona, 1957, inclusive. See DS.)

DBS   *Dictionnaire de la Bible (Supplément)*, edited by L. Pirot, A. Robert and others (Paris, 1928 ff.)

DS   Denzinger-Schönmetzer. *Enchiridion Symbolorum definitionum et declarationum de rebus fidei et morum quod primum edidit Henricus Denzinger et quod funditus retractavit Adolfus Schönmetzer S.I.* (DS = 32nd edition, Barcelona, Freiburg-im-Breisgau, Rome and New York, 1963. See DB.)

ETL   *Ephemerides Theologicae Lovanienses* (Louvain, 1924 ff.)

GCS   *Griechische Christliche Schriftsteller der ersten drei Jahrhunderte* (Leipzig and Berlin)

H.E.   Eusebius, *Historia Ecclesiastica*

JTS   *Journal of Theological Studies* (Oxford, 1899 ff.; New Series, 1950 ff.)

MG   J. P. Migne, *Patrologia Graeca* (Paris)

ML   J. P. Migne, *Patrologia Latina* (Paris)

N.F.   *Neue Folge* (= New Series)

NRT   *Nouvelle Revue Théologique* (Paris, Tournai and Louvain: 1869 ff.)

N.S.   New Series

NTS   *New Testament Studies* (Cambridge, 1954 ff.)

RB   *Revue Biblique* (Paris, 1892 ff.)

RSR   *Recherches de Science Religieuse* (Paris, 1910 ff.)

TWNT   *Theologisches Wörterbuch zum Neuen Testament*, edited first by G. Kittel, later by G. Friedrich (Stuttgart, 1933 ff.) References are always to the original German, but can easily be traced in the American translation edited by G. W. Bromiley, *A Theological Dictionary of the New Testament* (Grand Rapids, Michigan, 1964 ff.)

ZNW   *Zeitschrift für die neutestamentliche Wissenschaft und die Kunde der älteren Kirche* (Giessen and Berlin, 1899 ff.)

TO MY MOTHER AND FATHER

INTRODUCTION

'Holy Scripture containeth all things necessary to salvation: so that whatsoever is not read therein, nor may be proved thereby, is not to be required of any man, that it should be believed as an Article of the Faith, or be thought requisite necessary to salvation.'

This sixteenth-century formula, in the Sixth of the Thirty-nine Articles, accurately describes the faith of the Church of England, and indeed of all the Reformed Churches, on the normative role of Holy Scripture in establishing doctrine. A similar text is found at the beginning of the Lutheran confession of faith known as the *Formula Concordiae* (1583):

'We believe, confess and teach that the one and only rule and norm by which all dogmas and all teachers are to be assessed and judged is none other than the prophetical and apostolic writings both of the Old and of the New Testaments. . . . Other writings, whether of ancient or modern teachers, whatever they be called, are in no way to be regarded as equal to Holy Scripture.'[1]

A little later the doctrine is reiterated in these words:

'Holy Scripture alone is the judge, norm and rule by which all dogmas must be tested and judged, to see whether they are good or evil, true or false.'[2]

[1] 'Epitome Articulorum (initio): De Compendiaria Regula atque Norma' I, 1, in *Die Bekenntnisschriften der evangelisch-lutherischen Kirche*, second (revised) edition, Göttingen, 1952, pp. 767–8.

[2] *Ibid.*, III, 7, in *Die Bekenntnisschriften*, p. 769.

The first great Calvinist Confession of Faith, drawn up in 1559 by the French Protestants and adopted in 1571 by the National Synod at La Rochelle, affirms the same teaching:

'Since Holy Scripture is the norm of all truth, containing all that is necessary for the service of God and our salvation (Jn 15:11), it is not lawful for men, or even for Angels, to add to it, to subtract from it, or to change it.'[3]

And the Confession of Faith drawn up by John Knox and others, which was approved by the Parliament of Scotland in 1560, lays down the same principle:

'The doctrine taught in our churches is contained in the written word of God, to wit, in the Books of [the] new and old Testaments: In those books we mean which of the ancient have been reputed Canonical, in the which we affirm that all things necessary to be believed for the salvation of mankind, is sufficiently expressed (Jn 21:24, 25).'[4]

There is no need of further illustrations, for the position so firmly stated four centuries ago by the Churches of the Reformation in England, Germany, France and Scotland remains a principle of Protestant belief to this day, namely, that no Christian may ever be obliged to profess as an article of his faith a doctrine which is not attested by the evidence of Holy Scripture.

All the Churches which stand in the tradition of the Reformation therefore reject the teaching of the Roman Catholic Church concerning the Immaculate Conception and the Assumption of the Virgin Mary, on the ground that neither of these doctrines is attested in the Bible. Yet Pope Pius IX, in 1854, solemnly defined that Mary's freedom from original sin was 'a doctrine revealed by

[3] 'Confession de Foy', Art. I, n. 5, in *Bekenntnisschriften und Kirchenordnungen der nach Gottes Wort reformierten Kirche*, edited by Wilhelm Niesel, Zürich, 1938 (reprinted), p. 67, lines 18–21.

[4] 'The Confessioun of Faith', Chapter 18, in *Bekenntnisschriften und Kirchenordnungen*, pp. 102–4 (the spelling has been modernized).

God, and therefore one to be firmly and steadfastly believed by all the faithful';[5] and Pope Pius XII used almost the same words in 1950 ('it is a divinely revealed dogma') when he proclaimed the faith of the Roman Church concerning Mary's Assumption into heaven.[6] It is no exaggeration to say that the Roman Church's insistence on the acceptance of these two doctrines constitutes a complete road-block on the path to Christian unity. Is there any possible hope of removing it?

Logically, three solutions of the problem are possible, of which the first is obvious to everyone. If only the Roman Church would cease to insist on the acceptance of these two doctrines as a condition of reunion, the problem would simply disappear. Some see in the decree of the Second Vatican Council on Ecumenism, *Unitatis Redintegratio*, §11, an indication that this may not be impossible, for the Council there reminds Catholic theologians that there is a certain order or 'hierarchy' of truths, and that not all of them are equally closely connected with the foundations of the Christian faith. Many Christians hope and pray that reunion may be achieved through agreement on certain central and basic doctrines, leaving such matters as the Immaculate Conception and the Assumption of Mary as points on which Christians could legitimately differ while living in one communion. Roman Catholics would acknowledge that these two beliefs were not essential prerequisites for full communion, and Protestants would accept that they were not repugnant to the Christian faith. This is not, one hopes, an unfair presentation of the position held by many Anglicans and Protestants who are most sympathetic towards Rome, and it has been well expressed by Professor A. C. Piepkorn, an American Lutheran.

'With the maturing of certain insights in the Roman Catholic

---

[5] In the new edition of Denzinger's *Enchiridion Symbolorum*, edited by A. Schönmetzer, Barcelona, 1963, n. 2803; in the older editions by C. Bannwart, n. 1641. This work will hereafter be cited according to its two major revisions simply as DS (Denzinger-Schönmetzer) and DB (Denzinger-Bannwart), followed by the paragraph number.

[6] DS 3903 = DB 2333.

doctrine of the Church that have found seminal and nascent expression in *Lumen Gentium* and *Unitatis Redintegratio*, it may some day be realized and recognized that the *whole* Church was not consulted prior to 1854 and 1950, and that the *whole* Church did not concur in and consent to the definitions, and that whatever degree of canonical validity these definitions have for those who accept the authority of the Bishop of Rome, they are still open questions for the *whole* Church.'[7]

This is one view. But perhaps those who regard Rome as the Scarlet Woman are performing an equal or even greater service to the cause of Christian unity by reminding their brethren that hopes such as these are illusory. The decree on Ecumenism is concerned in §11 with the order and method of dialogue, and nowhere in the Second Vatican Council is there any hint that the less central doctrines are less essential; indeed, the same §11 of *Unitatis Redintegratio* makes the contrary quite clear.

Another approach to the problem raised by these two Marian doctrines must therefore be found, and it is not surprising that some Roman Catholic theologians have argued that the Protestant principle of *sola Scriptura* is untenable. They start from the principle that the Church derives its knowledge of the faith not from Scripture alone, but also from a living tradition of apostolic origin, and then reason as follows. Divine revelation is communicated to the Church in two distinct ways, through written tradition (*i.e.* the Bible) and unwritten tradition handed down from apostolic times. The Church therefore receives its knowledge of revelation through two channels, or (as they prefer to say) from two sources. These two sources are of equal authority, for both are of apostolic origin, and the accurate preservation and transmission of doctrine through oral tradition and customary practice is guaranteed by the abiding presence of the Holy Spirit in the Church; therefore either source on its own (Scripture or tradition) can provide sufficient evidence for a dogma. Therefore the Church may require that all its members should accept as an article of

[7] 'Mary's Place within the People of God', *Marian Studies* 18 (1967), p. 82.

faith a doctrine which is *de facto* unwitnessed in Scripture, provided only that this doctrine has been handed down by tradition from apostolic times, or is necessarily entailed in a doctrine so transmitted. It is clear that if the Reformed Churches could be convinced that there were two such distinct sources or channels of revelation, it would be possible to investigate whether certain teachings concerning the Virgin Mary had, though unnoticed in Scripture, been handed down over the centuries within the Church. Unfortunately for those who hold this theory of two distinct sources for our knowledge of revelation, the silence of early doctrinal tradition concerning Mary's Immaculate Conception and Assumption is just as disconcerting as the absence of clear biblical witness to these doctrines. On the patristic evidence available, it is impossible to prove that either of these doctrines had been handed down by oral tradition from apostolic times. In practice, then, the theory that the Church has two distinct sources for its knowledge of revelation does not support, but rather undermines, the Roman Catholic position on these two Marian doctrines, by exposing the woeful inadequacy of the 'proof from extra-biblical tradition'. And in any case, it is futile to expect the Reformed Churches to accept as dogma a teaching for which there is no biblical support at all. Just as those who ask Rome to withdraw her claim to doctrinal infallibility are asking not for a concession or compromise, but for an act of ecclesiastical suicide, so those who ask the Protestant Churches to accept a doctrine for which all biblical evidence is lacking are asking them, in effect, to forget the Reformation and to dissolve themselves.

There is, however, a third way of approaching the problem. *If* it could be shown that these doctrines about Mary are either plainly expressed or necessarily implied in Holy Scripture, a totally new situation would be created. They would then cease to be a primary obstacle to reunion. They are not, of course, plainly expressed there, but are they necessarily implied? This is a most difficult question, for the answer to it depends on two factors. First of all, Catholics and Protestants are not agreed on what the New Testament teaches about Mary. Secondly, even if they were agreed, they would then have to discuss whether the doctrines of the Immaculate Conception and the Assumption were necessarily entailed in what the New Testament teaches. This second step would presuppose some measure of agreement that development of doctrine is at least in theory possible, and can sometimes be justified. Historically, however, the main Christian Churches of the West have accepted the principle of doctrinal development by accepting the dogmas proclaimed at Nicaea, Constantinople, Ephesus and Chalcedon. Each of these councils declared that only one interpretation of certain biblical data was admissible; on no occasion was the doctrine defined 'plainly expressed' in the actual words of Scripture; but on each occasion the Church decided that it was 'necessarily implied' in the teaching of the Bible as a whole. One need not, therefore, be pessimistic about the prospects of agreement between Catholic and Protestant on the principle of doctrinal development.

The first task, however, is to decide what the New Testament teaches about the mother of Jesus, for without agreement on this, it is impossible to begin to discuss the legitimacy of later doctrinal developments. And today this first stage is more urgent than ever. For nowadays there are many Christians who reject or call into question not just the teaching of the Roman Church on the Immaculate Conception of the Assumption, but more basic doctrines as well. In particular, there are many who deny the historicity of the virginal conception of Jesus, the lifelong virginity of Mary, and the propriety of venerating her as mother of the Lord. Indeed, for many Protestants the main stumbling-block lies not in the dogmas defined in 1854 and 1950, but in the whole attitude of the Roman Church towards Mary, which they consider to be profoundly unbiblical. Quite clearly, as long as these fundamental issues remain in dispute, there is no point whatever in trying to reach agreement on the Immaculate Conception or the Assumption. The first task must be to seek agreement on what the New Testament teaches about Mary. Only when agreement is reached on this will it be possible to embark on further discussions. But if agreement could be reached on the teaching of the New Testament, this in itself would be no small achievement, and would mark a considerable advance in the ecumenical dialogue.

Of these three approaches, the first two seem foredoomed to failure. Those who hope that Rome will one day change her ways, and those Roman Catholics who trust that the Reformed Churches will eventually abandon their principle of 'Scripture alone', both make the same mistake: they hope and pray that with the passage of time the 'other side' will come to see the force of today's arguments and admit the fundamental error of its ways. These optimistic expectations might be justified if it were merely a matter of adjusting and amending a theological position of secondary importance; but what is at stake, on either side, is not a subsidiary issue—it is the *essence* of a particular religious tradition. For Roman Catholics, what is at stake is the very nature of Christ's Church, and whether the Holy Spirit continually guides its teaching from age to age; for Protestants, what is at stake is the authority of Scripture, and whether the revelation given in the New Testament is definitive for all future time. Roman Catholics, if they remain true to their tradition, cannot admit that the Holy Spirit has allowed their Church to pledge itself irrevocably to doctrinal error; Protestants, if they remain true to the Reformation, cannot admit that the revelation given in the Bible is capable of further additions. Reunion achieved by the abandonment of either or both of these principles would not be a fusion of the finest positive insights of the two traditions, Catholic and Reformed; it would spell the destruction of one tradition or both, and the absorption of at least one body of Christians into a Church whose doctrine would be totally alien to their tradition. A theologian might think that reunion at such a price was undesirable; the common man would judge it psychologically improbable; and one is on fairly safe ground in forecasting that the reunion of the Christian Churches will never be achieved by such means.

The third approach (examining the Scriptures to see if there is any biblical foundation for the Roman Catholic doctrines about Mary) is therefore at least worth exploring, since no one would wish to pronounce any road towards Christian unity impassable before anyone had made a survey of the terrain. For if some solid biblical evidence could be found in favour of these doctrines, the Roman Church might feel able to adopt officially a thesis which many Catholic theologians already accept privately, namely, that God's written Word in Scripture contains all truth that need be believed for salvation. Those who hold this view come very close to the Protestant principle of *sola Scriptura*, but would prefer to say *totum in sacra Scriptura*, so as not to exclude the validity of the witness of Church tradition. Moreover, the phrase *totum in sacra Scriptura* formulates more accurately than *sola Scriptura* the true function of the Bible as a source of revealed truth. To Catholic and Protestant alike, the Bible is presented within the context of a particular Church tradition; no man reads it (much less interprets it) in a religious vacuum. Today, all the leading Christian Churches agree that Scripture is holy because it enshrines the living tradition of the apostolic Church; could they not also agree that tradition too is sacred, because by it, and never without it, the message of Scripture is preserved and kept alive from one generation to another?

It may be of help to some readers to explain here the doctrine of the Roman Catholic Church concerning the relationship between Scripture and oral tradition, for its teaching on this point has often been misunderstood, and has sometimes been inaccurately presented by Catholic theologians, particularly in the course of this century. The discussion need not be lengthy, for there are only two official documents which need to be considered: the decree of the Fourth Session of Trent on Scripture and Traditions (1546), and that of the Second Vatican Council on Divine Revelation (1965).

The pertinent words of Trent read as follows:[8]

[*Evangelium*] 'quod promissum ante per Prophetas in Scripturis sanctis Dominus noster Iesus Christus Dei Filius proprio ore promulgravit,

[*The Gospel*] 'which had formerly been promised by the Prophets in the Holy Scriptures was first promulgated by our Lord Jesus Christ, the Son of God, in person (*proprio ore*).

[8] DS 1501 = DB 783.

deinde per suos Apostolos tamquam fontem omnis et salutaris veritatis et morum disciplinae "omni creaturae praedicari" (Mc 16:15) iussit;

He subsequently commanded his Apostles to "preach it to every creature" (Mk 16:15) as the source of all truth which avails unto salvation, and of every rule of conduct (*morum disciplinae*).

[*Sacrosancta Synodus*] perspiciensque, hanc veritatem et disciplinam contineri in libris scriptis et sine scripto traditionibus, quae ab ipsius Christi ore ab Apostolis acceptae, aut ab ipsis Apostolis Spiritu Sancto dictante quasi per manus traditae ad nos usque pervenerunt,

[*This Holy Synod*], therefore, observing that this truth and rule [*of conduct*] is contained in the written books and the unwritten traditions which the Apostles received from the mouth of Christ himself, or which the same Apostles learnt from the Holy Spirit, and which have been passed down as it were from hand to hand until they reached our own generation,

orthodoxorum Patrum exempla secuta,
omnes libros tam Veteris quam Novi Testamenti, cum utriusque unus Deus sit auctor,

and following the example of the orthodox Fathers,
accepts all the books both of the Old and of the New Testament, since the same God is author of both Testaments,

nec non traditiones ipsas, tum ad fidem, tum ad mores pertinentes, tamquam vel oretenus a Christo, vel a Spiritu Sancto dictatas et continua successione in Ecclesia catholica conservatas,

and the aforesaid traditions (whether appertaining to faith or conduct) as having been taught either orally by Christ, or by the Holy Spirit, and preserved by an unbroken succession in the Catholic Church.

pari pietatis affectu ac rever-
entia suscipit et veneratur.'

It accepts and reveres both
these holy books and these
unwritten traditions with an
equal sense of piety and with
equal reverence.'

During the first half of the twentieth century, the most commonly accepted interpretation of this text was that the 'unwritten traditions' mentioned in the decree differed in content from Holy Scripture, because they extended over a wider field and included matters not mentioned in the Bible. In other words, the Council was interpreted as having said that certain doctrines and (or) rules of conduct which were necessary for salvation had gone unmentioned in Scripture, but had nevertheless been handed down from apostolic times by oral tradition and customary practice. These doctrines and this code of Christian conduct (it was held) were ultimately of divine origin, having been taught by Christ or inspired by the Holy Spirit; and therefore they were to be received with the same reverence as Holy Scripture. As has already been mentioned, this theory has been invoked to support the doctrines of the Immaculate Conception and the Assumption. Here it is enough to mention that a refusal to assent to this 'Two Sources' theory was sometimes considered to be a rejection of Trent.

A very different interpretation has, however, been persuasively argued and has fast gained ground since about 1950. Its advocates point out that Trent did not by any means condemn the view that the whole deposit of faith was contained in Scripture, as well as in the living tradition of the teaching and believing Church. For before, during and after Trent, there were many Roman Catholic bishops and theologians who taught insistently that all truth necessary for salvation was contained (at least implicitly) in the words of Holy Scripture. Their contemporaries never re-garded them as having been condemned by the Council, since Trent's sole aim was to outlaw the Protestant view that oral tradition about doctrine carried no authority, or at least less authority than the written books of the Bible. In other words,

Trent was not concerned to draw a distinction between the doctrinal content of Scripture and of unwritten tradition; its sole intention was to affirm that the gospel message was conveyed just as fully and just as accurately through the preaching of the Church as it was through the Bible. According to the Reformers, the medieval Church had altered and corrupted the original message of the gospel, and the hour was come to return to the only uncontaminated source of truth, the Holy Bible. Trent replied that in every age the Holy Spirit continued to speak just as authoritatively through the voice of the Church as he had once spoken through the Bible. This was the issue in dispute between Trent and the Reformers, not the question whether oral tradition contained more than was in the Bible.

There is no need here to discuss at length which interpretation of Trent is the true one, for there are many excellent and up-to-date studies on the subject.[9] One point, however, must be made. The draft of the Tridentine decree stated that the gospel message was contained '*partly* in the written books, *partly* in unwritten traditions' ('*hanc veritatem* partim *contineri in libris scriptis*, partim *sine scripto traditionibus*')[10] To some of the Fathers at Trent, the disjunction involved in the words *partim . . . partim* seemed to imply that 'the truth which avails unto salvation' was *only partly* contained in Scripture. The General of the Servite Order, Bonucci, and the Bishop of Chioggia both criticized the draft on these grounds,[11] and several scholars think that the words *partim . . .*

[9] See especially the studies of J. R. Geiselmann listed in the Bibliography, and Y. M.-J. Congar, *Tradition and Traditions*, London, 1966, pp. 156–76.

[10] *Concilium Tridentinum. Diariorum, actorum, epistularum, tractatuum nova collectio*, published for the Görresgesellschaft at Freiburg-im-Breisgau from 1901 onwards. The text cited above is to be found in vol. 5, p. 31, lines 25–6. The work will be cited hereafter as *CT*, followed by the number of the volume (*e.g. CT* 5, p. 31).

[11] Bonucci: 'Iudico omnem veritatem evangelicam scriptam esse, non ergo *partim*' (*CT* 1, p. 525, line 18); Nachianti, Bishop of Chioggia: 'Nemo enim ignorat, contineri in sacris libris omnia ea, quae ad salutem pertinent' (*CT* 5, p. 18, lines 28–9), or 'Cum enim pro explorato habeamus omnia, quae ad nostram salutem pertinent, in libris scriptis scripta esse . . .' (*CT* 1, p. 33, lines 40–1).

partim were replaced by the simple conjunction *et* ('*in libris scriptis et sine scripto traditionibus*') in order to meet this objection.

The correction is an important one, and it is regrettable that no records have survived to tell us for certain why Trent made this change. It is unlikely that it was in deference to Nachianti, the Bishop of Chioggia, for he was something of a maverick at the Council,[12] and was frequently heckled during this speech.[13] It is even possible that the suppression of *partim . . . partim* and the substitution of *et* was merely a stylistic change to lighten an over-loaded sentence.[14] Nevertheless, the most probable explanation is that the amendment was accepted because of the intervention of Bonucci, who persisted in his opposition to the phrase until it was taken out:[15] he was much respected, and was chosen to preach at the Fourth Session (8 April 1546), when the definitive text was promulgated.[16] But whether this be the true historical explanation or not, it is quite certain that Trent did not in fact condemn those Catholic theologians who held that all truth necessary for salvation is to be found in Holy Scripture. Père Yves Congar summarizes well: 'Faced with two opposing currents of opinion among the Catholic theologians,—the one, perhaps the stronger, in favour of *partim . . . partim*; the other in favour of the sufficiency of Scripture—the council, seeing no adequate solution and ever

---

[12] On 5 April 1546, three days before the Fourth Session, Cardinal del Monte (later Julius III), one of the papal legates and presidents, said: 'Deus sit mihi testis, quod amo et diligo in fratrem (episcopum Clodianum) propter doctrinam et ingenium eius; verum Deum precor, ut det illi saniorem sensum' (*CT* 1, p. 45, lines 47–9).

[13] 'Reprehensus est a multis verbis ipsiusmet evangelii Ioannis ultimo' (Jn 21: 25) (*CT* 1, p. 494, line 22).

[14] *I.e.* assuming either that *partim . . . partim* meant nothing more than 'both-and' (thus J. Beumer, *Die mündliche Ueberlieferung als Glaubensquelle*, Freiburg–Basel–Vienna, 1962, pp. 83–4), or that *et* in the definitive text carries the full disjunctive meaning 'partly . . . and partly' (thus, though with very unconvincing arguments, N. Hens, 'Was sagt der vorliegende Text des IV. Sitzung des Tridentinischen Konzils über das Verhältnis von Schrift und Tradition?—Eine philologische Erklärung', in *Schrift und Tradition* (Mariologische Studien 1), Essen, 1962, pp. 85–8.

[15] As late as 1 April (*CT* 5, p. 47, lines 1–2), contrary to what Beumer says (op. cit.) on p. 83, n. 64.

[16] The sermon is given in *CT* 5, pp. 95–101.

careful to express itself only where Catholics were in agreement, contented itself with affirming, by juxtaposition and with no precision of their interrelation, the *two forms* under which the Gospel of Jesus Christ is communicated, in its plenitude and purity, as the source of all saving truth and of Christian discipline. This is also why the council insisted that the two forms should be received *pari pietatis affectu.*'[17]

It could well be, as Congar remarks,[18] that the Council Fathers (or the majority of them) believed that certain necessary truths had not been formulated in Scripture. This was certainly the view of some Catholic apologists of the time, and of many controversialists later, right down to our own day. All that need be stressed (against certain Catholic theologians of our own time) is that the Tridentine decree does not canonize this position, for 'the Council Fathers did not have in mind the question which interests *us*; in their first as in their second formulation, they had simply wished to oppose the exclusive and negative elements in the Protestant position with regard to Scripture, and to affirm the existence of apostolic traditions to which the faithful owed an absolute respect'.[19]

To sum up: whatever may have been the reason for the change in wording, and whatever view might have prevailed at Trent about the doctrinal content of Scripture and tradition, the definitive text of the Council does not commit the Roman Catholic Church to an assertion that there are certain doctrines necessary for salvation which are unattested in the Bible. That was not the object of the decree; it is nowhere formally and explicitly stated; nor does it follow from the text by logical necessity. Consequently, any Roman Catholic who respects the unbroken witness of the Church's teaching as of equal authority with Holy Scripture can (if he so chooses) maintain that all truth necessary for salvation is also contained in Scripture.[20]

[17] *Tradition and Traditions*, p. 165.　　[18] *Ibid.*, pp. 165–6.　　[19] *Ibid.*, p. 168.
[20] The most convenient summary of the question available in English is in *Tradition and Traditions*, pp. 164–9, where there is an excellent series of references. On p. 63, n. 2, Congar lists some of the Catholic theologians who uphold the view that everything necessary for salvation is in Scripture. On pp. 107–18 he has a

To understand the post-Tridentine development of Catholic theology, it is necessary to grasp the importance of a profound cultural change which had begun before the Reformation, but which was to have its full impact only after it, and because of it. 'A sort of ecclesiological positivism or fideism made itself felt from two different directions at the turn of the thirteenth and fourteenth centuries, amongst the theologians and amongst the canonists. In this way the theologians salvaged all the certitudes their critique of religious knowledge had destroyed. Nominalism and the Scotist criticism both came to the conclusion that all the articles of faith depend upon this one article, the first of all: *"Credo Ecclesiam regi a Spiritu Sancto"*.'[21] At the same time, as the renaissance of Roman Law (dating from the twelfth century) began to bear fruit, the principle accepted in the early Middle Ages, *'Omnes sub rege, et rex sub lege'*, was being steadily replaced by a new axiom, *'Quod principi placuit, legis habet vigorem'*. This new principle naturally thrust its way into the Church, where it was indeed welcomed by those theologians and canonists whose minds had been formed in an atmosphere of Scotist voluntarism and Nominalist positivism. Thus it was that when the Reformation came, many leaders in the Roman Catholic Church preferred to meet the problem by an appeal to the teaching authority of the Church rather than by debating each issue raised by the Reformers on its own merits. For the Church of Rome, Luther's insurrection was a disaster of the first magnitude: swift and effective action was called for, not calm and detailed academic debate. Thus 'the movement to exalt the authority of the Church,

---

well-documented *Excursus* 'On the Sufficiency of Scripture according to the Fathers and Medieval Theologians'; and on pp. 508–19, another *Excursus* on 'Scripture and the "Truths Necessary for Salvation"'. For fuller detail see J. Beumer, *Die mündliche Ueberlieferung als Glaubensquelle*, pp. 74–88; J. R. Geiselmann, 'Das Konzil von Trient über das Verhältnis der Heiligen Schrift und der nicht geschriebenen Traditionen', in *Die mündliche Ueberlieferung*, ed. by M. Schmaus, Munich, 1957, pp. 123–206, but especially pp. 133–67; *id.*, *Die Heilige Schrift und die Tradition* (= Quaestiones Disputatae 18), Freiburg–Basel–Vienna, 1962, especially pp. 91–107.

[21] *Tradition and Traditions*, p. 183, where Congar also notes: 'Those trained in the Thomist school reacted against this.'

and even, in fact, papal authority, continued and was even strengthened by the theology of the Counter-Reformation'.[22] The consequences of this invasion of Nominalism into the field of faith and the field of law were far-reaching, and two of them must now be described.

The meaning attached to the terms 'tradition', 'traditions', 'rule of faith', etc., underwent a subtle change. Until the eve of the Reformation, the primary meaning of these terms was simply the *content* of 'the faith once delivered to the saints'. The duty of the Church and its bishops was to preserve and to hand on this once-for-all deposit of faith, 'to hold fast to tradition'. With the advent of the new ideas mentioned in the last paragraph, the emphasis began to change, until 'tradition' began to mean the act of handing on the gospel; in such circumstances, it was only natural that 'tradition' should begin to include, as part of its definition, a clear statement about who handed on the deposit. Thus the word *traditio* slowly but inevitably became identified as a function of the *magisterium*, and its ancient meaning (*'that which is handed down'*), though never forgotten, slipped into second place.[23]

As the centre of gravity of the word 'tradition' moved over from 'content' to 'transmission', and as the supremacy of ecclesiastical authority became more firmly marked, a distinction familiar to the later medievals was lost to sight. They were accustomed to distinguish between 'truths necessary for salvation'[24] and 'teachings from which no Christian may lawfully dissent'. This is not simply a distinction between 'truths which there is an obligation

---

[22] *Ibid.*, p. 186.

[23] It is interesting to observe that though the Roman See has from ancient times acted as a judge on whether a thesis is compatible with the faith handed down, 'until modern times, [it] rarely exercised the active magisterium of dogmatic definition and constant formulation of Catholic doctrine in the way it has been exercised since the pontificate of Gregory XVI and especially since that of Pius IX' (Congar, *Tradition and Traditions*, p. 178). For the subject-matter of the paragraph above see pp. 177–83.

[24] It will be noted that this phrase or its equivalent occurs in the Sixth of the Thirty-nine Articles, in the French and Scottish Confessions of Faith cited above (pp. 1–2), and in the Fourth Session of Trent ('veritas salutaris').

to know and profess' and 'teachings which, if known, may not be
rejected' (though this thought is certainly included); hence it calls
for comment.

St Thomas Aquinas distinguishes between truths which are of
their nature directly connected with the attaining of eternal life
(*credibilia de quibus est fides secundum se, quasi per se intenta, et
principaliter, quae directe nos ordinant ad vitam aeternam*), and other
truths which are only indirectly connected with the attaining of
salvation (*credibilia in ordine ad alia, non quasi principaliter intenta*).
As examples of the former, he cites the doctrine of the Trinity,
the omnipotence of God, the mystery of the Incarnation, etc.;
as examples of the latter, the fact that Abraham had two sons, or
that a dead man was raised to life by contact with Elisha's bones
(2 Kgs 13:21). Stories like the latter, he says, are related not for
their own sakes, but simply to illustrate the majesty of God or the
Incarnation of Christ.[25] For St Thomas, the question whether a
truth is 'necessary for salvation' is decided by asking whether it is
intrinsically connected with that revelation which alone brings
eternal life.

William of Ockham (*c.* 1285–1347) relates that according to
some theologians 'only those truths are to be adjudged Catholic
and of necessity for salvation which are explicitly or implicitly
affirmed in the canon of the Bible', but a few pages later lists five
types of truth 'from which no Christian may lawfully dissent'.[26]
John Gerson (1363–1429), writing about 1417, lists six types of
truths, of which only the first two are required to be believed for
salvation: truth taught in the Bible, and truths taught by the
universal Church as necessary for salvation.[27] (The last-named
category, not found in Ockham, is a riposte to Wyclif.)

It is interesting to note that where St Thomas is mainly inter-

[25] 2–2ae, qu. 1, a. 6 ad 1um. For further references to St Thomas see Congar,
Tradition and Traditions, pp. 114 and 509–10.

[26] '. . . illae solae veritates sunt catholicae reputandae et de necessitate salutis
credendae quae in canone bibliae explicite vel implicite asseruntur' (*Dialogus*, lib.
2 primae partis, c. 1, initio, Lyons, 1494, f. VI recto), and 'Tenent isti quod quinque
sunt genera veritatum quibus non licet christianis aliter dissentire' (f. VIII verso).

[27] *Declaratio Veritatum quae credendae sunt de necessitate salutis*, in *Opera Omnia*,
vol. 1, Antwerp, 1706, c. 22.

ested in the content of the doctrine and its intrinsic connection with the central mysteries of the faith, Ockham and Gerson are mainly concerned with the obligation to give, or the freedom to withhold, assent. The change of emphasis was to prove of massive importance. For the distinction between 'truths which must be believed for salvation' and 'other truths from which no Christian may lawfully dissent' loses all real significance when men are interested only in knowing what truths the Church obliges them to profess. Hence it was that as the stress was ever more sternly placed on the duty of accepting whatever the Church teaches with authority, men gradually lost sight of, and then forgot about, this most important distinction.[28]

However, the distinctions made by Aquinas, Ockham and Gerson were not forgotten overnight, and as long as they were still alive in men's minds, the debate on whether all truth *necessary for salvation* was to be found in Scripture proved a rather academic exercise. No Catholic ever suggested that it could all be found there by private interpretation, without the aid of tradition; and all truth *necessary for salvation* was considered to have, *de facto*, a biblical basis. Some modern Catholic theologians have read the works of the Counter-Reformation writers without adverting to the importance which the words 'necessary for salvation' had for those writers; and they have in consequence ascribed to them a comprehensive 'Two Sources' theology which belongs more to the late nineteenth and twentieth centuries than to the sixteenth. For example, the famous Spanish Dominican Melchior Cano (1509–60) once wrote: 'There are many things belonging to the teaching and faith of Christians which are not contained, either plainly or obscurely, in Holy Scripture',[29] and on the strength of this sentence (and the chapter from which it is taken) he has been acclaimed (or denounced) as one of the

---

[28] For the whole paragraph see Congar, *Tradition and Traditions*, pp. 107–18 and 508–19, and J. Beumer, *Die mündliche Ueberlieferung als Glaubensquelle*, pp. 53–73.

[29] 'Multa pertinere ad Christianorum doctrinam et fidem, quae nec aperte nec obscure in sacris litteris continentur' (*De locis theologicis* III, c. 3, fund. 3, Cologne, 1605, p. 151. In Migne's *Theologiae Cursus Completus*, vol. 1, Paris, 1839, c. 191).

founding fathers of the 'Two Sources' theology. But Cano does *not* say that these 'many things' are necessary for salvation, and indeed a few pages later he writes that even the unwritten traditions which derive from Christ and his apostles 'are not additions (*additamenta*) to the divine Scriptures, but rather their complement, and a kind of commentary on them'.[30] By this Cano means that the Church's traditions (*e.g.* on the validity of infant baptism) should not be seen as adding something to the teaching of Scripture, but as the only sure guide by which the true meaning of Scripture may be discerned. Cano in fact held that Scripture did contain, if obscurely, all the truths which Christians must believe (or at least all those which are 'necessary for salvation'), *i.e.* the *veritates* (*de necessitate salutis?*) *credendae*, but subscribed to the *partim . . . partim* theory for the '*mores et consuetudines Ecclesiae*'.[31] He cannot therefore be cited, without severe qualification, as a supporter of the type of 'Two Sources' theology current in recent years.

But as these medieval distinctions were relegated to the background, and attention directed more to the magisterial authority of the Church, a new theology was bound to take shape. It was given classic form by the Italian Jesuit St Robert Bellarmine (1542–1621). Pressed by the need to find weapons for anti-Protestant controversy, Bellarmine stresses not what Scripture and tradition have in common, but the fact that tradition is a necessary supplement to Scripture, and goes so far as to write: 'When the universal Church embraces as a dogma of faith something which is not found in sacred Scripture, one must say that this comes from apostolic tradition. . . . Therefore everything which the Church holds by faith has been handed down by the Apostles or Prophets, either in writing or by

---

[30] 'Nec traditiones etiam huiusmodi divinarum scripturarum sunt additamenta: sed complementa sunt potius, et earum quasi commentaria' (*De locis theologicis* III, *Caput postremum*. In the Cologne edition, 1605, p. 172; in Migne's edition, c. 210).

[31] This reappraisal of Cano's teaching is the work of Ulrich Horst O. P., 'Das Verhältnis von Schrift und Tradition nach Melchior Cano', in the *Trierer Theologische Zeitschrift* 69 (1960), pp. 207–23 (see especially p. 222).

word.'[32] He instances the perpetual virginity of Mary and the canon of the Bible. The 'Two Sources' theory has arrived.[33]

Just as it would be foolish to underestimate the influence of Bellarmine after 1870 (he was declared *Beatus* in 1923, a saint in 1930 and a Doctor of the Church in 1931), so it would be a mistake to overvalue that influence in earlier times, when the Society of Jesus was often fighting not merely for its theology but for its very life.[34] Indeed, from Trent to the nineteenth century, Roman Catholic theologians seem to have been generally agreed that, apart from the doctrines of the canon and inspiration of Scripture, all the dogmas insisted on by Rome did in fact have a biblical basis. A German canonist, Georg Christophorus Neller, put it well when he asked, in 1746: 'Are there purely-oral dogmatic traditions, quite distinct from the written Word of God, to which there is not even a dark allusion in the Bible? . . . It seems to me that it could hardly be proved that there is any practical and basic dogma of the Christian religion which rests on merely-oral tradition.'[35] John Henry Newman judged no differently in 1845: 'Nor am I aware that later Post-tridentine writers deny that the whole Catholic faith may be proved from Scripture, though they would certainly maintain that it is not to be found on the surface of it, nor in such sense that it may be gained from Scripture without the aid of Tradition.'[36]

[32] 'Quando universa Ecclesia aliquid tamquam fidei dogma amplectitur, quod non invenitur in divinis literis, necesse est dicere, ex Apostolorum traditione id haberi . . . Igitur illa omnia, quae Ecclesia fide tenet, tradita sunt ab Apostolis, aut Prophetis, aut scripto, aut verbo' (*De Controversiis* I, lib. 4, c. 9: vol. 1, Prague, 1721, p. 118a).

[33] See J. R. Geiselmann, *Die Heilige Schrift und die Tradition*, pp. 184–221, especially pp. 193–5; J. Beumer, 'Die Frage nach Schrift und Tradition bei Robert Bellarmin', in *Scholastik* (Freiburg-im-Breisgau) 34 (1959), pp. 1–19.

[34] The case for his beatification, officially opened in 1627, was repeatedly and successfully opposed by the Jansenists and Gallicans: see P. Dudon, 'Pourquoi la cause de Bellarmin est-elle restée trois cents ans devant la Congrégation des Rites?' in *RSR* 12 (1921), pp. 145–67.

[35] *Principia Juris Publici Ecclesiastici Catholicorum*, Frankfurt and Leipzig, 1746, c. II, nn. 10 and 11, pp. 18–19.

[36] *The Development of Christian Doctrine*: in the standard edition by Longman, p. 342.

Nine years later, in 1854, came Pius IX's definition of Mary's Immaculate Conception. To an outside observer, it might seem self-evident that this was the moment at which the Roman Church finally declared itself free of any obligation to find, or to supply, a biblical justification for its dogmas; but that was not how most Catholics saw the issue at the time. The standard text-books of Catholic theology continued to put forward in support of the doctrine 'proofs' drawn from Scripture (principally Lk 1:28 and Gen 3:15), and though the exegesis was often by our standards unbelievably naïve, the very attempt to supply such a proof shows the importance then attached to the presentation of a biblical justification for the doctrine. But for all that, the outside observer would have been very near the truth.

The fact is, that among the more cautious theologians who perceived the weakness of the biblical justification, and in the text of the definition itself, a new approach to dogma was making itself felt. Leading scholars like Johannes Adam Möhler (1796–1838) in Germany[37] and Giovanni Perrone (1794–1876) in Rome had for some time been pressing the view that the living authority of the Church was the immediate criterion of religious truth *for the faithful*. An essay by Perrone, published in 1847, argued this position through to its logical conclusion: that the morally unanimous *faith* of the Church *in any age*—even the present—is *by itself* a sufficient criterion *for the bishops* to discern dogmatic truth, without the need to appeal either to Scripture or to past traditions.[38] His proof rests on the impossibility of the Holy Spirit's abandoning the Church to doctrinal error.[39] Newman had already acknowledged the force of a similar argument in 1845, and it had led him to the Church of Rome;[40] fourteen years later

[37] See his *Symbolism*, vol. 2, London, 1847, §§XXXVI–XLII, pp. 1–71. The work was first published in Germany in 1832, and the fifth edition (from which the English translation was made) appeared in 1838, the year of Möhler's death.

[38] *De Immaculato B.V. Mariae Conceptu an dogmatico decreto definiri possit Disquisitio Theologica*, Rome, 1847.

[39] He assumes, of course, that 'the Church' is identical with the Roman Catholic Church.

[40] See Congar, *Tradition and Traditions*, pp. 197, 209–11; J. H. Walgrave, *Newman the Theologian*, London, 1960, pp. 52–5, 57–8, 139–40, 184–8; H. Fries,

he was to expound it brilliantly in his now well-known essay 'On Consulting the Faithful in Matters of Doctrine'.[41] And Newman saw clearly what this principle entailed. In a letter of 15 November 1846 to his friend Dalgairns, he wrote: 'By the bye it is an encouraging fact, connected with the theory of development, that the said Perrone is writing a book to show that the immaculate conception may be made an article of faith.'[42] A few months later, in the spring of 1847, he presented to Perrone, at the latter's request, a paper entitled *De Catholici Dogmatis Evolutione*,[43] and Congar thinks that it was this contact with Newman which led Perrone to stress the *consensus fidelium* as a *locus theologicus*.[44] Be that as it may, it was certainly Perrone's essay and his arguments which turned the scales in Rome in favour of a definition of the Immaculate Conception. In 1850, a commission of bishops and theologians appointed to study the matter concluded that, *because of* the faith of the Roman Catholic Church at that time, the doctrine of Mary's sinless conception could be defined

---

'J. H. Newman's Beitrag zum Verständnis der Tradition', in *Die mündliche Ueberlieferung*, ed. by M. Schmaus, Munich, 1957, pp, 63–122, especially pp. 111–22; G. Biemer, *Ueberlieferung und Offenbarung: Die Lehre von der Tradition nach John Henry Newman*, Freiburg-im-Breisgau, 1961. For the influence of Möhler on Newman, see O. Chadwick, *From Bossuet to Newman*, Cambridge, 1957, pp. 102–19 (the influence was at secondhand); for Newman's differences from Perrone, see pp. 180–4.

[41] In *The Rambler* for July 1859, pp. 198–230. It has been edited and reprinted in book form by J. Coulson, London, 1961.

[42] *The Letters and Diaries of John Henry Newman*, ed. by C. S. Dessain, London and Edinburgh, vol. XI, 1961, p. 275.

[43] *Ibid.*, vol. XII, 1962, p. 40: '. . . quae à me pro tuâ solitâ benevolentiâ petiisti'. The full text (with Perrone's comments) was published by T. Lynch in *Gregorianum* 16 (1935), pp. 402–47.

[44] In *Tradition and Traditions*, p. 197, n. 4, Congar writes: 'Newman had complained that Perrone had made no mention, in his *Praelectiones* of 1842, of the *consensus fidelium* as a *locus theologicus*. In his *De immaculato B. Mariae Virg. Conceptu*, Rome, 1847, on the other hand, Perrone insists on the part played by the whole body of the faithful in the preservation of tradition. Mariological developments in the century following this work have not allowed theologians to forget this point.'

as a dogma.[45] Four years later, Pius IX, at the Secret Consistory held just a week before the definition (1 December 1854) put forward no argument for the definibility of the doctrine other than the belief of the universal Church, expressed principally in the consensus of the bishops.[46] It would seem that the Roman Church there accepted what Perrone had written in 1847: 'It must be frankly admitted that there is not a single biblical text which clearly decides the controversy in favour of one opinion or the other' (*i.e.* which clearly proves, or clearly excludes, the doctrine of Mary's Immaculate Conception).[47]

Nevertheless, as was said above, theological textbooks continued to set out biblical 'proofs' of the doctrine. But the scepticism engendered by the biblical criticism of the later nineteenth century could not fail to affect even the more remote fastnesses of conservative theology; and as the biblical 'proofs' of the Marian doctrine were seen to be too feeble to bear the weight placed upon them, theologians began to ground their case more and more on the faith of the living Church. This was easier than ever after the definition of Papal Infallibility in 1870, for the Bull of 1854 was the one perfect example of that doctrine in action. The year 1870 also saw the publication of a *Tractatus de Divina Traditione et Scriptura* by John Baptist (later Cardinal) Franzelin (1816–86). Franzelin was a Jesuit, a fellow-professor of Perrone at the Roman College from 1853 to 1876, and one of the principal theologians at the First Vatican Council. He had revolutionized the teaching of theology in Rome by virtue of his enormous

---

[45] The definitive work on the Bull of 1854 is that of Vincenzo Sardi, *La solenne definizione del dogma dell'Immacolato Concepimento di Maria Santissima: Atti e documenti pubblicati nel cinquantesimo anniversario della stessa definizione*, 2 vols., Rome, 1904. The influence of Perrone's thought is evident everywhere: in the arguments of the theologians (vol. 1, pp. 10–256), in the voting of the consultors (vol. 1, p. 793), in the first draft of the decree (vol. 2, pp. 36, 54), and in the voting of the bishops (*e.g.* Munich, Sydney, Amiens, Montauban and Westminster, vol. 2, pp. 216–35, 291).

[46] *Ibid.*, vol. 2, pp. 274–5.

[47] 'Fatendum prius ingenue est, nullum prorsus biblicorum testimoniorum suppetere, quod controversia pro alterutra sententia plane definiat' (*De Immaculato B.V. Mariae Conceptu*, p. 84).

learning, especially in the field of patristic theology, and the book on tradition and Scripture was his masterpiece. It remains to this day a work of rare merit and outstanding interest, and was destined to dominate Roman Catholic theology for seventy years. And on the relation of Scripture and tradition Franzelin was a firm follower of his fellow Jesuit and predecessor at the Roman College, Robert Bellarmine.[48]

The Modernist crisis only accelerated the movement to rest all dogma on the teaching authority of the present-day Church; and the anti-Modernist decrees certainly gave the impression (to put it mildly) that all biblical and patristic study had to be conducted in such a way that its findings would never be at variance with the accepted positions of post-Tridentine theology. A whole chapter of doctrinal history seemed to have been closed and sealed when in 1950 Pius XII appealed, for proof of the Assumption, only to the clearly manifested faith of the Roman Catholic Church. To those who were not within the Roman Communion, it seemed that neither Scripture nor past tradition could restrain the speculations of Roman Catholic teachers: the cheque-book handed to the papacy in 1870 was, they felt, being very freely used.

It was not, therefore, surprising that when the Second Vatican Council assembled in 1962, the Fathers were asked to approve a Dogmatic Constitution entitled *De Fontibus Revelationis*, in which it was stated that the Church

'has always believed and believes that the whole of revelation is contained not in Scripture alone, but in Scripture and Tradition, as in a double source, albeit in different ways. For the books of the Old and New Testaments not only contain revelation, but were also written under the inspiration of the Holy Spirit, so that they have God for their author.

---

[48] See his *Thesis XX* (1st ed., Rome–Turin, 1870, p. 207; 4th ed., Rome, 1896, p. 223), boldly entitled: 'De existentia traditionum divinarum, quae non continentur in Scripturis.' He cites as examples the validity of infant baptism, and the canon and inspiration of Scripture (1st ed., pp. 215–17; 4th ed., pp. 232–4). For an assessment of his influence see J. P. Mackey, *The Modern Theology of Tradition*, London, 1962.

But genuinely divine Tradition, preserved in the Church by uninterrupted succession, contains everything concerning matters of faith and morality[49] which the Apostles received either from the mouth of Christ or from the prompting of the Holy Spirit, and which they passed on to the Church as it were by hand, that they might be communicated through the preaching of the Church within the selfsame Church. . . . Let no one therefore make bold to set a lower value on Tradition, or to refuse it credence (*aut ei fidem denegare*). For although Holy Scripture, being inspired, provides us with a divine instrument to express and to illustrate the truths of faith, its meaning cannot be *certainly* and *fully* understood or even expounded except by apostolic Tradition; indeed, Tradition, and it alone, is the way whereby certain revealed truths become clear and known to the Church (above all, those which concern the inspiration, canonicity and integrity of each and every book in the Bible)'.[50]

[49] Note the contrast with the previous sentence about Scripture.

[50] 'Christi itaque et Apostolorum mandatis et exemplis edocta, sancta mater Ecclesia semper credidit et credit integram revelationem, non in sola Scriptura, sed in Scriptura et Traditione, tanquam in duplici fonte contineri, alio tamen ac alio modo. Nam libri Veteris et Novi Testamenti, praeterquam quod revelata continent, insuper Spiritu Sancto inspirante conscripti sunt, ita ut Deum habeant auctorem. Traditio autem vere divina, a Spiritu Sancto continua successione in Ecclesia conservata, in rebus fidei et morum ea continet omnia, quae Apostoli, sive ab ore Christi sive suggerente Spiritu Sancto, acceperunt atque Ecclesiae quasi per manus tradiderunt, ut in eadem per praedicationem ecclesiasticam transmitterentur. . . . Nemo ergo Traditionem exinde minoris facere aut ei fidem denegare audeat. Licet enim Sacra Scriptura, cum sit inspirata, ad enuntiandas et illustrandas veritates fidei instrumentum praebeat divinum, eius nihilominus sensus nonnisi Traditione apostolica *certe* et *plene* intelligi vel etiam exponi potest; immo Traditio, eaque sola, via est qua quaedam veritates revelatae, eae imprimis quae ad inspirationem, canonicitatem et integritatem omnium et singulorum sacrorum librorum spectant, clarescunt et Ecclesiae innotescunt.' The text of this draft is now published in the *Acta Synodalia SS. Concilii Oecumenici Vaticani II*, Vatican Press, vol. I, *Pars III*, pp. 14–26: the passages cited occur in §§ 4 and 5 (pp. 15–16). It is commonly believed that the architect of this first draft decree was Fr Sebastian Tromp, S.J., of the Gregorian University, a theologian standing firmly in the tradition of Franzelin and a noted authority on St Robert Bellarmine.

The implication of the last sentence is clear: there are other revealed truths, besides those connected with the inspiration and canon of Scripture, which are known to the Church only by unwritten tradition. We may note also that nowhere in this draft decree is there a word about the need for the Church of the present day to test its doctrines against the witness of Scripture and of past tradition. (Roman Catholic theologians all maintained the latter point, but the document never once made mention of it.)

The story of how this draft decree was rejected,[51] and a very different document substituted, is too recent and too well-known to call for repetition here. It is enough to say that in the decree which was finally approved, on 18 November 1965, by 2344 votes to 6, the Fathers of the Second Vatican Council left completely open the question whether all divine revelation is contained in Holy Scripture, and unambiguously declared that the teaching of the Roman Catholic Church today is subject to, and must be controlled by, the witness of Scripture and of past tradition.

'Sacred Tradition and Holy Scripture are closely joined and connected with each other, for both of them come to us from the same divine source, and in a way merge into one, and have the same purpose. For Holy Scripture is the utterance of God in that it is written down under the inspiration of the Holy Spirit; while Sacred Tradition hands on in its entirety the word of God that was entrusted by Christ the Lord and by the Holy Spirit to the Apostles. It hands it on to their successors so that they, enlightened by the Spirit of truth, may in their preaching faithfully preserve it, expound it, and spread it abroad. In this way it comes about that the Church does not derive from Holy Scripture alone the certitude she possesses on all revealed truths.[52] Therefore both

---

[51] The full texts of the speeches and written submissions are now available in the *Acta Synodalia*, vol. I, *Pars III*, pp. 27–110, 121–370.

[52] Cardinal Florit, Archbishop of Florence, in commending the final text to the Council on 22 October 1965, explained: 'In tuto ponitur doctrina catholica, constanti Ecclesiae praxi sancita, iuxta quam Ecclesia certitudinem suam de revelatis haurit per sacram Scripturam nonnisi cum Traditione coniunctam;

Scripture and Tradition are to be accepted with an equal sense of piety and with equal reverence.'[53]

'Sacred Tradition and Holy Scripture constitute a single sacred deposit of the word of God entrusted to the Church. . . . The office of interpreting authoritatively the word of God (whether scriptural or traditional) has been entrusted exclusively to the living magisterium of the Church, whose authority is exercised in the name of Jesus Christ. But this magisterium is not superior to the word of God; rather, it is at the service of the same, teaching only what has been handed down, insofar as it devoutly listens to, religiously guards and faithfully expounds the word, as God commands it to do, and as the Holy Spirit helps it to do. It is from this deposit of faith alone that the magisterium derives everything it proposes for acceptance as divinely revealed.'[54] The Church 'has ever held and holds that the Holy Scriptures, together with Sacred Tradition, are the supreme rule of her faith'.[55]

The first step in discussing the teaching of the Roman Catholic Church about Mary the mother of Jesus must be to find out what the New Testament tells us about her, for as long as there is disagreement between Catholics and Protestants on this point, it is impossible to talk about the legitimacy of later developments, such as the doctrines of the Immaculate Conception and the Assumption. And if this examination of the New Testament evidence is to be of any value in the ecumenical dialogue, it must be conducted according to the commonly accepted rules and conventions of critical scholarship. It is with this first step alone, not with any later development, that the present book is concerned. It is an attempt to answer the first and fundamental question: what does the New Testament teach about Mary, the mother of Jesus?

---

quapropter, ubi ad illam certitudinem assequendam Scriptura sola non sufficit, Traditio decisivum afferre potest argumentum. Sensus huiusmodi affirmationis ulterius diiudicandus est atque circumscribendus ex Schematis tenore. Ex quo quidem patet: nec Traditionem praesentari veluti quantitativum S. Scripturae supplementum; nec S. Scripturam praesentari veluti integrae revelationis codificationem' (*Schema Constit. Dogm. de Divina Revelatione: Modi a Patribus Conciliaribus Propositi et a Commissione Doctrinali Examinati,* Vatican Press, 1965, p. 73).

[53] The Dogmatic Constitution on Divine Revelation, *Dei Verbum,* § 9.

[54] *Ibid.,* § 10.   [55] *Ibid.,* § 21.

PART I

MOTHER OF THE SAVIOUR

(Luke 1–2)

'Legend may delight us with deep and gracious images, but we cannot build our lives on imagery, least of all when the very foundations of our belief begin to crumble away.'

(Romano Guardini, *The Lord*, Chapter 2.)

Chapter One

THE AUTHOR AND THE SOURCES OF LUKE 1–2

THE first two chapters of the Gospel according to St Luke differ remarkably, in content and in style, from all the following chapters. Nowhere else, except on Easter Day, does the reader encounter so many miracles in so short a time; in every episode the supernatural breaks through into the world of everyday life. Even the language of these two chapters is peculiar, for nowhere else in his writing does Luke so frequently employ strange phrases of Semitic origin such as 'walking in the commandments' (Lk 1:6) and 'advanced in their days' (Lk 1:7). To some of his Greek readers, many of these phrases must have sounded quite barbarous.

In order to explain the peculiar characteristics of Lk 1–2, several scholars have suggested that for these two chapters (as for the rest of his gospel) Luke had access to one or more written sources. Some have thought of a pre-Lucan document or documents written in Greek (and this would account for the difference in style from the remainder of the gospel); others have argued that the strongly Semitic phraseology is proof that Luke was here incorporating an account of Jesus' infancy that had been translated from a text (or texts) originally written in Hebrew or Aramaic. Having posited the existence of a pre-Lucan text (either in Greek or Hebrew or Aramaic), the same scholars proceeded to argue among themselves about its original language, its character, its content and its historical value. This debate continues today.

If such a document ever existed, it must have been written in

3

Greek or in Hebrew or in Aramaic. And since its existence is postulated principally to account for the many Semitic phrases and constructions in Lk 1–2, it would seem *a priori* that Greek should be excluded, and that the choice lies between Hebrew and Aramaic. The hypothesis of an Aramaic source has, however, failed to attract much support, and almost all who claim that the Greek of Lk 1–2 originates from a Semitic text add that this text was written in Hebrew.[1] The arguments in favour of this view are too complex to be examined here, and a study of this question is not essential to our purpose. It is sufficient to say that the main argument is that Lk 1–2 cannot be translated into Aramaic easily or gracefully, whereas the test of retranslation into Hebrew yields positive results. Clumsy Greek becomes natural Hebrew; word-play which escapes the reader of the Greek text comes to light in a Hebrew translation; and where Old Testament citations are found, the text of Lk 1–2 is seen to follow not the Greek Old Testament, much less the Aramaic Targums, but the original Hebrew.[2]

Yet many writers who are highly esteemed as literary critics of the gospels are not convinced: they continue to hold that, except for the Benedictus and the Magnificat, the first two chapters of Luke were from the first extant only in Greek.[3] Not all of them would agree that the original author was St Luke (some say there was a pre-Lucan text), but they do agree that this Infancy Gospel was written by a person who was consciously imitating the style and usage of the Greek Old Testament, the Septuagint. As a result,

[1] See Detached Note I: An Aramaic or Hebrew Source for the Lucan Infancy Gospel? (p. 435).

[2] The fullest modern statements of the arguments for a Hebrew source are found in E. Burrows, *The Gospel of the Infancy and other Biblical Essays*, London, 1940, pp. 1–58; H. Sahlin, *Der Messias und das Gottesvolk: Studien zur Protolukanischen Theologie*, Uppsala, 1945, pp. 70–311 *passim*; and in the articles of P. Winter listed in the bibliography.

[3] Winter himself cites (though without references) G. Dalman, J. H. Moulton, A. von Harnack, F. C. Burkitt and H. J. Cadbury, and allows that this opinion is still accepted by the majority of biblical scholars in England (*NTS* 1 [1954–5], p. 111). To these should be added the names of N. Turner, P. Benoit and H. Schürmann.

his writing contains many Semitic turns of phrase, and some oddly archaic expressions. It is as if a person of our own day were to write a religious story in the style and language of the Authorized Version: he could safely assume that most people would know what he was imitating, and that those who were thoroughly familiar with the Authorized Version would recognize literary allusions even to particular texts and themes. Those who hold that the author of the Lucan Infancy Gospel was deliberately writing in imitation of the Septuagint claim that the literary and syntactical peculiarities of these chapters are adequately explained by their theory, and that there is no need to postulate the existence of an original document in Hebrew. They answer, point by point, the arguments advanced against their own view, and conclude that the hypothesis of a written Hebrew text is neither necessary nor proved.[4]

The point at issue is not of purely academic interest, because of its implications. If Lk 1-2 (or part of it) is merely a Greek translation of a Hebrew document with little or no editorial revision, then allusions to the Old Testament will have to be explained by reference to the Hebrew of the Old Testament, not the Greek (and the two often differ considerably in meaning). Vice versa, if it were certain that the author of Lk 1-2 was making a pastiche of the Septuagint, his biblical allusions would have to be interpreted with the aid of the Septuagint rather than the Hebrew. The choice between the two views will therefore have repercussions on exegesis, and consequently on theology.

In this book, it is assumed that Lk 1-2 is, *on the whole*, to be interpreted by the aid of the Septuagint rather than the Hebrew. Many will no doubt query this principle, and will certainly raise objections against the interpretation of particular texts.[5] But neither the arguments for a Semitic substratum ('*Grundtext*') nor the arguments favouring an original composition in Greek seem totally convincing. It seems much more likely that stories about

---

[4] See especially the detailed studies of N. Turner, 'The Relation of Luke i and ii to Hebraic Sources and to the Rest of Luke-Acts' (*NTS* 2 [1955-6], pp. 100-9), and P. Benoit, 'L'Enfance de Jean-Baptiste selon Luc I' (*NTS* 3 [1956-7], pp. 169-94).

[5] *E.g.* the interpretation of Lk 1:28 in Chapter 4 (pp. 37-47).

the infancy of John the Baptist and of Jesus were recounted *orally* in Aramaic; that some of them were written down in Aramaic or Hebrew; that Luke either heard these tales in Aramaic or read them (probably in a Greek translation); and that Luke himself then selected what he needed, and wrote the final version with such great care that the original Semitic text (or tradition) has been transformed until it reads like a pastiche of the Septuagint, his own Bible.[6] If this is true, then Lk 1–2 should, *on the whole*, be interpreted by reference to the Septuagint rather than the Hebrew.

But there is another question of still greater theological import. If there was a written, pre-Lucan document, what did it contain? Many authors (mainly German)[7] think that St Luke came into possession of a document written by some followers of John the Baptist who had never heard of the Christian faith, or who were perhaps actively opposed to it. This document, in Hebrew or Greek, would have comprised (they say) the Annunciation to Zechariah, the birth and circumcision of the Baptist, and his departure to the desert, *i.e.* Lk 1:5–25, 57–66, 80. A few authors would include the Benedictus (Lk 1:67–79), and some others the Magnificat as well, which they ascribe to Elizabeth (Lk 1:46–55). These writers claim that St Luke modelled his own account of the Annunciation to Mary, of the birth and circumcision of Jesus, and his final remarks (*i.e.* Lk 1:26–38; 2:1–21, 39, 51–2) on this story of the Baptist's infancy, and that as he treated each parallel theme, he took care to stress the superiority of Jesus over the Baptist. Thus, where the 'Baptist' document told of John's miraculous conception in his parents' old age, Luke was moved to make the conception of Jesus even more wonderful and to present it as a virginal conception (Lk 1:5–25 compared with 1:26–38). At the birth of the Baptist, Zechariah was cured of his dumbness (Lk 1:64); at Jesus' birth, choirs of angels appeared to men, singing for joy (Lk 2:13–14). Other examples are easy to find.

[6] See, *e.g.*, G. B. Caird, *The Gospel of St Luke* (*Pelican Gospel Commentaries*), Harmondsworth, 1963, p. 20.

[7] Benoit lists among others (with references) A. von Harnack, E. Norden, M. Goguel, R. Bultmann, E. Lohmeyer, M. Dibelius, W. Bauer, Ph. Vielhauer and P. Winter (*NTS* 3 [1956–7], p. 169, footnote).

There are, however, three arguments (literary, critical and doctrinal) which compel one to treat this theory with caution, and not to assent to it without qualification. First, an analysis of the verses which allegedly belong to this document reveals that they contain just as many characteristically Lucan phrases and constructions as those other verses which are admitted to be Luke's own work.[8] Secondly, there is not a word in the so-called 'Baptist Infancy Story' which can fairly be interpreted as supplying positive evidence that its author was ignorant of, or hostile to, the Christian Church, Thirdly, the figure of the Baptist is there portrayed in exactly the same phrases as are used in later chapters of the Synoptic Gospels,[9] and the role assigned to him in Lk 1:15–17, 76–7 is exactly the role he plays afterwards: he is a messenger sent on in advance to prepare the way for a greater one who comes after him.[10] There are no positive grounds for asserting that behind part of Lk 1 there lies a document (or even a tradition) about the Baptist which was opposed to, or ignorant of, the Christian gospel.

This, and all the preceding arguments, lead by a convergence of probabilities to a conclusion which may be classed as certain, namely, that any written documents or oral traditions used must have been thoroughly revised by Luke before being incorporated into the gospel. Otherwise, there is no satisfactory explanation of the many distinctively Lucan phrases in these chapters. 'Thus, although Luke confesses the use of many sources and is the only synoptist who does so explicitly (1:1–4), he thoroughly assimilates them into his own authorship. As a consequence, analysts are quite unable to sunder sources from redaction except where other writers have preserved the same sources . . .[11] We may, of course,

[8] See Benoit, *NTS* 3 (1956–7), pp. 170–1.

[9] Compare Lk 1:15 with Lk 7:33 = Mt 11:18; Lk 1:16 with Lk 3:7–14; Lk 1:17, 76–7 with Lk 3:16–17; 7:27, etc.

[10] See Benoit, *NTS* 3 (1956–7), pp. 180–1.

[11] The continuation of the text is worth quoting: 'Scholars' inability to agree on the sources underlying Acts is a reminder of how difficult it would be to recover the sources of the Gospel if Mark and Matthew had not been preserved. Luke is so able an editor that many, if not most, of the marks of his pen are irrecoverable except where we have access to Mark and Q.'

be convinced, as I am, that there are sources, both written and oral, behind the birth stories. But that conviction does not entitle us to treat them in their present location as blocs of pre-Lucan tradition, relatively free of editorial revision. We may also be convinced, as I am, that the stories are thoroughly Lucan and are fully congenial in mood and motivation to his perspective as a whole. But this does not entitle us to treat them as an *ad hoc* composition, first produced by Luke to introduce the two volumes. Luke's typical fusion of tradition and redaction is of such an order that neither of the above conclusions is tenable'.[12] These words of Professor Paul S. Minear neatly summarize what is surely the most balanced judgment, and certainly the most widespread opinion today. Indeed, so competent is Luke's handling of his material that we might despair of ever detecting his sources precisely; fortunately, he has told us that his predecessors were 'those who had been from the beginning eye-witnesses and servants of the word' (Lk 1:2).

There are many traditions common to the Gospels according to Luke and John.[13] Some think that the author of the Fourth Gospel knew the Gospel according to Luke,[14] while others think that both Luke and the Fourth Evangelist drew upon a similar or identical body of oral traditions.[15] Whichever explanation be correct, the close resemblances between the opening chapters of Luke and John can hardly be attributed to mere coincidence.

The Prologue to the Fourth Gospel (Jn 1:1–18) and the Lucan Infancy Gospel have a number of themes in common, most of which are conspicuously absent from Matthew and Mark. Matthew, for example, does not have a word in his Infancy

[12] Paul S. Minear, 'Luke's Use of the Birth Stories', in *Studies in Luke-Acts. Essays presented in honour of Paul Schubert*, edited by L. E. Keck and J. L. Martyn, Nashville, New York, 1966, p. 112. Minear gives an excellent summary of the evidence for Luke's authorship on pp. 112–18.

[13] See R. Schnackenburg, *The Gospel according to St John*, vol. 1, New York and London, 1968, pp. 30–4.

[14] W. G. Kümmel, *Introduction to the New Testament*, London, 1966, pp. 144–5 gives a good survey of opinions; see also J. A. Bailey, *The Traditions Common to the Gospels of Luke and John*, Leiden, 1963.

[15] Thus Schnackenburg, *The Gospel according to St John I*, pp. 33 and 42.

Gospel about John the Baptist, whereas both Luke and John, *before* recording the birth of Jesus, stress that the Baptist was subordinate to him. He was but a messenger sent to point the way to Jesus (Lk 1:15-16, 76-7; Jn 1:6-8, 15), who alone was 'the true light', 'the light of the world' (Jn 1:8-9), and the 'light bringing revelation to the Gentiles' (Lk 2:32; 1:78-9). The titles here applied to Jesus were, in the Old Testament, used of God and of his faithful servant: thus Yahweh is called 'the light of Israel' (Is 10:17; *cf.* Ps 27:1), the everlasting light of Zion (Is 60:19-20), and appoints his servant to be 'the light of the Gentiles' (Is 42:6; 49:6; compare 51:5). Both Luke and the Fourth Evangelist must have been aware of this usage when they applied the term to Jesus; yet the title is given to Christ nowhere in Matthew or Mark, except for the citation of Is 9:1 at Mt 4:16, and is indeed hardly found in the New Testament outside the writings of St John.[16]

The Fourth Evangelist describes the Incarnation of the Word by a term which certainly refers to the Divine Presence in the Ark of the Covenant, when he writes that the Word *'encamped'* among us (Jn 1:14); Luke, as we shall see,[17] was also thinking the Divine Presence in the Ark and in the Temple when he wrote that the Power of the Most High would *'overshadow'* Mary (Lk 1:35). The only gospel parallel to either of these ideas occurs in the story of the Transfiguration, where the cloud which symbolizes the divine presence *'overshadows'* the disciples (Mt 17:5 = Mk 9:7 = Lk 9:34)[18] and Peter speaks of *'camping'* there for ever (Mt 17:4 = Mk 9:5 = Lk 9:33). It is significant that both Luke and John speak of this presence at the moment of the Incarnation.

Luke and John also speak of 'the Glory' of Jesus, a noun which to Jewish minds was primarily applied to God himself (Lk 2:32 and Jn 1:14; *cf.* Lk 2:9, 14); it is frequently used in descriptions of historic theophanies such as those during the Exodus (Ex

---

[16] See V. Taylor, *The Names of Jesus*, London, 1954, pp. 131-4: 'The Light of the World.'

[17] In Chapter 6, pp. 56-8.

[18] Apart from Lk 1:35, the verb occurs nowhere else in the gospels, and the only other occurrence in the New Testament is in Ac 5:15.

16:7, 10; 24:16–17; 33:18, 22, etc.). Both Luke and John stress that Jesus was abundantly blessed with God's grace (Lk 2:40, 52; Jn 1:14, 16, 17): 'grace' is a technical term which is never found in Matthew or Mark, and indeed nowhere in the gospels outside Lk 1–2 and Jn 1:1–18, though it is most common in the rest of the New Testament. This 'grace' which is the mark of the New Covenant is contrasted with the Law that came through Moses. Jn 1:17 makes the contrast explicit, but it is there implicitly in Luke: he portrays Zechariah and Elizabeth as righteous because they observed the Law, but presents Mary, by contrast, as endowed with grace freely given by God (Lk 1:16, 28, 30).

It is hard to believe that all these parallels between Luke and John are purely coincidental, particularly since they involve the very type of doctrinal concept on which the interest of the Church fastened during the second half of the first century. Their presence in two of the four gospels seems therefore to indicate that the two evangelists concerned are not here putting forward a purely personal estimate of Jesus, but are giving expression (at least to some extent) to beliefs held in the early Church. We shall return to this topic later[19] to see whether anything further can be deduced about the traditions common to Lk 1–2 and the Prologue of St John. For the moment it is sufficient to say that the substance of Luke's Infancy Gospel reflects traditions which were current somewhere in the Church at some time between A.D. 50 and A.D. 100. This accounts for the content of Lk 1–2, but it does not tell us *why* Luke chose to write this part of his gospel in a style so different from that which he uses elsewhere. To this problem we must now turn.

[19] See Chapter 14, pp. 147–8.

Chapter Two

THE LITERARY FORM OF THE LUCAN INFANCY GOSPEL

UNTIL modern times all Christians considered Lk 1–2 to be a trustworthy historical record of the events surrounding the birth and childhood of Jesus, and many prominent scholars of all Churches still hold this view. A later chapter will discuss this question at some length,[1] but a few preliminary remarks here at the beginning may assist the reader, for when modern theologians affirm that 'the Lucan Infancy Gospel is historical', the meaning attached to the term 'historical' is not quite what the non-theologian would expect. The term needs to be clearly defined if misunderstanding is to be avoided, and it will be convenient to set down a definition here.

It would be a mistake to infer (as the man-in-the-pew often does) that theologians who uphold the historicity of Lk 1–2 regard every detail narrated as a physical happening in the past. It would be quite wrong, for example, to regard the story of the Annunciation (Lk 1:26–38) as a verbatim report of a conversation between Mary and Gabriel, such as might have been taken down in shorthand by an observer or recorded on an electro-magnetic tape. It would be equally mistaken to think that Luke was trying to convey in words a general impression of what any third person (had one been present) might have seen or heard, for it is commonly admitted that God may reveal truths to men without there being any external phenomenon for an observer to see or to

---

[1] See Chapter 14, pp. 125–49.

hear.[2] It is necessary to restate these basic principles, for many Christians and many rationalists have in the past failed to observe them, and as a result their debates about the historical trustworthiness of Lk 1–2 have been off the real point. Opponents of Christianity have ridiculed the stories as no better than fairytales; more surprisingly, a large number of Christian scholars have, even in modern times, endeavoured to explain St Luke's narrative by treating it as if it were an account of an historical conversation between Mary and an angel. Both approaches rest on a false assumption. Theologians, when they say that the Lucan Infancy Gospel is historical, mean that it records events which really happened; but they do not thereby contend that the conversations narrated, or the imagery used, describe exactly how these events happened. They distinguish between the content (*i.e.* what the author meant to teach) and the literary form in which he presented his teaching.

How is this distinction between doctrinal content and literary presentation to be made? If Lk 1–2 cannot be regarded as history in the modern or Greco-Roman sense of the word, what kind of writing is it? Is it myth? Is it legend? How are we to discern the category of writing to which it belongs, and so be able to separate Luke's doctrinal content from its literary dress? Here another word of caution is required. Many modern writers think that Luke began with a doctrine which he wished to convey (*e.g.* that Jesus was the son of God); and they conclude that everything over and above this must be a literary dress for the doctrine (*e.g.* the story of the virginal conception is just a way of saying that Jesus had God for his father). Now one cannot start by presupposing that St Luke began with an abstract doctrine and then sought to express it in story; it may be that he did, but one cannot start by presuming that he did. Indeed, to approach the text with preconceived ideas of any kind is to run a very grave risk of misunderstanding what the author meant to say.

[2] See, *e.g.*, St Thomas Aquinas in the 2-2ae, qu. 173, a. 2. He certainly taught that Mary saw an angel in bodily form (3a, qu. 30, a. 3), but even there he does not say or imply that anyone else who had been present would have seen the angel or heard a voice.

In this context, it is worth quoting some words of Pope Pius XII, in his encyclical *Divino Afflante Spiritu*. 'Very frequently, the literal sense is not so obvious in the words and writings of ancient Eastern authors as it is in the writers of our own day. For *one cannot determine what they intended their words to mean* simply by applying the rules of grammar and philology, or *merely by looking at the content of a passage*.[3] It is absolutely indispensable for the interpreter to put himself back, mentally, into those far-off centuries in the Eastern world . . . in order to ascertain what literary forms writers chose to use, and did in fact employ, in those ancient days. For ancient Eastern writers did not always use the same forms and expressions as we use today in order to convey their ideas. Rather, they used those which were current among men of their own age and country; and what these were, the exegete cannot decide, as it were, *a priori*, but only by a careful study of ancient Eastern literature'.[4] St Luke was one of these writers, and therefore the literary form in which he cast his story can be determined only by examining the literary forms which writers of his own day, and of his cultural background, did in fact employ.[5] And in order to recognize these forms of literature, the reader must abstract from his own twentieth-century background and put himself, mentally, into the world in which the evangelist lived.

What literary form, then, did St Luke adopt in order to tell the story of the birth of Jesus? In the following chapters we shall see how Lk 1–2 is like a tapestry woven out of threads taken from the Old Testament. The threads are the various texts or ideas from the Old Testament which Luke weaves together in such a way as to produce a new pattern. Some of the ideas are quite obvious to anyone familiar with the Old Testament, while others are not so easily apparent to modern readers. For example, when the angel tells Mary that her son will inherit the throne of David, and will reign over the house of Jacob for ever (Lk 1:32–3), the

[3] My italics.

[4] *AAS* 35 (1943), pp. 314–15; in the English translation published by the Catholic Truth Society of London, §39.

[5] The argument still holds if Luke incorporated into his gospel an earlier document.

meaning is plain for all to see: her son will be the long-awaited 'son of David', the Messianic king. On the other hand, when the angel tells Mary that her kinswoman Elizabeth has conceived a child in her old age, and adds that 'Nothing is impossible for God' (Lk 1:37), relatively few modern readers will at once realize that the angel is quoting words from Gen 18:14, in which Sarah, the wife of Abraham, is informed that she will become a mother in spite of her advanced age. Yet once the allusion is pointed out, the parallel between Sarah and Elizabeth is evident. Examples could be multiplied, both of the obvious and of the more recondite parallels. Why did St Luke choose to write of the birth of Jesus in this particular way?

The answer to this question is that all four gospels 'were only occasional narratives, suggested by circumstances, and intended for the immediate use of particular persons'; they were not 'meant as historical records to convey to all future generations a faithful account of the actions and doctrines of our blessed Lord . . . [For] there is not in any of these works so much as a hint that the writers had in view the instruction of future generations, of men who were to exist many centuries afterwards, of men of different climes, and habits, and descent; there is nothing in them to warrant even a suspicion that they ever thought of any other readers than the converts of the day, the new Christians with whom they were more immediately connected'.[6] In short, Luke was writing for first-century Christians, and trying to answer their questions, not ours.

From the Pauline Epistles we know that many of the Christians in Rome, Corinth, Galatia and elsewhere were of Jewish stock; their mother-tongue was Greek, and they had been nurtured on the Greek Bible, the Septuagint. Once they had confessed Jesus as that Messiah for whom their people had waited, they re-read the Old Testament to see in ever closer detail how he had fulfilled the hopes of Israel. It was (at least partly) to this public that Luke addressed his work. He endeavoured to show them, often in the clumsy and archaic language of the Greek Bible they loved,

[6] [J. Lingard], *A New Version of the Four Gospels* . . . by a Catholic, London, 1836, pp. xvi–xvii.

how Jesus had fulfilled all the Old Testament prophecies about the Messiah, and had given to those prophecies a meaning deeper than their original authors had suspected.

The early Church set out to re-examine the message of the Old Testament in the light of Jesus' coming (*cf.* Lk 24:25–7, 32, 44–6), in order to uncover and to expound the deeper meaning which (it believed) lay hidden in the prophetical texts. Such searching of the Scriptures for hidden meanings was commonplace among the Jews of that time, and the technical name for an exposition of such hidden senses is a midrash. A midrash may therefore be defined as an interpretation and exposition of an Old Testament text which seeks to draw out the full import of that text by applying it to present circumstances and so discovering a message for the present which might not be obvious to the reader. Every midrash must start from the Old Testament scriptures, studied in the light of Israel's faith as a whole; but it does not correspond to scholarly, historical exegesis as practised in modern times, where the aim is to discover what the original author meant by what he wrote. On the contrary, its intention is above all homiletic, and its primary purpose is to bring home to ordinary people versed in the Scriptures the religious message of ancient texts by explaining those texts in the light of the circumstances of their own day.

A few examples will clarify the meaning of the term better than any definition, and will show how this type of writing has its origins in the Bible itself.[7] In Ez 16, the prophet describes in an allegory the history of Israel. Israel was like a newborn baby girl abandoned by her parents at birth (vv. 3–5); but then Yahweh passed by and adopted her as his own daughter (v. 6). When she grew up, Yahweh decked her out like a royal bride and made her renowned among the nations for her beauty (vv. 7–14). But then she became infatuated with her own beauty and gave herself to prostitution, flirting with the Egyptians and the Philistines and the Assyrians (vv. 15–34). Yahweh therefore determined to chasten her (vv. 35–43) as he had chastised her elder sister, the kingdom of

---

[7] The following pages are based on the article 'Midrash' by R. Bloch, in the *DBS* 5, cc. 1263–81.

Samaria, and her younger sister, the city of Sodom, neither of which had committed half the crimes committed by Judah (vv. 44–52). This, of course, is simply an allegory. Similar texts can be found in Is 60–2, where the prophet describes the New Jerusalem, and in the Song of Solomon, where the bride and bridegroom are clearly meant to typify Israel and Yahweh. These texts are not in the technical sense midrashim, but they are so many steps forward in the development of a certain kind of writing which was eventually to issue in the midrash.[8]

By the end of Old Testament times this development had reached perfection. As was to be expected, the symbolism became ever more sophisticated and complex, so that a close acquaintance with ancient biblical texts was often required in order to grasp all the subtle references, literary and doctrinal, in a midrashic exposition. The Book of Jesus, son of Sirach, commonly known as Ecclesiasticus, is a good illustration of this type of writing around the year 200 B.C. The author describes himself as 'a gleaner after the grape-gatherers', *i.e.* as one who has laboured to gather up aspects of biblical teaching which might otherwise have been left unnoticed.

> 'I was the last on watch,
>   like a gleaner after the grape-gatherers.
> By the blessing of the Lord I excelled,
>   and like a grape-gatherer I filled a wine-press.
> Know that I have not toiled for myself alone,
>   but for all who search for instruction' (Sir 33:16–17).

Two examples from this book will illustrate the author's method.

In chapter 24 Wisdom, personified, tells how she has dwelt in Israel throughout its history, especially through the presence of the divine law: the entire chapter is rich in allusions to earlier

[8] R. Bloch, 'Ecriture et tradition dans le judaïsme—Aperçus sur l'origine du midrash', in *Cahiers Sioniens* 8 (1954), pp. 9–34; *id.* 'Ezéchiel XVI: exemple parfait du procédé midrashique dans la Bible', in *Cahiers Sioniens* 9 (1955), pp. 193–223.

Old Testament writings. After two introductory verses Wisdom speaks and says:

'I came forth from the mouth of the Most High,
    and like a thick dark mist I enveloped the earth' (Sir 24:3),

where there is an evident allusion to Gen 1:2: 'Darkness covered the earth, and the spirit of God hovered over the waters'.

'I encamped in the high places,
    and my throne was in a pillar of cloud' (24:4).

The second half of this verse evidently refers to the cloud in which God led Israel out of Egypt (Ex 13:21–2), and the first half may therefore refer not directly to God's dwelling in the height of heaven, but to his presence on the summit of Sinai, from which he gave that Law which enshrined the Wisdom which gives life to men.

'I alone went round the circle of the sky,
    and walked round the depth of the abysses' (24:5).

Here the allusion is to Prov 8:27: 'When he made the firm foundations of the sky, I was there, when he traced a circle over the abyss . . .'. A few verses later we read:

'Then the Creator of the universe gave me a command,
    he who created me decreed that my tent should rest,
and said, "Pitch your tent in Jacob's land,
    and claim your inheritance in Israel"' (24:8).

Here the reference is probably to Ps 132:8, 13–14, or indeed to any texts in which the Ark of the Covenant is described as the focal centre of Israel's religion.

'Before time was, from eternity, he created me,
    and unto all eternity I shall exist' (24:9).

There is a clear allusion here to Prov 8:23, where Wisdom says: 'Before time was, he made me, in eternity'. And so the chapter continues, weaving together texts from Genesis and Proverbs, from the historical and prophetical books, to compose eventually a rounded picture of the biblical teaching about Wisdom. Job had asked where Wisdom was to be found (Job 28), and the son of Sirach answered that all Wisdom was to be found in the Book of the Covenant of the Most High God, in that Law which Moses gave to Israel, in the inheritance passed on in the synagogues of the Jews (Sir 24:23).

Authors differ considerably in their terminology, and many would refuse to classify Sir 24 as a midrash. Without entering into this debate, one may say that the techniques and procedures which were later to produce rabbinical midrashim are all present in Sir 24: whether this chapter be called a midrash or an anthology, it belongs within a stream of interpretation which may rightly and properly be termed midrashic. Sir 44:1–50:24 belongs to the same stream: there the author sings the praises of famous men from Enoch and Noah down to the high priest Simon II, son of Onias III, who lived around the year 200 B.C. and was therefore a contemporary of the author. On the basis of earlier books, the author gives seven chapters of Old Testament hagiography. The Book of Wisdom, too, written in Alexandria around the middle of the first century B.C., contains two splendid midrashim in chapters 10–12 and 16–19: the first explains God's manner of dealing with men from the creation to Israel's conquest of Canaan, and the second treats of the Exodus. These examples of midrashic writing are sufficient proof that such commentaries were not judged unworthy of a religious mind.

Between 200 B.C. and the beginning of the Christian era, midrashic exposition of the Old Testament became ever more common,[9] and whole books were written in this form. One of the

[9] During this period midrashim came to be described as 'midrash halakhah' or 'midrash haggadah', technical names which are still very much in use. The midrash halakhah is an exposition of the statutes of biblical law, and will not concern us in this book; the midrash haggadah embraces all that does not appertain to the law (see *The Jewish Encyclopaedia*, vol. 8, New York and London, 1904, p. 550b),

best-known is the Book of Jubilees, a work written (possibly by the Pharisees) in the second century B.C. 'The basic style of the book is midrashic, *i.e.* it takes the narrative from Gen 1 to Ex 14 [the first Passover], embellishes it with traditional lore, and infuses it with the spirit of late Judaism so that it is applicable to the author's time.'[10] One example will suffice to illustrate how the author fills out the biblical narrative with picturesque detail: here he openly adds to the biblical account a legend not preserved in the Bible. In describing Abram's departure from Ur (Gen 11:27-32), the author says that Abram tried to persuade his father Terah to abandon the worship of idols and to adore only the God of heaven: Terah confessed his faith in the Most High God, but, fearing that the people of Ur would kill him if he were to speak out against their paganism, asked Abram to leave matters there and not to denounce the gods of Ur. Abram, however, spoke to his brothers, but they would not listen; and then one night he himself set fire to the pagan temple. The people of Ur tried in vain to rescue their idols, and Abram's brother Haran was burnt to death in the attempt (*cf.* Gen 11:28: 'Haran died before his father Terah, in the land of his birth, in Ur of the Chaldees'). Terah then migrated with the rest of his family to Haran.[11] This is a representative example of midrashic exposition, and is cited here to show how the author does not shrink from inserting a popular story to help him put across the religious message of Genesis. This was a recognized procedure, and there are many other works of the

---

and it is with this type alone that we are concerned. Henceforward, when the term 'midrash' is used, the second type is always meant, the midrash haggadah (*i.e.* a study and exposition of the teaching in the Bible) and not midrash halakhah ('a study and exposition of the rules of conduct'). Some midrashim, of course, contain both types of exposition, when the biblical text itself contains both narrative and rules of conduct, as in the story of the Exodus (*cf. The Jewish Encyclopaedia*, vol. 8, pp. 554b-555a).

[10] R. E. Brown, 'Apocrypha', *The Jerome Biblical Commentary*, London, 1968, p. 539 = §68:20.

[11] The most accessible version of the Book of Jubilees is that printed in *The Apocrypha and Pseudepigrapha of the Old Testament in English*, edited by R. H. Charles, vol. 2, *Pseudepigrapha*, Oxford, 1913, pp. 1-82. The text summarized above is on pp. 30-1.

same kind: a number of previously unknown midrashim have been discovered at Qumran, but it would take too long to discuss them here.

Since the practice of midrashic commentary was so common, it is not surprising to find it in the New Testament. There is a fine example in Gal 4:21–31, where St Paul turns the biblical story about Abraham's two sons into an allegory relevant to the problem which was troubling the churches of Galatia: converts from Judaism to Christianity were insisting that circumcision and observance of the Jewish Law were essential for salvation. St Paul addressed himself to these Jews in a language and style they would understand. Consider, he said, the two women whom Abraham took to wife: one, Sarah, was a free woman, while the other, Hagar, was a slave. Hagar had a child, Ishmael, who was born in the ordinary course of nature, whereas Sarah's son, Isaac, was conceived only by the direct intervention of God. Now Hagar, from whom the Ishmaelites (an Arab tribe) were descended, at once puts us in mind of Mount Sinai, deep in the Arabian desert; her children, born in the course of nature, were also born to a life of slavery in that cruel desert. And in this, Paul adds, Hagar is a symbol of all who adhere to the Old Covenant of Sinai: they find life centred on Sinai a burden heavy as slavery. Sarah, on the other hand, was a free woman, whose son Isaac was born in defiance of nature, by the direct intervention of God: and Isaac's children inherited the Land of Promise. Sarah, there, is a symbol of the New Covenant established by Jesus Christ, in which men find favour with God not as a result of anything they themselves do, but by having faith that God fulfils his promises. Hagar and Sarah therefore stand for two types of covenant, one symbolizing Judaism, the other Christianity. And just as God commanded Abraham to banish Hagar and her son, and forbade him to allow Ishmael to share the inheritance with Isaac (Gen 21:10–12), so (St Paul says) the Christians of Galatia must not pretend that Judaism can share the inheritance which comes to us through Christ.

Another example of midrashic exposition is to be found in 1 Cor 10:1–13, where St Paul draws a moral lesson from the story of the Exodus. All those who left Egypt with Moses were protected by the cloud of the divine presence, and all passed safely through the sea: this can be compared with the baptism received by all Christians—they are overshadowed by the divine presence and brought to safety through the waters. In the desert, all the people without exception fed on the manna, a heavenly food, and (according to a rabbinical tradition) they were miraculously supplied with water from a rock which followed them across the desert (*cf.* Ex 17:5–6; Num 20:7–11): in the same way, all Christians are nourished in their earthly pilgrimage by the Holy Eucharist, and Christ himself continually travels by their side, alleviating their thirst for him. And yet, Paul warns, God was not pleased with most of the people whom he had freed from Egypt: only Caleb and Joshua lived to enter the Promised Land (Num 14:30). The whole story, St Paul concludes, is a warning to us (1 Cor 10:6) and was written down for our instruction (1 Cor 10:11): its message is that the gifts of faith and baptism, and even admittance to the table of the Lord, are not guarantees that, whatever our behaviour, we shall certainly attain eternal salvation.

Many other examples could be cited from outside the Bible and from the New Testament, but enough has been said to illustrate the essential point of midrashic exposition: it is essentially a homiletic exposition of an Old Testament text, as in Gal 4:21–31 or 1 Cor 10:1–13. Many of these midrashim contain popular stories and legends, like the story of Abraham's burning down the temple at Ur, or that of the water from the rock in 1 Cor 10. Unfortunately, the very frequency with which folklore is used has sometimes given rise to the erroneous notion that the word midrash denotes a legendary composition, a pious, popular and somewhat far-fetched story for which it would be foolish to seek a factual basis. Worse, the very charm of these popular tales has only strengthened this misapprehension. But it certainly will not do to label stories midrashim if all that is meant is that they are pious, far-fetched legends, for that is to miss the whole point of a midrash. The author of a midrash may use allegory and legend and fable as aid to a more lively presentation of his teaching, but such figures of speech are incidental, not essential, to his purpose. His writing must explore the significance of an Old Testament text, or it is not a midrash in any sense; but it need not contain any allegory, legend or fable.

What, then, is the literary form of Lk 1–2? It is an over-simplification to say (as many do) that it is a collection of Christian midrashim about the birth of the Saviour, unless the term be redefined, for it does not appear that Luke's primary concern was to expound the relevance of Old Testament texts for his own day. Yet the entire Infancy Gospel is so deeply penetrated by midrashic ways of thinking that it would be absurd to say, without quali-fication, that Lk 1–2 is not in any sense midrashic. It must be frankly confessed that there is no fixed technical term or sharply defined category which may serve as a label for the type of writing we find in the Infancy Gospel of Luke. What has happened is that the author of Lk 1–2 has stood midrashic exposition on its head: instead of looking to the past (an ancient text) and seeking to discover its lesson for the present, he looks at the present and seeks to express its full meaning by interpreting it in the light of the past (*i.e.* in the light of ancient texts and themes). Instead of an Old Testament text, he has taken as his starting-point the event of his own day—the birth of the Saviour—and then used midrashic procedure to illustrate the significance of this event. Thus he calls upon one Old Testament text after another to illuminate not a written text of the ancient Scriptures, but the living message of the Messiah's birth. 'We have here an example of the "Copernican revolution" which took place by the fact that from this moment God "has spoken to us by his son" (Heb 1:2). If the ancient midrashim "always kept Scripture as their fundamental point of reference . . . the earliest oral tradition and the gospels completely reversed the situation. The fundamental point of reference is Christ".'[12] But apart from this revolutionary alteration of the starting-point, from an Old Testament text to the event of Christ's coming, the literary procedure remained the same: parallel and

[12] R. Le Déaut, 'A propos d'une définition du midrash', in *Biblica* 50 (1969), p. 407. The second quotation within the citation ('always kept . . . Christ') is from C. Perrot, 'Les récits d'enfance dans la Haggada', in *RSR* 55 (1967), p. 515.

cognate texts were invoked, compared and combined (as in Sir 24, on Wisdom) in order to throw more light on the coming of Christ. Story and tradition, too, were pressed into service. There is no generally accepted name for this (Christian) 'searching of the Scriptures', but perhaps we could call it 'Christian midrash', provided that at least as much weight is attached to the adjective as to the noun. It was in this literary form that Luke (or someone before him) chose to describe the birth of Israel's Saviour.

Chapter Three

OLD TESTAMENT THEMES IN LUKE 1–2

LUKE's theme is Christ the Saviour: his aim is to show that Jesus by his coming has fulfilled at one stroke all the expectations of Israel. All the major themes of prophetic hope are therefore rehearsed in his Infancy Gospel, and it will facilitate the understanding of Lk 1–2 if some of the more frequently recurring themes are outlined once for all at the beginning.

There are many Old Testament texts which foretell the coming of an ideal king, a royal Messiah. The notion first appears when Nathan promises David that his dynasty will reign for ever (2 Sam 7), and Isaiah finds in this promise the certain guarantee of a glorious future for his people, even when Jerusalem is threatened by siege (Is 7:14), or when the Northern Kingdom is largely dominated by an Assyrian army of occupation (Is 9:1–6). This same confidence gave rise to those 'royal psalms' (*e.g.* Pss 2; 72; 89; 110) which sing of the permanence of David's line and which look forward to the day when an ideal monarch, a new David, will be born. Indeed, long after the house of David had ceased to reign in Jerusalem, the idea and the expectation lived on.

> 'An offspring will arise from the stump of Jesse,
>   and a flourishing branch will grow out of its roots,
>   and the Spirit of Yahweh will rest upon him . . .'
>
> (Is 11:1–2).

For a thousand years before the Christian era this dream of a new David lived on: in God's good time, he would restore the fortunes of Israel and bring its people peace. The thought is given forceful expression in the *Shemoneh Esreh* ('The Eighteen Benedictions'), the daily prayer of orthodox Jews from the fall of Jerusalem to the present day.

> 'And to Jerusalem, thy city, return in mercy,
> and dwell therein as thou hast spoken;
> rebuild it soon in our days as an everlasting building,
> and speedily set up therein the throne of David.
>
> Blessed art thou, O Lord,
> who rebuildest Jerusalem.
>
> Speedily cause the offspring of David, thy servant, to flourish,
> and let his horn be exalted by thy salvation,
> because we wait for thy salvation all the day.
>
> Blessed art thou, O Lord,
> who causest the horn of salvation to flourish.'[1]

The urgency of this plea shows the depth of the people's yearning, but never was this longing more intense than in those fateful years preceding the fall of Jerusalem in A.D. 70. It was around this time that St Luke began to write his gospel.

Luke's second theme is taken from those chapters of Daniel in which the prophet speaks of the coming of a new age, the age of 'the Son of Man' (Dan 7-12). The mere mention of the name Gabriel in Lk 1:19, 26 would be sufficient to alert a reader familiar with the Jewish Scriptures, for Gabriel's name occurs only twice in the Old Testament, in the second half of Daniel (Dan 8:16; 9:21): on both occasions his mission is to explain the import of a prophecy about the deliverance of Israel and the dawn of a new age. The close verbal similarities between Lk 1-2 and these chapters of Daniel leave no doubt that Luke is here consciously alluding to the Book of Daniel. In Lk 1:10, as in Dan 9:21,

---

[1] The translation is taken from *The Authorized Daily Prayer Book of the United Hebrew Congregations of the British Empire*, with a new translation by the late Rev. S. Singer, London, 12th ed., 1924, p. 49.

Gabriel appears at the hour of sacrifice. In Lk 1:12, we read that Zechariah 'was frightened when he saw [the angel], and fear fell upon him'; in Dan 10:7 the text runs, 'Only I, Daniel, saw this great vision ... but a terrible fear fell upon' the men who were with him. Again, in Lk 1:19, Gabriel identifies himself in the words 'I am Gabriel who stand before God, and I have been sent to speak to you'; in Dan 9:20-2, Gabriel is once more standing before God and comes out to inform the prophet of God's decree. The angel's opening greeting is almost identical: 'Zechariah, do not fear—your petition is heard'—'Daniel, do not fear—your word is heard' (Lk 1:13; Dan 10:12). Both Daniel and Zechariah are struck dumb, and when they recover the power of speech, it is said of each that 'he opened his mouth, and spoke', and that fear fell upon the listeners (Dan 10:16-17; Lk 1:64-5).[2]

Some writers even see in Luke a reference to Gabriel's prophecy that after Seventy Weeks deliverance would come to Israel (Dan 9:24-7).[3] Six months separate Gabriel's appearance to Zechariah from the Annunciation to Mary (Lk 1:26, 36), *i.e.* in biblical usage, 180 days. From Mary's conception to the birth of Jesus will be nine months, or 270 days; and from the birth of Jesus to the Presentation in the Temple will be 40 days (Lev 12:3). The total number of days, therefore, between Gabriel's first appearance and the entry of Jesus into the Temple will be 180 + 270 + 40, or 490 days, *i.e.* seventy weeks. The only flaw in this neat and ingenious calculation is that Lk 1:24 says that 'Elizabeth hid herself for five months', not six, and that the Annunciation to Mary took place *during* the sixth month after John's conception, not at the end of that month (Lk 1:26, 36): thus the figure 180 cannot stand, and the total period will therefore be somewhat less than 490 days. But the objection is not unanswerable. John's conception must have taken place some days after the angel's appearance to Zechariah, for we are told that Zechariah remained at the Temple until the rota of priests was changed (Lk 1:23), and during this period he could not have had intercourse with his wife, as that would have

[2] See R. Laurentin, *Structure et théologie de Luc I–II*, Paris, 1957, pp. 45-7.

[3] *E.g.* E. Burrows, *The Gospel of the Infancy and other Biblical Essays*, pp. 41-2; R. Laurentin, *Structure et théologie de Luc I–II*, pp. 48-56.

entailed ritual impurity (Lev 15:16). Thus a few days ought to be added between the apparition in the Temple and the conception of the Baptist, and the suggested reference to Daniel's Seventy Weeks can therefore stand. Certainly one cannot positively exclude the idea that Luke had it in mind, for at each of the significant stages in the history of the infancy we find the same refrain:

'*When the days* of his liturgical service *were fulfilled*' (1:23);
'*The days* for her to give birth *were fulfilled*' (2:6);
'*When eight days were fulfilled* for him to be circumcised' (2:21);
'*When the days* for them to be purified *were fulfilled*' (2:22).

Thus, even though Luke does not commit himself to an arithmetically exact reckoning of 490 days (the inexactitude would hardly have worried him or his contemporaries), he may well have had the symbolic import of this period of waiting in mind. In that case, the refrain just mentioned and the other references to the passage of time would have been intended to fix the reader's attention on the passing of the Seventy Weeks from Gabriel's first apparition, and to remind him continually that in only Seventy Weeks a climax would be reached. This brings us to the third theme.

The royal Messiah and the age of the Son of Man are the first two themes. The third is taken from the Book of Malachi, in which an anonymous writer of the fifth century B.C. urges a moral reform of the Levitical priesthood and of its worship 'before the great and terrible Day of Yahweh comes' (Mal 3:23 = 4:5). Malachi asks the priests of his own day to look back at the example of their predecessor Levi, who 'walked with me and turned many from unrighteousness' (Mal 2:6: Septuagint), and asserts that Yahweh, having sent a messenger before him to prepare his way, will all of a sudden come to his Temple (Mal 3:1). The book closes with a cryptic clue to the identity of the mysterious messenger: he will be Elijah the Thesbite, who will reconcile fathers and sons (Mal 3:23 = 4:5). This reference to Elijah's return before 'the great and terrible Day of Yahweh' stayed prominent in the Jewish mind as one of the principal signs which would herald the imminence of that day.[4]

In the Synoptic Gospels it is taken for granted that the prophet had to return before the Messiah came (Mk 9:11; Mt 17:10, etc.). So widespread and so deep-rooted was this conviction that, according to St Mark, the disciples themselves found it hard to understand Jesus' reference to the resurrection of the Son of Man because 'the scribes said that Elijah had to come' before there could be any resurrection (Mk 9:11).[5] Elijah, of course, would not be the Messiah, for he was not of the line of David; he would be only the forerunner of the Messiah (Mk 9:11 and parallel texts). His task would consist in restoring all things (Mk 9:12 and parallels) by preaching penance and conversion to Israel (Sir 48:10 and Apoc 11:3). Priests and Levites wondered whether the Baptist might not be Elijah (Jn 1:21, 25), and some Galileans thought that Jesus must be Elijah returned to earth (Mk 6:15 = Lk 9:8; Mt 16:14 = Mk 8:28 = Lk 9:19), for no other man had ever worked such astounding miracles (Lk 9:7 f.). Against the background of this expectation, it was clear to St Luke that if he wished to portray Jesus as the expected Messiah, he would do well to show that Malachi's prophecy about Elijah had been fulfilled. He does this by presenting the Baptist as the forerunner of Jesus, the new Elijah summoning God's people to repentance. He makes the Baptist the forerunner of Jesus not only in his preaching but also in his birth, and then goes on to show the fulfilment of the other part of Malachi's prophecy, by making the Presentation of Jesus the climax of his Infancy Gospel. For Luke, the day of the Presentation was the Day of Yahweh, when the Lord came into his Temple.

If Luke was seeking to describe the birth of Jesus as the coming of a new and glorious era, his fourth theme was inevitable. From the days of Amos, eight centuries earlier, an ever louder note of warning had been sounded by the Old Testament prophets: generation after generation they proclaimed more urgently that many, indeed most, Israelites would not live to enjoy the day of

[4] *Cf.* J. Jeremias in the *TWNT* 2, pp. 930–5.
[5] *Ibid.*, p. 938.

deliverance—only a remnant would be saved (Am 3:12; 5:15; 9:8–12; Is 4:2–3; 6:13; 10:19–20, etc.). Zephaniah indicated that this remnant would not be found among the rich and powerful, but among the poor and the lowly (Zeph 2:3; 3:11–13). After the exile, this belief became an integral part of the Jewish faith (Is 49:13; 66:2; Ps 22:25, 27; 34:3 ff.; 37:11 ff.; 69:33-4, etc.), and its truth was vindicated during the persecution under Antiochus Epiphanes. The Books of Maccabees tell how the upper classes readily apostatized for the sake of worldly advantage (1 Mac 1:11–15), while the poor remained staunch in the faith of their fathers (1 Mac 1:54–64; 2, etc.). In the minds of the prophets, as in history, there were two Israels: one embraced all the people without exception—the ethnic group—while the other, 'the true Israel of God', was restricted to that remnant of the race who were destined for salvation. St Luke, whose gospel abounds with compassion and love for the poor, could not fail to see that salvation had come, not to the great ones among the people, but only to those who were humble enough to accept it as an undeserved gift from God.

This brings us to a fifth Old Testament motif which may have been in the mind of St Luke when he prefaced his gospel with these two chapters: the theme of 'the Daughter of Zion'. I say 'may have been' because there is considerable dispute whether he did have this idea in mind; in order to judge this, it is essential to have a clear notion of what the Old Testament means by the phrase 'Daughter of Zion'.

Zion is popularly taken to be just another name for Jerusalem, but a careful examination of its use in the Old Testament reveals that this view is an oversimplification. Originally, Zion was the name of the south-eastern hill on which the Jebusite city stood before David's conquest (2 Sam 5:7; 1 Kgs 8:1; 1 Chr 11:5; 2 Chr 5:2), by contrast with Ophel, the north-eastern hill upon which Solomon's Temple would later be built. After David's time, as far as one can judge from the Bible, the 'Old Town' of Jerusalem on the south-eastern hill (i.e. the city of Zion) became more commonly known as 'The City of David' (2 Sam 5:7, 9; 1 Kgs 3:1; 8:1; 9:24; 11:27; Is 22:9; Neh 12:37), and the name

Zion seems to have fallen into disuse until around 750 B.C. Then it reappeared, though with a slightly different meaning: it was no longer used in its earlier topographical sense, but was restricted to poetry and used there to denote either the whole city or the (northern) Temple hill, with some very interesting nuances.[6]

In the pre-exilic prophets, Zion often stands for Jerusalem considered as the residence of the king and the political capital of the country (*e.g.* Am 6:1; Mic 3:10, 12 = Jer 26:18; Is 16:1; *cf.* Ps 110:2, etc.). When it is so considered, it often has the sense 'sinful city', and is harshly judged by the prophets (*e.g.* Is 1:21–7). At the same time, however, between 750 B.C. and the exile, the word had another connotation. The term Zion was used to denote Jerusalem as the site of Yahweh's presence on earth, because the Ark of the Covenant was housed there (Am 1:2; Mic 4:2 = Is 2:3; Is 8:18; 31:9; *cf.* Ps 20:3; 74:2, etc.). Thus it denoted also Jerusalem considered as 'the holy city', and indeed it is fair to say that the word Zion usually means Jerusalem considered as the religious capital of the nation. There is no conflict here with the idea of Zion as the residence of the king of Judah (*i.e.* with Zion as denoting the political capital), for Judah regarded itself as a theocracy. Under the monarchy, the king was regarded as Yahweh's viceroy on earth, and it was thought only fitting that he should live next door to the Temple.[7] Nor was there any contradiction in the minds of the prophets between the idea of Zion as the city where Yahweh dwelt, and Zion as a city corrupt with sin. On the contrary, precisely because Zion was held to be Yahweh's home, it could all too easily be defiled, and its guilt would be the greater, as the context often indicates (*e.g.* Is 1:21–7). It is against this background that we must examine the meaning of the term 'Daughter of Zion'.

It is in the prophecy of Micah of Moresheth that we first meet the expression 'Daughter of Zion'. M. Henri Cazelles has suggested that the phrase 'daughter of . . .' (applied to a town) originated in Transjordan, passed from there to the Northern

[6] *Cf.* G. Fohrer in the *TWNT* 7, pp. 292–4.

[7] *Cf.* R. de Vaux, *Ancient Israel: Its Life and Institutions*, London, 1961, pp. 316–17 and 320.

Kingdom, and from the north to Judah, when the refugees from Samaria flocked south after 721 B.C.[8] He further suggests that in Micah the term 'Daughter of Zion' denotes the new quarter of Jerusalem, north and north-west of the Temple, where these refugees were lodged close to the city wall, near the gate. This makes good sense of Mic 1:9, where the prophet, referring to the downfall of Samaria, writes:

> 'Her wound is incurable,
>   and it has come to Judah,
> it has reached to the gate of my people,
>   to Jerusalem.'

This new quarter of the city (north of the Temple) was an area quite distinct from, but totally dependent on, the old city (south and south-west of the Temple). This new quarter was, in northern parlance, a true 'Daughter of Zion', for (it will be remembered) at this time the name Zion denoted not the southern hill (the city of David), but the Temple hill. It is very likely that Hezekiah built a new, outer wall, to enclose and protect this extension of the city, for in 2 Chr 32:5 we read that he not only repaired the old wall of Jerusalem, but built another wall outside it. This would make good sense of the obscure text in Mic 5:1 (=4:14), which is perhaps an Assyrian taunt to the refugees: 'Now you are walled about with a wall!' It was probably a poor fortification, for in the time of Manasseh (687–42) it had to be rebuilt and raised in height (2 Chr 33:14), but it was better than nothing.[9] In this

[8] See Detached Note II: 'The Phrase "Daughter of Zion" in the Old Testament.' Nearly everything in the following paragraphs is taken from Cazelles, and the evidence for many of the statements made must be sought in this Detached Note.

[9] Cazelles does not say that such a wall was built around the new quarter, the 'Daughter of Zion', but refers the reader to the map of Jerusalem in Old Testament times at the end of *The Jerusalem Bible*. The area occupied was, he says, that which lies south of the Fish Gate and the Sheep Gate.

But Cazelles's argument is strengthened if such a wall was built by Hezekiah, as L.-H. Vincent held: 'Au Nord une muraille avancée couvrait le quartier neuf' (*Jérusalem de l'Ancien Testament* II–III, Paris, 1956, p. 647; *cf.* also p. 635 and Plate CXXIX).

new quarter north of the Temple, the remnants of Israel, 'driven from home, cast off by God, lame from their journey, sorely afflicted' (see Mic 4:6–7) awaited some form of deliverance. And it was to this group huddled in a corner of the city that Micah addressed his message of comfort and hope. If this interpretation is justified, then in Micah the phrase 'Daughter of Zion' stands not for the whole of God's people, but only for this last remnant of the Northern Kingdom, destitute refugees for whom all earthly hope was lost and whose only refuge was in God. Such was the origin of the expression 'Daughter of Zion'.

This interpretation also throws light on the prophecy of Zephaniah, written between 640 and 630 B.C. Zephaniah denounces the pro-Assyrian officials who rule Jerusalem (1:8) and oppress the poor (3:1–4), foretelling that for them the day of the Lord will be a day of wrath (1:12–15). But to the poor who lived in the new quarter of Jerusalem, 'the Second Quarter, near the Fish Gate', in slums where the mortar had not been allowed to set properly (1:10–11), he announces a message of hope. The day of the Canaanite traders and money-lenders is over (1:11), but the poor will be saved.

> 'Seek Yahweh, all you humble of the land,
>   who do his commands;
> seek righteousness, seek humility,
>   perhaps you may be hidden
>   on the day of Yahweh's wrath!' (2:3).

Later, after another promise that God will remove from the city the proud men who oppress it (3:11), there comes the verse:

> 'I will leave in the midst of you
>   a people humble and lowly' (3:12),

and the final message is addressed by name to the Daughter of Zion.

> 'Sing aloud, O Daughter of Zion!
>   Shout for joy, O Israel!

Rejoice and exult with all thy heart,
  O Daughter of Jerusalem!
Yahweh has annulled the judgments against thee,
  he has cast out thy enemies!
The King of Israel, Yahweh, is in thy midst,
  thou shalt fear evil no more!' (3:14-15).

Zephaniah's book is easily recognized as a message of comfort to the poor; but the whole prophecy comes to life and takes on a new dimension if these poor are considered as immigrants of northern origin, still enclosed after ninety years in an economic ghetto in the 'Second Quarter' of Jerusalem.

Whether Cazelles's exceedingly precise location and identification of the 'Daughter of Zion' be justified or not, it is a verifiable fact that in certain texts (*e.g.* Is 1:8 and especially Lam 1:6; 2:1, etc.) the phrase is virtually a synonym for Jerusalem. This does not invalidate Cazelles's thesis that the term first denoted the 'New Quarter' beside the Temple; for just as the word Zion was used by synecdoche for the entire city, so the phrase 'Daughter of Zion' could have been applied to the whole city and its population. In fact, it seems that the term became at the exile a sacral name for Jerusalem, because Zion was already a sacral name, and the 'Daughter of Zion' denoted that quarter of the city which stood closest to the Temple.

Cazelles's theory does, however, bring right in front of our eyes a truth which is too often overlooked, namely, that the expression 'Daughter of Zion' is closely (and perhaps intrinsically) linked with the notion of the remnant and of the poor. It reminds us too that the term is connected with the thought of the restoration of Israel (*cf.* Mic 4:8: 'the former dominion shall return to thee'): this thought dominates Mic 4-5, where the main references to the Daughter of Zion are found,[10] and this same theme was very much in the mind of St Luke, writing his gospel after the fall of Jerusalem in A.D. 70 (Lk 24:21; Ac 1:6). But above all, the expression must certainly be linked with the

[10] For a short discussion of these very obscure chapters see the Detached Note on the 'Daughter of Zion', pp. 439-42.

33

post-exilic theme of Zion as the mother of a new people (Is 54:1; 66:6–10, etc.).

This last theme is perhaps the most important of all, for it is as good as certain that Luke knew nothing of the pre-exilic use of the term 'Daughter of Zion' to denote a particular quarter of the city of Jerusalem. But he did know that the prophets had used the term as a sacral synonym for the poor, the righteous, the remnant, among the people of God. The historical and topographical connotation of the term was submerged after the exile in the deeper, religious meaning. 'Daughter of Zion' and 'Zion' became interchangeable words, and the ancient prophecies were read as foretelling an era of redemption for the lowly among the people (*cf.* Zech 9:9–10). At the same time, the concept of Zion as mother was developed. At first, it was as mother of a new Israel (Is 54:1; 66:6–10), but later, as the idea of the universality of God's salvation took hold of Israel, men began to think of Zion as mother of all the nations of the world. This idea reaches its climax in Ps 88, which is rightly entitled 'Zion as mother of all the nations'. It was this fully developed concept of Zion as mother of the world that Luke took over, but the ancient prophecies attached to the Daughter of Zion were a constant reminder that it was not the earthly, physical Zion which would be mother of the nations. It was to the lowly, the righteous, the remnant, that salvation would come; and from them, 'the true Israel of God', that redemption would come to the nations. The two great ideas of Luke, the universality of salvation and love for the lowly, are both contained in this symbol of the 'Daughter of Zion'. The themes of the Day of Yahweh and the salvation of a remnant are also intrinsically linked with the promise of salvation for the Daughter of Zion. Hence when we wish to speak of the salvation that comes to the poor and the remnant on the day of the Lord's coming, it will be convenient to speak of the coming of salvation to the eschatological Daughter of Zion, that is, to those who faithfully await the Lord on the day of his coming.

These, then, are the five main themes which go into the making of the Lucan Infancy Gospel: everlasting kingship in the dynasty of David, the age of the Son of Man, the Day of Yahweh's coming to his Temple, the salvation of a remnant of Israel, and the coming of redemption to the Daughter of Zion. There are many connections between these ideas even in the Old Testament, but there are many more in the New. Perhaps one may compare the first two chapters of Luke to an intricately-woven tapestry, in which these five themes are the weft and warp, each so intertwined with the others that to take out one of the threads would destroy the pattern and undo the fabric. Sometimes one idea, sometimes another, is visible on the surface; but though each thread may disappear from sight for a few verses, it is only to reemerge and so to preserve the pattern. Sometimes a double strand of two ideas combined runs through the narrative for a while, lending greater strength to the fabric and richer colour to the design. And sometimes, like an artist who wishes to introduce variety of illustration into his overall pattern, St Luke uses other Old Testament threads or colours in addition to those mentioned, to enliven certain parts of his work. Zechariah and Elizabeth, for example, are presented as a new Abraham and a new Sarah;[11] the Annunciation to Mary has many close affinities with the apparition to Gideon;[12] and there is a parallel, too, between Hannah, the mother of Samuel, and Mary, the mother of Jesus, which is certainly intentional.[13] There are many other allusions besides, which no Jewish reader of the stories could have failed to perceive, and which have serious doctrinal significance; they will be indicated later in the relevant places. For the present, it is sufficient to note that Luke does not restrict himself to the five leading themes to which attention has been drawn in this chapter. He works into his tapestry many other, shorter, threads, each of which lends new colour and further variety to the finished design.

The guiding thought in St Luke's mind was the conviction that

[11] Both couples are aged and childless (compare Lk 1:7 with Gen 11:30; 18:11); both fathers are told by God that they are to have a son (compare Lk 1:13 with Gen 17:16, 19); both Zechariah and Abraham are inclined to be incredulous (compare Lk 1:18 with Gen 17:17; 15:8).

[12] See J.-P. Audet, 'L'Annonce à Marie', in the *RB* 63 (1956), pp. 346–74.

[13] Compare 1 Sam 1:25 with Lk 2:22; 1 Sam 2:11 with Lk 2:39; 1 Sam 2:26 and 3:19 with Lk 2:52. The principal parallel lies, of course, in the themes of the Magnificat (see below, Chapter 9, pp. 73–9).

Jesus, the son of Mary, was also the son of God, whose coming had fulfilled the expectation of Israel. Luke therefore re-read his Old Testament and reassessed those expectations in the light of his Christian faith; and in his Infancy Gospel, he endeavoured to show his readers how all the Old Testament had pointed forward to the son of Mary in a way that previous generations could never have suspected (*cf.* Lk 24:27, 32). He selected events in the infancy of Jesus and chose his phrases in order to illustrate the great themes of Messianic hope: thus he stresses that the coming of Jesus had been prepared by God (2:31), and that it was the fulfilment of the divine promises to Abraham (1:55, 73) and the prophets (1:70). The whole Infancy Gospel is a Christian meditation on the birth of Jesus, in which the author expounds in quasi-midrashic form the message for which all Israel had waited so long: 'Today there is born to you a Saviour who is Messiah and Lord!' (2:11).

Chapter Four

'REJOICE, O DAUGHTER OF ZION!'

(Lk 1:28–30)

'WHEN the fullness of time came, God sent his son, born of a woman, born under a law, that he might redeem those who were under law, that we might receive adoptive sonship' (Gal 4:4). St Luke, like St Paul, saw the history of Israel as a long preparation for the day when the Son of God would take flesh from a woman, to redeem mankind from sin and to inaugurate a new covenant of grace (see Lk 2:29–32, etc.). But Israel was not meant to be an inert recipient of redeeming grace; it was to co-operate, at least by the willing acceptance of grace, in the work of the world's redemption. In particular, a Messiah was to come from the line of David; and therefore he had to be born of a Jewish mother, born under the Law. In Mary of Nazareth we find that daughter of Israel who was chosen to be the mother of the Messianic king.

Gabriel's first words to Mary are χαῖρε κεχαριτωμένη (Lk 1:28). Before 1939, nearly all writers took the word χαῖρε to be simply an everyday greeting, devoid of doctrinal significance, the Greek equivalent of the Hebrew *shalôm* or the Aramaic *shelam* ('Peace!'). Even Lagrange, who was so sensitive to Semitic usage in the gospels, is content to notice that there is alliteration, to observe that the turn of phrase is 'utterly Greek', and then to pass on to the next word.[1] The arguments in favour of this view are easily discerned: both in classical and in Hellenistic Greek χαῖρε is most commonly an everyday greeting, and it is found with this sense

[1] *Evangile selon s. Luc*, 7th ed., Paris, 1948, p. 28.

37

in the gospels;[2] the Latin translators took it to be an everyday greeting when they rendered it as '*Ave*', and most modern-language versions have done the same (as in the English 'Hail!').

In 1939 Père Stanislas Lyonnet S.J. published an article in which he challenged this rendering.[3] He began by pointing out that there are serious objections to the classical interpretation. On two other occasions where Luke wishes to express a greeting against a Semitic background, he employs the customary Semitic term 'Peace!': thus in Lk 10:5 the disciples are told to say 'Peace to this house!', and in 24:36 the risen Lord greets the Eleven with 'Peace to you!'.[4] Indeed, if we set aside 1:28, it is true to say that no-where in the gospel does Luke use χαῖρε as a greeting.[5] There are two places in Acts where the word is so used, but on each occasion Luke is quoting the text of a letter written to Greek-speaking persons (from the elders in Jerusalem to the Church at Antioch, Ac 15:23, and from Claudius Lysias to Felix, Ac 23:26). Now if Luke's only concern in 1:28 was to express a conventional greeting from Gabriel to Mary, why did he choose to write this greeting in the Greek, not the Semitic, form? Why did Luke not write 'Peace unto thee!', since he was so visibly striving to imitate a Semitic style and to imprint on the reader's mind a lively picture of a thoroughly Jewish world?

The suspicion that Gabriel's first word is not to be taken as a purely conventional greeting grows stronger when we consider the Septuagint usage of this word. In the books translated from the Hebrew, this imperative is never once found as the equivalent of the ordinary, everyday greeting *shalôm*: *shalôm* as a greeting is invariably rendered into Greek by the literal translation meaning 'Peace!' In these same books (*i.e.* those translated from the Hebrew,

---

[2] Thus Judas to Jesus in Mt 26:49, and Jesus to the women at the tomb in Mt 28:9.

[3] *Biblica* 20 (1939), pp. 131–41.

[4] There is some doubt on textual grounds about the presence of the greeting in Lk 24:36.

[5] It is interesting to note that Luke is the only one of the four evangelists who does not cite the phrase 'Hail, king of the Jews!' (Mt 27:29 = Mk 15:18 = Jn 19:3); but it is not significant, since (apart from an indirect reference to the scourging in 23:22) he omits the whole episode.

as distinct from those originally written in Greek), the imperative form χαῖρε, far from being a conventional greeting, always refers to the joy attendant on the deliverance of Israel; wherever it occurs, it is a translation of a Hebrew verb meaning 'Rejoice greatly!' It is therefore worth investigating whether this meaning ('Rejoice, for the day of salvation is here!') does not supply a more satisfactory interpretation of Gabriel's words to Mary in Lk 1:28 than is given by the customary rendering 'Hail!'.

We may begin by looking at the word in general. The verb χαίρω is found about eighty times in the Septuagint. About half the instances occur in those books which, like Tobit and Maccabees, were first written in Greek, and here (naturally enough) the verb is often used as a purely conventional greeting (e.g. 1 Mac 10:18, 25; 11:30, 32). These texts are not particularly informative to us. The other occurrences, in the books translated from the Hebrew, are of greater interest, for in about half of these texts (i.e. about twenty), the verb refers to the joy of the people as a whole at some striking act done by God for their salvation.[6]

Thus when Aaron, before approaching Pharaoh, worked miracles to persuade the people of his divine mission, 'the people were convinced and *rejoiced*[7] that Yahweh had visited the sons of Israel and had seen their misery' (Ex 4:31).[8] Jonathan said of David that 'he had taken his life in his hands when he killed the foreigner' (that is, the Philistine), 'and Yahweh performed a signal act of salvation, and all Israel saw it and *rejoiced*' (1 Sam 19:5). Hiram, when he was told of the plan to build a temple, '*rejoiced* and said, Blessed be God today, who has given David a wise son to rule over this great people' (1 Kgs 5:21); and after the consecration of the Temple, the people 'went off each to his own home *rejoicing* and of good heart because of all the good

[6] In the other half, the verb means simply 'to be glad': thus Pharaoh was glad when Jacob came to join Joseph in Egypt (Gen 46:16), and Aaron was glad to see Moses (Ex 4:14).

[7] In the following paragraphs, the verb *to rejoice* in italics translates the Greek χαίρειν.

[8] This and all the following texts are translated from the Septuagint, but for the sake of simplicity the names of the biblical books have been kept in their usual English forms.

things Yahweh had done for David his servant and for Israel his people' (I Kgs 8:66). In the mind of the historian of Israel, the consecration of Solomon's Temple was an act of God ensuring the permanent safety ('salvation') of Israel. The only other references in the books of Samuel and Kings record the rejoicing of the people at the death of Athaliah, for the end of her usurpation meant the restoration of David's true heir (2 Kgs 11:14, 20).

Some of the prophetical texts are extremely forceful. Is 13:3 describes how, at the fall of Babylon, 'strong men will come to accomplish my wrath, *rejoicing* and proudly triumphant'. In the famous oracle 'Go forth from Babylon', the Hebrew text 'there is no peace for the wicked' is rendered by the Septuagint as 'There is no *rejoicing* (χαίρειν) for the wicked' (Is 48:22); the same Hebrew text is rendered in the same way in the oracle which proclaims peace to those who are far off, and peace to those who are near (Is 57:21). But it is in the vision of the New Jerusalem that we find the most emphatic use of this verb:

> 'Be glad, Jerusalem,
>   and gather together within her,
>   all you that love her;
> *rejoice with joy* (χάρητε χαρᾷ)
>   all you that grieve over her . . .
> You will see,
>   and your heart *will rejoice*' (Is 66:10, 14).

There is no need to labour the point: other references in the prophets to the rejoicing of Israel at its salvation may be found in Jer 31:13 (= 38:13 in the Septuagint); Bar 4:37; Hab 3:18; Zech 4:10; 10:7, etc.

Three texts, however, are of peculiar interest, for in them we find the present imperative χαῖρε (Zeph 3:14; Joel 2:21; Zech 9:9),[9] and it could not be clearer that in these contexts the refer-

[9] The only other examples of this imperative are in Lam 4:21, where it is used ironically ('Rejoice and be glad, O Daughter of Edom, now dwelling in the land, for the cup of the Lord will most certainly come upon you . . .'); in Tob 7:1, where in the Codex Sinaiticus the plural occurs as a greeting; and in Prov 24:19 and Hos 9:1, where there is a negative, 'Do not rejoice'.

ence is to the rejoicing which accompanies the deliverance of Israel. What is of particular interest is that in each of these three texts Israel is either named or thought of as 'the Daughter of Zion' and as a mother. The texts in Joel and Zechariah are in all probability modelled on that of Zephaniah, which is the most ancient of the three. The Greek text and context of Zephaniah may be translated as follows:

14a   '*Rejoice*, O Daughter of Zion!
  b   Cry aloud, O Daughter of Jerusalem!
  c   Be glad, and be delighted with all thy heart,
  d   O Daughter of Jerusalem!
15a   The Lord has taken away thy wrong-doings,
  b   he has redeemed thee from the hand of thy enemies!
  c   The king of Israel is Lord in the midst of thee,[10]
  d   thou shalt no longer see evil.
16a   *At that time the Lord will say to Jerusalem:*
  b   Take heart,[11] Zion,
  c   do not let thy hands grow feeble!
17a   The Lord thy God is within thee,
  b   a Mighty One will save thee!
  c   He will bring thee gladness,
  d   and will renew thee in his affection,
  e   and he will be glad over thee
  f   with joy as on a feast day!'

The passage falls very clearly into two strophes (14–15 and 16b–17), each consisting of eight members, separated by 16a. Both begin with a call to rejoice (14a, 16b); both give as the reason for rejoicing the fact that 'the Lord is within thee' (15c, 17a) as 'king of Israel' (15c) and saviour (17b). Here, then, are two short poems in which the prophet envisages the day of salvation as already begun, and calls upon the Daughter of Zion to rejoice with all her heart, not to fear, because the Lord is with her, as her king and saviour. This is exactly the message of the angel in Lk 1:28–

---

[10] *Or*: 'The king of Israel, the Lord, is in the midst of thee.'
[11] The Hebrew reads: 'Do not fear.'

33: Luke envisages the two Annunciations as the dawning of the day of salvation (Lk 1:77–9), and Gabriel therefore tells Mary to rejoice, not to fear, because the Lord is with her, and because she will bear within her womb a son who will be the king of Israel and its saviour.

The texts of Joel and of Zechariah carry the same message in almost the same phrases. The passage in Joel 2 runs:

> 21a   'Take heart,[12] O land,
> b   *rejoice* and be glad,
> c   for the Lord has done great things . . .
> 23a   And you children of Zion
> b   *rejoice* and be glad in the Lord your God.'

Though Joel (unlike Zephaniah) does not explicitly name the 'Daughter of Zion', he does speak of 'the children of Zion', so that Israel is still considered as a mother rejoicing at her salvation.[13]

Zechariah 9:9 is very close in wording to the text from Zephaniah:

> 9a   '*Rejoice* greatly, O Daughter of Zion!
> b   Cry aloud, O Daughter of Jerusalem!
> c   Behold, thy king is coming to thee—
> d   a Righteous One and a Saviour, he!
> e   He is meek, and mounted on a beast of burden,
> f   upon a new-born foal.'

Here again 'the Daughter of Zion' is told to rejoice at the coming of her king and saviour. The last two lines of this verse were applied to Jesus by the early Church (Mt 21:5; Jn 12:15), and the verse which follows in Zechariah (9:10) recalls the classic theme

---

[12] In the Hebrew, 'Do not fear.'

[13] In the Hebrew, the verbs of verse 21*ab* are in the feminine, but the reason is that the noun 'land' is feminine: 23*a*, however, shows that the land is thought of as the mother of the people. The 'salvation' in this context is salvation from drought and pests.

of the peaceful reign of the Messiah, so that it is safe to infer that the entire context of Zech 9:9–10 was familiar to the early Christians.

Therefore, with the exception of Lam 4:21,[14] the imperative χαῖρε in the Greek Old Testament is always addressed to 'the Daughter of Zion', and is always an invitation to 'rejoice greatly' because 'the Lord is with her' as king and saviour. This use of the imperative harmonizes perfectly with what we know of the general usage of the verb: all the most impressive and memorable texts containing this verb use it to signify the joy that comes to the whole people of Israel when God actively intervenes to deliver them from distress and to bring them salvation.

Lyonnet concludes that Gabriel's greeting to Mary should therefore be translated not as 'Hail!', but as 'Rejoice!' This is the only rendering which does justice to the Old Testament background and language of the context; and it gives Gabriel the dramatic opening we should have expected, as he announces the fulfilment of the entire Old Testament in the words of the prophets: 'Rejoice, O lady full of grace, do not fear! The Lord is with thee, and thou wilt bear a holy child who will be Israel's king and saviour!' Moreover, this is the interpretation given by all the Greek exegetes and Fathers, from Origen to the Byzantine period.[15] It is not surprising, then, that the Greek Church takes the *Ave Maria* as a call to rejoice, the counterpart of the Latin hymn *Regina caeli, laetare*, and a hymn in the Divine Liturgy of St John Chrysostom for Easter Day interprets Gabriel's words in the same way:

---

[14] See above, p. 40, n. 9.

[15] See S. Lyonnet in *Biblica* 20 (1939), pp. 136–9. He cites Origen (*In Lucam*: GCS 9.40), Gregory of Nyssa (*In Cant.* 13: MG 44.1053, and *In diem natalem Christi*: MG 46.1140), Gregory Thaumaturgus (MG 10.1152), Sophronius (MG 87.3236), Andrew of Crete (MG 97.881, 885, 887, 904), Theophylactus (MG 123.704) and Euthymius Zigabenus (MG 129.868). To these one might add the *Sibylline Oracles*, Book III, lines 785–7: 'Rejoice, O virgin, and exult: for to thee the Creator of heaven and earth has given everlasting joy. And in thee shall he dwell, and thou shalt have eternal light' (translation by H. C. O. Lanchester in R. H. Charles, *The Apocrypha and Pseudepigrapha*, vol. 2, p. 392).

'The angel cried aloud to her that was full of grace,
Chaste Virgin, rejoice!
Again I say, rejoice!
For thy son has risen this third day from the tomb!
Shine forth, shine forth, thou new Jerusalem . . .'

Byzantine art, too, witnesses to the same interpretation. The angel
is not presented kneeling in veneration, as in Fra Angelico's
fresco: he stands upright to proclaim the good news loud to all
the world.

Lyonnet's thesis was received with enthusiasm among Roman
Catholics, but it was a Swedish Lutheran exegete, Harald Sahlin,
who elaborated the idea more fully. Apparently inspired by
Lyonnet, Sahlin argued that in the Hebrew source used by Luke
Mary was envisaged almost as an allegorical figure, certainly as a
living symbol of the Daughter of Zion.[16] Now while Lyonnet in
1939 did not expressly make this identification, and though Sahlin
is careful to state that Luke himself did not perceive that his source
was presenting Mary as the Daughter of Zion,[17] almost all who
have subscribed to their basic ideas have taken it that the evangelist
both perceived and intended the typological reference, and meant
his readers to see Mary as personifying the Daughter of Zion in
the day of eschatological salvation. In this form, the interpretation
has been accepted almost unanimously among Catholic writers,
and where Sahlin's hypothetical Proto-Luke presented Mary as a
literary symbol of Israel, later Catholic theologians have concluded that Luke saw Mary, the historical person, as embodying in
fact the whole 'corporate personality' of Israel.[18]

In this form, the thesis has been attacked in a long (and sometimes regrettably polemical) article by Dr August Strobel,[19] and

[16] *Der Messias und das Gottesvolk*, pp. 99–102; 'Jungfru Maria—Dottern Sion',
in the *Ny Kyrlig Tidskrift* 8 (1949), pp. 102–24. Sahlin's idea became known
principally through an article by A. G. Hebert, 'The Virgin Mary as the
Daughter of Zion', in *Theology* 53 (1950), pp. 403–10, and through a French
translation of it published in *La Vie Spirituelle* 85 (1951), pp. 127–39.

[17] *Der Messias und das Gottesvolk*, pp. 167, 275.

[18] For an explanation of the term 'corporate personality', see below, pp. 51–2.

[19] 'Der Gruss an Maria (Lk 1:28)', *ZNW* 53 (1962), pp. 86–110.

also rejected (though in a more irenic manner) by the Finnish scholar Dr Heikki Räisänen.[20] Strobel's main philological arguments in criticism of Lyonnet are three. If Lyonnet's thesis were true, he says, we ought to find an aorist, not a present, imperative, for 'the present imperative is found only where the manner of rejoicing is described or where joy is presented as a permanent condition and form of life'.[21] To this, the obvious rejoinder is that perhaps Luke meant to present Gabriel's message as a call to a permanent condition and form of life, especially if he had in mind the eschatological content of the prophetical texts just discussed. Secondly, Strobel points out that in 1:29 Luke expressly calls the phrase spoken by Gabriel a 'greeting'; to this one can only say that of course it is a greeting, but the question is, what kind of greeting. Does it have Old Testament overtones or not? Lastly, Strobel claims that the Fathers were moved by their theology of a parallel between Mary and Eve to read into the text of Luke a message of joy that would counterbalance Eve's condemnation to sorrow (Gen 3:16). The relevance of this argument becomes clear when we turn to Strobel's own explanation of the word, for it then becomes clear that the main thrust of his article is not to query the rendering 'Rejoice!', but to ensure that any reference to Mary as Daughter of Zion is put out of court.

Räisänen pleads the case better. He passes over in silence the arguments of Strobel set out in the last paragraph, and argues instead that a solitary χαῖρε is not sufficient evidence that Luke had the message of Zephaniah, Joel or Zechariah in mind. If Luke had really wanted the reader to think of these passages, then he ought to have used two verbs ('Rejoice and be glad!') or some more explicit phrase such as 'Rejoice, O Daughter of Zion!' The use of χαῖρε on its own is certainly not sufficient to justify the theory of Lyonnet and Sahlin.

Räisänen now rejoins Strobel, adopting his main argument and presenting it in a concise and attractive form. The word χαῖρε is an essentially Greek greeting, but it is by no means a merely

[20] *Die Mutter Jesu im Neuen Testament*, Helsinki, 1969, pp. 86–92.
[21] *ZNW* 53 (1962), p. 89.

conventional or purely formal greeting in Lk 1:28. For, depending on the context, the word can have a very forceful or even solemn connotation, in which the etymological sense breaks through. Strobel proves this with a wealth of examples from classical and Hellenistic usage,[22] but the evidence of early Christian literature would seem sufficient on its own. The opening verses of the Epistle of James (1:1–2) are clearly an invitation to rejoice, as well as a formal greeting; and every one of the Epistles of St Ignatius except that to the Philadelphians opens with a call to 'rejoice greatly' ($\pi\lambda\epsilon\hat{\iota}\sigma\tau\alpha$ $\chi\alpha\iota\rho\epsilon\iota\nu$) at the gifts which God has given us through Jesus Christ. In Ignatius, it could not be clearer that we are presented with a formal Greek greeting which is also a summons to great joy. Räisänen suggests[23] that Luke may have chosen $\chi\alpha\hat{\iota}\rho\epsilon$ rather than $\epsilon\iota\rho\eta\nu\eta$ in 1:28 in order to bring out the word-play between the verb and the following word $\kappa\epsilon\chi\alpha\rho\iota\tau\omega\mu\epsilon\nu\eta$, and that, though the primary meaning is 'Hail!', the subsidiary meaning 'Rejoice!' must not be excluded. Luke, however, is thinking not of the Old Testament call to the Daughter of Zion, but of his own more general theme, that the time of Jesus' life is a time of joy, and that the Christian community should be characterized by joy. Hence both Strobel and Räisänen retain one of Lyonnet's ideas, namely, that $\chi\alpha\hat{\iota}\rho\epsilon$ is not a purely conventional greeting, while rejecting the suggestion that it recalls the Septuagint usage of 'rejoicing' over the coming of salvation to the Daughter of Zion.

Who is right—Lyonnet, Sahlin and their followers, or Strobel and Räisänen? Did Luke intend Gabriel's greeting as a greeting to the Daughter of Zion? It must be conceded that if he had intended it to be taken in this sense, he might have made his purpose clearer—for example, by writing 'Rejoice and be glad, O Daughter of Zion!' But this is hardly Luke's style: in 1:31 his thought and his wording contain an unmistakable echo of Is 7:14, but he does not give a direct quotation, as Matthew does in 1:21–3. Similarly, Lk 1:32–3 echoes Is 9:7 and 2 Sam 7:12, 13, 16, but again Luke leaves the reader to work out the details for himself:

[22] *ZNW* 53 (1962), pp. 92–102.
[23] *Die Mutter Jesu im Neuen Testament*, pp. 90–1.

he does not provide direct quotation. The truth would seem to be that we cannot reason *simply* from Luke's use of the word χαῖρε that he *certainly* intended the reader to envisage Mary as the eschatological Daughter of Zion; but it is going too far in the other direction to affirm with real conviction that Luke did not envisage Mary in this role.

For we must consider the context. The first two chapters of Luke are tightly packed with Old Testament allusions; Mary is assigned, in these two chapters, a crucial role and a prominence which she is given nowhere else in the gospel; and in the immediate context, we are told that the Lord is with her, as king and saviour. And the more closely we examine the context, the more likely it seems that the idea of Mary as Daughter of Zion may well have been in Luke's mind. To clarify the issue, we must pass on to the next words spoken by the angel.

The second word of Gabriel's greeting, κεχαριτωμένη, has a fairly clear meaning. The verb occurs only once in the Septuagint, in the same participial form, but the text (Sir 18:17) is not of theological importance. Apart from Lk 1:28, the only instance of the verb in the New Testament is Eph 1:6, where the author speaks of 'that grace which God has *graciously bestowed* on us in the Beloved One'. There is no doubt that Luke uses the word in the same sense as the author of Ephesians, to denote that Mary was 'endowed with divine grace freely bestowed', and that is how the *gratia plena* of the Vulgate should be understood. The great Protestant exegete Johann Albrecht Bengel (1687–1752) probably thought he was making a very valid criticism of Roman Catholic doctrine when he commented on this word: '*non ut mater gratiae, sed ut filia gratiae*',[24] and even Plummer probably had the same thought in mind when he wrote: 'The *gratia plena* of the Vulgate is too indefinite. It is right, if it means "full of grace, *which thou hast received*"; wrong, if it means "full of grace, *which thou hast to bestow*"'.[25] Yet nothing could be more consonant with Catholic

[24] In his *Gnomon Novi Testamenti*, Tübingen, 1742; cited in A. Plummer, *A Critical and Exegetical Commentary on the Gospel according to St Luke (International Critical Commentary)*, 4th ed., Edinburgh, 1901, p. 22.

[25] *Loc. cit.*

teaching than these two statements, for the basic of all Catholic teaching about Mary is that she owes to God every grace, every blessing, every favour she has ever received; and wherever in hymnology she is addressed as '*mater gratiae*' or '*mater misericordiae*', the meaning is that Mary is an instrument of grace and mercy in the hand of the Almighty. Bede puts it neatly when he writes: 'Well is she called "full of grace", for she has received the grace which no other woman had deserved, namely, that of conceiving and bringing to birth the very author of grace'.[26] In this grace conferred, Mary is set in sharp contrast with the parents of the Baptist: they are described by Luke as 'righteous before God, walking in all the commandments and statutes of the Lord without blame' (Lk 1:6), and their son was to be the greatest of the prophets (Lk 7:26–8), and the last (Lk 16:16). Mary, on the other hand, is said to be 'favoured with divine grace' without reference to any law, and her son was destined to put an end to the Law with all its observances (Lk 16:16; *cf.* Eph 2:15). Luke's affinities with St Paul lead us to suspect that the contrast between Zechariah and Elizabeth, saints of the old dispensation, and Mary, the mother of Jesus, is not unintentional. If this contrast is intended, then both the χαῖρε and the κεχαριτωμένη imply that the era of grace is come, and that Mary is already endowed with that fullness of grace which God bestowed on mankind in his beloved Son.

'The Lord is with thee' (Lk 1:28). In the Old Testament, these words are never addressed to a person in ordinary circumstances, but always to someone for whom God has great plans, and they are an assurance that God will be constantly at his side in all his difficulties, enabling him to accomplish his mission.[27] Thus, after the death of Abraham, Yahweh said to Isaac at Beersheba:

[26] '*Bene gratia plena* vocatur *quae* nimirum *gratiam quam nulla alia meruerat* assequitur *ut* ipsum videlicet *gratiae* concipiat et generet auctorem' (*In Lucam* 1:28: *CC* 120, p. 31 = *ML* 92:316). Bede is here following (and in the italicized words, citing) Ambrose: 'Bene enim sola gratia plena dicitur, quae sola gratiam quam nulla alia meruerat consecuta est, ut gratiae repleretur auctore' (*In Lucam* II, 9: *CC* 14, Pars IV, p. 34 = *ML* 15:1556 or 1636).

[27] There is a very extensive study of the phrase by U. Holzmeister in *Verbum Domini* 23 (1943), pp. 232–7 and 257–62.

'I am the God of thy father Abraham. Fear not, for I am with thee . . .' (Gen 26:24). Later, when Jacob was on his way to Paddan-Aram, God appeared to him at Bethel, saying: 'I am with thee, and I will watch over thee wherever thou goest, and I will bring thee back to this land. I will not leave thee until I have accomplished what I have promised thee' (Gen 28:15; *cf.* 28:20). When God spoke to Moses at the burning bush, Moses was afraid and said: 'Who am I to approach the Pharaoh and to bring the Israelites out of Egypt?' God's answer was: 'But I will be with thee!' (Ex 3:12). Similarly, when Gideon objected that he could not possibly free his countrymen from the Midianites, Yahweh told him: 'But I will be with thee, and thou shalt crush the Midianites as if they were but one man' (Jdg 6:16). And when Jeremiah pleaded that he was unequal to the task to which he was called, the answer was: 'Do not be afraid . . . for I am with thee to deliver thee' (Jer 1:8).

In all these texts, the destiny of Israel is at stake. The person to whom the words are addressed is summoned by God to a high vocation, and entrusted with a momentous mission, and in the mind of the Old Testament writers, the religious history of Israel (and therefore of the world) depended, at that moment, on his response to God's call. Thus if Isaac or Jacob had abandoned the faith of Abraham, the people of Israel would not have been God's instrument in redemption. If Moses had not led the people out of Egypt, there would have been no covenant at Sinai. If Gideon had not gone to war, the loose federation of tribes might well have disintegrated politically and gone their separate ways in religion, to be ultimately absorbed into the general Canaanite culture. And if Jeremiah had not so effectively forewarned the people of impending doom, the disaster of 587 B.C. might well have been the final act in the drama of Israel's history, just as the fall of Nineveh in 612 brought to a close the history of the Assyrian Empire.

These Old Testament texts make the meaning of Gabriel's greeting plain. When he said to Mary, 'The Lord is with thee!', his words implied that God had a formidable task in hand for her, but that she would receive every assistance to perform it. The nature of the task is not stated at the outset, but the reader is at once alerted to its magnitude. For according to Luke, Mary at once understood from the angel's greeting that something extraordinary was to be asked of her, since in verse 29 we read that 'she was deeply disturbed at the message, and began to wonder what this greeting might portend'.[28] Like so many of the Old Testament figures who had heard such a message, she was afraid, and it was then that the angel said, 'Put aside thy fear, Mary, for thou hast found favour with God' (1:30).

We are now in a position to ask whether Luke in his Infancy Gospel did really wish to present Mary as the Daughter of Zion. It was pointed out above that the Old Testament teaching about the Daughter of Zion stressed above all her lowliness, her poverty and her helplessness, and that the idea is closely connected with the salvation of a remnant and the restoration of the nation.[29] Luke certainly presents Mary as a faithful and humble child to whom her Lord comes at the end of time, and certainly regarded her as dearly loved by God. This is clear not only from his use of the word κεχαριτωμένη, but also from the phrase in v. 30, 'Thou hast found favour with God'. These words in v. 30 reaffirm and clarify the sense of κεχαριτωμένη, for the phrase 'to find favour with God' is frequently used in the Septuagint with the meaning 'to be pleasing to God' (Gen 6:8; 18:3; 30:27; 32:5; 33:8, 10; 34:11, etc.). Mary is certainly presented as possessed of the fundamental quality (that is, in biblical thought, of *all* the qualities) which will characterize the Daughter of Zion at the end of time. In other words, there is nothing in the narrative to indicate that Luke positively excluded the thought that Mary as an individual might personify the Daughter of Zion.

But is there any positive evidence that he actually thought of her in this role, as the living embodiment and personification of the remnant of Israel? She was only a very young girl, and

[28] For a justification of this translation of ποταπὸς εἴη ὁ ἀσπασμὸς οὗτος, see W. Bauer's *Greek–English Lexicon of the New Testament*, translated and adapted by W. F. Arndt and F. W. Gingrich, p. 701: 'Sometimes the context calls for the meaning *how great, how wonderful*', as in Mk 13:1.

[29] See above, pp. 31–4 and 40–2.

throughout the Old Testament the term 'Daughter of Zion' always denotes the people, or a part of it. When the prophets address the Daughter of Zion, they are never thinking of an individual. Could Luke have reversed this usage?

One of the greatest English Old Testament scholars of the last generation, H. Wheeler Robinson, coined a technical term which is of first importance for the understanding of the Bible: *'corporate personality'*.[30] The Israelites did not, and could not, think of an individual as a solitary being, a person separate from all other men and without any essential relation to them. On the contrary, they regarded each individual as a living embodiment of the character and personality of his forefathers; he in turn would 'live on' in his children and descendants. And this bond which united the generations with their ancestors and descendants extended horizontally too: the individual was linked with his family, with his brothers and sisters and cousins, with the extended family and the clan, with his tribe and with the nation. The origins of this belief go back, of course, to the days when Israel lived in the desert, where all tribesmen consider themselves 'brothers' in a wide sense; but the belief itself persisted long after Israel had left the desert for a settled life in Canaan. The notion of 'corporate personality' is fundamental for a correct understanding of the Old Testament and it was applied above all to the person of the king. He embodied the nation's destiny, and it depended on him whether the nation fulfilled or rejected its vocation. The whole people could be punished for his personal sin, as when David took a census with the object of introducing conscription (2 Sam 24); and the nation could be saved by his faith, as happened when Hezekiah invoked the help of Yahweh against Sennacherib's forces at the gates of Jerusalem (2 Kgs 19). The king embodied the will of the people.

Though the monarchy passed away, the notion of 'corporate personality' lived on. To cite but one example, the concept is presupposed in St Paul's assertion that all men were made sinners

[30] In his essay on 'Hebrew Psychology' in *The People and the Book*, edited by A. S. Peake, Oxford, 1925, pp. 353–82; and in 'The Hebrew Conception of Corporate Personality' in *Werden und Wesen des Alten Testaments*, edited by J. Hempel, *BZAW* 66 (1936), pp. 49–62.

in Adam, and that all were redeemed in Jesus Christ (Rom 5:12–19). Did Luke, according to tradition a Gentile, have this notion of corporate personality, and if so, did he apply it to Mary? He must have seen that at the moment before the Incarnation, Mary held in her hands the destiny of Israel, and of the world, for only when Mary utters her *Fiat* does the angel depart from her (Lk 1:38). He must have seen, then, that Mary at that moment personified Israel, and that the Messiah came to Israel only by coming to her, to be born of a woman, born under the Law.

In Luke's narrative, therefore, all the preconditions are present which need to be there if Mary is to be envisaged as the Daughter of Zion. Mary as described by Luke can appropriately be called, in Old Testament language, 'the Daughter of Zion at the end of time'. But did Luke himself consciously think of Mary as this Daughter of Zion? Perhaps a judicious answer needs to be phrased in three statements. It cannot be proved merely by examining the text that Luke did have this symbol in mind; equally, there is nothing in the text which tells against the idea, and it cannot be proved that Luke did not intend this symbol. But if anyone had asked him outright, 'Do you mean that Mary is the Daughter of Zion foretold by the prophets?', he would have replied that this title summed up perfectly all that he meant to say.

Chapter Five

MOTHER OF CHRIST
(Lk 1:31–33)

THE word 'Christ', like the Hebrew term 'Messiah', means 'Anointed'. 'Jesus Christ' therefore means 'Jesus the Messiah, Jesus the Anointed One', though it is more usual nowadays to think of the word 'Christ' as a proper name of Jesus of Nazareth. Indeed, non-Christians in the Greek world thought of the word 'Christ' as a proper name from very early times (see Ac 11:26), but the followers of Jesus themselves at first used the terms 'Christ' and 'Messiah' more in the sense in which they were used by the Jews, then as now. And for a Jew, the word 'Messiah' has always had a closely defined meaning: it is not just a broad synonym for any kind of divinely-appointed saviour (Is 45:1 is notable as a unique exception to this rule), but a technical term for the ideal king who comes from the line of David. For the sake of clarity, this strict and formal usage of the Old Testament and of Judaism will be observed, and the words 'Messiah' and 'Christ' reserved for the son of David as the ideal king. It is in this sense that Lk 1:31-3 states that Mary is to be the mother of the Christ, the mother of Israel's long-awaited king. There is already a hint of this in Lk 1:27, where Mary is said to have been betrothed to a man named Joseph, 'of the house of David': any child of Mary would trace his legal ancestry through Joseph, and would therefore be a member of the house of David. But the full revelation comes only in Lk 1:31-3, where the angel explains to Mary the nature of the task to which God is calling her.

Mary was deeply perturbed at the words of the angel's greeting, and wondered what it portended. Gabriel at once explained: 'Behold, thou shalt conceive in the womb, and give birth to a son, and thou shalt call his name Jesus. He shall be great, and shall be called the Son of the Most High. And the Lord God will give him the throne of his father David, and he will reign over the house of Jacob for ever. And of his kingdom there will be no end' (Lk 1:31-3). These verses recapitulate the promises about the Messianic king:[1] he will be of the line of David, a saviour to his people ('Jesus' means 'saviour'), and of his kingdom there will be no end. Gabriel's message here is that Mary is to be the mother of this Messianic king.

Two points call for comment. Lk 1:31 is a virtual citation of the Greek text of Is 7:14, except that the child's name is not Immanuel ('God with us'), but 'Jesus' (that is, 'Saviour'). Thus when Mary was wondering what God was going to ask of her, Gabriel began by saying that she was called to fulfil the national destiny of Israel by becoming the mother of the Messiah.

The second point looks, at first, a minor one. Nathan's prophecy about the royal Messiah (2 Sam 7:12-14) mentions first that he will be a king, and secondly that he will be God's son, whereas Luke, in 1:32-3, reverses the order. The text of 2 Sam 7:12-14 reads: 'When thy days are over, and thou art laid to rest with thy fathers, I will raise up thine offspring after thee, one born from thy own body, and I will make his kingdom secure. He shall build a house to my name, and I will make his royal throne secure for ever. I shall be to him a father, and he will be my son.' In this text, David's royal rank is that which entitles his heir to be considered as God's son. Luke, however, states first that 'He shall be called the Son of the Most High', and secondly that 'the Lord God will give him the throne of his father David' (1:32-3). Is there a hint, in Luke's order of words, that Jesus' divine sonship is his title to be considered the king of Israel? It would certainly harmonize well with Luke's theology elsewhere (see Ac 2:36), and the kingdom would be of its nature universal and everlasting. Perhaps Luke did imply this when he wrote 'Of his kingdom there shall be no end' (1:33).

[1] See above, pp. 24-5.

The central theme of these verses, then, is that Mary is to be the mother of 'the Son of the Most High', and one must ask what this phrase means. Here the contrast between the Baptist and Jesus is most enlightening. It is said of John the Baptist that 'he will be great before the Lord' (Lk 1:15), but of Jesus that 'he will be great'—without any addition or qualification (Lk 1:32). In verse 32 there is an emphatic pronoun (οὗτος), but not in verse 15: the greatness of Jesus is stressed more than that of the Baptist. Again, the greatness of the Baptist lies in his consecration from birth, and in his predestined task of preparing people for the Lord (1:15*b*–17), whereas the greatness of Jesus lies in the fact that he will be called the Son of the Most High (1:32). This last phrase does not, of itself, declare divine sonship in the sense in which divine sonship is understood in the works of St John, or in a Trinitarian sense, but it certainly does not preclude those meanings; indeed, it leaves the way open for such explanations. In Lk 1:17 and 76 it is written of the Baptist that he will go 'before the Lord God' to prepare his paths, and Luke then shows John fulfilling this mission by preparing the way for Jesus (*e.g.* Lk 3:1–18, especially verse 16).

In these verses, then (Lk 1:31–3), the angel tells Mary that she is to be the mother of the Messiah, of a king whose reign will know no end, of a more than ordinary mortal, of a great Saviour —in short, of a child who will be, in some sense still to be defined, the Son of the Most High God.

Chapter Six

ARK OF THE COVENANT
(Lk 1:35)

THE meaning of Lk 1:34 will be discussed later.[1] It will be more in keeping with the arrangement of this book's arguments to pass now to Lk 1:35, to see if it is possible to define more closely the sense in which Mary's child was to be God's son. Gabriel's words in Lk 1:35 are the most momentous in his message:

'A Holy Spirit will come upon thee,
   and a Power of the Most High will overshadow thee;
that is why the Holy Child
   will be called God's son'.[2]

This verse is the biblical basis for a title given to Mary in the Litany of Loreto—'Ark of the Covenant'.

The first half of the verse consists of two parallel members: 'a Holy Spirit' corresponds to 'a Power of the Most High', and the advent of this Holy Spirit corresponds to an 'overshadowing' of Mary. The definite article is omitted before both nouns (*a* Spirit, *a* Power), and the most likely explanation of this fact (particularly in view of the general context) is that Luke here wishes to maintain an Old Testament atmosphere.

In the Old Testament, the Spirit of God is seen as the source of life, hovering over a shapeless creation (Gen 1:2), quickening

---

[1] See Part II, Chapters 3–5, pp. 173–99.

[2] Another, less probable, rendering is 'that is why the Child will be called holy, God's son'.

into life the inert body of the first man (Gen 2:7), and thereafter giving life to all that breathes on earth (Ps 104:30). Ezekiel was sure that the least breath of God could inaugurate a new creation, bringing back to life all that was dead (Ez 37), and Job proclaimed the faith of Israel when he said: 'It was the Spirit of God which made me' (Job 27:2–3; 33:4; 34:14). But the Spirit of God did not finish its work at creation: it was also the source, the only source, of a full and rich life. A divine Spirit descended upon judges like Othniel, Gideon, Jephthah and Samson, enabling them to perform superhuman deeds (Jdg 3:10; 6:34; 11:29; 14:6; 15:14), and Ezekiel regarded possession of such a Spirit as an essential charism for his prophetic mission (Ez 11:24–5). Hence it was generally believed that the kingdom of the Messiah and the coming of the Messianic age would be characterized by an un-paralleled outpouring of the Spirit (Joel 3:1–5 and Ac 2:17–21), and that possession of God's Spirit in the fullest measure would be the mark of the Messianic king (Is 11:1–2). The Spirit of God, then, is seen throughout the Old Testament as a creative force, life-giving, strengthening and enlightening; it is, as Luke's parallel implies, the creative power of the Most High. The instructed Christian reader of the gospel would of course see more in the term, but for Luke's purpose it was sufficient if he understood it, at the beginning, in this limited Old Testament sense. As with the title 'son of God' in Lk 1:32, the way lay open for further precision and clarification later on.

Verse 35 asserts that this creative, life-giving Power of the Most High will overshadow Mary. Luke's choice of the word 'over-shadow' is of first importance. Several recent writers, Lutheran, Anglican and Roman Catholic,[3] have stressed the significance of this verb in this context: they see in it an indication that the Divine Presence descended on Mary as it had once descended on the Ark of the Covenant. At the very end of the Book of Exodus, when the Tent has at last been completed, the writer adds: 'Then the Cloud enveloped the Tent of Witness, and the Tent was filled

---

[3] See especially H. Sahlin, *Der Messias und das Gottesvolk*, pp. 186–9; A. G. Hebert in *Theology* 53 (1950), pp. 405–6; S. Lyonnet in *L'ami du clergé* 66 (1956), p. 44; and R. Laurentin, *Structure et théologie de Luc I–II*, pp. 73–7.

with the Glory of the Lord. And Moses could not enter the Tent of Witness, *because the Cloud was overshadowing it*, and the Tent had been filled with the Glory of the Lord' (Ex 40:34-5, translated from the Septuagint). In the Greek Old Testament, words meaning 'to overshadow' are comparatively rare, and they are nearly always found in passages which speak of the presence of God. Thus the cloud *cast its shadow over* the Tent (Num 9:18, 22) and the camp (Num 10:34 = 10:36 in the Septuagint; Wis 19:7); the cherubim *cast their shadow over* the Ark (Ex 25:20; 1 Chr 28:18); and God himself is said to *overshadow* those whom he protects (Deut 33:12; Ps 91:4; 140:7 = Ps 90:4 and Ps 139:7 in the Septuagint). In Is 4:2-6 the prophet says that on the Day of Yahweh, God's glory will shine over all the land, to exalt and glorify the remnant of Israel; that remnant will be called holy, for the Lord will then have washed away the sins of the daughters of Zion. Then Yahweh himself will come to Mount Zion (v. 5, according to the Septuagint) and a cloud *will make a shadow over* the mount and its surroundings during the daytime. In brief, Isaiah promises that on the Day of Yahweh, the Divine Presence will once again overshadow the purified Daughter of Zion with its glory.

St Luke, when he wrote the word 'overshadow', must have known what associations it would evoke in the Jewish mind. No Jew, reading the words 'A Power of the Most High will overshadow thee', could fail to think of the Divine Presence or *Shekinah*. The meaning of Lk 1:35, therefore, is that the creative Power of God's Holy Spirit is going to descend upon Mary, as the Glory of the Lord had once descended upon the Tent of Witness and filled it with a Divine Presence. The implication is that Yahweh is going to visit his people by what he does in Mary: and what he does is to create in her womb, without the intervention of any human father, a child. That is why her Holy Child is called God's son.

St Matthew also states that Mary's child was conceived 'of the Holy Spirit', not by the intervention of man (Mt 1:20), but Matthew (as we shall see)[4] is mainly concerned to show that Jesus

[4] See Part II, Chapter 2, pp. 167–72.

was truly of the line of David. Luke had a different purpose in mind: for him, it was not the Davidic sonship, but the divine sonship of Jesus which was central to his story. One must therefore ask what exactly Luke himself understood, and intended to convey, by saying that Mary's child would be called God's son.

Here it is necessary to recall how slow the disciples were to realize who Jesus was, and how gradual was the formulation of the faith of the early Church. The most primitive outline of the early kerygma still available to us is probably to be found in St Peter's speech at Pentecost, in which he asserts that Jesus has been 'made' Lord and Christ by being raised from the grave (Ac 2:36); St Paul, too, states that Jesus was 'constituted son of God in power' by his Resurrection (Rom 1:4; Ac 13:33),[5] and the Epistle to the Philippians says that God bestowed on him the title 'Lord' because of his obedience unto death (Phil 2:9–11). On any interpretation of these texts, it would seem that the unique quality of Jesus' divine sonship was not manifest to the disciples until after the Resurrection. In other words, it was not until his earthly life was over that the disciples realized that he was in a unique sense the son of God. This raised the same questions for them as it does for us: did Jesus become the son of God only after his death, and if so, who was he, what was he, before the Resurrection?

The early Church gave its answer to these questions by telling of two theophanies in Jesus' earthly life, the Transfiguration and the Baptism. On both occasions a voice from heaven had proclaimed: 'This is my beloved son' (Mt 17:5 = Mk 9:7 = Lk 9:35; Mt 3:17 = Mk 1:11 = Lk 3:22). The gospels say that on the mountain three of the Twelve (Peter, James and John) heard the voice and saw his glory: this is equivalent to asserting that the divine sonship of Jesus was attested to these three at the Transfiguration. The early Church therefore taught that Jesus had been the son of God before the Resurrection, at the time of the Transfiguration. Something similar had happened at the Baptism, and so the question arises: did Jesus first become God's son, in an utterly unique way, by virtue of a divine call at his Baptism?

[5] For the interpretation of this very difficult phrase from Romans, see M.-E. Boismard, 'Constitué Fils de Dieu (Rom 1:4)', in the *RB* 60 (1953), pp. 5–17.

The early preaching of the Church, as exemplified in Mark's Gospel and in the Acts, apparently did not deal with the Lord's life before his Baptism (*cf.* Ac 1:22; 10:37; 13:24), but once the question had been asked, it demanded an answer. Luke gives his answer, and the answer of the Church to which he belonged, in 1:35, where he asserts that the divine sonship of Jesus goes back long before the Baptism: Jesus was the son of God from the first instant of his conception in Mary's womb. The Fourth Gospel would later give clear utterance to an even more striking doctrine by saying that the Word who became flesh had existed before creation with God the Father (Jn 1:1).

Was Luke, in 1:35, asserting eternal sonship in the same sense as Jn 1:1-18? He certainly meant to affirm that Jesus was in a unique sense the son of God from the moment of his conception; but was this simply because of the virginal conception, or did it also involve, for Luke, pre-existence before creation 'in the bosom of the Father'? There can be no doubt that Luke knew what Paul had preached to the Philippians (Ac 16:11-15),[6] and what had been written in the letter to the Colossians (*cf.* Col 4:14).[7] Now the epistles to these two churches contain two hymns which proclaim in the most explicit language that Christ Jesus existed before the creation of the world in absolute equality with the Father (Phil 2:6; Col 1:15-17). Consequently, it is not unreasonable to say that Luke, when he wrote that Jesus was called God's son at the Baptism and at the Transfiguration, would have expected his Christian readers to understand the title in the sense in which the Christians of Colossae and Philippi would have understood it; and from the hymns quoted in the letters to these churches, it is legitimate to conclude that at Philippi, Colossae and elsewhere, the title would have been taken to mean that Jesus was equal with

[6] It is at this point that Luke, the author of Acts, begins to tell the story in the first-person plural. He accompanied Paul to Philippi, and perhaps stayed there, for the first 'We-section' of Acts ends in Philippi (16:17), and the second one begins there (20:5-6).

[7] The phrasing of this last clause is not intended as an implicit denial of the Pauline authorship of Colossians; it is meant to imply that even those who deny that Colossians was written by Paul ought to agree that Luke was acquainted with the contents of the letter.

God, and had existed eternally with the Father before his earthly life began. And it is this classical doctrine of the Incarnation which is presupposed and implied in Lk 1:35.

In this verse, Luke's purpose is to assert that Jesus was God's son from the moment of his conception. He therefore takes two formulas which were used in the catechetical teaching of the Church to describe the Baptism and the Transfiguration respectively. These formulas must have been commonly used in preaching about the two episodes, for they are found in all three Synoptic Gospels to describe these happenings, and nowhere else in the gospels. At the Baptism 'the Holy Spirit descended on Jesus' (Mt 3:16 = Mk 1:10 = Lk 3:22; *cf.* Jn 1:32); at the Transfiguration, a cloud 'overshadowed' the group (Mt 17:5 = Mk 9:7 = Lk 9:34); on both occasions a divine voice proclaimed Jesus the son of God. So, in order to say that Jesus was the son of God from the moment of his conception, Luke combined the two ideas in the words:

> '*A Holy Spirit will come upon thee,*
> and a Power of the Most High *will overshadow* thee.'

The Holy Spirit did not first descend on Jesus at the Baptism, nor did God's shadow first fall on him at the Transfiguration. What Jesus was at the Resurrection, he had been from the first instant of his conception—the son of God. And underlying this text, though not explicitly stated (as in John), is the thought that he who was exalted at the right hand of the Father had existed before his conception in the virgin's womb. This is discreetly conveyed in the imagery invoked. Like the Dwelling in the desert and the Temple of Solomon, Mary was overshadowed by the Divine Presence and filled with the Glory of Israel (Ex 40:34-5; 1 Kgs 8:10-11; Lk 1:35; 2:32); like the Ark of the Covenant, she became the Dwelling-place of the Most High.

One or two authors (they are not many)[8] see in the scene which follows the Annunciation a confirmation of this identification of

[8] Laurentin holds this view (*Structure et théologie de Luc I-II*, pp. 79-81), but cites only E. Burrows on his side (*The Gospel of the Infancy*, p. 47).

Mary with the Ark of the Covenant. The story of the Visitation, they argue, makes a charming and subtle use of the parallel between Mary and the Ark by describing her journey to the hill country of Judah in terms which recall David's transfer of the Ark to Jerusalem. Lk 1:39-45 would in that case be a Christian midrash on 2 Sam 6.

The two stories open with the statement that David and Mary 'arose and made a journey' (2 Sam 6:2; Lk 1:39) up into the hill country, into the land of Judah. On arrival, both the Ark and Mary are greeted with 'shouts' of joy (2 Sam 6:12, 15; Lk 1:42, 44). The verb used for Elizabeth's greeting in Lk 1:42, (ἀνεφώνησεν) is, in the Septuagint, used only in connection with liturgical ceremonies centred round the Ark; it is best translated as '*intoned*'.[9] The Ark, on its way to Jerusalem, was taken into the house of Obededom, and became a source of blessing for his house (2 Sam 6:10-12); Mary's entry into the house of Elizabeth is also seen as a source of blessing for the house (Lk 1:41, 43-4). David, in terror at the untouchable holiness of the Ark, cried out: 'How shall the Ark of the Lord come to me?' (2 Sam 6:9); Elizabeth, in awe before the mother of her Lord, says, 'Why should this happen to me, that the mother of my Lord should come to me?' (Lk 1:43). Finally, we read that 'the Ark of the Lord remained in the house of Obededom three months' (2 Sam 6:11), and that Mary stayed with Elizabeth 'about three months' (Lk 1:56).

The comparison is undoubtedly ingenious, but was it intended by St Luke? The verbal affinities between the two stories are not so close as to be convincing beyond dispute, and the idea itself may seem too far-fetched to be true. The real test is to ask whether there was any doctrinal reason for presenting Mary's journey to Judaea in terms of the transfer of the Ark to Jerusalem. Here the theme of Malachi may help: Luke's Infancy Gospel builds up to a climax in the Presentation, when 'the Lord comes to his Temple' and Simeon can say '*Nunc Dimittis*'. When we recall how Luke

[9] 1 Paral (= Chr) 15:28; 16:4, 5, 52; 2 Paral 5:13. The last two texts refer to the transfer of the Ark to Jerusalem and to the Temple. For further comment on this verb see below, p. 72.

describes the Divine Presence in terms certainly applicable to the Ark of the Covenant, it does not seem beyond the bounds of credibility that Mary's three-month stay in the hill country was intended as a parallel to the Ark's halt before it was first installed in Jerusalem. But the argument as a whole is not fully convincing. Perhaps Luke adapted an early Christian midrash about the Ark of the Covenant; the verbal similarities between his story and 2 Sam 6 might then be surviving traces of an earlier, perhaps oral, midrash whose symbolism he toned down, possibly in order to imply that his story was truly historical.

Chapter Seven

'BEHOLD THE HANDMAID OF THE LORD!'
(Lk 1:38)

THE classical interpretation of Lk 1:38 makes this verse the logical conclusion to vv. 31–7, in the following manner. When Gabriel told Mary that she was to be the mother of the Messiah (vv. 31–3), Mary asked, 'How shall this be, since I do not know man?', *i.e.* since I am, and intend to remain, a virgin (v. 34). From the time of St Augustine, it has been commonly held in the Latin West that these words are evidence that Mary had made a vow of virginity before the Annunciation, and this has given rise to the idea that Mary here queried how she could be the mother of the Messianic king without breaking her vow. This seems to lead in well to v. 35, where the angel in reply explains that she is to conceive a child by the Power of the Most High, *i.e.* that hers is to be a virginal conception, without the intervention of any earthly father; and as proof of his message, Gabriel offers the news that Elizabeth, Mary's relative, has conceived a child in her old age (vv. 35–7). Though Luke does not expressly say so, he certainly implies that Mary had not previously heard of Elizabeth's conception, for Elizabeth had hidden herself for five months (vv. 24–5, *cf.* 26, 36). Mary is then presented by Luke as the exemplar of perfect, undoubting faith, believing without further evidence in the word of God's messenger, quietly accepting the fact of Elizabeth's conception, and humbly consenting to her own vocation in the words 'Behold the handmaid of the Lord! May it be done unto me according to thy word!' (v. 38).

It is clear that this interpretation of this passage revolves around the understanding of v. 34: do Mary's words there really mean 'How can I be a mother, for I have resolved to remain a virgin?' There are many good reasons for rejecting this view, and they will be explained later;[1] for the moment, it is sufficient to note that this, the classical interpretation of v. 34, has affected the interpretation of v. 38. As long as the words 'How shall this be . . .?' are thought to imply a certain reluctance or hesitation to accept the role of mother of the Messiah, there is a danger of interpreting v. 38 as nothing more than an expression of humble submission to God's will, as if Mary acquiesced in the divine plan out of obedience, but without joy. Her *Fiat* is then taken in the same sense as Jesus' *Fiat voluntas tua* in Gethsemane (Lk 22:42, *cf.* Mt 26:42 = Mk 14:36), and the same notion of submissive resignation is even applied to the *Fiat voluntas tua* of the Lord's Prayer (Mt 6:10, *cf.* Lk 11:2 in many manuscripts). The identity of the Latin translation *Fiat* in all three contexts has certainly assisted, and perhaps even been responsible for, this interpretation of Mary's words, but the Greek will not bear this meaning in Lk 1:38. In the Lord's Prayer and in Gethsemane, the Greek text has the aorist imperative, whereas Lk 1:38 has the optative, which can only be translated as an earnest wish or prayer. Latin cannot accurately render this distinction, but it remains true that the only correct translation of Lk 1:38 is as a cry of joy—'O may it be so for me, according to thy word!'

It is not only Roman Catholics who have failed to perceive the full significance of this optative. Plummer, for example, comments on this text:

'This is neither a prayer that what has been foretold may take place, nor an expression of joy at the prospect. Rather it is an expression of submission,—"Gods' will be done" . . . Mary must have known how her social position and her relations with Joseph would be affected by her being with

[1] See below, Part II, Chapter 3, pp. 173–87 for the full statement and critique of this position. It owes its popularity in no small measure to the influence of St Bernard, whose exposition of the verse is set out on p. 175.

child before her marriage . . . and what likelihood was
there that he would believe so amazing a story?'[2]

It should be said quite bluntly that this interpretation is positively
excluded by the fact that the verb is in the optative; Luke's
choice of this mood means that Mary's words are both a prayer
and an expression of joy, not just a declaration of humble
submission.

St Bernard of Clairvaux, in spite of his interpretation of v. 34,[3]
catches the feel of the Lucan narrative better than most modern
commentators when he comes to this verse, in which Luke sets his
first climax. Bernard, though writing in medieval style and
preaching a meditation, grasps the essential message and supplies
all the background with consummate imagination: Bernard
sees that Luke is here presenting Mary as the eschatological
Daughter of Zion.

'The angel waits for the answer, for it is time for him to return
to the God who sent him. And we too, Lady, crushed down
by the sentence of damnation, are waiting for the word of
compassion. See, held out before you is the ransom that will
be our salvation; if you consent, we shall at once be set free.
. . . Poor Adam with his wretched family, exiled from Paradise, implore you, dear Virgin. Abraham and David, and
the other holy Patriarchs—your own ancestors, no less,
who now dwell in the land of the shadow of death—most
earnestly beg this of you. Indeed, the whole world falls
down at your knees awaiting your answer, and rightly so,
for on your reply depends the comfort of the afflicted, the
redemption of [Satan's] prisoners, the liberation of a race
condemned to die. In a word, on your response depends
the salvation of all the children of Adam, of all your race.

Answer quickly, O Virgin; Lady, say the word for which
earth and underworld and heaven are waiting. The very
King and Lord of all has desired your beauty, and is now

[2] *The Gospel according to St Luke*, p. 26.
[3] See above, p. 65, n. 1.

awaiting with equal eagerness your answer, your consent, through which he has designed to save the world. You have pleased him hitherto through your silence, but you will please him still more by one word, for he cries to you from heaven, "O fairest among women, let me hear your voice!" . . . Behold, the Desired of all nations stands knocking at the door. . . . Arise and run and open to him!'[4]

These words of St Bernard give the true sense in which Mary's response is to be taken, as the 'Yes!', as the 'Amen!' of humanity to God's offer of a Saviour, as an unconditional affirmation of complete willingness to accept, humbly and thankfully, God's unmerited offer of redeeming grace.

Thus Mary's *Fiat* rounds off and closes the story of the Annunciation. Gabriel's first word had been a call to rejoice. Mary closes the scene in words which return to this theme of rejoicing: 'Behold the handmaid of the Lord! O may it be so with me, according to thy word!'

[4] *Hom. 4a in 'Missus est'* 8 (ML 183.83–4).

Chapter Eight

BLESSED AMONG WOMEN
(Lk 1:39–45)

THIS theme of joy rings out again in the story of the Visitation (Lk 1:39–45). As soon as Elizabeth heard Mary's greeting, the child in her womb 'leapt for joy' (1:41, 44). The noun here used for 'joy' and its cognate verb ($\dot{\alpha}\gamma\alpha\lambda\lambda\iota\dot{\alpha}o\mu\alpha\iota$) are found only in biblical and ecclesiastical Greek, and in the New Testament are always used to stress God's eschatological salvation: he has *at last* fulfilled his promises and redeemed his people (see especially Apoc 19:7 and Jn 8:56).[1]

The episode closes with a verse (45) in praise of Mary: 'And blest is she that has believed that there will be fulfilment of what has been said to her by the Lord.' It is surprising that Elizabeth here uses the third person ('to her') when in verse 42 she had used the second person ('Blessed art thou among women'), and the Clementine edition of the Vulgate does in fact keep the second person in v. 45, but without any support among the Greek manuscripts.[2] Räisänen comments: 'The first saying (v. 42) applies only to Mary personally. The latter (v. 45) can be taken out of its context, and thereupon becomes universally valid, and an expression of the fundamental attitude of the *Christian* to the word of God. Mary is here taken as the model of the Christian.'[3]

No one would wish to contest the validity of this comment.

---

[1] Thus R. Bultmann in the *TWNT* I, pp. 19–20.
[2] 'Beata quae credidisti, quoniam perficientur ea quae dicta sunt tibi a Domino.'
[3] *Die Mutter Jesu im Neuen Testament*, p. 110.

Unfortunately, Räisänen proceeds to draw a conclusion which does not seem to be justified by the text. He continues: 'Luke stresses that the important thing is not Mary's motherhood (v. 42) but her *faith*. This stress is not an invention of the evangelist, for he certainly found v. 45 in his source. He does not, however, repeat the traditional saying (*die überlieferte Aussage*) unthinkingly, but undoubtedly assents to it himself. This can be seen from his insertions in 1:48*b* and 2:19, which will have to be discussed later. The traditional beatitude praising the faith of Mary became a cornerstone of Lucan "Mariology".'[4] The assertion that Luke considered Mary's faith more important than her motherhood is not self-evident, and certainly does not follow from the fact that in her faith she is a model for all Christians (v. 45), whereas in her motherhood she is unique (v. 42). Indeed, one wonders whether Luke would have understood the point of asking which was the more important, for it seems a singularly irrelevant question, in that it is difficult to see what is meant by 'more important'. It will be more profitable to examine what Luke has in mind in verse 42.

'Blessed art thou among women, and blessed is the fruit of thy womb' (Lk 1:42). Laurentin has suggested[5] that these words are modelled on words in the Book of Judith (13:18): 'Blest art thou, my daughter, by God Most High, above all the women on the earth . . .' Did Luke have this text, or some similar text, in mind?

To answer that question, one must look rather closely at the Book of Judith. Few people, if any, would hold that the book recounts historical events, though there may be some facts about a Jewish woman at the origin of the legend. It is impossible to tell, but at least the lesson of the book is wonderfully lucid. The name 'Judith' means 'the Jewish woman', 'the Jewess', and the story has obvious parallels with that of an earlier woman who proved herself a saviour of Israel, Jael the wife of Heber (Jdg 4:17-22; 5:24-7). When Judith made her way unescorted to Holofernes' camp, the destiny of Israel was in her hands. She is presented as a model of piety (Jdt 8:5-6), symbolizing all that was best in the

---

[4] Pp. 110-11.

[5] *Structure et théologie de Luc I–II*, pp. 81-2; but he does not develop the idea.

nation, and after the death of Holofernes, she is saluted in the words:

> 'Thou art the glory of Jerusalem,
> the great pride of Israel,
> the great boast of our race!' (Jdt 15:9, Septuagint).[6]

It has already been argued that Luke thought of Mary in very similar terms: chosen to be the mother of the Messiah, of the Son of the Most High, she willingly consented to the role. A certain parallelism exists, therefore, between Mary and Judith in that each of them, though in very different ways, is considered to have made a signal contribution to the salvation of Israel. Can one go further?

Judith, upon her return from the enemy camp, was welcomed into the city by the high priest with these words:

> 'Blest art thou, my daughter, by God Most High,
> above all the women on the earth!
> And blessed be the Lord God,
> who created the heavens and the earth,
> and guided thee to smite the head
> of the leader of our enemies!' (Jdt 13:18).

These words of the high priest echo the words in which Melchizedek, an earlier priest of Jerusalem, addressed Abram after that victory which gave him the freedom of the Promised Land:

> 'Blessed be Abram by God Most High,
> who created the heaven and the earth!
> And blest be God Most High,
> who has delivered thine enemies into thy hand!'
>
> (Gen 14:19–20)

Like Abram, Judith had secured for the chosen people the freedom of the Promised Land. Jael, too, had been saluted as 'most blessed of women' (Jdg 5:24) for saving her people from the enemy.

[6] Here, as elsewhere in Judith, the Vulgate has a different text which expresses the same ideas.

Abraham, Jael and Judith had all been saviours of their people in war, and Judith in particular is portrayed as the personification of valiant Jewish womanhood. But could Luke have thought of Mary, the meek and obedient servant of the Lord (Lk 1:38) as a woman winning victory in battle? It must be said at once that the idea seems highly improbable in itself, and since there is no evidence that Luke knew the Book of Judith, the suggestion that 1:42 is somehow modelled on Jdt 13:18 may be confidently rejected. That, however, is not the end of the argument, for even if the words in 1:42 are not modelled on Jdt 13:18, they may still be the words of a hymn of a type used to salute those who had made an outstanding contribution to the salvation of Israel ('Blessed art thou . . . and blessed is God . . .').[7]

There is nothing improbable in the suggestion that the early Christians sang hymns of praise in honour of Mary. We know that St John's disciples in particular 'searched' (*darash*) the Scriptures (Jn 2:22; 5:39; 7:38, 42; 10:35; 13:18; 17:12; 19:24, 28, 36, 37; 20:9) to discover hidden references to Jesus in the Old Testament; indeed, many authors think that the Fourth Gospel and the Apocalypse look upon Mary as filling the role assigned to the woman mentioned in Gen 3:15.[8] That her special rank was acknowledged by the Church is implied by the text of the Magnificat, where Luke says that 'from this present time' (1:48*b*) all generations will call her blessed. Could Luke have written that phrase if, at the time when he was writing (A.D. 70–80), his own generation had not begun to call her blessed?

The text of Lk 1:42 would seem conclusive proof that the early Church expressed its reverence for the mother of its Lord by singing hymns in her honour. We can discount the idea that Luke is here reporting the actual words which Elizabeth used on the occasion of Mary's visit, for to him and to his contemporaries

---

[7] The idea that Lk 1:42 has liturgical overtones is mentioned by A. R. C. Leaney, *The Gospel according to St Luke* (*Black's New Testament Commentaries*), London, 1958, p. 86; P. S. Minear, *The Interpreter and the Birth Narratives* (= Symbolae Biblicae Upsalienses 13), Uppsala, 1950, p. 15; and by A. Strobel, *ZNW* 53 (1962), pp. 109–10.

[8] See below, Part III, pp. 374–6, 383–7 and 429–30.

the actual words would have been of no importance. It was important, though, that Elizabeth should greet Mary in a worthy manner. What was more obvious or more appropriate than to place on her lips a prayer commonly used by Christians of the day to the mother of Jesus?

Hence Elizabeth welcomes Mary as 'the mother of *my Lord*'—an ancient title which takes us back to the first days of the Christian Church (*cf.* Jn 20:13, 28; Phil 3:8) before it gave way to '*our* Lord'. Such a title would never have been used by Elizabeth before the birth of the Baptist, for the name 'Lord' was given to Jesus only after the Resurrection (Ac 2:36), and its very solemnity is a hint that Elizabeth is here speaking the language of the early Christian community. This harmonizes well with the idea that in Lk 1:42 we have preserved for us the opening words of an early liturgical hymn in honour of Mary; and only by taking v. 42 as the first words of a hymn can one explain why Elizabeth is said to have '*intoned*' the words '*in a loud voice*'. The verb there used (ἀνεφώνησεν) means in classical Greek 'to cry aloud, to proclaim, to declaim', and occurs only five times in the Septuagint, always in conjunction with religious ceremonies around the Ark (1 Paral = 1 Chr 15:28; 16:4, 5, 42; 2 Paral 5:13). These texts from the Septuagint are all concerned with making music or song around the Ark, and if we therefore translate the word at Lk 1:42 as '*intoned*', we have an explanation of what is otherwise inexplicable, namely, why Elizabeth is said to have used '*a loud voice*'. If Luke is citing a liturgical formula, all becomes clear. Elizabeth then greets Mary in the words of a hymn which the Christian community addressed to 'the mother of its Lord' in apostolic times:

> 'Blessed art thou among women,
> and blessed is the fruit of thy womb!'

Chapter Nine

THE MAGNIFICAT
(Lk 1:46–55)

MARY responds to this praise from Elizabeth by declaring that all the glory is due to God: this is the theme of the Magnificat.

There are basically three theories about the origin of the Magnificat. The most ancient is that it is a canticle composed by Mary herself, possibly on the occasion of her visit to Elizabeth. Another theory, of relatively modern origin, is that it is a canticle written by St Luke and placed on Mary's lips to show forth her gratitude and humility at the honour she had received.[1] Yet a third theory, which is fairly generally accepted nowadays, is that Luke took over, and possibly adapted, a previous composition. This third theory appears in various forms, but by far the most attractive suggestion is that the Magnificat was a hymn celebrating God's redemption of the 'the lowly' and 'the poor', composed in the early Jewish-Christian Church and later applied to Mary by the insertion of v. 48.[2] If its words were applicable to the Christian community of Palestine, they were supremely true of that 'humble servant of the Lord' who had been blessed and exalted more than all others.

[1] We need not discuss the theory usually associated with the name of A. von Harnack, that the Magnificat was originally (*i.e.* in Luke's own manuscript) ascribed to Elizabeth. See Detached Note III: Should the Magnificat be Ascribed to Elizabeth?

[2] This seems preferable to the opinion that it was originally a Jewish psalm which the Christian Church adopted, for in vv. 54–5 the fulfilment of the promises to Abraham is spoken of as having already taken place: compare Lk 1:68–73.

But whatever the origin of the Magnificat may have been, there is no doubt that as it stands in the gospel, it is meant to be read as the expression of Mary's joy and thanksgiving for her virginal conception of the Messiah. And when she praises God in this canticle for the great things he has done to her, she praises and thanks him not merely on her own behalf, but also in the name of all the 'lowly' in Israel, whom she personifies. The theme is that the God of Abraham has in these last days fulfilled his promises and sent salvation to the lowly.

The hymn begins (vv. 46*b*–7, 49–50) with praise of God for his gracious condescension in mercifully sending salvation to Israel; the second part (vv. 51–3) stresses that he has shown this mercy not to the noble and powerful, but to the lowly and humble of heart; the conclusion (vv. 54–5) recalls that he has thereby fulfilled his promises to Abraham and his descendants. Verse 48, the only verse in the first section which speaks of the lowly, and the only verse in the hymn which refers directly to Mary as an individual, makes far better sense if it is regarded as an interpolation into an earlier psalm, inserted to make Mary the spokesman of the 'lowly' because on her, more than on any other, the blessings promised to the lowly were bestowed. Moreover, if v. 48 is taken as a later insertion, the first two parts of the hymn are perfectly balanced, with three couplets in each.[3]

46*b* My soul proclaims the greatness of the Lord,
47   and my spirit has rejoiced in God my Saviour.
48*a* [*Because he has looked graciously on his servant in her lowliness:*
  b   *for behold, henceforth all generations shall call me blessed.*]
49*a* For he that is mighty has done great things to me,
  b   and holy is his name.
50*a* From generation to generation his mercy never fails
  b   towards those who revere him.

[3] In this analysis and in the commentary, I follow J. T. Forestell, 'The Old Testament Background of the Magnificat', in *Marian Studies* 12 (1961), pp. 205–44.

51a He has done mighty deeds with his powerful arm,
b   scattering those with proud dispositions of heart,
52a Deposing sovereigns from their thrones,
b   making the lowly renowned,
53a Granting the hungry their fill of good things,
b   while the rich are sent empty away.[4]

54a He has come to the aid of Israel, his child,
b   remembering that mercy
55a Which he promised he would show to our fathers,
b   to Abraham and his children, for ever.

In the first part, Mary's personal thanksgiving is made up of
phrases which are used in the Old Testament to express the
collective thanksgiving of Israel for some signal act of grace
towards the nation. In the psalmody of Israel, it was a regular
practice of the writers to associate with themselves all the lowly,
or the whole nation, or even all the peoples of the earth (*e.g.*
Ps 34:3–4; 40:17; 57:10–11), and this is the underlying assumption of the Magnificat: that all may join with Mary in her praise.
The closest parallels to its opening couplet are 1 Sam 2:1 (Hannah's
thanksgiving for her child) and Hab 3:18. The canticle of Habak-
kuk is not the prayer of an individual for a personal favour, but
an impassioned plea for God to ride forth in glory as saviour of
the nation, and to scatter its enemies as he had once scattered
Cushan and Midian. Then, says the prophet, 'I shall sing for joy
in the Lord, and shall rejoice in God my Saviour' (Hab 3:18).
The words he uses, and which the Magnificat adopts, are classical
expressions to describe the deliverance of Zion (Ps 69:30–1, 36–7;
70:5–6), and especially of the poor and lowly in Zion (Ps 9:1–2,
10–19; 31:8; 40:16–17). Hannah, too, praises God not only on her
own behalf, but in the name of all the poor and lowly in Israel
(1 Sam 2:1–10). So also Mary begins her canticle by thanking God
her Saviour for the deliverance of Israel.

---

[4] The present participles in vv. *51b–3*, and the indicatives in vv. *51a* and *53b*,
translate what are in the Greek gnomic aorists, *i.e.* which express a perennial
truth.

Verse 48*a* continues this theme of thanksgiving: 'He has looked graciously on the lowly estate of his servant.' The nearest verbal parallel to this verse is Deut 26:7: 'We cried out to the Lord, the God of our Fathers, and the Lord listened to our voice, and saw our lowly estate', but the similarity there lies in the thought rather than in the words. Yet the full richness of this line of the Magnificat can be grasped only by a careful examination of each word. The verb ἐπιβλέπω is often used of God's consideration for human distress,[5] whether individual[6] or national;[7] and in Ps 102:14–21 God's response to the prayer of the afflicted is nothing less than the restoration of Zion.[8] All these ideas are present when Mary says, 'He has *looked graciously* on his servant in her lowliness'. God has seen her lowly estate, the distress of the nation, and the prayers of the afflicted; and by sending his Redeemer, he has begun the work which will culminate in the restoration of Zion. The nouns used ('the lowly estate of his servant') are also significant. In the Old Testament, the words 'poor', 'lowly' and 'needy' generally refer either to Israel as a whole, or to a faithful remnant of the people: in either case, they refer to Israel considered in all its helplessness, as a mere creature before God. Likewise, in the Old Testament, Israel or its faithful remnant is also called 'the servant of God'. By combining the two terms in the phrase 'the lowly estate of his servant', Mary asserts that 'the Lord has sent redemption to his people, secured his covenant for ever' (Ps 112:9). When she speaks of what God has done for her, she speaks of what God has done for Israel: that is, she speaks of herself as the Daughter of Zion.

'Behold, henceforth all generations shall call me blessed' (48*b*). The parallel usually cited is Leah's cry in Gen 30:13: 'All women will call me blessed', but there is another parallel in Mal 3:12:

---

[5] In the Septuagint Psalter, see Ps 12:4 (of the soul in sorrow) = 13:4 in the Hebrew; 24:16 (of the afflicted) = 25:16 in the Hebrew; 68:17–18 (God's servant in distress) = 69:17–18 in the Hebrew.

[6] *E.g.* Hannah's sterility in 1 Sam 1:11.

[7] *E.g.* 1 Sam 9:16 (when Israel had no king to fight its wars).

[8] Note the title of this psalm: 'A prayer of one afflicted, when he is weary and pours out his complaint before the Lord.'

'All the nations will call you blessed.' The parallel from Genesis has this in its favour, that Leah is there rejoicing over the birth of a child to her servant; but on the other hand the text of Malachi is closer in thought to the Magnificat. Malachi's text refers to the Day of Yahweh, whereas Gen 30:13 has no eschatological reference. Leah, moreover, rejoices over her own good fortune as an individual, whereas Mary rejoices because God has sent salvation to the entire people.

Verses 49–50 need not detain us. The closest parallel to 49*a* is Deut 10:21: 'He is thy boast, and he is thy God, who has done great things in thee'—again, a text addressed to the whole community of Israel. The nearest verbal parallel to 50*a* is Ps 89:2: 'I shall sing of thy mercies, O Lord, for ever; to generation after generation I shall proclaim thy fidelity', as the Greek text translates it. There is also the refrain of Ps 136: 'His mercy endures for ever', and the whole series of texts asserting that his 'mercy' or 'loving-kindness' (*hesed*) is only for those who fear him (Ps 101: 11, 13, 17, etc.).

God's gracious love, however, far surpasses the highest range of human concepts: no human mind can grasp its richness, no human words are adequate to express it. This is the meaning of v. 49*b*: 'Holy is his name!' When the Israelites called God 'holy', they meant that he was utterly different from everything else in existence: in philosophical terms, they meant that he was transcendent. This phrase therefore summarizes the whole first part of the Magnificat: God has done greater things than the human mind can imagine or express, in making Mary the mother of his Son. And what he has done for Mary, he has done, through her, for his people.

The second part of the hymn (vv. 51–3) develops the idea of v. 50*b*: God has not performed these wonders, or sent this salvation, to those who are noble by birth or powerful in this world, but to those who are meek and humble of heart. 'He has done mighty deeds with his powerful arm' (51*a*). The phrase, so reminiscent of Deuteronomy, recalls how Yahweh had once led an oppressed people out of the land of Egypt, where they were living in slavery; he led them out 'with a mighty hand and an outstretched arm' (Deut 6:21; 26:8 and *passim*). The same term recurs in Is 51:9, where the prophet is praying for deliverance from Babylon:

> 'Awake, awake, employ thy strength,
>   O arm of Yahweh!
> Awake as in days of old,
>   as in generations of long ago!'

In other words, Lk 1:51*a* expresses in classical terms the redemption of Israel. Verses 51*b*–3 simply stress, by various metaphors, that this redemption is reserved to the poor in spirit, to the meek and humble of heart.[9]

God made three promises to Abraham: that his children would be a great nation (Gen 12:2; 13:16; 15:5; 17:6, 19; 22:17); that his descendants would possess the land of Canaan (Gen 12:7; 13:15; 15:18–21; 17:8); and that in him all the nations of the world would count themselves blessed (Gen 12:3; 22:18). In Mary's child, the last of the three promises was fulfilled, and it is not surprising that Luke draws out many parallels between Mary and Abraham. Like Abraham (Gen 18:3), Mary found favour with God (Lk 1:30); like Abraham (Gen 12:3; 18:18; 22:18), she is a source of blessing for, and is blessed by, all nations (Lk 1:42, 48); like Abraham (Gen 15:6), she is praised for her faith in the promise that, by a miracle, she would have a son (Lk 1:45).

Thus, in the Magnificat, Mary begins by voicing the praise and gratitude of Israel in Messianic days (vv. 46–50); then she reflects that God has sent this salvation not to those whom the world esteems, but to the lowly, in whom the spiritual destiny of Israel was centred from the time of Jeremiah, *i.e.* from the end of monarchical times (vv. 51–3); and finally her thoughts move back further still, to the very beginning of Israel's history, and she sees her virginal conception as the final accomplishment of the

---

[9] See especially Jdt 9:11–12. The verbal cross-references are: for v. 51, Ps 89; 11, 14; 118:15–16 and 2 Sam 22:28; for v. 52*a*, Sir 10:14; 11:1, 5–6, 11–13; Job 12:19; for v. 52*b*, Job 5:11; Ps 147:6; for v. 53, Ps 107:9; 34:11; 1 Sam 2:5, etc.

promises made to Abraham himself (vv. 54–5). Just as Abraham, one man, had received the promises at the beginning on behalf of the entire nation, so one woman, Mary, received the fulfilment of those promises on behalf of the nation at the end of time.

Chapter Ten

THE SAVIOUR IS BORN
(Lk 2:1–20)

MARY, by giving birth to Jesus, gave to Israel its Saviour, its Messiah and its Lord (Lk 2:11). The day of his birth was the day of salvation for the faithful remnant of Israel, *i.e.* for those who, according to God's design, were to carry a message of peace and reconciliation to the ends of the earth (this is the plan of Luke–Acts).[1] Thus the birth of Jesus inaugurated a new age of glory to God, and of peace among men (Lk 2:14; *cf.* Is 9:5–6).

Some authors divide the Lucan Nativity Story into two parts, vv. 1–7 (the birth) and vv. 8–20 (the shepherds), and see vv. 1–7 as relating the fact, and vv. 8–20 the interpretation. Professor Heinz Schürmann in particular stresses this division: according to him, the first part is a description of Jesus' birth as the fulfilment of prophecy, while the second part explains the significance of this birth by the well-known apocalyptic literary form of a vision of angels.[2] The division is convenient, provided one remembers that both halves belong together: for it is quite certain even on literary grounds that the entire passage is thoroughly Lucan,[3] and the central point both of vv. 1–7 and of vv. 8–20 is the fact that the

---

[1] See any introduction to the New Testament, and especially Ac 1:8; 28:30–1. Note also how Lk 3:4–6 continues the citation of Is 40:3 ff. down to the words 'and all flesh shall see the salvation of our God' (contrast Mt 3:3; Mk 1:3 and Jn 1:23).

[2] *Das Lukasevangelium*, vol. 1, Freiburg–Basel–Vienna, 1969, pp. 97–8.

[3] R. Morgenthaler, *Statistik des neutestamentlichen Wortschatzes*, Zürich and Frankfurt-am-Main, 1958, pp. 62–3 and 187.

child is found in a manger. The passage must be seen as a unity.

In narrating this story, Luke may have had in mind certain verses from the book of Micah which were accepted as Messianic prophecies in the early Church.[4] The first of these occurs in Mic 5:2–5 (= 5:1–4 in the Septuagint). It looks forward to the coming of a royal Messiah from the line of David.

1a 'And thou, Bethlehem, house of Ephrata,
 b   art the least among the clans of Judah.
 c   From thee shall come forth
 d   one who is to be my ruler in Israel,
 e   and his origins will be from the beginning,
 f   from the days of eternity.[5]
2a Therefore he [*viz.* the Lord] will abandon them
 b   until the time when a mother gives birth,
 c   and the remainder of their brothers return
 d   to the sons of Israel.
3a And he will arise and look around[6]
 b   and will shepherd his flock with the strength of the
        Lord,
 c   and they will live in the glory of the name of the Lord
        their God.
 d   Therefore he shall henceforth be exalted to the ends of
        the earth.

[4] It is not necessary, for this chapter, to decide whether these texts formed part of Micah's own message, or were added later (after the exile?) to his book, for it is unlikely that Luke asked this question. For a view on this point, and an interpretation of Mic 4–5, see Detached Note II, on pp. 440–2. But there is another difficulty which cannot be avoided, and which affects the interpretation of Luke. The Hebrew text of Micah is in very bad repair, and the Septuagint is often more intelligible. Since Luke was certainly more familiar with the Septuagint than with the Hebrew, the texts from Micah will be translated from the Septuagint, with significant discrepancies from the Hebrew recorded in the footnotes. Those who think Lk 1–2 was originally written in Hebrew will of course look for parallels with the Hebrew text.

[5] The Hebrew runs: 'He will be of ancient origin, from timeless days.' The reference in the Hebrew is to the ancient origin of David's line, but the Greek translator has rendered 'ancient' and 'timeless' by words which imply eternity.

[6] The Hebrew omits: 'and look around'.

4a And there shall be this peace . . .' (Mic 5:1–4a, Septuagint).

In Micah's picture, the ruler who was to come from the house of
David and from the town of Bethlehem would be of eternal
origin (5:1ef), and the day of his birth would be the signal for the
return and conversion of 'many brothers' to Israel (5:2). These
'brothers' would constitute, along with the people of Israel, a
flock over which the Messiah would reign; and the birth of this
shepherd-king would initiate a reign of peace to the ends of the
earth (5:3–4a).

It is quite certain that in the second half of the first century this
text from Micah was interpreted by the Jews as referring to the
Messiah, and by Christians as referring to Jesus. Mic 5:1 and 3 are
cited in Mt 2:6. When Herod inquired of the scribes where the
Messiah would be born, they gave the answer: 'In Bethlehem,
in Judaea. For so it is written by the prophet: "And thou,
Bethlehem, land of Judah, art by no means the least among the
leaders of Judah, for out of thee shall come a prince who will be
the shepherd of my people Israel".' There is also an unmistakable
allusion to Mic 5:1 in Jn 7:42: 'Does not the Scripture say that
the Messiah will come from the line of David, and from Bethlehem, the little town where David lived?' It is assumed in these
texts that Jews as well as Christians expected the Messiah to be
born in Bethlehem, and the allusions must be to Mic 5:1, for
there is no other text in the Old Testament which states that the
Messiah will come from Bethlehem. That Christians saw in
Micah a prophecy of the birth of the Messiah in Bethlehem is
self-evident. But the Jews also must have accepted that the
Messiah would be born there, or the apologetic value of the
gospel texts (Mt 2:6 and Jn 7:42) would have been nil, and it is
interesting to note that even after Christians had begun to use the
text from Micah as a powerful apologetic argument, the rabbis
did not deny that the Messiah would be born in Bethlehem.[7]

[7] See Strack-Billerbeck, *Kommentar zum Neuen Testament aus Talmud und Midrasch*, vol. 1, Munich, 1926, p. 83, for the texts. See also Justin, *Dialogus* 78
(MG 6.657).

It would seem certain that Luke had this text in mind, even though he does not cite it explicitly.[8] He stresses that Jesus was born in Bethlehem and (as if to underline the fact that this is not just a piece of topographical information) adds 'in the city of David' (2:4). This was truly so, he says, even though his mother's home was at Nazareth; and he gives very precise details to explain why it was that Mary had to make the journey to Bethlehem (2:1–5). Later, he adds that her son was both Messiah and Lord (2:11). In asserting that Jesus was the Messiah born in Bethlehem, Luke implicitly claims that the prophecy of Mic 5:1–4a has been fulfilled. In calling him 'Lord' (the word by which the Septuagint translates the name Yahweh), Luke further implies that 'his origins are from the beginning, from the days of eternity' (cf. Mic 5:1ef).[9] Micah's oracle ends with the statement that men will live 'in the glory of the name of the Lord their God . . . and there shall be peace' (5:3–4a); Luke closes the story of the apparition to the shepherds with the words 'Glory to God in the highest heavens, and peace on earth among men of his good will' (2:14).[10]

There is, however, another text in Micah (4:6–10) which, according to some authors,[11] was also in Luke's mind. The passage, in its original context, is generally taken to foretell exile for Israel, and then deliverance by Yahweh, and this certainly seems to be the meaning of the Greek text.[12] The Septuagint gives basically the sense of the Hebrew, except that in nearly every line the nation is personified as a woman. Where the Hebrew, for example,

[8] Very often Luke does not cite an Old Testament text explicitly when he could do so: see above, p. 46.

[9] This is accepting, in Lk 2:11, the reading 'Christ and Lord'. There is some very feeble support for the alternative 'Christ of the Lord'. See H. Schürmann, *Das Lukasevangelium I*, pp. 111–12 for a discussion of the textual problem.

[10] For the reading 'men of his good will', see below, p. 97, n. 42.

[11] Notably P. Winter, 'The Cultural Background of the Narrative in Luke I–II', in the *Jewish Quarterly Review* 45 (1955), pp. 238–41, and R. Laurentin, *Structure et théologie de Luc I–II*, pp. 87–8.

[12] For a different interpretation which diverges from this more common view, and seems far more convincing, see the Detached Note on the Daughter of Zion on pp. 440–2. But here we are concerned only with the sense in which Luke understood Micah.

has 'I will gather the lame', the Greek reads 'I will take back her who has been crushed'. The Septuagint text may be translated as follows:

6a 'On that day, says the Lord,
 b   I will take back her who has been crushed,
 c   and I will welcome her who has been banished,
 d   and those whom I drove away.
7a And her that was crushed I will make into a remnant,
 b   and her that was driven away into a mighty nation,
 c   and the Lord will reign over them on Mount Zion,
 d   from this time forward and for ever.
8a And thou, waterless tower of the flock,
 b   Daughter of Zion,
 c   to thee shall come and shall return the sovereign power
          of yesterday,
 d   a kingdom from Babylon for the Daughter of
          Jerusalem!'

In addition to the personification of Israel, one point is noteworthy: in the very last line (8d) the Septuagint inserts two words not found in the Hebrew text: 'from Babylon'. This may be of significance for the Lucan Infancy Gospel—that a kingdom comes *from Babylon* to the Daughter of Jerusalem.

Micah next describes in very cryptic language how Yahweh will deliver his people from their enemies. The words are explicitly addressed to the 'Daughter of Zion'.

9a 'And now, why hast thou known evil fortune?
 b   Was there no king in thee?
 c   Or did thy plan come to nothing
 d   because pains like those of childbirth seized thee?
10a Writhe and struggle,[13] O Daughter of Zion,
 b   like a woman in labour,
 c   for now thou art going to leave the city

[13] This is probably the sense of the Hebrew text. The Greek version is here most obscure: it reads 'Groan and play the man and draw near, O Daughter of Zion'.

d   and camp in the open country,
e   and thou shalt go far away to Babylon.
f   Thence the Lord thy God will deliver thee,
g   thence he will redeem thee,
h   from the hand of thy enemies' (Mic 4:6-10, Septu-
                                                agint).

In this second half of the passage, the first six lines (9*a*-10*b*) speak of some terrible disaster, probably because of the incompetence or sinfulness of a king (9*bcd*); the next two lines (10*cd*) foretell the deportation of the people—they must leave the city and camp in the fields on the way to exile; 10*e* names the place of exile— Babylon. The last three lines promise deliverance from Babylon (10*fgh*).

There is no clear evidence that these verses were regarded as a Messianic prophecy in the apostolic Church.[14] One possible argument to support such a view would be that when Gabriel says that Mary's son 'will reign over the house of Jacob for ever' (Lk 1:33), the allusion is to Mic 4:7: 'The Lord will reign over them on Mount Zion, from this time forward and for ever.' But the idea expressed in Gabriel's words could just as easily be Luke's own paraphrase of the whole content of Messianic hope. The only other New Testament texts of interest are Jn 16:21 and Apoc 12:2, which speak of a woman in labour and are therefore similar to Mic 4:9-10*b*. But again these texts could be based on Is 66:7 or some other passage, and in any case they are not necessarily a direct citation of the Old Testament. There is no convincing proof (as there was for Mic 5:1-4*a*) that Mic 4:6-10 was used as a Messianic prophecy in apostolic times.

Yet one must beware of going to the other extreme, as if it were quite certain that Luke did not have Mic 4:6-10 in mind. For if Micah's message there be closely examined, it comes very near to a *theologia crucis*. Artur Weiser, after observing that the text portrays the helplessness of Israel, makes this very pertinent comment: 'The comparison with the pains of a woman in labour is (as elsewhere in the Old Testament, *cf.* Hos 13:13;

[14] Justin, however, does cite Mic 4:1-7 in the *Dialogus* 109 (MG 6.728).

Jer 6:24; Ps 48:7) meant first and foremost to bring home to the listeners the quite painful depth of their need. Nothing is screened from sight, nothing is made light of—the bitter reality is soberly faced and accepted. But at the same time the image of childbirth is given a deeper meaning, as is clear from v. 10. There is a crisis which is a matter of life and death; but distress is not the last word in this bitter and critical hour. Distress is but a transit-point at which God intervenes afresh; his intervention leads to a future beyond distress, and with his help something entirely new is brought into existence. That is why the suffering must first be accepted with the utmost seriousness, and positively engaged in, by faith'.[15] In other words, the pain of childbirth is not a metaphor denoting unqualified agony, for 'when the woman is delivered of the child, she no longer remembers the anguish, for joy that a man is born into the world' (Jn 16:21). One cannot, at this stage, wholly exclude the possibility that Luke saw in the birth of Jesus in poverty, far from his mother's home at Nazareth, a fulfilment of Mic 4:6–10.

It is difficult, probably impossible, to decide for certain whether Luke had Mic 4:6–10 in mind. Against the idea that he had this text in mind, one could argue as follows. It is hard to see how the journey to Bethlehem could have been, in Luke's mind, both a joyful, 'eschatological', journey to 'royal David's city' where the Messiah was to be born, and at the same time a sad 'going away to Babylon', to exile and suffering; the two images are mutually exclusive, and Bethlehem can hardly do duty for both, in one and the same text. One must therefore choose between seeing Lk 2: 1–20 as the fulfilment of Mic 5:1–4a, and seeing it as the fulfilment of Mic 4:6–10. The relevance of Mic 5:1–4 is proved beyond all doubt; and therefore it is all but certain that Luke did not intend his story to be read as the fulfilment of Mic 4:6–10.

On the other hand, both Mic 4 and 5 are concerned with the coming of eschatological salvation to the remnant of Israel.[16] In Mic 4:7–10 the prophet is concerned with the reign of Yahweh,

[15] Das Buch der zwölf Kleinen Propheten I (= Das Alte Testament Deutsch, Teilband 24), 4th revised edition, Göttingen, 1963, pp. 269–70.

[16] For this paragraph see Laurentin, Structure et théologie de Luc I–II, p. 88.

the deliverance of Israel, and the 'eschatological' child-bearing of the Daughter of Zion; in Mic 5:1–4, he is concerned with the reign of the Messiah, who is born of a woman (though it is impossible to decide whether he is thinking of the mother of the Messiah as an individual, or of Israel as a community, or of both without distinction). Now Luke is concerned not to distinguish between the kingship of Yahweh and the kingship of Jesus, but to stress their identity (cf. Lk 1:32–3);[17] for him, Jesus is both 'Christ' and 'Lord' (2:11). Therefore it is permissible to look upon Mary as that Daughter of Zion through whose child-bearing in poverty and homelessness (Mic 4:8–10) there came great joy to all the world (Mic 5:1–4).

With this Old Testament background in mind, and remembering above all the perennial Lucan theme that salvation comes to the poor and the lowly, and that only by suffering does man enter into glory (cf. Lk 24:26–7), it is possible to ask what is the doctrinal message of Lk 2:1–20. The inquiry may be conveniently phrased in three questions, corresponding to the three major points of interest in the narrative. What is the message conveyed by the sign of the child in the manger? What was Luke's purpose in mentioning the census? What did Luke intend to say by the story about the shepherds?

The central point of the narrative (as Christian tradition has always perceived) is that when Jesus was born, his mother 'wrapped him in swaddling clothes and laid him in a manger' (Lk 2:7). The angel told the shepherds 'This will be a sign to you' (2:12), and the shepherds verified the fact for themselves (2:16–17). Now why should a child lying in a manger (v. 12) be a *sign* that this infant is both Christ and Lord (v. 11)?[18] We may note first that the formula 'And this shall be a sign [for you]' is taken verbatim from the Old Testament (Ex 3:12; 1 Sam 2:34; 14:10; 2 Kgs 19:29; 20:9; Is 37:30; 38:7), and one is therefore tempted to look for something similar to the Old Testament signs alluded to in these texts. But in these Old Testament texts,

---

[17] See above, pp. 54–5.

[18] For what follows see L. Legrand, 'L'évangile aux bergers', in the RB 75 (1968), pp. 169–73.

the sign given is an extraordinary or miraculous event which is intended as a guarantee that a divine promise will be fulfilled in the future; and it is given in response to doubt, to strengthen faith. Now there is nothing particularly miraculous about a child lying in a manger, and the 'sign' is offered to the shepherds spontaneously, not in response to any doubt. We must therefore look outside the Old Testament for a solution to the problem.

In the New Testament, 'signs' are a distinctive characteristic of the mission of the apostles, as the summaries in Acts stress (Ac 2:43; 4:33, *cf.* v. 30; 5:12, 15–16; 8:6–8, 13; 14:3). These signs of the mission of the apostles are, contrary to what happens in the Old Testament, given spontaneously, and not in answer to some doubt. 'Henceforth, signs have acquired a different internal structure. From this time onwards, they are not so much phenomena intended to guarantee a promise about the future as the spontaneous irruption of a new reality within history—what the Synoptics term the Kingdom, or what Luke, from his own particular angle, calls the Spirit. The function of these signs is no longer to stimulate confidence in a promise, but to support the appeal to conversion which the gospel contains. Accordingly, their value henceforth depends less on their "surprising" character than on their ability to condense the gospel-message (*de leur densité kérygmatique*), on their power to "pierce the heart" (Ac 2:37). It is no longer, then, a question of things unheard of being performed, but of putting across the message of conversion. And in this sense, the most effective sign is the sign of the cross (cf. 1 Cor 1:22–5)'.[19] So, in Lk 2:34, Jesus is 'a sign that will be contradicted'.[20] So also the infant lying in a manger is a sign— not an extraordinary or a miraculous sign, but a sign 'to pierce the heart'—already preaching in the humility of his birth the lesson he would preach on Calvary. The manger is the mirror of

[19] L. Legrand, *RB* 75 (1968), pp. 170–1. He adds, on p. 171, that in Lk 11:29–32, by contrast with Mk 8:11–12 (where any sign is totally refused) and with Mt 16:1–4 (where the only sign offered is Jonah as a type of the Resurrection), Jonah is presented simply as the type of a preacher calling for repentance. Thus, for Luke, is Jesus a sign.

[20] See below, pp. 104–12.

the cross, the *res et sacramentum* of the gospel. This is the interpretation given by St Ambrose,[21] and by the Venerable Bede. Bede writes: 'He was wounded for our transgressions, he was bruised for our iniquities (Is 53:5). It should be carefully noted that the sign given of the saviour's birth is not a child enfolded in Tyrian purple, but one wrapped round with rough pieces of cloth; he is not to be found in an ornate golden bed, but in a manger. The meaning of this is that he did not merely take upon himself our lowly mortality, but for our sakes took upon himself the clothing of the poor. Though he was rich, yet for our sake he became poor, so that by his poverty we might become rich (*cf.* 2 Cor 8:9); though he was Lord of heaven, he became a poor man on earth, to teach those who lived on earth that by poverty of spirit they might win the kingdom of heaven'.[22]

In this sense, it is easy to understand that the child in the manger is a sign to pierce the heart, a summons to conversion; but in what sense can the presence of this child in a manger be a sign to the shepherds that 'Today there is born to you a saviour who is Christ and Lord, in the city of David' (2:11)? To answer this question, we must consider Luke's purpose in writing of the census.

It is commonly assumed in modern commentaries that Luke's purpose was to explain how Jesus came to be born in Bethlehem, though his mother's home (and Joseph's) was in Nazareth; and that perhaps Luke also intended to give a date for the birth. The first assumption is certainly true, the second possibly so. But the leading patristic commentators see a deeper significance in the mention of the census, and may well point the way to Luke's real message. Origen sets the tone:

'I can imagine someone saying: Evangelist, what use to me is the story that the *first registration* of the entire world took place under Caesar Augustus, that along with everyone else

---

[21] *In Lucam* II, 41 (ML 15.1649). Ambrose sees in the scene an anticipation of Is 53:5 and a realization of 2 Cor 8:9. It is from him that Bede takes these two texts.

[22] *In Lucam* I, commenting on Lk 2:12 (*CC* 120.51-2 = ML 92.333).

Joseph too with Mary his betrothed (she being with child) put his name on the census-book, and that, before the registration was completed, Jesus was born? But if you look more closely, you will see that a great mystic sign is set before us: for in the registration of the entire world, Jesus Christ had to be included. His name was written down with all the others in the world so that he might sanctify the world, and transform this roll of registration into the book of life, so that the names of those who were registered with him and who believed in him might be written down in heaven.'[23]

Ambrose follows Origen, adding that the prime mover in the census was in the end not Augustus, but Christ himself, for 'the earth is the Lord's, and the fullness thereof'.[24] Gregory the Great puts this tradition neatly when he writes:

'Why was there a census of the world when the Lord was about to be born? Surely the plain meaning is that he was appearing in the flesh in order to record the names of his elect for eternity.'[25]

Bede makes the same point.[26]

In the light of these patristic commentaries, it is fair to ask whether this may not have been Luke's primary purpose in mentioning the census. Untold quantities of ink have flowed on the dating of the 'first census' under Quirinius in Syria,[27] but may not Origen point the way to a better understanding of the text by his statement that this was the first time there had been a census of the entire world? Luke's passionate interest in the universality of salvation is well-known, and it is worth examining his text to

[23] *In Lucam*, Hom. 11, translated from the Greek where extant (*GCS* 49 [35], Berlin, 1959, p. 71 = MG 13:1828).

[24] *In Lucam* II, 37: 'non enim Augusti, sed domini est terra et plenitudo eius' (ML 15.1647).

[25] *XL Hom. in Evangelia*, Lib. I, Hom. 8 (ML 76.1103).

[26] *In Lucam* I, commenting on Lk 2:1 (*CC* 120.45–7 = ML 92.328–9).

[27] For a brief summary of the *status quaestionis* and an up-to-date bibliography, see H. Schürmann, *Das Lukasevangelium I*, pp. 99–101.

see whether he may not have been more interested in the religious significance of the census than in supplying a date for the birth of Jesus.

'In those days there went forth a decree from Caesar Augustus' (Lk 2:1). Schürmann has observed that Luke distinguishes very carefully between the phrase 'in *these* days', where the reference is simply to the time at which an event takes place (Lk 1:39; 6:12; 23:7; 24:18; Ac 1:15), and the words 'in *those* days': the latter always refers to days in which some great eschatological and salvific event takes place (as in Lk 2:1; 4:2; 5:35; 9:36; Ac 2:18).[28] He therefore comments on Lk 2:1: 'It was in those days so full of significance, so pregnant with apocalyptic promises and fulfilments (*cf.* 1:5–80)'[29] that there went forth a decree from Caesar Augustus. In other words, Luke sees the decree as part of God's salvific plan, at least in the sense that it brought Joseph and Mary to Bethlehem. 'And it came to pass that *while they were there, the days were fulfilled* for her to give birth' (2:6): here the very wording stresses the fulfilment of prophecy.[30] The decree of Augustus is not cited merely to give chronological information; it was the immediate occasion of the birth of Jesus in Bethlehem.

'Joseph too went up from Galilee, from the city of Nazareth, to Judaea, to the city of David, which is called Bethlehem, because he was of the house and family of David, to be registered with Mary his wife,[31] she being with child' (Lk 2:4–5). The word-order makes it plain that Luke is not simply saying that Mary accompanied Joseph from Galilee to Bethlehem; rather, he is saying that Joseph went to Bethlehem *in order to be jointly registered with Mary*, she being with child.[32] Whatever may have been the custom about the registration of women and children (and this is much debated), the intention of the evangelist is to affirm that

[28] *Das Lukasevangelium I*, p. 65, fn. 162.

[29] *Ibid.*, p. 98.

[30] See above, pp. 27 and 81–3.

[31] 'His wife', though not strongly attested, is almost certainly the original reading (rather than 'his betrothed'): see Schürmann, *Das Lukasevangelium I*, p. 103, fn. 37.

[32] This is even clearer in the Greek than in English.

Mary was indubitably in Bethlehem when Jesus was born. What Luke is saying is therefore this: that though Augustus was surveying his dominions and listing his subjects, God used this imperial census to bring about in Bethlehem, the city of David, the birth of one who, though wrapped in swaddling clothes and lying in a manger, was the true king for whom the Gentiles would be an inheritance, and whose possessions would reach to the ends of the earth (Ps 2:7–8). Luke makes this point in the words 'Today there is born to you a saviour who is Christ the Lord, in the city of David' (2:11): this sentence is astonishingly close to the terms in which the birth of a royal prince was officially announced in the courts of the Hellenistic world.[33] But at once he adds a qualification; this new-born child, though truly heir to the throne of David, was not destined to rule over an earthly empire by force of arms, as Augustus did. 'This shall be the *sign* to you' of the nature of his kingship, and of the means whereby he will bring the world under his sway: 'you will find the child wrapped in swaddling clothes and lying in a manger' (2:12). And precisely because Jesus came to establish a new kind of kingdom by peaceful means, and a kingdom open to all the nations of the world, the episode can close with the hymn

'Glory to God in the highest heavens,
 and on earth peace among men of his good will' (2:14).

It was said above[34] that stories about the infancy of Jesus were first recounted orally in Aramaic, and that when Luke selected what he needed, he transformed the stories which he had heard or read until they were wholly adapted for his Greek (and probably Gentile) readers. Certainly Lk 2:1–20 is through and through Luke's own composition,[35] and the birth of Jesus is presented as the birth of a prince who was to inherit Augustus' world. Could there be, *behind* Luke's own interpretation of Jesus' birth, an

[33] See L. Cerfaux and J. Tondriau, *Le culte des souverains dans la civilisation gréco–romaine*, Paris and Tournai, 1957, pp. 320, 332, 380, 450.

[34] See above, pp. 5–6.

[35] See above, p. 80, and fn. 3.

older, Palestinian story which Luke has transposed for the Greek world? In the nature of the case, this (hypothetical) Palestinian story will be difficult to discover, and the only clue we have is that it must make the same point as Luke's Greek version. In all likelihood, it will be based on Old Testament prophecy.

I would suggest that Laurentin and Winter are fundamentally right in asserting that behind Lk 2:1–20 there is a wealth of allusion to Mic 4:6–10; and that this was (in *oral* tradition) the ultimate source of Luke's thought. We may begin by recalling part of the passage:

> 8a   'And thou, waterless tower of the flock,
>   b   Daughter of Zion,
>   c   to thee shall come and shall return the sovereign power
>   of yesterday,
>   d   a kingdom from Babylon for the Daughter of
>   Jerusalem!
> 9a   And now, why hast thou known evil fortune?
>   b   Was there no king in thee? . . .
> 10a   Writhe and struggle, O Daughter of Zion,
>   b   like a woman in labour,
>   c   for now thou art going to leave the city
>   d   and camp in the open country,
>   e   and thou shalt go far away to Babylon.
>   f   Thence the Lord thy God will deliver thee,
>   g   thence he will redeem thee,
>   h   from the hand of thy enemies.

In the Apocalypse, 'Babylon' is simply a name for imperial Rome, a city devoted to the pursuit of material wealth and the enemy of the Christian Church (Apoc 14:8; 16:19; 17:5; 18:2, 10, 21; *cf.* I Pet 5:13). Those first-century Christians who thought of imperial Rome as 'Babylon' could hardly fail to see in the many threats uttered against the ancient Babylon (*e.g.* Is 13–14) a divine assurance that the new Babylon, Rome, would meet the same fate as the city in southern Mesopotamia. For a person with this attitude towards imperial Rome, a decree from Caesar

Augustus ordering a census of the entire world would have been a decree issuing from Babylon. Now Luke states that as a result of Augustus' decree, Mary had to leave her home in Nazareth and travel to Bethlehem, where she gave birth to her child in abject poverty, in some place which was used as a stable. Is he perhaps thinking of the Daughter of Zion 'leaving her city, going far away to Babylon, and encamping in the open country' (Mic 4:10)? If he did have this text in mind, the remainder of Mic 4:10 would have been most apposite: 'From there the Lord thy God will deliver thee, from there he will redeem thee from the hand of thy enemies'—words which are echoed in the opening verses of the Benedictus (Lk 1:68–71). Moreover, if Luke really did see Mary's journey to Bethlehem as fulfilling Mic 4:10, then he certainly would have perceived that on the occasion of the Roman census, 'the sovereign power of former days returned to David's line, and dominion passed from Babylon to the Daughter of Jerusalem' (Mic 4:8cd).

So we come to the third question: what did Luke mean to convey by his story of the apparition to the shepherds, and of their visit to the new-born child (Lk 2:8–20)? Origen asks: 'Do you think the message of the Scriptures is nothing more divine than the bare affirmation that an angel came to some shepherds and spoke to them? Open your ears, you shepherds of the churches, you shepherds of God, to the fact that his angel is always coming down from heaven and proclaiming to you that "this day there is born to you a saviour who is Christ and Lord".'[36] In other words, is Luke merely relating a factual event, or is he using the story to convey to 'the shepherds of the churches' a truth about Jesus of Nazareth? And if it is the latter, what truth does Luke wish to convey?

In Micah, the shepherd-motif is mentioned three times. The Daughter of Zion is referred to as 'a tower of the flock' (4:8); the Messiah will shepherd his flock with the strength of the Lord (5:3b); and the remnant of Israel will be saved 'like sheep in distress, like a flock in the middle of its pen they will be saved from men' (2:12, in the Greek). It seems highly probable that

[36] *In Lucam*, Hom. 13 (= GCS 49 [35], pp. 72–3 = MG 13.1828–9).

Luke means to recall this prophetical theme by portraying Jesus as 'the shepherd of Israel', for it is a theme which would have been readily understood not only in Palestine or among Jews, but also among the Greeks.

Throughout the ancient world the king was regarded as the shepherd of his people. In Babylonia and in Assyria, in Egypt and in Homeric Greece, the king was given this title;[37] even Plato uses it of the rulers of the city-state.[38] It is astounding, therefore, to find that Israel seems to have deliberately refused to call its king 'the shepherd of his people', especially when one remembers its general enthusiasm for adopting the court protocol of neighbouring nations.[39] There is one exception. David, the idealized king of the past, is said 'to have shepherded' his people (2 Sam 5:2 = 1 Chr 11:2; Ps 78:71 f.), and he himself speaks of them as a flock (2 Sam 24:17 = 1 Chr 21:17), though even in these texts the noun 'shepherd' is not applied to David. Apart from these five texts referring to David, no king of Judah or Israel is ever called 'the shepherd of his people'. Later, the word is used in the plural for all kinds of other leaders in Israel: it is used of the Judges (2 Sam 7:7 = 1 Chr 17:6), of the priests (Jer 2:8) and of teachers of the Law (Jer 3:15), and it is applied once (in the singular) to Cyrus, the emperor of Persia (Is 44:28 in the Hebrew text, though the Greek omits this word).[40] One may reasonably ask whether it is purely by accident that not a single text refers to any king except David as the shepherd of Israel.

In the above-mentioned texts where the word is used of leaders other than David and Cyrus, the context is almost always one of condemnation (2 Sam 7:7 is an exception): these leaders have

[37] *Cf.* J. Jeremias in the *TWNT* 6, 485–6 for the references. The information on which this and the following paragraph are based comes from this article, though the facts are given a slightly different interpretation.

[38] Jeremias, *art. cit.*, p. 486, fn. 16 refers to the *Republic* I, 343b–45a; III, 416ab, and the *Laws*, V, 735 b–e.

[39] *Cf.* R. de Vaux, *Ancient Israel*, pp. 100–32, *passim*.

[40] Perhaps the Greek translator read the same Hebrew text as we do, and deliberately suppressed the title. It is hard to say why the author of Second Isaiah used it, but perhaps it was because of the influence of his own Babylonian background.

proved disloyal, wicked or foolish shepherds. Apart from David (and Cyrus, if the Hebrew text of Is 44:28 be accepted in preference to the Greek), there is no instance of an historical individual ever behaving as a good or wise shepherd. By contrast, the title 'Shepherd of Israel' is frequently given to Yahweh himself. 'Listen, O Shepherd of Israel' (Ps 80:2) and 'Yahweh is my shepherd' (Ps 23:1) are phrases which give utterance to a concept deeply rooted in the mind and heart of Israel (cf. Is 40:11; 49:10–11, etc.): it was no earthly king, but God himself who cared for, and looked after, his people. It is all the more impressive, therefore, to find that the same title is given to one man other than David—to the future Messiah, the new David for whose coming the nation was always waiting. The central and classic text dealing with this theme (Ez 34) contains all the three ideas just mentioned. Wicked shepherds have been feeding themselves and neglecting the flock (Ez 34:1–6); therefore Yahweh will intervene, dismiss the shepherds and himself take charge of the flock (vv. 7–16). Verse 23 reads: 'And I will set up over them one shepherd, my servant David, and he shall feed them; he shall feed them, and be their shepherd.' Thus, according to Ezekiel, both Yahweh and his Messiah would be faithful shepherds of the flock. In the light of this text, contrasted with the others, it is fair to say that among men only David, seen as an idealized figure of the past, and the new David, seen as an idealized figure of the future, could be called 'shepherds of Israel', because they alone perfectly obeyed Yahweh, the 'Chief Shepherd'.

The angel who first appeared to the shepherds near Bethlehem proclaimed that the saviour who was born was both 'Christ and Lord' (Lk 2:11). These two titles, 'Lord' and 'Christ', are those which Peter proclaimed after the Resurrection (Ac 2:36). It is not fanciful to think that Luke, the author of Acts, is here asserting once more (as in Lk 1:35)[41] that Jesus did not begin to be 'Lord and Christ' after the Resurrection, but that he had been such from the moment of his birth. By either title, he was to Jewish Christians the Shepherd of Israel and its saviour; to Gentile ears, he who was 'Lord' and 'Saviour' was truly the shepherd of the entire world.

[41] See above, pp. 59–61.

The angel who gave this message to the shepherds was suddenly joined by a great multitude of the heavenly host singing

'Glory to God in the highest heavens,
   and on earth peace among men of his good will'
                                  (Lk 2:14).[42]

Not only Micah, but many other prophets and psalmists had foretold that the reign of Yahweh and the reign of the Messiah would bring peace on earth among those who loved and served God.[43] In Ez 34, this message is paramount: the prophet affirms that Yahweh, the true Shepherd of Israel, will himself come to search out his sheep; that he will rescue them from all dangers and bring them to pasture on the mountains of Israel; and that he will set over them 'one shepherd, my servant David', who will feed them and be their shepherd (Ez 34:11, 13–14, 23).

This is the heart of Luke's message: that Yahweh himself, the Good Shepherd, comes to seek out his sheep. And it is to the humble, the poor and the lowly, to shepherds still busy in the night looking after their flocks, that heaven itself announces the coming of 'the covenant of peace' (Ez 34:25). The hymn in the Roman Liturgy for Lauds on Christmas Day catches the mood and the thought of St Luke to perfection when, after dwelling on the poverty in which the Saviour was born, it says that all heaven rejoiced when the Creator and Shepherd of all that lives made himself known to the poorest in the land.[44]

---

[42] *I.e.* among men whom God has freely chosen to receive his grace and peace. The parallels from Qumran make it all but certain that v. 14 should read 'men of his good will' rather than 'good will to men', or 'men of good will'. See Schürmann, *Das Lukasevangelium I*, pp. 114–15, fn. 142, 143, 146 for some references to periodical literature.

[43] See W. Eichrodt, *Die Hoffnung des ewigen Friedens im alten Israel*, Gütersloh, 1920; H. Gross, *Die Idee des ewigen und allgemeinen Weltfriedens im Alten Orient und im AT*, Trier, 1956; J. J. Stamm and H. Bietenhard, *Der Weltfriede im Alten und Neuen Testament*, Zürich, 1959; H. W. Wolff, *Frieden ohne Ende: Jesaja 7:1–17 und 9:1–6 ausgelegt*, Neukirchen, 1962.

[44] Thus Ambrose, *In Lucam* II, 53 (ML 15.1653).

Feno iacere pertulit,
praesepe non abhorruit,
parvoque lacte pastus est
per quem nec ales esurit.

Gaudet chorus caelestium
et angeli canunt Deum,
palamque fit pastoribus
pastor, creator omnium.

Chapter Eleven

THE LORD COMES TO HIS TEMPLE

(Lk 2:22–38)

THE major themes underlying St Luke's thought were nearly all interwoven in the story of the Nativity. Jesus was there presented as the Davidic Messiah; and behind the census decreed by Augustus we may surely see an allusion to the heaven-born Prince of Peace, that Son of Man whose empire was to embrace all peoples, nations and tongues, whose dominion was to be an everlasting dominion that shall not pass away (Dan 7:14). The day of his birth was therefore the day of salvation for the remnant of Israel, when Yahweh himself sought out the remnant of his flock to set over them the shepherd-king, the new David (Ez 34:11–31). Luke had already told his readers that Mary was 'Blessed among women', destined to be honoured by all generations, because in her motherhood the promises to Abraham had been fulfilled; through her, and her alone, Israel gave the world its Lord and saviour. It is not absurd, therefore, to say that Mary was, in those eschatological days, the living embodiment of the Daughter of Zion. Thus of the five major themes described in Chapter 3,[1] four are found in the story of the Nativity. Only one is still lacking: the reader still awaits the fulfilment of Malachi's prophecy that 'the Lord whom you seek will suddenly come to his temple' (Mal 3:1). Luke closes his account of the infancy of Jesus by recording the fulfilment of this prophecy. In the story of the Presentation Mary (one may well think, *qua* Daughter of

[1] Pp. 24–36.

Zion) takes Jesus to the Temple and there presents him to the Lord.

'When the days of their[2] purification were completed'—that is, seventy symbolic weeks after Gabriel's first appearance in the Temple[3]—'they took him up to Jerusalem to present him to the Lord' (Lk 2:22). If Luke had Daniel's prophecy in mind,[4] the day was now come 'to make atonement for iniquity, to bring in everlasting righteousness, to set the seal on vision and prophet, and to anoint the Most Holy' (Dan 9:24).[5] Jesus, the son of God, was going to hallow the sanctuary by his presence; in the Temple, Jesus the son of Mary would himself be openly dedicated to the service of God.

[2] Thus the Greek text, while the Vulgate has *'purgationis eius'*, which can refer either to Jesus or to Mary. (The old Roman Missal, in the Mass for 2 February, expressly stated *'purgationis Mariae'*.) Certainly *'their* purification' cannot refer to Mary and Joseph. It is usually understood to refer to Jesus and Mary, though some authors do take it to refer to the Jews (*cf.* R. Laurentin, *Structure et théologie de Luc I–II*, p. 90, fn. 4). P. Benoit comments: 'The Law prescribed the purification of the mother (Lev 12:1–8) and the ransoming of the first-born (Ex 13:11–16). The mother had to go in person to the sanctuary, but it is not so clear that the child had to be taken in person (Num 18:15–16). The five silver shekels which were paid to ransom the child were quite distinct from the sacrifice of two turtle-doves offered by the mother. Luke combines the two rites into one, makes a presentation of the Child the centre of the scene—which is in any case quite plausible, either by reason of devotion (1 Sam 1:22–8) or because of a pious desire to do more than the Law demanded (Neh 10:37)—and gives the impression that the sacrifice was of avail for the Child as well as for the mother (hence "*their* purification"). The reason is that in his eyes Jesus, rather than Mary, stands at the centre of the scene. "Anyone unacquainted with the Law would not even suspect that she (Mary) had any part to play in this ceremony. What was important for Luke was to present Jesus in the Temple, where he had to be recognized as Messiah" (Lagrange)' (*CBQ* 25 (1963), p. 258, fn. 27).

[3] See above, pp. 26–7.

[4] See above, p. 27.

[5] The phrase in Daniel, here translated 'the Most Holy', is literally 'a Holy of Holies'. The term can mean either the innermost room of the Temple building, or (very rarely) a gift to God. (In 1 Chr 23:13 Aaron and his sons are set apart 'to consecrate the most holy things'.) Perhaps the two ideas were present in Luke's mind, and this is the sense taken in the final sentence of the paragraph above, namely that Jesus would hallow the Temple by his presence, and would himself be dedicated by being formally and in the sight of men presented to God.

St Luke gives, as the reason for this presentation, a precept of the Law of Moses: '*Every male child opening the womb* shall be called holy *to the Lord*.' There is in fact no such precept in the Pentateuch. Luke's words are a loose citation of three separate verses in Ex 13:2, 12, 15; these verses contain the words in italics, but not the words 'shall be called holy'. The precept of Exodus reads: 'Every first-born of man among your children you shall redeem' (Ex 13:13), and this is a verse which Luke does not cite. Instead, he takes three other verses. The words 'every male opening the womb' occur in vv. 12 and 15, and v. 2 reads: 'Sanctify to me every eldest thing, every first-born opening every womb among the children of Israel, from men to beast: it is mine.' The precept of the Law is therefore quite clear: every male child who was the first-born had to be consecrated to God (v. 2) and to be redeemed (v. 13). Luke, however, has altered this to a statement that every male child opening the womb had to be 'called holy to the Lord'.

The reason for his alteration is not far to seek. Jesus, who had been conceived by the power of the Holy Spirit, could not be consecrated or '*made* holy' by being presented to God; from the first instant of his existence in Mary's womb he was by nature holy. Nor could he be 'redeemed' like any other child. In the Old Law, the concept of 'redeeming' creatures was rather subtle. Everything which belonged to God belonged to him exclusively, but by paying to the Temple some substitute offering (a sacrifice, or money) it could be 'redeemed' and thereby became, in some sense, 'desacralized', so that it could serve a profane use. Now Jesus could never have been 'redeemed' in this sense: no substitute-offering could ever have released him from a total, undivided and everlasting consecration to God. Like the Levites (Num 3: 12–13; 8:14–18), Jesus was irrevocably consecrated to God for the whole of his life. It is impossible to think of him as being (in the Mosaic sense) 'redeemed'.

Jesus could neither be '*made* holy to the Lord' nor 'redeemed'. And yet his parents took him to the Temple in order to observe the legal prescriptions. Luke therefore finds a different reason for this presentation by citing Exodus as far as he can ('Every male child opening the womb . . . to the Lord') and altering the verb; looking back to his statement of the virginal conception, he completes the sentence with Gabriel's words ('shall be called holy', 1:35).[6] This in turn harmonizes perfectly with Dan 9:24: it was the day awaited for seventy weeks by the people and the Holy City, the day appointed 'to make atonement for iniquity, to bring in everlasting righteousness, to set the seal on vision and prophet, *and to anoint the Most Holy*' (Dan 9:24). 'The Lord came to his temple' (Mal 3:1), and the last prophecy was fulfilled. It is true that in the actual description of the scene (Lk 2:22–38) there is no direct citation of, or overt allusion to, this prophecy of Malachi, but when we recall that Luke has already cited Malachi more or less explicitly in 1:17 and 76, and that he will do so again in 7:19 and 27, the reader can be expected to remember that John the Baptist is the new Elijah going before the Lord. 'Behold I send my messenger to prepare the way before me': the reader is therefore already alerted for the imminent fulfilment of the second part of this verse: 'and the Lord whom you seek will suddenly come to his temple; the messenger of the covenant in whom you delight, behold he is coming, says the Lord of hosts' (Mal 3:1). Indeed, a recent study has shown that whereas in the Old Testament the Temple is the place of the presence of God, in Luke and in Acts (as in St John) Jesus himself is the new temple where men come face to face with God.[7]

St Luke tells how Simeon, a prophet inspired to believe that he would live to see the Messiah, was that day guided to the Temple by the Spirit of God (Lk 2:25–7). When Mary and Joseph entered, he took the child Jesus into his arms, and said the Nunc Dimittis. In this canticle, which is doubtless another hymn from the early Christian liturgy, the major themes of Messianic salvation recur. In the infant Jesus, all mankind sees God's promised Saviour (Is 40:5; 52:10), for he is that Servant of Yahweh destined

---

[6] On p. 56, Lk 1:35 was translated as 'the holy child shall be called God's son', though an alternative rendering is 'the child will be called holy, God's son'. Whichever version be adopted, Jesus can still be called 'holy'.

[7] K. Baltzer, 'The Meaning of the Temple in the Lukan Writings', in the *Harvard Theological Review* 58 (1965), pp. 263–77.

to bring revelation to the Gentiles (Is 42:4; 49:6) and glory to Israel (Is 46:13). The insertion of Simeon's canticle at this point underlines the eschatological significance of the context: 'the Lord has come to his temple'.

Chapter Twelve

SIMEON'S PROPHECY ABOUT THE SWORD
(Lk 2:34–5)

THE final chapter of Malachi's prophecy states that the day of
Yahweh's coming will be a day of judgment for Israel (Mal 3:2,
3, 5, 16–18, 19–20 [=4:1]), and St Luke stresses the same idea.
Immediately after the Nunc Dimittis, Simeon 'blessed them and
said to Mary his mother:

34a   Behold, this (child) is destined for the downfall and
        resurrection of many in Israel,

  b   to be a sign that will be opposed [or: disputed];

35a   and thou thyself wilt feel a sword pass through thy
        soul,

  b   that the secret thoughts of many hearts may be re-
        vealed.'

Professor Black voices the opinion of most commentators when
he remarks: 'The verses are among the most difficult in the Greek
Bible; it is virtually impossible to find a logical connexion of
thought running through the passage. How, for instance, are
we to connect the first and second parts of verse 35?'[1] The interpretation set out in this chapter is that of Père Benoit; he seems
to have offered the most satisfactory elucidation of the many
obscurities which the text contains.[2]

[1] M. Black, *An Aramaic Approach to the Gospels and Acts*, 3rd ed., Oxford, 1967,
p. 153.

[2] P. Benoit, ' "Et toi-même, un glaive te transpercera l'âme" (Lc 2:35)', in the
CBQ 25 (1963), pp. 251–61. For a different view see J. Winandy, 'La prophétie
de Syméon (Lc 2:34–5)', in the *RB* 72 (1965), pp. 321–51.

'This (child) is destined for the downfall and resurrection of many in Israel' (34*a*). These words echo the thought of Is 8:14, where Yahweh Sabaoth is said to be 'a sanctuary, and a stone of offence, and a stumbling-block to the two houses of Israel'.[3] Isaiah, in chapters 6–8, confronts the people with a choice between alternatives. Either they must believe his message without reservation, and place their trust in Yahweh alone, or they must with open eyes reject their God. If they believe, they will be saved; if they refuse to believe, their cause is lost. That was the message Isaiah himself had received on the day he was called to be a prophet (Is 6:9–13); that too was his message to Ahaz (7:9). Is 8:5–8 tell of the consequences that will follow Judah's rejection of the prophet's message: because the people refuse to trust the gently-flowing waters of Shiloah (the only source of water in Jerusalem, and therefore the symbol of Yahweh's care for Zion), their land will be flooded by the river-waters of the Euphrates (the symbol of Assyria, to which Ahaz had turned for help). Thus Isaiah's offer of salvation, precisely because it was so clearly presented, proved a trap and a snare to Judah: many stumbled, fell into the trap, and were lost. Lk 2:34*a* describes an exact parallel to this event. Jesus brought a message of salvation for men, on the one condition that they would believe; and precisely because it was so clearly presented and because it demanded wholehearted acceptance, his message resulted in the downfall of many in Israel. 'Whoever is not with me is against me, and whoever does not gather with me is scattering things around' (Lk 11:23).

'This child is destined to be a sign that will be opposed' or 'disputed' (Lk 2:34*b*). Some would accept him as a prophet sent from God, while others would bitterly contest his claims and

[3] Thus the Hebrew. The Septuagint is rather different: 'And if you trust in him, he will be a sanctuary for you, and you will come to him not as to a stone of offence or a rock of stumbling.' The message of the Hebrew and the Septuagint does not differ (for the latter expressly says '*If* you trust in him'), contrary to Winandy's assertion in the *RB* 72 (1965), p. 328. Another Isaian text with the same message occurs in 28:16: 'Behold, I am laying in Zion ... a precious corner-stone, and he who believes in him will not be put to shame.' For examples of various forms in which this text was quoted, see Rom 9:33 and 1 Pet 2:4.

oppose him. Again the text of Luke has a parallel in the same part of the Book of Isaiah. The prophet, when first commanded to challenge Ahaz (Is 7:3), was expressly told to take with him his son Shear-jashub ('A remnant shall return'); the boy's name was to be a silent warning to court and king. After the failure of this mission and the king's hypocritical refusal to believe (7:12), Isaiah was commanded (8:1-4) to give his next son the name Maher-shalal-hash-baz (that is, 'Speed, spoil! Hasten, plunder!'); whereas the name of the first son was a warning, the naming of the second son spelt judgment on Judah's infidelity. A few verses later, Isaiah speaks of himself and 'the children whom Yahweh has given him' as 'signs and portents in Israel from Yahweh Sabaoth who dwells on Mount Zion' (8:18). According to Simeon, Jesus too was destined to be a sign that would be disputed and opposed.

'And thou thyself wilt feel a sword pass through thy soul' (Lk 2:35a). The word here translated 'sword' is used several times in the Old Testament as a metaphor for God's devastating anger (e.g. Wis 5:20: 'He will sharpen stern wrath into a sword'). The metaphor occurs mainly in Ezekiel, where we read, for example: 'Mountains of Israel, listen to the word of the Lord. . . . See, I am bringing a sword against you, and your high places will be destroyed' (Ez 6:2-3). The 'sword' here referred to is the devastation wrought by the Babylonian armies in 588-587 B.C. Similar texts occur in Ez 5:1-3; 12:14; 14:17; 17:21. In each of these texts, however, Ezekiel mentions that a remnant of the people will escape destruction: e.g. 'When some of you are saved from the sword among the Gentiles, when you are scattered through the lands, those of you who are saved will remember me among the Gentiles' (Ez 6:8-9; cf. 5:3-4; 12:16; 14:12-23; 17:21). For Ezekiel, the sword is not merely an instrument of punishment, but also an instrument whereby God divides his people into the remnant and the dead.

Among these five passages from Ezekiel, the closest parallel to Lk 2:35a is Ez 14:17. The prophet is there expounding the truth that each individual is responsible for his own acts. If God were to punish the country by famine (vv. 12-14), by an invasion of wild beasts (vv. 15–16), by war (vv. 17–18), or by a plague (vv. 19–20), and three upright men like Noah, Daniel and Job were found, these three and they alone would be spared. Verses 17–18 read: 'Suppose I were to bring a sword against that country, and were to say, "Let a sword pass through the country and I will rid it of man and beast!"; if these three men were in the middle of it—as I live, says the Lord Yahweh, they would not save their own sons and daughters—they alone would be saved!' Here, as in the other passages, the sword is a symbol for war, but in the war itself God discriminates between the upright and the wicked.

'Thou thyself wilt feel a sword pass through thy soul.' How can war be said to pass through Mary's soul? One interpretation which has gained considerable favour recently among exegetes of various churches deserves to be expounded at some length.[4] According to these writers, Luke is considering Mary once more as the personification of Israel, and Simeon's prediction of a terrible judgment is addressed to Mary as the representative of the people, and should therefore be glossed as follows:

'Behold, this child is destined for the downfall and resurrection of many in Israel,
    to be a sign that will be opposed;
and thou thyself, *O Israel*, shalt feel a sword pass through thy soul,
    that the secret thoughts of many hearts may be revealed.'

The abrupt change from the third- to the second-person singular is disconcerting to a Western mind, but such sudden changes of person are a regular idiom of Semitic poetry (*e.g.* Deut 32:15),[5] and if the saying in 35a is taken as referring to Israel, then a coherent pattern of thought begins to emerge. Jesus, like Yahweh in the

[4] Thus H. Sahlin, *Der Messias und das Gottesvolk*, pp. 273–5; A. G. Hebert, in *Theology* 53 (1950), pp. 406–7; R. Laurentin, *Structure et théologie de Luc I–II*, pp. 89–90; A. R. C. Leaney, *The Gospel according to St Luke*, pp. 100–1; P. Benoit, *CBQ* 25 (1963), pp. 252–6. So also M. Black, *An Aramaic Approach to the Gospels and Acts*, 3rd ed., pp. 154–5 and M.-E. Boismard in the *RB* 66 (1959), p. 140.

[5] See M. Black, *An Aramaic Approach to the Gospels and Acts*, 3rd ed., p. 154. For examples of changes of person in Hebrew poetry, see *Gesenius' Hebrew Grammar*, 2nd English ed., by A. E. Cowley, Oxford, 1909, §144, *p.*

days of Isaiah, will confront men with an inescapable dilemma (Lk 2:34a and Is 8:14); Jesus, like Isaiah himself, is destined to be a sign that many will oppose (Lk 2:34b and Is 8:18). A sword will pass through the nation, bringing to light the moral character of every individual, dividing the good from the bad, and bringing disaster to the wicked (Lk 2:35a and Ez 14:17); as a result, the deep-rooted qualities of sincerity or insincerity which might otherwise continue hidden in men's hearts will be brought into the open light of day (Lk 2:35b). It only remains to ask why Luke, in 35a, chooses to say that a '*sword*' will pass through the nation. What does he mean by this word, and how can a sword reveal the hidden thoughts of many hearts?

In Is 49:2 the Servant of Yahweh says: 'He has made my mouth like a sharp sword.' The Septuagint here translates μάχαιρα, not ῥομφαία (the word used in Lk 2:35a), but the difference is not significant, for the image from Second Isaiah is taken up in the Apocalypse with the word ῥομφαία. Thus 'a sharp two-edged sword' comes forth from the mouth of the Son of Man (Apoc 1:16). John is ordered to write to the angel of the church at Pergamum a letter beginning: 'Thus says he who wields the sharp two-edged sword' (2:12), and ending: 'Repent, then, or else I shall come quickly and make war on them with the sword of my mouth' (2:16). Again, at the end of the book, a Horseman rides out from heaven to execute the final judgment, with *a sharp sword* issuing *from his mouth*: his name is 'the Word of God' (19:11, 13, 15, 21). In all these texts from the Apocalypse the sword is a symbol for the word of revelation which comes from the Son of Man, and this sword becomes, by reason of men's reactions to it, an instrument of God's judgment. One may add that in Eph 6:17 the word of God is called 'a spiritual sword' (μάχαιρα), and that in Heb 4:12 it is called 'a sharp two-edged sword' (again μάχαιρα) which penetrates into the furthest depths of the human soul, bringing to light the sentiments and the thoughts of the character which is there. In the New Testament, then, the sword can be a metaphor for divine revelation as an instrument of judgment, whereby God compels men to reveal their true characters.

The preaching of Jesus is such a two-edged sword. His preaching allowed no one to be neutral: 'Whoever is not with me is against me, and whoever does not gather with me is scattering things around' (Lk 11:23). It stirred up strife within the family: 'Do you think I came to bring peace in the country? No, I tell you—only strife! There shall be strife between father and son . . . between mother and daughter . . .' (Lk 12:51–3). The parallel text in Matthew reads: 'I did not come to bring peace, *but a sword*' (Mt 10:34).

The meaning of Simeon's prophecy, therefore, is that the word of revelation brought by Jesus will pass through Israel like a sword, and will compel men to reveal their secret thoughts. Thus, just as Jesus will fulfil the prophecy of Is 49:6 by being 'a light bringing revelation to the Gentiles' (Lk 2:32), so he will fulfil the role assigned to the Servant of Yahweh in Is 49:2, for his message will be felt as a sharp sword.

The advantage of this interpretation is that it makes verse 35*a* fit the context. Since the time of Robert Stephanus (1551), many editors of the New Testament have placed the words 'A sword shall pass through thy soul' in parentheses, as if they interrupted the sequence of thought,[6] but there is no need for this. The interpretation just given makes this phrase not an interruption, but a link in the development of thought: Jesus' preaching is destined to bring about the fall and resurrection of many in Israel precisely because it will force men to reveal their inmost thoughts.

Furthermore, this interpretation gives a real unity to the wider context, Lk 2:29–35, for the sayings of Simeon are seen to fall into two contrasting and complementary halves. In vv. 29–32 (the Nunc Dimittis) Simeon proclaims that Jesus will be a light bringing revelation to the Gentiles and salvation to all the nations of the world; his mission will therefore be, in itself, the glory of God's people, Israel. Unhappily (vv. 34–5) this preaching will provoke a crisis in Israel, splitting the nation apart, for the majority of God's people will reject him. Thus the destiny of Jesus and the tragedy of his rejection are predicted by Simeon on the very day when Mary, the Daughter of Zion, brings the Lord to his Temple.

[6] For a survey of the punctuation at this verse, see *The Greek New Testament* edited by Kurt Aland and others, London, 1966.

This modern explanation of Lk 2:35a was, it seems, quite unknown in ancient times. The Fathers were, however, very conscious of the obscurity in the words 'A sword shall pass through thy soul', and put forward many widely different interpretations of the phrase.[7] Nearly all their attempted explanations have long been abandoned, but one has become classical in the Church: the sword signifies the suffering felt by Mary as she stood by the cross, watching the death-agony of her son. This classical interpretation is obviously attractive, but there is one decisive objection to it: 35b becomes almost impossible to explain. How can the mental sufferings of Mary on Calvary 'reveal the secret thoughts of many hearts'? It is this apparent *non sequitur* between 35a and 35b which leads so many authors to put 35a in parentheses, but this amounts to an admission that there is nothing in the context to justify the classical interpretation.

And yet the context does justify this classical interpretation, provided that it is correctly understood. Simeon states that a sword will pass through Mary's soul. His words have in the past been usually taken to refer to Mary *solely* as a private individual, and to refer *solely* to that moment in her life when she stood at the foot of the cross. The biblical text, however, gives no positive grounds for the conviction that Simeon's words are concerned with Mary merely as a private individual, and only with her sufferings at the foot of the cross.

A fair amount of evidence has been adduced to show that Mary, as presented by Luke, can aptly be called (in Old Testament terms) the 'Daughter of Zion', for she is the representative *par excellence* of Israel in Messianic times:

'Blessed art thou among women,
and blessed is the fruit of thy womb.'

[7] There is a complete survey of the patristic evidence, Greek and Latin, and a good survey of the Latin medieval writers, in A. de Groot, *Die schmerzhafte Mutter und Gefährtin des göttlichen Erlösers in der Weissagung Simeons*, Kaldenkirchen, 1956, pp. 1–64. A list of opinions ancient and modern is also available, and more accessible, in T. Gallus, 'De sensu verborum Lc 2:35 eorumque momento mariologico', in *Biblica* 29 (1948), pp. 220–39.

And just as one series of Old Testament prophecies prepared the way for the coming of the Messiah, so another series spoke of the Messianic community from which, and into which, the Messiah would be born (*e.g.* Mic 5:1–4*a*). The first series pointed to Jesus; and I would suggest that Luke in his Infancy Gospel regards the second series as pointing above all to Mary, the true 'Daughter of Zion'. He is certainly well aware that Mary had a role to play as an individual (*cf.* Lk 1:45); but in Luke's perspective Mary as an individual embodied within herself the destiny of Israel and the hope of the world (*cf.* the entire story of the Annunciation, 1:26–38 and the Magnificat, 1:46–55).

The 'classical interpretation' of Lk 2:35*a* may therefore be restated with this perspective of Luke in mind. 'Thou thyself, O *Israel*, shalt feel a sword pass through thy soul.' Mary as an individual had rejoiced to be the mother of him who would fulfil the promises made to Abraham; as the Daughter of Zion, more aware than anyone else of the destiny of her child,[8] she welcomed his coming for the joy it would bring to Israel and to the world (*cf.* once more the Magnificat). Yet in the course of Jesus' public life she had to watch the mounting opposition to her son, and knew that the leaders of Israel were thereby turning against their saviour. Her mental sufferings reached a climax on Calvary,[9] but they had begun long before. And even at the foot of the cross, she suffered a double agony. She watched the physical torment and heard the mockery directed at Jesus, her son; but in addition she had the far greater sorrow of knowing that the appointed leaders of God's chosen people had refused the message of salvation.

Simeon's prophecy that a sword would pass through Mary's soul thus takes on a far richer meaning, which is still fully in line

[8] This may be asserted, without seeking to determine further the extent of Mary's knowledge, if one accepts the virginal conception as an historical fact. The historicity of the virginal conception will be discussed in Part II.

[9] That Luke thought of Mary as having been present on Calvary seems a legitimate inference from 23:49 (*cf.* Ac 1:14), taken in conjunction with his affinities to the Fourth Gospel. But even if she had not been physically present, the argument above would still hold.

with the classical interpretation. And provided that his words are not referred to Mary merely as an individual or only at one moment in her life, they fit the context excellently: there is no need to place this half-verse, 35*a*, in parentheses. The sword which passed through Israel was the preaching of Jesus: it brought about the downfall of many, because it compelled men to reveal their secret thoughts. This same sword passed through Mary's soul in that she, feeling for her people, felt the tragedy of the rejection of Jesus; and nowhere was this tragedy more painful than when she stood beside the crucified. Simeon's words make a sad climax to the scene in which Israel brings its Messiah to the temple.

One might have expected St Luke's Infancy Gospel to end on a note of triumph. Triumph is not absent in the story (Lk 2:28–33, 36–8), but the tale ends on a note of foreboding, with this dark allusion to sorrows yet to come (Lk 2:34–5). Thus the story of the Presentation is St Luke's way of teaching the reader yet another lesson found in the Prologue of St John. The Lord came to his Temple; but when he came to what was his own domain, his own people did not accept him (Jn 1:11).

Chapter Thirteen

THE BOY JESUS IN JERUSALEM
(Lk 2:41–52)

CANON LAURENTIN has published a monograph on the episode in which Jesus as a boy of twelve years is found by his parents in the Temple (Lk 2:41–52). Laurentin's book is enormously impressive in its documentation, setting out every interpretation given from patristic times to the present day, and this chapter quarries freely in it.[1]

What is the real point of this solitary narrative about Jesus in those years before he began his public ministry? According to Bultmann, the story belongs to the realm of 'legend';[2] according to Dibelius, it is a typical example of 'a legend about the person'[3] (the word 'legend' being taken to mean, in both cases, an edifying story which is half-way towards a myth). Both these authors think its purpose is to portray the intelligence and the piety of Jesus. Laurentin, however, following Professor Van Iersel,[4] points out that the real emphasis is not on Jesus' piety or intelligence; rather, the whole narrative hinges on the saying 'I must be in my Father's house' (Lk 2:49). It should therefore be classed not as a legend, but rather among those stories which Bultmann calls 'apophthegms' (akin to what Dibelius calls 'paradigms'), or (to use the more meaningful English term) as a 'pronouncement

---

[1] *Jésus au Temple: Mystère de Pâques et Foi de Marie en Luc 2:48–50* (*Etudes bibliques*), Paris, 1966.

[2] *The History of the Synoptic Tradition*, pp. 300–1, 302, 304, 307.

[3] *From Tradition to Gospel*, Cambridge and London (reprint of 1971), pp. 106–9.

[4] 'The Finding of Jesus in the Temple', *Novum Testamentum* 4 (1960), pp. 161–73.

story'.[5] All the interest is on the saying. (This is particularly evident if, with Van Iersel, one regards vv. 44 and 47 as later editorial insertions in the story; but the conclusion holds good even if these two verses formed part of the original narrative.)

Classical literature supplies some interesting parallels in the lives of its great men. These are the more noteworthy in that ancient writers were not as a rule very interested in the formative years of their heroes; yet there are a number of cases where a story is told about a future king who, around the age of twelve years, uttered some particularly significant words that gave an indication of his future life and character. Where these stories are found, the classical authors normally select just one episode, and that around the age of puberty, to set in relief the central trait of the hero's personality.

Herodotus has a good example about Cyrus. Cyrus had been condemned to death at birth by his grandfather because of an oracle that he would reign in his grandfather's stead; so he was exposed, but saved from death by a cowherd who substituted for the baby Cyrus the dead body of his own son. When Cyrus was ten years old, he was playing with some other boys who in a game elected him king: everybody else had to do what he told them, but a certain nobleman's son refused to play the part given him. Cyrus thereupon ordered the other boys to seize him and give him a thrashing. The boy's father complained to the king, who summoned Cyrus and asked how he had dared to have the nobleman's son beaten. To this Cyrus replied:

'Master, what I did to him I did with justice. The boys of the village, of whom he was one, chose me in their play to be their king; for they thought me the fittest to rule. The other boys then did as I bid them: but this one was disobedient and cared nothing for me, till he got his deserts. So now if I deserve punishment for this, here am I to take it.'[6]

[5] *Jésus au Temple*, pp. 158–9.
[6] *History* I, 114 (translation by A. D. Godley in the Loeb edition, vol. 1, pp. 149–51).

Naturally, the secret of Cyrus' parentage was thereupon discovered, but the point of the tale is self-evident. Cyrus here gives proof both of his aristocratic lineage and of his future firmness and fearlessness as a ruler.

Plutarch, in his accounts of Alexander's youth, has a similar story. He relates it in two slightly different versions, one in the *De viris illustribus*,[7] the other in the *Opera Moralia*. The latter runs as follows:

> 'Once, when ambassadors came from the Persian king to Philip, who was not at home, Alexander, while he entertained them hospitably, asked no childish questions, as the others did, about the vine of gold, or the Hanging Gardens, or how the Great King was arrayed; but he was completely engrossed with the most vital concerns of the dominion, asking how large was the Persian army; where the king stationed himself in battle . . . and which roads were the shortest for travellers going inland from the sea, so that the strangers were astounded and said, "This boy is a great king".'[8]

The whole life of Alexander is presaged in these questions.

In the Bible, the closest parallel to Lk 2:41-52 is the dedication of the boy Samuel (1 Sam 2:1-11). Both Luke and 1 Samuel mention an annual pilgrimage (Lk 2:41; 1 Sam 2:19); according to a rabbinical tradition (see Josephus, *Ant.* V, x, 4 = §348), Samuel was at the time of his dedication twelve years old (*cf.* Lk 2:42); and Samuel's mother had vowed that her son would 'dwell for ever in the presence of the Lord' (1 Sam 1:22). Both in 1 Samuel and in Luke we are told at the conclusion of the story that the boy 'grew in stature and in favour with God and with men' (1 Sam 2:26; Lk 2:52).[9] It is to be noted, however, that

[7] *The Life of Alexander* 5, 666 E–F (in the Loeb ed., vol. 7, p. 235).

[8] *De Alexandri Magni fortuna aut virtute* II, 11, 342 B–C: the translation is by F. C. Babbitt in the Loeb edition of the *Moralia*, vol. 4, p. 471.

[9] The fullest documentation of the parallels between Lk 1-2 and 1 Sam 1-2 is in E. Burrows, *The Gospel of the Infancy*, pp. 6-26.

Samuel does not make any significant pronouncement and indeed (in spite of the rabbinical tradition) seems to have been a good deal less than twelve years old.[10]

There is one passage of slight interest in Josephus' autobiography,[11] but it does not contain a saying. More relevant is the way in which Luke's sober narrative has been rewritten by the (second-century, Christian) *Infancy Story of Thomas*. After quoting Lk 2:42-6 almost verbatim, this apocryphal gospel continues:

> '*And all* paid attention to him and *marvelled* how he, a child, put to silence the elders and teachers of the people, expounding the sections of the law and the sayings of the prophets. *And his mother* Mary came near *and said* to him: "*Why have you done this to us, child? Behold, we have sought you sorrowing.*" *Jesus said to them: "Why do you seek me? Do you not know that I must be in my Father's house?*" But the scribes and Pharisees said: "Are you the mother of this child?" And she said: "I am." And they said to her: "Blessed are you *among women* because the Lord has *blessed the fruit of your womb*. For such glory and such excellence and wisdom we have never seen or heard . . .'[12]

Here indeed we see the evolution of true legend, attributing to the hero of the story 'glory, excellence and wisdom' of a degree never seen before. The *Arabic Infancy Gospel* improved on the *Infancy Story of Thomas*, making up the questions and answers, and portraying Jesus as fully conversant with astronomy and medicine.[13] Indeed, the more closely one examines the apo-

[10] 1 Sam 2:19 says that 'his mother used to make for him a little robe and take it to him each year, when she went up with her husband' to Shiloh.

[11] *Life*, §2: 'While still a mere boy, about fourteen years old, I won universal applause for my love of letters; insomuch that the chief priests and the leading men of the city used constantly to come to me for precise information on some particular in our ordinances.' (Translation by H. St.J. Thackeray in the Loeb ed., vol. 1, p. 5.)

[12] E. Hennecke, *New Testament Apocrypha*, ed. by W. Schneemelcher, English trans. edited by R. McL. Wilson, I, London, 1963, pp. 398-9.

[13] See *Evangile arabe de l'enfance*, 50-2, in P. Peeters, *Evangiles apocryphes II*,

cryphal parallels the more one is struck by the contrast with Luke's narrative, in which (as Laurentin neatly puts it) there is 'neither mythomania nor megalomania'.[14] Jesus is simply presented sitting in the middle of the teachers, and his first recorded words imply that God is his father. Luke thereby shows Jesus as 'the teacher' and 'the son of God', but conveys his message merely by a subtle hint and by quiet implication. Jesus' saying dominates the episode.

'(My) child, why hast thou done so to us? Behold, thy father and I were in pain as we searched for thee' (Lk 2:48). Many have seen in these words a reproach, however gentle,[15] and some have drawn from this premiss the conclusion that Mary at this time understood little or nothing of Jesus' greatness. To draw this conclusion, however, is to ignore the literary form of the narrative. The question is certainly couched as a mild reproach, but it is so phrased simply to elicit the answer of Jesus. And Jesus' reply ('Why were you searching for me? Did you not know . . .?') quite evidently implies that Mary and Joseph ought not to have been anxious, because they already knew something about him which should have been sufficient to preserve them from anxiety. Only, they had failed to perceive its full implications.[16]

'Did you not know that I must be in my Father's house (ἐν τοῖς τοῦ πατρός μου δεῖ εἶναί με)' (Lk 2:49)? The force of the

---

Paris, 1914, pp. 62–3. Questioned by a master of astronomy, Jesus 'told him the number of the spheres and of the heavenly bodies, their natures, their powers, their oppositions, their combinations in three, four and six, their ascensions and declinations, their positions in minutes and seconds, and other things which surpass reason.' Similarly on medicine (he spoke 'of nerves, bones, veins, arteries and tendons', etc.).

[14] *Jésus au Temple*, p. 157.

[15] Beautifully expressed by Aelred of Rievaulx, in *De institutione inclusarum* 31: 'O quanta copia fluent lacrymae, cum audieris matrem dulci quadam increpatione Filium verberantem' (*CC. Continuatio medievalis* 1.664–5 = ML 32.1466 among the works of St Augustine: but cf. ML 32.1451 and ML 195.701).

[16] Laurentin, *Jésus au Temple*, pp. 199–201, cites four fragments (nn. 29–32) from Greek writers (not found in Migne) in which the authors dwell on the fact that Mary and Joseph ought to have deduced from the virginal conception that Jesus would be found with his heavenly Father.

verb 'I must' was well observed by Alford in the nineteenth century: '. . . that δεῖ so often used by Our Lord of his appointed and undertaken course . . .', as also by Dean Farrar: '*I must* lays down the law of devotion to His Father by which he was to walk even to the Cross'.[17] The words here translated 'in my Father's house' have caused more difficulty. We need not delay over the theories that the phrase means 'among the things of my Father',[18] or 'among those who serve my Father',[19] or 'in the domain of my Father'.[20] A very common translation, however, consecrated in English by the Authorized Version, is 'about my Father's business'.[21] Laurentin has shown that this rendering arose in the thirteenth century with the Dominican Hugues de Saint-Cher (*d.* 1263) and was taken up by St Albert (*c.* 1200–80) and Ludolph of Saxony (*c.* 1300–78), also Dominicans. By the sixteenth century it had become almost commonplace, and in England the translation 'about my Father's business' is found in Tyndale (1534), Coverdale (1535), Matthew (second edition, 1549), the Geneva Bible (1560), the Bishops' Bible (1574), the Rheims New Testament (1582) and the Authorized Version (1611). On the Continent, it was the interpretation accepted by Erasmus, Beza and Calvin, to name only three.[22] In view of this wide-ranging acceptance, it is little wonder that until modern times few authors questioned the accuracy of the rendering; after all, it was good Christology and excellent for preaching.

[17] H. Alford, *The Greek Testament I: The Four Gospels*, 7th ed., 1874, p. 466; F. W. Farrar, *St Luke*, Cambridge, 1884, p. 124. Both are cited in Laurentin, *Jésus au Temple*, p. 102, fn. 9.

[18] See Laurentin, *Jésus au Temple*, pp. 39–42.

[19] *Ibid.*, pp. 42–6. This, like the preceding interpretation, stems from a misreading of Origen. Since the argument is not of direct interest for this book, it is enough to refer the readers to Laurentin's discussion. The texts of Origen and his successors are printed in the Appendix to Laurentin.

[20] This rendering hardly differs in meaning from 'in my Father's house', but is preferred by W. Grundmann, *Das Evangelium nach Lukas*, Berlin, 1961, pp. 93 and 96.

[21] It was abandoned in the Revised Version (1881) and in the Revised Standard Version (1946).

[22] For all the references, see Laurentin, *Jésus au Temple*, pp. 48–51.

Modern writers, however, are overwhelmingly in favour of the view that the phrase can only mean 'in my Father's home' ('*chez mon Père*'). Apart from classical, Hellenistic and biblical examples of this usage of ἐν τοῖς,[23] it is the interpretation given by all the Greek Fathers, the Latin Fathers, and the medievals up to the thirteenth century.[24] It would be pedantic to labour the point; we may simply affirm that Jesus' answer to Mary's question was 'Did you not know that I must be *in my Father's home*?'[25]

'And they did not understand the word which he spoke to them' (Lk 2:50). This sentence means that neither Mary nor Joseph understood the saying of Jesus in verse 49,[26] and it may be significant that Luke calls this saying not a λόγος but a ῥῆμα. The latter is a word used several times by Luke in his Infancy Gospel to denote either an event which is pregnant with *heilsgeschichtlich* meaning, or the word of revelation which calls attention to the deeper significance of some event which is externally observed. Like the Hebrew *dabar*, it connotes both the thing and the word; in scholastic terms, it denotes '*non rem tantum, sed rem et sacramentum*'. It is in this doubly significant sense that the term is used by Gabriel of Elizabeth's conception (Lk 1:37), and about the child in the manger ('Let us see this *fact* which has happened', 2:15; 'They understood about the *word* which had been

[23] For the references, see Laurentin, *ibid.*, pp. 56–9.

[24] *Ibid.*, 59–66.

[25] One should mention here that P. Winter ('Lk 2:49 and Targum Yerushalmi', *ZNW* 45 [1954], pp. 145–79) has argued that Jesus' words do not imply any special or transcendent relationship to the Father, for Jewish children were taught to call God 'our Father'. But as elsewhere in the gospels, the distinction between 'my Father' and 'our Father' is important. See also Laurentin, *Jésus au Temple*, pp. 73–6.

[26] One may safely ignore the view that this verse refers to the bystanders, or to Joseph but not to Mary. Similarly, we may set aside the idea that the verbs should be translated as pluperfects ('They *had not* understood the word which he had (previously) spoken to them'), as if Jesus had told them beforehand that he would see them 'in his father's house' (he meaning the Temple, they taking it to mean at Nazareth). For details of these views, see Laurentin, *Jésus au Temple*, pp. 13–17.

spoken', 2:17). Again, when Simeon said, 'Now, Lord, thou callest on thy servant to depart, according to thy *word*' (2:29), the word of promise had been fulfilled by a fact. So also when we read that 'all these *things* were talked about over the entire hill-country of Judaea' (1:65), the many prophetic utterances are certainly included; and above all, when we read that 'Mary kept all these ῥήματα in her heart' (2:19, 51), the meaning is not restricted to the words spoken, but extends to the events as well. So in 2:50 'They did not understand the *word* which he spoke to them' means that Mary and Joseph did not grasp the *fact implied* in the words which Jesus uttered, 'I must be in my Father's home'. That is to say, they did not understand the *truth contained* in these words. Yet in no sense is Luke's comment intended as an adverse criticism of Mary or Joseph. Rather, there is here an instance of a theme found elsewhere in Luke (9:45; 18:34; 24:25-7, 45-6) and very frequently in John, according to which men failed to see the significance of various events and utterances in Jesus' life until after the Resurrection. The next step, therefore, is to ask what was the full significance of Jesus' words. What is the content of that fuller understanding which Mary and Joseph did not have at the time, and which came only later?

The significance of Jerusalem in Luke's Gospel and in Acts is well-known. The Infancy Narrative begins in the Temple and ends in the Temple. From 9:51 to 19:28 Luke presents Jesus as 'making a journey up to Jerusalem' (*cf.* 9:51; 13:22, 33-4; 18:31; 19:28) there 'to achieve his departure' (9:31) because 'it cannot be that a prophet should suffer outside Jerusalem' (13:33).[27] After the Resurrection, the disciples are commanded to remain in the city until they have been endowed with power from on high (24:49; Ac 1:4), and the Book of Acts then takes up the message. The disciples will be witnesses to Jesus in Jerusalem (Ac 1-7),

[27] It is noteworthy that from Lk 3:1-9:50 there is frequent mention of place-names scattered round Galilee, and that from 9:51-19:28 this precision ceases until Jesus reaches Jericho (one reads of 'a village', 'on the road', etc.). That this 'Lucan Travel Narrative' is an artificial composition is evident; a better title would be 'The Following of Christ' (to Calvary) (*cf.* Lk 9:57-62; 10:25, 42; 11:1, 9; 14:27, etc.).

in all Judaea and Samaria (Ac 8–12) and even to the ends of the earth (Ac 13–28): this is the plan of Acts outlined in 1:8. Everything in the gospel leads up to Jerusalem; and in Acts, all salvation flows outward from it.

Hardly less important in Luke's theology is the Temple. Bede, after recalling the significance of the Temple in the infancy narratives, and quoting the words 'I must be in my Father's house', adds: 'And after many similar remarks, Luke at the end of his gospel gathers the disciples in the Temple to praise God.'[28] More eloquent still are the words with which he closes his great commentary: 'Luke has expounded the priesthood of Christ more fully than the others, and his ending is striking in its beauty. Having begun his gospel with the ministry of the priest Zechariah in the Temple, he ends it with a story of Temple devotion. There he depicts the apostles (that is, the future ministers of the new priesthood) gathered together not to shed the blood of animal victims, but to praise and to bless God.'[29]

It would therefore seem that the deeper meaning of Jesus' words, 'I must be in my Father's home', which his parents did not understand, was not to become clear until the Resurrection. In those words of the twelve-year-old child was concealed the assertion that ultimately he was called by his heavenly Father to Jerusalem, there to accomplish the salvation of the world.[30] Thus this story of the young boy (like the tales about Cyrus and Alexander) encapsulates in one sentence all his future destiny.

[28] *In Lucam I* (at 2:41): 'Et post cetera talia laudantes Deum in templo discipulos in evangelii sui fine conclusit' (*CC* 120.71 = ML 92.348).

[29] *In Lucam VI*: '. . . eo quod ipse sacerdotium Christi ceteris amplius exponendum susceperit pulcherrime qui evangelium suum a ministerio templi per sacerdotium Zachariae coepit hoc in templi devotione complevit cum apostolos inibi ministros videlicet novi sacerdotii futuros non in victimarum sanguine sed in laude Dei et benedictione conclusit.' (*CC* 120.424–5 = ML 92.634).

[30] The translation 'in my Father's *house*' is at this point misleading, for the Greek does not have the word 'house', and the meaning is not that Jesus was to accomplish his divine mission in the Temple itself. But it was to be accomplished in Jerusalem. The French '*chez mon Père*' catches the idea perfectly, but the English equivalent ('at my Father's') is too familiar (and too vague) as a rendering of the Greek.

That is why Luke includes this narrative of Jesus' first recorded words.[31]

This interpretation is confirmed not only by Luke's picture of Jesus 'setting his face towards Jerusalem' (9:51-3) there to 'achieve' all his work (13:22, 32-3), but also by the Lucan versions of the sayings in which Jesus foretells his passion. After the first prediction (Lk 9:22) comes the story of the Transfiguration; and whereas Matthew (17:3) and Mark (9:4) merely state that Moses and Elijah talked with Jesus, Luke (9:31) says that they 'spoke about his departure (ἔξοδος) *which he was to accomplish in Jerusalem*'. After the second prediction, Luke expands a Marcan saying (Mk 9:32) into the following statement: 'But they did not grasp this word (ῥῆμα). It was concealed from them, so that they should not perceive it, and they were afraid to ask him about this word' (Lk 9:45). A similar observation (this time without a parallel in Matthew or Mark) follows the third and last prediction of the passion: 'And they did not understand anything of these things. This word (ῥῆμα) was hidden from them, and they did not know what was said' (Lk 18:34). If Luke can make such assertions about the disciples during the public ministry of Jesus, and after such unambiguous predictions, it is sensible to think that in 2:49-50 he means to affirm the same about Mary and Joseph: they did not grasp the import of Jesus' saying.

This interpretation is further confirmed by certain details of the narrative. The episode took place at Passover (2:41): in Luke's Gospel, Jesus' next Passover in Jerusalem will be the one at which he is crucified. In 2:49 we meet for the first time in Luke's Gospel, the δεῖ of divine necessity: 'I *must needs be . . .*'. It occurs elsewhere usually with reference to the destined suffering of Jesus (9:22; 13:33; 17:25; 22:37; 24:7, 26, 44, and perhaps

[31] R. Bultmann, *The History of the Synoptic Tradition*, pp. 300-1, affirms that the episode has a double point: (1) the surprising wisdom of the youthful Jesus, and (2) his tarrying in the Temple (which makes known his religious destiny). He implies, too, without expressly saying it, that the first motif is dominant. But the explanation given in the text above, which treats the episode not as a legend but as a pronouncement-story, seems to fit the text much better, for there is little emphasis on the extraordinary wisdom of Jesus (contrast the apocryphal gospels cited above on pp. 116-7).

22:7), once with reference to his preaching (4:43)[32] and once with reference to the evils that must precede the fall of Jerusalem (21:9). Again, it is sensible to think that Luke is hinting at a great mystery connected with 'his Father's home', which is yet to be disclosed.

Bede,[33] followed by Bernard[34] and other medieval writers,[35] states that Mary and Joseph had failed to grasp that Jesus was true God.[36] Others say that Mary and Joseph did not fully understand the sense of Jesus' words, without defining what full comprehension would entail.[37] Yet others say that they did not understand his mission.[38] None of these interpretations seems wholly satisfactory except the last, and even that calls for further definition.

[32] This theme, of course, supplies another minor parallel to the scene in the Temple. Jesus 'must needs be' among the teachers in the Temple.

[33] *In Lucam I* (on Lk 2:50): 'Parentes eius non intellegunt verbum quod de sua divinitate loquitur ad illos' (*CC* 120.73 = ML 92.350); *Homeliarum I*, 19: 'Cuius multum est miranda magnae dispensatio pietatis qui, dum.parentes suos mysterium divinae suae maiestatis necdum capere vidisset, exhibuit eis humanae subiectionem humilitatis, ut per hanc eos paulatim ad agnitionem divinitatis institueret' (*CC* 122.137 = ML 94.66).

[34] *Sermones de Tempore:* In tempore Resurrectionis III, 4 = ML 183.291 ('Verbum non capiebatur in se').

[35] See Laurentin, *Jésus au Temple*, p. 21.

[36] An article by E. F. Sutcliffe ('Our Lady and the Divinity of Christ', in *The Month* 180 (1944), pp. 347–51), in which the author followed Bede on Luke 2:50, sparked off a very lively controversy among Roman Catholics in England, Ireland and the U.S.A. A full list of references to the exchanges is given in R. Laurentin, *Jésus au Temple*, pp. 23–4.

The interpretation given by Bede has in recent years been put forward in Europe by J. Guitton, *La Vierge Marie*, Paris, 1949, p. 40 (but see Laurentin, *Jésus au Temple*, pp. 24–5); by R. Guardini, *Die Mutter des Herrn*, 2nd ed., Würzburg, 1956, pp. 48–9; by J. Galot, *Marie dans l'Evangile*, Paris, 1958, pp. 61–2; and by M. Schmaus, *Katholische Dogmatik 5: Mariologie*, Munich, 1958, pp. 213–14; 2nd ed., 1961, pp. 234–5. All the texts are cited in Laurentin, *Jésus au Temple*, pp. 24–5.

[37] This view has found constant support from medieval to modern times. For examples, see Laurentin, *Jésus au Temple*, pp. 27–9.

[38] This view again has found support from the sixteenth century to the present day: see Laurentin, *Jésus au Temple*, pp. 29–31. The best presentation of it (on which the text above is partly based) is by J. Dupont, 'Luc 2:41–52: Jésus à douze ans', in *Assemblées du Seigneur*, Bruges, 1961, pp. 25–43.

It seems much more likely that what Mary and Joseph did not understand was this: that in those first fateful words, 'I must be in my Father's home', Jesus was darkly alluding to his future passion and Resurrection in the Holy City.

Chapter Fourteen

TRADITION AND INTERPRETATION
IN LUKE 1–2

THE argument of the preceding chapters rests upon the conviction that the Lucan Infancy Gospel represents a type of writing akin to the Jewish midrash, and that the interpreter is therefore justified in looking for a profound doctrinal message beneath the apparently simple narrative.[1] Most modern scholars would agree that Lk 1–2 were written to express doctrine, but many conclude that these chapters cannot be taken as a record of historical events.

The general line of argument against the historicity of Lk 1–2 may be summarized as follows. There are so many alleged miracles in these two chapters that it is reasonable to think the author's purpose was to teach doctrine rather than to record events as they really happened: for instance, Luke could hardly have expected his readers to believe that a choir of angels really hovered in the skies over Bethlehem. Secondly, the words ascribed to Gabriel, to Elizabeth and to Simeon are so evidently careful compositions based on Old Testament themes that they must have been written to express doctrine; certainly there are no positive grounds for claiming that they represent even the substance of words uttered on the occasions indicated. For example, if Elizabeth's greeting, the Magnificat and the Nunc Dimittis[2] are in fact hymns taken from the early Christian liturgy, it must be admitted that these hymns have no true historical connection with the events to which they are attached in the gospel story.

[1] See above, Chapter 2, pp. 22–3.
[2] One could mention also the Benedictus, which has not been discussed.

Thirdly, it is evident from everything that has been written in the preceding chapters that Luke was guided by doctrinal motives in the overall planning and in the detailed presentation of his narrative. It would seem beyond doubt, therefore, that Luke's intention was not to recount facts 'as they really happened', but to give a doctrinally significant interpretation of the birth of Jesus. Thus Luke's teaching may be a valid expression of the faith of his own generation around A.D. 65–80, but one cannot pretend that his account represents historical fact, at least not here in the Infancy Gospel.

Such is the general line of argument against the historicity of Lk 1–2. The first step in discussing it must be to examine the accuracy, or rather the applicability, of Leopold von Ranke's description of the purpose of history: 'to record facts as they really happened'. Must the historian be content to narrate externally observable *facts as* they really happened, or would it be more correct to say that he should record *events which* really took place? Von Ranke (1795–1886) was defining, in the positivist climate of the early nineteenth century (to be exact, in 1824[3]) what was soon to be regarded as the only truly scientific way of writing history, in which value-judgments and interpretation were always suspect, and often suspended. The twentieth century, under the influence of existentialist philosophy, is more ready to admit that the meaning and significance of a 'happening' are part and parcel of an 'event'.[4] Were it not so, Thucydides himself would have to be erased from the list of the world's historians. Interpretation is essential to genuine historical writing, but there are many ways in which it may be conveyed. For example, the ancient world

[3] In the first volume of his first work, *Geschichte der römischen und germanischen Völker*, Berlin, 1824.

[4] Here the word 'happening' is used to denote an ascertainable fact (*e.g.* that Luther posted 95 theses at Wittenberg in 1517), and the word 'event' to denote that fact in so far as it is interpreted and seen with all its causes and consequences. It is an endeavour to reproduce the distinction between what the Germans call the object of *Historie* (the 'happening') and the object of *Geschichte* (the 'event'). For a full explanation of the distinction between *Historie* and *Geschichte* see A. Malet, *The Thought of Rudolf Bultmann*, Irish University Press (Shannon), 1969, pp. 61–80.

had different conventions from ours, and to convey interpretation, its historians readily wrote speeches for their *dramatis personae*, as Thucydides and Livy did. Yet here another distinction must be made. Thucydides warns his readers that 'the speeches are not, and could not be for reasons stated, the *ipsissima verba* of the speakers', but he does assure the reader that he will give 'the overall purport or purpose of what was actually said'.[5] Some of the speeches he had heard himself; for others, he relied on reports from men who had been present; and it seems highly improbable that he ever inserted a speech which was wholly imaginary and without any basis in fact.[6] Thus Thucydides may be said to have recorded *events which* really happened, though not (in positivist terms) *exactly as* they really happened. With Livy the reader stands on very different ground, for Livy could not possibly have had access to written accounts or trustworthy oral traditions of speeches delivered two hundred years earlier; the speeches in Livy are as fictional as those in Shakespeare, but they are indispensable as interpretation. The contrast between the speeches in Livy and those in Thucydides is instructive not least because it demonstrates that the modern reader cannot deduce, merely from the fact that an ancient author placed a speech on the lips of one of his characters, *either* that the speech is devoid of historical foundation *or* that it necessarily rests upon some sound historical tradition. To decide that issue, other criteria must be employed. What can be deduced from the speeches both in Thucydides and in Livy is that in ancient times interpretation was respected as a most important part of truly historical writing.

St Luke was neither a fifth-century Athenian historian nor a Roman writer, but his cultural background was far closer to theirs than to that of a twentieth-century scholar, and he does not present fact and interpretation separately in the way that modern Western scholars do. Like Thucydides, Luke set out to record events which really happened (Lk 1:1-4), but in order to do so, he quite naturally chose 'those literary forms which were current

---

[5] F. E. Adcock, *Thucydides and his History*, Cambridge, 1963, p. 27. The reference to Thucydides is to I, 22, 1.

[6] *Ibid.*, pp. 28-31.

among his own contemporaries and countrymen'.[7] The form he chose for the Infancy Narrative was, as we have seen, a Christianized version of the Jewish midrash;[8] but it does not follow that what is described in these stories has no historical basis, any more than the existence of midrashim about the Exodus proves that no Exodus ever took place. What does follow is that great care must be exercised in interpreting the text when one is trying to find out if some factual content can be distilled from the narratives. In other words, although Luke wrote his story in words, concepts and images taken from the Old Testament, this does not necessarily mean that he had no facts to clothe in this language, or that in so clothing them he has disguised the original happenings beyond all possibility of recognition. The question at issue is this: can one discern, beneath the 'midrashic' exposition in Lk 1–2, the true nature of any happenings which once took place, or not?

Let us take as an example the Annunciation to Mary. The ordinary modern reader untrained in theology will certainly regard the story as an account of a 'vision': that is, he will take it to be a narrative of something *seen* and *heard* rather than of something *understood*. Yet Luke does not have a single word describing what the angel looked like, or how he approached: we are not even told whether the scene is set indoors or out of doors. Luke has restricted the visual details to the bare essentials needed to relate the message he wishes to teach, and his caution should be remembered when one is tempted to visualize the scene in the imagination. Some people might be inclined to think, for example, that had anyone else been present, he too would have seen an angel in bodily form, and overheard a conversation. No theologian and no hagiographer claims that this normally happens in the case of a vision,[9] and it is therefore reasonable to begin by asking whether the Annunciation to Mary is not Luke's way of presenting to the reader an account of some more spiritual and

---

[7] *Divino Afflante Spiritu*, §39 (*AAS* 35 [1943], p. 315).

[8] See above, Chapter 2, pp. 22–3.

[9] Compare, *e.g.*, the accounts of the apparitions at Lourdes in 1858, all of which stress that the bystanders neither saw nor heard anything from the grotto.

wholly interior experience, of which no bystander could have been a witness.[10] In classical theological terminology, Luke would be saying that Mary received a revelation through a mystical experience. Some who hold this view would say that the essence of Luke's narrative (the 'factual content') is the assertion that Mary learnt from God that she was to bear a child without loss of her virginity, and that this child was to be the Messiah and (in some sense) the son of God. Others might say that Mary experienced an invitation to make an act of total self-surrender to God, and to undertake in total faith whatever God might ask of her: she consented ('Behold the handmaid of the Lord!'), and the next thing she knew, she was going to have a baby.

Suppose that Mary did have a mystical experience, the reality and the genuineness of which she could not doubt, because she was directly and unmistakably aware of its divine origin. In that case, one must ask whether the figure of the angel is not a literary convention. But before discussing whether 'Gabriel' represents a really existent angelic being who actually 'conversed' with Mary, we may note that anyone who admits that Mary had a mystical experience (even though he denies the intermediary role of any angel) admits that Luke's story of the Annunciation is in some sense historical, in that it gives an account of something which really happened.

Is the mentioning of the Angel Gabriel a mere literary convention? In the Old Testament, and particularly in the most ancient narratives, an angel may be a figure of speech employed by the writer in order to highlight the transcendence and the inaccessibility of God: this is especially true of the Elohistic traditions in the Pentateuch (e.g. Gen 21:17; 31:11). But that does not mean that throughout the Old Testament angels are never anything but a literary convention. On the contrary, there is ample evidence (especially in the later books) that the Israelites regarded them as powerful creatures, spiritual beings who formed the heavenly court of God (Job 1) and who acted as God's messengers. Some of them were even called by particular names, such as Gabriel and Michael (Dan 8:16; 12:1), and the question

[10] Cf. J.-P. Audet in the RB 63 (1956), p. 355.

at issue is whether St Luke, in the first century of the Christian era, meant us to think of Gabriel as a distinct individual angel who (in some way) conversed with Mary.

Luke's mention of the name Gabriel does not decide the issue, for though the name Gabriel indicates an individual, it does not necessarily follow that this individual really exists. In the Old Testament, Gabriel features only in Dan 7–12, where the author is not concerned to teach men about the existence of angels, but to inspire them by a message of consolation in a time of dire persecution. It did not matter, for the author of Daniel, whether Gabriel was a really existent individual or not, just as it does not matter to the reader of *David Copperfield* whether Mr Micawber and the rest of the characters ever existed or not. And if it did not matter for the author of Daniel, we may reasonably ask whether it mattered for St Luke. Did he want his reader to think of Gabriel as a really existent individual? Did he expect him to do so?

Here the gospel accounts of the Temptations provide a helpful parallel. Very few scholars nowadays would regard the accounts in Matthew and Luke as anything other than a vivid description of the three temptations which confronted Jesus from the start of his public ministry; yet the literary presentation carries the hallmark of genius, and is admirably suited for catechetical teaching. The fact that Luke has incorporated this story into his gospel is of high significance, for if he used a story-form once in order to teach an abstract truth, he may have done it on other occasions too. In other words, it could be that Luke wrote his story about the Annunciation in the form of a conversation with an angel because that was the most effective and eloquent way of conveying to his readers what he wanted to say, but without meaning that Mary was, as a matter of historical fact, once engaged in dialogue by an angel of the name Gabriel.

In this context, it is pertinent to appeal to two great writers on mystical experiences, St Teresa of Avila and St John of the Cross. These two Carmelite saints frequently warn their readers against the perils of attaching too much importance to visions and apparitions, and stress that the closer a soul is to God, the more direct is God's communication with it. St John of the Cross writes, in *The Ascent of Mount Carmel*, of 'the hindrance and harm that may be caused' by paying too much attention to what is supernaturally represented to the bodily senses:[11]

'. . . there may come, and there are wont to come, to spiritual persons representations and objects of a super-natural kind. With respect to sight, they are apt to picture figures and forms belonging to the life to come—the forms of certain saints, and representations of angels, good and evil, and certain lights and brightnesses of an extraordinary kind. And with the ears they hear certain extraordinary words, sometimes spoken by these figures that they see, sometimes without seeing the person who speaks them.
'. . . And it must be known that, although all these things may happen to the bodily senses in the way of God, we must never rely on them or admit them, but we must always fly from them, without trying to ascertain whether they be good or evil; for, the more completely exterior and corporeal they are, the less certainly are they of God. For it is more proper and habitual to God to communicate Himself to the spirit, wherein there is more security and profit for the soul, than to sense, wherein there is ordinarily much danger and deception . . .
'And the more exterior are these corporeal forms and objects in themselves, the less do they profit the interior and spiritual nature . . . [for] the soul goes after them, abandoning faith and thinking that the light which it receives from them is the guide and the means to its desired goal, which is union with God. But the more attention it pays to such things, the farther it strays from the true way and means, which are faith'.[12]

What St John of the Cross says of visions in general may certainly be applied to Luke's account of the Annunciation. St

11 Book II, Chapter 11, title.
12 *Loc. cit.*, nn. 1, 2 and 4. The translation is by E. Allison Peers, *The Works of St John of the Cross*, vol. 1, London, 1943, pp. 102–4.

John of the Cross, like St Teresa of Avila, frequently insists on the difficulty of describing the stages by which the soul draws closer to God: he attempts to describe it as an *'Ascent of Mount Carmel'*, she as an entering into the *'Interior Castle'* of the soul. Both are convinced that visions or apparitions, though they may sometimes be of divine origin, are more often than not illusory, and that 'the more completely exterior and corporeal they are, the less certainly are they of God'. Both stress that the normal way to God is by faith; and both regard a direct awareness of God's presence in the soul as the supreme blessing that man can experience during his earthly life. This is what is meant by a 'mystical experience' (a direct awareness, either transient or habitual, of God's presence in the soul), and both St John and St Teresa acknowledge that no human language can adequately describe it. In the light of this exceedingly conservative, Roman Catholic, traditional teaching, it is not rash to suggest that Luke, in the story of the Annunciation to Mary, may only be stating, in simple and unsophisticated language readily comprehensible to his readers, that Mary had a mystical experience. It could be that she learnt at this time that she was to be the virgin mother of God's son. But it is far more plausible to think that Mary, who would have been only a young girl of thirteen at the time, simply felt an overpowering call to place herself entirely at God's disposal, no matter what it might entail. She was ready to commit her ways to the Lord; and there followed the virginal conception. Thus Mary is presented as the model of the Christian believer: almost the first words she utters are 'Behold the handmaid of the Lord!'

It does not follow, if this interpretation be accepted, that the episode should be dismissed as 'unhistorical' (on the ground that no angel appeared to Mary). Quite the contrary is true, for Luke would only be relating in a comprehensible form 'what really happened', according to 'those literary forms which were current among his own contemporaries and countrymen'.[13] How *does* one describe an interior call from God such as Mary is said to have experienced? Isaiah described his vocation to the prophetical

[13] *Divino Afflante Spiritu*, §39 (*AAS* 35 [1943], p. 315).

office in terms of a vision in the Temple (Is 6); Jeremiah and Ezekiel had recourse to symbols in the same way (Jer 1; Ez 1-2). The Christians for whom Luke was writing would have been to some extent at least familiar with these Old Testament descriptions of the prophetical call, and there is no reason to believe that they thought of them as anything other than symbolic descriptions of an otherwise inexpressible experience. The fact that a prophet describes his vocation in terms of a vision does not lead us to doubt the reality of his call; and the fact that Luke narrates the story of the Annunciation as an angelic apparition is not sufficient ground for denying that there is any historical basis for the story. This point does need to be stressed, because the episode is often dismissed as unhistorical simply on the ground that it records the apparition of an angel. But if Mary experienced in some way a divine call to be the virgin mother of God's son, and if all the details about the angel and the conversation are literary dress and theological interpretation, then Luke's account is still (by the standards of his contemporaries) a truly historical narrative, in that it is a record of something which really happened.

The Annunciation to Zechariah might seem at first sight to be on a par with the Annunciation to Mary, since the content of the story is again a divine revelation given by the Angel Gabriel. Yet it is very difficult to think that Luke here intended to describe a mystical experience, for Zechariah's response is not joy, but disbelief, and the story ends with his punishment (Lk 1:18-20). On the other hand, the precise details about the Temple observances (*e.g.* the remark about the class of Abijah in 1:5) and the tone of much of the narrative seem to indicate that we are here dealing with a story of Palestinian provenance which probably existed long before Luke's Gospel was written.[14] Can one discern behind the narrative any inherently credible factual basis?

Martin Dibelius comments: 'It is impossible and also unimportant to determine how much historically reliable information is contained in this legend. For in the face of such a legend, every attempt in that direction seems to be equally devoid of objective criteria (*unmethodisch*): whether one reduces the legend, on

---

[14] See A. Loisy, *Les évangiles synoptiques*, vol. 1, Ceffonds, 1907, p. 277.

critical grounds, to those parts which remain when the miracles have been excised, or whether one uncritically assigns everything narrated to the field of history, or (finally) whether one simply denies the possibility that particular information about the origins of the Baptist could be reliable'.[15] Dibelius is surely right when he asserts that there are no universally acceptable criteria which would enable one to decide with certainty what facts (if any) lie behind the story. He is also right when he states that 'it is unimportant to determine how much historically reliable information is contained in this legend', for in this case the historicity of the details can hardly be classed as an essential part of, or intrinsically connected with, 'that truth which God for our salvation willed to be recorded in the Bible'.[16] The doctrine expressed in this passage, namely, that the Baptist is to prepare the way for Jesus, holds good whether the story is factually historical or merely legend.[17] And one can only applaud Dibelius' strictures against those who would simply cut out the miracles, against those who without proof take everything as a record of fact, and above all against those who reject the very possibility that information about the Baptist's birth could be reliable. Yet men will doubtless continue to ask whether there is anything historical behind the story, and it is certainly legitimate to advance a suggestion which seems to avoid the three pitfalls stigmatized by Dibelius.

The conception of John the Baptist when his parents had for years been childless is well within the bounds of credibility, and it is perhaps noteworthy that Luke gives as the first reason for their

[15] 'Jungfrauensohn und Krippenkind', in *Botschaft und Geschichte*, vol. 1, Tübingen 1953, pp. 8–9.

[16] Second Vatican Council, 'On Divine Revelation', *Dei Verbum*, § 11. On the importance of the qualification 'truth *necessary for salvation*' (*veritas salutaris*), see the Introduction, pp. xxxvii–xl.

[17] In this, the story differs from the account of the Annunciation to Mary. For the burden of the latter (Lk 1:26–38) is not that Jesus will be the Messiah (this occupies only two verses, 32–3), but that Mary consented to be the virginal mother of Jesus (vv. 27–31, 34–8). In Part II we shall discuss whether this account of the virginal conception represents historical fact or edifying legend (see Chapters 12–16, pp. 278–329).

childlessness the fact that 'Elizabeth was barren'. Only afterwards does he mention that both parents were of advanced years (Lk 1:7), but what exactly is meant by 'advanced years'? One may simply observe that the birth of a child after years of waiting is not by any means unheard of; it is not inherently incredible.

The dumbness of Zechariah and his subsequent cure are not beyond the bounds of possibility, provided that the dumbness was of psychic (not organic) origin. Shock at learning of his wife's conception, and joy at the relief afforded by her safe delivery, could therefore account for Zechariah's dumbness and cure. This too (if it happened) could (indeed, would) have been a matter of public knowledge.

The principal difficulty lies in the apparition of the angel, but it is perhaps noteworthy that the angel is not named when he first appears in the narrative (vv. 11, 13, 18), contrary to what happens in the story of the Annunciation to Mary (v. 26). It may also be significant that the role of Zechariah's son is spelt out in a cento of Old Testament quotations from v. 14 to v. 17; and that it is possible to omit vv. 14–17, or vv. 18–22 (where the angel pronounces the sentence of dumbness) or even the whole of vv. 14–22, and still to retain a coherent narrative which flows on without interruption.

I would suggest that there was originally a story, which came into Luke's hands, about the conception of the Baptist. This story told how Zechariah and Elizabeth were childless and old, and that when Zechariah was serving in the Temple he had a vision of an angel telling him that his wife Elizabeth would bear him a son (i.e. the substance of Lk 1:5–13, but without the final clause 'You shall call his name John'[18]). Since we are expressly told in v. 13 that Zechariah's prayer was heard, it is legitimate to suggest that Zechariah had prayed for a son, and that the acceptance of his prayer was related in legend by the tale that an angel had appeared to him in the Temple. The creation of this legend would have been inspired by reflection on the greatness of the Baptist. I would further suggest that the story which came into

---

[18] For the reason behind this suggestion about the absence of the name, see below, p. 141.

Luke's hands then continued with the remarks given in vv. 23, 24–5 (perhaps omitting 'for five months' in 24) and 57, in the following manner.

> (13) 'The angel said to him, "Do not be afraid, Zechariah, for thy prayer is heard, and thy wife Elizabeth will bear thee a son". (23) And when his time of service was over, he went to his home. (24) After these days, his wife Elizabeth conceived, and hid herself [for five months?], saying, (25) "Thus has the Lord done to me in the days when he has looked upon me, to take away my reproach among men". (57) And the time came for Elizabeth to be delivered, and she gave birth to a son . . .'

If this reconstruction is legitimate, then we should indeed have here a legend about the birth of the Baptist, possibly independent of Christian tradition, but certainly showing no marks of hostility to Christianity, and containing no positive indication that its proponents were ignorant of the Christian gospel.[19]

Let us now examine the second tradition about Zechariah, namely, the story that he was struck dumb in the Temple. Lk 1:18–22 make a self-contained unit. The text runs on smoothly if we omit these verses, either from v. 17 to v. 23, or (as above) from v. 13 to v. 23. It is therefore possible that Luke (or his source) added the story of Zechariah's temporary dumbness to a different story which spoke only of the angelic apparition in the Temple. It is therefore legitimate to suggest first that Luke has here incorporated into his gospel two ancient stories about the birth of the Baptist; and secondly, that he has brought forward the commencement of Zechariah's dumbness and placed it in the context of the angel's appearance in the Temple.[20] One may

---

[19] *I.e.* the legend could have originated in Christian circles, and therefore this is not the same theory as that rejected above on pp. 6–7.

[20] Luke does not hesitate to change the time and place of an event in order to draw a theological lesson. For instance, it is commonly admitted that in 5:1–11 he has inserted, at the first call of Peter, the miraculous catch of fish recorded as a post-Resurrection event in Jn 21:6–11 (and significantly absent from the parallel

then think that Luke took over these old Palestinian traditions about the Baptist's conception and birth, and carefully rewrote them to suit his own purpose. Thus I suggest that he himself added vv. 14-17, to spell out the relationship of the Baptist to Jesus; that he himself gave the angel the name Gabriel (v. 19), to call attention to the fulfilment of Dan 9 (the Seventy Weeks); and that he then used this story of the angel's appearance to Zechariah as a literary model for his own account of Mary's virginal conception.[21]

The appearance of the angels to the shepherds provides a third problem. If Jesus really was born in Bethlehem, then it is by no means improbable (quite the contrary) that some of the ever-inquisitive Beduin would have come to visit him, especially if Mary and Joseph were in some hut or cave frequented by the shepherds (cf. the manger, Lk 2:7). Any difficulty lies not in a visit by some shepherds, but solely in the apparition of the angels. But a mind steeped in the Old Testament would see the hand of God directly at work in the most mundane or trivial decisions; and if some shepherds had visited Jesus on the very night of his birth, a Jewish Christian would have regarded those men as having been supremely blessed and guided by God himself to see the new-born Messiah lying in a manger (and what modern Christian would disagree?). There, seeing him helpless, weak and born in poverty, they had been privileged to glimpse the mystery of Calvary. The description of this event in terms of an angelic

---

versions of Peter's call in Mt 4:18-22 and Mk 1:16-20). Compare also the way in which he deals with time and place when relating the appearances of the risen Lord in Lk 24 and Ac 1:1-11.

If Zechariah was in fact struck dumb by shock at finding his wife pregnant (see above, p. 135), it would have been natural to regard this as a divine punishment for not having believed that his prayer would be heard.

[21] Some say that Luke made up the story of the virginal conception as a way of asserting Jesus' superiority to the Baptist in the manner of his birth (see above, Chapter 1, p. 6). To say that Luke took the story of Gabriel's appearance to Zechariah as the *literary* model for his account of the Annunciation to Mary does not, of course, necessarily mean that one assents to this thesis and refuses to accept the virginal conception as an historical fact. The historicity of the virginal conception will be discussed in Part II.

apparition may therefore be Luke's way of saying that there was joy in heaven at the message of glory to God and peace to men revealed by the presence of the child in the manger.

It is not, therefore, satisfactory to dismiss the Lucan Infancy Gospel as devoid of historical basis simply because it records apparitions of angels, or because nearly all the text is theological reflection on the basic truths of the Christian gospel. There is nothing inherently incredible in the suggestion that Elizabeth conceived a child after years of infertility, or that Zechariah was for a time speechless with shock, or that Mary received a divine revelation in the course of a mystical experience, or that some shepherds visited Jesus on the night of his birth. It must be conceded that the above interpretation is a tenable hypothesis. The question remains, is it true? Or is it more reasonable to think that Lk 1–2 represent a collection of legends without historical basis (or at least without any ascertainable historical basis)?

Many modern authors are sceptical about the historical value of the Lucan Infancy Gospel; they think that Luke is there merely recording legends created to express in story the Christian faith of his own generation. Some trace the origins of certain motifs in the Infancy Gospel to Hellenistic mythology: Rudolf Bultmann, for example, claims that the idea of the virginal conception is (at least ultimately) derived from Hellenistic myths, as are the ideas of the 'Saviour', the 'good tidings' and the 'shepherds' in Lk 2: 1–11.[22] Those who detect such Hellenistic motifs claim that Luke is there asserting, to his Greek readers, that Jesus was greater than all the heroes and demi-gods of the Hellenistic world. Others think these two chapters are devoid of historical basis on the ground that everything in them can be explained as a theological message in cipher to be decoded by reference to the Old Testament.[23] For example, the placing of Jesus' birth in Bethlehem would be an invention of the Christian mind: the early Christians, once they had accepted Jesus as Messiah, would either have con-

---

[22] *The History of the Synoptic Tradition*, pp. 291–301 and 304.

[23] The most extreme example of this type of exegesis is the article by M. D. Goulder and M. L. Sanderson, 'St Luke's Genesis', in the *JTS* (N.S.) 8 (1957), pp. 12–30.

cluded that he must therefore have been born in Bethlehem (because Mic 5:2–5 or 1–4 had foretold that the Messiah would be born there), or have made up the story as part of their creed that Jesus was the Messiah. Certainly an attitude of scepticism or agnosticism about the historical value of Luke's stories is very widespread today.

Yet if one analyses closely these chapters of Luke, it becomes apparent that the expression of specifically Christian doctrine is (with one exception) conveyed not through the events related, but only through the conversations and speeches. If we set aside the assertion of the virginal conception, none of the 'happenings' which Luke relates in the Infancy Gospel is of such a nature as to convey a doctrinal message about Christ when detached from the speech or conversation accompanying it.

Thus in Lk 1:5–7 we are told that Zechariah and Elizabeth were childless and old, and in 1:24–5 we read of the conception of the Baptist. A Christian could have had no doctrinal motive for inventing this story that John was born to childless parents in their old age; it makes no difference whatever to the role of the Baptist; and to ascribe this episode to a 'Baptist document' is to admit as much.[24] But would the author of a Baptist legend, intent on exalting John, have made up without any evidence the story of Zechariah's disbelief and punishment (1:18–20)? The externally observable 'happenings' in Lk 1:5–25 do not give any ground for suspecting that they were invented to put across Christian doctrine, and what there is of Christian teaching in this passage occurs only in the speech by the angel, where he explains the role of the Baptist *vis-à-vis* Jesus (vv. 14–17).[25] It is therefore more reasonable to think that we are here dealing with an old tradition than with a legend invented for doctrinal motives.

---

[24] See above, Chapter 1, p. 6, and also the note in H. Schürmann, *Das Lukas-evangelium I*, pp. 95–6: 'Zur Vorgeschichte des Täufererzählung 1:5–25, 57–80'.

[25] Against Schürmann (*loc. cit.*) and others, one must stress that John fulfils his role of 'going before the Lord God' (Lk 1:17, 76) by going before Jesus (3:4; 7:27). It is pure and unproved hypothesis to say that Lk 1:17 (and 76) indicate a document according to which John was not the forerunner of Jesus, but only of 'the Lord'.

The historicity of the virginal conception will be examined in Part II. The episode following it is the Visitation, with its appendix, the Magnificat (Lk 1:39–45, 46–56). There are certainly no motifs in Hellenistic mythology, or in the Old Testament, which might have led an early Christian to invent this episode. For if it had been invented, the more natural idea would have been to portray Elizabeth as making pilgrimage to Nazareth, there to salute the mother of her Lord, and thus to show the older woman making obeisance to the younger. This could hardly have been done, of course, without suppressing the detail that Elizabeth was far advanced in her pregnancy. But if John and Jesus were more or less of the same age, and if one was simply making up a story for doctrinal reasons, uninhibited by the evidence of historical traditions, then it would have been easy to place the birth of the Baptist later than that of Jesus, and to have Elizabeth going to greet Mary in Galilee. Besides, the whole episode is so unnecessary, and so peripheral to the central themes of Christianity, that it is impossible to conceive why any Christian should have invented it to express doctrine.[26] What Christian doctrine is there contained is all in the words spoken, except for the 'leaping' of the child in Elizabeth's womb.

It is self-evident that the account of the birth of the Baptist (1:57–66) was not invented to express any Christian truth, and that it is not based on Hellenistic or Old Testament motifs. Its Christological significance is (once again) set forth only in the words which follow it, the Benedictus (1:67–79). It could be argued that the story is a legend invented by followers of the Baptist, and then turned in a Christian direction by Luke (or his source) through its inclusion in the Infancy Gospel. Against this, however, stands the fact that the central issue is the disagreement over the boy's name (1:59–63), with its underlying stress that Zechariah, the father of this great child, was still under the

---

[26] *A fortiori*, this episode would never have been invented by followers of the Baptist ignorant of, or hostile to, the Christian Church.

I do not think one can take seriously the suggestion that the episode was invented (with *no* basis in fact) as a midrash on 2 Sam 6, on the transfer of the Ark of the Covenant. See above, pp. 61–3.

punishment of God. A legend made up to exalt the Baptist might have chosen a happier way of proclaiming his greatness. The most reasonable suggestion would seem to be that we have here an utterly authentic tradition, based on fact, about the birth of the Baptist: at his circumcision, there was a quarrel over the boy's name, and Zechariah determined that it should be John. Later, it was said that Gabriel in the temple had ordered him to call the boy John.

It is hard to believe that Luke's mentioning of a 'registration' under Augustus and his deliberate naming of Quirinius (Lk 2:1–2) are not intended as historical references. Nevertheless, it has been suggested that these two statements are a mere device to 'stage' the birth of the Christ at Bethlehem, as prophecy (Mic 5:1–4 or 2–5) demanded. According to this theory, Luke telescoped the great census which took place in Palestine under Quirinius between A.D. 6 and A.D. 9[27] into the reign of Herod the Great, who died in 4 B.C., in order to provide an appropriate *mise en scène* for the birth of the Saviour: the census would then explain why Joseph and Mary were not in Nazareth but in Bethlehem when Jesus was born. To this suggestion several replies may be made. First, if Luke had deliberately advanced the date of the census by some ten years, would he have written that Jesus was about thirty years old in the fifteenth year of Tiberius Caesar (Lk 3:1, 23)? His readers would have been familiar with the taxing of Judaea in A.D. 6–9 (*cf.* Ac 5:37), and would have known that the fifteenth year of Tiberius came twenty, not thirty, years after it. Secondly, if Luke advanced the date of the census by ten years, why did he give away the true date of Jesus' birth by mentioning that Herod was king in Judaea (Lk 1:5)? There was no need to mention Herod, who plays no part in the story, and even if he had figured in Luke's source, it would have been simple to suppress his name. Thirdly, the word ἀπογραφή, usually translated 'census', has as its primary meaning the *registration* of land or property, and Josephus, in describing the work of Quirinius and Coponius in A.D. 6–9, writes instead of a 'valuation' or 'raising of taxes' (ἀποτίμησις).[28] There are a number of ancient texts which

[27] Josephus, *Ant.* XVII, xiii, 5 = §355 and XVIII, i, i = §§1–3.   [28] *Loc. cit.*

state that for the registration of property, each one had to go to his own home, at least in some of the provinces and particularly in Egypt:[29] it is not therefore incredible that a first register of land and property was made, at the request of the Romans, at the very end of the reign of Herod the Great: Josephus tells us that Herod made his subjects swear an oath of loyalty to Augustus in 7 B.C., and the registration of property might have taken place soon after.[30] There is nothing *a priori* incredible in the assertion that Jesus was born in Bethlehem, even though his parents' home was at Nazareth.

Furthermore, the tradition that Jesus was born in Bethlehem is not confined to Luke: indeed, apart from the virginal conception, it is the only detail in his Infancy Gospel which is also to be found in Matthew (Mt 2:1–23). Jn 7:41–2, 52 is even more persuasive, because less explicit. 'Some of them began saying, "Surely the Christ is not going to come out of Galilee? Has not Scripture stated that the Christ will come from the line of David, and from Bethlehem, the little town where David lived?"' As so often in the Fourth Gospel, the irony is evident; yet it is equally clear that, according to the evangelist, many of the contemporaries of Jesus did not know the true place of his birth. There is, then, a solid tradition, much older than Matthew, Luke or John, affirming that Jesus was born in Bethlehem; and since this could be considered to have arisen from the belief that Jesus was the Messiah, we shall have to consider whether there are any clues which might indicate whether this tradition is based on fact or is merely a *theologoumenon*. For the present, we may simply note that the theological explanation of the significance of the birth in Bethle-

---

[29] U. Istinsky, *Das Jahr der Geburt Christi*, Munich, 1957, pp. 33–4 and especially H. Braunert, 'Der römische Provinzialzensus und der Schätzungsbericht des Lukas-Evangeliums', in *Historia* 6 (1957), pp. 192–214.

[30] *Ant.* XVII, ii, 4 = §42. It is interesting to note that Lk 2:2 is the only sentence in Lk 1–2 (except, obviously, 1:1) which is not introduced by a connective particle. Should it not then be read as a parenthesis (as in the Authorized Version), with the meaning 'This first registration took place *in Syria*' (as distinct from Palestine) *only* 'when Quirinius was governor there'. For this distinction between Syria and Palestine in the Lucan writings see Ac 15:23, 41; 18:18; 20:3; 21:3, and compare the distinction between Syria and Judaea in Gal 1:21–2.

hem (and of the child in the manger) occurs (once again) in the words of the angel to the shepherds.

The story of the Presentation in the Temple follows the same pattern. The specifically Christian doctrine is to be found almost entirely in the words of Simeon (2:29-32, 34-5), though there are a few editorial touches as well ('he was led by the Spirit into the Temple'). The details about Anna, the daughter of Phanuel (2:36-8) can only come from pre-Lucan tradition, and it is therefore reasonable to think that some of the details about Simeon come from the same, or a similar, source. Anyone who wishes to argue that the whole episode is a Christian legend devoid of historical foundation has to explain why the totally irrelevant details about Anna are included in the gospel story; and if it is argued that these details about Anna are a truncated version of an earlier legend in which she also prophesied, one has to explain why Luke did not omit the whole legend instead of suppressing just the interesting part.

There is enough evidence here to justify the claim that many of the events narrated in Lk 1-2 cannot be explained as legends created by the Christian community to express doctrine. There is nothing to suggest that the main inspiration of these chapters came from Hellenistic mythology, and there is much evidence against that view. The only two events narrated which might arguably have been invented for doctrinal motives are the virginal conception and the birth of Jesus in Bethlehem; it could be argued that the former was an attempt to express in story the belief that Jesus was the son of God, the latter an assertion that he was the Messiah. Are we then faced, in Lk 1-2, with a number of historical traditions (to which Luke or his source has attached a profound Christian interpretation)? Or are we faced, at least at some points, with legend (profound in its Christian message) for which there is no historical basis?

It is sometimes argued (more often assumed) that the Lucan Infancy Gospel cannot rest on trustworthy evidence because it was written too long after the events it purports to narrate (say, at the earliest between A.D. 65 and 70): at a distance of seventy years, it is claimed, all testimony is notoriously unreliable. Though at first hearing this argument seems very plausible, there can be few people who have not accepted as true what their parents or grandparents have told them about events which took place seventy years before. Admittedly, memory may play tricks, and stories improve in the telling, but there must be many alive today who have accepted without scruple stories of something that happened in the 1890s. Old people, whose memory of recent events may be confused or non-existent, can frequently astound a younger generation by the precision with which they remember details of their childhood; and those who make a hobby of collecting oral traditions from the elderly are, far more often than not, impressed by the accuracy and fidelity of their memories —especially when the same story is heard from the same individual after a lapse of several years. One may add that women in particular have an astonishing memory for important family events, especially those connected with the birth of children. It is therefore not unreasonable to ask that anyone who seeks to assess the trustworthiness of the Lucan Infancy Gospel should judge the evangelist by the criteria he would employ when listening to a friend's account of what he had heard on good evidence; and it is certainly not the mark of an impartial mind always to treat Luke as a hostile witness. Most of the Lucan Infancy Gospel is in fact a family history, *i.e.* an account of events which would have been regarded within the family as all-important, but which would have passed unnoticed in the world at large. It is not to be expected, therefore, that external evidence will ever enable men to decide either that Luke's narrative here has an historical basis, or that it is merely a tissue of unfounded legends. Family history is not of this type, and Luke's Infancy Gospel must be judged on purely internal grounds, as it stands.

The only fact recorded in these chapters which might have qualified for inclusion in the annals of the time as an historic event is the registration of Palestine (or of Judaea) under Augustus; and this is neither confirmed nor positively disproved by external evidence. The only fact, apart from the virginal conception, which might arguably have been thought up by Christians for an apologetic motive is the placing of Jesus' birth in Bethlehem. Yet both these incidents are set in the framework of a family history in which there is much evidence to indicate that we are not dealing with legends created, with no historical basis, to exalt Jesus or the Baptist. There is nothing *a priori* incredible in the narrative; and there is no positive evidence against any of the incidents recorded.

It can be objected, of course, that 'infancy legends' were bound to grow around the figure of Jesus; that this actually happened can be proved from the apocryphal gospels. This objection cannot be answered by saying that the canonical Infancy Gospels (Mt 1-2; Lk 1-2) are sober and restrained where the apocryphal Infancy Gospels are wildly fantastic. It is true that the Infancy Gospels of Matthew and Luke are very sober when compared with the apocryphal Infancy Gospels, but when compared with the rest of Matthew and Luke, the infancy stories look anything but restrained. We must therefore ask why the Church accepted as canonical the books of Matthew and Luke (including their Infancy Gospels) at the very time when it was waging an unrelenting war on what Jerome calls the *deliramenta apocryphorum*. There must have been some criterion by which the Church distinguished, and in the end the only possible answer is that the Church decided that the books of Matthew and Luke possessed, in some sense, apostolic authority.[31] And since the second-century Church drew no distinction between the authority of the Infancy Gospels and that of the rest of the gospels, it is legitimate to infer that it regarded the teaching contained in the Infancy Gospels as proceeding, in some sense, from the apostolic generation. As far as the Lucan Infancy Gospel is concerned, it would appear to have accepted the author's claim that his narrative and interpretation of events were guaranteed by trustworthy sources (Lk 1:1-4).

If we allow that the speeches and dialogues in Lk 1-2 are (in their present form) almost entirely the work of the evangelist, and are intended as an interpretation of the happenings narrated, then, in judging the claim to historicity, our attention must be directed to the incidents recorded. And here we see why Lk 1-2

[31] *Cf.* M.-J. Lagrange, *Histoire ancienne du Canon du Nouveau Testament*, Paris, 1933, pp. 8-43.

differs from the rest of the gospel: it is a family history, not a record of a public ministry. This means that of their nature the events narrated in Lk 1–2 would have been quickly forgotten, or even overlooked by the world at large; forgotten or overlooked, that is, except by the family, and above all by Mary, whom we should expect to have remembered in detail many incidents connected with the birth of her son. Quite clearly, Mary alone could have known of the Annunciation and of her own virginal conception; and if the virginal conception is accepted as an historical fact, the argument is virtually closed, for then there is an overwhelming case for accepting her as the witness and the source for the entire narrative. But even if we abstract for the moment from this presupposition about the factuality of the virginal conception, we find that Luke tells the story as seen through Mary's eyes.

Here and there in the narrative there are graphic touches such as might have been introduced by a sensitive writer. What is interesting is that, with one exception (Lk 1:22), they figure only when Mary is, so to speak, on stage. Thus, for example, there are no vivid touches in the story of the Annunciation to Zechariah, except for the remark that he made signs to the people outside the Temple (Lk 1:22); and if Luke combined the story of Zechariah's dumbness with another story that did not mention it, he himself may have introduced the 'speaking in sign-language' at v. 22. And he could have been moved to make this insertion by the 'sign-language' mentioned in v. 62. This is the only exception to the rule that pictorial touches occur only when Mary is present.

There are no vivid touches of this kind in the Annunciation to Mary, which, it has been suggested, is a free composition by Luke.[32] But in the story of the Visitation, Mary 'rose and went with haste to a city of Judah' (1:39), and the infant in Elizabeth's womb leapt for joy (1:41, 44). The description of the scene at the circumcision of the Baptist is the most pictorially vivid in the whole narrative (1:57–66); and Luke tells us (without any apparent theological motive for doing so) that 'Mary remained

[32] See above, pp. 132–3 and 137.

146

with Elizabeth about three months' (1:56), *i.e.* until the birth of the Baptist. 'She wrapped him in swaddling clothes and laid him in a manger, because there was no room for them in the lodging' (2:7): this is the birth of Jesus seen through Mary's eyes, just as 'Simeon took him into his arms' (2:28) is the arrival in the Temple, through Mary's eyes. There is no need to spell out her part in the story of the finding of Jesus in the Temple (2:41-52). Of course it could be argued that the lively touches in these scenes are just the invention of Luke, or of some other writer or story-teller; but in that case, why are there no similar details in the verses which describe the shepherds in the fields (2:8-15), and why does Luke elsewhere suppress vivid touches found in Mark (contrast Mk 4:35-41 with Lk 8:22-5)? It is more reasonable to think that Luke has retained these details from one of his sources because the details themselves point to Mary, and because he perceived that his own account of Jesus' infancy could have no solid claim to be regarded as historical unless its source were Mary. Twice Luke tells us that she pondered things in her heart (2:19, 51, *cf.* 33), two statements that cannot be explained as mythology or typology, and which cannot be dismissed as empty of meaning: Luke must have meant to say something by these words. It is not absurd, therefore, to suggest that Luke had reason to believe that his own sources or informants were relating what they had learnt (ultimately) from Mary.

Thus we return to our starting-point. The affinity between Luke's Gospel and the Fourth Gospel is nowhere more marked than in the Infancy Narrative,[33] and the Fourth Gospel cannot be wholly detached from John the son of Zebedee.[34] Luke himself begins by affirming that he is going to relate 'traditions handed down to us by those *who were from the beginning eye-witnesses* and servants of the word' (Lk 1:2), and according to Luke, the first disciples were Simon, James and John (5:1-11). Now the Fourth Gospel asserts that after the death of Jesus, Mary went to live with the beloved disciple (Jn 19:27);[35] unless it is assumed that the

[33] See above, Chapter 1, pp. 8-10.
[34] See below, Part III, Chapter 1, pp. 358-60.
[35] See below, p. 378.

writer was either grossly misinformed, or utterly indifferent to fact, or speaking purely figuratively, or that the beloved disciple was someone other than the son of Zebedee (all of which are assumptions requiring positive proof), this verse must mean that after the crucifixion Mary went to live with John the son of Zebedee. It is legitimate to conclude that Luke learnt the story of the birth of the Saviour from a Johannine source, and that John in turn learnt them from Mary herself.

There is no need to argue that Mary's own witness would have been truthful and informed. The disciples would surely have accepted her witness. It is *a priori* likely that Mary gave some account of the infancy of Jesus to the first disciples, and that they believed her account, as they had believed the teachings of her son. Moreover, it is hardly conceivable that John and the other disciples should, consciously or unconsciously, have later distorted or misrepresented Mary's account of the birth and conception of Jesus, so that her original account has perished without trace, and been replaced by a different one; for the central point of the apostolic preaching was 'We are witnesses of these things' (1 Jn 1:1-3). On the other hand, it is very likely indeed that John and his friends pondered and discussed the facts which Mary told them, and so came to realize ever more clearly how the Scriptures had been fulfilled in those events.[36] But this later theological reflection (of which Lk 1-2 is an outstanding example) must have been an interpretation of things which really happened, or the disciples would have been conscious that they were misrepresenting the true reality, and that the Scriptures had not in fact been fulfilled.

This argument is not rebutted by affirming that the disciples (or the evangelists) argued to the 'incidents related' (*e.g.* the birth in Bethlehem) because they were already convinced that the Scriptures had been fulfilled, and that 'facts' could therefore be deduced from the Old Testament. For the question then arises, 'Why was the evangelist convinced, how was he convinced, that Scripture had been fulfilled?' And if Luke was deducing 'facts' from Old Testament prophecy without any historical evidence,

[36] See above, p. 71 and below, p. 359.

why does he put so much stress on the virginal conception (which is not foretold in the Old Testament), when the very idea of a virginal conception would seem to undermine the claim that Jesus was 'of the seed of David'? The slogan of Form Criticism is *Im Anfang war die Predigt.* It is wiser to keep to Goethe and say *Im Anfang war die Tat.*

The doctrine recorded in Lk 1-2 was not created *ex nihilo sui et subiecti* by the theological speculation or the religious experience of the early Church. Reflection and prayer, and the enlightening grace of the Holy Spirit, no doubt influenced the early Christians and guided them to a fuller realization of the implications of their beliefs. But the tradition they accepted was that Mary by a virginal conception was the mother of the son of God. Luke could not have failed to perceive that his account of the infancy of Jesus would be trustworthy if, and only if, the basic factual content (as distinct from the literary and theological presentation) came originally from Mary herself. He conveys this discreetly by relating the story as seen through Mary's eyes. And by giving not merely major facts, but also certain minor details which are of no doctrinal significance, he implicitly appeals to her as to his ultimate authority—to her word, her character and her life.

Chapter Fifteen

MARY THE DAUGHTER OF ZION

It will not be out of place to conclude this first part of the book by attempting, not to summarize Luke's teaching about Mary, but to determine its central motif. This problem can be conveniently raised by asking the question which divides exegetes today: is it correct to say that Mary is presented in Lk 1-2 as the (eschatological) Daughter of Zion? Ever since Sahlin's epoch-making book in 1945,[1] many writers (especially Roman Catholic theologians) have answered with an unconditional 'Yes', and the Second Vatican Council bestowed a mild blessing on this view when it said:

> 'She stands out among the lowly and the poor of the Lord who confidently hope for, and receive, salvation from him. Lastly, it is with her, the glorious Daughter of Zion (*praecelsa Filia Sion*), that the times are fulfilled after long ages of waiting for the promise, and that the new Dispensation is inaugurated.'[2]

Not surprisingly, other exegetes (principally Lutheran) have rejected any identification of Mary with the Daughter of Zion on the ground that it reads more into the text than is said there, and mistakes shadows of allusions for substantial reality.

There can be no doubt that some writers (especially Roman

[1] See above, p. 44.
[2] The Dogmatic Constitution on the Church, *Lumen Gentium*, Chapter VIII, § 55.

Catholics) have been carried away by enthusiasm and have read into Luke's text far more than is really there; but *abusus non tollit usum*, and the identification cannot be rejected simply because some of the arguments in its favour have rightly been found wanting. At the other extreme, it is not unfair to say that some of the less ecumenically minded among German Protestants appear to reach for weapons of war whenever the name of the mother of Jesus is mentioned by a Roman Catholic. One may without lack of charity suspect that these Catholics and these Protestants are prompted more by fidelity to their own doctrinal traditions than by a critical and open-minded reading of Luke's text.

To avoid embroilment in the more exaggerated views for and against the thesis that Luke identified Mary with the Daughter of Zion, it will be sufficient to quote the case against the identification as it is set out, with customary moderation, by Räisänen.

'It is not because of her motherhood, but only because of her faith, that Mary is blessed (1:45; 11:28). Tradition had already emphasized the faith of Mary. Luke made of her a kind of *Prototype of the Christian* [the italics are the author's]. She is not—not once in the sources of Luke—the personification of the "Daughter of Zion", as some have claimed. Instead, she is made into an ideal representative of the Christian community, in whose experiences the Christian readers could recognize their own. In Mary, characteristic traits of the "poor" of the Old Covenant (1:51-5) are united with those of Christians in the New. She is the object of grace, of the great deeds of God (1:48-9). The grace of God, and the eschatological joy that springs from it, are the hall-mark of her life (1:28). The Spirit which works in manifold ways within the community breaks into her life at the decisive point (1:35). Mary is a maid who casts herself obediently down under the will of her Lord (1:38). Throughout, Luke speaks of Mary in the same tone as he speaks later of the first Christians.

But above all, Mary is a typical *Hearer of the Word*. With her, the "seed" does not fall on rock or among thorns.

Mary listens to the word, keeps it and ponders it in her heart (2:19, 51). In this, all hearers should imitate her.

The portrait of Mary given by Luke can therefore be summarized in one word as "exemplary" (*paradigmatisch*). Mary is the exemplar and type of the believer. Both her experiences and her behaviour are exemplary for Christians. In spite of a slight trace of human incomprehension (2:50), she appears as an exemplary and ideal figure, and she belongs to the preaching of the evangelist.'[3]

In this summary by a Lutheran exegete, everything that is said in praise of Mary may (and should) be accepted by all Christians, whatever their confessional creed. The only point with which one might wish to quarrel is the assertion that Mary is nowhere presented as the Daughter of Zion.[4]

For when one considers the portrait of Mary given by Räisänen himself, one finds that he has stressed precisely those traits which in the Old Testament delineate 'the faithful Daughter of Zion' as she will be 'at the end of time'. Mary, he says, is the ideal representative of the Christian community—that is, of the Messianic community; she unites in her person characteristic traits of the poor of the Old Covenant, and of the New. This is exactly what Roman Catholic writers mean to say when they call Mary 'the eschatological Daughter of Zion'. 'The grace of God', says Räisänen, 'and the eschatological joy that springs from it, are the hall-mark of her life.' The grace of God and the eschatological joy that springs from the coming of Zion's king are themes of Zeph 3:14–17 and Zech 9:9: they are the hall-marks of the eschatological Daughter of Zion.

Secondly, as far as Mary is concerned, the key event in Lk 1–2 is the Annunciation. In Luke's account, the Incarnation itself is made dependent on Mary's acceptance. As soon as she says

[3] *Die Mutter Jesu im Neuen Testament*, p. 154.

[4] The fact that Räisänen here says that Mary is not presented as the Daughter of Zion 'in the sources used by Luke' is not significant, since he takes the sources to mean 'the content of the chapters' (pp. 77–80), and since he does not agree that Mary is so presented by Luke himself (*e.g.* p. 91: 'Für Lukas verkörpert also Maria nicht die "Tochter Zion" ').

'Behold the handmaid of the Lord', the angel departs from her (1:38); and Luke's final comment on the episode, through the mouth of Elizabeth, is, 'Blessed is she for her belief that there will be fulfilment of what has been spoken to her by the Lord' (1:45). In accepting to be the mother of Zion's king, Mary as an individual becomes that Daughter of Zion who brings to birth the Messianic age; by the very fact of carrying Jesus in her womb, she was ushering in 'the end of [Old Testament] time'.

The truth of the matter would seem to be that those writers (especially Roman Catholic dogmatic theologians) who have argued in favour of the identification of Mary with the eschatological Daughter of Zion have placed all the emphasis on the fact of Mary's motherhood. This, for them, is (rightly) the central 'dogmatic' fact of the narrative. The Lutheran writers like Räisänen who reject this identification are mainly exegetes; and they (again rightly, on their terms) point out that Luke's picture of Mary stresses above all her faith (1:38, 45; 2:19, 51). But these two positions are not, in the last analysis, in any way opposed to each other. The notion of Mary as the ideal or prototype of the Christian believer, the faithful and lowly servant of the Lord, corresponds in every single detail with the Old Testament concept of the faithful Daughter of Zion at the end of time; and there is no exegetical (much less dogmatic) reason why Lutherans should refuse her this title. And it is because of her faith, and through her faith (itself a freely bestowed gift from God), that she becomes the mother of the Redeemer. Thus to ask whether Mary's faith or her motherhood is the central notion in Luke's mind is to place a dichotomy where Luke saw none; her motherhood of Jesus was entirely dependent on her faith, and God gave her that immeasurable faith in order that she might be the mother of Jesus. The two gifts are inseparable, because each is essentially related to the other. A prayer formerly much used in the Roman Breviary states the thought perfectly:

Omnipotens, sempiterne Deus, qui gloriosae Virginis Mariae corpus et animam, ut dignum Filii tui habitaculum effici mereretur, Spiritu Sancto cooperante, praeparasti . . .

PART II

VIRGIN AND MOTHER

(The Virginity of Mary in the New Testament)

'Anyone who wants to undo a knot must first look at it very closely, to see how it is tied. Similarly, anyone who wants to unravel a problem must first consider all the knotty points, to see how they were caused.'

(St Thomas Aquinas, *Commentary on Book III of Aristotle's Metaphysics*, Lecture 1.)

Chapter One

THE BETROTHAL OF MARY TO JOSEPH
(Mt 1:18)

THE genealogy of Jesus Christ at the beginning of St Matthew's gospel is followed by eight verses concerning his virginal conception (Mt 1:18–25). These verses are evidently meant to explain why Mt 1:16 does not read (as one would have expected) that 'Joseph was the father of Jesus', but that 'Joseph was the husband of Mary, of whom Jesus was born'.[1] All commentators are agreed that verses 18–25 are intended as an explanation of this last link in the genealogy,[2] or that the awkward turn of phrase in v. 16 is an introduction to the story which follows, but there are two verses (18 and 19) about which there is widespread disagreement. What is the meaning of the phrase 'before they came together' in Mt 1:18? And how should one interpret v. 19: 'Joseph, being an upright man and not wanting to expose her, was thinking of giving her a secret divorce'? These two points will be discussed in two separate chapters.

Mary was already betrothed to Joseph when, 'before they came together', she was found to be with child from the Holy Ghost.

---

[1] There is no need to discuss here the textual variations: see any critical edition of the New Testament, or any good commentary.

[2] Thus K. Stendahl, 'Quis et Unde? An Analysis of Mt 1-2', in W. Eltester, *Judentum–Christentum–Kirche* (Festschrift für J. Jeremias), Berlin, 1960, pp. 94–105. He calls it 'the enlarged footnote to the crucial point in the genealogy' (p. 102), and translates v. 18a: 'But as for this last link in genealogy "Jesus Christ" his origin was this wise' (p. 101). His judgment is cited with approval by A. Vögtle, 'Die Genealogie Mt 1:2–16 und die matthäische Kindheitsgeschichte', in the *Biblische Zeitschrift* (N.F.) 8 (1964), pp. 242–4.

Many exegetes, ancient and modern, have taken the phrase 'before they came together' to mean 'before they had known each other as man and wife': this is the interpretation given by St John Chrysostom[3] and St Jerome,[4] for example. If it is correct, then these words are a formal assertion of the virginal conception of Jesus, and Mt 1:18 describes it in two ways: first negatively ('Mary and Joseph had not yet come together'), stressing the absence of human fatherhood, and secondly in a positive manner ('she was found to be with child of the Holy Ghost') pointing to the divine cause of Jesus' conception. The Greek verb used in the phrase 'before they came together' ($\sigma\upsilon\nu\acute{\epsilon}\rho\chi o\mu\alpha\iota$) does sometimes bear the meaning 'to have sexual intercourse',[5] but most modern scholars deny that it carries this sense in the phrase under discussion. Here, they say, the sense is that Mary and Joseph had not yet begun to live together under the same roof, and therefore this verb (in contrast to the last words of v. 18 and to v. 25) does not say anything about the virginal conception. In order to decide which of these two interpretations is correct, it is necessary to consider the Jewish law concerning betrothal and marriage, and some of the social customs in Palestine during New Testament times.

The customary procedure of betrothal can be gathered from various treatises in the Mishnah, particularly from the two entitled *Kiddushin* ('Betrothals') and *Ketuboth* ('Marriage Deeds').[6] The young man would approach the father (or the legal guardian) of the girl he wished to marry, and make a formal proposal of marriage: he could make this offer 'either by his own act or by

---

[3] *In Matt.*, Hom. 4, n. 2 (MG 57.42).

[4] *In Matt.*, Lib. I (*CC* 77.11 = ML 26.24 or 25A).

[5] *Cf.* Liddell and Scott, *A Greek–English Lexicon*, 9th ed., Oxford, 1940, *s.v.*; and especially W. Bauer's *Greek–English Lexicon of the New Testament*, *s.v.*

[6] The Mishnah, a code of Jewish Law, was compiled in its present form towards the end of the second century of the Christian era. It is generally acknowledged as a conservative and trustworthy record of legal prescriptions dating back some centuries before that time, and can often be used to determine the laws and customs which obtained during New Testament times. There is an excellent English translation by the late Canon Herbert Danby (*The Mishnah*, Oxford, 1933) containing brief, but very valuable notes. All the citations in this book are taken from Danby's edition.

that of his agent'.[7] On the girl's side, the arrangements were usually in the hands of an agent (*e.g.* her father or her brother), but she had some say in the acceptance or rejection of the offer, though the laws are very complex.[8] When the terms had been arranged, the formal betrothal took place, but the girl remained under her father's authority from the time of betrothal to the time of her marriage.

> 'The father has control over his daughter[9] as touching her betrothal whether it is effected by money, by writ, or by intercourse [whereby betrothal is effected];[10] and he has the right to aught found by her and to the work of her hands, and [the right] to set aside her vows, and he receives her bill of divorce . . .'.[11]

It was her father too to whom the *Ketubah* or 'brideprice' was paid: this was a sum of money which the man paid over in case the girl should be left without husband, and it was meant to provide for her if her fiancé should die or divorce her. If he died or divorced her *before* the marriage,[12] this money became the property of her father (who then remained financially responsible for her); but if the girl was divorced or widowed *after* the marriage, the money was her own.[13] The system of the *Ketubah* and the need for a formal divorce even before marriage are clear evidence that a Jewish betrothal had far wider consequences than an engagement has in western Europe today.

[7] *Kiddushin* 2:1; *cf.* 2:4; 3:1 (Danby, pp. 323–5).

[8] *Yebamoth* ('Sisters-in-law') 13 (Danby, pp. 237–40).

[9] The Hebrew word implies that the girl is not yet twelve and a half years old (Danby, p. 250, fn. 3).

[10] The man who raped or seduced a virgin not yet betrothed could be compelled either to marry her or to pay money equivalent to the brideprice for a virgin; and it was the girl's father who decided whether to insist on marriage or not (*cf.* Ex 22:15–16; Deut 22:28–9). This is the meaning of 'betrothal by intercourse'.

[11] *Ketuboth* 4:4 (Danby, p. 250).

[12] Once a girl had been betrothed, she needed a formal bill of divorce from her fiancé before she could marry another man: *cf. Kiddushin* 1:1 (Danby, p. 321).

[13] *Ketuboth* 4:2 (Danby, p. 249).

Among the consequences, some say,[14] was the right to sexual intercourse, so that betrothal was practically what we mean by marriage; and there are certain laws, expressions and customs which at first sight seem to support this view. A fiancée who gave herself to any man other than her betrothed was to be treated in exactly the same way as a married woman who had committed adultery, according to the law of Deut 22:23-8, *cf.* v. 22.[15] An engaged couple were often referred to as 'man and wife': thus in Mt 1:19 Joseph is called Mary's husband, and in v. 24 Mary is called his wife (*cf.* also v. 20).[16] And after the Jewish Revolt of A.D. 132–5 it was the custom in Judaea for betrothed couples to sleep together before the marriage, so that the Roman soldiers would nọt be tempted to seize the girl on the occasion of the wedding procession.[17]

On the other hand, there is abundant evidence that a virgin bride was both esteemed and honoured.[18] The *Ketubah* paid for a virgin was 200 denars, whereas that for a widow was only 100 denars; and if after the wedding a girl was discovered not to be a virgin, her husband could lodge a suit either for annulment of the marriage or for repayment of the difference in the *Ketubah*.[19] This law assumes that a husband will not discover whether his wife is a virgin during the period of betrothal, but only after the marriage. It is also an established fact that outside Judaea it was at all times considered unseemly, not to say immoral, for two fiancés to be alone together, or even to spend the night under the same roof.[20] These and similar laws presuppose that during the period

---

[14] Thus C. G. Montefiore, *The Synoptic Gospels*, vol. 1, London, 1927, p. 5; P. Dausch, *Die drei älteren Evangelien*, 4th ed., Bonn, 1932, p. 46.

[15] In the *Encyclopaedia Judaica*, vol. 2, c. 313 (Jerusalem, 1971) adultery is defined as 'voluntary sexual intercourse between a married woman or one engaged by payment of the brideprice, and a man other than her husband'.

[16] *Cf.* Jerome on Mt 1:16: 'Recordare consuetudinis Scripturarum, quod sponsi viri et sponsae uxores vocantur' (*CC* 77.9 = ML 26.23 or 24).

[17] See below, n. 20.   [18] *Ketuboth*, *passim* (Danby, pp. 245 ff.).

[19] *Ketuboth* 1:1-5 (Danby, p. 245); *cf. Kiddushin* 2:5 (Danby, p. 323).

[20] *Ketuboth* 1:5 reads: 'If in Judea a man ate in the house of his father-in-law and had no witnesses he may not lodge a virginity-suit against her, since he had [already] remained alone with her' (Danby, p. 245). Further, the normal rule was

of betrothal the two fiancés lived apart, and that the girl normally remained a virgin until the day of the wedding.

It is therefore an oversimplification to assert without qualification that Jewish betrothal gave the fiancés the right to marital intercourse,[21] and the arguments put forward to justify this statement do not prove the point. Admittedly, a fiancée who gave herself to a man other than her betrothed was to be treated in the same way as an adulteress;[22] but this proves only that she

---

that a widow or a betrothed girl whose fiancé died might not marry again, or be betrothed, for three months (in case she had conceived a child). Around A.D. 150 R. Judah sought to ease this ruling when he said: 'They that had been married may forthwith be betrothed, and they that had been [only] betrothed may forthwith be married, excepting betrothed women in Judea, since [there] the bridegroom is less shamefast before her' (*Yebamoth* 4:10; Danby, p. 224). From these two texts it is clear that in Judaea there was a custom of consummating the union before the wedding procession, *i.e.* during the period of betrothal; and from other sources it is known that the reason for this was to prevent the Roman troops from claiming the *ius primae noctis* (*cf.* Babylonian Talmud, *Ketuboth* 3b; Jerusalem Talmud, *Ketuboth* 1, 25c). Hence R. Judah held that a girl who had been betrothed in Judaea might not marry until three months after the death of her fiancé, because it was very possible that a young girl would have conceived a child; but a girl who had been betrothed elsewhere did not have to wait, because she was presumed to be a virgin. K. H. Rengstorf comments on this text: 'The strict moral code of the time comes forcibly before our eyes in this Mishnah. . . . As we can clearly see, the Galilean rabbis were anxious to protect the morals of their little homeland, and yet they had to take into account the moral code which obtained in Judaea. All the same, the contempt with which Galileans looked down on the "lax" relations in Judaea is evident' (*Die Mischna* III, 1, Giessen, 1929, p. 61).

[21] The *Encyclopaedia Judaica*, vol. 11, c. 1048 ('Marriage'), referring admittedly not to New Testament times but to later Talmudic law, states: '*Kiddushin* alone, however, does not serve to call into being the mutual rights and duties existing between husband and wife . . . and, in particular, cohabitation between them is forbidden'.

[22] Though capital punishment was enjoined by Deut 22:22–8 for both cases, it was rarely enforced in New Testament times for breaches of the Jewish religious law (*cf.* G. F. Moore, *Judaism* II, Cambridge, Mass., 1932, pp. 186–7, and also Jn 18:31); according to the Babylonian Talmud (*Sanhedrin* 41a), the death penalty for adultery was suppressed forty years before the fall of Jerusalem. The treatise in the Mishnah entitled *Sotah* ('The Suspected Adulteress') makes no mention of the death penalty: the guilty woman was to be divorced (*Sotah* 1:5: Danby, p. 293). For further detail see the *TWNT* 7, pp. 739–40.

had an obligation of fidelity to her partner, not that she had the same rights as a wife. It is also true that fiancés were often referred to as man and wife; but it is not significant. Both in Greek and in Aramaic, one and the same word is used for 'woman' and 'wife' (like the French *femme* or the German *Frau*), and in both languages the word for 'man' is the normal word for 'husband'. Thus, when Jewish fiancés are said to be 'man and wife', the words used are simply 'man and woman', and one cannot argue from this linguistic usage to the conclusion that fiancés had exactly the same rights as a married couple.[23] Lastly, it was only in Judaea, and even there only after A.D. 135, that consummation of the union during the period of betrothal was regarded as normal; and though the practice was tolerated in that district, a virgin bride remained the ideal of rabbinical Judaism, so that in later centuries a compiler of the Jerusalem Talmud could complain that 'although the persecution was over, this custom [of anticipating the marriage union] did not cease'.[24]

The legal effect of betrothal was to give the man the right to marry this particular woman, and to impose upon the woman the duty of marrying this man; in a monogamous society, such a right and such a duty are of their nature exclusive. From the moment of her betrothal, a girl was pledged to her fiancé and could not withdraw from the marriage without his consent. But in all other matters she remained under the authority of her father or guardian until, on the day of the wedding, she passed under the authority of her husband. On that day, she was escorted in solemn procession from her father's house to the home of the bridegroom, the Wedding Blessing was pronounced, and the couple were thereafter free to live as man and wife.

Mary and Joseph were betrothed in Galilee about seventy years before the First Jewish Revolt (A.D. 66–70), and it is natural to

[23] Aramaic does have a separate word for 'husband', and Greek has several (mainly poetic); but 'man' is the usual term, as in Mt 1:19. In any case, to prove that this linguistic usage demonstrates that intercourse before marriage was lawful, one would have to prove that these words could not be understood, by prolepsis, as 'husband-to-be' and 'wife-to-be'.

[24] *Ketuboth* 1, 25c.

presume that they observed the Jewish code of morals puncti-
liously, *i.e.* to presume that Mary remained a virgin during the
period of betrothal. But this presumption does not rest only on a
reverential estimate of their characters. For if even after A.D. 135
the Galileans regarded intimate relations before marriage as
unseemly or wrong, there is every reason to believe that, at the
beginning of the Christian era, a small Galilean town would
have been particularly insistent on correct behaviour between
fiancés: the social background gives a presumption that Mary
would have remained a virgin during the period of betrothal.
Thus, though the modern interpreters of Mt 1:18 rightly assert
that the phrase 'before they came together' refers not to sexual
intercourse but to the ceremony of escorting the bride to her
future home, it is incorrect to conclude that the phrase tells us
nothing about Mary's virginity. It does not state the fact explicitly,
but contemporary Jewish law and Galilean custom imply that
Mary, like any other pious Jewish girl, would have remained a
virgin until she went to live in her husband's house.

This interpretation is confirmed by the wording of the story.
First, the negative side (namely, that 'to come together' does not
here refer to the consummation of the union) is confirmed by Mt
1:25, which states that Joseph refrained from 'knowing' Mary[25]
until she gave birth to Jesus. 'To know a woman' is the normal
Semitic expression to denote sexual intercourse, and there is no
reason why the author should have avoided it in Mt 1:18, if that
was all he wanted to say. Secondly (on the positive side), the
verb 'to come together' is frequently used in Hellenistic Greek
with the sense 'to marry', perhaps because the ceremony of leading the bride to her future home (*deductio in domum*) was a normal,
though not an essential, feature of Roman marriage. With the
Jews, however, this ceremony was essential, and συνέρχομαι
is the obvious Greek word to denote this ceremony.[26]

[25] Note the imperfect.

[26] J. H. Moulton and G. Milligan, *The Vocabulary of the Greek Testament*,
London, 1952, p. 606; M.-J. Lagrange, *Evangile selon s. Matthieu*, 8th ed., Paris,
1948, p. 9.

Chapter Two

JOSEPH THE FATHER OF JESUS
(Mt 1:19)

DURING the period of betrothal, Mary was discovered to be with child, and as a result Joseph began to think of divorcing her (Mt 1:18–19). Most exegetes have taken these verses to imply either that Joseph suspected Mary of unfaithfulness,[1] or that, being firmly convinced of her chastity, he was utterly bewildered and sought to extricate himself by a divorce from a situation he could not understand.[2] The first alternative can claim the support

[1] The view that Joseph suspected Mary of unfaithfulness was held by St Justin (*Dialogus* 78: MG 6.657 C), St John Chrysostom (*In Matt.*, Hom. 4, n. 6: MG 57.47 B), St Ambrose (*De Instit. Virginum* 5: ML 16.315; cf. *In Lucam* II, 5: CC 14.32 = ML 15.1554 C), and expressed very strongly by St Augustine, who writes: 'Ioseph cum eam comperisset praegnantem cui se noverat non esse commixtum et ob hoc nihil aliud quam adulteram credidisset, puniri tamen eam noluit nec approbator flagitii fuit' (*Ep.* 154, c. 4, n. 9: ML 33.657 B). Admittedly Augustine is there replying to a correspondent, a civil servant in Africa, and arguing that there is nothing improper in a bishop's pleading for mercy for a convicted criminal. But he also preached this opinion: 'Quia enim de se gravidam non esse sciebat, iam velut consequenter adulteram existimabat' (*Sermo* 51: ML 38.338 C).

[2] Thus St Jerome (*In Matt.*, Lib. 1, on Mt 1:19: CC 77.11 = ML 26:25), the *Glossa Ordinaria* (ML 114.70) and many of the medievals, especially the preachers such as St Bernardine of Siena (1380–1444: *Sermo* 1 *de s. Ioseph*, in his *Opera*, vol. 4, Venice, 1745, p. 235). There is a classic statement of this view in a work by Conrad of Saxony (d. 1279) which was widely read in the Middle Ages and for centuries attributed to St Bonaventure. 'O ineffabilis laus Mariae, magis credebat Ioseph castitati eius quam utero eius, et plus gratiae quam naturae, possibilius credebat mulierem sine viro concipere, quam Mariam posse peccare' (*Speculum*

164

of Chrysostom and Augustine, but the second is usually favoured by Roman Catholic exegetes, partly out of reverence for Joseph and partly because of the formidable authority of Jerome. It is to be noted, however, that nearly all writers, ancient or modern, here make an assumption which will shortly be questioned: they assume that, according to Matthew, Joseph began to think of divorcing Mary because he did not know how her child had been conceived.

Having made that assumption, they argue as follows. A fiancée who conceived a child not fathered by her future bridegroom could be condemned to death, in accordance with the law of Deut 22:23-8; but (contra Jerome)[3] this was not obligatory, and was not the practice in New Testament times.[4] Rather, three courses lay open to Joseph. He could denounce Mary and publicly divorce her; he could withdraw from the betrothal without denouncing her and, by giving her a bill of divorce privately, leave her free to marry another; or he could take her to be his wife.

Some exegetes say that Joseph had a legal, or at least a moral, obligation to divorce Mary, once he had discovered that she was going to bear a child that was not his.[5] They point, on the other hand, to his generosity in choosing to fulfil this obligation of the law as discreetly as possible. Thus he would both discharge his duty and spare Mary's reputation so far as he could.[6] This, they say, gives a natural sense to Mt 1:19: 'Joseph, her husband, being an upright man and having no desire to bring the matter into the open, was thinking of divorcing her without publicity'. The first weakness of this interpretation is that it implies a certain conflict in Joseph's mind between the obligation of obeying the law and

---

b. *Mariae Virginis*, Lect. 17 *in fine*: in the *Opera s. Bonaventurae*, vol. 6, Rome, 1696, p. 482. For the authorship see *Opera Omnia s. Bonaventurae*, vol. 9, Quaracchi, 1901, pp. xiii–xiv, and vol. 10, 1902, p. 24).

[3] CC 77.11 = ML 26.25.   [4] See above, p. 161, n. 22.

[5] J. Knabenbauer even writes 'Hic est sensus verborum obvius' (*Commentarius in Matthaeum*, Paris, 1892, p. 53).

[6] Lagrange says this view is held by '*la plupart des modernes*' (*Evangile selon s. Matthieu*, p. 11).

the desire to spare Mary's reputation; yet the gospel text contains no hint of any conflict. Matthew does not write 'being an upright man, *but* not wishing to bring the matter into the open'; on the contrary, the text reads 'being an upright man *and* not wishing to bring the matter into the open', as if the two ideas were parallel, not contradictory. It was because of his integrity, not in spite of it, that Joseph wished to keep the divorce quiet. Secondly, there was no legal or moral obligation to divorce an unfaithful wife or fiancée; indeed, the prophecy of Hosea implies that the husband who pardoned an errant wife would be closer to God (Hos 2: 18–19, 21–2, 25). Thirdly, if Joseph had planned to keep the divorce secret in order to spare Mary's reputation, it would have been a singularly inept plan, for anyone would have realized that the story was bound to come out very soon. Matthew could not possibly have expected his readers to think this.

Hence other authors[7] stress that Joseph did not wish to expose Mary to public disgrace precisely because he was an upright man, that is, a kind, compassionate and God-fearing man. He believed, against all appearances, in her chastity, and therefore in an effort to be just to her, intended to keep the inevitable divorce as secret as he could. This interpretation escapes the first two objections raised against the previous explanation, but it is equally vulnerable to the third criticism: the story was bound to become known, questions would be asked, and it is hardly satisfactory to say that whatever followed after the divorce was none of Joseph's business. This is such an obvious objection that it is hard to believe that Matthew would not have thought of it himself; and therefore if any more satisfactory meaning can be given to his text, it ought to be preferred.

Nearly all commentators on St Matthew's gospel adopt one or other of these positions, neither of which is wholly satisfactory. The basic error is that these commentators assume without proof that, according to Matthew, Joseph was in total ignorance of the

[7] St Jerome (*CC* 77.11 = ML 26:25 AB); Lagrange, *Evangile selon s. Matthieu*, p. 11. The most learned defence of this position (in an article written against Léon-Dufour's thesis set out below on pp. 167–70) is by C. Spicq, 'Joseph, son mari, étant juste . . . Mt 1:19', in the *RB* 71 (1964), pp. 206–14.

virginal conception until he was informed by the angel (Mt 1:20). *A priori*, this could be Matthew's meaning; alternatively, it may not. Is it reasonable to assume that Matthew means us to think that Mary never told Joseph, her fiancé, about the fact of the virginal conception? Or that Joseph suspected her of unfaithfulness and was yet too shy to ask her about the child? Or that she told him of the manner of her conception, and that he refused to believe her? Yet at least one of these three assumptions must be accepted (without any proof), or the entire foundation of the two common interpretations is destroyed.

The inadequacy of these two theories has led a small number of Catholic scholars[8] to revive in very recent years an almost forgotten solution which was vigorously championed four centuries ago by the great Jesuit theologian Salmerón. If one assumes that, according to Matthew, Mary told Joseph about her virginal conception and that Joseph believed her, then the whole passage becomes clear. Joseph was an upright man, that is, a man who observed the Mosaic Law scrupulously, out of reverence for God. When he learnt that Mary had miraculously conceived a child who was to be the son of God,[9] his first reaction must have been to withdraw from his engagement to marry this singularly favoured woman. As an upright man, full of reverence for God, he would fear to take such a woman as his wife, sincerely believing that there was now no place for him at Mary's side. Salmerón writes:

'In his modesty, he thought he was unworthy of so great an honour, of living with so great a Virgin. He wanted to give the Incarnate Word and his most holy Mother their

[8] X. Léon-Dufour, 'L'annonce à Joseph', in *Mélanges Bibliques rédigés en l'honneur de André Robert*, Paris, n.d. (1957), pp. 390–7; 'Le juste Joseph (Mt 1:18–25)', *NRT* 81 (1959), pp. 225–31; K. Rahner, 'Nimm das Kind und seine Mutter', in *Geist und Leben* 30 (1957), pp. 14–22. Others have followed these.

[9] Salmerón, of course, assumes that Mary knew of the divinity of her son from the beginning, and that Joseph acknowledged it. But his argument holds good even if Mary's knowledge at the time be restricted down to the mere fact of the virginal conception: this would still give Joseph sufficient ground for withdrawing from the marriage out of reverence.

rights, *i.e.* to pay them that honour and reverence to which they were entitled. That is why he thought of releasing Mary from her engagement. . . . This was the thought and the motive in Saint Joseph's mind. He recognized his own insignificance and his own unworthiness, and contrasted them with the excellence and the eminence of his spouse, who had been made Mother of the Messiah and of God. And so, in his modesty and humility, he began to think of divorcing her, for he feared that to share a house and a home with her might be offensive to God.'[10]

Joseph wanted to release Mary from the obligation of marrying him because of his reverence for her and for God. In addition, 'he had no desire to expose her', and therefore decided to keep the divorce secret. The verb translated 'to expose' ($\delta\epsilon\iota\gamma\mu\alpha\tau\acute{\iota}\sigma\alpha\iota$) means simply 'to expose what is hidden', and therefore the text does not necessarily imply that Joseph's motive was 'not to expose her to public disgrace',[11] as so many commentators assume; it can mean that Joseph had no desire 'to divulge her secret', as at least two of the Greek Fathers insist.[12] Hence a less misleading

[10] *Commentarii in Evangelia*, vol. 3, Cologne, 1612, p. 237a. Alfonso Salmerón (1515–85) was one of the original band of men who joined Ignatius of Loyola to found the Society of Jesus in 1534. A most influential figure at the Council of Trent, a papal diplomat and a considerable theologian, he spent the last years of his life preparing for publication his lectures on Scripture. They were published only after his death, first in Madrid between 1597 and 1601.

[11] The word for this would be $\pi\alpha\rho\alpha\delta\epsilon\iota\gamma\mu\alpha\tau\acute{\iota}\zeta\omega$. Liddell and Scott's *Greek–English Lexicon* gives examples from the papyri of the simplex verb $\delta\epsilon\iota\gamma\mu\alpha\tau\acute{\iota}\zeta\omega$ where there is no question of disgrace; and though ordinary lexicons of New Testament Greek cite Mt 1:19 as meaning 'to expose to disgrace or shame', the more common meaning of the word is simply 'to expose what is hidden' (see the *TWNT* 2, p. 31, lines 26–35, and contrast the discussion of Mt 1:19 in lines 36 ff.). Räisänen (*Die Mutter Jesu im Neuen Testament*, pp. 62–3, n. 3) protests that Liddell and Scott, Bauer and Moulton-Milligan lend no support to Léon-Dufour's translation '*divulguer*', but seems to have missed the point that the Greek verb is quite neutral in meaning, and therefore can bear, in this context, the sense 'to divulge what is secret'.

[12] Pseudo-Basil, *Hom. in Christi generationem*, 4: 'He did not dare to make public what had happened to her' (MG 31.1464 D). Eusebius of Caesarea insists most

translation would be: 'he had no desire to bring the matter into the open'. This rendering does not prejudge the choice between the two rival interpretations; like the Greek verb it translates, it can mean either that Joseph wished to spare Mary any public dishonour, or that he did not wish to divulge her secret. If the second meaning is assigned to the verb (and there is nothing against this, since the verb itself, meaning simply 'to expose what is hidden', is quite neutral as between the two interpretations), then a fresh light is thrown on the context. If according to Matthew Joseph was planning to withdraw from the marriage out of reverence and humility, then the implication is not that he considered Mary to have failed in her duty of faithfulness, but that he himself felt obliged to waive his right of marrying her in order to leave the way free for God to proceed with the matter in his own good time and in his own manner.

This third interpretation is completely satisfactory. It explains the gospel text; it assumes only what is *a priori* probable, namely, that when Mary told Joseph about the virginal conception, he believed her;[13] and it satisfies that Christian piety which has ever regarded Joseph as a worthy partner of the Blessed Virgin and a worthy foster-father of Jesus Christ. It is therefore reasonable to ask why it has not been more widely adopted before. One reason is that Mt 1:20 seems to imply that the angel (not Mary) first revealed to Joseph the fact of Jesus' supernatural conception. It is true that this appears to be the sense if one reads the passage (as most people do) with the unconscious assumption that Joseph knew nothing about the mystery until the angel appeared to him; but it is precisely this assumption which is in question. Against this assumption, one may point out that v. 18 says that 'Mary was

---

strongly on the difference between the two verbs: 'He did not say "not wishing to defame her", but "not wishing to bring her before the public eye" ' (*Quaest. Evangelicae* I, 3: MG 22.884 D).

[13] The only assumption here is that the virginal conception really took place. but even those who deny its historicity ought to admit that Matthew's story assumes it, and therefore that Matthew's story (implicitly) assumes that Mary told Joseph about it: for the proof of this, see pp. 170-2.

discovered to be with child *by the Holy Ghost*', and that in v. 19 this fact is given as the motive for Joseph's decision. There is no reason to suppose that in v. 18 Matthew means to say only that Joseph discovered the fact that Mary was with child, and added 'by the Holy Ghost' solely to clarify the story for the reader. The angel's words in v. 20 would have been sufficient for that purpose, and could have been lengthened if necessary, to tell the reader about the virginal conception at that point. The natural sense of v. 18 is that Joseph learned that Mary had conceived a child by the power of the Holy Spirit; unfortunately, most readers unconsciously assume that Joseph discovered only that Mary was with child, and that he knew no more.

The fact is that the combined authority of Chrysostom, Jerome and Augustine has conditioned men to approach St Matthew's story with this presupposition: all three presume that Joseph knew nothing of God's intervention until the angel appeared to him, and this view has been preached and taught for so many centuries that it is commonly read into Matthew's text. But the contrary interpretation adopted by Salmerón can also claim respectable patristic support: it was held by Eusebius of Caesarea[14] and Ephraem,[15] by the Pseudo-Basil[16] and the Pseudo-Origen.[17] It was accepted by Rabanus Maurus[18] and by Theophylactus,[19] to mention only earlier medieval writers. Nothing, however, could avail against the authority of St John Chrysostom and St Jerome, especially when Jerome's commentary was incorporated into the Roman Breviary, and when they were supported by the master of the Latin West, Augustine. This would seem to be the historical reason why the interpretation favoured here failed to win wide acceptance and was eventually forgotten.

It has been shown that there are no grounds for presuming that

[14] *Quaest. Evangelicae* I, 3 (MG 22.884 BD).

[15] *Commentaire de l'Evangile concordant*, translated from the Armenian by L. Leloir (*Corpus Scriptorum Christianorum Orientalium*, vol. 145), Louvain, 1954, pp. 18–19.

[16] *Hom. in Christi generationem*, 4 (MG 31.1464).

[17] *Hom.* I *in Matt.* (GCS *Origenes Werke*, vol. 12, 1), Leipzig, 1941, p. 241.

[18] ML 107.749 A.

[19] MG 123.156 D.

Joseph (in Matthew's story) was ignorant of the virginal conception until the angel appeared to him. But one can go further,
and say that the text gives positive reasons for asserting that
Matthew's account assumes that he knew about it before the angel
appeared. The clue lies in the use of the particle γάρ in Mt 1:20.
J. D. Denniston writes that the first meaning of γάρ is 'confirmatory
and causal, giving the ground for belief, or the motive for action.
This usage may be illustrated from any page of any Greek author.
It is, however, commoner in writers whose mode of thought is
simple than in those who logical faculties are more developed . . .
Γάρ gives the motive for saying what has just been said: "I say
this because . . .".'[20] If we apply this principle to Mt 1:20, the
full depth of meaning in the verse comes to light. When Joseph
was thinking of divorcing Mary secretly, an angel appeared to
him and said: 'Joseph, son of David, do not be afraid to take Mary
as your wife. *I say this because* her child has been conceived by the
Holy Ghost, but she will bear a son and you will give him the name
Jesus, for he will save his people from their sins'. Joseph is told
'not to be *afraid*' of taking Mary as his wife: the assumption is
that he was *afraid* to do so, not that he suspected her of infidelity,
or that he was perplexed and confused. The following sentence
'gives the motive for saying what has just been said', *i.e.* it gives
the reason why Joseph is not to be afraid of taking Mary as his
wife: because, although her child has been conceived by the power
of the Holy Ghost, it is God's will that Joseph should be its legal
father. The particle δέ here carries its full adversative force, as
the translators of the Latin and Syriac versions perceived ('*Pariet
autem filium*'), so that both Mary's giving birth to the child and
Joseph's adopting of it[21] are contrasted with the conception, which
is the work of the Holy Spirit. Thus a rather free, but very accurate, translation would be: 'Joseph, son of David, do not be afraid
to take Mary as your wife. I say this because, although her child
has been conceived by the Holy Ghost, she will bear a son to

[20] *The Greek Particles*, 2nd ed., Oxford, 1954, pp. 58, 60.

[21] Räisänen (*Die Mutter Jesu im Neuen Testament*, pp. 62–3, n. 3) seems to have
missed this double contrast, and this invalidates the argument he there brings
forward against Léon-Dufour.

whom you must give the name Jesus'. That is why the angel stresses his lineage, saying 'Joseph, son of David' and not (as one would have expected after v. 16) 'Joseph, son of Jacob'. By taking Mary as his wife, Joseph would make Jesus a son of David.

Thus the point of this pericope is not to affirm the virginal conception. Matthew assumes it, and seeks to resolve the consequent problem: if Jesus was virginally conceived, how could he be of the line of David?

Two minor points may be noticed. Joseph, by obeying the angel, showed that he was prepared to play his part in God's plan, and to be the adoptive father of Jesus. It is not therefore surprising to read in Mt 1:25 that he respected Mary's virginity throughout the whole period preceding the birth of her son (the verb is in the imperfect tense).[22]

[22] For further comment on this imperfect see p. 204.

Chapter Three

LK 1:34 (I): A VOW OF VIRGINITY?

THE words of Lk 1:34 ('How shall this be, since I know not a man?') are of classic difficulty for exegetes, and no one interpretation has yet secured universal acceptance.[1] A number of writers, following Harnack, have even suggested that vv. 34–5 (or a part of them) are a later interpolation into Luke's own narrative of the Annunciation;[2] but there is not the slightest evidence in the Greek manuscripts to support this suggestion,[3] and the excision of these two verses would in fact destroy the delicate literary balance of the story. If these two verses are suppressed, so is Luke's witness to the virginal conception; but then the miraculous conception of John the Baptist would stand out as a far more wonderful event than the conception of Jesus, and this is scarcely in the spirit of the narrative. The literary parallelism between the two Annunciations is clearly intended; but if the statement about the virginal conception in 1:34–5 did not form part of Luke's

[1] G. Graystone, *Virgin of All Virgins: The Interpretation of Luke* 1:34, Rome, 1968, gives an exhaustive survey of all opinions from patristic times to the present day. The author himself thinks the text implies a vow of virginity. This work will be cited in this and the next two chapters simply as 'Graystone'.

[2] The suggestion was first advanced by H. Usener, *Religionsgeschichtliche Untersuchungen I: Das Weihnachtsfest*, Bonn, 1889, but the fullest and best-known exposition is by A. von Harnack, 'Zu Lk 1:34–35', in the *ZNW* 2 (1901), pp. 53–7.

[3] The only manuscript evidence to support it is the fact that one Old Latin manuscript, the Codex Veronensis (fourth–fifth centuries) omits all v. 34 except 'Dixit autem Maria' and continues 'Ecce ancilla Domini'. See Graystone, pp. 95–101 for a full discussion of the text.

own narrative, then the relative silence of Lk 1-2 on Joseph becomes rather difficult to explain, when one considers how prominent is the role assigned to Zechariah. Furthermore, the words of Lk 1:37 ('Nothing is impossible to God') lose half their point, as does Mary's *Fiat* in Lk 1:38. Lastly, if the original text of St Luke contained no mention of the virginal conception, why does Lk 1:27 say that Mary was a virgin at the time of the Annunciation? Harnack himself is consistent enough to say that the word 'virgin' should be deleted in v. 27, and the phrase 'as was thought' suppressed from Lk 3:23. Others have practised even more daring surgery in an endeavour to secure a coherent text which contains no mention of the virginal conception,[4] but such drastic measures are rather out of fashion today. Recent writers all accept that Lk 1:34-5 are an authentic part of Luke's Gospel, and are agreed that these verses intend to affirm the virginal conception of Jesus.

There is disagreement, however, about the further implications of the words in v. 34, 'How shall this be, since I know not a man?' It has often been held that these words imply that Mary had already made a resolution, or taken a vow, to remain a virgin for ever. Indeed, this is the classical interpretation of these words, and it deserves to be discussed fairly thoroughly.[5]

This interpretation owes its success, in very large measure, to the authority of St Augustine, who was the first to put it forward in the Latin West.[6]

[4] See Graystone, pp. 97-101 for full details.

[5] From the eleventh century onwards, most authors speak of this resolution as 'a vow of virginity', and though some would regard the term 'vow' as an anachronism in this context, there is no need to delay over the terminology, for whatever word they prefer or use, all these authors assume that Mary's resolve to remain a virgin was taken out of love for God.

[6] The idea had, however, been put forward at least once before, in a sermon preached on 25 December 386, by St Gregory of Nyssa (*In diem natalem Christi*: MG 46.1140 ff.). The authenticity of this sermon, which was formerly denied or at least questioned, is nowadays generally admitted (see J. Quasten, *Patrology*, vol. 3, Utrecht-Antwerp and Westminster, Maryland, 1960, p. 277, and J. Daniélou, 'Chronologie des sermons de s. Grégoire de Nysse', in the *Revue des Sciences Religieuses* 19 (1955), pp. 365 ff.).

Augustine, however, was probably inspired rather by Ambrose, who paints

'Before he was conceived, he chose to be born of a woman already consecrated to God. This is the meaning of the words with which Mary replied to the angel's message that she was to bear a child ("How shall this be, etc."). Surely she would not say that, unless she had previously vowed her virginity to God (*quod profecto non diceret, nisi Deo virginem se ante vovisset*)?'[7]

From the eleventh century to the Reformation, this explanation was adopted everywhere in western Europe. St Bernard of Clairvaux expounded it in a form that became the classic expression of the theory:

'She does not inquire whether it will happen, but how. It is as if she were saying: My Lord, who is witness of my conscience, knows of his maidservant's vow, not to have knowledge of a man. By what law, or in what manner, will he be pleased to bring it about [that I shall bear this son]? If I must break my vow in order to bear such a son, then I rejoice over the son, and grieve for my resolution; but his will be done! If, however, I am to conceive as a virgin, and to give birth as a virgin—which will not be impossible if he pleases—than I shall most surely know that he has looked graciously on the lowliness of his maidservant.'[8]

St Thomas Aquinas[9] and St Albert the Great,[10] St Bonaventure[11]

---

such a picture of Mary in his *De virginibus ad Marcellinam* that a firm resolution of perpetual virginity even before the Annunciation is evidently implied (II, 2: ML 16.220–3). Yet neither there nor in his commentary on Lk 1:34 (*In Lucam* II, 14: CC 14.37 = ML 15.1638–9) does Ambrose use the word 'vow' with reference to Mary; indeed, he does not even speak of a *propositum castitatis* (a term he uses in *Exhortatio virginitatis* 8:54: ML 16.356 A). Hence one may rightly say that Augustine was the first to put forward the idea in the Latin West. For further detail on the Fathers see Graystone, pp. 6–13.

[7] *De sacra virginitate* 4 (ML 40.398); cf. also *Sermo* 291, 5: 'Si enim fieret, quomodo de omnibus infantibus fieri solet, non diceret, quomodo fiet? Sed illa propositi sui memor et sancti voti conscia, quia noverat, quid voverat . . .' (ML 38.1318).

[8] *Hom. 4a in 'Missus est'* 3 (ML 183.80).   [9] *Summa theol.*, 3a, qu. 28, a. 4.

[10] *In IV Lib. Sent.* Dist. 30, qu. 2, especially a. 11.

[11] *In IV Lib. Sent.* Dist. 30, qu. 2.

and Duns Scotus[12] all accept that Lk 1:34 is evidence that Mary had made a vow of virginity, and Suarez in his day could write: 'It is not disputed among Catholics that Mary had made a vow of virginity'.[13] Indeed, among Roman Catholics this interpretation went virtually unchallenged until the beginning of the twentieth century.[14]

At first sight, this interpretation is extremely attractive, for it seems to explain everything in the text. When the angel tells Mary that she is to bear a son, she asks, 'How shall this be, since I have made a vow of virginity before God?' Only then does the angel inform her that she will conceive miraculously, while remaining a virgin (Lk 1:34-5), and Mary cries out in joy, 'May this be so, according to thy word!' (Lk 1:38).

Yet there are two serious objections to St Augustine's interpretation, one theological and one historical, each of which must be examined.

The most obvious objection to the suggestion that Mary had made a vow of virginity was discussed at length by all the great medieval theologians:[15] if Mary had made such a vow to remain a virgin for ever, why was she betrothed to Joseph, and was not her marriage null and void? Both her betrothal and her marriage would seem to be proof that she had made no such vow or resolution.

All the medieval masters were alive to this difficulty, but the Dominicans felt it keenly, for it was the common teaching of their

[12] *In IV Lib. Sent.* Dist. 30, qu. 2.

[13] *In Tertiam Partem S. Thomae*, qu. 28, a. 4, Disput. 6, sect. 2, n. 1; *cf.* the whole of sections 1 and 2.

[14] For further references to medieval writers, see Graystone, pp. 13-17, and for the period 1500-1900, pp. 18-28. There is some dispute whether Cajetan (1469-1534) in later life, in his Commentary on the Gospels (1528), withdrew his earlier support, in his commentary on the *Summa* (*In Tertiam Partem*, qu. 28, a. 4), for the theory of a vow. If he did, he stands as a solitary exception to the general stream of Roman Catholic exegesis. The matter is unimportant for present purposes. Details are given in Graystone, pp. 22-3.

It is perhaps not superfluous to point out that this theory, however well supported in history, forms no part of Catholic *dogmatic* tradition. See Detached Note IV: Mary's Vow of Virginity, on pp. 446-7.

[15] In their commentaries *In IV Lib. Sent.* Dist. 30.

Order that a vow of virginity, pronounced before marriage, rendered any subsequent marriage contract null and void.[16] St Albert the Great therefore states explicitly that Mary never made an absolute vow of virginity at any time in her life, though she always desired to remain a virgin if that would be pleasing to God;[17] consequently, he interprets Lk 1:34 as expressive only of a very conditional vow which amounts to little more than an intense desire.[18] St Thomas Aquinas, on the other hand, departs a little from the common teaching of his Order, stating that Mary always wished to remain a virgin, but accepted betrothal to Joseph because to remain unmarried was apparently contrary to the law; after the betrothal, she then made, along with Joseph, an unconditional vow of virginity, before the Annunciation and before her marriage:

'Since the Law (Deut 7:14) seemed to forbid both men and women to abstain from procreation, the Mother of God did not make an unconditional vow of virginity before she was betrothed to Joseph, although she would have wished to do so. But she did make a conditional vow, "if it should be pleasing to God" (*si Deo placeret*). Afterwards, when she had been betrothed, and had learnt that it was pleasing to God, she made, along with Joseph, an absolute vow of virginity, at some time before the angelic Annunciation.'[19]

[16] The Franciscans solved the difficulty more simply. Holding that the marriage of Mary and Joseph was undoubtedly valid, and that Mary had made an unconditional vow of virginity before it, they concluded that such a vow did not invalidate a marriage contract. Thus Bonaventure, *In IV Lib. Sent.* Dist. 28, qu. 6, a. 1; Dist. 30, qu. 2, a. 1, and Duns Scotus, *In IV Lib. Sent.* Dist. 30, qu. 2.

[17] *In IV Lib. Sent.* Dist 30, qu. 2, a. 11 (*cf.* also aa. 8–10). See also *De Bono*, Tr. III, qu. 3, a. 9 ('De virginitate gloriosae virginis Mariae'), where he writes that Mary was so humble that she entrusted herself to God 'ut haberet, si vellet, virginem, et si vellet, haberet propagatricem usque ad conceptum' (*Opera Omnia*, vol. 28, Münster-in-Westf., 1951, p. 171).

[18] See *Postillae super evangelium Lucae*, on Lk 1:34: '. . . quod maxime in voto habuit, dicens, *Quoniam virum non cognosco*, hoc est, non cognituram propono' (*Opera Omnia*, vol. 22, Paris, 1894, p. 91b).

[19] For clarity, phrases from the text of 3a, qu. 28, a. 1c have here been conflated into the reply given (in the same article) ad 1um. Strangely, Thomas thought this

Thomas then argues that the marriage between Mary and Joseph was nevertheless valid first because the fact of physical consummation is not essential to a marriage,[20] and secondly because every other 'perfection' of marriage was there realized: both Mary and Joseph renounced marriage with any other party and agreed to share a home with the other for life, consented to consummate the marriage 'if God should wish it', and undertook the upbringing of the child Jesus. Thomas ends his exposition with a quotation from Augustine:

'Every perfection of marriage (*omne nuptiarum bonum*) was realized in those parents of Christ: offspring, fidelity and sacrament. As offspring, we recognize the Lord Jesus himself; fidelity we see, for there was no adultery; and a sacrament, for there was no divorce. The only thing not found there was marital intercourse.'[21]

Thomas is thus able to accept the classical, Augustinian interpretation of Lk 1:34 as indicating that Mary had vowed virginity

---

joint vow was taken while Mary and Joseph were still fiancés, before their marriage, and yet thinks they were living in the same house (qu. 29, a. 2, ad 3um); it is strange, because he was quite aware of the contrary opinion, as his last lines ad 3um show.

[20] Thomas is here appealing ultimately to a principle of Roman Law phrased by Ulpian as 'Nuptias non concubitus, sed consensus facit'. Ambrose was the first to introduce this principle into the Christian Church (*De institutione virginis* 6:41: ML 16.331 A) in the words 'Non enim defloratio virginitatis facit coniugium, sed pactio coniugalis'. This text of Ambrose, as cited by Gratian, *Decretum*, Pars 2a, Causa 27a, qu. 2, cap. 5 (*Corpus Iuris Canonici* edited by A. Friedberg, I, Leipzig, 1879, col. 1064, or ML 187.1394 B), became one of the foundations of medieval marriage law. The marriage between Mary and Joseph was therefore *matrimonium vere ratum* (*licet non consummatum*). In 3a, qu. 29, a. 2, however, Thomas quotes not this text of Ambrose, but a very similar one from the commentary on Luke (II, 5: *CC* 14.33 = ML 15.1555 A) which is marginally more apt for his purpose.

[21] 3a, qu. 29, a. 2c. The citation from Augustine comes from *De nuptiis et concupiscentia* I, 11:13 (ML 44.421 CD).

before her marriage, and at the same time to uphold, by the arguments stated, the validity of Mary's marriage.

In similar ways, within their own terms of reference and within the framework of their own theology, all the medieval masters found a satisfactory and logically coherent answer to the difficulty arising from Mary's vow of virginity. This kind of answer is often still accepted by Roman Catholics today, but there is a serious flaw in the very foundation of this classical explanation. The medievals assumed that both Mary and Joseph had been inspired by God, *before* their marriage, to resolve on a life of virginity. This is openly stated in the most widely used of all medieval textbooks, Peter Lombard's *Liber Sententiarum*. Admittedly, Peter Lombard puts the idea forward only with a fairly strong qualification ('*Sane credi potest*'),[22] but the qualification tended to be overlooked by later writers, and a direct divine inspiration for the vows of Mary and Joseph became accepted as a fact, since it was an essential link in the argument. The fundamental weakness here is that in order to defend one supposition (that Mary had made a vow of virginity before her marriage) it is necessary to introduce another supposition (that God had inspired both her and Joseph to make such a vow). Yet it is reasonable to ask whether even the first and basic supposition is really necessary.

In fact, modern Roman Catholic exegetes are more and more inclined to reject the hypothesis of a vow made before the Annunciation, partly because they consider it unnecessary and partly because it seems historically improbable. It is unnecessary, they argue, because there are other and better ways of explaining the text (these will be examined in the next two chapters). It is improbable, they say, because Jewish tradition looked upon children as the greatest blessing of marriage, and regarded childlessness as a disgrace. The latter point deserves to be considered in some detail.

Is such a vow historically possible or likely? It is beyond all doubt that the Jews considered it a great honour and blessing

[22] *IV Lib. Sent.* Dist. 30, a. 2 (ML 192.917). The phrase *Sane credi potest* can perhaps best be rendered as 'It is not, of course, impossible to believe . . .'

to have many children, and that they regarded a childless marriage as a trial, a punishment, or a disgrace.[23] This attitude was very much alive in New Testament times (Lk 1:25), and the Mishnah states that marriage is a sacred duty so binding that no man is exempt from the law (although a woman was not obliged to marry):[24]

'No man may abstain from keeping the law *Be fruitful and multiply*, unless he already has children: according to the School of Shammai, two sons; according to the School of Hillel, a son and a daughter. . . . The duty to be fruitful and multiply falls on the man but not on the woman'.[25]

Granted this cultural environment, and granted this deeply religious attitude to the procreation of children, it is reasonable to ask whether it was possible for Mary to have made a vow of virginity, and to have thought she could honour God by doing so.

It must be admitted that the idea of a celibate life consecrated to the service of God was not unknown among the Jews during the first century of the Christian era. Pliny the Elder (*d.* A.D. 79) records that at the time of the First Jewish Revolt there was a kind of monastic community called Essenes living near the West shore of the Dead Sea: he was astounded to learn that they had freely chosen to pass their lives in penance, celibacy and poverty.[26] In the last twenty-five years, this monastery has been identified with the settlement at Qumran, where the Dead Sea Scrolls were written; both the excavations at Qumran and the evidence of the texts found there confirm Pliny's statement, for many of the community lived a celibate life.[27] Philo of Alexandria (*c.* 30 B.C.– *c.* A.D. 45) also gives some interesting information. In a fragment

[23] *Cf.* R. de Vaux, *Ancient Israel*, p. 41.

[24] It is obvious that women could not be bound by the law since they were not able to make a proposal of marriage (see above, p. 159).

[25] *Yebamoth* 6:6 (Danby, p. 227).

[26] *Hist. naturalis* V, 17.

[27] R. de Vaux, *Archaeology and the Dead Sea Scrolls* (Schweich Lectures of the British Academy), London, 1973, pp. 128–9.

preserved by Eusebius, he says that the Essenes abstained from marriage out of contempt for women,[28] but elsewhere he stresses that they chose celibacy from love of God.[29] Philo also knew of a similar group called the Therapeutae, who lived in the region of Lake Mareotis near Alexandria, and who were perhaps connected with the community of Qumran. The Therapeutae had convents of women next door to those of the men, and separated from the latter only by a wall:

'The majority are virgins of advanced age, who have pre-served their chastity not because they were constrained to (like some of the Greek priestesses), but by their own free decision. It was to seek and to love Wisdom that they chose to live together, and disdained bodily pleasures . . .'[30]

It is true that Philo is not always accurate in his information, and that he is given to idealizing a picture; but this text does at least show that the concept of serving God by a life of consecrated celibacy was not unthinkable to the Jews of Alexandria in his day. Yet another witness is Flavius Josephus, who had spent some time with the Essenes in his youth,[31] and who was well informed about their life. Josephus relates that some of the Essenes lived a celibate life,[32] though others were married.[33] Finally, the saying of Jesus in Mt 19:12 would seem conclusive proof that to remain unmarried in order to serve God was not an unknown concept in New Testament times.

[28] *Praep. evang.* 8:11 (MG 21.644 AB); but (as this passage and others prove) Philo was a misogynist.

[29] *Quod omnis probus liber sit* 84 (Loeb ed., vol. 9, pp. 58–9, though the editor, F. H. Colson, gives a different interpretation and translation of this phrase).

[30] *De vita contemplativa* VIII, 68 (Greek text in the Loeb ed., vol. 9, p. 154).

[31] *Life* 2.

[32] *Jewish War* II, 8, 2, §§119–21.

[33] *Ibid.*, II, 8, 13, §§160–1. The existence of these married Essenes is attested also by the so-called Damascus Document, of which several copies have been found at Qumran; many of these communities lived in isolated Jewish villages in southern Syria. *Cf.* J. T. Milik, *Ten Years of Discovery in the Wilderness of Judaea* (Studies in Biblical Theology 26), London, 1959, pp. 90–2.

This evidence, however, is not of itself sufficient to justify the conclusion that Mary might have made a vow (or a resolution) of virginity, for all the texts listed above concern people who had chosen not to marry. All but one of the instances cited refer to men (not women) living in a religious community; and the solitary exception (the Therapeutae of Mareotis mentioned by Philo) refers to women who had entered a convent in order to live a life of virginity. None of these examples gives any indication that a life of virginity outside a convent was conceivable as a religious ideal for a young Jewish woman, especially if she was betrothed and intended to marry.

Roman Catholic dogmatic theologians, however, bring forward other arguments in favour of a vow. The mother of Jesus, they say, is not to be judged merely by the normal and customary standards of the society in which she lived. Many saints have bewildered their friends and their own families by highly unconventional decisions, and one cannot decide whether Mary made a resolution of virginity merely by finding out whether other young girls did. Hence a number of dogmatic theologians argue that Mary must have had a quite unique perception of the intrinsic spiritual value of consecrated virginity, particularly by reason of her Immaculate Conception.[34] To one who accepts the Immaculate Conception as a dogma of faith, this is a powerful consideration; and though it may be of no interest to Protestant exegetes, a Catholic exegete cannot just ignore it, for he acknowledges that the teaching of the Church in a later age may enable him to perceive in Scripture truth which he himself would not (perhaps could not) have deduced merely by a critical examination of the text.[35]

---

[34] *E.g.* J. Galot in the *NRT* 79 (1957), pp. 470–4. E. Schillebeeckx writes against those who reject the idea of a vow before the Annunciation: 'But if this is so, we are leaving out of consideration the enormous reality which . . . we simply cannot ignore—the fact of her immaculate conception and the potentialities inherent in this fact' (*Mary, Mother of the Redemption*, London, 1964, pp. 57–8).

[35] The best illustration of this is the *homoousion* of Nicaea. All orthodox Christians accept that this term expresses a truth contained in the New Testament.

Are there, then, dogmatic (as distinct from purely exegetical) reasons for affirming that even before the Annunciation Mary had resolved to remain a virgin all her life? On this point, Roman Catholic dogmatic theologians are themselves divided today.

Some are quite adamant in their assertions that Mary could not have entertained the idea of consummating marriage. They argue that if Mary had chosen perpetual virginity only after the Annunciation and in consequence of her divine motherhood, her self-consecration to God as a virgin would have been less than total, less than complete. Moreover, if before the Annunciation she had intended to contract a normal marriage and to consummate it, she would have been less completely committed to virginity than many other Christian virgins who have from an early age dedicated themselves to the service of God by an unwavering resolution of perpetual virginity. How then could the Church salute her as *Virgo virginum*, as the unequalled exemplar of all other consecrated virgins?[36] Theologians who hold this opinion recognize that Mary's betrothal to Joseph constitutes a real difficulty against their theory (not to mention the subsequent marriage). Some suggest that she was betrothed because in those days there was no more efficacious way of safeguarding her virginity; others suggest that she was perhaps an only child, heiress to the family property, and therefore morally bound to marry someone, according to the law of Num 36:6, so that she was not free to choose virginity outside marriage. If Mary had in fact resolved to remain a virgin, these conjectures supply a reasonable explanation why she was betrothed. But had she made such a resolve? When one reads that she was betrothed to Joseph, the natural inference is that she intended to lead a normal married life at some time in the future.

The fact of her betrothal therefore leads other dogmatic theologians (and many exegetes) to affirm that Mary had not committed

---

But would any individual exegete claim that he personally would have been able to deduce the consubstantiality of the Second Person of the Holy Trinity merely by studying the text of the New Testament?

[36] Galot argues this point eloquently in the *NRT* 79 (1957), pp. 468–9.

herself absolutely and irrevocably to a life of virginity at the time of her betrothal. Thus Fr Karl Rahner has argued that Mary may at one time have contemplated living a normal married life, because consecrated virginity is not conceivable as a religious ideal except after the Incarnation:

'Christian virginity is a response to the eschatological kingdom of God when it has already arrived; it is not to be thought of as a preserving of oneself from the power of sexuality considered as dangerous or even as sinful.'[37]

Rahner stresses, however, that if before the Incarnation Mary had intended to consummate her marriage at some future date, this intention would have been subsumed under an overriding and absolute determination to place herself unreservedly at the service of God. Thus her intention, before the Incarnation, of living a normal married life does not detract in any way from her total and absolute response, in a life of virginity, to God's call after the Incarnation: she is still the first and unequalled 'Virgin among virgins'.[38] This is a good specimen of a modern attempt to explain how Mary could still be the perfect model for all Christian virgins, even if she had at one time intended to live a normal married life (as seems historically probable, and as her betrothal implies). And it requires only a little reflection to perceive that this is a modern presentation of Mary's marriage in the tradition of St Thomas Aquinas, just as the position set out in the paragraph before this is a modern presentation of the theology of St Bonaventure and Duns Scotus.

Rahner's argument, however, has been challenged (on grounds which again bring to mind the medieval disputes about Mary's Immaculate Conception). He maintains that the acceptance of virginity as a religious ideal must follow (not only logically, but also in time) the coming of the eschatological kingdom of grace. To this, some Catholic theologians reply that the eschatological kingdom of grace was in fact already inaugurated, in Mary, some

[37] *RSR* 42 (1954), p. 517, fn. 73.
[38] *RSR* 42 (1954), p. 518, fn.

years before the Incarnation, by the fact of her Immaculate Conception, and that there is consequently no reason why Mary should not have made an absolute resolution of virginity even before the Annunciation: it would have been the proper response to her own Immaculate Conception.[39] But this argument is not conclusive. It is true that the eschatological kingdom was already inaugurated in Mary by her sinless conception, but this does not prove that Mary herself, as soon as she came to the age of reason, at once realized that the proper response (for her) to the coming of the eschatological kingdom was to make a vow of perpetual virginity. She may well have been at first uncertain whether such a vow would be pleasing to God, as the medieval Dominicans, Albert and Thomas, rightly observed:[40] the religious tradition of her people was against it, and humility would counsel a prudent hesitation.

Historical considerations confirm this view. In Palestine, during New Testament times, the normal age for the betrothal of a girl was between twelve and twelve and a half years;[41] at this age, the girl was still under the authority of her father, and he decided all questions concerning her marriage.[42] Every effort was made to ensure that a girl was betrothed before the age of twelve and a half,[43] for the moral dangers to a girl older than this were greatly feared (cf. Sir 42:9-11). If it is assumed that Mary was betrothed at the customary age, she would have been subject to her father before the betrothal, and to her fiancé as well after it.[44] Before the betrothal, she could not have chosen to remain unmarried unless her father agreed, and such a choice would have deprived her of physical protection and support once her father was dead. Prudence would have led the father to advise his daughter to marry, and

[39] This point is excellently made by Galot in the *NRT* 79 (1957), p. 471.

[40] See above, p. 177.

[41] Strack-Billerbeck *Kommentar zum Neuen Testament aus Talmud und Midrasch* vol. 2, Munich, 1924, p. 374c.

[42] *Ketuboth* 4:4 (Danby, p. 250), cited above on p. 159.

[43] Strack-Billerbeck, *loc. cit.* in note 41. The same custom obtained among the native Arab population of Palestine forty years ago (cf. H. Granqvist, *Marriage Conditions in a Palestinian Village I*, Helsingfors, 1931, p. 38).

[44] See above, pp. 159, 162.

Mary could not have refused without sinning against the law of God, 'Honour thy father and thy mother' (Ex 20:12). After her betrothal, she could not have chosen perpetual virginity without the consent of her husband. Hence both before and after the betrothal, Mary could not have resolved to remain a virgin for ever unless someone else agreed. Thus any resolution of virginity on her part must have been at first conditional, not absolute, for it would have depended on whether her father or her husband would consent to it.

The Immaculate Conception, Mary's subsequent sinlessness, and her perpetual virginity are for Roman Catholics dogmas of faith. It might be argued that Mary's complete consecration to God from the moment of her conception would lead inexorably to a firm resolution of perpetual, consecrated virginity; but her sinlessness would seem to entail a strictly conditional resolution— 'provided my father and my husband consent'. If this second consideration constitutes a valid argument, then in practice the opinion of St Thomas Aquinas is reinstated in an amended form. Thomas held that Mary first desired, and later vowed, virginity on condition that such a life would be pleasing to God.[45] The restrictive condition he mentions ('*si Deo placeret*') was rightly dismissed by Scotus as nugatory, for every vow, however absolute, presupposes this qualification;[46] but the condition now put forward ('if others consent') is far from inconsequential. For if Mary had desired, and resolved on, a life of perpetual virginity subject to this condition, then her self-consecration to God through virginity would have been total and absolute as far as lay in her power: she would still be the unequalled exemplar of all Christian virgins. On the other hand, her desire to embrace such a life would not have been so total or so absolute as to exclude under all circumstances the possibility of a normal married life.

It has been pointed out that Roman Catholic exegetes are more and more inclined to reject the idea of a vow or resolution of virginity made before the Annunciation.[47] Dogmatic reasoning,

[45] See above, p. 177.
[46] Scotus, *In IV Lib. Sent.* Dist. 30, qu. 2.
[47] See above, p. 183.

however, seems to give at least a strong indication that Mary would have chosen perpetual virginity if it had been possible to do so. Are we to conclude that an interpretation of the Bible which is exegetically improbable is strongly recommended to Roman Catholics by dogmatic reasoning? Are we even to say that an unlikely explanation of the New Testament *must* be accepted by Roman Catholics on dogmatic grounds?

In fact, the idea that the words recorded in Lk 1:34 may be evidence of a resolution of virginity is not as absurd as it may seem, provided that one distinguishes between the words placed on Mary's lips by Luke, and the attitude of Mary at the time. We shall return to this theme later,[48] but meanwhile another explanation of the text must be considered.

[48] See below, pp. 194–6.

Chapter Four

LK 1:34 (II): A MISUNDERSTANDING?

Dissatisfaction with the classical theory that Mary had made a vow or resolution of virginity has led a number of Roman Catholic exegetes to seek an alternative explanation of the words 'How shall this be, since I know not a man?' The first significant departure from the mainstream came in an article by a German Benedictine, Simon Landersdorfer, in 1909.[1]

Landersdorfer suggested that Mary misunderstood the angel's words in Lk 1:31 ('Behold... thou wilt bear a son'), and imagined that the angel was telling her that she had already conceived a child, and would give birth to a son. In her astonishment, Mary exclaimed, 'How can this be, since I have not known a man?'[2] Landersdorfer based this conclusion on the following considerations.

There are four Old Testament passages closely parallel to the words in Lk 1:31: 'Behold, thou wilt conceive in the womb, and give birth to a son, and call his name Jesus.' All four texts in the Old Testament begin with 'Behold'; two of them contain the words 'to be with child, and bear a son, and call his name...' (Gen 16:11; Is 7:14); the other two have 'to be with child, and bear a son' (Jdg 13:5, 7). Now in each of these four texts the

---

[1] 'Bermerkungen zu Lk 1:26–38', in the *Biblische Zeitschrift* [First Series] 7 (1909), pp. 30–48, especially pp. 36–44. The author, who was primarily an Old Testament scholar and an Assyriologist, became Bishop of Passau in 1936, and died only in 1971, aged ninety-one.

[2] This is almost a return to the position of Cajetan in 1528, but see below, note 5.

Hebrew has an adjectival form, *harah*, meaning 'pregnant', and the Hebrew construction reads, literally, 'Behold, thou with child!' (One may compare the French construction *Te voilà enceinte!*) The Hebrew text (like its French parallel) can be understood grammatically as referring either to the past or to the present or to the future, according to the circumstances in which it is spoken. Thus when the angel said to Hagar *hinnak harah* (Gen 16:11), the sense was 'Behold, thou art already with child!', as is clear from Gen 16:4; but when another angel said to the mother of Samson *hinnak harah* (Jdg 13:5, 7), the sense was 'Behold thou wilt conceive!' In other words, with this phrase *hinnak harah* only the context enables the reader to determine whether the reference is to past, present or future: in Is 7:14, for example, the meaning is much debated.

Landersdorfer argued that Mary, hearing the angel say (in Hebrew) *hinnak hárah*, took the words to mean 'Behold, thou art *already* with child!' Her astonishment was understandable, and her exclamation in v. 34 is a most natural reaction. 'How can this be,' she asks, 'since I have never known a man?' (This is a very defensible translation of Lk 1:34 if we assume that the verse represents words of a conversation in Hebrew.) The reason why Christians have failed to see the ambiguity of the angel's words is that the Greek text of v. 31 has an unequivocal future indicative: 'Behold, thou wilt conceive . . .' But in Mary's own conversation with the angel, in Hebrew, there would have been a real ambiguity in the angel's words, provoking her cry of astonishment in v. 34.

In this form, the theory has never attracted any followers. Even within the author's fundamentalist framework, it is not wholly satisfactory. If the words in v. 31 were ambiguous, it would have been more natural for Mary to take them as referring to the future than to think the angel was saying she was already with child. Further, the meaning which Landersdorfer ascribes to the angel's words in v. 31 is certainly not the meaning intended by Luke, who uses not a past or a present tense, but a future ('Behold, thou wilt conceive...'). But above all, the theory presupposes that the Lucan story is a verbatim account of a conversation (and that in Hebrew) between Mary and Gabriel, whereas all the evidence indicates that it is a free composition written long afterwards.

There is, however, another interpretation of Lk 1:34 which is very similar to this, and which has been advanced by a number of German-speaking Roman Catholics, in particular by Donatus Haugg and Paul Gaechter.[3] These writers assert that Mary understood the angel to mean that she was to conceive a child in the immediate future, and argue as follows.

In the Hebrew construction *hinnak harah*, the adjective *harah* ('pregnant') has the force of a participle. Now the Hebrew participle is used as a predicate to announce future happenings. This usage is common when the subject is introduced by the word *hinneh* ('Behold!'), more frequent still if the word *hinneh* has a pronominal suffix attached to it (as in *hinnak*), and extremely common when the event is announced as imminent and sure to happen, when it is called *futurum instans*.[4] This argument from Hebrew usage is incontrovertible, and there is nothing in the Greek text of the gospel which does not harmonize with it perfectly. Indeed, the whole context of Luke's account implies that Mary understood from the angel that the conception of the child was imminent; and the context implies, too, that she had understood the message correctly. Thus far, one may agree with the thesis: up to this point it is in fact exactly the same interpretation as that given by Cardinal Cajetan (without benefit of Hebrew) in 1528.[5]

---

[3] D. Haugg, *Das erste biblische Marienwort*, Stuttgart, 1938, pp. 61–73; P. Gaechter, *Maria im Erdenleben*, Innsbruck–Vienna–Münster, 1953, pp. 92–8. Graystone, p. 30, observes that J. Schmid changed from the classical view to that of Haugg and Gaechter in the third edition of *Das Evangelium nach Lukas*, Regensburg, 1955, pp. 42–3, as did M. Schmaus in the fifth volume of his *Katholische Dogmatik* (contrast vol. 2, 4th ed., Munich, 1949, p. 621, where he takes the classical view, with vol. 5: *Mariologie*, 1955, pp. 117–20, = 2nd ed., 1961, pp. 127–9, where he follows Haugg and Gaechter).

[4] Cf. *Gesenius' Hebrew Grammar*, §116 p.

[5] Cajetan's text reads: 'Rationem quare quaesivit modum, subiungit, quia expers sum virilis commercii. Non dixit, non cognoscam, sed, non cognosco: quia intellexerat verba angeli tunc implenda, dicente angelo, ecce concipies. Maximam affero rationem inquirendi modum quo nunc concipiam: quamvis usque in praesens viri cognitionem non habeo; hoc est, quia virgo sum.' *Cf. Evangelia cum commentariis Rmi. D. D. Thomae de Vio Caietani: In Lucam* I, 7 on Lk 1:34, Paris, 1536, p. 103 c.

The modern German Catholics, however, go one step further.[6] At the time of the Annunciation, Mary was only betrothed, not married (Lk 1:27). She understood the angel correctly in thinking that the conception was both imminent and sure to happen; but she misapprehended his message by inferring that she was going to conceive this child by Joseph before they were legally married. Hence her astonishment, and her exclamation: 'How shall this be, since I am only betrothed, not married, and therefore have no right to know a man?' Thereupon the angel announces that hers will be a virginal conception: 'A Holy Spirit will come down upon thee . . .' (Lk 1:34–5).

The explanation is clear, but it has not been widely welcomed. Many would refuse to accept it on the ground that fiancés did have the right to live as man and wife: in other words, the basic postulate of the theory is wrong. This view, however, has already been rejected,[7] and therefore cannot be invoked against the present interpretation.

The real weakness of the theory, within its own terms of reference, is that it lays too much stress on the fact that Mary and Joseph were only fiancés at the time. Suppose that Mary did understand the angel correctly in thinking that the conception of the child was imminent and sure to happen; and suppose that she did conclude (erroneously) that this child was to be conceived in the natural way. There was still no need for her to infer that the angel was counselling her to have immoral intercourse before marriage, for the date of the wedding could easily have been brought forward. The period of betrothal lasted normally about twelve months, but such a delay was not of strict obligation; the interval was designed to give both parties a reasonable time to prepare for the marriage, and could easily be shortened by mutual agreement.[8] If the date of the wedding had been advanced, no moral dilemma would have arisen, and Mary could have conceived a child in the natural way. Surely she would have been more likely to assume that this was the angel's intention than to infer that he

---

[6] Detailed scholarly support for the hypothesis is to be found in the studies of J. B. Bauer and H. Quecke listed in the bibliography.

[7] See above, pp. 160–2. [8] *Ketuboth* 5:2 (Danby, p. 251).

was counselling or commanding her in the name of God to have intercourse before marriage? Thus, even within its own terms of reference, the theory is not logically irreproachable.

One may mention here, for the sake of completeness, a rather unusual suggestion by Père Jean-Paul Audet.[9] He argues that there is a special literary form which may be termed an 'Annunciation-story': thus in Jdg 6:11-24, when all Israel is groaning under the oppression of the Midianites (cf. vv. 1-10), an angel appears to tell Gideon that he is to be the nation's deliverer. Audet draws out many parallels between this passage and Lk 1:26-38, and then reasons as follows. Luke means us to assume that Mary was awaiting the coming of the Messiah who would deliver Israel, and she knew that the mother of this Messiah would be a virgin (Is 7:14).[10] Consequently, when she heard the angel say 'Behold, thou shalt conceive and bear a son, and call his name . . .' (Lk 1:31), Mary at once realized that she herself was called to be the mother of this Immanuel. Puzzled to know how she could be both a virgin and a mother, she asked: 'How shall this be, since in that case I must not know a man?' (This translation is grammatically possible.) Mary, in other words, simply asks how it will happen, and the angel replies that the conception will take place by the direct intervention of the Power of the Most High. Audet's idea has not found any real support, principally because he assumes that the virginity of the mother of Immanuel was fairly clear from Is 7:14. Furthermore his translation of Lk 1:34, though grammatically possible and defended with erudition, seems highly improbable in the context. All in all, his interpretation seems to strain the meaning of Lk 1:34 to breaking-point.

The flaw in all the theories discussed in this chapter (even in Audet's) is that they treat the story of the Annunciation too much as a record of Mary's mind at the time, instead of seeing it as a theological composition written long afterwards.

[9] 'L'annonce à Marie', RB 63 (1956), pp. 365-74.

[10] 'Une prophétie d'Isaie, qui avait déjà attiré l'attention de la foi commune, devait retenir également sa pensée' (p. 363). Audet gives no evidence to support this assertion about the common understanding of Is 7:14, and almost everyone rejects it (see below, pp. 281-2).

Chapter Five

LK 1:34 (III): AN ASSERTION BY LUKE

THE theory that Mary, before the Annunciation, had decided to remain a virgin all her life is fraught with difficulties arising directly out of the biblical text; and there are equally cogent objections to the idea that she had somehow misunderstood Gabriel's words. These two facts, together with the revaluation of the literary forms employed in the gospel, have led an ever-increasing number of modern exegetes to the conclusion that the words in Lk 1:34 are simply a literary device, a question placed on Mary's lips by St Luke in order to give Gabriel an opening for the second part of his message, that Mary's will be a virginal conception (Lk 1:35).[1]

This view is not open to any of the objections raised against the interpretations discussed in the last two chapters. Indeed, it is so free of difficulty and has so much to commend it that many commentators who accept it hardly bother to examine its implications. One point, however, cannot be overlooked. Luke was presumably trying to say something meaningful when he wrote

[1] The view first appears in a developed form in H. J. Holtzmann, *Die Synoptiker I:4: Das Evangelium nach Lukas*, 1892, *cf.* 3rd ed. Tübingen–Leipzig, 1901, p. 309. Thereafter it quickly became commonplace among German Protestant exegetes (see Graystone, pp. 26–7), and has slowly but surely found acceptance in other lands and other confessions.

During the last twenty years it has become widely accepted among Roman Catholic exegetes also, principally as a result of the studies by S. Muñoz-Iglesias, 'El Evangelio de la Infancia en San Lucas y las infancias de los héroes biblicos', *Estudios Biblicos* (Madrid) 16 (1957), pp. 329–82, and by J. Gewiess, 'Die Marienfrage Lk 1:34', *Biblische Zeitschrift* (N.F.) 5 (1961), pp. 221–54 (summarized in *Theology Digest* 11 [1963], pp. 39–42).

'since I do not know a man'. If he had merely wanted to provide Gabriel with an opening which would lead smoothly to the announcement of the virginal conception, he had no need to write anything except the main clause 'How shall this be?' There was no need to add the words 'since I do not know a man': they must at least be there in order to underline the fact of Mary's virginity for the benefit of readers who would not otherwise have grasped that v. 35 was describing a virginal conception. Do they imply anything more than this?

Loisy points the way to a more satisfactory solution. He insists that 'one must consider above all the thought of the evangelist', and doubts 'whether Luke's thought is here restricted (as Protestant exegetes readily believe) to the virginal conception of Jesus'. Catholic exegetes down the centuries have always favoured the view that these words imply that Mary was determined to remain a virgin all her life; and this attitude of Catholic scholars, says Loisy, cannot be called arbitrary, for it is evident that Luke thought of Mary and Joseph as abstaining from sexual intercourse after their marriage.[2] These perceptive and judicious remarks deserve more attention than they have received, for the whole problem is to determine the exact import of the clause 'since I do not know a man'. I would suggest that these words mean that Mary did not envisage sexual intercourse as probable at any time in her life.

To interpret the clause as meaning 'since I am *at the moment* a virgin' is inadequate. It is inadequate first because the clear precision of this rendering is purchased only by interpolating into Luke's text a phrase ('at this moment') which is not found there; the meaning is clear, but it is not what Luke actually says. Secondly, if that really was what Luke intended to say, he could quite easily have written 'since I do *not yet* know a man'. This he does not write, and therefore it is permissible to think that there is more to Mary's words than a simple affirmation that she was at that moment a virgin.

[2] A. Loisy, *Les Evangiles Synoptiques I*, pp. 290–1. Later, in *L'évangile selon Luc*, Paris, 1924, pp. 88–9 he omits much of this exegesis and practically returns to the position of Holtzmann (see p. 193, note 1).

On the other hand, her words do not in strict logic pos
exclude the consummation of marriage at some future
Just as 'I do not smoke' is a different proposition from 'I shall
never smoke', so 'I do not know a man' is not the logical equivalent of 'I shall never know a man'. The person who says 'I do not
smoke' means that here and now he has a habit of not smoking,
and implies that he does not contemplate ever starting—rather,
the reverse. True, he may have been a smoker in the past, or he
may start smoking in the future, but here and now he has an attitude of mind which does not positively entertain the idea of
starting to smoke (though his words do not in strict logic preclude
it).

If therefore Mary's words contain more than an affirmation of
her present virginity, and less than a positive proposal of lifelong
virginity, what exactly do they imply?

I would suggest that in Lk 1:34 the present tense is employed
with the force of a future. This is a regular usage in New Testament Greek: for example, Mt 26:18 is best translated as 'I am to
celebrate the Passover'. The classic grammar by Blass and
Debrunner states that 'in confident assertions regarding the future
a vivid, realistic present may be used for the future'.[3] Nigel
Turner comments that these present tenses 'are confident assertions intended to arrest attention with a vivid and realistic tone or
else with imminent fulfilment in mind',[4] and Moulton says: 'We
may define the futural present as differing from the future tense
mainly in the tone of assurance which is imparted'.[5] Thus the
most accurate translation of Lk 1:34 would be: 'How shall this
be, *since I am not to know a man?*'

Mary was at the time betrothed, and normally any girl already
betrothed would regard the consummation of marriage as probable

[3] F. Blass and A. Debrunner, *A Greek Grammar of the New Testament and Other
Early Christian Literature*, translated and revised by R. W. Funk, Chicago and
London, 1961, p. 168, §323.

[4] In *A Grammar of New Testament Greek* by J. H. Moulton, vol. 3 (Syntax) by
N. Turner, Edinburgh, 1963, p. 63.

[5] *Ibid.*, vol. 1 (Prolegomena), Edinburgh, 1906, p. 120. See also C. F. D.
Moule, *An Idiom-Book of New Testament Greek*, Cambridge, 1960, p. 7.

or certain in the not too distant future. One would therefore expect Luke to have written 'since I do not yet know a man', if his *sole* purpose was to state and to underline the fact of the virginal conception. This he does not write. The words he attributes to Mary are so absolute and so devoid of qualification that they represent Mary, even though betrothed, as one who does not regard the consummation of her marriage as imminent or positively probable. Why did Luke, after stating that she was a virgin, and betrothed, place such words on her lips? There seems to be only one possible explanation. When Luke composed this dialogue some seventy years after the birth of Jesus, he must have written these words because he believed that Mary had been *destined* to remain a virgin for ever, *i.e.* because he firmly believed that Mary had in fact remained a virgin all her life, before and after the birth of Jesus. In short, the words which Luke places on Mary's lips are a formal and deliberate assertion by the evangelist, *after* the event, of Mary's perpetual virginity.

This interpretation offers many advantages. It avoids all the difficulties inherent in the idea of a vow *before* the Annunciation, while preserving intact all the positive teaching about consecrated virginity which that theory enshrines. For example, there were two objections to the theory of a vow before the Annunciation: such a vow would seem to cast doubt on the validity of Mary's marriage, and if she had made such a vow, why was she betrothed? These objections cannot be urged against the present interpretation. If Luke wrote 'How shall this be' merely to introduce Gabriel's reply, and added 'since I am not to know a man' in order to assert Mary's perpetual virginity, he is not affirming that Mary had already determined to remain a virgin all her life even before the Annunciation took place. On this interpretation, it is quite possible to hold that Mary at first contemplated a normal marriage with Joseph, and to say that her choice of virginity dates only from the time of the Incarnation. This would be sufficient justification for Luke's attributing to her a resolution of virginity during the Annunciation itself.

Another objection to the theory of a vow before the Annunciation is that it is historically improbable, indeed for a married woman unthinkable. This argument also fails to conclude if one postulates that it was only after the Annunciation that Mary realized that for her the perfect response to the coming of the eschatological kingdom was to consecrate herself, body and soul, to the service of her son by a life of perpetual virginity.

Furthermore, it is in practice hard to uphold the theory of a vow made before the Annunciation without at least indirectly disparaging the state of marriage. It is all too easy for those who defend the idea of a vow to present virginity as something good in itself, irrespective of its motive, as if the value of virginity consisted in its purely negative aspect of abstaining from sexual pleasure. Not all preachers have avoided this danger, but the proposition is frankly Manichaean, and a blasphemy against the Creator. Assuredly, these consequences are not foreseen or intended by preachers who are rightly concerned to stress the possible dangers of sex; but if they use the argument that, before the Incarnation, Mary had already totally renounced the use of sex, they may easily give the impression that God prefers his children to abstain from sexual activity, whatever the motive. If that were true, we should have to admit that a bachelor or a spinster who remained unmarried for purely selfish motives was making a choice that was pleasing to God.

For a thousand years Catholic exegetes and theologians have explained that Mary had made a vow of virginity before the Annunciation, and on the basis of this interpretation they have enriched the Church with much fruitful and constructive thought concerning the value of consecrated virginity. None of this teaching need be abandoned if the interpretation set out here is adopted. If Mary's choice of virginity came after the Annunciation, not before it, and if this choice was a consequence of her divine motherhood, not an antecedent decision unconnected in her mind with the historical Incarnation, then the positive value of Mary's perpetual virginity is enhanced, not diminished. For then Mary is the first person in the history of the world to choose perpetual virginity out of a personal love for her Incarnate Lord, and Joseph is the second. Mary and Joseph, bound to each other inseparably by their consuming love for Jesus, teach the world by their example what life will be for all men in the glorious resurrection (*cf.* Mt 22:30).

Further, if we assume that until the moment of the Incarnation both Mary and Joseph intended to consummate their marriage, and that they changed their plan after it, the full richness of the Christian theology of marriage is revealed. First, the holiness of the physical union between man and wife is proclaimed for all time, in conjunction with the central mystery of the Incarnation. The Word of God chose to be born of a woman who was aspiring to serve God through marriage; and Roman Catholics will add that she who was conceived without any trace of original sin betrothed herself to Joseph with every intention of living a normal married life. There is thus no place for a Manichaean attitude to sex within the framework of orthodox Christianity. Secondly, the still higher value of a love transcending sex is also demonstrated. No Christian will pretend that the supreme value of marriage (its *summum bonum*) is to be sought or found in the physical pleasure of sexual union; all will agree that it consists in the deep personal spiritual love of which physical endearments are but the imperfect expression and the sign, so that the greater love is often to be seen in illness and at the approach of death. Mary and Joseph, by their embracing of virginity, call attention to the primacy of this greater love. By their first intention of consummating the marriage, the positive religious value of physical love is set before the world for ever; by their subsequent choice of virginity in order to serve Jesus with all their heart, a still nobler and wholly unselfish love is made known.

Mary and Joseph thus become models for all Christian parents, whose love for their children so often demands immeasurable self-sacrifice, and a dying to oneself. By their total commitment to Jesus, 'their' son, Mary and Joseph show how the mutual love of husband and wife may be expressed and deepened through the love of God and one's children, so that those who lose their life in this way are the only ones who truly find it (Lk 9:24; Jn 12:25).

For the same reason, Mary and Joseph are models for all who choose celibacy for the sake of the kingdom (Mt 19:12). The essence and the motive of Christian virginity is to dedicate oneself completely and unconditionally to the service of God and one's fellow-men without seeking anything in return. By making a vow of celibacy or virginity a person binds himself irrevocably to the life-long service of mankind in the name of Jesus. If the exegesis of Lk 1:34 given here is correct, then Mary and Joseph were the first ever to dedicate themselves in this way to the service of Jesus, for the furthering of his task of redeeming mankind from all its sins and selfishness. The lives of those who have followed in their footsteps over the centuries have been in each generation a reminder to the world that all things pass away except charity (1 Cor 13).

One final advantage of this interpretation of Lk 1:34 cannot go unmentioned. Outside the Roman Catholic and Eastern Churches it is widely accepted that the brothers of Jesus mentioned in the gospels were sons of Mary and Joseph. Now if Lk 1:34 is understood as a vow or resolution, there is no proof that Mary did not retract this resolution later in her life. If the verse is taken to mean 'since I have not known a man' or 'since I am at the moment only betrothed' (the second theory), it is impossible to prove from Scripture that Mary did remain a virgin all her life; indeed, on these interpretations it would be most reasonable to conclude that the brothers of Jesus were sons of Mary and Joseph. And if the verse is taken merely as a literary device concerned solely with the virginal conception, it is no argument against the view that Mary later gave birth to other children, by Joseph. Lastly, even if one were to show that the 'brothers' of Jesus were not children of Mary, this would not of itself prove that Mary remained a virgin to the end of her life. In short, all these interpretations leave the perpetual virginity of Mary an open question as far as Holy Scripture is concerned.

If, however, the interpretation put forward in this chapter is the true one, then (without appealing to the witness of ecclesiastical tradition) the Church has in Lk 1:34 a formal and explicit statement by the evangelist, made after the event, that Mary did in fact remain a virgin to the very end of her life.

Chapter Six

THE BROTHERS OF JESUS
(I): THE HELVIDIAN VIEW

A NUMBER of New Testament texts mention certain 'brothers of Jesus', or name someone as 'a brother of the Lord'. There are three interpretations of this phrase which are sometimes called (after their fourth-century protagonists) the 'Helvidian', the 'Epiphanian' and the 'Hieronymian' theories. According to the first theory, the 'brothers of Jesus' were children born to Mary and Joseph after the birth of Jesus; according to the second, they were children born to Joseph by a previous marriage; and according to the third theory (St Jerome's), the 'brothers' were in fact cousins of the Lord.[1]

In or around the year 382 a certain Helvidius wrote a small book asserting that after the birth of Jesus, Joseph and Mary consummated their marriage, and that Mary later gave birth to other children, the 'brothers of Jesus' mentioned in the gospels.[2] The Roman Catholic and Eastern Churches have always condemned this theory as heretical because it contradicts the traditional doctrine that Mary remained ever a virgin, both before and after the birth of Jesus. On the other hand, this 'Helvidian' view is nowadays generally adopted by Protestant scholars, on the ground that there is no other satisfactory explanation of the biblical texts. Their conviction rests on the following considerations.

[1] For this and the following three chapters J. Blinzler, *Die Brüder und Schwestern Jesu*, Stuttgart, 1967, provides a rich mine of information.

[2] The book has not survived, but its arguments are well known from St Jerome's reply to it (*Adversus Helvidium de perpetua virginitate beatae Mariae*: ML 23.193–216). Almost nothing is known about Helvidius himself.

When the gospels mention certain 'brothers' of Jesus, the obvious and natural inference is that Mary and Joseph had other sons beside Jesus. Moreover, this inference would appear to be confirmed by the Infancy Gospels of Luke and Matthew. When Luke writes that Mary 'gave birth to her first-born son' (Lk 2:7), does not his use of the word 'first-born' imply that he knew of at least one other son born later to Mary? And in Matthew's Infancy Gospel, the passage concerned with the virginal conception ends with the statement that Joseph 'did not know her (Mary) until she gave birth to a son' (Mt 1:25); surely this turn of phrase would have been avoided by a writer who believed in the perpetual virginity of Mary? Thus, it is argued, Mt 1:25 implies that Joseph and Mary consummated their marriage after the birth of Jesus; Lk 2:7 implies that they had at least one other son, younger than Jesus; and both texts confirm the view that the brothers of Jesus named later in the gospels were in fact sons of Mary and Joseph.[3]

Later in the gospels, during the public ministry, four brothers of Jesus are mentioned by name: James and Joseph, Simon and Judas. Sisters, too, are spoken of, though none is mentioned by name. When Jesus preached in the synagogue at Nazareth, many were astounded at his wisdom and said, 'Is not this the carpenter, the son of Mary, and a brother of James and Joses[4] and Judas and Simon? And do not his sisters live here among us?' (Mk 6:3; cf. Mt 13:55–6). This is the basic text which is always cited in favour of the Helvidian view. It is clear from this text (so the argument runs) that the people of Nazareth regarded Jesus as one of several brothers; that Mark himself shared this view; and that these brothers were Mary's children can be inferred from the fact

---

[3] Helvidius appealed also to the text of Mt 1:18 ('before they came together'), which he understood to refer to the consummation of the marriage: 'Nemo de non pransuro dicit, antequam pranderet' (in Jerome's *Adversus Helvidium* 3: ML 23.195 A). Modern authors, however, are nearly all agreed that the phrase used in Mt 1:18 refers rather to the ceremony of leading the bride to her husband's home. See above, pp. 158, 163.

[4] Joses, a short form for Joseph (like the English 'Joe'), was apparently an abbreviation common in Galilee. See G. Dalman, *Grammatik des jüdisch–palastin-ischen Aramäisch*, 2nd ed., Leipzig, 1905, §15, 6 d, p. 106, and §35, p. 175; and J. Blinzler, *Die Brüder und Schwestern Jesu*, p. 22, n. 6.

that they are constantly shown as being in attendance on her (Mk 3:31–5; Mt 12:46–50; Lk 8:19–21; Jn 2:12; Ac 1:14). Writers who support this position add that if these men were not true blood-brothers of Jesus, the evangelists would surely have warned their readers about the fact; and since no such warning or hint is ever given, one must conclude that Mary gave birth to other children besides Jesus. This is not merely the natural and obvious meaning of the text, but the only satisfactory one.

A number of modern writers stress that this interpretation is of a respectable antiquity, that it was held by Tertullian, and in the fourth century by Helvidius, Bonosus, Jovinian and others.[5] Thus, they claim, the argument from antiquity is not all on one side, for the Helvidian view is in fact older than Jerome's suggestion that the brothers were really cousins of the Lord; and Bishop Lightfoot observes that in his bitter polemic against Helvidius, Jerome, for all his erudition, could not cite a single ancient authority in favour of his own interpretation.[6]

Finally, it is often said that the sole reason for not admitting that the brothers were Mary's children is a doctrinal conviction (or prejudice) about Mary's perpetual virginity. Some even assert that this belief has no basis in Scripture at all.[7] Others point out that even the doctrinal arguments are not all on one side. For

[5] For the precise references to these ancient authors see pp. 205–6.

[6] J. B. Lightfoot, *Saint Paul's Epistle to the Galatians*, 10th ed., London, 1896, pp. 258–9. Lightfoot, himself a strenuous defender of the Epiphanian view, insists very strongly that the notion of cousins is entirely Jerome's own idea, and was unheard of before his day.

[7] *E.g.* 'There is no more baseless, nor, for that matter, more prejudiced theory, in the whole range of biblical study, that that which makes Jesus the only child of Mary' (E. P. Gould on Mk 6:3, in *The Gospel according to St Mark* [*International Critical Commentary*], Edinburgh, 1896, p. 104). 'Both views [*i.e.* Epiphanian and Hieronymian] are obviously motivated by the desire to defend the doctrine of the perpetual virginity of Mary, and have no warrant in the earliest evidence' (B. H. Branscomb, *The Gospel of Mark*, London, 1937, p. 101). 'This is but another example of making doctrinal fitness do duty for historical evidence and it is of no authority whatever. It is not suggested by anything in Scripture' (C. J. Cadoux, *The Life of Jesus*, London, 1948, p. 34). Or M. Goguel (*Jésus*, 2nd ed., Paris, 1950, p. 200): 'Il n'y a pas de problème des frères de Jésus pour l'histoire; il n'y en a que pour la dogmatique catholique.'

many Christians, they say, the knowledge that Jesus had brothers (and sisters) underlines the reality and the completeness of the Incarnation;[8] and though the abandoning of belief in Mary's life-long virginity might diminish the status of Christian virginity in the minds of some believers, by the same token the holiness of marriage would be notably enhanced. The converging evidence of these different arguments leads many modern exegetes to conclude that, all in all, 'there can be little doubt that the Helvidian view stands as the simplest and most natural explanation of the references to the brothers of Jesus in the Gospels'.[9]

Nevertheless, the Helvidian view is open to several grave objections on purely exegetical grounds, one of which may be mentioned immediately. It was argued in the last chapter that Lk 1:34 is an assertion by the evangelist, after the event, that Mary remained a virgin to the end of her life.[10] Either this inter-pretation of Lk 1:34 or the Helvidian theory must be rejected, for Luke was well aware of the fact that some men were known as brothers of Jesus (Lk 8:19–20; Ac 1:14) and had himself met James (Ac 21:18; cf. Gal 1:19). Yet unless one starts by assuming that these brothers of Jesus were sons of Mary and Joseph, the interpretation of Lk 1:34 given above is not absurd. Further bib-lical evidence against the Helvidian theory will be produced later,[11] but in this chapter it will be enough to show that the case in its favour is not proven. This can be done by examining those biblical texts set out above[12] which at first reading seem to imply that Mary had other children besides Jesus.

'She gave birth to her first-born son' (Lk 2:7). The word used here for 'first-born' ($\pi\rho\omega\tau\acute{o}\tau\omega\kappa\omega\varsigma$) is very rare in non-biblical writings, and in fact is never found in any Greek work written before the Septuagint.[13] By contrast, it is fairly common in the Septuagint (130 occurrences), where it is almost always a transla-tion of the Hebrew word $b^{e}k\hat{o}r$ or of a cognate word; vice versa, $b^{e}k\hat{o}r$ is almost everywhere rendered by $\pi\rho\omega\tau\acute{o}\tau\omega\kappa\omega\varsigma$, so that the

[8] V. Taylor, *The Gospel according to St Mark*, pp. 248–9.

[9] *Ibid.*, p. 249.   [10] See above, p. 196.

[11] See Chapter 9, pp. 235–50.   [12] Pp. 201–2.

[13] W. Michaelis in the *TWNT* 6, pp. 872–3.

two words are evidently synonymous. To a Jew familiar with the Old Testament, the idea conveyed by the term 'first-born' would be not the birth of other children, or sons, afterwards, but the special consecration of this one: God had chosen the first-born males for himself (Ex 13:12-15; 34:19-20, etc.). 'Thus "first-born" does not necessarily suggest "later-born", any more than "son" suggests "daughter".'[14]

The second text brought forward in support of the Helvidian theory is Mt 1:25: Joseph 'did not know her (Mary) until she gave birth to a son'. Those who see in this phrase a hint that the marriage was later consummated overlook a most significant fact: the verb used for 'know' (ἐγίνωσκεν) stands in the imperfect tense, not in the aorist, and therefore lays the stress on the duration of the period throughout which Joseph and Mary abstained from intercourse.[15] The meaning is that Joseph had no carnal knowledge of Mary during the period which preceded the birth of her son. This interpretation suits the context perfectly, for the whole of Mt 1:18-25 is concerned with the virginal conception of Jesus and its consequences for paternity.[16] If (as those who uphold the Helvidian view maintain) the author had wished to imply that after the birth of Jesus, Joseph and Mary consummated their marriage, it is more likely that he would have used here the Aorist (ἔγνω). His choice of the imperfect implies rather that he did not exclude the possibility that Joseph and Mary lived a life of virginity after the birth of the Lord.

The principal text advanced in support of the Helvidian view is Mk 6:3: 'Is not this the carpenter, the son of Mary, and a brother of James and Joses and Judas and Simon? And do not his sisters live here among us?' (cf. the parallel text in Mt 13:55-6). This verse will be examined in detail later, but two remarks are called for immediately. First, one cannot cite this text in favour of the Helvidian position without a *petitio principii*, for the question at issue is *whether* this text implies that James and Joses, Judas and

[14] J. B. Lightfoot, *Galatians*, p. 271. See also W. Michaelis in the *TWNT* 6, p. 875.
[15] M. Zerwick, *Analysis philologica Novi Testamenti Graeci*, Rome, 1953, p. 2.
[16] See above, pp. 167-72.

Simon were children of Mary and Joseph. Secondly, according to Mk 15:40, among the women who witnessed the death of Jesus was 'Mary the mother of James the little and of Joses'. Vincent Taylor writes:

'Presumably James and Joses were well known in the primitive community (*cf.* the references to Simon, Alexander, and Rufus in 15:21), but it is difficult to identify them. *They are clearly not the brothers of Jesus (6:3), for Mark would not have designated Mary the Virgin in this roundabout manner*'[17] (italics mine).

It is obvious that Mark would never have referred to the mother of Jesus in this way; but it is by no means obvious that the 'James and Joses' of Mk 15:40 are different persons from the James and Joses of Mk 6:3. Neither Taylor nor anyone else as far as I know has brought forward any solid evidence to prove that they are different people; and unless such proof is forthcoming, one cannot exclude the possibility that there was but one pair of brothers, who were not children of Mary the Virgin. Moreover Luke (24:10) speaks simply of 'Mary the mother of James'; it is hard to accept that he is referring to anyone except the mother of James the bishop of Jerusalem, the brother of the Lord. A more detailed discussion of Mk 6:3 will follow later.[18] For the present, it is enough to note that a large question mark is placed against the Helvidian interpretation of this verse by the evidence of Mk 15:40 and Lk 24:10.

A further argument adduced to support the view that the 'brothers of Jesus' were children of Mary is the evidence of certain ancient writers. If we omit for the moment apocryphal writings,[19] the earliest witness invoked is Tertullian. Tertullian, however, nowhere openly states or directly implies that the brothers mentioned in the gospels were children of Mary and Joseph,

[17] *The Gospel according to St Mark*, p. 598.
[18] See below, pp. 239–41 and 247–8.
[19] These and other early testimonies about the brothers of the Lord will be examined later: see pp. 211–8, 220–1, 244–6 and 251–3.

and therefore the examination of his views can be more suitably treated in an appendix.[20] The other ancient writers whose names are invoked need not detain us either, for they all belong to the closing years of the fourth century, and their opinion was decisively rejected by the Church as soon as it was voiced, on the ground that it was contrary to all tradition. Helvidius was apparently the first to shock the faithful with his novel theory, in or around the year 382;[21] his booklet at once provoked an explosion of invective from Jerome, writing in Rome.[22] A few years later, the same idea was put forward by a certain Jovinianus, a rather worldly monk living first in Rome and later in Milan, and by one Bonosus, bishop of Sardica in Illyricum (the modern Sofia). Jovinianus was condemned in the year 390 at a synod held in Rome under Pope Siricius,[23] and by another held in Milan under St Ambrose.[24] Bonosus was condemned in a synod held at Capua in 391,[25] and in another synod held shortly afterwards at Thessalonica.[26] Epiphanius records that similar views were being voiced in Arabia about the same time: he labels the men who put forward these views '*Antidikomarianitae*' or 'Opponents of Mary' because they denied the perpetual virginity of the mother of Jesus, and he evidently regards their views as a heresy previously unheard of, 'a novel madness'.[27] Thus every time the Helvidian theory was put forward in antiquity, it was at once firmly rejected; it can claim no support in ecclesiastical tradition, and therefore it

[20] See Detached Note V: Some Texts of Tertullian Invoked by Supporters of the Helvidian Interpretation.

[21] Jerome, *Adversus Helvidium* 1: ML 23.193.

[22] 'Dum adviveret sanctae memoriae Damasus, librum contra Helvidium "de Beatae Mariae virginitate perpetua" scripsimus' (Jerome, *Ep.* 48, *Ad Pammachium*, n. 18: ML 22.508).

[23] J. D. Mansi, *Sacrorum Conciliorum nova et amplissima Collectio*, 3, Florence, 1759, pp. 663 and 687–8 (cited hereafter simply as Mansi, with the number of the volume and page).

[24] Mansi, 3, pp. 664–7 and 689–90. For both these episodes in notes 23 and 24, see the *Histoire des Conciles par Charles Joseph Hefele, traduite . . . par Dom H. Leclerq, et continuée jusqu'à nos jours*, vol. 2, Part 1, Paris, 1908, pp. 78–80.

[25] Mansi, 3, pp. 685–6.

[26] Mansi, 3, pp. 689–90: see also Hefele-Leclerq (*cf.* n. 24), *loc. cit.*, p. 81.

[27] *Haer.* 78, 6: MG 42.708 A; also *ibid.* 78, 25: MG 42.738 C.

must stand or fall on its own intrinsic merits as an explanation of the gospel texts.

The one remaining argument in favour of the theory is the doctrinal one: the Helvidian interpretation, it is said, underlines the reality and the completeness of the Incarnation. Though at first sight this seems to be true, the facts of history and of experience disprove it. The belief that Joseph and Mary had several children all too often leads (not logically, but psychologically) to an acceptance of the view that Jesus himself was not virginally conceived, and that the biblical narrative is meant to point a theological truth, not to record an historical happening. And from believing that Jesus was the son of Joseph and Mary, it is a short step (again, not in strict logic, but psychologically) to abandoning the traditional doctrine that he is the consubstantial, coeternal Son of the Father. Thus the Jesus of history is eventually seen as being quite other than that Christ-figure who is the object of faith. In this way, many who might at first have claimed that the Helvidian view underlines the reality and the completeness of the Incarnation have been led in the end to affirm that there was never any Incarnation at all.

The biblical texts put forward in support of the Helvidian theory do not supply adequate proof of that position; nor do the arguments from antiquity and from doctrinal suitability. It may appear the simplest and most natural explanation of the gospel texts, but that does not mean it is the most satisfactory one, or the true one.

Rejecting the Helvidian view does, of course, leave the exegete face to face with a real difficulty: if the brothers of Jesus were not Mary's children, why are they called brothers of Jesus? One very old theory is that they were sons of Joseph by a previous marriage, and to this we must now turn.

Chapter Seven

THE BROTHERS OF JESUS
(II): THE EPIPHANIAN THEORY

THE interpretation according to which the 'brothers of Jesus' were sons of Joseph by a previous marriage is sometimes labelled the 'Epiphanian' view, for it was warmly advocated by St Epiphanius of Salamis in Cyprus towards the end of the fourth century.[1] The obvious argument in its favour is that it safeguards the perpetual virginity of Mary while at the same time assigning an intelligible and very natural meaning to the words 'brothers of the Lord'. In modern times it has been brilliantly expounded by

[1] Theophylactus, an archbishop in Bulgaria during the eleventh century, explains that they were sons of Joseph by a levirate marriage. 'The Lord had brothers and sisters, whom Joseph fathered by the wife of his brother Klopas: for when Klopas had died childless, Joseph, in accordance with the law, took his wife and had six children by her, four boys and two girls' (*In Matt.* 13:55: MG 123.193 A; *cf.* his commentary *In Gal.* 1:19: MG 124.1188 C). Since no other writer seems to have adopted this idea, and since it is merely stated (without proof) by Theophylactus, there is no need to discuss it. It may be noted, however, that if the Kleophas mentioned in the story of Emmaus (Lk 24:18) is the Klopas of Jn 19:25, the whole theory collapses: he was alive at the time of the crucifixion.

A much more bizarre theory was put forward by G. M. de la Garenne, *Le problème des 'Frères du Seigneur'*, Paris, 1928. He suggested that Joseph died after his betrothal to Mary, and that his brother Klopas then made a levirate marriage with Mary. The first son of this union, Jesus, was therefore counted as the son of Joseph, the others as sons of Mary and Klopas. The author blithely overlooks the gospel tradition that Joseph was still alive when Jesus was twelve years old! For further detail see J. Blinzler, *Die Brüder und Schwestern Jesu*, pp. 15–16.

J. B. Lightfoot as the more probable solution of a very question.[2]

Lightfoot argues with great erudition that this explanation has the support of most orthodox writers of antiquity, citing in its favour Clement of Alexandria, Origen, Eusebius of Caesarea, St Hilary, 'Ambrosiaster', St Gregory of Nyssa, St Epiphanius, St Ambrose and St Cyril of Alexandria. Early apocryphal writings, such as *The Gospel of Peter* and *The Protevangelium of James*, are called as witnesses to the same tradition; the Greek, Syrian and Coptic liturgies, and all later Greek writers are also said to follow this interpretation. Against such a cloud of witnesses, Jerome (though followed by Augustine and the Latin West) stands almost alone; and though Jerome based his view on a most ingenious study of the relationships within the family of the Lord, his arguments have been demolished by later scholars. Thus, according to Lightfoot, both the biblical texts and the consensus of patristic opinion point to one conclusion: that the Epiphanian view is the most reasonable explanation of the gospel texts because it retains a natural sense for the term 'brothers' and preserves the doctrine of Mary's perpetual virginity.

This interpretation is not accepted by anyone nowadays, except in the Orthodox Church.[3] Modern Protestants reject it because they usually take for granted that it was invented for a doctrinal reason, namely, to safeguard the perpetual virginity of Mary. Some add that the Epiphanian theory, like St Jerome's explanation, originated also from a desire to underline the religious value

[2] In his Dissertation on 'The Brethren of the Lord', printed in his commentary on *The Epistle to the Galatians*, pp. 252–91. Precise references to the patristic texts are given there, and will be found later in this chapter (together with the references to Migne, absent from Lightfoot's work) as each one is discussed.

[3] V. Taylor, *The Gospel according to St Mark*, p. 248, mentions as supporters of the Epiphanian theory in modern times only J. B. Lightfoot, C. Harris ('Brethren of the Lord', in the *Dictionary of Christ and the Gospels*, vol. 1, Edinburgh, 1906, pp. 232–7), and J. H. Bernard (*The Gospel according to St John* [*International Critical Commentary*], vol. 1, Edinburgh, 1928, pp. 84–6), all of whom are long dead. J. Blinzler, *Die Brüder und Schwestern Jesu*, p. 15, fn. 16, cites four Orthodox authors writing since 1900, one in 1950 and another (the Bishop of Corcyra) in 1962.

of virginity. Roman Catholic writers are not much more sympathetic: in general they ignore the Epiphanian suggestion on the ground that it has been rejected by nearly all scholars for many centuries. But there are good exegetical reasons against it too. If these brothers of Jesus were in fact older than he, having been born of an earlier marriage, why are they never mentioned in the Infancy Narratives? The impression left both by Matthew and by Luke (including Luke's story of Jesus in the temple, Lk 2:41–52) is that even twelve years after Jesus' birth the Holy Family consisted of three persons only. Again, the impression left by Mt 1:18–25 is that Jesus was to be the heir of Joseph, 'the son of David';[4] but if Joseph already had a number of sons, Jesus would not have been his heir. Thirdly, if James the brother of the Lord who was bishop in Jerusalem is the same person as that James mentioned in Mt 13:55 and Mk 6:3, then his mother was surely alive at the time of the Resurrection. For Luke could never have designated any woman other than this man's mother by the simple words 'Mary (the mother) of James'.[5] (What Luke actually writes is 'Mary of James', but that he means the mother—not the wife or daughter—of James is clear from the parallels in Mt 27:56; Mk 15:40.) Consequently James the brother of the Lord cannot possibly be the son of Joseph by a wife who died before the birth of Jesus.

On the other hand, it is a pity that the Epiphanian interpretation has not been taken more seriously by those who reject it, and the evidence in its favour examined more closely. For it would then have been discovered that this theory was not invented simply to safeguard the perpetual virginity of Mary (though Epiphanius and some others like Lightfoot and the Greek Orthodox may have been attracted to it partly for this reason); on the contrary, it arose from a misreading of some ancient and valuable texts. To these texts we must now turn.[6]

[4] See above, Chapter 2, pp. 171–2.

[5] For Lightfoot's answer to this powerful and obvious objection, see below, p. 213, fn. 13.

[6] The fullest study of the question is in Th. Zahn's 'Brüder und Vettern Jesu' in *Forschungen zur Geschichte des neutestamentlichen Kanons und der altkirchlichen*

The principal witnesses whom Lightfoot calls in favour of the Epiphanian interpretation may be divided into four classes: (1) apocryphal works of the second century; (2) Hegesippus; (3) Clement of Alexandria and Origen; (4) witnesses from the fourth century. They will be considered in this order.

(1) *Apocryphal works of the second century.* Origen writes in his commentary on Mt 13:55:

'Some persons, on the ground of a tradition in *The Gospel according to Peter*, as it is entitled, or *The Book of James* (*i.e.* the *Protevangelium*), say that the brothers of Jesus were Joseph's sons by a former wife to whom he was married before Mary . . .'.[7]

The Gospel according to Peter is one of the oldest of the apocryphal gospels; it dates in all probability from the early years of the second century. Though its existence was known of from early times, not a single quotation from it was known until, in the winter of 1886-7, a large fragment of it was discovered in Upper Egypt. This fragment, however, deals only with the crucifixion and the Resurrection, and contains no mention of the 'brothers of Jesus'. On the other hand, there certainly could have been such a mention in the original work, for Origen's second reference, to '*The Book of James*', is perfectly accurate.[8]

According to *The Protevangelium of James*, Mary was brought up in the Temple until she was twelve years old; the high priest then assembled all the widowers of Israel, and a miraculous sign designated Joseph as the man who was to take the young virgin under

---

Literatur 6, Leipzig, 1900, pp. 225-364; when the very conservative Zahn came down in favour of the Helvidian view, most German Protestants abandoned the view of Luther and Calvin and regarded the issue as closed.

[7] *In Matt.* 10, 17 (MG 13.876-7).

[8] *The Gospel according to Peter* (that is, the extant fragment of it) is printed, with a long introduction by Chr. Maurer, in E. Hennecke's *New Testament Apocrypha* edited by W. Schneemelcher, English translation edited by R. McL. Wilson, vol. 1: *Gospels and Related Writings*, London, 1963, pp. 179-87. *The Protevangelium of James* is given in the same volume, with an introduction by O. Cullmann, on pp. 370-88.

his care. Joseph at first objected, 'I have sons and am old, but she is a girl. I fear lest I should become a laughing-stock to the children of Israel' (*Prot. James* 9:2). Later, Joseph says, 'All the children of Israel know that she is not my daughter' (*Prot. James* 17:1). The original form of this work, and the passages just mentioned, may with reasonable confidence be dated to the latter half of the second century, and several later apocryphal narratives repeat these stories, with various modifications and generous embellishments. Sometimes Joseph's daughters are named, sometimes his first wife (Salome); but these later narratives are by universal consent pure fabrications, and of no historical value at all.[9] In comparison with them, *The Protevangelium of James* has considerable literary merit, being both lively and relatively restrained. The book was obviously written to glorify Mary, and its popularity is proof that from very early times Christians had a warm devotion to the mother of Jesus. But literary merit is no substitute for historical veracity, and though no tradition about its authorship has survived, Professor Cullmann remarks that its ignorance of Palestinian geography and of Jewish custom point to an author who was a non-Jew.[10] Since it is a work of fiction, composed between A.D. 150 and 200, reflecting neither Palestinian nor Jewish–Christian traditions, its historical value as a witness in favour of Joseph's earlier marriage is nil. If the Epiphanian theory is to stand, it needs a more solid basis than *The Protevangelium of James*. So we come to Lightfoot's principal and most impressive witness, Hegesippus.

(2) *Hegesippus* was a Palestinian Christian, perhaps of Jewish stock, who around A.D. 180 wrote down his *Memoirs*. Although the work is now lost,[11] several valuable quotations have been preserved in the *Historia Ecclesiastica* of Eusebius of Caesarea, a number of which are very pertinent to our inquiry.

Lightfoot presents his case in the following words:

---

[9] See Detached Note VI: The Brothers of Jesus in Apocryphal Writings and the Influence of the Protevangelium of James.

[10] *New Testament Apocrypha I*, p. 372.

[11] B. Altaner, however, in his *Patrology*, Edinburgh, 1960, p. 149, remarks that some manuscripts of the work were probably still extant in Greek monasteries even in the sixteenth and seventeenth centuries.

'Hegesippus . . . writes as follows: "After the martyrdom of James the Just on the same charge as the Lord, his paternal uncle's child Symeon the son of Clopas is next made bishop, who was put forward by all as the second in succession, being cousin of the Lord" (μετὰ τὸ μαρτυρῆσαι Ἰάκωβον τὸν δίκαιον ὡς καὶ ὁ κύριος ἐπὶ τῷ αὐτῷ λόγῳ, πάλιν ὁ ἐκ τοῦ θείου αὐτοῦ Συμεὼν ὁ τοῦ Κλῶπα καθίσται ἐπίσκοπος, ὃν προέθεντο πάντες ὄντα ἀνεψιὸν τοῦ Κυρίου δεύτερον, Eusebius, H.E. 4:22 [MG 20.380 A]). If the passage be correctly rendered thus (and this rendering alone seems intelligible), Hegesippus distinguishes between the relationships of James the Lord's brother and Symeon his cousin . . .'[12]

Lightfoot is here saying that according to Hegesippus, the relationship of Jesus, James and Simeon should be construed thus:

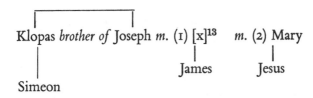

Klopas *brother of* Joseph *m.* (1) [x][13]   *m.* (2) Mary

                                       James   Jesus

Simeon

---

[12] *Galatians*, pp. 276–7.

[13] Lightfoot does not give a table of family relationships, but this one represents his thought. Note that the James who is the brother of the Lord is here taken to be a different person from that James whose mother Mary witnessed the crucifixion. Lightfoot sees that the references to 'Mary the mother of James and Joses' constitute a powerful reason for rejecting both the Helvidian and the Epiphanian theories, and writes as follows. 'When a certain Mary is described as "the mother of James", is it not highly probable that the person intended should be the most celebrated of the name—James the Just, the bishop of Jerusalem, the Lord's brother? This objection to both the Epiphanian and Helvidian theories is at first sight not without force, but it will not bear examination. Why, we may ask, if the best known of all the Jameses were intended here, should it be necessary in some passages to add the name of a brother Joses also, who was a person of no special mark in the Church (Mt 27:56; Mk 15:40)? Why again in others should this Mary be designated "the mother of Joses" alone (Mk 15:47), the name of his more famous brother being suppressed? In only two passages is she called simply "the mother of James"; in Mk 16:1, where it is explained by the fuller description which has gone before "the mother of James and Joses" (15:40); and in Lk 24:10,

In a footnote, Lightfoot explains and defends his rendering of the Greek text:

'A different meaning however has been assigned to the words: πάλιν and δεύτερον being taken to signify "*another* child of his uncle, *another* cousin," and thus the passage has been represented as favouring the Hieronymian view . . .'

I.e. some have construed the relationships as follows:

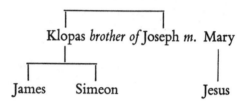

Lightfoot rightly objects that if James and Simeon were brothers, no more clumsy way of stating such a simple fact could have been found:

'To this rendering the presence of the definite article alone seems fatal (ὁ ἐκ τοῦ θείου not ἕτερος τῶν ἐκ τοῦ θείου);[14] but indeed the whole passage appears to be framed so as to distinguish the relationships of the two persons; whereas, had the author's object been to represent Symeon as a

---

where no such explanation can be given. It would seem then that this Mary and this James, though not the most famous of their respective names and therefore not at once distinguishable when mentioned alone, were yet sufficiently well known to be discriminated from others, when their names appeared in conjunction' (*Galatians*, pp. 269–70).

If this Mary and this James were sufficiently well known to be identified when their names appeared in conjunction, why in some passages should it be necessary to add the name of a brother Joses? And Lk 24:10 can only refer to the mother of the bishop of Jerusalem. Lightfoot's attempt to extricate himself (and the Epiphanian theory) from the problem raised by 'the mother of James' is sadly unconvincing.

[14] *I.e.* 'the son of his uncle', not '*another* of his uncle's sons'.

brother of James, no more circuitous mode could well have been devised for the purpose of stating so very simple a fact. Let me add that Eusebius (*loc. cit.*) and Epiphanius . . . must have interpreted the words as I have done.

Whether αὐτοῦ should be referred to Ἰάκωβον or to Κύριος is doubtful. If to the former, this alone decides the meaning of the passage. This seems the more natural reference of the two, but the form of expression will admit either.'[15]

Lightfoot continues:

'Hegesippus distinguishes between the relationships of James the Lord's brother and Symeon his cousin. So again, referring apparently to this passage, he in another fragment (Euseb. *H.E.* 3:32 [MG 20.284 B]) speaks of "the child of the Lord's paternal uncle, the aforesaid Symeon son of Clopas" . . . to which Eusebius adds, "for Hegesippus relates that Clopas was the brother of Joseph." Thus in Hegesippus Symeon is never once called the Lord's brother, while James is always so designated. And this argument powerful in itself is materially strengthened by the fact that, where Hegesippus has occasion to mention Jude, he too like James is styled "the Lord's brother": "There still survived members of the Lord's family (οἱ ἀπὸ γένους τοῦ κυρίου) grandsons of Judas who was called His brother according to the flesh" (τοῦ κατὰ σάρκα λεγομένου αὐτοῦ ἀδελφοῦ); Euseb. *H.E.* 3:20 [MG 20.252-3]. In this passage the word "called" seems to me to point to the Epiphanian rather than the Helvidian view, the brotherhood of these brethren, like the fatherhood of Joseph, being reputed but not real. In yet another passage (Euseb. *H.E.* 2:23 [MG 20.196-7]) Hegesippus relates that "the Church was committed in conjunction with the Apostles to the charge of . . . the Lord's brother James, who has been entitled Just by all from the Lord's time to our own day; for many bore the name of James." From this last passage however no inference can be safely drawn . . . Thus the testimony

---

[15] *Galatians*, p. 277, fn. 2.

of Hegesippus seems distinctly opposed to the Hieronymian view, while of the other two it favours the Epiphanian rather than the Helvidian. If any doubt still remains, the fact that both Eusebius and Epiphanius, who derived their information mainly from Hegesippus, gave this account of the Lord's brethren materially strengthens the position. The testimony of an early Palestinian writer who made it his business to collect such traditions is of the utmost importance'.[16]

It cannot be too firmly stressed that this is Lightfoot's main witness: he himself admits that Eusebius and Epiphanius are not independent authorities, but in this matter wholly reliant on Hegesippus. Nowhere, however, is there even a hint, much less a direct statement, that James the brother of the Lord or Jude was the son of Joseph by a first marriage.

What we learn from Hegesippus is rather that Jude was 'called' the Lord's brother. The same phrase is used of James in the *Clementine Homilies*;[17] and Lightfoot rightly observes that the word 'called' seems to indicate that the brotherhood in question was reputed rather than real.

(3) *Clement of Alexandria and Origen* are more specific. Two quotations from Clement are relevant. The first occurs in a passage from a work now lost, the *Hypotyposeis*, which has survived only in a Latin translation by Cassiodorus (*c.* A.D. 540). Lightfoot's version of this text runs:

'Jude, who wrote the Catholic Epistle, being one of the sons of Joseph and [the Lord's] brother (*frater filiorum Joseph exstans*), a man of deep piety, though he was aware of his relationship to the Lord, nevertheless did not say that he was His brother; but what said he? *Jude the servant of Jesus Christ*, because He was his Lord, but *brother of James*; for this is true; he was his brother, being Joseph's [son] (*frater erat eius, Joseph*)'.[18]

[16] *Galatians*, pp. 277–8.
[17] See below, p. 252.
[18] MG 9.731.

The Latin translation by Cassiodorus leaves much to be desired, for the two phrases cited in Latin and in brackets are crucial to the sense of the passage, and they could hardly be more obscure. Why does the text read *'frater filiorum Joseph exstans'*, and not simply *'filius Joseph'*, if that is what the author meant to say? Lightfoot inserts here 'the Lord's', as if the text were *'frater Domini, filiorum Joseph exstans'*. This gives good sense, but it is not what the Latin version says. In the final phrase, too (*'frater erat eius, Joseph'*), Lightfoot inserts *'filius'*. The passages are undoubtedly obscure, but all that can be deduced with certainty is that Clement believed a number of people were known as sons of Joseph.

A second text from Clement is often cited to prove that he held the Hieronymian view; but as Lightfoot rightly says, the passage proves nothing one way or the other. All it states is that there were two men called James, the brother of the Lord and the son of Zebedee; but Clement neither states nor implies that there were two only, and therefore one cannot infer that James the brother of the Lord was (as some maintain) the son of Alphaeus.[19] (This view will be explained and discussed later.)[20]

Origen is much clearer, declaring unambiguously in one place that the brothers of Jesus were sons of Joseph by a deceased wife. In his commentary on Jn 2:12 he writes:

Jesus 'had no brothers by nature, for the virgin did not give birth to any other child and he himself was not the son of

[19] *Galatians*, p. 280. The text of Clement occurs in Eusebius, *H.E.* 2:1 (MG 20.136): 'Clement, in the sixth book of the Hypotyposeis gives the following account: Peter and James and John, he tells us, after the resurrection of the Saviour were not ambitious of honour, though the preference shown them by the Lord might have entitled them to it, but chose James the Just Bishop of Jerusalem. The same writer too in the seventh book of the same treatise gives this account also of him (James the Lord's brother); the Lord after the resurrection delivered the gnosis to James the Just and John and Peter. These delivered it to the rest of the Apostles. . . . Now there are two Jameses, one the Just who was thrown down from the pinnacle (of the temple) and beaten to death with a club by a fuller, and another who was beheaded' (Lightfoot's version).

[20] See pp. 223–8.

Joseph. It was legally, therefore, that they were counted as his brothers, being sons of Joseph by a predeceased wife'.[21]

Elsewhere he writes:

'These sons who were said to be Joseph's were not born of Mary',[22]

and in the passage already cited in part on p. 211 he says:

'Some persons, on the ground of a tradition in *The Gospel according to Peter*, as it is entitled, or *The Book of James* (i.e. the *Protevangelium*), say that the brothers of Jesus were Joseph's sons by a former wife to whom he was married before Mary. Those who hold this view wish to preserve the honour of Mary in virginity throughout. . . . And I think it reasonable that as Jesus was the first-fruit of purity and chastity among men, so Mary was among women: for it is not seemly to ascribe the first-fruit of virginity to any other woman but her.'[23]

Origen therefore plainly rejects the Helvidian view, and regards the 'Epiphanian' interpretation as giving a good interpretation of the term 'brothers of Jesus'. It is the only explanation he gives, and he seems quite satisfied with it.

(4) *The witness of fourth-century writers*. Eusebius of Caesarea is the first in order of time and, because of his familiarity with Palestinian traditions, the first in importance. He speaks of

'James, who was referred to as the Lord's brother, for he too was called Joseph's boy, and Joseph, to whom the virgin was betrothed, was the father of Christ' ('Ιάκωβον τὸν τοῦ Κυρίου λεγόμενον ἀδελφόν, ὅτι δὴ καὶ οὗτος τοῦ Ἰωσὴφ ὠνόμαστο παῖς κτλ.).[24]

---

[21] *The Commentary of Origen on S. John's Gospel*, [edited] by A. E. Brooke, vol. 2, Cambridge, 1896, p. 244, Fragment 31.

[22] *In Lucam*, Hom. 7 (MG 13.1818 B).

[23] *In Matt.* 10, 17 (MG 13.876–7).   [24] *H.E.* 2:1 (MG 20.133–6).

Grammatically, this text is as ambiguous in the original Greek as in the above English rendering. Who was called Joseph's boy—Jesus or James? If the words 'he too' refer back to 'the Lord' ('he too was called Joseph's boy'), the second half of the sentence simply repeats what the first part has stated with perfect clarity. This interpretation, though grammatically defensible, seems logically absurd, and it is difficult to see why Lightfoot adopts it.[25] If, on the contrary, the words 'he too' refer to James ('he too was called Joseph's boy'), then everything makes perfect sense: that is why James was called the Lord's brother.

Writers from the Western Church next provide two unequivocal assertions that the brothers of Jesus were sons of Joseph. St Hilary of Poitiers writes in his commentary on St Matthew (c. 350–5):

'It is recorded that our Lord had several brothers . . . yet if these had been sons of Mary and not rather sons of Joseph, the offspring of a former marriage, she would never at the time of the passion have been transferred to the Apostle John to be his mother'.[26]

Some twenty years later the anonymous Roman exegete known as Ambrosiaster says:

'This James was the son of Joseph, and he was called the brother of the Lord because Joseph his father was also called the father of the Lord.'[27]

A few sentences later, Ambrosiaster makes it clear that he did not regard James as the only son of Joseph by this first marriage.

So we come to St Epiphanius, whose views are unmistakable. Not very long before Jerome wrote his work against Helvidius, Epiphanius came forward as the champion of the perpetual

---

[25] *Galatians*, p. 283, fn. 1. On the other hand, he makes a valuable comment when he writes that 'to be called' the son of someone is a good Greek phrase to denote both real and reputed sonship.

[26] *In Matt.* 1:4 (ML 9.922 B).   [27] ML 17.344–5.

virginity of Mary against an obscure group of Christians in Arabia who interpreted the phrase 'brothers of Jesus' in the same way as Helvidius. The long pastoral letter in which he denounces their teaching forms the substance of his '78th Heresy' in his great encyclopaedia of heresies. There, as far as one can judge today, he follows the apocryphal gospels quite closely. Joseph, he states, was eighty years old when the virgin was betrothed to him. By his former wife he had six children, four sons (James, José, Simeon and Jude) and two daughters (Mary and Salome). Jesus was brought up along with them, and that is how they came to be called his brothers. Epiphanius does not seem to have observed that if Joseph had been eighty years old before the birth of Jesus, the brothers and sisters would presumably have grown up long before![28]

What is the value of all this ancient testimony? It is impossible to evaluate the evidence of *The Gospel according to Peter*, because the relevant section is not extant; but since Origen brackets it with *The Protevangelium of James*, its historical value may not be very high. The *Protevangelium* in turn is a work of fiction; its aim is edification, not history, and consequently its evidence is not to be taken as true unless it is confirmed from more reliable sources. Hegesippus, however, does not confirm this account of the brothers of the Lord: he takes for granted that James the Just, bishop in Jerusalem, was *called* the brother of the Lord, and says too that Jude was '*called* his brother according to the flesh'.[29] But this much we know from the New Testament, and the question at issue is what the phrase 'brother of the Lord' means. Clement of Alexandria (it is claimed) and Origen (certainly) took it to mean that these brothers of Jesus were sons of Joseph by a first marriage: Clement's meaning is hard to discern with certainty because of the obscurity of the Latin translation, but Origen mentions the theory as if it were a reasonably satisfactory explanation of a difficult phrase. However, when he writes that 'some say,

---

[28] *Haer.* 78 (MG 42.699–740 *passim*: *cf.* especially 708–9,711). The same interpretation is put forward in *Haer.* 28:7 (MG 41.385 D), 29:3–4 (MG 41.393–6), 51:10 (MG 41.908) and 66:19 (MG 42.58 D).

[29] See above, p. 215.

on the ground of a tradition in *The Gospel according to Peter*, or in *The Book of James . . .*', he is surely warning the reader not to attach to this explanation more credence than it merits. He himself evidently regarded the explanation as reasonably satisfactory, but without committing himself fully, because he knew the suggestion came from a suspect source.

Of the fourth-century writers cited, only Hilary, Ambrosiaster and Epiphanius speak unequivocally. Epiphanius' evidence is wholly based upon apocryphal gospels, and everyone knows that for all his diligence in collecting fragments of tradition and local gossip, he was not exactly critical in his assessment of the material collected. Ambrosiaster and Hilary mention the matter only once each: and Hilary wrote his commentary on St Matthew (his first work) *before* his exile to Asia Minor, when he had not been a bishop for very long.[30] All in all, the patristic evidence in favour of the view that the brothers of Jesus were older children of a previous marriage is very flimsy indeed.[31]

But, it will be objected, if the ancient evidence for this theory is so fragmentary and so unsubstantial, why did Bishop Lightfoot accept it? Rarely, if ever, has anyone brought a sharper or a more critical mind to the study of the early Fathers, and it is unthinkable that Lightfoot could have held the Epiphanian interpretation on the basis of the evidence so far quoted. In fact, it was not the evidence set out above which, in Lightfoot's judgment, tipped the balance in favour of the Epiphanian interpretation, but evidence not so far mentioned. A number of patristic texts either assert or clearly imply that James the brother of the Lord and later first bishop of Jerusalem was not one of the Twelve;[32] and this fact (as will be seen in the next chapter) appears to be securely established from the biblical texts. Now St Jerome, while still a relatively young man, dashed off a violently polemical essay, his *Adversus Helvidium de perpetua virginitate beatae Mariae*,[33] in which

[30] See P. Galtier, *Saint Hilaire de Poitiers*, Paris, 1960, pp. 13–33.

[31] For a much fuller list of ancient writers holding the Epiphanian view, see J. Blinzler, *Die Brüder und Schwestern Jesu*, pp. 131–3.

[32] See the list in Lightfoot, *Galatians*, p. 291.

[33] ML 23.193–216.

he argued that James the brother of the Lord was one and the same person as James the son of Alphaeus, who was one of the Twelve. In the Western Church, Jerome's position came to be identified with doctrinal orthodoxy, for many believed that Jerome had proved beyond refutation that the 'brothers of the Lord' were in fact his cousins. Bishop Lightfoot rejected the arguments of Jerome, on the ground that scripture and patristic witness alike show that James the brother of the Lord was not the same person as James the son of Alphaeus. And if he was not (so it is generally believed) Jerome's case falls to the ground, and the Epiphanian interpretation is the only remaining alternative to the Helvidian. The real reason why Lightfoot committed himself to the Epiphanian theory was that he could see no other way consistent with scholarship in which the doctrine of Mary's perpetual virginity could be upheld.

Chapter Eight

THE BROTHERS OF JESUS
(III): ST JEROME'S THEORY

ST JEROME held that the brothers of Jesus were in fact his cousins, and this interpretation has ever since been accepted in the Latin Church. Jerome first expounded his theory in his treatise against Helvidius,[1] and the argument runs as follows.

Two of the twelve apostles were called James—the son of Zebedee and the son of Alphaeus. Now James the brother of the Lord who became bishop in Jerusalem (Ac 15:13; 21:18; Gal 1:19) was either one of the Twelve or not. If he was one of the Twelve, then he must be identified as James the son of Alphaeus, for the son of Zebedee had been put to death by Herod before the Council of Jerusalem (Ac 12:2). If he was not one of the Twelve, then there were (at least) three prominent persons in the early Church named James; but in this case, how could a certain James be called '*minor*' ('the less, the younger'), as in Mk 15:40, since the Latin term '*minor*' implies a comparison between two and two only? How could a woman be distinguished as 'the mother of James the younger' if there were in fact three men called James? Moreover, St Paul writes that he 'saw none of the apostles except James the brother of the Lord' (Gal 1:19), and so James the brother of the Lord must have been one of the Twelve. Consequently, he must be one and the same as James the son of Alphaeus.

If he was the son of Alphaeus, why was he called Jesus' brother? For this Jerome has a most ingenious explanation. Among the brothers of Jesus mentioned in the gospels we find a certain James and Joseph (Mt 13:55 = Mk 6:3), and it is recorded

[1] *Adversus Helvidium de perpetua virginitate beatae Mariae* (ML 23.193–216).

...at Mary the mother of James (the younger) and of Joseph was present at the crucifixion (Mt 27:56 = Mk 15:40). This Mary, then, must have been the wife of Alphaeus, the father of James. But Jn 19:25 states: 'There stood by the cross of Jesus his mother and his mother's sister, Mary of Clopas and Mary Magdalen.' If therefore Mary of Clopas, the wife of Alphaeus and the mother of James and Joseph, was the virgin's sister, then her child James would in fact be Jesus' first cousin.

Jerome himself deals with two rather obvious objections against his theory. If Jesus and James were first cousins, why are they called brothers? Jerome replies that the term 'brothers' is used in Scripture for (1) blood brotherhood or (2) common nationality or (3) blood relationship in a very wide degree or (4) friendship: he expresses the different senses in the words 'natura, gente, cognatione, affectu'.[2] In the case of the Lord's brothers, the third meaning applies: James was his 'relative', and Jerome reminds the reader that Abraham called his nephew Lot his 'brother' (Gen 13:8), and that Laban used the same term of his nephew Jacob (Gen 29:15). The second objection is almost equally obvious: why is Mary the wife of Alphaeus called Mary of Clopas in the gospel according to St John? Jerome admits that he does not know, but reminds his reader that many people in the Bible were known under two names, from Moses' father-in-law (Raguel and Jethro) to the son of Jonah (Simon, Peter and Cephas). Alternatively, he suggests that Clopas may have been the name of her father or her clan.[3] In the end, however, he confesses that he does not know the answer to this question, and adds that he is not going to trail his coat over the issue.[4] He is quite content to allow that Mary of Clopas and Mary the mother of James and Joseph may be different persons, provided that the latter (the mother of James and Joseph) is not identified with the mother of the Lord.[5]

[2] Adversus Helvidium 14 (ML 23.206 C).

[3] '. . . sive a patre sive a gentilitate familiae' (ML 23.206 A).

[4] 'Verum in hac parte contentiosum funem non traho, alia fuerit Maria Cleophae, alia Maria Iacobi et Iosetis, dummodo constet, non eamdem Mariam Iacobi et Iosetis esse, quam matrem Domini' (ML 23.206 D).

[5] Cf. Adversus Helvidium 12–15 (ML 23.204–9).

This is the argument given by Jerome, who started the theory, but as worked out by other writers and as generally stated, it includes two additional particulars which are also of interest.

The two proper names Alphaeus and Clopas are, it is said, alternative ways of transcribing the same Aramaic word *hlpy*: the initial letter of this word, the Aramaic *Heth*, might be omitted in Greek transcription (as in Alphaeus) or replaced by the Greek *Kappa* or *Chi* (hence Clopas or Klopas). This identification would of course considerably strengthen the case in favour of Jerome's view, for it would explain why Mary the wife of Alphaeus is also called Mary of Clopas (Jn 19:25); but it was apparently quite unsuspected by Jerome himself.[6] Lightfoot writes:

'It occurs first, I believe, in Chrysostom, who incidentally speaks of James the Lord's brother as "son of Clopas", and after him in Theodoret who is more explicit (both on Gal 1:19).[7] To a Syrian Greek, who, even if he were unable to read the Peschito version, must at all events have known that Chalphai was the Aramaean rendering or rather the Aramaean original of Ἀλφαῖος, it might not unnaturally occur to graft this identification on the original theory of Jerome.'[8]

And yet another identification unsuspected by Jerome has been added to his theory, namely, that of Judas the apostle with Judas the brother of the Lord. In St Luke's lists of the Twelve, the name 'Judas of James' occurs (Lk 6:16; Ac 1:13); on the assumption that the various lists refer to the same twelve men, this Judas must be identical with the Thaddaeus of Mt 10:3 and Mk 3:18. Now a certain Judas is mentioned as one of the four brothers of the Lord in Mt 13:55 = Mk 6:3, and the writer of the Catholic Epistle styles himself 'the brother of James' (Jude 1). Hence it is suggested that the ellipsis in 'Judas of James' should be supplied by '*brother*' (as in the Authorized Version, etc.) and not by '*son of*', which

[6] See the last paragraph but one, where he simply makes guesses as to why this Mary is called Mary of Clopas.

[7] MG 61.632 (Chrysostom) and MG 82.468 CD (Theodoretus).

[8] *Galatians*, p. 257.

would be more regular (and which is found in the Revised and Revised Standard Versions). Thus Judas the brother of the Lord is also made one of the Twelve, and some authors have even identified Simeon the brother of Jesus with that Simon who is listed among the Twelve.

> 'Now it is remarkable that these three names occur together in St Luke's list of the Twelve: James (the son) of Alphaeus, Simon called Zelotes, and Judas (the brother) of James. In the lists of the other Evangelists too these three persons are kept together, though the order is different and Judas appears under another name, Lebbaeus or Thaddaeus. Can this have been a mere accident? Would the name of a stranger have been inserted by St Luke between two brothers? Is it not therefore highly probable that this Simon also was one of the Lord's brothers? And thus three out of the four are included among the Twelve.'[9]

This interpretation of St Jerome's (together with the identification of Alphaeus and Clopas) has been generally adopted in the Western Church from A.D. 400 until modern times, and in the Roman Catholic Church many think that the doctrine of Mary's perpetual virginity cannot be effectively defended except by this explanation. Yet in all honesty it must be conceded that a large part of this theory has been demolished by Bishop Lightfoot (whom no one can accuse of rationalism or contempt for tradition!); on the other hand (as the next chapter will show) Lightfoot's arguments do not demolish the Hieronymian theory as completely as he claimed.

[9] Lightfoot, *Galatians*, p. 258. He suggests that the first author to include Simon (brother of the Lord and bishop of Jerusalem) among the Twelve was St Isidore of Seville (*De vita et obitu Patrum* 139: ML 83.153 C), but confesses that he does not know exactly when the identification of the two Judas's was made (p. 257).

For a discussion of more modern literature on this topic, see J. Blinzler, *Die Brüder und Schwestern Jesu*, pp. 119–26 ('Die These von der Apostolizität des Jakobus und änderen Herrenbrüder') and pp. 126–9 ('Waren die Apostel Jakobus, Judas und Simon Brüder?'). The last hundred years have added nothing of value to what Lightfoot wrote.

Lightfoot begins by making two very valid points.[10] Before criticizing the theory itself, he seeks to divest it of all fictitious advantage by placing it in its true light. He points out that St Jerome claims no traditional support for his views in the treatise against Helvidius; that indeed he sets aside the appeal to ancient patristic authority in one of those sweeping generalizations of which he is so fond when engaged in polemic;[11] and that in his later writings he regards the interpretation as only his personal opinion.[12] Secondly, Jerome does not even hold his own theory staunchly and consistently. The reference in his works, taken in chronological order, speak for themselves. His main point in the treatise against Helvidius, written when he was still quite a young man, is that Mary remained ever a virgin, and to this his own special solution is quite subordinate. He speaks of himself as 'not caring to fight hard' ('*contentiosum funem non traho*') for the identity of Mary of Clopas with Mary the mother of James and Joseph, though this is the pivot of his theory (according to Lightfoot).[13] (*Aliquando bonus dormitat Homerus!* Here Lightfoot has nodded badly, for if Mary the mother of James and Joseph was the virgin's *sister* [Jn 19:25], but a different person from Mary of Clopas, Jerome's argument would still stand.) It is true, however, that as time advances Jerome holds to the details of his theory less firmly. In his commentary on the Epistle to the Galatians (1:19), written about A.D. 387, he speaks very vaguely. He remembers, he says, having when at Rome written a treatise about the brothers of the Lord with which (such as it is) he ought to be satisfied,[14] but then goes on rather inconsistently:

[10] *Galatians*, pp. 258 ff.

[11] 'Verum nugas terimus, et fonte veritatis omisso opinionum rivulos consectamur' (*Adversus Helvidium* 17: ML 23.211 B).

[12] '. . . ut *nonnulli* existimant, Ioseph ex alia uxore; ut autem *mihi* videtur Mariae sororis matris Domini filius' (*De viris illustr.* 2: ML 23.639 A); 'Quidam fratres Domini de alia uxore Ioseph filios suspicantur . . . Nos autem, sicut in libro quem contra Helvidium scripsimus continetur, fratres Domini non filios Ioseph sed consobrinos Salvatoris Mariae liberos intelligimus materterae Domini . . .' (*In Matt.* Lib. 2, on Mt 12:49: CC 77.100–1 = ML 26.84–5 or 87–8).

[13] *Galatians*, p. 259. Jerome's statement is in ML 23.206 D.

[14] 'Qualiacumque sunt illa quae scripsimus his contenti esse debemus.'

'Suffice it now to say that James was called the Lord's brother on account of his high character, his incomparable faith and extraordinary wisdom: the other Apostles are also called "brothers" (Jn 20:17; *cf.* Ps 22:22), but he pre-eminently so, to whom the Lord at his departure had committed the sons of his mother' (*i.e.* the members of the Church of Jerusalem).[15]

Immediately after this passage Jerome explains at length that the title 'apostle' was by no means restricted to the Twelve. In *De viris illustribus* (A.D. 392) and in his commentary on St Matthew (A.D. 398), he adheres in the main to his earlier opinion set out in the treatise against Helvidius, though now affirming only that the brothers were sons of the Virgin's sister, the Lord's aunt, another Mary: the identification of this woman with Mary of Clopas has disappeared.[16] Similarly in his commentary on Isaiah (A.D. 398) he speaks of the fourteen apostles, 'the Twelve who were chosen, and the thirteenth, James the brother of the Lord, and Paul, the chosen vessel'.[17] Lastly, in a still later essay, the Letter to Hedibia, written about A.D. 406–7, he speaks of Mary of Clopas the maternal aunt of the Lord, and Mary the mother of James and Joseph as two distinct persons 'although *others* contend that the mother of James and Joses was his mother's sister (*matertera*)'.[18] Yet this identification, of which he here writes with such indifference and indeed ascribes to 'others', had once been the keystone of his own theory, and his use of the words 'others' certainly seems to imply that he no longer believed the mother of James and Joses to have been Jesus' aunt on his mother's side.

Lightfoot seems to have proved conclusively that Jerome's interpretation in the *Adversus Helvidium* was a purely personal one without any support in earlier tradition, and that Jerome

[15] Lightfoot's slightly condensed translation (*Galatians*, p. 260): see ML 26.330–1 or 354–5 for this text and the remarks about the meaning of the word 'apostle'.

[16] The texts are given on p. 227, fn. 12.

[17] *In Isaiam*, Lib. 5, on Is 17:7 (CC 73.185 = ML 24.175 or 180). Most of the commentary on Isaiah was written about A.D. 408–10, but the fifth book was already completed in A.D. 398 (see CC 73, p. v).

[18] *Ep.* 120 (ML 22.987–8).

himself eventually abandoned the details of the theory. It can therefore hardly be regarded as a sheet-anchor of doctrine, and Lightfoot himself has argued the case against it most eloquently.

The sense which Jerome gives to the word 'brother' is not satisfactorily supported by biblical usage.

'In an affectionate and earnest appeal to move the sympathies of the hearer, a speaker might not unnaturally address a relation or a friend or even a fellow-countryman as his "brother", and even when speaking of such to a third person he might through warmth of feeling and under certain aspects so designate him. But it is scarcely conceivable that the cousins of any one should be commonly and indeed exclusively styled his "brothers" by indifferent persons; still less, that one cousin in particular should be singled out and described in this loose way, "James the Lord's brother".'[19]

Again, Jerome's theory, when completed,[20] supposes that two or even three of the Lord's brothers are to be counted among the Twelve. This scarcely suits the gospel narrative, where they appear as distinct from the disciples and as not believing in Jesus.

'Only a short time before the crucifixion they are disbelievers in the Lord's divine mission (Jn 7:5). Is it likely that St John would have made this unqualified statement, if it were true of one only or at most of two out of the four? Jerome sees the difficulty and meets it by saying that James was "not one of those that disbelieved".[21] But what if Jude and Simon also belong to the Twelve? After the Lord's Ascension, it is true, His brethren appear in company with the Apostles, and apparently by this time their unbelief has been converted into faith. Yet even on this later occasion, though with the Twelve, they are distinguished from the Twelve; for the latter are

[19] *Ibid.*, p. 261.
[20] As described above on pp. 225–6.
[21] *Adversus Helvidium* 11 and 13 (ML 23.194 A and 195 C).

ST JEROME'S THEORY AS COMPLETED BY OTHERS AND
A SUMMARY OF LIGHTFOOT'S OBJECTIONS

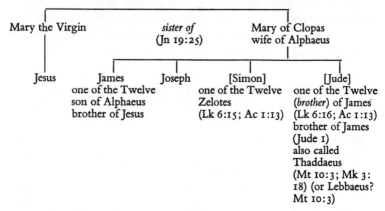

Lightfoot's objections to the above scheme:
1. (a) Does this justify calling them brothers of Jesus?
    (b) If so, why are Simon and Jude not referred to as such in the lists of the Twelve? Why is James singled out?
2. Why are the brothers presented as unbelievers (Jn 7:5) if James (and Simon? and Jude?) belonged to the Twelve? And they are distinguished from the Eleven in Ac 1:14.
3. (a) The title 'apostle' (Gal 1:19) does not prove that James was one of the Twelve.
    (b) Jude seems to disclaim the title (Jude 17).
4. If Mary of Clopas was the mother of these four sons and also sister to the Virgin, it is strange that she is never mentioned as their mother.
5. Jerome assumes that there were only two prominent disciples called James.
6. Why in Lk 6:15–16; Ac 1:13 is Jude alone referred to as (brother) of James, if Simon was also the brother of James?
7. If Lk 6:16; Ac 1:13 should rather be translated Jude 'son of James', then Jude was not the son of Alphaeus.
8. Mt 10:3 Thaddaeus–Lebbaeus; Mk 3:18 Thaddaeus; Jn 14:22 'Jude, not the Iscariot'. Are such designations thinkable if the reference is in fact to 'Jude the brother of the Lord'?
9. The whole scheme assumes that Jn 19:25 refers to three women, not four, and that two sisters were named Mary.

described as assembling in prayer "with the women and Mary the mother of Jesus and [with] His brethren" (Ac 1:14).'[22]

Furthermore, the fact that James appears sometimes to be called an apostle (e.g. in Gal 1:19—though not one of the passages alleged is free from ambiguity) is not decisive, for this title is

[22] Lightfoot, Galatians, pp. 261–2.

by no means confined to the Twelve: Paul was most certainly called an apostle, and Barnabas too (compare Ac 13:2, 3 with 14:4, 14). Again, Jude the author of the Epistle seems to disclaim the title (Jude 17); if so, this is an argument against his having been one of the Twelve.

Moreover, the brothers are mentioned in the gospels in connection with Joseph and Mary the mother of Jesus, but never once in connection with Mary of Clopas, who is assumed to have been the wife of Alphaeus. Surely it would have been otherwise if the latter Mary were really their mother?

Jerome lays great stress on the epithet 'minor' applied to James (Mk 15:40) as if it implied two only.[23] The Greek, however, gives not 'James the Less' but 'James the Little' (ὁ μικρός); is it not most natural to explain this epithet of his height? Hegesippus tells us that 'there were many of the name of James',[24] and the short stature of one of them might well have served as a distinguishing mark. At any rate this explanation is distinctly the more probable.[25]

Moreover, if Jerome's theory be extended to make Jude the brother of the Lord also one of the Twelve and the blood-brother of James the son of Alphaeus, then why, in Luke's lists of the Twelve (Lk 6:16; Ac 1:13) do we read 'James (the son) of Alphaeus, Simon called Zelotes, and Judas (the brother) of James'? It would have been more natural to write 'James and Judas, the sons of Alphaeus', as in the case of the other pairs of brothers. Then again, if Simon Zelotes was not a brother of James, why was he placed by Luke between two brothers? And if he was their brother, why is the designation of brotherhood attached to James alone? The more rational course is to supply the ellipsis in 'Judas of James' by rendering the phrase not 'Judas the

[23] Thus Lightfoot, ibid., p. 262: cf. Adversus Helvidium 13 (ML 23.196 A): 'cum maior et minor non inter tres, sed inter duos soleant praebere distantiam'. But Jerome is here taking up a distinction admitted by Helvidius (ibid. 12: ML 23.195 A) to make a retort.

[24] In the passage cited by Eusebius, H.E. 2:23 (MG 20.197 A).

[25] The argument of this paragraph (from Lightfoot's Galatians, pp. 262–3) is, as the author sees, not all that strong.

brother of James' but 'Judas *the son* of James'. This is the obvious translation; it is supported by two ancient versions (the Syriac Peschitta and the Sahidic), while two others (the Old Latin and the Bohairic) leave the ellipsis unsupplied and thus preserve the ambiguity of the original. Needless to say, if the father of this James was called Alphaeus, and the father of Jude was called James, these two disciples cannot have been blood-brothers.

Again, in the different lists of the Twelve Jude is designated in three different ways (once more we have to assume here that the lists all refer to the same twelve men). In Mt 10:3 he is called Thaddaeus (or Lebbaeus); in Mk 3:18, Thaddaeus; and in Luke 'Jude of James'. St John, when he has occasion to mention him (14:22), distinguishes him by a negative: 'Judas, not the Iscariot'. Is it thinkable that if he had been the Lord's brother, he would never have been so designated, when this title would have forestalled any confusion?

Finally, in order to maintain St Jerome's theory, it is essential, in Jn 19:25, to take the words 'his mother's sister' and 'Mary of Clopas' as being in apposition, and to understand this verse as enumerating three women, not four. But it is at least highly improbable that two sisters should have borne the same name, Mary.[26] Hence it is not unlikely that a sound tradition underlies the Syriac rendering, which inserts a conjunction: 'There stood by the cross of Jesus his mother and his mother's sister, and Mary of Clopas and Mary Magdalen.' Lagrange comments on this text:

> 'After long hesitation,[27] I cast my vote without reservation in favour of four women. If Mary of Clopas was the sister of Jesus' mother, then the same name had been given to two sisters, which is not usual. Furthermore, why such precise nomenclature for this woman? And should not her proper

[26] Lightfoot here remarks: 'The case of the Herodian family is scarcely parallel, for Herod was a family name, and it is unlikely that a humble Jewish household should have copied a practice which must lead to so much confusion' (*Galatians*, p. 264).

[27] Here he is referring to his *Evangile selon s. Marc*, Paris, 1911 (4th ed., 1928), p. 80.

name have preceded the words 'sister of his mother'? Besides, names are often cited in couples, as for example in Matthew's list of the Apostles (10:3 ff.) . . .'.[28]

Lightfoot also points to this arrangement of names in couples in Mt 10:2–4.

It has been shown, then, that Jerome pleaded no traditional authority for his explanation; it was entirely his own idea, and in later life he did not attach too much importance to it, provided that the virginity of Mary was not impugned. It must stand or fall on its own intrinsic merits, and this chapter may conclude with Lightfoot's verdict.

'Though this hypothesis, supplemented as it has been by subsequent writers, presents several striking coincidences which attract attention, yet it involves on the other hand a combination of difficulties—many of them arising out of the very elements in the hypothesis which produce the coincidences—which more than counterbalance the arguments in its favour, and in fact must lead to its rejection, if any hypothesis less burdened with difficulties can be found'.[29]

[28] *Evangile selon s. Jean*, Paris, 1925, p. 493.
[29] *Galatians*, pp. 264–5.

Chapter Nine

THE BROTHERS OF JESUS
(IV): CONCLUSION

IF the interpretations given by Helvidius, Epiphanius and Jerome are all to be rejected, some new explanation of the phrase 'brothers of Jesus' must be found. The biblical evidence in particular must be closely re-examined, for the witness of later writers must always remain subordinate to this. The complete list of New Testament references runs: Mt 12:46–50 = Mk 3:20–1, 31–5 = Lk 8:19–21; Mt 13:55–6 = Mk 6:3; Jn 2:12; 7:3, 5, 10; Ac 1:14; 1 Cor 9:5 and Gal 1:19.

The two texts from St Paul are not very helpful. In 1 Cor 9:5 the 'brothers of the Lord' could be fairly numerous, since they are compared with the apostles as a group, or they could be as few as two, since they are contrasted with Paul and Barnabas (in v. 6). And in Gal 1:19 James is called 'the brother of the Lord' simply to distinguish him from any other James. Neither of these texts, taken by itself, gives any clue about the relationship of these brothers to Jesus. And even if Gal 1:19 is compared with other texts, no conclusion can be drawn. Paul writes that three years after his conversion he visited Jerusalem and stayed with Peter for fifteen days. Then he adds: 'But I did not see any other one of the apostles, except James, the brother of the Lord'—a sentence which can equally well be translated: 'But I did not see any other one of the apostles—*only* James, the brother of the Lord' (Gal 1:19). If the first version correctly represents Paul's thought, then he regarded James as an apostle; if the latter version is correct, he distinguishes James from the apostles. But there is no way of deciding which of the two English translations gives the meaning intended by Paul. Furthermore, even if this matter could be settled, it might not assist the present inquiry, for the title 'apostle' was not restricted to the Twelve. Paul and Barnabas were also called apostles (Ac 14:4, 14), and therefore even if James had a right to the title, this would not prove he was one of the Twelve. Only if it were proved that he was not called an apostle could one conclude that he was not one of the Twelve. But the matter cannot be settled, and therefore nothing can be deduced from the Pauline texts.

Ac 1:14 relates that the Eleven disciples persevered in prayer 'along with the women and Mary the mother of Jesus, and with his brothers'. The Greek text here is uncertain, but if this translation represents the true reading, Mary is grouped with the women and mildly contrasted with the brothers (the preposition 'with' occurs twice): this might be considered strange if the brothers were in fact her sons. On the other hand, it is flimsy evidence for any conclusion, and the better reading of the Greek manuscripts is 'along with the women and Mary the mother of Jesus and his brothers' (omitting the second 'with'). Nothing can be based on this text. This leaves only the two passages in the Synoptics and the references in John.

The Synoptic references are the crucial ones, and in each case the most important text is that of Mark. It will be helpful to set out the first text according to Mark in a slavishly literal translation (Mk 3:20-1, 31-5):

'And he goes into a house; and again a crowd assembles so that they cannot even eat a meal. And when his people (οἱ παρ' αὐτοῦ) heard, they went out to get hold of him, for they were saying that he had lost control of himself.'

[Here Mark inserts the dispute with the scribes from Jerusalem on whether Jesus is in collusion with Satan, vv. 22-30. He then continues the story: Jesus is still talking to the scribes.]

'And his mother goes, and his brothers, and standing outside they sent to him, calling for him. And a crowd was seated around him, and they tell him, "See, thy mother and thy brothers [*some texts add:* and thy sisters] are outside looking for thee". And by way of answer to them he says, "Who is my mother and [my] brothers?" And looking round at those sitting in a circle around him, he says, "See here my mother and my brothers. [For] whoever does the will of God, he is my brother and sister and mother"'.[1]

The second part of this passage (vv. 31-5), that part which is related also by Matthew (12:46-50) and Luke (8:19-21), is a paradigm example of what British scholars call a 'Pronouncement Story'. Vincent Taylor writes:

'These are the short narratives in which everything is subordinated to the desire to give a saying of Jesus which was of interest and importance to the earlier Christian communities . . . It is in the isolating and description of this kind of narrative that Form Criticism has achieved its greatest success'.[2]

In such a passage, the whole pericope leads up to a noteworthy saying or 'Pronouncement' of Jesus which is the very soul of the passage, giving point to the rest of the story and providing the key to its interpretation. Thus when the Pharisees criticize the disciples for plucking ears of corn on the sabbath, the story reaches its climax in Jesus' answer that 'The sabbath was made for man, not man for the sabbath' (Mk 2:23-8). It is the saying of Jesus which provides the point of the story, and in the episode about the brothers there can be no doubt that the climax lies in the final lines: 'Whoever does the will of God, he is my brother and sister and mother' (Mk 3:35).

The saying is undoubtedly metaphorical, but where precisely does the force of the comparison lie? Jesus rounds off the whole episode very neatly by drawing a contrast between his physical

---

[1] The passage is translated from the text given in *The Greek New Testament*, edited by K. Aland and others, London, 1966. The words in square brackets are of doubtful textual validity.

[2] *The Gospel according to St Mark*, p. 78.

mother and brothers who stand outside, and those who are his 'brother and sister and mother' because they do the will of God. It is to be noted, however, that the contrast is not directly between those who stand outside the house, the physical relations, on the one hand, and those inside the house, listening to Jesus, on the other. That this is not the real contrast intended is very clear from the context, for those inside listening to Jesus include the scribes from Jerusalem (Mk 3:22), Pharisees (Mt 12:24) who were positively hostile to his teaching and at that very moment accusing him of collusion with Satan. It is too simple a comment merely to say that the contrast is between those outside and those inside. Jesus is rather contrasting the few entitled to call him son and brother by reason of their blood-relationship with the many who can claim a spiritual relationship because they do the will of God. Matthew brings this point out well when he writes that Jesus *pointed to his disciples* and said, Here are my mother and brothers' (Mt 12:49). The lesson is that *all* who do the will of God can count Jesus as their brother.

The whole story must be interpreted in the light of this pronouncement. The immediate problem is to discern the relationship between Jesus and the brothers mentioned in vv. 31–5. At first reading, it seems self-evident that they were Mary's children, since they are in her company, but this first impression needs to be tested against v. 21. There what is evidently the same group[3] is denoted by the words οἱ παρ' αὐτοῦ, translated above as 'his

[3] M.-E. Boismard, *Synopse des Quatre Evangiles*, vol. 2, Paris, 1972, p. 173, §117, II 2 a, draws attention to the unity of Mk 3:20–35 by pointing to its chiastic structure:

A	Jesus' relatives look for him	3:20–1
B	Accusation: he is possessed by Beelzebul	3:22a
C	Accusation: it is by the Prince of demons . . .	3:22b
D	The saying about Satan	3:24–6
C'	Answer to the second accusation	3:27
B'	Answer to the first accusation	3:28–9
A'	The true relations of Jesus	3:31–5

This scheme is even more attractive if 3:21 means that Jesus' relatives thought he was out of his mind, for the text would then give three accusations, in crescendo, and three replies. But for the meaning of Mk 3:21 see below, p. 238, fn. 9.

people'.[4] Taylor has an excellent note on this phrase[5] which must be reported.

In classical Greek the phrase is used to denote 'envoys' or 'ambassadors'. In the Septuagint, it denotes 'adherents' or 'followers' (1 Mac 9:44;[6] 11:73; 12:27, 28;[7] 13:52; 15:15; 16:16; 2 Mac 11:20), but also 'parents' and other relatives (Prov 31:21, where the Hebrew has 'all her house'; Susanna 33 = Dan 13:33). In the papyri the phrase is used freely to describe 'agents', 'neighbours', 'friends' and 'relatives'.[8] In other words, the Greek phrase chosen by Mark denotes rather vaguely the 'family circle' at Nazareth, and can therefore best be rendered as 'his people'.

Report reached this family circle that Jesus had gone into a house, but that such a crowd had gathered that no one could take a meal. Hearing this, 'his people' set off to rescue Jesus, or at least to persuade him to take more care of himself,[9] and it is the arrival

[4] On p. 235. The colloquialism is intentional.

[5] *The Gospel according to St Mark*, p. 236.

[6] Thus in the Codices Sinaiticus and V, though the Codex Alexandrinus here reads 'to the brothers'.

[7] The Codex Sinaiticus here reads 'fathers'.

[8] For evidence of the usage in the papyri, Taylor (p. 236) refers to F. Field, *Notes on the Translation of the New Testament*, Cambridge, 1899, pp. 25–6; J. H. Moulton and G. Milligan, *Vocabulary of the Greek Testament*, London, 1914–29, pp. 478–9; and to J. H. Moulton, *A Grammar of New Testament Greek*, vol. 1, *Prolegomena*, Edinburgh, 1908, p. 106.

[9] This seems the obvious motive, but it is hard to fix the exact meaning of the final words in Mk 3:21: ἔλεγον γὰρ ὅτι ἐξέστη. Were Jesus' own relatives saying that he had gone out of his mind, or was it that other people were making this charge? The former interpretation seems rather more likely (*cf.* Taylor), but the latter cannot be excluded. And is the version 'He has gone out of his mind' (Vulgate: *in furorem versus est*) too strong, as some think? Or is it permissible, but only as hyperbole? Or does it refer to '*une exaltation mystique*' (Loisy, *Les évangiles synoptiques* 1, p. 698)? Or is it a simple statement that since Jesus' closest relatives did not believe in his mission (*cf.* Jn 7:5), they concluded that he was mad? Fr Henry Wansbrough, O.S.B., of Ampleforth Abbey, makes the radical and novel suggestion that the subject of ἐξέστη is not Jesus, but the crowd: 'they went out to rescue him, for they were saying "It has got out of control!"' (*NTS* 18 [1971–2], pp. 233–5). It seems impossible to decide between the above interpretations, but all of them, including Fr Wansbrough's, appear to make good sense of the phrase.

of this group which is recorded in Mk 3:31: 'his mother and his brothers arrive'. It is natural to wonder why the phrase 'his people' (v. 21) has become 'his mother and brothers' (v. 31). If the brothers were sons of Mary, it is difficult to see why Mark did not write 'his mother and his brothers' in v. 21; it would seem clear that Mark at this point (v. 21) is referring to a wider family circle. All the same, there is a real difficulty in v. 31. Modern Roman Catholics sometimes argue that if the saying which occurs in v. 35 ('Whoever does the will of God, he is my brother and sister and mother') is to have its full literary effect, there needs to be some mention of mother, brothers (and sisters[10]) earlier on. So, they continue, Mark changed the phraseology of v. 21 ('his people') when he came to v. 31, in order to give himself the opening for a Pronouncement Story, writing 'And his mother comes, and his brothers',[11] employing there the term 'brothers' in its wider sense as meaning 'kinsmen'; for he could not use the term 'his people' without wrecking the build-up to the saying in v. 35. This explanation certainly sits well with Roman Catholic doctrine, but to those who have already accepted the Helvidian theory, it will seem strained, if not far-fetched.

The second Synoptic text about the brothers of Jesus occurs in Mt 13:55–6; Mk 6:3. When Jesus began to preach in Nazareth, his fellow-townsmen were astonished and said:

'Is not this the carpenter, the son of Mary and brother of James and Joses and Judas and Simon? And are not his sisters here with us?' (Mk 6:3).[12]

---

[10] In Mk 3:31 only the mother and brothers are mentioned, but in v. 32 some texts insert 'and his sisters'. Is it not likely that this phrase was added in order to secure a gradual transition to the saying about the true 'brother and sister and mother' in v. 35? If so, these interpolators were moved by the motive ascribed above to Mark himself. At the same time, one has a far more impressive climax if there is no mention of sisters until Jesus himself uses the word in v. 35.

[11] The fact that the verb of v. 31 is in the singular ('his mother comes, and his brothers') could be taken as a slight indication that Mary and the brothers are not here considered as one homogeneous group, but separately, if one were to accept the interpretation given in the text above.

[12] On the Greek text of Mk 6:3 see Taylor, *The Gospel according to St Mark*, p. 300, supplemented by J. Blinzler, *Die Brüder und Schwestern Jesu*, pp. 28–30.

Matthew's text (13:55-56) is different in its wording, though its meaning is the same. It reads:

> 'Is not this the carpenter's son? Is not his mother called Mary and his brothers James and Joseph and Simon and Judas? And his sisters, are they not all with us?'

Points to notice are that Matthew, a more Jewish and more Palestinian gospel than Mark, says that 'his mother *is called* Mary, his brothers James and Joseph' etc., when one would more naturally have expected the verb 'to be'; that he employs the form 'Joseph' rather than 'Joses';[13] and that the order of the last two names is not the same as in Mark. Above all, his final remark about '*all* his sisters' is interesting. Jerome observes that 'all' denotes a considerable number—what he in his youthful enthusiasm dubbed

> 'a team of four brothers and a heap of sisters . . . we don't say "all" unless we're talking about a crowd'.[14]

Were these brothers and sisters children of Mary?

It will be observed that in Mark (but not in Matthew) Jesus is described as '*the* son of Mary and brother of James etc.', or as '*the* son of Mary and *a* brother of James etc.', with no definite article before 'James' (only four Greek manuscripts have the article here). On the other hand, Matthew (who does insert the definite article before 'brothers') uses not the verb 'to be', but 'called'. These details may be an indication that Mark wished to draw a distinction between Jesus' relationship to Mary and his relationship to James and the rest, a distinction superfluous in Matthew because of his choice of verb. If so, this casts suspicion on the Helvidian theory.

Apart from Matthew's mention of 'all' Jesus' sisters, and Mark's omission of the definite article before 'brother', a third element in Mark gives ground for thought.

---

[13] For the distinction, see above, p. 201, fn. 4.

[14] '. . . quadrigam fratrum et sororum processisse congeriem . . . omnes, nisi de turba, non dicitur' (*Adversus Helvidium*, ML 23.200).

'Jesus said to them that a prophet is not without honour
except in his own country and *among his kinsmen* and in his
home' (Mk 6:4).

Why does Mark not write 'in his own country and *among his
brothers* and in his home'? Perhaps it was to maintain a crescendo
from 'his own country' through a narrower circle (his kinsmen)
to a still smaller group (his own home). All the same, the choice
of 'kinsmen' in v. 4, coming straight after v. 3, might be an
indication that the brothers just mentioned could also be described as 'kinsmen', *i.e.* not full blood-brothers. Thus this second
Synoptic pericope does not supply clear and irrefutable evidence
for the Helvidian theory; it might even find a more satisfactory
interpretation if that theory were untrue. At all events, a solution
must be sought elsewhere.

Among the women who stood by the cross was Mary the
mother of James and Joseph (Mt 27:56 = Mk 15:40[15]). It has
already been pointed out that, unless there is proof to the contrary, this pair of brothers must be identical with the James and
Joseph mentioned earlier in the same gospels (Mt 13:55; Mk 6:3).[16]
It is possible to retort that the designation 'James the little' in
Mk 15:40 was inserted precisely to guard against this identification; but in that case, why did Matthew not enter a similar *caveat*
when writing 'the mother of James and Joseph'? His readers
would have been equally liable to make the identification. It is
possible to retort also that since in Mt 13:55 and Mk 6:3 James
and Joseph are certainly brothers of Jesus, whereas in Mt 27:56
and Mk 15:40 they are certainly not, no confusion was possible.
Against this, the fact that Matthew on both occasions refers to
'James and Joseph', Mark to 'James and Joses', gives grounds for
suspicion that the evangelists are concerned with only one pair of
brothers. This suspicion is not dispelled when Mt 13:55 continues
'and Simon and Judas', whereas Mk 6:3 reverses the order ('Judas

[15] There are slight variations in the manuscripts which do not affect the
argument. For full details see J. Blinzler, *Die Brüder und Schwestern Jesu*, pp.
82–6.

[16] See p. 205.

and Simon'), with every single manuscript supporting the variation in order. This may be an indication that Simon and Judas
are not full blood-brothers of the first couple (James and Joseph);
and if Simon and Judas, not being full blood-brothers of James
and Joseph, are called brothers of Jesus by the same title as they,
this raises the question whether the James and Joseph of Mt 13:55
and Mk 6:3 are truly blood-brothers of the Lord.

Let us assume as a hypothesis that the James and Joseph named
in Mt 13:55 and Mk 6:3 were not children of the Blessed Virgin,
but of another Mary, a woman so close to Jesus and his mother
that she accompanied them on the last journey to Jerusalem. Her
home was in Galilee, for all three Synoptics record that she was
one of those women who 'when he was in Galilee, followed him
and served him, and went up with him to Jerusalem' (Mk 15:41;
cf. Mt 27:55-6; Lk 23:49, 55 in conjunction with 24:10). She
is that 'other Mary' who on the Friday evening stayed behind after
the funeral, watching with Magdalen beside the sealed tomb
(Mt 27:61; Mk 15:47, where she is called 'Mary (the mother) of
Joses'), and who returned early on the Sunday morning to complete the funeral anointing (Mt 28:1, 'the other 'Mary'; Mk 16:1
and Lk 24:10, 'Mary (the mother) of James'). It remains to be shown
that her children, James and Joses, were for some reason so close
to the Holy Family that they were known as brothers of Jesus.

The three Synoptics agree that the women who followed Jesus
to Calvary 'watched from a distance' (Mt 27:55-6; Mk 15:40-1;
Lk 23:49), but it could hardly have been a very great distance, for
the site of Golgotha is only a few yards west of the wall of
Herodian Jerusalem. Hence there is no incompatibility between
their accounts and that of the Fourth Gospel, which relates that a
little group stood near to the cross just before Jesus died (Jn 19:25).
Those who accept the four accounts as a true record of what
happened will find no difficulty in thinking that the soldiers
might have allowed four or five people, relatives and close friends,
to go close up to the cross when the end was near and inevitable;
there could be no disturbance and no irregularity to fear from
such a group at that late moment. Those who are sceptical about
the value of the gospels as history will even more readily admit

that the group mentioned in the Synoptics must be distinguished from the group mentioned in John. A distinction may be drawn, therefore, between the women who watched from a distance (Mt, Mk, Lk) and the four who were allowed to approach the cross at the end (Jn).

Among the women who watched from afar, Matthew names Mary Magdalen, Mary the mother of James and Joseph, and the mother of the sons of Zebedee (27:56); Mark mentions Mary Magdalen, Mary the mother of James and Joses, and Salome (15:40). Many commentators identify Salome as the mother of the sons of Zebedee, and it is highly likely, but of no interest for the present argument. Luke does not at this point mention any of them by name, but in 24:10 speaks of Mary Magdalen, Joanna, and Mary the mother of James.

The reason that the Synoptics mention these names becomes clear immediately: these women are the witnesses of Jesus' death and burial, and they are the first witnesses of the empty tomb. In Matthew, it is Mary Magdalen and 'the other Mary' who find the tomb empty and hear the message of the angel (28:1–8); in Mark, it is Mary Magdalen, Mary the mother of James, and Salome (16:1). Luke names his witnesses for the first time in 24:10. Matthew and Mark both record that when Jesus was arrested, his disciples abandoned him and fled (Mt 26:56; Mk 14:50). The women, however, who remained faithful to the end, became on the third day the privileged witnesses that Jesus had truly died and had risen again. This is the centre of interest in the Synoptic Gospels.

The point of interest in the Fourth Gospel is rather different. There we read that Mary Magdalen found the tomb empty and went to tell Simon Peter and the disciple whom Jesus loved (Jn 20:2); Magdalen and the beloved disciple had been near the cross, and to this extent the Johannine version coincides with the viewpoint of the Synoptics. But Magdalen apart, the other women mentioned on Calvary are not cited in John as witnesses of the empty tomb, so that John must have had some other motive for recording their names. They are mentioned in a context (Jn 19:25–7) of which one obvious meaning is that Jesus was providing a home for his mother after his departure;[17] and there-fore the tradition here is a tradition concerned with Jesus' family. In that case, it is easy to see why the evangelist records that the mother of Jesus and her sister stood near to Jesus as he was dying; what of Mary of Clopas? Was she perhaps a member of the family too, or was she unrelated, like Mary Magdalen?

A firm distinction has been drawn between the women who watched from a distance (the Synoptics) and those who were near at the end (John). Only Magdalen belongs for certain to both groups. Many writers, because they regard the two groups as much the same, have identified Mary the mother of James and Joses with Mary of Clopas (because both are called Mary). But it is equally reasonable, as a hypothesis, to distinguish the two, for why should Matthew and Mark identify her by her sons, and John by the name of her husband (or father)? If the woman mentioned by John was the mother of James and Joses, it is hard to see why he did not call her such. But if Mary of Clopas was not the mother of James and Joses, a credible table of the relation-ships within the family of Jesus can be formulated.

Suppose that Clopas was (as Hegesippus says)[18] the brother of Joseph; and that Mary the mother of James was Joseph's *sister*.

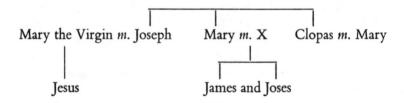

Mary the Virgin *m.* Joseph   Mary *m.* X   Clopas *m.* Mary

Jesus   James and Joses

I suggest that this hypothesis, and this one alone, explains all the references in the gospels; and that it is confirmed by the testimony of early tradition.

'There stood by the cross of Jesus his mother and his mother's *sister-in-law*, Mary of Clopas and Mary Magdalen' (Jn 19:25).

[17] That the text is not purely symbolic is clear from the mention of 'his mother's sister' and 'Mary of Clopas'. Neither of these has any symbolic role in the Fourth Gospel.

[18] Eusebius, *H.E.* 3:32 (MG 20.284 B): see above, p. 215.

This translation of ἀδελφή by 'sister-in-law' is quite defensible.[19] Four women are then referred to, all called Mary; but since four Mary's would be rather a litany, the evangelist has divided them into pairs, giving the first pair anonymously, in their family relationship, and the second pair (unrelated by blood) by name.[20]

If the above scheme is accepted, and Simeon's name added as the child of Clopas, the text of Hegesippus discussed on pp. 213–5 becomes clear:

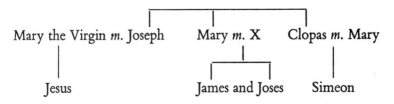

Mary the Virgin *m.* Joseph Mary *m.* X Clopas *m.* Mary

Jesus   James and Joses Simeon

'After the martyrdom of James the Just (*nephew of Joseph and of Clopas*) on the same charge as the Lord, his uncle's child Simeon, the son of Clopas, is next made bishop. He was put forward by everyone, he being yet another cousin of the Lord'.[21]

Lightfoot thought the word θεῖος was restricted to the paternal uncle, but it can also mean a mother's brother,[22] and this is the

[19] The suggestion is made by K. Endemann, 'Zur Frage über die Brüder des Herrn', in the *Neue kirchliche Zeitschrift* 11 (1900), pp. 833–65 (defending the Reformation tradition against Zahn's essay: see above, p. 210, fn. 6). I have not been able to consult Endemann, nor have I been able to find specific and non-poetic texts in which ἀδελφή certainly denotes a sister-in-law, but everyone admits that the word can denote a family relationship wider than that of consanguinity. By her marriage with Joseph, the Virgin would have become the 'sister' of the mother of James.

[20] For full details of the various views on 'his mother's sister' see J. Blinzler, *Die Brüder und Schwestern Jesu*, pp. 111–18.

[21] Alternatively, one could translate: 'After the martyrdom of James the Just on the same charge as the Lord, once again his (*i.e. Jesus'*) uncle's child, Simeon the son of Clopas is made bishop', and so defend the table given on p. 214. This seems less probable, for there would then be no need to repeat in the next sentence that he too was a cousin of the Lord.

[22] See Liddell and Scott, *A Greek–English Lexicon, s.v.*

meaning taken in the above translation. James the Just is then legally[23] the first cousin of Jesus, and Simeon yet another first cousin.

If James was the first cousin of Jesus, why in Mk 6:3 is he called his brother? Most Roman Catholics are content with Jerome's explanation (which stands independently of Jerome's ideas about the exact relationships) that the word 'brother' here means 'a close relative'. Honesty compels us to admit that this 'interpretation' of the term 'brother' at Mk 6:3 stretches its meaning to breaking point, and one cannot seriously expect those unconvinced of the perpetual virginity of Mary to accept it. There is, however, one meaning of 'brother' not explicitly alluded to by Jerome in his *'natura, gente, cognatione, affectu'*[24] which gives a very normal sense to the word, and yet permits one to think that James was in fact a first cousin: namely, 'foster-brother'. Lightfoot mentions a nineteenth-century German scholar who suggested that Joseph undertook the charge of his brother Clopas' children after their father's death;[25] if so, the presence of Simon among Jesus' brothers (Mk 6:3) would be explained. But on the genealogical table given above, it would have been the children of Mary, Joseph's sister, who were brought up in the same household as Jesus (with or without Simon and Judas). If Joseph's brother-in-law had died, and James and Joses had been brought up with Jesus, then it is reasonable to think that they would have called each other brothers, and that the people of Nazareth would have talked about them as brothers. And this is all that the gospel text (Mk 6:3) says.

There is, I think, evidence to support this view both in the gospels and in early Christian writings. Twice in Matthew we read the words 'the other Mary' (Mt 27:61; 28:1). She is so designated to distinguish her from Mary Magdalen (*ibid.*), and has already been introduced unmistakably as 'the mother of James and Joseph' (Mt 27:56). But could it be that she was called 'the other

---

[23] Though not, of course, in the strict sense, by blood, because of the virginal conception of Jesus.

[24] See above, p. 224.

[25] *Galatians*, p. 254. The reference is to an article by a certain Lange in Herzog's *Real-Encyclopädie* ('Jakobus im N.T.') which I have not been able to consult.

Mary' to distinguish her not primarily from Magdalen, but from the mother of Jesus? The term occurs only in Matthew, and Palestinian Christians might have referred to her thus to avoid confusion when speaking of the family of Joseph.

Again, why does Mark talk about 'James the little' and 'Joses' (not Joseph)? Could the reference to 'James the little' not refer to his age (as well as to his stature)? And might not the diminutive form Joses (in Aramaic José) have been a convenient and familiar way of distinguishing within the home between the virgin's husband, Joseph, and the little nephew he had adopted?[26] Joseph's sister might well have called one of her children after his uncle.

The Pronouncement Story in Mk 3:20–1, 31–5 is well explained by this hypothesis. Mark speaks first, with perfect accuracy, of 'his people' ($o\hat{\iota}$ $\pi\alpha\rho$' $\alpha\dot{\upsilon}\tau o\hat{\upsilon}$), and introduces the more forceful phrase 'his mother and brothers' only in v. 31 as he moves towards the climax of v. 35.[27] If those who accompanied Mary were foster-brothers, but living in the same house, it is very reasonable to describe them as 'his people'; and it is not surprising to read that at this period of the public life they had not come to believe in Jesus. It is very likely that they would not at this time have been admitted by Mary and Joseph to the secret of the mystery of Jesus' birth, and this would explain why they said, 'He is out of his mind' (or 'He is beside himself', Mk 3:21).[28] (Perhaps one ought to mention also that there is nothing in the text to indicate that Mary shared this unbelief.)

The peculiarities of the second Synoptic text about the brothers are also accounted for, if the brothers were foster-brothers: '*the* son of Mary, and *a* brother of James etc.' in Mk 6:3, the refer-

---

[26] That this is not a wholly fanciful argument may be seen from a charming note by J. Blinzler about his own family (*Die Brüder und Schwestern Jesu*, pp. 116–17, fn. 20). Of his mother's seven sisters, two were called Mary and two Margaret: in each case the younger one was known by a diminutive form. Of his father's five brothers, two were baptized John: the elder was known as Johann, the younger (naturally) as Hans. For it was the custom in Franconia always to give the child the name of its god-parent.

[27] See above, pp. 238–9.

[28] See above, p. 238, fn. 9.

ence to kinsmen, not brothers, in Mk 6:4, and Matthew's use of the verb 'called' in 13:55. Indeed, we can now see that the common translation of Mt 13:55 is absurd. To write 'Is not his mother called Mary?' is pointless in the context, for there was never any dispute about his mother's name. The question is rather (Mt 13:54): 'Where did this man acquire this wisdom and these mighty works?' Vv. 55–6 continue the thread of the same argument: 'Is not this the son of the carpenter? Is not Mary *said to be* his mother, James and Joseph and Simon and Judas his brothers? And his sisters, are they not all here around us? Whence then did he acquire all this?' Matthew is here writing apologetic, heaping up objections voiced against the idea that Jesus was the Messiah; and to formulate the charge that Jesus was nobody exceptional, he points to a very ordinary mother and father, and wants as many brothers (and sisters—Jerome's *sororum congeries*)[29] as he can find. This is the purpose of the pericope, as also in Mark, and therefore one can see why Mark has the order 'Judas and Simon' (6:3) while Matthew has 'Simon and Judas'. They were not blood-brothers to James and Joses, or to each other, and there was no customary order for citing their names. Indeed, it could well be that Simon and Judas were far younger than Jesus, and never lived in the same house as he. But they were just as much relatives by blood as James and Joses, and in the context of apologetic, especially when Simon was bishop in Jerusalem (say, from A.D. 60 onwards), well worth mentioning as proof that Jesus was nobody all that extraordinary.[30]

Jn 2:12 reads: 'He went down to Capernaum, he and his mother and his brothers and disciples'. Nothing can be deduced from this text, but it provides no obstacle against the theory of foster-brothers. One may recall, however, that in Jn 2:11 'his disciples believed in him': no such remark is made about the brothers. Indeed, in Jn 7:3–10 the evangelist affirms that 'even his

---

[29] See above, p. 240, fn. 14.

[30] One may compare here the story told by Hegesippus (Eusebius, *H.E.* 3:20: MG 20.253) about the relatives of Judas, 'members of the Lord's family', who in the reign of Domitian (A.D. 81–95) were just ordinary hard-working peasants, as they proved by the callouses on their hands.

brothers used not to believe in him' (v. 5). No indication is given of the precise relationship between these men and Jesus, but it is easy to ascribe non-belief to them if they were not sons of Mary and Joseph, and were all too familiar with Jesus.[31]

Immediately after the Ascension, however, the brothers form part of the primitive Christian community 'along with the women and Mary the mother of Jesus' (Ac 1:14). Since no women are mentioned in Acts before this verse, Luke must be referring to those who watched the crucifixion (Lk 23:49), assisted at the burial (23:55), and witnessed the empty tomb (24:10), among whom he names 'Mary the mother of James' (24:10). How did it come about that those brothers who six months previously did not believe in him (Jn 7:2-10) were so soon after the Resurrection counted as honoured members of the Church in Jerusalem, as Ac 1:14 implies? The crucifixion and death of Jesus would, one might think, have confirmed them in their unbelief.

An incidental statement of St Paul explains all: 'Then he appeared to James' (1 Cor 15:7). At the time St Paul wrote, there was but one person eminent enough in the Church to be called James without any distinguishing epithet: the brother of the Lord who was bishop of Jerusalem.[32] This is confirmed by *The Gospel according to the Hebrews*, which seems to have preserved more than one true tradition, and which expressly relates the appearance of the Lord to his brother James after the Resurrection. It too introduces him simply as 'James' without further detail, yet later makes clear that he is the brother of Jesus who was bishop of Jerusalem.[33] It was the appearance of Jesus to James which brought the brothers from belief to unbelief, as the total mystery of Jesus was unfolded to them.

If these brothers were somewhat younger than Jesus, it is understandable that they should have been slow to comprehend his

---

[31] Compare the comment on Mk 3:21, given on p. 247.

[32] See Detached Note VII: The Name 'James' in the New Testament.

[33] The above two paragraphs are condensed from Lightfoot, *Galatians*, pp. 265-6. The passage from *The Gospel to the Hebrews* is preserved by Jerome in *De viris illustribus* 2 (ML 23.642-3). It is translated in *New Testament Apocrypha I*, p. 165, with an informative introduction by P. Vielhauer on pp. 158 ff.

person and his mission; that they should at one time have thought he was neglecting himself unduly in order to preach the word (Mk 3:21); and that at another time they should have been eager for him to display his power in Judaea in order to attract proper attention (Jn 7:3-4), even though 'they did not believe' in his real (i.e. his religious) mission. Lagrange comments on this episode:

'Nothing indicates that the brothers were in bad faith, and were trying to trap Jesus so that he might fall into the hands of the Jews. Assuredly, they judged him according to their own ideas; they thought he had ambition, a love of glory, but lacked the necessary boldness; they wanted him to take a chance, and were apparently decided to take the risk together with him, for after all they invited him to go with them. They still had the attitude of the crowd after the multiplication of the loaves (Jn 6:14 f.), but did not want to assume the main responsibility. All that, however, is not faith in the sense in which it is understood by John. Even they, although relatives, and therefore daily witnesses, did not believe that Jesus was the envoy of God, and that it was therefore necessary to have complete confidence in his behaviour, and to be, like him, firmly committed to doing the will of God'.[34]

Even so, such an attitude is not actively hostile to the light. Further evidence that the brothers were perhaps younger than Jesus is found in extra-biblical sources;[35] and their youthfulness

[34] *Evangile selon s. Jean*, Paris, 1925, p. 199.

[35] According to Josephus (*Ant.* XX, ix, 1 = §200), James was martyred by the Jews when a certain Albinus was procurator in Judaea. A Christian tradition relates that he was thrown down from the pinnacle of the Temple, in the seventh year of Nero, *i.e.* A.D. 60 (Clement of Alexandria, cited in Jerome, *De viris illustr.* 2: ML 23:642; Eusebius, *H.E.* 2:1: MG 20.133 ff., 195 ff.).

Hegesippus says that James was succeeded by Simeon, the son of Clopas, who was martyred under Trajan (*i.e.* between 98 and 117) at the age of 120 years (Eusebius, *H.E.* 3:32: MG 20:281-4): his death is sometimes placed in A.D. 107. Even though the age ascribed to him at death is absurdly high, the statement about Trajan's reign would indicate that he was distinctly younger than James.

would account not only for their 'unbelief', but also for the fact that they lived at home in Nazareth (Mt 13:55–6; Mk 6:3).

If Mary the mother of James was a sister of Joseph and Clopas, the evidence of the second and third century writings becomes much easier to understand.

Two apocryphal works of the second century, cited by Origen, were referred to above, *The Gospel of Peter* and *The Protevangelium of James.*[36] Their assertion that the brothers of Jesus were sons of Joseph by a first marriage can be dismissed, for the author of the *Protevangelium* betrays an alarming ignorance of Palestinian geography and Jewish custom.[37] But perhaps there lies behind these works a lingering memory that the 'brothers' were *known as* children of Joseph. Alone, this suggestion is worthless, but if it harmonizes with other evidence, it may not be groundless.

It has already been shown that the testimony of Hegesippus harmonizes to perfection with the theory that James was the son of Joseph's sister, and that Simeon was cousin both to Jesus and to James.[38] But Hegesippus also mentions Jude 'who was called his brother *according to the flesh*', a phrase which both in Eusebius and in other early Christian writers stresses that the relationship is a true relationship of blood, not a purely spiritual relationship ('brothers according to the spirit');[39] yet Hegesippus also says '*called*', not simply '*was* his brother according to the flesh'. This is surely an indication that though there was a family relationship between Jude and Jesus, they were not full blood-brothers.[40]

Two other works may be mentioned along with the second century writings: *The Clementine Homilies* and *The Clementine Recognitions*. They are works pseudonymously attributed to Clement, bishop of Rome, and tell of St Peter's travels and missionary work. There is considerable dispute about the date of their composition (many ascribe both to the fourth century), but there

---

[36] See pp. 211–2.   [37] *Ibid.*   [38] Pp. 244–6.

[39] See J. Blinzler, *Die Brüder und Schwestern Jesu*, pp. 108–11: 'Verwandte "dem Fleische nach"'. The references to Eusebius are *H.E.* 1:7 and 3:11 (MG 20.93 C and 245 B); *cf.* also Rom 9:3; 4:1; 1 Cor 10:18.

[40] The text of Hegesippus on Jude occurs in Eusebius, *H.E.* 3:20 (MG 20.252–3): see above, p. 215.

is a measure of agreement among scholars that both are based on an Ebionite text which was current by the end of the second century.[41] In the *Homilies* we read that James the bishop of Jerusalem was '*called* the brother of the Lord' (ὁ λεχθεὶς ἀδελφὸς τοῦ κυρίου, 11:35).[42] This is a turn of phrase which occurs more than once in second and third century writings: James was *called* the brother of the Lord, while, outside Origen and the apocryphal gospels,[43] there is not a single example of a plain statement that he *was* the brother of the Lord or that he *was* the son of Mary or of Joseph.

A text from Clement of Alexandria caused difficulty earlier.[44] 'Jude, who wrote the Catholic Epistle, being a brother of the sons of Joseph (*frater filiorum Joseph exstans*), a man of deep piety, though he was aware of his relationship to the Lord, nevertheless did not say he was his brother; what did he say? *Jude the servant of Jesus Christ*, because he was his Lord, but *brother of James*; for this is true—he was his brother, being Joseph's (*frater erat eius, Joseph*)'.[45]

The passage becomes clear if one posits that Jude, like James, was a relative, but not a blood-brother, of the Lord. This would explain why Clement does not call him 'a son of Joseph', but uses the extraordinary circumlocution 'a brother of the sons of Joseph' (*i.e.* a relative of James and Joses); why Jude calls himself 'the servant of Jesus Christ, because he was his Lord, but brother of James'; why Clement adds that Jude was truly the brother of James (not because both were born of the same parents but) because he was (in some way we do not know) related to Joseph. Clement's obscure text remains obscure if he is thought to have

---

[41] *Cf.* B. Altaner, *Patrology*, Edinburgh–London, 1960, pp. 104–5. The Ebionites were a Jewish–Christian sect who recognized Jesus as Messiah, but not as divine.

[42] MG 2.301 A.

[43] See above, pp. 211–2 and 218.

[44] Pp. 211–2.

[45] The Latin is untranslatable unless something be supplied: but there is no problem in presupposing that the original Greek read ὢν τοῦ ᾽Ιωσήφ, or (better still) ὄντος τοῦ ᾽Ιωσήφ (meaning 'Jude was *James*' brother, and James [was the son] of Joseph').

held the Epiphanian theory; but if he regarded James as the cousin and foster-brother of Jesus, and Jude as a relative of both Jesus and James, obscurity gives place to light.

Origen may be passed over, for his statement that the brothers were sons of Joseph by a first wife clearly originates from the apocryphal gospels, and he does not stand firmly by it.[46] But Eusebius of Caesarea is worth noticing.

> 'James *was referred to* as the Lord's brother, for he too (*i.e.* James) *was called* Joseph's boy, and Joseph, to whom the virgin was betrothed, was the father of Christ'.[47]

Once again the hypothesis of foster-brothers explains why Eusebius says that James 'was referred to' as the Lord's brother (not, 'he was'), and that he 'was called' (not 'was') Joseph's boy. Neither James nor Jesus was in fact Joseph's offspring, but both were called such.

Eusebius is the last writer worth considering as a reliable witness of early Palestinian traditions. St Hilary and Ambrosiaster, like Epiphanius after them, undoubtedly thought the brothers were sons of Joseph by a previous marriage, but neither Hilary nor Ambrosiaster was a historian, and Epiphanius must have possessed one of the most gullible minds in the early Church. Their evidence may be discounted, but enough has been said to show that the hypothesis of foster-brothers is by no means absurd.

St Jerome's theory as expounded in the *Adversus Helvidium* cannot stand. Its presentation of the relationships within the Lord's family has been demolished by Lightfoot,[48] and in any case Jerome himself abandoned this theory in the end.[49] But even the second strand of his theory (namely, that in the Bible the word 'brothers' means 'cousins') is to be rejected. It is often said, in support of this theory, that neither Hebrew nor Aramaic has a special word to denote a 'first cousin'; but they do have a word for 'uncle' (*dodh*: Lev 10:4; Num 34:11 etc.) and for 'aunt'

---

[46] See above, pp. 217–8 and 220–1.

[47] *H.E.* 2:1 (MG 20.133–6). The Greek is given above on p. 218.

[48] See pp. 227–33.   [49] See pp. 227–8.

(*dodhah*: Ex 6:20; Lev 20:20), so that a word for 'cousin' is not needed, for it is always possible to talk about 'my uncle's son' or 'the daughter of my aunt'. Moreover, the gospels were written not in Hebrew or Aramaic, but in Hellenistic Greek, which has the very precise word ἀνεψιός (in the New Testament, only in Col 4:10) and the three rather general words συγγένεια, συγγενής and συγγενίς. It was not for lack of a wider vocabulary that the evangelists wrote about the 'brothers' of Jesus.

In the New Testament, the term 'brothers' does not mean 'cousins'. It *means* 'brothers'. But that is not to say that it *denotes* blood-brothers; it can denote first cousins who were known as brothers; who ever refers to his foster-brother (outside a legal context) as anything but his 'brother'? These 'brothers' were, as this chapter has shown, the first cousins of Jesus on his father's side, and not (as the *Adversus Helvidium* suggested) on his mother's.

Thus the hard core of St Jerome's theory stands, and with it the Roman Catholic and Orthodox dogma (or, to those who prefer it, the ancient Lutheran and Calvinist tradition) of the perpetual virginity of Mary the mother of Jesus.[50]

[50] Here I cannot resist the temptation to add a Detached Note (VIII) on 'A Much Needed Reform in the Liturgical Calendar of the Latin Church' (p. 455).

Chapter Ten

'HE WAS BORN OF GOD'

(Jn 1:13)

ONE of the commonest arguments against the virginal conception of Jesus is that neither St Paul nor St John ever refers to it. The evidence of the Pauline epistles will be considered in the next chapter,[1] but the alleged silence of John raises a more serious difficulty. He, after all, wrote a gospel, in which one might reasonably expect to find some mention of the virginal conception, if its author was aware of the doctrine; yet even so cautious a scholar as Professor Dodd can affirm that John does not betray 'any knowledge of, or interest in, the doctrine of the virgin birth of Christ, as it meets us in the First and Third Gospels and in Ignatius'.[2] The contention of this chapter is that John's silence is not absolute, and that the Fourth Gospel makes a clear allusion to the virginal conception of Jesus at 1:13.[3]

The Greek text of Jn 1:11–14 may be translated as follows:

11*a* He came to what was his own,
   b   and his own people did not accept him.

---

[1] Pp. 273–6.

[2] *The Interpretation of the Fourth Gospel*, p. 260. To be fair, Dodd adds in a footnote that 'it is possible that the evangelist was acquainted with the tradition of the miraculous birth, but regarded it as an esoteric mystery which he would not divulge'.

[3] All previous studies on this text have been eclipsed by that of J. Galot, *Etre né de Dieu* (*Jean 1:13*) (=Analecta Biblica 37), Rome, 1969, but the articles by F.-M. Braun and A. Houssiau (cited in the Bibliography) are still worth consulting.

12a But to as many as did accept him
  b   he gave the power to become children of God,
  c   to those who believe in his name;
13a who were born not of blood-streams,
  b   nor of the will of flesh,
  c   nor of the will of a husband [*lit.* 'of a male'],
  d   but of God.
14a And the Word became flesh,
  b   and encamped among us . . .

There is, however, a variant reading in v. 13, with the verb in the singular, not the plural, and this would give the meaning:

12a But to as many as did accept him
  b   he gave the power to become children of God,
  c   to those who believe in the name of him
13a who was born not of blood-streams,
  b   nor of the will of flesh,
  c   nor of the will of a husband,
  d   but of God.
14a And the Word became flesh . . .

If this second reading is the true one, then Jn 1:13 contains a fourfold affirmation of the virginal conception of Jesus, and in the very clearest terms. This alone justifies a thorough discussion of the evidence for and against the variant reading.

The controversy over this text dates back to Tertullian, and Pierre Sabatier two hundred years ago gave an admirable *status quaestionis* in his great work.[4] The majority of scholars in modern times, and all translations, I think, except the Jerusalem Bible, prefer the accepted reading with the verb in the plural, but an imposing group of twentieth-century writers (including more Protestants than Catholics) have pronounced themselves in favour of the singular: *qui non ex sanguinibus . . . sed ex Deo natus*

---

[4] *Bibliorum sacrorum latinae versiones antiquae seu Vetus Italica*, vol. 3, Rheims, 1749, pp. 388–9.

est.[5] Those who defend the received text with the plural (*'qu nati sunt'*) do so because the manuscript evidence in its favour is overwhelming, and because they think it harmonizes well with the general theme of the Fourth Gospel. Those who defend the singular and see in Jn 1:13 a witness to the virginal conception argue that there is sufficient patristic evidence to outweigh the unanimous testimony of the Greek manuscripts, and that the construction with the singular fits to perfection the immediate context of the prologue.

All the Greek manuscripts of the gospel without exception have the verb in the plural: ἐγεννήθησαν or ἐγενήθησαν. In addition, all the ancient versions (with the exception of some witnesses of the Old Latin and Old Syriac versions: see below) give the plural. And the majority of Christian writers, at least after A.D. 300, read the text with the verb in the plural.[6]

In fact, the main manuscript evidence in favour of the singular rests on two Latin codices which read *qui ex deo natus est.* There is in the Chapter Library at Verona one of the finest, if not the finest, manuscript of the Old Latin text of the gospels, the Codex Veronensis: it was copied in letters of silver on purple at some time in the fifth century, before Jerome's revision of the gospels was in wide circulation. This manuscript (known as *b*) has *ex deo natus est.* Most of the other Latin manuscripts which contain the gospel in a pre-Vulgate version cannot be taken into account.

[5] Galot, *Etre né de Dieu*, pp. 5–6, lists as supporters of the singular (with precise references): A. Resch, F. Blass, A. Loisy, A. von Harnack (with qualifications), Th. Zahn, R. Seeberg, C. F. Burney, F. Büchsel, M.-E. Boismard, F.-M. Braun, J. Dupont, D. Mollat, etc. But nearly all modern commentators on the gospel prefer the reading with the plural (Galot, p. 6, fn. 18, cites as examples C. K. Barrett, R. H. Lightfoot, A. Wikenhauser, R. Schnackenburg and R. E. Brown).

[6] Galot, *Etre né de Dieu*, gives a thorough survey, with full references, of the patristic evidence both Greek (pp. 50–63) and Latin (pp. 64–79). In favour of the plural he cites Clement of Alexandria (allusions), Origen (who is explicit), and then Eusebius of Caesarea, Athanasius, Pseudo-Athanasius, Epiphanius, John Chrysostom, Cyril of Alexandria and Procopius of Gaza; and among Latin writers, Cyprian, Eusebius of Vercelli, Hilary, Optatus, Ambrosiaster, Tyconius, Jerome and Sulpicius Severus. Ambrose and Augustine seem to have been acquainted with both readings, singular and plural.

Some, like the Codex Bobiensis (*k*), dating from the fourth or fifth century, and the Codex Bezae (*d*), dating from the fifth or sixth century, lack the leaf, or part of the leaf, containing this verse. Others are of so late a date that the possibility of their having been influenced by the plural *nati sunt* in Jerome's Vulgate cannot be excluded.

The only other manuscript which contains the reading *ex deo natus est* is an eleventh-century lectionary from the Church of Toledo now in the Bibliothèque Nationale in Paris (Nov. acq. lat. 2171).[7] So late a manuscript from the south of Spain may seem worthless as a witness to the text of the Old Latin Bible, but this particular lectionary often differs from the Vulgate on which it is based, and its reading at Jn 1:13 may well represent a traditional text dating back to St Hildefonsus, bishop of Toledo from 657 to 667. Jerome's Vulgate made its way into liturgical use only slowly, and everyone knows from experience that to alter a familiar and well-loved text in the liturgy is the surest way to provoke an ecclesiastical storm: perhaps, then, the lectionary of Toledo retained *ex deo natus est* because that was the reading the faithful were used to before Jerome's Vulgate was adopted in their church. These two witnesses, the Codex Veronensis and the lectionary of Toledo, at least raise the question whether the Old Latin version did not read *ex deo natus est*.

There is some evidence too that the Old Syriac version which preceded the Peshitta[8] may have had the singular ('he was born of God'). Of the two manuscripts containing the Old Syriac Gospels, one (the Syro-Sinaitic) has the plural and the other (the Curetonian) has the singular. However, even in the Curetonian text the antecedent relative pronoun stands in the plural, so that

[7] It has been edited by D. G. Morin, O.S.B. in the *Anecdota Maredsolana* under the title *Liber Comicus, sive Lectionarius Missae quo Toletana Ecclesia ante annos mille et ducentos utebatur*, Maredsous, 1893.

[8] 'Peshitta' means literally the 'Simple (Edition)' (cf. our '*editio vulgata*' or 'Authorized Version') which was in general use in the ancient Syriac Church from the fifth century onwards. Its translation of the New Testament was probably made about the beginning of the fifth century. Before this there was an Old Syriac version in use. For further detail see F. Kenyon, *Our Bible and the Ancient Manuscripts*, 5th (revised) ed., London, 1958, pp. 229–31.

the literal translation would be 'those who . . . was born of God'. More curious still is the fact that this grammatical howler recurs in half a dozen manuscripts of the Peshitta, dating from the fifth to the tenth century. On the basis of this evidence, strenuous efforts have been made to prove that the original Syriac reading was in the singular[9]; but since Tatian's Diatessaron, composed in Syriac around A.D. 175–80, has, in all its many versions, the plural, it would seem incontrovertible that Tatian, in his copy of John's Gospel, read the plural. The simplest explanation of the Curetonian text would seem to be that the final *waw* at the end of the verb for 'born' (*'ethiledu*), which would make the verb plural, has fallen out by haplography because the next verse began with the same letter ('And the Word became flesh', *umeltha'*). Indeed, Lagrange remarks that such plural terminations are often omitted by Syriac scribes in any case.[10]

More important is the evidence that the anonymous author of an apocryphal work called the *Epistula XI Apostolorum* had almost certainly read the singular in his text of St John. In a kind of profession of faith ascribed to the Eleven after the Resurrection he writes:

'We believe that he, the Lord, son of the Lord, is *the Word who became flesh*, of the holy Virgin Mary, that he was carried in her womb, conceived of the Holy Spirit, that it was *not by lust of the flesh but by the will of the Lord that he was begotten* . . .'.[11]

The reference to Jn 1:13 is evident. The place of origin of this work is debated—Egypt, Palestine, Syria and Asia Minor have all been suggested; the date of its composition is also uncertain,

[9] Particularly by Th. Zahn, *Das Evangelium des Johannes*, 6th ed., Leipzig, 1921, pp. 713–14, and by F.-M. Braun, 'Qui ex Deo natus est', in *Aux sources de la tradition chrétienne* (= Mélanges Maurice Goguel), Neuchâtel, 1950, p. 14.

[10] *Evangile selon s. Jean*, Paris, 1925, p. 18.

[11] The text has survived only in a Coptic and an Ethiopic version (and in two Latin fragments), but this passage is extant only in Ethiopic. The quotation above is taken from the French translation of the Ethiopic text published by L. Guerrier in the *Patrologia Orientalis* 9, fasc. 3, p. 190.

though everyone agrees that it was at the outside between A.D. 140 and 210. The conclusion therefore is that its author had, at this time, read in his gospel of John the text equivalent to *qui ex deo natus est*, in the singular; and if no Syriac translation existed before he wrote,[12] then he must have found this reading in a Greek manuscript.[13] So the question is this: what was the reading of the Greek text of Jn 1:13 in the second century, before the great uncials were written? The only way to answer this question is to examine the citations in the early Christian writers.

This is not the place to discuss all the various patristic texts which cite or presuppose one reading or the other,[14] but some particularly significant authorities must be quoted, of whom Tertullian is the most important because of his unequivocal support for the reading *natus est*. He writes in *De carne Christi* 19, 1:

'What is the meaning of the text "*He was born not of blood, nor of the will of the flesh, nor of the will of a husband, but of God*"? Before I deal with this text, it will be advisable to prove wrong those who falsify it. For they contend that the text reads: "They were born not of blood, nor of the will of flesh or of man, but of God", as though it referred to those mentioned previously as believing in his name'.[15]

Later, in chapter 24,2 of the same work Tertullian says of the evangelist:

---

[12] The *Epistula XI Apostolorum* cannot have been based on Tatian's Diatessaron (written before A.D. 180) because the order of events is not the same in the two works.

[13] The case is well argued by F. M. Braun, 'Qui ex Deo natus est', pp. 14–16.

[14] Full details can be found in the studies of Boismard and Houssiau cited in the Bibliography, or in Galot, *Etre né de Dieu*, pp. 12–94.

[15] 'Quid est ergo *non ex sanguine neque ex voluntate carnis neque ex voluntate viri, sed ex deo natus est?* Hoc quidem capitulo ego potius utar, cum adulteratores eius obduxero. Sic enim scriptum esse contendunt: "Non ex sanguine nec ex carnis voluntate nec ex viri, sed ex deo nati sunt", quasi supra dictos credentes in nomine eius designet' (*CC* 2.907 = ML 2.784 B).

'He replies to Ebion that *he was born not of blood nor of the will of flesh or of man, but of God*'.[16]

Without going into the details of Tertullian's argument, we may simply note that he regards the plural reading as nonsensical, since all those who believe in the name of Christ are in fact born of blood and of the will of the flesh and of man, *i.e.* through sexual intercourse; and therefore, he asserts, the reference must be to the virginal conception of Christ's human body.[17] He certainly regarded the reading in the singular as the true one, and though he may have been wrong in suggesting that the plural was of Valentinian origin, one must reckon with the fact that he was acquainted with Rome as well as North Africa; one cannot therefore exclude the possibility that around the year 200 *qui ex deo natus est* was a reading known in the Western Empire.

Four or five passages from the Latin parts of St Irenaeus' *Adversus Haereses* can be cited in support of the reading *natus est*. All of them are rather free citations of Scripture, but it seems reasonably certain that Irenaeus did read the singular.[18] On the

[16] 'Et *non ex sanguine neque ex carnis aut viri voluntate, sed ex deo natus est* Hebion respondit' (*CC* 2.915-16 = ML 2.791 A).

[17] 'Quomodo autem ita erit, cum omnes, qui credunt in nomine eius, pro communi lege generis humani ex sanguine et ex carnis et ex viri voluntate nascantur, etiam Valentinus ipse?... Intellegimus igitur ex concubitu nativitatem domini negatam...' (*De carne Christi* 19, 2 and 4: *CC* 2:907-8 = ML 2.784-5).

[18] The texts are: (1) 'non enim ex voluntate carnis, neque ex voluntate viri, sed ex voluntate Dei, Verbum caro factum est' (*Adv. Haer.* III, 17, 1 = in Harvey's edition, Cambridge, 1857, vol. 2, p. 83, lines 25-6, or in Migne III, 16, 2 = MG 7.921-2); (2) 'cognoscit autem illum, is cui Pater qui est in caelis revelavit ut intelligat, quoniam is qui non ex voluntate carnis, neque ex voluntate viri natus est, filius hominis, hic est Christus Filius Dei vivi' (III, 20, 2 = Harvey, vol. 2, p. 103, lines 25-8; Migne III, 19, 2 = MG 7.940 A); (3) perhaps also the text: 'circumscripsit igitur genitalia viri in promissione Scriptura: imo vero nec commemoratur, quoniam non ex voluntate viri erat, qui nascebatur' (III, 26, 1 = Harvey, vol. 2, p. 117, lines 8-10; Migne III, 21, 5 = MG 7.952 A); (4) 'et propter hoc in fine non ex voluntate carnis, neque ex voluntate viri, sed ex placito Patris manus eius vivum perfecerunt hominem, uti fiat Adam secundum imaginem et similitudinem Dei' (V, 1, 3 = Harvey, vol. 2, p. 317, lines 8-11, or MG 7.1123 B); (5) perhaps also the short remark 'quod enim est Deo natum est, Deus est' in I, 8, 5 (Harvey, vol. 1, p. 77, line 7 or MG 7.534 B). There is a good discussion of the

other hand, attempts to trace this reading further back by showing that Justin and Ignatius of Antioch read the singular are at best inconclusive, for every one of the texts invoked can be explained otherwise (e.g. as inspired by Lk 1:35); the most that can be said is that there is nothing to exclude the possibility that Justin and Ignatius read the verb of Jn 1:13 in the singular.[19] Finally, the recently published Papyri Bodmer II and XIV (P 66 and P 75), both dating from around A.D. 200, have the plural: ἐγεννήθησαν in P 66 and ἐγενήθησαν in P 75.

The evidence of the Greek manuscripts is unanimous in favour of the plural, taking Jn 1:13 to refer to the spiritual birth of those who believe in his name. In the Greek world, only Irenaeus and the *Epistula XI Apostolorum* provide positive support for the singular; and Tertullian in the West may well have adopted this reading from Irenaeus.[20] Ambrose and Augustine, who sometimes

---

texts and their contexts in A. Houssiau, 'Le milieu théologique de la leçon ἐγεννήθη (Jn. 1:13)' in *Sacra Pagina* II, Gembloux–Paris, 1959, pp. 177–81, and in J. Galot, *Etre né de Dieu*, pp. 29–40.

[19] The texts of Justin and Ignatius are listed and discussed in Houssiau's article (see n. 18), pp. 173–6, and in Galot, *Etre né de Dieu*, pp. 11–27. The two examples from Ignatius will show the fragility of the evidence in favour of Ignatius' having read the singular. In the Epistle to the Smyrnaeans 1, 1 the text runs: 'that he [our Lord] is in truth of the family of David *according to the flesh, God's son by the will and power of God*, truly born of a virgin . . .' (Kirsopp Lake's rendering in the Loeb edition of *The Apostolic Fathers*, vol. 1, p. 253). The words here italicized are more easily explained as reminiscent of Rom 1:3–4 than by a reference to Jn 1:13. Ephesians 18, 2 reads: 'For our God, Jesus the Christ, was conceived by Mary by the dispensation of God, as well of the seed of David as of the Holy Spirit: he was born (ὃς ἐγεννήθη) . . .' (Kirsopp Lake, vol. 1, pp. 191–3). This text also contains as much of Rom 1:3–4 as of Jn 1:13. The various texts from Justin can similarly be explained as stemming from Lk 1:35 or from some general statement about the virginal conception, and one must confess that Galot, pp. 18–27, seems rather to overplay his hand in arguing for Justin's having read the singular.

[20] Tertullian, in his *Adversus Valentinianos* 5, 1 (CC 2.756 = ML 2.548–9), names Irenaeus as one of his sources, among those 'quos optaverim adsequi'. The *Adversus Valentinianos* was written between 208 and 211; and the *De carne Christi*, in which alone he cites Jn 1:13, was not written until 212, so that Tertullian could easily have been moved to adopt the reading *natus est* because that was the text he had found in Irenaeus.

take the text as *natus est*, may well have been influenced, directly or indirectly, by Tertullian. The external evidence, therefore, is overwhelmingly against the idea that Jn 1:13 is a direct assertion of the virginal conception of Jesus.

Yet the internal evidence is just as certainly in favour of that idea, and Galot has argued the case at great length.[21] It will be sufficient to set out only his most powerful arguments.

If the verb in Jn 1:13 is read in the plural, so that the reference is to the spiritual birth of believers, one has to explain why such great stress is laid on the negative aspects of this birth: why should John assert three times over that the spiritual birth of believers does not come about as a result of sexual intercourse? Who ever suggested that it did? This threefold negation is all the more strange in that it throws no light at all on the nature of this spiritual birth, and in no way prepares the reader for the statement immediately following that 'The Word became flesh'. In other words, the affirmation itself is so self-evident as to be pointless, and in its context disrupts the progression of thought. Worst of all, to read the verb in the plural is to put oneself in a logical quandary: how can those who have been once for all begotten of God (v. 13) be given by Christ the power to *become* children of God (v. 12)? Those who are already his children cannot be given the power to become his children. Galot rightly remarks that 'We are so accustomed to reading the plural that we no longer notice how bewildering it is, how difficult to accept'.[22]

On the other hand, if the verb be read in the singular, and taken as referring to the earthly birth of Jesus, it is very easy to explain the threefold negation ('not of blood-streams, nor of the will of flesh, nor of the will of a husband') as a triple affirmation of the virginal conception against its first opponents (probably Ebionites).[23] Irenaeus in particular seems never to have suspected

---

[21] *Etre né de Dieu*, pp. 95–124. On pp. 123–4 he summarizes thirteen arguments in favour of the singular.

[22] *Etre né de Dieu*, p. 96.

[23] Some authors, while accepting the reading with the singular, think the reference is not to the virginal conception but to the eternal generation of the Word *apud Patrem* (*e.g.* Augustine in the *Confessions* 7, 9, 13 = ML 32.740–1; A. Loisy,

that the text could bear any other meaning.[24] If this is the true interpretation, then v. 13 throws light on v. 12: the reason that believers are enabled to become children of God is that they are one by faith with him who had no human father, but was wholly and exclusively the son of God. In addition, v. 13 then leads quite naturally to v. 14: the triple denial of human paternity is followed by the assertion of divine fatherhood and so leads up to the statement that 'The Word became flesh'. Both in itself and in its context, the reading with the singular gives excellent sense.

Further evidence in support of the singular is that the tense employed in Jn 1:13, the aorist, denotes a once for all event, and is therefore eminently suitable to denote the birth of the Word in flesh. Elsewhere, when he speaks of Christians as 'having been born of God', John uses not an aorist but a perfect passive, in order to stress the continuance of the state which spiritual rebirth brings with it (Jn 3:6, 8; 1 Jn 2:29; 3:9 [bis]; 4:7; 5:1 [bis], 4, 18), and indeed 1 Jn 5:18 switches from the perfect participle (denoting the Christian) to an aorist participle in order to designate Christ (πᾶς ὁ γεγεννημένος ἐκ τοῦ θεοῦ οὐχ ἁμαρτάνει, ἀλλ' ὁ γεννηθεὶς ἐκ τοῦ θεοῦ τηρεῖ αὐτόν).[25]

A final argument for the singular is that the Fourth Gospel often asserts that the Word made flesh gives to those who believe in him the power to become what he himself already is *par excellence* (e.g. Jn 11:25; 12:36; 14:12).[26] This idea gives an

---

Le quatrième évangile, Paris, 1903, pp. 180–2; J. Dupont, *Essais sur la christologie de s. Jean*, Bruges, 1951, p. 56, n. 1). But apart from the fact that in that case a three-fold negation would hardly be necessary, v. 13 seems far too closely linked with v. 14: if one is going to read the singular, v. 13 must refer to the virginal conception of the Word in the flesh.

It is fairly certain that the Ebionites, a Jewish group who confessed Jesus as the Messiah but not as son of God, denied that he was virginally conceived.

[24] See the texts cited above on p. 261, n. 18, and the commentary by Galot in *Etre né de Dieu*, pp. 29–32.

[25] The aorist passive is used of the rebirth of Christians in Jn 3:3, 4 (*bis*), 5, 7, but only in reference to the once for all event of baptism *in the future*. John, when he writes of Christians as *already* born of God, always uses the perfect.

[26] Galot, *Etre né de Dieu*, p. 109, citing M.-E. Boismard, *Le Prologue de s. Jean*, Paris, 1953, p. 57.

additional argument in favour of the singular: believers are given the power to become children of God because of their faith in him who is *par excellence* the son of God,[27] the 'only-begotten son who is in the bosom of the Father' (Jn 1:18).

There is therefore a head-on collision of evidence. That by the year 200 the Greek text of Jn 1:13 read ἐγεννήθησαν ('they were born') cannot be questioned without abandoning all the canons of textual criticism. On the other hand, the structure, wording and context of the sentence clamour for the singular ἐγεννήθη ('he was born'). Can these opposing facts be reconciled?

Braun argues that the external witness of Irenaeus (and perhaps of Justin) should be preferred above all other external authorities inasmuch as Irenaeus (and Justin) were closely connected with Ephesus, where the Fourth Gospel may well have originated.[28] Galot suggests (less convincingly) that the original text had the singular; that between A.D. 160 and 190, largely under the influence of Gnosticism, the text was applied to the spiritual regeneration of Christians, particularly in Egypt; that this application of the text seemed to call for a plural reading; and that once the plural became the generally received text in the Church of Alexandria, it came to dominate completely the manuscript tradition.[29] But it is hard to believe that not a single manuscript escaped such contamination.

Most commentators follow the opposite course, and seek to explain how the reading *natus est* could have arisen as a variant from the true text (with the plural). Professor Barrett states the case succinctly and clearly:

'The origin of the text of b [*Veronensis*] is readily understandable; the threefold negation (not of blood, nor of the will of flesh, nor of the will of a husband) seemed to correspond exactly with the Church's belief about the birth of

[27] Note that John, unlike the Synoptics (*e.g.* Mt 5:45), never refers to Christians as 'sons of God', but always as 'children of God'. In John, the title 'son' is reserved to Jesus.

[28] See the article cited on p. 259, n. 9, pp. 26–30.

[29] *Etre né de Dieu*, pp. 87–9.

Jesus, and since the Virgin Birth is nowhere expressly mentioned in John it was natural to introduce a reference to it here. The reading which refers explicitly to the birth of Jesus is to be rejected; but it remains probable that John was alluding to Jesus' birth, and declaring that the birth of Christians, being bloodless and rooted in God's will alone, followed the pattern of Christ himself.'[30]

Thus even if the reading *natus est* is rejected, there is still a probable allusion to the virginal conception in this verse, and it is too much to assert without qualification that there is no evidence in the Fourth Gospel to indicate that its author had ever heard of the virginal conception.

One must choose, it seems, between the position adopted by Braun or Galot and that taken up by Barrett, while noting that either view gives some positive evidence in favour of the virginal conception. There is, however, a third possibility, though it will not commend itself to many readers. C. F. Burney[31] and C. C. Torrey[32] have argued eloquently, if not always convincingly, that the Fourth Gospel was originally written in Aramaic; and even if their arguments are far from conclusive, it does seem that a good case can be made out for the assertion that parts of this gospel were first set down in writing in Aramaic. Now if Jn 1:13–14 had been written in Aramaic, the copulative *waw* at the beginning of v. 14 could, by dittography, have been repeated at the end of the last word in v. 13, thereby turning a singular (*'ithyeled*) into a plural (*'ithyel^{e}du*).[33] Thus the original author would have written in Aramaic 'who *was* born', and his Greek translator, working perhaps from a defective copy, would have rendered the text as 'who *were* born'. This would explain how the

---

[30] *The Gospel according to St John*, London, 1960, pp. 137–8.

[31] *The Aramaic Origin of the Fourth Gospel*, Oxford, 1922. For Jn 1:13 see p. 34.

[32] *Our Translated Gospels*, London, n.d., pp. 151, 153; see also 'The Aramaic Origin of the Gospel of John' in the *Harvard Theological Review* 16 (1923), pp. 305–44.

[33] *I.e.* reversing the argument about the Curetonian Syriac, given on p. 259.

internal evidence can be all in favour of the singular, while all the Greek manuscripts without exception (but not the Curetonian Syriac!) have the plural.

Furthermore, if the Gospel of John does incorporate passages originally written in Aramaic, this would perhaps explain why Irenaeus took the reading of Jn 1:13 to be a singular: he could have been in contact with a living tradition at Ephesus, or he could have known an Aramaic or Syriac version of parts of the gospel older than the text represented in our Greek manuscripts. Here a remark by Harvey, the editor of Irenaeus, is very relevant. In his preface he writes:

'A point of some interest will be found of frequent occurrence in the notes; which is, the repeated instances that Scriptural quotations afford, of having been made by one who was as familiar with some Syriac version of the New Testament, as with the Greek originals. Strange *variae lectiones* occur, which can only be explained by referring to the Syriac version. It will not be forgotten that S. Irenaeus resided in early life at Smyrna; and it is by no means improbable that he may have been of Syrian extraction, and instructed from his earliest infancy in some Syriac version of Scripture'.[34]

On this hypothesis (which to the present writer seems the likeliest of all), we have a full explanation why all the internal evidence points to the singular ('who was born') as the original reading, and why all the external evidence of the Greek manuscripts points the other way. We see, too, why Irenaeus has the singular, and it is reasonable to conclude that Tertullian adopted this reading from him,[35] even though the majority of the Fathers, and all the Greek manuscripts, read the plural. And with Tertullian, the phrase *qui ex deo natus est* gained a foothold, albeit a precarious one, in the Latin West. And if this hypothesis is correct, we can see why the *Epistula XI Apostolorum* also has the

---

[34] *Sancti Irenaei . . . Libros Quinque adversus Haereses . . . edidit* W. Wigan Harvey, Cambridge, 1857, vol. I, Preface, p. v.

[35] See p. 363, n. 20.

singular—because it originated perhaps in Syria or in Palestine, but not in Egypt (where all the manuscripts had the plural reading). This would seem to be a reasonable explanation of all the data of the problem; but, as was said above, it is not likely to commend itself to many.

Chapter Eleven

'BORN OF THE VIRGIN MARY'

IT is impossible to deny that the New Testament affirms that Jesus was born of a virgin mother. Such a denial can be sustained only by taking extreme liberties with the text of Mt 1 and Lk 1 in defiance of every rule of textual criticism, and though at the beginning of this century some scholars suggested that Lk 1:34-5 might have been interpolated into a pre-existent document either by Luke or by some other early Christian,[1] there is no need to delay over this now ancient and long abandoned argument. A more contemporary objection is that since Matthew and Luke relate the story of the virginal conception only in their Infancy Narratives, they must be expressing in mythological form their conviction that Jesus was the son of God. For, it is argued, the story plays no further part in the first or third gospel, is never again alluded to except at Lk 3:23, and is significantly absent from the rest of the New Testament. Hence, it is claimed, the New Testament as a whole does not regard the matter as important; certainly, it does not belong among the central doctrines of the gospel, and is nowhere taught as an historical fact.

Whether the Infancy Narratives are at this point relating history or a doctrinally significant myth or legend is a question to be discussed later,[2] but before that discussion begins, one must first decide whether, outside the Infancy Gospels, the New Testament is really so silent as is claimed.

[1] See above, Chapter 3, p. 173.
[2] See below, Chapters 12-16, pp. 278-329.

'Arguments [from silence] inevitably look much stronger than they are, and it is a commonplace that beginners are easily misled by them'.[3]

It cannot be stressed too often that the New Testament is not an orderly compendium of Christian doctrine, setting out in magisterial form a comprehensive synthesis of all items like the *Summae* of the medieval schoolmen; and indeed it is *a priori* possible that an item of historical fact—even an important item, which was widely known in the early Church—could have failed to find a place or mention in the apostolic writings by pure accident. Such a total silence (*e.g.* on the martyrdom of James, the bishop of Jerusalem) is no proof that it never happened.

But when we consider the virginal conception, we are not faced with total silence. Douglas Edwards well remarks that there can be no absolute and utterly convincing argument from silence against the doctrine, for 'unless the silence is complete, the argument cannot so much as start.'[4] The question is rather whether there is a relative silence, *i.e.*

'whether the doctrine of the Virgin Birth is so conspicuously absent from the New Testament writings as to make it reasonable to conclude that the Apostles themselves knew nothing of it. Critics hostile to the doctrine claim that, if the New Testament writers had known of it at all, they would have been certain to refer to it; that (except, of course, for St Matthew and St Luke in their Birth Narratives) they do not refer to it; and that the only conceivable explanation of their silence in regard to a matter so unusual and so significant is that they had no knowledge of it'.[5]

What is this argument worth?

[3] D. Edwards, *The Virgin Birth in History and Faith*, London, 1943, p. 43. Those who know this highly original book will easily recognize how much this and some of the following chapters owe to it.

[4] Edwards, *The Virgin Birth*, p. 49.

[5] *Ibid.*, p. 48.

Fortunately, there is in the New Testament a fairly close parallel which proves that such a 'relative silence' is of no value at all. If only the Christians of Corinth had been better behaved, it would have been very difficult to maintain that Jesus commanded his disciples to celebrate the Supper, after his departure, in memory of him. Matthew and Mark do not mention any such command in their accounts of the meal (Mt 26:26–9; Mk 14:22–5); and one could argue that Luke's testimony (in 22:19) may therefore represent a Hellenistic accretion to the primitive gospel, particularly since John, though he expressly mentions the Supper (13:1), makes no reference to this command. In other words, had the Corinthians shown more propriety in their assemblies, we should have had an 'argument from relative silence' indicating that Jesus never said 'Do this in memory of me', on the ground that Matthew, Mark, John or Paul would have been sure to mention so important a command. The firm wording of 1 Cor 11:24 ('I received from the Lord that which I also passed on to you') and the universal practice of the infant Church shows how feeble such an argument is; and correspondingly, a 'relative silence' in the New Testament on the subject of the virginal conception cannot reasonably be construed as a positive indication that the apostles had never heard of it.

But are the New Testament writings as silent as is claimed? It has often been observed that Mark, who alone of the Synoptics does not record the virginal conception, is the only evangelist who does not name Joseph as the father of Jesus during his narrative of the public ministry. Mt 13:55 reads 'Is not this the son of the carpenter?' and Lk 4:22 has 'Is not this the son of Joseph?' By contrast, Mk 6:3 has 'Is not this the carpenter, the son of Mary?', a text which is often cited as evidence for the virginal conception.[6]

'The very fact that he [Mark] had no Birth Story in his Gospel meant that he could mention a human father of Jesus

[6] These texts have already been more fully discussed on pp. 239–41 and 247–8. For a full discussion of the textual variants in Mk 6:3 see J. Blinzler, *Die Brüder und Schwestern Jesu*, pp. 28–30 or (more briefly) V. Taylor, *The Gospel according to St Mark*, pp. 299–300.

only at the cost of creating in the inquirer's mind the impression that Jesus was born in the ordinary way, or of making an awkward and almost unmanageable digression to explain that he was not'.[7]

It is true that to refer to a man, and particularly to a rabbi or teacher, by his mother's name is distinctly unusual for this epoch in Palestine; but one may query whether it is so unusual as to justify the inference that Mark is here darkly alluding to the virginal conception.

It is sometimes said (with a cross-reference to Jdg 11:1) that the phrase is as a rule, insulting, implying illegitimate birth; and some conclude that the people of Nazareth are here casting doubt on Jesus' parentage. But apart from the fact that Mark would have been unlikely to record such a slur unless he was going to refute it, the basic premiss of the argument is wrong. There are several instances in the Old Testament where a man is referred to as the child of a particular mother and without disparagement;[8] and it would seem that in New Testament times it was a fairly regular usage when the father was dead and the widow had no other sons (compare Lk 7:12: 'the only son of his mother, and she was a widow').[9] In all probability, then, Mark here refers to Jesus as 'the son of Mary' because Joseph was dead and Mary had no other children, and Jesus was therefore known in Nazareth as 'the son of Mary'. Thus this Markan phrase gives no direct or positive support to the doctrine of the virginal conception, though it does confirm the view that James and Joses, Simon and Jude were not sons of Mary. On the other hand, there is nothing in the phrase to indicate that Mark was ignorant of the virginal conception, for it is self-evident that he could not have placed

[7] Edwards, *The Virgin Birth*, pp. 58–9.

[8] *E.g.* in Gen 36:10 Eliphaz is called the son of Adah, and Reuel the son of Basemath, simply to inform the reader that they were only half-brothers, Adah and Basemath both being wives of Esau.

[9] For further detail see J. Blinzler, *Die Brüder und Schwestern Jesu*, pp. 71–2: 'Zur Beinamen "der Sohn Marias" Mk 6:3'. He points out also that in the Qoran 'the son of Mary' is a regular term for Jesus, and used without any trace of contempt.

on the lips of the people of Nazareth an explicit testimony to it.

The Fourth Gospel, however, is not completely silent, as the last chapter has shown.[10] One may note also that Jn 7:26, 41, 42, 52 presuppose that the reader knows Jesus was born in Bethlehem, not in Galilee (the Johannine irony is evident). From what source did John expect his readers to have learnt of the birth in Bethlehem? The only extant records of it, in Matthew and in Luke, include also the story of the virginal conception. If this passage in Jn 7 is considered along with Jn 1:13, it is surely not improbable that John's readers, who are presumed to have known of the birth in Bethlehem, are presumed to have heard also of Jesus' virginal conception.

But, it will be said, if the story of the virginal conception was so widely told, why does St Paul never mention it in connection with the Incarnation? It is possible to answer this by putting a parallel question: if the story of the empty tomb was as widely told as the gospels imply, why does St Paul never mention it when writing of the Resurrection? Many, of course, would hold that both the story of the virginal conception and that of the empty tomb found their way into the gospel at a very late date, and would adduce as proof the silence of St Paul on both matters. But *whether* these two stories were added to the gospel at a very late stage is the question in dispute; and there seems no particular reason for holding that whatever is not mentioned in St Paul's purely occasional writings is necessarily, or even probably, an unwarranted addition to the preaching of the primitive Church. Paul, after all, was not the only preacher in early times, and his epistles tell us very little about the historical facts of Jesus' earthly life. He does not even mention that Jesus once preached in Galilee, but it can hardly be doubted that Paul believed he did (Ac 13:31). An argument from 'Pauline silence' is very feeble indeed, especially where the silence concerns the earthly life of Jesus. But is Paul totally silent on the virginal conception?

In none of the classical Pauline texts concerning the Incarnation is there any attempt to prove the fact or to describe the manner

---

[10] Pp. 255–68. At the very least, one must subscribe to the judgment of Professor Barrett quoted on pp. 265–6.

of it (Rom 9:5; 1 Cor 8:4–6; 2 Cor 8:9; Phil 2:5–7; Col 1:13–17). In all these texts, Paul is writing about something familiar to his hearers, and to have introduced a statement about the virginal conception would not have assisted his argument at all.

There are, however, three texts deserving of close examination, for in each of them Paul is speaking of the pre-existent Lord's entry into the world of time: Gal 4:4, Rom 1:3 and Phil 2:7. In these three texts Paul uses the verb γίνομαι to denote Christ's birth, and not γεννάομαι, which is the normal New Testament word meaning 'to be born'. Thus in Gal 4:4 we read that 'when the fulness of time came, God sent his only son γενόμενον ἐκ γυναικός, γενόμενον ὑπὸ νόμον; in Rom 1:3, τοῦ γενομένου ἐκ σπέρματος Δαυὶδ κατὰ σάρκα; and in Phil 2:7, ἐν ὁμοιώματι ἀνθρώπων γενόμενος. Now although the verb γίγνομαι is frequently found both in classical and in Hellenistic Greek with the meaning 'to be born', it is at least debatable whether it ever carries this meaning in the New Testament. The only text (apart from the three Pauline ones under discussion) which can be so translated is Jn 8:58: πρὶν 'Αβραὰμ γενέσθαι, ἐγὼ εἰμί. Yet in Jn 8:58 Jesus is not speaking of the moment of Abraham's birth,[11] but referring rather to the whole time-span of his earthly life. The most accurate rendering would be 'Before Abraham existed, I am'. This would correspond with the meaning of the verb in Jn 1:15 and 30—ἔμπροσθέν μου γέγονεν ('he *existed* before me').

Of the three Pauline texts, the most significant appears to be Gal 4:4, and it is worthy of note that the Latin here translates 'factum *ex muliere*, factum *sub lege*', and not 'natum *ex muliere*, natum *sub lege*', though at first reading the latter version would seem to suit the context better. The basic meaning of the verse is that God's son began life with a woman for his mother, under the Mosaic Law. But is there any evidence that Paul was here thinking of a virginal conception? It might seem significant that he uses the phrase 'of a woman', with no mention of a human father; but this does not imply an extraordinary conception, only the reality of the human nature referred to, as in Job 14:1 ('man born

---

[11] If the evangelist had wished to say that Jesus existed before Abraham *was born*, it would have been more natural to write πρὶν 'Αβραὰμ γεννηθῆναι.

of woman') and Mt 11:11 ('among those born of women'). Yet though nothing can be deduced from the phrase 'of a woman', it is otherwise with the verb used there (γενόμενον), for later in the same chapter Paul three times uses the word γεννάομαι when referring to the birth of Ishmael (Gal 4:23, 24, 29). One may note also that in Job 14:1 and Mt 11:11 the participle employed is γεννητός. Is there something significant in Paul's having avoided this verb at Gal 4:4, when writing of the birth of God's son? Douglas Edwards argues that the verb γίνομαι was chosen in opposition to γεννάομαι precisely because Jesus was not 'begotten' in the ordinary way, and therefore sees this text, along with Rom 1:3 and Phil 2:7, as evidence that Paul was anxious to stress the extraordinary character of Jesus' birth.[12]

There is force in Edward's contention, but it does not follow that the extraordinary character of Jesus' birth is necessarily to be sought *in the fact of a virginal conception*. Indeed, Phil 2:7 might be thought to militate against such an interpretation:

> ἐν ὁμοιώματι ἀνθρώπων γενόμενος,
> καὶ σχήματι εὑρεθεὶς ὡς ἄνθρωπος.
> 'Being made in the likeness of men,
>   and found, in outward form, like a man'.

In the first half of this phrase, the stress does not fall on the participle γενόμενος, for this could be replaced by a synonym without altering the meaning at all (*e.g.* φανερωθείς); the whole emphasis is on the words 'in the likeness of men'. In Phil 2:7 the leading idea is that the pre-existent Lord enters a new mode of existence, and it is the birth on earth of this heavenly Being which gives cause for wonder and astonishment. Phil 2:7 does not refer directly to the virginal conception; rather, in the language of St Leo and Chalcedon, it contrasts the *nova nativitas secundum carnem* with the *aeterna generatio apud Patrem*. Yet the fact remains that Phil 2:7 (like Gal 4:4) does not use the verb 'begotten' when it could easily have done so; that the Latin is again sensitive to the distinction ('*in similitudinem hominum* factus', and not 'natus');

[12] *The Virgin Birth*, pp. 68–78.

and that one cannot exclude altogether the possibility that Paul wrote γενόμενος because he believed that Christ Jesus' *nova nativitas secundum carnem* took place without the intervention of a human father.

Rom 1:3 is the most important text of all, for at first sight it seems to be a blunt denial of the virginal conception: 'he was (born) *of the seed of David* according to the flesh'. Yet at a second reading the flaw in this interpretation is disclosed, for was there ever a phrase which clamoured more loudly for the verb γεννηθείς—'begotten of the seed of David according to the flesh'? Thus Paul, on every occasion where he refers even distantly to Christ's entry into this world of time, never once uses the verb 'to be begotten'. Is this purely by accident, even in Rom 1:3? Or is it because Paul wished to avoid any suggestion that the son of God had a human father on earth? When one considers Paul's emphasis on the fact that we were saved 'by the free gift of God', 'through a new creation in Christ Jesus', it is difficult to believe that he, Luke's friend and fellow-traveller, had never even heard the story of the virginal conception.

What, then, can be said of the New Testament as a whole? First, it is false to say that the only witnesses of the virginal conception are a handful of verses in the Infancy Gospels of Matthew and Luke; Jn 1:13 is certainly an additional witness to the belief of the early Church. Secondly, the texts of Gal 4:4; Phil 2:7 and Rom 1:3 cannot simply be set aside as of no significance; when they are considered along with Matthew, Luke and John, and when one recalls the joint travels of Luke and Paul, it is hard to think that Paul had never heard of the virginal conception. One could argue that the doctrine was only invented after the death of St Paul, and is a very late addition to the gospel. But this theory collapses as soon as one reflects on the central theme of Jewish Messianic hope. If one fact is certain from the Old Testament, it is that the Jews believed a Messiah would come from the stock of David. And if one fact is certain from the New Testament, it is that the early Christians believed Jesus was this Messiah. Now since at that time everyone believed that generation took place simply by the implanting of the male seed in the mother's womb, which was as it were the soil in which the seed grew and matured, the obvious logical step for the early Christians was to prove by every possible means that Jesus was 'of the seed of David according to the flesh', and to concentrate all their apologetic on his *paternity*. That they were not insensitive to this need is proved by dozens of texts in the New Testament. Could the idea of the virginal conception, without male seed of the line of David, have made its way into the Church, and into the Palestinian Church, if it had first been heard of after A.D. 70, when it seems to destroy the very possibility of Jesus' having been of the seed of David? Would it ever have been accepted by the Church if it had not been founded on indisputable fact?

Chapter Twelve

THE VIRGINAL CONCEPTION
(I): A LEGEND OF JEWISH DERIVATION?

OUTSIDE the Roman Catholic Church, the majority of contemporary exegetes regard the story of the virginal conception of Jesus as a pious legend devoid of historical foundation but of abiding religious value inasmuch as it affirms graphically and unequivocally that Jesus of Nazareth was first and foremost the son of God. Indeed, of recent years a small number of Roman Catholic writers have embraced the same view,[1] and when in 1966 the first edition of the new Dutch Catechism, while not denying the historicity of the virginal conception, seemed to go out of its way to avoid affirming it, the Holy See insisted that in future editions the Catechism should openly affirm in clear language that Jesus was in reality born of a virgin.[2] The fact that this ancient doctrine is today so frequently represented as a myth or legend both justifies and necessitates a rather lengthy examination of the question.

Before the discussion begins, two preliminary observations are called for. Many modern Christians judge that certain narratives in the gospels cannot be historical because of their content,

---

[1] The best presentation of the various views (with an excellent bibliography) is by H. M. Köster, 'Die Jungfrauengeburt als theologisches Problem seit David Friedrich Strauss', in *Jungfrauengeburt gestern und heute* (= Mariologische Studien 4), Essen, 1969, pp. 35–87. I am grateful to Dr Köster for permission to reproduce his Appendix listing the main defenders and opponents of the virginal conception as an historical fact (see Detached Note IX, pp. 456–8).

[2] See Detached Note X: The New Dutch Catechism and the Virginal Conception.

because the events narrated are contrary to the laws of nature. This judgment rests upon the presupposition that God never intervenes in human history against the course of nature. Now this presupposition is not something which science or history has firmly established, for many very capable scientists and historians reject it. It is in fact nothing more than a postulate of rationalist or deist philosophy, and it would be equally reasonable to postulate the contrary, namely that God does sometimes intervene in history against the course of nature. Both presuppositions are equally incapable of proof by *a priori* reasoning (*e.g.* by an analysis of the terms involved), and neither can be accepted as a starting-point. The only possible way of discovering whether or not God does interfere in history against the course of nature is to examine the empirical evidence, *i.e.* to see whether there are good grounds for believing that God has at times wrought miracles, or good reasons for believing that he has not.

The more conservative-minded Christian, however, needs to beware of a different danger, coming from the very opposite quarter: he may be tempted to assert *a priori* that there are no myths or legends in the New Testament. Yet nowadays almost everyone admits that they are to be found in the Old Testament; and if God could speak to our fathers in times past through myth and legend, it is absurd to maintain *a priori* that he could never have tolerated the use of such literary forms under the covenant of grace. Many who are sincerely shocked by the suggestion that the New Testament contains myths and legends (because they feel such an admission would undermine the historical basis of their faith) fail to reflect that they are in fact placing limits on God's freedom of action. They do not realize that they are in practice insisting that the only proper and correct way for God to speak to man is by factual statement and unadorned narrative. Indeed, the rationalist who refuses to accept the possibility of miracles, and the fundamentalist who refuses to entertain the possibility of legend in the New Testament, are very much alike. Both seek to dictate, on the basis of their own presuppositions, the limits within which God may reveal himself to man.

This and the following chapters will therefore proceed on two presuppositions which are the opposite of those rejected in the last two paragraphs. It will be assumed that there is nothing *a priori* impossible in the idea of a miraculous and virginal conception through the direct intervention of the Creator; and it will also be assumed that there is nothing *a priori* impossible or unfitting in the suggestion that the biblical story of the virginal conception is a legend devoid of historical foundation, related by the evangelist in order to teach the religious truth that Jesus is first and last the son of God. In other words, it will be assumed that the debate about the historicity of the virginal conception cannot be settled on *a priori* principles, but only *a posteriori*, by an examination and evaluation of the literary evidence supplied in the Bible.

Because of its length, the argument needs to be divided over several chapters. If the virginal conception belongs to the realm not of history but of myth, there are four, and only four, possible explanations of its origin: *either* it was derived from Jewish sources *or* from pagan sources *or* from both *or* it was a Christian invention. These theories will be discussed in four successive chapters. First, then, is the doctrine ultimately inspired by Jewish ideas?

It is sometimes said that the Old Testament stories about Isaac, Samson and Samuel, all three born to childless women in old age, may have inspired the idea of assigning to Jesus a virgin mother,[3] for the Baptist was born to Elizabeth in similar circumstances, and Luke's intention was to portray Jesus as greater than the Baptist. And (so the argument runs) if the superiority of Jesus over John was to be manifested in the manner of his birth, and if John was born of aged parents by an extraordinary miracle of divine grace, what was more natural than to exclude human paternity altogether in the case of Jesus?[4]

Despite the plausibility of the argument, one must answer that it was not a natural step at all, for in Judaism paternity was all-

[3] It is this theory which seems to underlie the text of the first edition of the Dutch Catechism. The full text is printed on pp. 459–60.

[4] The argument is summarized by J. Gresham Machen, *The Virgin Birth of Christ*, Grand Rapids, Michigan, 1965 (a reprint of the edition of 1932), on pp. 280–1. The following chapters rely heavily on this classic work in defence of the historicity of the doctrine.

important: in Lk 1, for example, there can be no doubt that Zechariah, not Elizabeth, has the more prominent role. If Luke had merely wanted to show the superiority of Jesus over the Baptist, one would have expected him to stress the superiority of Joseph, the descendant of David, over Zechariah, an idea of which there is no trace at all in his narrative. Indeed, such was the emphasis in the Old Testament on the fact that the Messiah would be 'of the seed of David' (*e.g.* Ps 132:11) that the very notion of a *virginal* conception would seem to a Jew to debar Jesus from any claim to the title of Messiah. Matthew perceived this very clearly, and that is why, in 1:18-25, he is at such pains to point out that Joseph took Jesus as his son, thus explaining how, in spite of the virginal conception, Jesus was truly 'the son of David'. Matthew assumed the fact of the virginal conception and sought to resolve the consequent difficulty.[5]

And there is a second general objection to the theory that the story of the virginal conception is a legend of Jewish derivation. To a Jew, anything that might diminish or compromise the transcendence of God was anathema. Now if a pre-Christian Jew had been asked whether a woman could give birth to a child without a human father, he might conceivably have thought of a devil as having intercourse with a woman; but it would have been to him unthinkable that the All-Holy could be in any carnal sense the father of a human child. This reflection enables us to perceive the essence of the story told by Matthew and Luke: the virginal conception is presented as a pure creative act of God, a work analogous to the creation of man and woman in the Garden of Eden. This a Jew could have accepted without scruple, though he would hardly have thought of the idea without prompting. However one looks at the problem, the notion of the creation of a child in Mary's womb without any human father is not solely inspired by, or directly traceable to, the tales of miraculous births in the Old Testament.

The only text which could possibly be alleged as the source of the idea is Is 7:14: 'Behold, the virgin shall conceive and bear a son, and shall call his name Immanuel'. It is sometimes asserted

[5] See above, Chapter 2, pp. 170-2.

that the Jews interpreted these words as a prophecy of the virgin birth of the Messiah, particularly if they heard the text read in Greek (ἰδοὺ ἡ παρθένος . . .). But there is not a scrap of evidence to show that pre-Christian Jews understood Is 7:14 as foretelling a virgin birth: in the words of Paul Billerbeck, 'Mt 1:18 represents something absolutely new to Jewish thought'.[6]

This leaves only one possible way of pleading a Jewish origin for the doctrine. It could be said that although the Jews never interpreted Is 7:14 in the manner described, the early Christians did. In other words, it could be argued that the early Christians held Is 7:14 to be a prophecy of the birth of the Messiah and (since all prophecy had to be fulfilled) drew from it the conclusion that Jesus the Messiah must have been born of a virgin mother.[7]

The fatal flaw in this argument is that it assumes that the early Christians, *before* they had ever heard of the virginal conception, understood the text of Is 7:14 to imply birth from a virgin mother, and were indeed so convinced of this meaning that they built upon it the doctrine of the virginal conception. Yet they could not have taken this interpretation of Isaiah from Judaism, where the passage was taken to refer to Hezekiah and was not understood to involve virginal motherhood. More important, they would never have been led to it by the text itself. For it is incontrovertible that the Hebrew word employed in Is 7:14 ('almah) denotes only a young girl of marriageable age with no particular stress on her virginity; indeed, the word 'almah is used in Gen 34:3 of a young woman who is certainly not a virgin, and if Isaiah had wished to speak of a virgin giving birth, he would surely have chosen the very common and unequivocal Hebrew term for a virgin (bethûlah). Those Christians who heard Isaiah

[6] *Kommentar zum Neuen Testament*, vol. 1, p. 49. By way of confirmation, one may note that in Justin's *Dialogus*, Trypho the Jew, who voices the arguments of second-century Judaism against the Christian faith, does not argue that although prophecy required the Messiah to be born of a virgin, Jesus was not so born. On the contrary, his argument is that the Old Testament never predicted the virgin birth at all, and particularly not at Is 7:14. See chapters 43 and especially 67–8 in MG 6.568–9 and 629–36.

[7] *Cf.* D. Fr. Strauss, *The Life of Jesus*, English tr., London, 1898, p. 142, from whom many others have taken up the idea.

read in Hebrew (or in the Aramaic Targum, where the cognate word is used) would never have suspected that the prophecy of 7:14 alluded to a virginal conception if they had not previously been acquainted with the idea from another source. Similarly, those Christians who heard Isaiah read in Greek would never have suspected that the word παρθένος there implied physical virginity; for (like 'almah in Hebrew) the Greek noun denotes only a young unmarried girl, who is normally presumed to be a virgin, but with no particular stress on this fact. It also is used in Gen 34:3, in the story of the rape of Dinah. Only with the Syriac and Latin versions did Is 7:14 come to be rendered by a noun denoting physical virginity.

There was, then, no Old Testament text or Jewish tradition from which the early Christians could have been led to believe that Jesus was born of a virgin mother. Indeed, the many plain prophecies that the Messiah would be born 'of the seed of David' would have prejudiced them most strongly against that belief. The fact that the idea took root, and survived, and won the day against these prophecies, means that they must have thought it rested on very substantial ground. But it was certainly not a legend of Jewish derivation.

Chapter Thirteen

THE VIRGINAL CONCEPTION
(II): A LEGEND OF HELLENISTIC ORIGIN?

BULTMANN writes, in *The History of the Synoptic Tradition*:

'It seems clear to me that an Hellenistic origin has to be assumed for the motif of the Virgin Birth . . . Admittedly this motif could have entered Palestinian Judaism in pre-Christian times and could also have been taken over by the Palestinian–Christian tradition. But all attempts to prove this seem to me to have been unsuccessful so far; so I think it much more likely that the idea was taken over from an Hellenistic environment.[1]

'It was first added in the transformation in Hellenism, where the idea of the generation of a king or hero from a virgin by the godhead was widespread.'[2]

The only argument that Bultmann himself presents in favour of this opinion is that since the idea is not of Jewish origin, it must be of Hellenistic provenance:

'The idea of a divine generation from a virgin is not only foreign to the O.T. and to Judaism, but is completely

---

[1] In the English translation, Oxford, 1963, p. 304. In this and the following two quotations, Bultmann is rejecting the theory defended principally by Gunkel, according to whom the idea originated in Greek mythology, but took root in Judaism, in the shape of a belief that the Messiah would be born of a virgin mother.

[2] *Ibid.*, pp. 291–2.

impossible... The idea of the Virgin Birth of the Messiah in particular is foreign to Judaism.'[3]

It is much to be regretted that Bultmann does not specify whether any arguments other than this negative one persuade him to adopt the view that a Hellenistic origin for the doctrine of the virginal conception is 'much more likely'. He does, however, refer in a footnote to a number of standard works on the topic,[4] and one must therefore be content with examining the classic presentation of the theory as given in these German studies on comparative religion: they all date from the early years of this century, but it does not appear that any significant new arguments have been advanced in recent years to support the suggestion of a Hellenistic origin.

J. G. Machen has summarized the case with his customary clarity:

'In the earliest years of the Christian Church—so the theory runs—Jesus was called "Son of God". This title in the Jewish Christian Church was of course as far as possible from excluding a human father or involving a special physical derivation from God; the Jewish Christians used the term, no doubt, in a sense analogous to its Old Testament usage by which it could be a title of the Messiah, or they used it to designate that warm filial relationship of a moral kind in which Jesus felt Himself to stand toward God. But when the Gentile Christians, as distinguished from the Jewish Christians, heard this title applied to Jesus in the instruction that they received in their new faith, they would naturally interpret it in accordance with their previous habits of thought. Those previous habits of thought of the Gentile Christians attributed a very different sense to the title, "Son of God", from that which was attributed to it in Judaism; the Gentile Christians found implied in the title an actual physical sonship analogous to the

[3] *Ibid.*, p. 291, n. 4.
[4] *Ibid.*, p. 292, fn. 1. The authors there cited are in the main those whose views are examined in the present chapter.

relation of a man to his physical father. Zeus, according to the previous beliefs of these Gentile converts, was father of gods and men; and both he and other gods are represented as begetting children by human mothers. Similar stories were current with regard to the birth of great men of historic times; Alexander, Plato, Augustus and others were regarded as having been begotten by gods. These great men were "sons of gods". Could Jesus, in the mind of the Gentile converts, be less than they? And if they were sons of pagan gods, must not Jesus, in somewhat similar fashion, be the Son of the one true god in whom these converts had at their conversion come to believe?'[5]

This argument must be considered first in general, and then in detail.

Before the theory is considered in detail, it should be observed that three very powerful antecedent objections can be lodged against it. First, it attributes to those apostles who preached to the Gentiles a quite singular lack of pedagogic skill, not to say obtuseness. Are we seriously expected to believe that they allowed their converts to think that, when Jesus was called the son of God, the title was used in much the same way as when Alexander or Augustus was called the son of God? That they allowed them to think he had been physically begotten by God in much the same way as the Greek heroes were said to have been begotten? Or that they never noticed the interpretation the Greek converts were putting on their words? Or that the true doctrine was firmly inculcated in the first generation, but that around A.D. 80 the Greeks managed to substitute for the Jewish idea of divine sonship a more colourful, more physical, more Hellenistic notion derived from pagan mythology, and that the entire Church

[5] *The Virgin Birth of Christ*, pp. 324-5. Machen adds in a footnote: 'This theory was presented in classic form by Usener (whose *Weihnachtsfest* appeared, in its original first edition, in 1889), though of course the theory is far from having been originated by him. It has subsequently been supported, in varying forms, by a large number of recent scholars, particularly by Eduard Meyer (*Ursprung und Anfänge des Christentums*, i, 1921, pp. 54-7).'

meekly accepted this 'transformation in Hellenism' without a word of protest on any side? Are we really expected to believe this, when one recalls the violence of the controversies over minutiae of the Law which bedevilled the life of St Paul?

Secondly, those Gentile Christians who had turned their backs on paganism were just as resolutely opposed to the earthy mythology of Olympus as any Jew or Jewish Christian. 'You turned to God from idols, to serve the living and true God' (1 Thess 1:9). Is it likely that these converts would have wanted to implant at the very centre of their new faith an idea stemming from the least spiritual and least lovable features of that polytheism they had so recently abjured? I say 'the least spiritual features' because the elements in paganism which are alleged to have given rise to the doctrine of the virginal conception are those which speak of the sexual union of gods with mortal women; and 'the least lovable' because these same stories as often as not are tales of rape or deception.[6] The more closely one looks at classical mythology, the harder it is to accept the notion that a Greek mind of the first century could have thought up the idea of a genuinely virginal conception.

And thirdly, if this story is of Hellenistic origin, how does one explain that it is (according to Bultmann and his followers) nowhere alluded to in the more Greek parts of the New Testament, but only in the least Hellenistic, the most Palestinian and the most completely Jewish parts of the New Testament, namely, in the Infancy Gospels of Matthew and of Luke? All in all, the view that the idea of the virginal conception is of purely Hellenistic origin places considerable strain on the reader's credulity.

But where the argument really comes apart is at the point where the reader begins to test in detail the alleged parallels. Obviously, stories about the birth of mythological heroes who

---

[6] To be fair, it must be recorded that one protagonist of the theory, Hermann Gunkel, not only sees but stresses this difference. 'The early Christian Infancy stories are distinguished from these heathen myths first and foremost by their greater tenderness and reverence: in place of the god who goes into the girl, the divine spirit enters and "overshadows" the virgin' (*Zum religionsgeschichtlichen Verständnis des Neuen Testaments*, 3rd ed. [unchanged], Göttingen, 1930, p. 66).

were born of divine mothers and begotten by divine fathers lie well outside the scope of the present inquiry, for no one says that Jesus was conceived and born in heaven of the union between a god and a goddess. The only stories which are relevant are those which tell of the birth of a son as a result of the union between a divine father and a human mother. Perseus was such a man: his mother Danaë, though locked up behind bronze doors by her father, was loved by Zeus, who changed himself into a shower of gold, came to her, and so gave her a son.[7] Hercules was another: he too was the child of Zeus and of a mortal mother, Alcmene.[8]

Usually, however, much more stress is laid on the stories that relate not to the demi-gods of antiquity, but to historical persons. The most famous of these is about Plato. There was a story in Athens that Plato's mother, Perictione, conceived this genius of a child not by union with her husband Ariston, but by union with the god Apollo. Apollo then appeared to Ariston, advising him to refrain from relations with Perictione until the child was born, an injunction which Ariston duly obeyed.[9] (Not surprisingly, this tale is cited as the perfect parallel to the narrative in Mt 1: 18-25.[10]) A somewhat similar story is related by Plutarch about Alexander the Great. His mother Olympias, on the night before her marriage with Philip was due to be consummated, heard a

[7] R. Graves, *The Greek Myths*, vol. 1, Pelican, Harmondsworth, 1960, §73: 'Perseus', pp. 238 and 242, n. 4, cites the following classical references: Hyginus, *Fabula* 63; Apollodorus, ii, 4, 1; Horace, *Odes*, iii, 16, 1 ff.

[8] R. Graves, *The Greek Myths*, vol. 2, §118: 'The Birth of Heracles', pp. 85 *c* and 87, n. 3, cites: Hesiod, *Shield of Heracles*, 1-56; Apollodorus, ii, 4, 7-8; Hyginus, *Fabula* 28; Tzetzes, *On Lycophron* 33 and 392; Pindar, *Isthmian Odes*, vii, 5.

[9] The story is recorded in the third century after Christ by Diogenes Laertius, iii, 2 (Loeb ed., vol. 1, p. 277) and by Origen, *Contra Celsum* 1:37 (MG 11:729–33), but Diogenes quotes three sources, including Speusippus, Plato's nephew, and Clearchus, both of whom lived in the fourth century B.C., so that the story must be considerably older, and can safely be assigned to pre-Christian times. Certain other writers who mention the tale are listed in H. Usener, *Das Weihnachtsfest*, 2nd ed., 1911, pp. 72–3.

[10] Notably by Ed. Meyer in *Ursprung und Anfänge des Christentums*, vol. 1, pp. 56–7: 'The parallel between Matthew and the birth-legend of Plato could scarcely be more perfect.'

loud clap of thunder and felt as it were a thunderbolt entering her womb, which then became a raging fire within her. Another story told that a serpent once appeared stretched out beside Olympias as she slept, and that thereafter Philip did not approach her 'either because he feared that certain sorceries might be practised on him, or on the ground that she belonged to one greater than he'.[11] Similar stories circulated about Scipio Africanus, who laid the foundations of the Roman Empire,[12] about Augustus,[13] and Apollonius of Tyana.[14]

[11] *The Life of Alexander*, iii, 2.

[12] Livy (xxvi, 19) records the tale with a certain cynicism. While grudgingly admitting Scipio's very real virtues ('*non veris tantum virtutibus mirabilis*'), he wonders whether his habit of visiting the Capitol every day before beginning work was not perhaps the act of a shrewd politician commending himself to a superstitious people. Livy continues: 'This custom, which he observed all his life, was (whether by accident or design) proof to some of the common people that he was of divine race; and the rumour went round that had previously been circulated about Alexander the Great. It is as foolish as it is fictitious, but it told how he had been conceived by intercourse with a great serpent: they said that something prodigious of this kind had frequently been seen in his mother's bedroom, though as soon as anyone entered it suddenly disappeared and vanished from sight.'

[13] Suetonius writes (*Augustus* 94): 'There is a story which I found in a book called *Theologoumena*, by Asclepias of Mendes. Augustus's mother Atia, with certain married women friends, once attended a solemn midnight service at the Temple of Apollo, where she had her litter set down, and presently fell asleep as the others also did. Suddenly a serpent glided up, entered her, and then glided away again. On awakening, she purified herself, as if after intimacy with her husband. An irremovable coloured mark in the shape of a serpent, which then appeared on her body, made her ashamed to visit the public baths any more; and the birth of Augustus nine months later suggested a divine paternity' (translation by Robert Graves, Penguin Books, Harmondsworth, 1965, p. 101). The story is mentioned also by Dio Cassius, xlv, 1, 2 and by Apollinaris of Sidon (a Christian writer, *obiit* A.D. 488) in his *Carmina*, ii, 121.

[14] In the *Life* by Philostratus we read (i, 4): 'To his mother, just before he was born, there came an apparition of Proteus, who changes his form so much in Homer, in the guise of an Egyptian demon. She was in no way frightened, but asked him what sort of child she would bear. And he answered: "Myself". "And who are you?" she asked. "Proteus," answered he, "the God of Egypt." Well, I need hardly explain to readers of the poets the quality of Proteus and his reputation as regards wisdom . . .' (translation by F. C. Conybeare in the Loeb ed., vol. I, pp. 11–13).

One last example may be cited from Josephus, not because it supplies a good parallel, but because it shows that the idea of sexual union with a god was not considered wholly impossible by the more credulous people of his day.[15] In the time of Tiberius, he writes, there was a noble Roman lady named Paulina, married to one Saturninus, who was deeply attached to the worship of Isis. A young man named Decius Mundus became infatuated with her beauty and endeavoured to seduce her by bribery. When all his advances had been spurned, Mundus persuaded the priests of Isis to assist him. They, bribed by Mundus, sent a message to the pious Paulina saying that she was beloved by the god Anubis, who wished that she should share his bed. The credulous Paulina accepted the invitation, and her husband, knowing his wife's reputation for chastity, readily consented that she should spend a night in the temple. This she did, and gave herself to Mundus, who pretended to be the god. After the event, Paulina boasted openly of the favour she had received, so that her husband and all her lady friends, knowing her reputation for chastity, hesitated between incredulity and reverent astonishment. Unfortunately Mundus met her two days after the incident and cruelly disillusioned her.

In reading these stories, one is moving in a different world from that of St Luke's Infancy Gospel. Yet these so-called parallels are presented as evidence compelling us to treat the gospel story of the virginal conception as a myth. The more closely one examines them, the more evident it becomes that these tales are parallel to Luke's account of the virginal conception only in the sense that the stories will never converge even in infinity. It is true that Justin and Origen use these pagan tales in their presentation of the faith to pagans, pointing out that the story of Jesus' birth is no more incredible than the story of Danaë's conception. Thus Justin writes:

'And if we too hold that he was born of a virgin, think of this as something which he has in common with Perseus'.[16]

[15] *Ant.* XVIII, 3, 4 = §§ 66–80 (Loeb ed., vol. 9, pp. 50–9).
[16] *1 Apol.* 22 (MG 6.361 B).

This remark could conceivably be cited (out of its general context) as evidence that the more intelligent among the early Christians looked upon the virginal conception as an item in their mythology, but not as historical fact. It is therefore important to stress (as Origen does) that these tales are simply used as *argumenta ad hominem* when presenting the faith to pagans:

'there is nothing unreasonable in using Greek stories when arguing with Greeks'.[17]

What Justin and Origen are in fact saying is this: 'You claim that the virginal birth of Jesus is unbelievable; well, is it any more unbelievable than the stories you yourselves accept?' That Justin had in fact a very low opinion of the Greek stories can be seen from his *Dialogus*. There, when he is arguing with Trypho the Jew, he takes great care to stress that the heathen myths (including expressly those about the birth of Hercules and Perseus) were inspired by the devil. The devil, just as he had worked miracles through the wise men of Egypt in order to prevent Pharaoh from recognizing Moses as a prophet, and just as he had led Israel astray in the time of Elijah, had also inspired these Greek myths in order to prevent men from seeing the truth of the virginal conception of Christ.[18] Faced with Gentile or Jew, Justin seems to find the *argumentum ad hominem* irresistible, appealing to mythology when it suits him, and wholeheartedly condemning it when it does not. Origen is much more academic and cautious, reminding his readers that 'the Greek stories really are myths',[19] and though useful for rebutting *a priori* objections from the Greeks, are not true parallels. We may note, for example, that Origen, by contrast with Justin, never refers to Danaë as a 'virgin'; is this perhaps a result of Origen's more careful scholarship?[20]

[17] *Contra Celsum* I, 37 (MG II, 732 AB).

[18] *Dialogus* 69 (MG 6.636 C). The entire passage from 67–70 should be read (MG 6.629–41).

[19] *Contra Celsum* I, 37 (MG II.732 B).

[20] This observation is taken from J. G. Machen, *The Virgin Birth of Christ*, p. 336, fn. 43. All his pages from 332 to 336 are well worth reading.

The more one looks at these stories (on which Bultmann's case must ultimately rest), and the more often and carefully one reads them, the clearer it becomes that there is nothing in Hellenistic mythology which even remotely approaches the idea of a *virginal* conception. In every single case the god who is said to be the father begets his son by a material impregnation of the woman, either by a shower of gold or by a thunderbolt or by a serpent. In no case do we read anything distantly comparable to the theme: 'He spoke, and they were made.' It is tragic that the founding father of all Form Criticism, Hermann Gunkel, should have stated more clearly than anyone else what is the issue at stake, and then have opted for the wrong alternative.

> 'The Judaism which stems from the Old Testament could (men rightly say) talk of the miraculous *creation* of the child, but not of the miraculous *begetting* by a divine element.'[21]

That is the whole point; and it is hard to resist the thought that Gunkel's choice of a mythological explanation in preference to the idea of direct creation is dictated not by a study of what the New Testament actually says, but by a firm and unassailable conviction that miracles do not happen.

The plain fact is that nowhere in the New Testament is Jesus said to have been 'begotten' of Mary,[22] and the only alternative is that he was created in her womb. Nowhere in the mythology of Greece is there even a hint of such an origin by direct creation in a virgin's womb. The idea of the virginal conception cannot, therefore, be derived solely from Hellenistic sources.

[21] *Zum religionsgeschichtlichen Verständnis des Neuen Testaments*, p. 66.
[22] See above, pp. 274–6.

Chapter Fourteen

THE VIRGINAL CONCEPTION
(III): A LEGEND DERIVED FROM BOTH
HELLENISTIC AND JEWISH MOTIFS?

IT has been shown that the story of the virginal conception could not have originated from Judaism alone, or from Hellenism alone; could it be, though, that the idea arose from a fruitful combination of Jewish and Hellenistic motifs?

Hugo Gressmann argued, in *Das Weihnachts-Evangelium* (1914), that the origin of the story is to be found partly in an Egyptian legend about the finding of Osiris by a poor water-drawer near the Nile;[1] this, he said, led to the creation, in pre-Christian times, of a legend about shepherds finding a child in a cave near Bethlehem. His proof runs as follows. The Semitic character of Lk 2:1–20 is evidence that some such story about shepherds finding a child in a cave near Bethlehem circulated in Palestinian Judaism: the child is a divine child, without human parents, wrapped in swaddling-clothes and lying in a manger, and the angels who guided the shepherds to him sang of him as 'Saviour' and 'Lord'. This story, with its crass mythology, could not have been ultimately of Jewish origin. Therefore it must have originated elsewhere, and the legend of Osiris provides the closest parallel. The story must therefore have originated in Egypt, and passed from there to Bethlehem; and since there was no river near Bethlehem, it was natural to substitute shepherds for the water-drawer, and the parallel is then clearly seen. Like Osiris, the child in the Bethlehem-legend had no visible parents; he was a foundling;

[1] The story is told in Plutarch, *Isis and Osiris*, xii.

and he was a royal child of divine origin. After all, foundling-legends are mostly about kings (often of divine birth) who are discovered in lowly circumstances by humble folk. And if we grant that such a legend about a nameless foundling existed at Bethlehem in pre-Christian times, the origin of the Lucan story is explained. What was more natural than that the Church should take up this story and apply it to Jesus, whom it acclaimed as 'son of David', as 'Christ and Lord'?

Gressmann is adamant that in the gospel accounts of the virginal conception, Lk 1:26-38 and not Mt 1:18-25 reflects the more ancient tradition (and no one would disagree). Now the Lucan account stresses both Mary's virginity (Lk 1:27, 34) and the fact that Jesus owed his Davidic descent to his being the son of Joseph (Lk 1:27, 32-3; cf. 2:4). These two facts are plainly contra-dictory. How, then, did the contradiction arise? Gressmann sug-gests that Mary and Joseph were introduced into a narrative in which they had originally no place. The old legend, he says, had originally told about a virgin mother and a divine father, whose child was both human and divine, and destined to be a king. That legend was in pre-Christian times applied by some Jews to the Messiah; and when the early Jewish Christians adopted it to do honour to Jesus, they seized on these two ideas of virginal motherhood and divine fatherhood. Yet Mary and Joseph were well known to have been the parents of Jesus, and therefore had to be brought into the story. So Christians, when they applied the legend to Jesus, made Mary the virgin mother, and Joseph the purely legal father (cf. Lk 3:23), and the contradiction in Lk 1:26-38 is the inevitable result.

In order to justify his theory, Gressmann obviously needs to produce some evidence that the old Bethlehem-legend spoke of a virgin mother and a divine father. Once more, he appeals to Egyptian mythology, principally because, according to the New Testament, the divine-human child is destined to be a great *king*.

'In Egypt, both in ancient times and during the period of the Ptolemaic dynasty, it was the current belief that every new king sprang from a human mother and from the highest god, Amon-Ra, who appeared to the young queen in his divine form, had intercourse with her, and then promised that she should bring forth a son who should be king over Egypt.'[2]

'The power of the Most High' (Lk 1:35) corresponds to 'the Most High God', Amon-Ra, the sun-god of Egypt; and the Egyptians believed that a 'divine spirit' (cf. 'a holy spirit' in Lk 1:35) could have intercourse with a woman and so beget a child. And so all the Pharaohs from ancient times · were held to be 'sons of Amon-Ra, the Most High God'. It is true, of course, that the Egyptian myth contains no mention of the virginity of the mother, because in Egypt it was dogma that the god had physical intercourse with the queen; but when the legend was transferred to a land where intercourse on the part of God was unthinkable, there needed to be emphasis on the virginity of the mother. Thus we have reflected in Luke, and then in Matthew, a legend of Egyptian origin suitably censored in pre-Christian times by the Jews to make it applicable to their Messiah.

The postulates in Gressmann's theory are too numerous to be counted, and they remain unconfirmed at the end. Three comments will have to suffice. First, Osiris was in no sense the child of unknown parents,[3] and was not in this sense a foundling. The most that can be said in favour of Gressmann's interpretation is that Osiris was found abandoned. Secondly, nowhere in Lk 2:1–20 is there a single remark that might remotely suggest that Jesus was a foundling-child: his parentage is openly declared, and there is nothing to indicate that his parents ever left his side. Thirdly, Gressmann has to *postulate* that his story of a foundling-child near Bethlehem existed in pre-Christian times, that it was applied by some Jews to the Messiah, and that it included the details about a virgin mother and a divine father. There is not a shred of

---

[2] J. G. Machen, *The Virgin Birth of Christ*, pp. 357–8. For further detail see J. G. Frazer, *The Golden Bough: The Magic Art and the Evolution of Kings*, 3rd ed., vol. 2, London, 1913, pp. 130–2.

[3] For the myth of Osiris see J. G. Frazer, *The Golden Bough: Adonis Attis Osiris*, 3rd ed., vol. 2, London, 1914, pp. 3–23. The story of his birth is told on p. 6.

evidence to support any one of these three postulates. It is difficult to believe that this (completely hypothetical) legend had as profound an influence on Lk 1:26–38 and 2:1–20 as Gressmann claims.[4]

A similar hypothesis was put forward by Eduard Norden in *Die Geburt des Kindes* (1924), which is primarily a study of Virgil's Fourth Eclogue; but Norden argues the case in a more subtle way. According to him, Virgil was not thinking of some contemporary noble Roman child, but stating an ancient myth, when he wrote the famous lines so loved in the Middle Ages as a pagan prophecy of the birth of Christ:

> Ultima Cumaei venit iam carminis aetas;
> magnus ab integro saeclorum nascitur ordo.
> iam redit et virgo, redeunt Saturnia regna,
> iam nova progenies caelo dimittitur alto . . .
> ille deum vitam accipiet divisque videbit
> permixtos heroas et ipse videbitur illis,
> pacatumque reget patriis virtutibus orbem.[5]

The original home of this myth, says Norden, was Egypt, from which the story travelled abroad to various countries, and in Virgil we have the two essentials to make a parallel to Luke,

[4] I have not been able to consult Gressmann's book, but there is a long summary and critique in J. G. Machen, *The Virgin Birth of Christ*, pp. 349–55, on which the above paragraphs are based.

[5] *The Fourth Eclogue*, lines 4–7 and 15–17. In John Dryden's translation it runs:
> 'The last great age, foretold by sacred rhymes,
> Renews its finished course: Saturnian times
> Roll round again; and mighty years, begun
> From their first orb, in radiant circles run . . .
> A golden progeny from heaven descends . . .
> The son shall lead the life of gods, and be
> By gods and heroes seen, and gods and heroes see.
> The jarring nations he in peace shall bind,
> And with paternal virtues rule mankind.'
>   (*The Works of Virgil*, Oxford, 1961, p. 16).
Dryden, unfortunately, does not manage to capture the all-important reference 'Iam redit et virgo'.

the virgin mother and the divine child. That the idea was not unknown in Egypt can be proved from Plutarch, who writes in his *Life of Numa*:[6]

'And the Egyptians seem to think, not unreasonably, that it is possible for a spirit of God to fill a woman and to engender certain beginnings of generation.'

Philo, too, writing of God's converse with human beings, says:

God 'is the father of all things, for He begat them, and the husband of Wisdom, dropping the seed of happiness for the race of mortals into good and virgin soil. For it is meet that God should hold converse with the truly virgin nature, that which is undefiled and free from impure touch; but it is the opposite with us. For the union of human beings that is made for the procreation of children, turns virgins into women. But when God begins to consort with the soul, He makes what was before a woman into a virgin again, for He takes away the degenerate and emasculate passions which unmanned it and plants instead the native growth of unpolluted virtues.'[7]

Thus Plutarch attests that the Egyptians thought of God's begetting a human body in a mortal woman by the intervention of his spirit, but does not mention virginity; and Philo, the Jew of Alexandria, says that God sows the seed of immortal virtues in the virgin soul, but does not mention the spirit.

Norden concludes that the two ideas were crossed in the Greco-Egyptian religion of the Ptolemaic period, to affirm that God's spirit engendered a body (the Egyptian contribution) in a pure virgin (the Greek contribution), and that when the myth was transplanted to Jewish soil, it was suitably emended to conform with

[6] iv, 4.

[7] *De Cherubim*, xiv = 49–50. The entire passage from xii–xiv (= 40–52) should be read (in the Loeb ed., vol. 2, pp. 35–41). The passage translated above (by F. H. Colson and G. H. Whitaker) occurs on pp. 38–9.

the Jewish idea of God. Virgil, however, has preserved the older form of the myth, in which a virgin gives birth to a child who ushers in the final age of mankind, a truly divine child come down from heaven, and therefore a king bringing peace to all the world. The Jewish version of the myth attained its final form in Luke and in Matthew, according to whom God begets a son through non-carnal ('pneumatic') union with a virgin. But it is still the ancient myth, applied to Christ.

There is no need to delay over an elementary weakness in Norden's theory, but it should be recorded that the text from Philo is very clearly allegorical, referring to purity of soul; it cannot therefore be invoked as evidence that the Egyptians or the Alexandrians of the Ptolemaic period believed in the possibility of human parthenogenesis. Better evidence than this is required to locate the origin of Virgil's reference '*Iam redit et virgo*', and of St Luke's Annunciation story, in Egypt.

A far more important criticism, as Norden himself admits, is that the Egyptian texts all refer to a theogamy, *i.e.* to the sexual union of a god with a mortal woman. (This is also the mortal weakness in Gressmann's attempt to discover an Egyptian prototype for the virginal conception.) Sir James Frazer has described well what the Egyptians meant when they said that the Pharaoh was the son of Amon-Ra:

'At Thebes in Egypt a woman slept in the temple of Ammon as the consort of the god, and, like the human wife of Bel at Babylon, she was said to have no commerce with a man (Herodotus I, 182). In Egyptian texts she is often mentioned as "the divine consort", and usually she was no less a personage than the Queen of Egypt herself. For, according to the Egyptians, their monarchs were actually begotten by the god Ammon, who assumed for the time being the form of the reigning king, and in that disguise had intercourse with the queen. The divine procreation is carved and painted in great detail on the walls of two of the oldest temples in Egypt, those of Deir el Bahari and Luxor; and the inscriptions attached to the paintings leave no doubt as to the meaning of the scenes ... The nativity is depicted in about fifteen scenes, which may be grouped in three acts: first, the carnal union of the god with the queen; second, the birth; and third, the recognition of the infant by the gods.'[8]

Frazer then cites a long passage from the inscriptions setting forth the physical joy of the queen at this embrace.[9] Whether Virgil had these ideas in mind is more than debatable, and it is hard to believe that they lie at the origin of his Fourth Eclogue; but could anything be further removed from the Christian doctrine of the virginal conception? Norden himself admits the weakness of his own theory when he writes:

'Wherever trustworthy tradition is extant, the mystery is without exception clothed in the form that the god himself appears to the mortal woman with whom he desires to enter into the marital relationship. "I will descend into thy bosom" —thus or in some similar way he speaks to her, and she gives herself willingly to him. The Gospel narrative exhibits by its peculiarity a conscious departure from a type.'[10]

This final sentence is by itself an admission that the Christian story is not derived solely from a combination of Greek and Egyptian motifs.

Nor is this conclusion invalidated by the text from Plutarch's *Life of Numa* cited above,[11] for what Plutarch understands by the 'spirit' or 'breath' of God is something material or physical, like air or light, as Norden himself hints.[12] The most that can be said is that Plutarch himself glimpsed the possibility that God could create not in the manner of a human father 'through seed', but

[8] *The Magic Art*, vol. 2, pp. 130–1.

[9] *Ibid.*, p. 132.

[10] *Das Geburt des Kindes*, p. 91. The translation is taken from Machen, *The Virgin Birth of Christ*, pp. 360–1.

[11] P. 297.

[12] *Das Geburt des Kindes*, p. 80. See also the following note.

'by a different power';[13] but whether he thought of this power as totally spiritual ('He spoke, and they were made') is more than open to question.

A third attempt to explain the biblical story of the virginal conception by reference to both Jewish and Hellenistic ante-cedents is that of Hans Leisegang, whose *Pneuma Hagion* was published in 1922.[14] His is the most elaborate argument among those which seek to derive the doctrine partly from Jewish and partly from Greek sources, and the following outline is of neces-sity oversimplified.

The New Testament account of Jesus' birth appears in two versions, one in Matthew and one in Luke. If we had only Matthew, the explanation might be very simple, for Mary is there 'found with child of *a* holy spirit' (note the absence of the definite article). Now among the more superstitious tribes of modern Arabia, it is popularly believed that a woman may conceive a child by a *weli, i.e.* by a spirit, and barren women are said to have recourse to places known to be haunted by such spirits.[15] The 'holy spirit' mentioned in Matthew (1:18, 20) would therefore be a good spirit, different in moral quality from the unclean spirits whom Jesus cast out, but belonging to the same order of being. By this story, the transcendence of God would be preserved (he would have no direct part in the begetting of Jesus) and yet the super-natural origin of Jesus would also be safeguarded. Hence this idea would have commended itself to the early Jewish Christians. It is true that extant literary sources do not bear witness to the existence of a similar superstition in first-century Judaism; but we should hardly expect the *literary* sources to do so. Yet popular religion is very conservative, and it seems plausible to postulate

[13] *Quaest. Conv.*, viii, 1, 2 f. Further detail can be found in the article by Her-mann Kleinknecht in the *TWNT* 6, particularly on pp. 337–41 ('*Pneuma* in Mythology and Religion: I Life-creating Spirit'). The references to Plutarch are on pp. 340–1.

[14] The full title is *Pneuma Hagion: Der Ursprung des Geistesbegriffs der synoptischen Evangelien aus der griechischen Mystik*, Leipzig, 1922.

[15] Leisegang's authority for this statement is S. J. Curtiss, *Primitive Semitic Religion Today*, 1902. There is a careful and detailed review, by L. H. Vincent, of its German translation in the *RB* 14 (1904), pp. 279–83.

that such beliefs did exist among the less sophisticated Jews of that time, just as they survive today after thirteen centuries of Islam.

Yet just as this theory would have been altogether too crude for official Judaism, so (in the form stated) it was utterly repugnant to the early Christians. Hence we encounter a more refined and developed wording in St Luke (1:35), which thereafter became the accepted interpretation of Matthew's story. In the Lucan Infancy Gospel Zechariah (1:67), Elizabeth (1:41), John the Baptist (1:15, 80) and the aged Simeon (2:25) are all said to have received a holy spirit[16] and (except of course for the infant Baptist) to have prophesied.[17] Of Mary too it is said that 'a holy spirit will come upon her' (1:35); only, in her case the result is not prophecy, but the conception of a child. Luke, at least in his phrasing at 1:35, is different from, and perhaps more refined than, Matthew at 1:18 ('she was *found to be with child* of a holy spirit'). Where did Luke find the inspiration for this new approach?

Leisegang has no hesitations. The notion of a divine power 'overshadowing' men is well attested in Philo;[18] and the position of the prophetess at Delphi, seated on a tripod over a cavern from which the 'prophetic spirit' came, leaves no doubt that it was considered to enter her womb. It is true, of course, that Philo is concerned not with physical birth, but with the need for God's spirit to overshadow men in order that they may conceive upright ideas. It is also true that the priestess at Delphi brought forth only oracles, not a child. A wide gulf therefore remains between these texts and the New Testament. To bridge that gulf, Leisegang appeals to the Dionysiac mysteries, and here is the most original part of his theory.

[16] In all these texts (as in 1:35) there is no mention of '*the* holy spirit' (with the definite article). True, it occurs at 2:26 and 27, but there it is the only possible usage in Greek, since the term refers back to that holy spirit received by Simeon and just mentioned in 2:25.

[17] Note that Zechariah, Elizabeth and Simeon are said to be filled with a holy spirit only in the moment before they 'prophesy'. Zechariah, for example, is not 'filled with a holy spirit' in the Temple.

[18] In *Pneuma Hagion*, pp. 25–6, Leisegang quotes three passages from Philo. The references are given below on pp. 305–6.

According to the Greeks, the mother of Dionysus (Semele) was thrown into a state of ecstasy as soon as she had conceived this child by Zeus; and so were all who touched her body.[19] Here

> 'Leisegang finds a special similarity to the Lucan narrative in that in both cases the mother during her pregnancy is represented as being herself in an enthusiastic condition and as transferring this condition to all who come into contact with her.'[20]

Here, in the Dionysiac myth, the idea of possession is already combined with the idea of divine begetting; and according to Leisegang, this thoroughly Greek combination entered Judaism through the work and thought of Philo.

For Philo was a mystic, and had personally experienced the thrill of a new power and enlightenment suddenly descending into his soul. In seeking to describe this condition, Philo turns to the language of the mystery-religions and (like many later Christian mystics) to the language of human love. Two examples will have to suffice as illustrations at this point. The first is couched in the language of childbirth and of mystery-religions: after the futility of his own attempts to philosophize, he describes the feeling of enlightenment from above.

> 'For the offspring of the soul's own travail are for the most part poor abortions, things untimely born; but those which God waters with the snows of heaven come to the birth perfect, complete and peerless. I feel no shame in recording my own experience, a thing I know from its having happened to me a thousand times. On some occasions, after making up my mind to follow the usual course of writing on philosophical tenets, and knowing definitely the substance of what I

[19] In *Pneuma Hagion*, p. 41, n. 1, the author cites a scholion on Apollonius Rhodius: 'Aeschylus introduced her as a woman with child and possessed by a god, as were all who touched her womb' (i, 636). *Cf.* Apollodorus III, iv, 3 and Hyginus, *Fabula* 179.

[20] J. G. Machen, *The Virgin Birth of Christ*, p. 368.

was to set down, I have found my understanding incapable of giving birth to a single idea, and have given it up without accomplishing anything, reviling my understanding for its self-conceit, and filled with amazement at the might of Him that IS to whom is due the opening and closing of the soul-wombs. On other occasions, I have approached my work empty and suddenly become full, the ideas falling in a shower from above and being sown invisibly, so that under the influence of the Divine possession I have been filled with corybantic frenzy and been unconscious of anything, place, persons present, myself, words spoken, lines written.'[21]

The second passage uses more tempestuous language, in which, says Leisegang,[22] we can almost hear the rhythmic chant of initiates to a mystery-religion as they pray for a 'pneumatic' or virginal conception:

'For rich in offspring is this wedlock, seeing that it does not bring one body to the embraces of another but mates well-endowed souls with perfect virtues.

Mount then, all ye right thoughts and reasonings of wisdom,
impregnate, impart seed,
and whenever you catch sight of a soul
of deep rich virgin soil,
pass it not by,
but inviting it to union
and intercourse with yourselves,
render it pregnant
and so effect its consummation.'[23]

[21] *De migratione Abraham*, vii = 33–5 (translation by F. H. Colson and G. H. Whitaker in the Loeb ed., vol. 4, pp. 150–1).

[22] *Pneuma Hagion*, p. 50. I have arranged the second part in strophic form, following Leisegang's division of the lines as far as the English version allows it. The rhythm is, of course, far more pronounced in the original Greek.

[23] *De somniis* I, xxxiv = 200 (again translated by F. H. Colson and G. H. Whitaker, Loeb ed., vol. 5, pp. 402–5).

It is, then, in utterly sexual imagery that Philo describes the implanting of ideas by God in the virgin soul of the man who is pure of heart. Elsewhere, he speaks of God's begetting the Logos, in texts too numerous and too complex to be examined here,[24] but enough has been said to show that Philo is not unfamiliar with the notion that God may bring something to birth in the virginal soul.

We are now in a position, says Leisegang, to trace the full development of the birth narratives in Matthew and in Luke. In ancient Greece, in early times, the wild orgiastic religion of Dionysus was widespread, and was particularly attractive to women. It was not unnatural that in such circumstances the belief also gained currency that a demon could enter a woman's body and perform with her the sacred act of begetting a child. In the mystery-religions the same belief was at least suggested, and perhaps symbolically performed; for though the poets and philosophers might protest emphatically and endeavour to stress the essentially spiritual nature of the divine, their protests were at the popular level of no avail. The author of St Matthew's gospel was in such respects a layman, seized upon material that came to him from the Hellenistic world, understood it in accordance with popular Semitic superstitions and inserted the idea as best he could into his narrative. St Luke was rather more sophisticated, and included with his story various elements originating in Greek prophetism, laying great stress on the creative and prophetical power of the Spirit of God. Both have in fact followed the inherent logic of Philo's argument to its inevitable conclusion, for why should one restrict God's creative power to the implanting of spiritual ideas in the soul? But in doing so, they have left far behind the ethereal world of the Alexandrine philosopher and come down to an extremely material plane.

Leisegang's theory has been expounded at length because his book, though published in 1922, remains to this day the most imposing and scholarly attempt to explain the origin of the gospel story by recourse to Hellenistic mythology as interpreted by

[24] The most convenient summary in English (with references) is to be found in C. H. Dodd, *The Interpretation of the Fourth Gospel*, pp. 66–73.

Jewish thought. And since nowadays there are many who affirm that the biblical story of the virginal conception is derived from Greek mythology, it was necessary to present the strongest case possible in favour of this view, and to present it as fairly and as fully as possible.

Nevertheless, the case contains a number of weaknesses in detail. It is difficult to take seriously the suggestion that even the less sophisticated and more superstitious Jews of that time would have accepted the idea that a woman might conceive by a *weli*. Certainly, it is unreasonable to base this assertion on what a nineteenth-century American traveller reports about Arab superstitions in his day. And it passes belief how anyone can be tempted to explain St Matthew's story by this means when even for an out-and-out rationalist far simpler, clearer and more credible interpretations lie to hand. Leisegang, however, is far too intelligent to rest his case on such unsubstantial ground, and since the hypothesis about popular belief in *welis* is in no way essential to his thesis, one is in the end left puzzled to know why he ever mentioned it at all.

A further weakness lies in his interpretation of Philo. Of the three main passages referred to, not one uses the verb 'to overshadow' in the sense which is found at Lk 1:35. The first text reads:

'When the light of God shines, the human light sets; when the divine light sets, the human dawns and rises. This is what regularly befalls the fellowship of the prophets. The mind is evicted at the arrival of the divine Spirit, but when that departs the mind returns to its tenancy. Mortal and immortal may not share the same home. And therefore the setting of reason and the darkness which surrounds it produce ecstasy and inspired frenzy.'[25]

Here the verb 'to overshadow' does not occur at all; the arrival of the divine spirit brings divine light, not a shadow; the darkness

[25] *Quis rerum divinarum heres?* liii = 264-5 (translation by F. H. Colson, Loeb ed., vol. 4, pp. 418-19).

of human reason which results from the advent of the divine spirit is an obscuring of human reason, by which man is caught up into ecstasy and inspired frenzy. Could anything be further removed from that 'overshadowing' of Mary spoken of in Lk 1:35? She is hardly portrayed as losing her reason 'in ecstasy and inspired frenzy'. The second passage is no more helpful: it too speaks of the setting of 'the mortal and human light', but contains no mention of the verb 'to overshadow'.[26] The third alone contains this verb, but again in the sense of losing the light of divinely-given wisdom:

'When the light of the understanding is dimmed and clouded [literally, "*overshadowed*"], they who are of the fellowship of darkness win the day.'[27]

It seems clear that in each of these three passages, cited to illustrate the meaning of Lk 1:35, we have the exact opposite of what Luke meant by 'A holy Spirit shall overshadow you.'[28] Those exegetes who find the meaning of this verse illustrated in the Old Testament and the gospels have, on purely literary grounds, a far more reasonable case.[29]

Nor is the appeal to Greek prophetism any happier in its results, whether we think of Delphi or of the Dionysiac mysteries, as Leisegang himself admits.

'The Phthias', he writes, 'the Sibils, the Gnostic prophetesses, the participants in the mysteries receive the spirit likewise in their body, come thereby into an enthusiastic condition, and bring forth—well, certainly not a child.'[30]

---

[26] *De somniis* I, xix = 118–19 (Loeb ed., vol. 5, pp. 360–1).

[27] *Quod Deus sit immutabilis* i = 3 (Loeb ed., vol. 3, pp. 10–11).

[28] Bultmann makes a similar remark in his review of Norden, *Die Geburt des Kindes* in the *Theologische Literaturzeitung* 49 (1924), col 322 (cited in J. G. Machen, *The Virgin Birth of Christ*, p. 376, fn. 149).

[29] See Part I, Chapter 6, pp. 57–61.

[30] *Pneuma Hagion*, p. 35, translated by Machen in *The Virgin Birth of Christ*, p. 375.

After this admission, we need proceed no further, and may end with a quotation from Bultmann's review of Leisegang which is cited by J. G. Machen:

'The crucial point in the argumentation [of Leisegang] is, however, the question whether in Lk 1 there is really to be found a connection between the Spirit as "prophetic Spirit" and as power of fructification. This is in my judgment not the case. That which in Lk 1 (aside from verses 34–7) is said concerning the Spirit does not seem to go beyond Old Testament–Jewish ideas; moreover, neither is Mary represented as a pneumatic prophetess (even if verses 46ff. belong in her mouth), nor is Jesus, the miraculously conceived child, represented as a prophet, as ought to be the case according to the analogies. Above all, however, the verses 34–7 (or 34–5), which contain the *motif* of the miraculous conception, are probably an insertion into the source, so that the connection which Leisegang maintains does not exist at all.[31] In my opinion the *motif* of the supernatural conception in Luke as well as in Matthew comes from a very much more primitive sphere than that of Hellenistic mysticism; and it seems to me to be a very artificial proceeding to explain Mt 1:18–21 from crassly-misunderstood Greek pneuma-speculation adapted to Semitic popular beliefs.'[32]

Thus we are once more driven back in the end to the conclusion that Luke was thinking of direct creation, to which there is no parallel in Hellenistic Judaism. For Leisegang, in spite of his vast erudition and wide-ranging investigations, has failed to produce

[31] One does not have to accept Bultmann's opinion about the interpolation of these verses to agree with his previous criticisms, but it is part of his theory about the Lucan Infancy Narrative (see *The History of the Synoptic Tradition*, pp. 295–6 and 304).

[32] *Theologische Literaturzeitung* 47 (1922), col. 426, translated by Machen, *The Virgin Birth of Christ*, p. 378. It should be noted, of course (see the final sentence), that Bultmann criticizes Leisegang not for defending a Hellenistic origin for the story of the virginal conception (which Bultmann himself affirms: see above, p. 284), but for finding it in Hellenistic *mysticism*.

a single clear and unmistakable example from the Hellenistic world of a spirit's producing a child in a mortal woman without carnal union.

In short, however the story of the virginal conception may have arisen, it was not an idea present in the Old Testament or in Jewish tradition which was later applied to Jesus Christ. It was not an invention of the Greek Christians thought up as a parallel to the Greek myths, for the early Church would never have tolerated such a misrepresentation of the historical character of the Incarnation. And it was not the natural product of the cross-fertilization of Jewish and Hellenist ideas. Whatever explanation be sought for the doctrine, one must in the end concede that it is a purely Christian idea.[33]

[33] It seems pointless to examine alleged parallels from ancient Babylonia, from Persia or India until someone has shown, by historical evidence, that these tales could have found their way into first-century Judaism or Christianity. Those interested will find some of the relevant stories discussed in J. G. Machen, *The Virgin Birth of Christ*, pp. 339-48.

Chapter Fifteen

THE VIRGINAL CONCEPTION
(IV): A CHRISTIAN THEOLOGOUMENON?

THE biblical narrative of the virginal conception is a story unique in the ancient world, and of Christian origin; and there is good evidence that by the end of the first century Christians understood it as a record of historical fact.[1] Hence it is misleading to speak of it as a myth or legend, for that is to set the biblical story on a level with the myths and legends of Greece and Rome, tales which the Greeks and Romans of the first century treated with considerable scepticism. To use the same terms (myth and legend) about the virginal conception is to fail to do justice to the earnestness with which the early Christians regarded the story. If it is considered that the biblical account of the virginal conception should be interpreted as an expression of Christian belief, but not as a record of an historical happening, then a term is needed which brings out the seriousness of this belief, and the most suitable one is a Christian *theologoumenon*, *i.e.* a deduction reached by theological reasoning from other accepted religious truths, or the expression in another form (here, by story) of a religious truth (here, of the more abstract truth that Jesus is the son of God).

---

[1] Even so convinced and vigorous an opponent of the historicity of the doctrine as Hans von Campenhausen writes: 'For Ignatius the virgin birth is a piece of the Church's recognized tradition, to which he refers in fixed phrases reminiscent of confessional formulae (Eph. 7, 2; Trall. 9, 1; Smyrn. 1, 1). But that does not mean that this point of doctrine was merely part of his mental luggage; it has its place in the centre of his conviction' (*The Virgin Birth in the Theology of the Ancient Church* = Studies in Historical Theology 2, London, 1964, p. 29).

This approach was suggested many years ago by Ferdinand Kattenbusch in his classic work on the Apostles' Creed,[2] and once more J. G. Machen supplies an excellent summary of the argument. Kattenbusch suggests that the doctrine of the virginal conception developed within the Church on the basis of Pauline teaching. In the development of the doctrine, he says, two stages are to be distinguished.

'In the former stage came the idea of conception by the Holy Spirit; in the second stage the idea of the virgin birth. The former idea, which is the dominant one in the Lucan narrative,[3] might well have been suggested, Kattenbusch thinks, by the Pauline intimation that the Spirit was active in the entrance of Jesus into the flesh; the latter idea, the idea of the virgin birth, was fostered by Paul's doctrine of Christ as the second Adam, had its final form imparted to it by the prophecy in Is 7:14, and then was important in making acceptable the Pauline doctrine of the pre-existence of Christ.'[4]

In other words, the early Christians first believed that the Holy Spirit was active in the advent of Jesus: they soon came to believe that 'he was conceived of the Holy Ghost'. Then St Paul began to speak of him as 'the second Adam' (1 Cor 15:45, cf. 22, and Rom 5:14). Once this concept of the second Adam had taken root, men began to ask why Christ was so called; and reading the Immanuel prophecy in Is 7:14, they concluded that this second Adam had, like the first Adam, come straight from the hand of God—or, as Isaiah says, had been virginally conceived.

It should be observed at once that Kattenbusch has put his

[2] *Das apostolische Symbol*, vol. 2, Leipzig, 1900, pp. 620–4. He upholds essentially the same position in a review of J. G. Machen's book entitled 'Die Geburtsgeschichte Jesu als Haggada der Urchristologie' in *Theologische Studien und Kritiken* 102 (1930), pp. 454–74.

[3] Machen observes (*The Virgin Birth of Christ*, p. 317, fn. 3) that Kattenbusch suggests, though he does not expressly propose, that the idea of the *virginal* conception (as distinct from conception *by the Spirit*) entered the Lucan narrative only by the interpolation of 'since I know not man' in Lk 1:34.

[4] *The Virgin Birth of Christ*, p. 317.

finger on the central point which needs developing—Christ, the second Adam. Only, as Machen points out, 'it would be more plausible, if the choice had to be made, to suppose that the designation of Christ as the second Adam grew out of the fact of the virgin birth than that the story of the virgin birth grew out of that designation'.[5] This theme will need to be discussed later,[6] but first we must examine the most able, scholarly and balanced argument against the historicity of the virginal conception, and in favour of its being a Christian *theologoumenon*. Its author is Martin Dibelius, whose *Jungfrauensohn und Krippenkind* was published two years after J. G. Machen's book, in 1932.[7]

Dibelius opens his case by affirming (what all must admit) that Lk 1–2 is a collection of early Christian traditions. Next, he argues, the story of the Annunciation to Mary in Lk 1:26–38 is very evidently from a different source than the story of the birth in Bethlehem recorded in Lk 2:1–20, for the following reasons. (1) In Lk 2:4–5 Joseph and Mary are introduced with biographical details as if they had never been mentioned before. Joseph is 'of the house and family of David', Mary is 'his betrothed', and Nazareth is 'a town in Galilee'. Now precisely the same information has already been given in Lk 1:26–7: Nazareth is a town in Galilee, Joseph is of the house of David, and he is betrothed to a woman named Mary. Surely this is proof that the Lucan stories of the Annunciation and the Nativity were originally totally separate from each other? (2) In Lk 2:4–5 Joseph and Mary are represented as an ordinary couple living in Nazareth and travelling together to Bethlehem because of the census. This story, taken on its own, clearly gives one to understand that Joseph is the father of the child. This is in flat contradiction to the story recounted in 1:26–38. (3) In 1:31–3 it is openly stated that Mary's child will 'inherit the throne of David his father and reign over the house of Jacob for ever', *i.e.* the stress falls on the greatness of the earthly kingdom that will be

---

[5] *Ibid.*, p. 318.   [6] See below, pp. 332–8.

[7] For the full title and details see the Bibliography. Page references in this chapter are to the reprint in Dibelius' collected essays, *Botschaft und Geschichte*, vol. 1, Tübingen, 1953.

his. By contrast, 2:11–12 affirm that he is 'Christ the Lord, the Saviour', and the stress falls on the spiritual salvation brought by the lowly child 'wrapped in swaddling clothes and lying in a manger' (2:7, 12). From every point of view, says Dibelius, we are dealing with two separate traditions.[8]

Moreover, these two traditions do not complement each other. First, there is no sequel to Gabriel's Annunciation—no record of Mary's conception (as in Mt 1:18, or as in Lk 1:24 for Elizabeth), no record of Joseph's taking her to his own home (as in Mt 1:24). The whole Annunciation-story is rounded off and closed by Mary's words in Lk 1:38: 'Be it done unto me according to thy word!' Secondly, the Nativity story in Lk 2:1–20 is perfectly intelligible without the Annunciation. The most that can be said is that Luke has supplied a connection between the two traditions by inserting, in 1:27, the words 'betrothed to a man whose name was Joseph'. But if these words are suppressed at 1:27, nothing is lost, for Joseph plays no part at all in the story of the Annunciation. On the contrary, all is gain, for then we have a perfectly coherent narrative beginning (1:26–7): 'The angel Gabriel was sent by God to a town in Galilee called Nazareth, *to a virgin of the house of David*, and the virgin's name was Mary'. At one stroke all the difficulties vanish. There is no need to ask why Joseph should be mentioned in 1:27; the promise of David's kingdom (1:32–3) fits the context excellently; and the reader is fully prepared for the assertion of the virginal conception.[9]

And indeed, Dibelius continues, this restoration of the original version of the story brings to the fore the true nature of the narrative, where the primary interest is not in the virginal conception, but in the fact that Mary's son will be the Messianic king (1:31–3). It is only in the second place, and as proof of the child's Messianic destiny, that the angel asserts that he will be conceived of a holy spirit. Now if Mary is a virgin, unattached to any man (the word 'betrothed' having been suppressed from v. 27), the promise of a son to an unwedded and unbetrothed virgin is a most singular and convincing sign. But the words in which this sign is promised ('Thou shalt conceive in the womb and bear a son and call his

[8] *Botschaft und Geschichte I*, pp. 9–10.   [9] *Ibid.*, pp. 11–13.

name' Jesus: 1:31) are quite evidently taken from Is 7:14 (in the Septuagint version) and are therefore eminently suitable to introduce the theme of the virgin birth of the Messianic king.[10]

Dibelius then goes on to stress that both Matthew and Luke are concerned above all to affirm the supernatural origin of Jesus, and he interprets Lk 1:35 in much the same way as was done in Part I of this book.[11] He insists that 'the main thing for the narrator is therefore *not the upholding of Mary's virginity*; what is essential for him is the *divine origin* as is defined by the word ἐπισκιάζειν'.[12] He condemns entirely Leisegang's misinterpretation of the verb 'overshadow' in the works of Philo, on the grounds given above, adding three more texts where the verb is found which also tell against Leisegang.[13] Finally, he rejects the idea that the New Testament story could have originated from rabbinical parallels: for example, when in Gen 21:1 God is said to have 'visited' Sarah, the rabbis stressed that it was God who took away her barrenness, but with their strong conservative attachment to history they could never have entertained the idea that this excluded the fatherhood of Abraham.[14]

Where, then, did the idea of the virginal conception originate? Dibelius turns to Gal 4:21–31, where Paul inserts his midrash about the birth of Isaac and Ishmael,[15] and in particular to 4:29: 'just as then the one begotten according to the flesh persecuted him [begotten] according to the spirit, so it is now'. Here Isaac is said to have been begotten not by flesh (κατὰ σάρκα) but by spirit (κατὰ πνεῦμα). It is not said that God took away the barrenness of his mother, in the way that the Old Testament and the rabbis understood this phrase; rather, the whole stress falls on the fact that Isaac was begotten 'in spiritual manner', by

---

[10] *Ibid.*, pp. 15–17.

[11] *Ibid.*, p. 18, and see above, Part I, Chapter 6, pp. 57–61.

[12] *Ibid.*, p. 20. The italics are the author's.

[13] *Legum Allegoriae* II, viii = 30 (Loeb ed., vol. 1, pp. 244–5); *De confusione linguarum* xiv = 60 (Loeb ed., vol. 4, pp. 44–5); *De Josepho* x = 49 ('Lust is powerful to *becloud* even the keenest of senses': Loeb ed., vol. 6, pp. 166–7). See above, pp. 301 and 305–6 for Leisegang's theory.

[14] *Botschaft und Geschichte* I, pp. 24–5.

[15] See above, p. 20.

direct contrast with 'the natural manner, by the flesh'. Abraham's part in Isaac's birth has receded totally into the background. To what degree, may be seen from Paul's citation at this point of Is 54:1: 'the children of *the woman without husband* are more numerous than those of *her who possesses a husband*' (Gal 4:27). Paul, by applying this oracle (originally referring to Zion) to two individual women, Sarah and Hagar, has almost denied the physical fatherhood of Abraham at this point (though elsewhere, of course, he readily affirms it, Rom 4:18-21). What is interesting is that when Paul is writing midrash, he more or less affirms that Isaac had no human father![16]

Paul could never have taken this idea from the Old Testament or from his rabbinic schooling. And, says Dibelius, he did not get it from the Christian community, because *he never applied it to Jesus Christ!*[17] There is nothing mythological in the account, no hint of any sexual union between God and woman (for which the aged Sarah would be an ill-chosen example!); the whole picture is of *direct creation* by the Spirit of God. Now in Hellenistic Judaism the idea of direct creation by the Holy Spirit of God, with all co-operation of the husband excluded, was not unknown. Leisegang, when interpreting Philo, erred by tracing the origin of Philo's thought back to Hellenistic mysticism and Greek prophecy;[18] he overlooked the text of Gal 4:21-31. Had he considered it, he would perhaps have seen that both Paul and Philo are drawing on a common idea, namely, that God can create a child in the womb without the co-operation of a husband. The idea must therefore have been present in Hellenistic Judaism; and if in the school of Alexandria, why not in Tarsus too?

It remains to be shown that Philo was acquainted with this idea of direct creation in the womb by the Holy Spirit of God. The decisive text occurs in *De Cherubim* xiii = 44-7,[19] where we read:

---

[16] *Ibid.*, pp. 27-9.

[17] *Ibid.*, p. 29. Italics and exclamation mark by the author.

[18] See above, pp. 302-4.

[19] Translation by F. H. Colson and G. H. Whitaker in the Loeb ed., vol. 2, pp. 34-7.

'Who then is he that sows in them the good seed save the Father of all, that is God unbegotten and begetter of all things?' (44).

A few lines later, with reference to Sarah, Leah and Rebecca, we read that

'virtue receives the divine seed from the Creator' (46),

and that Moses found Zipporah

'pregnant through no mortal agency' (47).

Dibelius places great stress on this text from Philo, writing:

'No further proof is needed that Hellenistic Judaism could ascribe to God the births of famous holy men which, for one reason or another, are represented as miraculous, and could indeed exclude the human father.'[20]

One may query whether Philo really meant to exclude human paternity (he could, for example, mean that it is God alone who makes human seed fruitful), but this question is not important for a correct understanding of the argument. For Dibelius rightly sees that the Hellenistic Jews could not think of God physically begetting a child, but only of direct creation.

'In Hellenistic Judaism these births are attributed to the *activity of the creative "holy spirit" to the exclusion of the husband* . . . God brought them about without any anthropomorphism, as a Creator, not as a lover.'[21]

And, he concludes, for such a child a divine origin was attested.[22]

It is easy to see how the argument then develops. The early Christians, firmly believing that Jesus was the son of God, deduced that he must have been born of the spirit of God:

[20] *Ibid.*, p. 32.
[21] *Ibid.*, pp. 30 (italics by the author) and 35.
[22] *Ibid.*, p. 35. The argument of the last two paragraphs summarizes pp. 30–5.

'It was as a *theologoumenon*, not as a story (whether legend or myth) that the wonderful conception of Jesus made its first entry into Christian preaching.'[23]

Dibelius utterly rejects the principle that simple tales or narratives necessarily precede in time more abstract *theologoumena*, and points to the development of the Resurrection stories and to the doctrine of Christ's descent *ad inferos*. In the former (he claims) belief that Jesus was still living, unconquered by death, gave birth to the story of the empty tomb; in the latter, the knowledge that Jesus had been for a time in the realm of the dead gave rise to the story that he preached to them (*cf.* 1 Pet 4:6 and 3:19), or broke open the gates of Limbo to set them free.[24] One need not assent without reservation to these examples in order to concur in his judgment that the simple tale is not necessarily anterior in time to the theological affirmation, and we may therefore rapidly summarize the remainder of his argument.

The early Christians, believing that Jesus was the son of God, naturally deduced that he was 'born of God', and the question then arose, 'But how?' The notion of a theogamy, of the wedding of God to a mortal woman, was as abhorrent to them as it was to the Jews. In explaining the divine conception of Jesus, the first step was taken when they began to preach that an angel announced it (compare the angelic announcement of the Resurrection): that is to say, all happened by God's word. Then, to emphasize still further the transcendence of the Creator, they affirmed that it was not God himself, but his spirit or his power that came upon Mary; and those who read or heard this story would by these words understand that it was God's creative power which brought Jesus into existence. Once this stage had been reached, we cannot

---

[23] *Ibid.*, p. 35. Elsewhere, however, he does refer to the virginal conception as a 'legend': *From Tradition to Gospel*, pp. 124, 132, 269, and *The Message of Jesus*, London, 1939, p. 179. There is no contradiction here: he means that the idea began as a *theologoumenon* and later developed into a legend as details were added. See below, p. 317, n. 27.

[24] See *Botschaft und Geschichte I*, pp. 35–8, where many references to the early Fathers and apocryphal writings are given.

totally exclude the possibility that Is 7:14 began to play a part in the development of the doctrine. That text, read in the Septuagint, probably influenced those early Christians to take a further step, and to affirm that Jesus had been *virginally* conceived through the Holy Spirit of God. This was all the more likely since certain texts from Philo which hint at the possibility of God's creating a child without human intercourse speak of his doing so in a *virginal* nature,[25] on the ground that only such a soul is capable and worthy of union with God. This last idea (Dibelius thinks) Philo absorbed from Egypt.[26] Thus reflection upon the heavenly origin of Jesus led to the affirmation that he was born 'not according to the flesh, but *according to the Spirit*' (*cf.* Gal 4:29), and this is the distinctive contribution of Hellenistic Judaism to the doctrine; this in turn led to the affirmation that he was conceived by the power of the Holy Spirit *in the womb of a virgin*, and this is an idea which stems, ultimately, from pagan Egypt.[27]

Dibelius' case is enormously impressive, brilliantly argued, calm and scholarly in its assessment of texts and in its general

[25] *De Cherubim* xiii = 45; xiv = 49, citing Jer 3:4: 'Didst thou not call upon me as thy house, thy father and the husband of thy virginity?'; xiv = 50, 'It is meet that God should hold converse with the truly virgin nature, that which is undefiled and free from impure touch; but it is the opposite with us' (in the Loeb ed., vol. 2, pp. 34–9). In *De congressu eruditionis gratia* ii = 7, it is said of Leah (Gen 29:31) that God 'opens the womb which yet loses not its virginity' (Loeb ed., vol. 4, pp. 460–1); in *Quaestiones in Exodum* II, 3, that 'when souls become divinely inspired, from (being) women they become virgins' (Loeb ed., Supplement II, p. 38); and in *De Somniis* II, xxviii = 185 that the virgin wife of the high priest 'strange paradox, never becomes a woman' (Loeb ed., vol. 5, pp. 526–7).

[26] On the ground that two feasts are attested in Egypt, one for the 25 December and one on the night of the 5–6 January, each containing the liturgical acclamation 'The Virgin has given birth!' See *Botschaft und Geschichte* I, pp. 41–2, fn. 66 for the references. For fuller documentation see the footnotes in J. G. Frazer, *The Golden Bough: Adonis Attis Osiris*, vol. 1, pp. 303–7 (though Frazer does not draw Dibelius' inferences).

[27] For the whole paragraph see *Botschaft und Geschichte* I, pp. 39–42. There is no need to summarize here the remainder of Dibelius' essay (pp. 42–78), which is concerned to show how the full 'legend' contained in the Bible developed from this basic *theologoumenon*. Quite a number of the points he makes have in fact been discussed earlier in this book, in other contexts.

presentation. One thing it has almost certainly achieved: it has closed the case for ever against the theory that the doctrine of the virginal conception is simply a copy or an imitation of stories from Greek or Egyptian mythology. If one wants to explain the origin of the biblical story without admitting an historical basis and supernatural intervention, this is surely the most logical and coherent way to do it. And Dibelius himself is far from insensitive to the religious message of the doctrine. After observing that the story of the child in the manger is meant to show how the Redeemer appears in the most straitened circumstances, not in glory, he concludes his essay with these words:

> 'The two legends of the Virgin's son and the Child in the manger thus clearly express the two trends of Christian preaching: to describe at one time the astounding fact of the redemption as a superhuman phenomenon repealing the law that governed previous human history, and to represent it at another time as a gift from God within the straitened confines of earthly existence.'[28]

Is this powerfully argued case sufficient by itself to explain how the doctrine of the virginal conception originated?

It is evident that Dibelius' case rests to a very considerable extent on his contention that some circles of Hellenistic Judaism (as attested by Paul and Philo) had already positively envisaged the idea that God was capable of creating a child by a virginal conception. There is nothing *a priori* impossible in this suggestion, when one reflects on the exalted notion of the Godhead in all Judaism. But it is debatable whether even the Jewish philosophers of Alexandria ever put the question to themselves. The obscure text of Philo's *De Cherubim* xiii–xiv (= 43–50)[29] is certainly patient of Dibelius' interpretation, but it seems preferable to explain it as meaning that it is God alone who implants the good seed of virtue in the offspring of men: it was God alone who bestowed on Abraham a child so wise as Isaac, and on Isaac and Rebecca

[28] *Botschaft und Geschichte I*, p. 78.
[29] Loeb ed., vol. 2, pp. 34–9.

the steadfast, all-enduring Jacob. For when Philo asks 'Who is he that sows in them the good seed save the Father of all?' (44), the pronoun 'them' refers to virtues 'whose offspring may not have to do with mortal man' (43). Throughout this passage (as in the others cited)[30] Philo is speaking not of the creation of a human body, but of the virgin soul.

A more serious weakness is the appeal to Gal 4:21-31. It is surely significant that in v. 23, where Paul is speaking directly of the physical begetting of Ishmael and Isaac, he does not say that Isaac was born 'by the spirit': 'the son of the slave-girl was begotten *according to the flesh*, the son of the free woman *by means of a promise*'. If Paul had really believed he could talk about Isaac as 'begotten by the spirit', here was the point to assert it: as it is, he changes both the preposition and the case. Ishmael was born κατὰ σάρκα, Isaac δι᾽ἐπαγγελίας. In v. 25 he writes that '*the figure of* Hagar (τὸ δὲ ʽΑ.) represents Mount Sinai in Arabia', but in v. 26 moves directly to a consideration of the heavenly Jerusalem *without any mention of Sarah*. It is to the heavenly Jerusalem which is our mother that Paul applies the text of Is 54:1, and in this he is utterly faithful to its original, collective, meaning. In no way does Paul apply the text of Isaiah 54:1 to Sarah (who, after all, did not have any more children than Hagar!); it is the heavenly Jerusalem alone which, in Paul's eyes, is bride and mother. His first conclusion is that 'you, brethren, are children *of a promise, after the manner of Isaac*' (v. 28): note that he does *not* write 'you, like Isaac, are *born according to the spirit*' (ὑμεῖς δέ, καθὼς καὶ ὁ Ἰσαάκ, κατὰ πνεῦμα τέκνα ἐστέ), as one might reasonably have expected on Dibelius' hypothesis. Only in v. 29 does Paul introduce the phrase on which Dibelius' case rests: 'just as then the one born κατὰ σάρκα persecuted the one born κατὰ πνεῦμα, so it is now'. Here Paul's choice of the phrase κατὰ πνεῦμα seems to be evidently dictated by the content of the second clause ('so it is now'). The spiritual regeneration of Christians takes place κατὰ πνεῦμα, οὐ κατὰ σάρκα, and it was therefore an obvious invitation to refer to the birth of Isaac at the very end of the allegory as being κατὰ πνεῦμα. Dibelius' appeal to Philo is of

[30] P. 317, n. 25.

doubtful validity; his appeal to Paul is, I suggest, most certainly wrong. And in that case he has failed to show that the notion of a virginal conception was known in Hellenistic Judaism before the Christian gospel was preached.

But that does not mean that Dibelius' whole case is destroyed. One could take the argument set out above on pp. 315–7 and say that it stands firm on its own, even without the supporting evidence of Philo or Paul. That is, one could argue that just as the early Christians created many stories and legends about the Resurrection in order to affirm that Christ was unconquered by death, so they made up the story of the virginal conception to affirm that he was wholly and entirely the son of God. The only difference would be that in the first case those early Christians did have a Jewish idea of resurrection to start with, whereas they did not have a Jewish idea of virginal conception to start with in the second. But even a little reflection on the power of God the Creator would have convinced them that a virginal conception is not for him impossible; and once the possibility was grasped, it would have been a short step to asserting that Jesus was virginally conceived, by the power of the Holy Spirit. It would have been an attractive and colourful way of affirming their belief that he was, from the first moment of his earthly life, the son of God.

This is the form in which the 'legendary' character of the story is nowadays most often presented, and it has the merit of avoiding all the errors of earlier writers who sought to trace the origin of the virginal conception to Judaism, mythology or Greek mysticism. But there is one objection which seems to have conclusive force. It is an argument used before against the theory of Jewish derivation.[31] If there is one thing certain from the Old Testament, it is that the Jews believed the Messiah would be 'of the seed of David'. And if there is one thing certain from the New, it is that the early Christians believed that Jesus of Nazareth was this promised Messiah. Any early Christian who had simply thought up the idea of a virginal conception as an attractive way of expressing his belief that Jesus was the son of God would have seen at once that this would entail denying that he was truly 'of the seed

[31] See pp. 276–7 and also p. 283.

of David', and that this new idea would destroy the credibility of the claim that Jesus was the Messiah, at least among the Jews. Are we to believe that purely for the sake of a colourful but quite unnecessary story, the Christians (of Palestine?) were prepared to put at risk the Messianic status of Jesus among the Jews?

Chapter Sixteen

THE VIRGINAL CONCEPTION
(V): AN HISTORICAL FACT

ONLY three serious objections remain against the view that the biblical narrative of the virginal conception records a biological fact, the first of which is philosophical, the second historical, and the third theological.

It may be asserted on philosophical grounds that a virginal conception is impossible. For an atheist (though not for an agnostic) such a judgment is logically consistent. But on the assumption that the only people likely to read this book believe in the existence of God, it is legitimate to observe that for them such a judgment is impossible. If the story of the virginal conception is a myth or legend, may one not say that the traditional doctrines of the Incarnation, of the Redemption of the world through Christ's passion and death, of the Resurrection and of the Parousia (*i.e.* all the major items in the Creed) are also nothing more than myths and legends? Of course, there are many today, especially in North-West Europe and North America, who would wholeheartedly concur in this conclusion. But in that case what is the objection to saying that the idea of God the Creator is yet another myth? Or (to turn the argument round), if one admits the objective existence of a Creator-God, on what principle can one deny to him the ability to create by a virginal conception?[1]

Among Christians, however, the more usual reason for not regarding the virginal conception as a biological fact is that there

[1] This point is adapted from H. M. Köster in *Jungfrauengeburt gestern und heute* p. 57.

is not sufficient evidence to justify such a conclusion. Douglas Edwards comments on this in his usual trenchant style. Those who hold this view, he says, have

> 'never asked themselves precisely what evidence they would have been prepared to regard as *sufficient*. Had they done so, they would probably have discovered that the kind of evidence which they were all this time desiring was impossible evidence —the evidence, for example, of a medical board. Yet clearly, if evidence of that kind should prove to be forthcoming, the same critics would be among the first to protest—and this time with justice—that such evidence is its own condemnation.'[2]

Whether in fact those who refuse to accept the story as historical would be quite so exigent as Edwards suggests is questionable, but at least his main point stands. No opponent of the historicity of the narrative, as far as I know, has ever put down in writing what evidence he would regard as convincing (*e.g.* the testimony of four gospels instead of two; an explicit statement by St Paul, or an assertion in the early kerygma). But Chapter 11 has already shown that there is in the New Testament more evidence to support the doctrine than is often admitted; and even if there were more still, one sometimes feels that what the critics really want is a clear affirmation in the New Testament that 'this is not a legend or a myth, but a record of historical fact'. Yet even when such statements are made (about the Resurrection: Ac 2:32; 3:15; 5:32; 10:39–40; 13:31), the same critics refrain from discussing in detail the precise import of these assertions, so that in the end anyone who would defend the historicity of the virginal conception can only present his case as persuasively as he can and challenge those who disagree to find a better explanation of the texts.

The principal reason given for not accepting the virginal conception as an historical (*i.e.* biological) fact is that there is not enough evidence in the New Testament to support this conclusion. Those who take this view fail to appreciate the peculiarly intimate

[2] *The Virgin Birth*, p. 149.

nature of the doctrine, for if Jesus was in truth virginally conceived, how could this fact have been manifested during his earthly life without exposing him, and his mother, and Joseph, to a barrage of obscenity and ridicule? Is it not obvious that if the virginal conception really took place, it could never have been made publicly known until after the Resurrection?

Secondly, if Jesus was in fact virginally conceived, is it not likely that Mary, during her earthly life, would have entrusted such a secret only to those who were closest to her, and to Jesus? Luke puts ample stress on the humility of this handmaid of the Lord; for him, it is her characteristic virtue. Because of this humility, it is hard to think that Mary would ever have acquiesced in the public proclamation during her earthly life of the great things done to her by him that is mighty. Indeed, it is highly questionable whether she would have informed all the Twelve, or all her own family, of the mystery of Jesus' conception. Yet (still assuming the fact) her virginal conception stood out among the *magnalia Dei*, and it is equally unthinkable that one so humble should have wished this great mystery to remain eternally concealed. The most probable explanation of the relative silence of the earlier books of the New Testament is that Mary during her earthly life entrusted this secret only to one who was exceedingly close to her, as he had been to Jesus, to the beloved disciple, *i.e.* to John the son of Zebedee.

If this was in fact so, it is easy to see why the records of Jesus' public life contain no direct allusion to his virginal conception; why the early kerygma as presented by Luke in Acts passes over the mystery in silence; and why the most striking testimony to the doctrine is found in Jn 1:13 and in those pages of Luke which are closely related to the Fourth Gospel.[3] Indeed, it is worth calling attention at this point to a singular omission in Jn 1:13. If the evangelist had there wished to speak of the eternal generation of the Word (as some have maintained),[4] or if he had wished to deny in every possible way that Jesus took his human origin from men, he could have written:

[3] See above, pp. 8–10 and 147–8.
[4] See above, pp. 263–4, n. 23.

'He was born not of blood-streams,
nor of the will of the flesh,
nor of the will of man,
nor of the will of woman,
but of God.'

Is it not perhaps legitimate to see, in the absence of the phrase 'nor of the will of woman', an intimation that Jesus was born solely of the will of woman, and from God? 'Behold the handmaid of the Lord! Be it done unto me according to thy word!' (Lk 1:38).[5]

The last three paragraphs have treated the virginal conception as an historical fact. Let us now consider it as if it were a legend ('like the Resurrection'). If it was a legend, why should it not have been used (at least by reference or allusion) to exalt the person of Jesus in the records of his public ministry? Why was it not incorporated into the early kerygma in Acts, where it would have made such a colourful counterbalance (entrance and exit) to the 'legend' of the Resurrection? Why above all did Luke, that supreme artist, not seize upon the literary possibilities of drawing a parallel between these two 'legends'? And if it was a legend of Hellenistic origin, why did Luke not insert it into the speeches of Paul to the Greeks? If it was of Jewish-Hellenistic origin, why did he not use it when Paul was speaking in the synagogues of Hellenistic Jews? And if it was a *theologoumenon*, an affirmation in story that Jesus was wholly and exclusively the son of God, but not an historical fact, why was Matthew (1:18–25) so concerned to stress that this purely fictitious tale about the virginal conception of Jesus did not invalidate his claim to be the Messiah?[6]

It was said above that the principal reason given for not accepting the virginal conception as an historical fact is that there is not enough evidence in the New Testament to support this conclusion.[7] I would suggest that the relative paucity of clear evidence in the New Testament is a very good reason for *not* treating it as a

[5] *Cf.* J. Galot, *Etre né de Dieu*, p. 100.
[6] See above, Chapter 2, pp. 167–72, especially p. 172.
[7] P. 270.

legend or a *theologoumenon*, but for asserting that it was an historical fact, a secret kept hidden by Mary until the end of her life and only subsequently revealed through the agency of John.

So we come to the latest objection against the view that the virginal conception should be regarded as an historical event. I do not know that any fresh exegetical arguments have been brought forward since Dibelius' essay of 1932;[8] contemporary exegetes seem to repeat, in varying combinations, the old arguments already discussed. But since 1950 or thereabouts a number of dogmatic theologians have affirmed (not on exegetical grounds, but on the basic of their systematic theology) that the story is only a symbol (unfounded in a biologically virginal conception) of the divine sonship of Jesus. A powerful and even necessary symbol in the past, especially among the unsophisticated, it no longer speaks meaningfully to twentieth-century man, and may therefore be discarded insofar as it is an assertion about the biological origin of Jesus. In other words, these theologians ask whether the evangelists (given their cultural background) had at their disposal any more eloquent concept to affirm that Jesus was exclusively the son of God, the gift of God to man.

For theologians who approach the matter in this way the story of the virginal conception was, if not the indispensable, certainly the ideal way of presenting the message of Jesus' divine sonship to the Greco-Roman world: for it clothed the religious truth in the powerful and persuasive language of myth.

'The Christian concept of the virgin birth of Jesus had as its background the total experience of the early Christian community, which consisted of and came into contact with and desired to proclaim a message to peoples of diverse historical traditions. The narratives of Jesus' birth in the New Testament reflect a milieu of Jewish, Gentile, and Christian elements (Jewish: miraculous birth motif, the Septuagint translation of Is 7:14, reflection of other Old Testament passages, the double meaning of *pais* as servant and child; Gentile: the universal child-savior motif; Christian, the

[8] See above, pp. 311–8.

several primitive Christologies). In order to bring about contact with non-Christians, the story of Jesus' birth had to be similar to the stories of the births of the heroes of the other traditions . . .

The canonical narratives of the virgin birth may be generally described as Christian stories in a primarily Hellenistic mode of thought cast in a Jewish setting and designed to make a universal appeal . . .

The myth of Jesus' origin and the legends that comprise this vignette present in primitive concrete form what New Testament authors record elsewhere in philosophical and abstract modes of thought. By the very nature of the story, the myth in addition encompasses a number of elements, individual ones of which have always been relevant and pertinent to different audiences . . . Because of the mythical form into which this truth was cast, Christianity was able to evangelize the ancient world. The story of Jesus' origin in its Biblical form established a natural bridge between the Christian community and non-Christian society. The closest association between Christian and pagan tradition was at the point of the narratives of the birth of gods and heroes. Not only were these traditions the most comparable, they were also the most popular. The Christian story made it possible for God's Word concerning incarnation to be communicated to the hearts of the masses of men.'[9]

In short, the argument is that it was principally by this supremely clear and attractive myth of the virginal conception that the ancient Church was able to express to the non-Christian world the all but ineffable mystery of the Incarnation.

Yet, as Paul Tillich has written, 'symbols are born and die':[10] a symbol which speaks the truth to one generation or culture may be meaningless, or may even convey a totally different message, to another. If the story of the virginal conception is

---

[9] T. Boslooper, *The Virgin Birth*, Philadelphia, 1962: extracts from his Conclusion, on pp. 227–37.

[10] *Der verlorene Dimension*, Hamburg, 1962, p. 44.

simply a myth or a *theologoumenon* thought up in the ancient Church in order to proclaim to non-Christians in the Roman Empire the message that God was incarnate in Jesus, has it not now ceased to serve its purpose, so that it could with profit be discarded? For the story that Jesus was born of a virgin does not express to non-Christians of the twentieth century the message that in Jesus God is incarnate. 'Let us look dispassionately at today's real cultural situation: if a modern man who has not been brought up as a Christian hears the words "Jesus is God made man" he will straightaway reject this explanation as mythology which he cannot begin to take seriously nor to discuss, just as we do when we hear that the Dalai Lama regards himself as the reincarnation of Buddha.'[11] To such a modern man, the doctrine of the virginal conception is simply the most perfect example of the mythological character of the Christian faith. Clearly, everyone must admit that *if* the story of the virginal conception was a symbol invented to assist the presentation of the gospel to non-Christians two thousand years ago, it has outlived its purpose. But was it simply invented as a symbol, for this purpose? That is the question at issue.

Tillich has put forward another argument for rejecting the historicity of the virginal conception. This symbol, he says, has not only outlived its purpose in that mythology no longer conveys truth to modern man. This particular symbol 'stands theologically on the boundary of the heretical. For it abrogates one of the fundamental doctrines of the Council of Chalcedon, the classical Christological doctrine, that the full humanity of Jesus must be maintained beside his full divinity. A human being who has no human father does not possess full humanity. Hence this symbol must be rejected, not on historical grounds, but because of what is involved in the symbol.'[12] But again, Tillich *assumes* that he is here dealing with a symbol, not with an historical fact. And *whether* the doctrine is purely symbolic is precisely the point at issue.

[11] K. Rahner, 'Theology and Anthropology', in *Theological Investigations*, vol. 9, London, 1962, on p. 40.

[12] *Der verlorene Dimension*, p. 54.

Myth, legend, *theologoumenon* or record of historical fact? Every attempt so far made to find a parallel to the story of the virginal conception in the myths and legends of the ancient world has, within the space of a few years, been fiercely criticized and decisively rejected even by those scholars who do not admit the historicity of the narrative. That is to say, there is a consensus of opinion even among rationalist critics that no positive explanation for the origin of the story has yet been found in the realm of ancient mythology. Today, the only alternatives left are the theory that the story is a *theologoumenon* (*i.e.* a Christian myth created within the community) and the ancient tradition that the story records an historical event.

There is no historical evidence that the story began life as a *theologoumenon*. It need only be added that as long as one holds that the early Church believed Jesus to be the Messiah, and believed that the Messiah would be of the seed of David, the road is firmly closed to any *future* demonstration that the early Christians made up this story with no prompting in terms of historical testimony.

The reasons for retaining the ancient belief that the narrative is a record of historical fact are that the events in Lk 1–2 (as distinct from the theological interpretation given there) point to Mary as the primary witness, through John as her intermediary;[13] that the relative silence of the New Testament is not merely well, but excellently, explained on this hypothesis;[14] and that there is no reasoned objection (as distinct from an *a priori* denial) on literary, historical or theological grounds to this view. All this together is not, of course, sufficient to provide an apodictic demonstration that Jesus was in truth virginally conceived; such a demonstration, sufficient to convince even the most stubborn sceptic, is never to be found in any of God's dealings with men. But anyone who accepts the New Testament as the revelation of God in word, narrating his self-revelation in deed, has every reason for accepting, and none for rejecting, the historicity of the virginal conception.

[13] See above, pp. 143–8.
[14] See above, p. 324.

Chapter Seventeen

THE RELIGIOUS SIGNIFICANCE OF
THE VIRGINAL CONCEPTION

EVER since the beginning of the third century, it has been the custom to require that candidates for baptism should make a profession of faith in the virginal conception of Jesus. There is clear evidence of this practice in the *Apostolic Tradition* of St Hippolytus, written about A.D. 217, in which we read:

'Do you believe in Christ Jesus, the son of God,
   who was born of the Holy Spirit from the virgin Mary?'[1]

A similar formula is found in the Old Roman Creed, the prototype of what is generally known as the Apostles' Creed:

'He was conceived of the Holy Spirit
and born of the virgin Mary.'[2]

This profession of faith has survived in most Western baptismal liturgies to the present day.

In modern times, however, more and more Christians have begun to ask whether the virginal conception of Jesus (taken as an historical fact) is really an integral part of the gospel message, a doctrine by which the Church's faith stands or falls. Many quite ordinary Christians complain that they cannot see its relevance, much less its importance. In this, they may sometimes have a

[1] 'Credis in Christum Iesum, Filium Dei, qui natus est de Spiritu Sancto ex Maria virgine . . .?' (DS 10).

[2] For the many variations in the wording of the Greek and Latin texts see DS 11 ff.

legitimate grievance, for all too often preachers have treated this article of the Creed as if it were merely a demand for intellectual assent to the statement that such a miracle once took place. They may have added that it also shows forth the glory of Mary's virginity, in that the Word of God chose to be born of a woman who had firmly resolved to remain a virgin for ever.[3] The result has been, particularly in the Roman Catholic Church, that the doctrine has come to be regarded at a popular level as being primarily a Marian doctrine, the principal purpose of which is to call attention to the religious significance of Mary's virginity. Parallel to this has been the alienation of Protestant sympathy for the doctrine; since 1900, many members of the Reformed Churches have felt no doctrinal scruples in abandoning it, thinking that such a step was fully in the spirit of the Reformers' protest against 'Roman Mariolatry'. And with the modern insistence on the holiness of sex within marriage, and the disappearance within the Churches of the last traces of Manichaeism and Jansenism, the doctrine that Jesus was virginally conceived has lost much of the ascetic appeal that it had in earlier times.

Those who have abandoned this doctrine, or adopted an attitude of scepticism towards it, are nearly always convinced that in the end it does not matter whether or not Jesus was in reality conceived and born of a virgin mother. There is a certain element of truth in this, but only because the statement is ambiguous. One can certainly say 'It did not matter whether Jesus was virginally conceived' if the meaning is that God was utterly free to bring about the Incarnation of his Son in a child conceived naturally: even so conservative a theologian as Suarez could write that 'without doubt God could have been conceived and begotten by union between a man and a woman'.[4] But if anyone says that it *does* not matter whether Jesus was born of a virgin, meaning that the New Testament witness to the virginal conception carries no religious message of any importance, then the assertion is false.

When men say that the fact of the virginal conception is of no real importance within the general framework of the gospel

[3] In the manner described above on pp. 174–6.
[4] *In Tertiam Partem S. Thomae*, qu. 32, a. 4, Disput. 10, sect. 3, n. 2.

teaching, they are nearly always considering it as a *Marian* doctrine, as if it were purely a statement of a biological fact. But to adopt such narrow terms of reference is to regard the matter very differently from the way it is viewed in the Creeds. There it is not a Marian doctrine, but first and last a *Christological* statement in which Mary's part is mentioned only in the second place: the wording of the Apostles' Creed is, 'He was *conceived of the Holy Ghost*, and born of the Virgin Mary', while the Creed of Nicaea and Constantinople has 'He was *incarnate of the Holy Ghost*, from Mary the Virgin'.[5] The virginal conception is placed among the Church's basic dogmas not because it says something about Mary, or about the value of virginity, but because it is an assertion that the birth on earth of Jesus Christ the Redeemer is due exclusively to the direct intervention of God. It is a firm denial that he was born in the course of nature from our own sinful race.

It does not require much reflection to perceive that a Jew would have found it very foolish to suggest that an entirely sinless redeemer might have been born in the course of nature from the sinful race of men:

> 'Who can bring a clean thing out of an unclean?
> There is not one . . .
> What is man, that he can be clean?
> Or he that is born of woman,
> that he can be righteous?' (Job 14:4; 15:14).

St Paul in particular lays great stress on the fact that all men, Jew and Gentile alike, stand in need of redemption (Rom 1:18–3:20, especially 3:9–12), for all without exception are one with Adam in sin (5:12–21); yet he speaks of Jesus Christ as 'him who had not known sin' (2 Cor 5:21; *cf.* Heb 4:15). Are we to think that Paul never noticed the latent problem—how a sinless human being could have been born of Adam's race?

I would submit that Paul did see the question, but did not regard it as a problem because he knew that he already had the solution,

[5] See DS 10–36 for the variations in the text of the *Apostolicum*; DS 150 for that of Nicaea–Constantinople.

in the doctrine of the virginal conception. Christ was indeed of Adam's race (*i.e.* the same kind of being as Adam), because he was born of woman. But he was not born in the course of nature from Adam's stock: he was 'a new creation'. And this doctrine of the new creation is the very heart and soul of Paul's soteriology.

That Paul could have learnt of the virginal conception, from John, before he wrote the Epistle to the Romans, is indisputable, if one accepts the theory proposed in the last chapter (that Mary revealed the fact of the virginal conception to the son of Zebedee[6]); for the visit to Jerusalem at which he met John the son of Zebedee (Gal 2:1–10) took place many years before Romans was written. All one need postulate is that Mary had already died, or that Paul too was entrusted with the secret of the virginal conception.[7]

In two of his best-known doctrinal passages, Rom 5 and 1 Cor 15, St Paul draws a parallel between Christ and the first man, Adam. It is generally accepted that in the first passage (Rom 5: 21–21) the parallelism lies in this: that just as the first man's disobedience made all men sinners, so the obedience of Christ made all men righteous. It is also generally accepted that in the second text (1 Cor 15:42–9) the parallelism consists in this: that just as we inherit from the first Adam our earthly bodies, so we shall receive from the Risen Christ (the Second Adam) the bodies that will be ours at the general resurrection. On these interpretations, it is fairly clear that the parallel between Christ and Adam in Romans is by no means as close as that in 1 Corinthians, which was written only a few months earlier. More surprisingly, the two parallels have little in common.

Adam 'is a type of him that was to come' (Rom 5:14). All the writers who comment on Rom 5 in Migne's *Patrologia Graeca* adopt the interpretation given above. They are nearly all conscious of the anomaly in it: how can Adam's *dis*obedience typify and foreshadow Christ's obedience? When we speak of Old Testament types, we refer to people or institutions that bespeak

[6] See above, p. 324.

[7] If Paul was entrusted with the story as a secret to be kept hidden for the time being, this might account for the allusive nature of the phrases in Gal 4:4 and Rom 1:3 and, as we shall soon see, in Rom 5:14 also.

a promise of something far greater to be revealed in the New Covenant (*e.g.* manna in the desert is a type of the Holy Eucharist, Melchizedek a type of Christ the High Priest). How can Adam's *sin* possibly be considered as a foreshadowing and promise of Christ's obedience? Most of the Greek Fathers are content to say that there is here a 'parallelism by contrast'.[8] Only Origen, the greatest exegete of them all, seems really aware of the difficulty, but admits that he can think of no better solution:

> 'I do not see how one can explain his disobedience and his sin, and the fact that through him death came to all men, as if these things prefigured Christ,—unless perhaps by way of contrast.'[9]

The few Latin writers who commented on Romans do not seem to have been at all worried by the problem which vexed Origen, and as a result the theory of 'parallelism by contrast' has held the field until this day.

Yet it was not as if the likeness between the creation of Adam and the virginal conception totally escaped them. St Irenaeus had seen it[10]; so had Tertullian[11] and St Ambrose.[12] It was possibly

[8] *E.g.* Photius, *Fragmenta in Romanos* (MG 101.1233) and Theophylactus, *In Romanos* 7 (MG 118.421 AB), two authors of late date who simply summarize the undisputed tradition of earlier commentators.

[9] *In Romanos* 5 (MG 14.1020).

[10] *Adv. Haer.* III, 30 and 31, 1 in Harvey, vol. 2, pp. 120–1 = Migne III, 20, 10 and 21, 1 = MG 7:954–6; and especially the *Proof of the Apostolic Preaching* 1, 32: 'Whence, then, comes the substance of the first man? From God's Will and Wisdom, and from virgin earth. For *God had not rained*, says the Scripture, before man was made, *and there was no man to till the earth*. From this earth, then, while it was still virgin, God took dust and fashioned the man, the beginning of humanity. So the Lord, summing up afresh this man, reproduced the scheme of his incarnation, being born of a virgin by the Will and Wisdom of God, that He too might copy the incarnation of Adam, and man might be made, as was written in the beginning, *according to the image and likeness of God*' (translation by J. P. Smith, in the series *Ancient Christian Writers* vol. 16, Westminster, Maryland 1952 and London, 1953, p. 68).

[11] *De carne Christi* 17 (CC 2.904 = ML 2.782).

[12] 'Ex terra virgine Adam, Christus ex virgine; ille ad imaginem Dei factus, hic imago Dei' (*In Lucam* IV, 7: CC 14.108 = ML 15.1614).

from Ambrose in Milan that St Maximus of Turin took the idea. In a Lenten sermon he writes:

'He willed to be born in every detail like Adam . . . For Adam was born of virgin soil, and Christ procreated of Mary the Virgin. The ground that was Adam's mother had not yet been disturbed by any hoe; the womb of the mother of Christ had never been disturbed by sexual contact. Adam was formed from mud by the hands of God; Christ was formed in the womb by the Spirit of God. Both therefore come from God as father, both had a virgin mother, both (as the evangelist says) are sons of God.'[13]

Maximus, though not preaching directly on the text of Romans, certainly had Rom 5:12–21 in mind, for he uses this parallel to underscore the different paths subsequently taken: Adam went on to sin by gluttony and disobedience, Christ began his ministry by fasting (it is a Lenten sermon), and by obedience recovered for mankind the gift of immortality.[14] This text from St Maximus of Turin is, as far as I know, the only one in the Latin Fathers where the birth of Adam from virgin soil is used in conjunction with the themes of Rom 5:12–21.

It is all the more remarkable, therefore, that St Thomas Aquinas grasped the possibility of explaining Rom 5:14 (Adam 'is a type of him that was to come') in terms of the virginal conception. In his commentary on the Epistle to the Romans, he first gives the standard explanation that Adam is a type of Christ only by contrast, but then adds:

'There are, however, other similarities between Christ and

[13] '. . . per omnia secundum similitudinem Adae nasci voluit. . . . Adam enim de terra virgine natus est, et Christus de Maria virgine procreatus: illius maternum solum necdum rastris scissum fuerat, istius maternum secretum numquam concupiscentia violatum. Adam dei manibus plasmatur e limo, Christus dei spiritu formatur in utero. Uterque ergo oritur deo patre, uterque virgine utitur matre, uterque, sicut evangelista dicit, filius dei est' (*Sermo* La, 2 in *CC* 23.203 = Sermo 19 in ML 57.571).

[14] *CC* 23.202–3 = ML 57.570–1.

Adam: namely, that just as the body of Adam was formed without sexual intercourse, so was the body of Christ, from a virgin . . .'[15]

Connoisseurs of Aquinas' Latin may be able to judge whether the introductory phrase used here ('*Sunt autem et aliae similitudines . . .*') does not indicate a certain scepticism about the idea of typology by contrast, and a distinct preference for some better explanation. It certainly feels so, but Thomas was always reluctant to challenge a customary interpretation of Scripture, and is content to leave the reader with this suggestion of his own.

Adam 'is a figure of him that was to come' (Rom 5:14). Was Paul here alluding to the virginal conception? Here St Luke's genealogy is informative. Jesus was, at the time of his baptism, about thirty years of age, 'being the son, *as was thought*, of Joseph' (Lk 3:23). The genealogy that follows ends with 'the son of Enos, the son of Seth, the son of Adam, the son of God' (Lk 3:38, Revised Standard Version). In the Greek, all the names are in the genitive, with the definite article. It seems that what Luke is saying is that Jesus was not physically the son of Joseph, but (like Adam) the direct or immediate creation of God. If this was, for Luke, the heart of the message of the virginal conception, then one cannot exclude the possibility that Paul had the same idea in mind when he wrote of Adam as 'the figure of him that was to come'.

Douglas Edwards has argued this case most forcefully,[16] but his argument needs rephrasing today. He rightly observes that it is not enough to say that Christ is the Second Man because he gave the human race a fresh start, or because (like Adam) he is the Head of a new race. For the further question then arises: why was Jesus, if he was born in exactly the same way as other men, able to give the human race this fresh start? Why was he, unlike other men, totally unaffected by hereditary sinfulness and able to com-

---

[15] 'Sunt autem et aliae similitudines inter Christum et Adam: quod scilicet sicut corpus Adae formatum fuit sine coitu, ita et corpus Christi de virgine . . .' (*In Romanos*, cap. 5: *Lect. 4a in fine*).

[16] *The Virgin Birth*, pp. 106–7.

municate righteousness to all mankind? Many Christians would answer 'because of his Godhead'. But then one has to ask, 'Did his Godhead "cleanse" his human nature from the hereditary sin passed on to all humanity?' This would seem contrary to 2 Cor 5:21: 'he had never known sin'. Or was he 'preserved' from sin, in the way the Roman Catholic Church teaches that Mary was preserved from all sin, original and personal? In that case, he would have been 'preserved' from sin by the special intervention of God. The doctrine of the virginal conception renders all this theorizing unnecessary, for once it is accepted, Jesus Christ as man is from the first instant of his existence the new and immediate creation of God in the womb of Mary, 'filled with the Holy Spirit' from the first moment of his earthly existence.

If one reads Rom 5:12–21 with the virginal conception in mind, the text takes on new depths of meaning. 'By one man sin came into the world, and by sin, death . . .' The children of Adam all inherited death, but the message of hope rings out at once. For Adam was a figure of another that was to come, from whom a new race would inherit instead of sin, righteousness, and instead of death, life. Christ directly created by the power of the Spirit in the womb of the Virgin was God's 'great gift', 'the grace of God and his free gift in grace' (χάρισμα; ἡ χάρις τοῦ θεοῦ καὶ ἡ δωρεὰ ἐν χάριτι). The virginal conception is all too often regarded, by defender and opponent alike, as if it were a doctrine which spoke primarily of the exaltation of Mary. Nothing could be further from the biblical reality. It is, of all the doctrines of the Christian Church, the one which proclaims most loudly the central tenet of Calvinism—'Soli Deo gloria!'

1 Cor 15:42–9 also yields better sense if Paul is thought to have had the virginal conception in mind. 'The first man was out of the earth, made of dust; the second man is from heaven' (v. 47). Of course the primary reference here is to the Risen Lord as the Final Adam; but why does Paul call him 'Adam'? Clearly, one reason is that there is a parallel between the first Adam from whom we inherit an earthly body, and the Risen Lord from whom we shall inherit a heavenly body (vv. 48–9). But if mere flesh and blood cannot inherit God's kingdom (v. 50), and if Jesus

while on earth was merely (like us) flesh and blood, how did he himself inherit the kingdom? In other words, if Jesus was by natural descent a man of Adam's race, how did he enter heaven in the first place and so acquire the ability to be the head and source of a new race? Paul's reference to Gen 2:7 ('the first Adam became a living soul') shows that he has in mind the creation of man 'from the slime of the earth'; he contrasts with this the fact that Christ, the Final Adam, is 'a life-giving spirit' (v. 45). Now if in speaking of the first Adam Paul had in mind his origin by direct creation from the earth, may it not be that in referring to the Final Adam Paul had in mind that he too was the immediate creation of God? The whole passage becomes much clearer if we assume that Paul had in mind not just the Resurrection of Christ, but also his virginal conception. On this hypothesis, Paul saw Jesus as passing into the heavenly realm because, far from being flesh and blood of the old, sinful world (v. 50), he was 'conceived of the Holy Ghost', the beginning and the first-fruits of God's new creation.[17]

No modern theologian has spoken up more eloquently for the virginal conception than Karl Barth.[18] Though many (especially Roman Catholics) would be unable to assent to his negative state-ments about the radical incapacity of human nature to approach God without grace, Barth's positive assertions about the gratu-itousness of God's gift in Christ should commend themselves without reservation to all Christians. Of the virginal conception he writes:

'It is *such an event* that to every Why? and Whence? and How? we can only answer that here God does it all Himself.'[19]

This is the first and primary message of the doctrine: the event

[17] The last three paragraphs are adapted from D. Edwards, *The Virgin Birth*, pp. 104–16.

[18] *Church Dogmatics*, vol. 1, Part 2, Edinburgh, 1956, pp. 172–202: 'The Miracle of Christmas'.

[19] *Loc. cit.*, p. 177.

itself spells out discontinuity with the history of sinful man, proclaiming that salvation comes only by the direct intervention of God. This is the point of the first assertion of the Creed: 'he was conceived of the Holy Ghost'.

But there is in the Creed a second phrase: 'born of the Virgin Mary'. This phrase defines the part taken or place occupied by humanity in the mystery of the Incarnation. It is in the first place an affirmation that Jesus is true man, truly born of Mary:

> 'By its *natus ex Maria* it states that the person of Jesus Christ is the real son of a real mother, the son born of the body, flesh and blood of his mother, both of them as real as all the other sons of other mothers'.[20]

But the Creed does not stop there: it says 'of Mary *the Virgin*'. The mention of Mary's virginity is an affirmation that the part played by the human race in the Incarnation is that of accepting God's gift, and nothing more. It is an affirmation that man considered as a being who wills, achieves, creates, and exercises sovereignty over his own actions did not, for all his striving and for all his achievements, positively contribute to his own redemption. *Ex Maria virgine* is a credal affirmation that humanity's part in the work of redemption lay solely in freely accepting salvation from the hand of the Omnipotent: 'Behold the handmaid of the Lord! Be it done unto me according to thy word!' (Lk 1:38).[21]

The doctrine of the virginal conception is thus an outward sign or sacrament of the mystery of the Incarnation. It affirms first and foremost that the earthly life of Jesus owes its origin to God alone, not to man; secondly, that he was true man; thirdly, that man's only contribution to the Incarnation consisted in accepting the gift of Jesus from God. The credal affirmation is a profession of faith in all three aspects of the mystery. It is obvious that anyone who confesses as historical fact that Jesus Christ was 'conceived of the Holy Ghost and born of the Virgin Mary'

[20] *Ibid.*, p. 185.
[21] *Ibid.*, pp. 188–96.

accepts all three aspects of the Incarnation. But what about the man who does not accept the virginal conception as an historical happening? Is it possible for him to hold on to the three elements of the mystery of the Incarnation which the Creed affirms? Barth replies:

'When two theologians with apparently the same conviction confess the mystery of Christmas, do they mean the same thing by that mystery, if one acknowledges and confesses the Virgin birth to be the sign of the mystery while the other denies it as a mere externality or is ready to leave it an open question? Does the second man really acknowledge and confess that in His revelation to us and in our reconciliation to Him, to our measureless astonishment and in measureless hiddenness the initiative is wholly with God? Or does he not by his denial or declared indifference towards the sign of the Virgin birth at the same time betray the fact that with regard to the thing signified by this sign he means something quite different? May it not be the case that the only one who hears the witness of the thing is the one who keeps to the sign by which the witness has actually signified it?'[21]

The doctrine of the virginal conception is *the* outward sign or sacrament in which the mystery of the Incarnation is spoken of in the New Testament and in the Creeds. Similarly, one might say that the New Testament describes the mystery of the Resurrection by pointing to the empty tomb: not that the empty tomb is a proof of the Resurrection, or describes the content of the mystery, but it is *de facto* the externally visible sign under which the glory of the Lord is revealed.

'It is no accident that for us the Virgin birth is paralleled by the miracle of which the Easter witness speaks, the miracle of the empty tomb. These two miracles belong together. They constitute, as it were, a single sign, the special function of which, compared with other signs and wonders of the New

[22] *Ibid.*, pp. 179-80.

Testament witness, is to describe and mark out the existence of Jesus Christ, amid the many other existences in human history, as that human historical existence in which God is Himself, God is directly the Subject, the temporal reality of which is not only called forth, created, conditioned and supported by the eternal reality of God, but is identical with it. The Virgin birth at the opening and the empty tomb at the close of Jesus' life bear witness that this life is a fact marked off from all the rest of human life, and marked off in the first instance, not by our understanding or our interpretation, but by itself. Marked off in regard to its origin . . . And marked off in regard to its goal.'[23]

In these last six lines, Barth has raised the ultimate question, and it is this. Was the earthly life of Jesus, the Word Incarnate and the world's Redeemer, *in truth and in reality* utterly different from every other human life in its origin, or is it simply that the New Testament, the Creeds and the Churches have in the past understood it as different, whereas in fact it was the same? Anyone who adopts the second alternative may discover that his unbelief in the virginal conception will lead him by force of logic to reappraise and perhaps to abandon the traditional Christian doctrine of grace. And to change one's attitude to that doctrine is not merely to adjust one's theological stance, but to change one's religion; for to reappraise or to abandon those central tenets of the doctrine of grace which have hitherto been confessed with equal firmness by Catholic and Protestant alike is to adopt an entirely different view of man's status and condition before God.

At the centre of the Christian revelation, as traditionally understood, stands this truth, that man is incapable of achieving, or even contributing to, his own redemption by his own unaided efforts. The virginal conception is the sign and sacrament both of the Incarnation and of the Redemption. That is why every candidate for baptism is required to profess belief in this doctrine; for by confessing this belief, he says in effect of the Incarnation and of the Redemption, 'Soli Deo gloria!'

[23] *Ibid.*, p. 182.

'*Humana hic merita conticescant, quae perierunt per Adam, et regnet quae regnat Dei gratia per Iesum Christum Dominum nostrum, unicum Dei Filium, unicum Dominum.*'[24]

[24] 'Let all human merits here fade into silence, for they came to an end through Adam, and let the grace of God hold sway (as it always does) through Jesus Christ our Lord, the one and only Son of God, the one and only Lord' (Augustine, *De praedestinatione Sanctorum* 15, 31: ML 44.983).

Chapter Eighteen

THE RELIGIOUS SIGNIFICANCE OF
MARY'S LIFE-LONG VIRGINITY

It has been argued above that Mary and Joseph originally intended a normal marriage, physically consummated; that their joint decision to live together in virginity was taken only after the Incarnation; and that this decision was motivated solely by the fact of the Incarnation. It was a resolve to devote all their lives to the service of this miraculously conceived child.[1] It has also been argued, in the last chapter, that the doctrine of the virginal conception is in all its dominant elements a Christological, not a Marian, doctrine.[2] Since the first of these theses is relatively new in Roman Catholic theology, and since the second has at a popular level often been neglected, it would not be surprising if at this point many Catholic readers felt uneasy. True, the fact of the virginal conception and the fact of Mary's life-long virginity have been unambiguously defended, but some Catholics may wonder whether in the process the virginity of Mary has not been down-graded. Can one hold the theses put forward in this book and at the same time retain unimpaired that respect and reverence for the virginity of the mother of the Lord which the Church from the earliest ages has always inculcated?

At the risk of stating the obvious, one must first explain why the Church holds virginity in such esteem, for even today there is some confusion on this point. Perhaps relatively few modern Christians are prey to Manichaeist or Jansenist fears of sex as something inherently evil, but there are many, as in the age of the

[1] See above, Chapter 5, pp. 196-9.
[2] See especially pp. 330-2 and 338-42.

Fathers, who are much attracted by (ultimately Stoic) ideals of self-discipline, and who may therefore be tempted to think that the positive value of virginity consists principally in the self-control and self-denial entailed by the renouncing of marriage. Against this view, it must be unequivocally affirmed that the value of Christian virginity lies neither in the purely material non-use of sex, *nor in the self-control entailed*, but solely in the motive for which virginity is chosen and in the use to which it is put. In the classic words of St Augustine, virginity 'is honoured not because it is virginity, but because it is dedicated to God'.[3]

But why, one may ask, is virginity consecrated to God so highly esteemed in the Church? The traditional answer, based on 1 Cor 7:32-4, is that such a life makes it easier to give oneself totally and directly to the service of God, either by prayer and contemplation, or by putting oneself entirely at the disposal of others, or by a life which combines both. Now it is obvious that the mere fact of not being married is only a condition of life which facilitates the practice of charity in one of the three ways described; it is no guarantee that the celibate will inevitably be led to ever greater charity. Consequently, the mere fact of not being married is not in itself of any particular spiritual value; it acquires spiritual value only when it is chosen and used as a means to the practice of charity. These considerations are of first importance, for if they are overlooked, there will be a real temptation to revert to the idea that the principal value of Christian virginity lies in self-control, *i.e.* in the purely negative aspect of abstaining from sex. And that is to place man in the centre of the picture, 'the man or woman of self-control', and to forget all about God.

There can be no question of saying that the glory of Mary's virginity is to be sought in her self-control. For then her virginity would be no different from that of any other chaste unmarried person, Christian or not; and it is certainly not the reason that the Church addresses her as 'Holiest of all virgins'. It is self-evident that the reason behind the Church's reverence for her virginity is to be sought in connection with Jesus.

Yet this reverence and respect is not to be founded on the

[3] *De sacra virginitate* 8 (ML 40.400).

purely physical fact of the virginal conception considered as a biological fact. That has its importance, an immeasurable importance, as the last chapter has shown: it is an assertion and a sign that in the work of the Incarnation and Redemption, God did everything by himself. But if the Word of God had become incarnate in a child conceived by Mary through union with Joseph, her divine motherhood would have been just as real, and she would have been entitled to the same reverence that she now receives. There is no reason why the Church should give her *more* honour because she was a *virgin* mother, *as long as we consider only the biological fact of the virginal conception on its own.*

'*Semper virgo*', 'ever-virgin', is one of Mary's most ancient titles, and it is in this that the religious significance of her virginity is to be sought. That is why the question of the brothers of Jesus is not theologically irrelevant or unimportant, and why the Roman Catholic and Orthodox Churches have always taken such a firm stand against the suggestion that Mary had several children. It is not just that they object to the idea that after the birth of Jesus Mary ceased to be *physically* a virgin; it is rather that, in line with the ancient Church, they perceive very clearly the need to stress the *total* virginity of Mary, physical and spiritual, with the latter the more heavily underlined. For this is how the Bible presents 'the humble handmaid of the Lord' (Lk 1:38), and this is how the ancient Church understood its message. In the words of St Augustine, 'Mary's relationship as mother would have been of no profit to her if she had not more joyfully borne Christ in her heart'.[4]

When Mary (and Joseph), after the miraculous conception, decided on a life of virginity, their motive was to put themselves entirely and exclusively at the service of Jesus, and to renounce everything that might conceivably divert or distract them from playing their full part in his mission. Their motive was not lack of esteem for the married life (unthinkable in Judaism), or even the prizing of continence as a higher ideal than the consummation of marriage. Their choice was motivated exclusively by the fact

---

[4] 'Materna propinquitas nihil Mariae profuisset, nisi felicius Christum corde gestasset' (*De sacra virginitate* 3: ML 40.398).

of the virginal conception, by the desire to serve *this* child. Indeed, the choice of virginity would seem to have been for them an existential necessity, *i.e.* given all the circumstances, it was in practice impossible for them to choose otherwise. For the situation was unique. In a normal family, each child adds something of its own which enriches the family; but this was not a normal situation. In Jesus 'there dwelt all the fullness of the Godhead bodily' (Col 2:9). May we not add, 'In him there dwelt all the fullness of humanity too'? What additional desirable qualities could any further children bring? And the virginal conception itself, being a word of God to man, was both an invitation and a call, to her who was to be the mother of the Lord. What possible response could Mary have made except that of exclusive dedication to the work of him that is mighty, who had done such great things for her?

When we are considering Mary, then, the title 'ever-virgin' takes precedence over 'virgin mother'. For her virginal motherhood cannot be correctly understood except in conjunction with her life-long virginity. The glory of her virginal motherhood lies not in the purely physical fact that Jesus was virginally conceived, but in the fact that Mary responded to this greatest of graces by giving her life exclusively to the service of this son. Her physical virginity is a sign, and a precious sign, of her spiritual love, but it is the latter which needs to be stressed more. Certainly, it is not so much because of her physical virginity as because she gave Jesus the undivided love of her soul that the Church extols her as *Virgo veneranda, Virgo praedicanda, Virgo fidelis*.

Both in ancient and in modern times, denials of the life-long virginity of Mary have spurred Catholics to defend and to stress the physical virginity of the mother of Jesus. There is nothing regrettable in this reaction provided that even more emphasis is placed on the virginal love of Mary for her son. But the temptation in controversy is to concentrate all attention on the precise point which is denied, and it cannot be said that Catholics have always put the spiritual values of Mary's virginity in the first place, with her physical virginity as a consequence and a manifestation of the deeper and more important truth.

The text of Lk 11:27 spells out this truth most eloquently, and it is regrettable that some commentators read this text as if it were pointing away from Mary as a model for all Christians. In fact, the Lucan text is saying exactly the opposite of this, for Jesus is there saying that blessedness is not restricted to her who bore him, but available for all who hear the word of God and keep it. Mary's physical motherhood is unique, and therefore inimitable; not so her love. Bede rightly interprets Lk 11:27 as an invitation to all Christians to see Mary's glory partly in the fact of her physical motherhood, but most of all in the response she made by her eternal love.

'*A woman in the crowd raised her voice and said to him, "Blessed is the womb that bore thee, and the breasts which thou hast sucked!" But he said, "Blessed rather are those who hear the word of God and keep it!"* How beautifully our Saviour replies to this woman's word of witness! He points out that she who had the merit of being the bodily mother of the Word of God is not the only one who is blessed. Rather, all who have striven to conceive the same word spiritually by faith, who have striven by good works to bring it to birth in their heart, or in the heart of their neighbours, and as it were to give it nourishment—all these too he proclaims blessed. For the mother of God herself, though she is assuredly blessed because she was the minister of the Word's Incarnation, is far more blessed because she never ceased to keep that Word, never ceased to love him.'[5]

In the final sentence, the word-play on the text of St Luke is more evident in Bede's Latin than in an English translation:

'. . . *eadem Dei genetrix et inde quidem beata quia verbi incarnandi ministra est facta temporalis sed inde multo beatior quia eiusdem semper amandi custos manebat aeterna*'.

[5] 'Pulchre salvator attestationi mulieris annuit non eam tantummodo quae verbum Dei corporaliter generare meruerat sed et omnes qui idem verbum spiritaliter auditu fidei concipere et boni operis custodia vel in suo vel in proximorum corde parere et quasi alere studuerint asseverans esse beatos quia et eadem Dei genetrix et inde quidem beata quia verbi incarnandi ministra est facta temporalis sed inde multo beatior quia eiusdem semper amandi custos manebat aeterna' (*In Lucam IV*, on 11:27: *CC* 120.237 = ML 92.480).

PART III

MOTHER OF THE WORD INCARNATE

(Mary in the Theology of Saint John)

'Among all the Scriptures, the gospels have pride of place; and among the gospels, pride of place belongs to that according to John. Yet no one can grasp its meaning unless he has leaned upon the breast of Jesus, and also accepted from Jesus Mary, to be his own mother.'

(Origen, *Commentary on St. John, I, 6.*)

Chapter One

THE UNITY OF JOHANNINE THEOLOGY

FROM the second century until modern times, it was generally accepted that the Fourth Gospel, the three Epistles of John and the Apocalypse were all written by John the son of Zebedee. Those Christians who today still hold this view will obviously find no problem in using any one of these books as a guide to the interpretation of the others. In fact, the origin of these writings was rather more complex, and though this is not the place to discuss in detail all the arguments about their authorship, some basic information must be given to show why it is still legitimate to regard these very diverse books as forming a homogeneous group within the New Testament.[1]

To illustrate the problem, it will be useful to begin by saying something about the composition of books in ancient times. Authors did not as a rule write in their own hand, for the simple reason that it was technically so difficult. The materials employed (parchment or papyrus, a reed pen, ink that was a mixture of soot and glue) made writing a slow and delicate process, so that even a professional scribe could write only one hundred words an hour, and one hundred lines a day.[2] One can readily comprehend

[1] The general argument of this chapter, and most of the details, are taken from F.-M. Braun, *Jean le Théologien et son Evangile dans l'Eglise ancienne* (*Etudes Bibliques*), Paris, 1959, pp. 3–62. It will be cited as *Jean le Théologien I.*

[2] Writing on wax tablets was faster, but was used only for notes of an ephemeral nature (*cf.* Lk 1:63) because the words could so easily be smudged, altered or erased. For this reason Quintilian advises their use in preparing a script, unless feeble eyesight makes it necessary to use parchment; the trouble with parchment, he says, is that the process is so slow that one loses the train of thought. 'Scribi

THE MOTHER OF JESUS IN THE NEW TESTAMENT

the reluctance of a non-professional to engage in such laborious work, since he would inevitably be both slower and less legible. With this background in mind, it is easy to accept that most, if not all, of the New Testament books must have been dictated to a professional scribe. In Romans the fact is expressly mentioned (16:22: 'I Tertius who have written this letter send you my greetings'); 1 Corinthians (16:21), Colossians (4:18) and 2 Thessalonians (3:17) end with 'The signature is in my hand— PAUL', implying that the rest was not. Galatians make the same point even more vividly: 'SEE WHAT GREAT LETTERS I HAVE TRACED FOR YOU IN MY OWN HAND' (6:11). Paul evidently did not think very highly of himself as a calligrapher!

At the rate of one hundred words an hour, dictation was a painful procedure. Cicero was fortunate enough to have a scribe who could take down whole paragraphs (presumably by stenography) and then go off to write them; but at least once, in his absence, he was compelled to use another man who could take down 'only one syllable' at a time.[3] Moreover, it was not until around A.D. 150 that a type of stenography was used for Greek (as distinct from Latin).[4] In such a world, the skilled professional

---

optime ceris, in quibus est facillima ratio delendi: nisi forte visus infirmior membranarum potius usum exiget: quae ut iuvant aciem, ita crebra relatione, quoad intinguntur calami, morantur manum, et cogitationis impetum frangunt' (*De institutione oratoria* 10, 3).

[3] *Ad Atticum* 13, 25 *in fine*. According to Plutarch (*Cato Minor* 23), it was Cicero who first introduced stenography into the Senate: he had Cato's speech against Catiline taken down as it was delivered. The practice soon became widespread in Rome at government level. Several speeches of Julius Caesar were so recorded (Suetonius, *Julius Caesar* 55), and Titus was so fast at stenography that he would challenge his own scribes (Suetonius, *Titus* 3). See C. Blanc, in her introduction to Origen, *Commentaire sur s. Jean*, vol. 2 (= Sources Chrétiennes 157), Paris, 1970, pp. 18–19.

[4] In the Greek world too the practice spread. Eusebius (*H.E.* VI, 23, 2 = MG 20.576) records that Origen had more than seven 'fast writers' working in relays, backed up by seven copyists, and a team of young girls who specialized in calligraphy. Only with such a team could Origen have achieved his monumental output.

scribe was much more important than a copy-typist, and was often equivalent to a confidential secretary. In writing a letter, a man might simply outline his ideas, leaving the scribe to formulate them and to bring back the text for revision and approval. In writing a long work, especially one which took several years, an author could find himself changing secretaries, and according to his personal preferences they would play a larger or a smaller part in his work. For if the author was the source of the ideas and of their expression, he was bound to be influenced (after perhaps years of collaboration) by his secretary and friend, just as surely as the secretary would be influenced by him. Hence, when one thinks of an ancient author, one must not forget his secretary. It is against this background that one must evaluate the evidence for the authorship of the writings ascribed to John.

The literary unity of the Fourth Gospel is now so generally admitted that it would be superfluous to discuss it. With the exception of the story of the woman taken in adultery (Jn 7:53–8:11) and the final chapter (Jn 21), the entire gospel is the work of one author. Certainly, he incorporated material from older sources, and there are good reasons for believing that some of these were originally written or spoken in Aramaic. But he mastered all this material, made it his own, and finally gave shape and structure to the book as a whole. The coherence of his thought is evident even in translation, where the same leading ideas such as light and darkness continually recur,[5] and where the pattern of event and explanatory discourse can so easily be discerned.[6] But in the Greek text, the homogeneity of a distinct style is strikingly evident: no less than fifty positive characteristics and eleven negative ones have been detected—tiny points of grammar, syntax and vocabulary which are notably different from the usage

[5] Dodd, in *The Interpretation of the Fourth Gospel*, p. ix, lists as the leading ideas Eternal Life, Knowledge of God, Truth, Faith, Union with God, Light, Glory, Judgment, Spirit, Messiah, Son of God, Son of Man, and Logos.

[6] *E.g.*, the Samaritan woman at the well and the discourse on living water (Jn 4); the Feeding of the Five Thousand and the discourse on bread from heaven (Jn 6); the Raising of Lazarus and the discourse on Resurrection and Life (Jn 11), etc.

of non-Johannine New Testament writers.[7] Though in its final form the work seems to have been retouched, and perhaps to some extent arranged for publication, by another man (whom we may call the editor), today the literary unity of the Fourth Gospel is unassailable.

Did the man who composed the gospel, and whom we shall call henceforward 'the evangelist' (leaving aside for the moment his identity), also write the three epistles ascribed to John? Let us consider first the anonymous work known as 1 John. Though earlier in this century its unity was strongly contested, it is now more commonly admitted that 1 John is just as truly the work of a single author as is the Fourth Gospel, and for the same reasons. Like the Fourth Gospel, it is permeated from beginning to end by well-defined themes and by a characteristic style. Moreover, the leading ideas are exactly those which occur in the Fourth Gospel; and of the fifty positive characteristics found in the gospel, no less than nineteen are found in the relatively short pages of the first epistle. Those not found there occur mainly in historical narrative; and the negative characteristics of both writings are the same.[8] Dodd argued many years ago that the evangelist was not the author of 1 John,[9] but if allowance is made for the difference of literary form between a gospel and an epistle, and for the difference of content too, everything indicates that the evangelist (or someone exceedingly close to him) was the author of the first epistle, and that if he used a secretary, it was the same man in both cases.[10]

[7] They are listed in Braun, *Jean le Théologien I*, pp. 401–3. Braun in fact gives fifty-one positive characteristics, but by an oversight has listed one twice (Nos. 3 and 47 are identical.) Compare also E. A. Abbott, *Johannine Vocabulary*, London, 1905, and *Johannine Grammar*, London, 1906, two splendid works, the latter of which is still of inestimable value.

[8] See Braun, *Jean le Théologien I*, pp. 33 and 402–3.

[9] 'The First Epistle of John and the Fourth Gospel', in the *Bulletin of the John Rylands' Library* 21 (1937), pp. 129–56; also *The Johannine Epistles (The Moffatt New Testament Commentary)*, London, 1945, pp. XLVII–LVI.

[10] See W. F. Howard, 'The Common Authorship of the Johannine Gospel and Epistles', *JTS* 48 (1947), pp. 12–25, and W. G. Wilson, 'An Examination of the Linguistic Evidence Adduced against the Unity of Authorship of the First Epistle of John and the Fourth Gospel', *JTS* 49 (1948), pp. 147–56.

2 John and 3 John are such short letters that any statement about their linguistic peculiarities might justifiably be received with extreme caution. Yet even in so limited a space there is considerable evidence that 2 John was written by the same man as 1 John. For in the body of the letter (2 Jn 4–11), *i.e.* apart from the initial greeting and the ending, four of the eight verses correspond in content, syntax and vocabulary (though not in style) to statements in 1 John.

2 John	1 John
(5) . . . not as though I were writing to thee a new commandment, but that which we had from the beginning, that we should love one another.	(2:7) I do not write to you a new commandment, but an ancient commandment, which you had from the beginning.
(6) And this is love, that we walk according to the commandments; this is the commandment, as you heard from the beginning, that you should walk in it.	(5:2) . . . when we love God and do his commandments. (5:3) For this is love of God, that we should keep his commandments.

So also 2 Jn 7 corresponds to 1 Jn 4:2–3; 2 Jn 9 to 1 Jn 2:23–4; and 2 Jn 12 to 1 Jn 1:4. The statements of 2 John are those of 1 John, and though the form of expression is sometimes rather different, may not this be due to the fact that the letters were written by two different secretaries?

The points of contact between 1 John and 3 John are not so immediately obvious. In fact, it is the second letter which makes the connection clear. Even if 3 Jn 9 ('I have written a line to the Church') does not refer to the letter to the 'Lady Elect' (2 Jn 1), the greeting is the same in 2 Jn 1 and 3 Jn 1, as is the ending (2 Jn 12–13 = 3 Jn 13–15). The most plausible explanation of the facts is that 1, 2 and 3 John were all the work of one man, and that the evangelist; but that 2 and 3 John were not penned by the secretary who was responsible for 1 John and the gospel. One may add that even if the three letters were not written by one man, or not written by the evangelist, the close relationship of thought and expression between the Fourth Gospel and the Johannine Epistles fully justifies their classification as a homogeneous group within the New Testament. Even those who question the unity of author-ship must admit that all four writings originate from the same school of thought.

The Apocalypse takes us into another world. It represents a type of book fairly common in Palestine between 200 B.C. and A.D. 200, all known examples of which were originally composed either in Hebrew or in Aramaic. Everything indicates that the author of the Johannine Apocalypse owed far more to Palestinian Judaism than to Hellenistic Judaism or Hellenistic Christianity, and that he was therefore by origin a Palestinian Jew, though resident in Asia Minor. His Greek is barbaric. He seems incapable of using correctly the most elementary particles other than 'and', 'but' and 'for'; he ignores basic rules on the agreement of adjec-tives and nouns; and he is often quite careless about verb endings. It is true that Greek of this type can be abundantly paralleled from contemporary papyri, but in the Apocalypse these traits are carried to the point of idiosyncrasy.[11] The style is indeed so far removed from that of the Fourth Gospel and the Johannine Epistles that it is almost unthinkable that one man could have written all five books. Any commentary on the Greek text will supply ample illustrations to support this statement.

Yet for all that, the Apocalypse presents some remarkable affinities with the Fourth Gospel and the Johannine Epistles. Even in its grammar and syntax, analogies are not altogether wanting, but the main similarities are found in its doctrinal content. Jesus is presented as the Lamb of God (Jn 1:51; Apoc *passim*), and the One whom they pierced (Jn 19:37; Apoc 1:7). His judgment is righteous and true (Jn 5:30; 8:16; Apoc 19:11). In the gospel, Jesus announces that the Temple of Jerusalem must pass away, and

[11] See, *e.g.*, E. B. Allo, *L'Apocalypse* (*Etudes Bibliques*), 3rd ed., Paris, 1933, pp. CXLIV–CLXXX, or R. H. Charles, *A Critical and Exegetical Commentary on the Revelation of St John* (*International Critical Commentary*), Edinburgh, 1920, vol. 1, pp. XXIX–XXXIV.

be replaced by the temple of his body (Jn 2:19, 22; 4:22); in the Apocalypse (21:22) we read of the New Jerusalem, 'I saw no temple therein, for the Lord God almighty is its temple, and the Lamb'. The list of parallels could easily be prolonged. Two facts therefore stand out. Many of the themes are common, and characteristically Johannine; yet the Greek of the gospel is so different from that of the Apocalypse that it is impossible to believe both works were penned by one man. Should one therefore say that the Apocalypse comes from the same school of thought as the gospel, or is it sufficient to postulate two different secretaries?

Not to delay unduly over this problem, one can say for certain that the Apocalypse originates from proconsular Asia (Apoc 1:9 and the letters to the Seven Churches). And according to tradition, it was there too that the Fourth Gospel was published. Nevertheless, both works are profoundly influenced by Palestinian Judaism, both in their language and in their ideas. The author of the Apocalypse writes exactly like a Palestinian Jew; and the author of the gospel was familiar not only with Palestinian geography, but also with the very details of the topography of Jerusalem as it was before the destruction of the city in A.D. 70.

It is of course possible that the author of the Apocalypse and the author of the Fourth Gospel were two different men, both Jews from Palestine, both resident in or near Ephesus at the end of the first century. But at least they shared the same ideas, and to a large extent the same way of expressing them, so that the writing of the one may be used to elucidate obscurities in that of the other. In that case, we should regard the Apocalypse and the Fourth Gospel as works coming from the same school.

Nevertheless, the whole history of human thought, from the time of Socrates or Origen down to that of Lagrange or Bultmann, shows that a homogeneous school of thought normally arises under the impact of one dominant personality. (The history of the Oxford Movement, with Keble, Pusey and Newman as three leaders might seem a counter-example; but the fragmentation of the group would seem to confirm the thesis.) Some of those who hold that the Apocalypse and the gospel were written by the same man explain the vast differences of language by saying that he wrote the Apocalypse first, and years later, when his Greek was much more fluent, composed the gospel. Against this there is the general consensus of opinion that the Apocalypse was written towards the end of Domitian's reign (*i.e.* about A.D. 95), and the gospel not much later; would an author have had time so to transform his mastery of Greek prose in the interval?

The most satisfactory explanation would seem to be that one author was responsible for all five Johannine books, but that not all were written by the same secretary. The secretary who wrote the Apocalypse during or after the exile on Patmos may have been either himself unskilled in Greek, or very particular to put down unaltered exactly what the author told him. 2 John and 3 John were probably set down in writing by another man, more sensitive to the canons of literary Greek, yet scrupulous to retain certain Semitisms used by the author (*e.g.* 2 Jn 6, 'to walk in the commandment'; 3 Jn 4, 'to walk in the truth'). And yet a third secretary would seem to have been responsible for penning the first epistle, a man who felt at ease in taking liberties with the dictated word where Greek usage called for it. Thus in 1 Jn 1:6, 7; 2:11 we read of 'walking in the light' or 'in the darkness', but nowhere in this epistle of 'walking in the truth' (2 Jn 4; 3 Jn 3, 4); in 1 Jn 2:3, 4; 3:24 and 4:21 we read of 'keeping the commandments', but not of 'walking in them' (contrast 2 Jn 6). There is nothing improbable in the idea that one author called on the services of three different secretaries, if at one time he was on Patmos (Apoc 1:9), if 2 and 3 John were despatched together (*cf.* 3 Jn 9) at a time when he was travelling and staying as a guest in a town not his own (2 Jn 12–13; 3 Jn 14–15), and if 1 John was written by his usual secretary, at his home. But behind all three secretaries stands the dominating personality of the author.

The secretary who penned 1 John was, I believe, the man responsible for the 'writing' (not the 'composition') of the Fourth Gospel; and it would make good sense to think of him as the editor who finally retouched it and arranged it for publication. The gospel itself is quite certainly the fruit of long years of meditation on the life of Jesus, and broadly speaking it seems to have originated in this way. Ancient traditions about events in the life of Jesus and about his teaching, guaranteed by an eye-witness who was among the closest of the disciples (*cf.* Jn 19:35), were jealously treasured by a group of Christians who knew this eye-witness. During his lifetime, they questioned him about the meaning of Jesus' teaching and in these discussions the disciple himself was led to an ever deeper understanding of Jesus' words (Jn 14:26 = 15:26–7 = 16:12–15, *cf.* 16:25). Some of his re-collections and meditations may well have been written down in Aramaic, and this would account for the irregularly dispersed Aramaisms in the Fourth Gospel. Among his own disciples was a highly intelligent Jew, who began to collect and to arrange the memoirs of the eye-witness and theologian, and to spell out their meaning; and it is he whom we should regard as 'the evangelist'. But the process of collecting, arranging and perfecting the present-ation of Jesus' doctrine occupied him for years, and the work, though substantially ready for publication, was not completed at his death. This man, the evangelist, spent the last years of his life in or near Ephesus, working at the book with the assistance of a secretary whose Greek was better than his own. He was an important figure in the Church of proconsular Asia, an elder who could write with authority (2 Jn 1; 3 Jn 1) in the full confidence that he interpreted rightly the teaching of his master. From Patmos he could rebuke six of the Seven Churches of Asia, showing an intimate knowledge of them all (Apoc 1–3); and why should not the name 'John' in Apoc 1:9 be a pseudonym, ascribing the teaching of the book to that son of Zebedee whose message the author had made his own?

This position seems to do full justice to the demands of ancient tradition, internal evidence and modern critical scholarship. Ancient tradition attributes the gospel, the first epistle, and (with less certainty, on the grounds of millenarianism) the Apocalypse, to John the son of Zebedee; it hesitated over 2 and 3 John,[12] as if they did not possess the same degree of apostolic authority. This harmonizes to perfection with the above thesis, for 2 and 3 John are just short letters. Internal evidence points to ancient and

[12] For the references see Braun, *Jean le Théologien I*, pp. 31–2.

revered sources within the gospel, accompanied by a richly developed theology aimed at displaying the message before the Greek world. The situation of the Apocalypse is different. This book is an urgent word of comfort to those already within the Church, summoning them to stand firm under persecution. What was more natural than that the author should seize upon the classic form for such a message of consolation; that in such an emergency he should write it rapidly and send it out without waiting for a scribe who could polish the Greek; and that, certain of his heavenly patron and anxious to affirm that he spoke with his authority, he should, in the tradition of apocalyptic writers, issue it under the name of John? And as we have seen, linguistic arguments against unity of authorship for all five Johannine writings are hard to sustain, if one postulates three different secretaries. In the position adopted here there is nothing, one hopes, that offends critical scholarship.

If, then, one asks who was the author of the Johannine writings, a distinction is needed. If the word 'author' is understood in the sense of the Latin *auctor*, *i.e.* as denoting 'the originator, the initiator, the person who supplies the main inspiration of an enterprise', then the author of the gospel, of the first epistle and of the Apocalypse was John the son of Zebedee. But if the word 'author' is taken in its modern sense as 'the person who wrote the book, who collected the ideas and put them into shape', then the author of all five writings was an anonymous Christian of Jewish origin, an elder of the Church in Asia towards the end of the first century. A disciple of 'John the Theologian', he is the man we should call 'the evangelist'; but at a literary level, he was much indebted to the services of a secretary who was responsible for publishing the gospel in its final form.

Chapter Two

THE MOTHER OF JESUS IN THE FOURTH GOSPEL (I): A MODERN ROMAN CATHOLIC INTERPRETATION

THE most important and most interesting study of the mother of Jesus in the writings of St John is by the Belgian Dominican, Père F.-M. Braun. First published as an article in 1950-1,[1] then rewritten to reach a wider public, it was issued in book form in 1953 under the title *La mère des fidèles*.[2] A scholarly work, equally sensitive to the demands of modern exegesis and ancient tradition, it has rightly come to be regarded as a masterly exposition of its theme. With some qualifications and amendments, Braun's interpretation of St John has been widely accepted among Roman Catholic theologians, not least because it seems to furnish a solid biblical basis for the doctrine that Mary is the spiritual mother of all Christians. The intrinsic interest of the book and its wide influence make a presentation and a critique of its theory doubly justified. Its argument runs as follows.

It is noteworthy that John nowhere mentions the name of Mary. For him, she is simply 'the mother of Jesus' (Jn 2:1, 3, 5; 19:25, 26), as if the evangelist meant to stress that her role in the

[1] 'La mère de Jésus dans l'œuvre de s. Jean', in the *Revue Thomiste* 50 (1950), pp. 429-79 and 51 (1951), pp. 5-68.

[2] Tournai and Paris, 1953; 2nd ed. (revised, with additional notes, some of which are replies to criticisms), 1954. It seems pointless to give references paragraph by paragraph to the pages of this work, since anyone who possess it will know how simple it is to find the relevant passage from the table of contents, with its multiple headings.

gospel lay only in her relationship to her son. The term is in no way meant to diminish Mary's importance: even today, the Arabs refer to a woman very respectfully as (*e.g.*) 'the mother of Abdullah', especially if the son is a famous man. In the Fourth Gospel, Jesus is always seen as 'the Word by whom all things were made, who was in the beginning with God', and who walked among us (*cf.* 1 Jn 1:1–2). Hence in the Fourth Gospel the choice of the phrase 'mother of Jesus' in preference to 'Mary' is an indication not of her relative unimportance, but of the contrary. It was through her that 'the Word became flesh and dwelt among us, that we might see his glory, the glory as of the Only-begotten of the Father, full of grace and truth' (*cf.* Jn 1:14). Consequently, if we wish to bring out by paraphrase in meaningful English the full content of the Johannine term 'mother of Jesus', the only correct equivalent is 'mother of the Word Incarnate'.

The mother of Jesus is mentioned on only two occasions in the Fourth Gospel, once at Cana (Jn 2:1–11) and then on Calvary (Jn 19:25–7). The interpretation of Mary's intervention and Jesus' reply at Cana is of notorious difficulty, for it poses three major problems. Why does Jesus address Mary not as 'Mother', but as 'Woman'? How should one interpret the phrase, 'What is that to me and to thee?' What is meant by 'My hour is not yet come'?

In years gone by, Protestant polemists pointed to the choice of the term 'Woman' rather than 'Mother' as indicative of a certain coldness on Jesus' side. Their Catholic counterparts were not slow to retort that the same term is used in Jn 19:25–7, where Jesus is showing both care and affection. Indeed, some in their enthusiasm deduced that the term must have been a highly respectful way of addressing one's mother, just as Victorian boys in certain classes of society were brought up to address their father as 'Sir'. This is a very gratuitous contention, for apart from Cana and Calvary there is not a single instance anywhere in the Bible or in any of the rabbinical writings of a son's addressing his mother as 'Woman'.[3]

[3] R. E. Brown, *The Gospel according to John* (*The Anchor Bible*) New York, 1966 or London, 1971, vol. 1, p. 172 comments thus on Jn 4:21: 'Jesus normally uses this form of address. "Woman" is not an entirely happy translation and is some-

In fact, Jesus in the gospels uses this form of address to several women, including those whom he had never met before. Thus he uses it to the Samaritan woman (Jn 4:21) and to Mary Magdalen (Jn 20:13), to the Canaanite woman (Mt 15:28) and to the woman crippled with arthritis (Lk 13:10). He also uses it to the woman caught in the act of adultery (Jn 8:11). From these examples it is fair to conclude that it was a normal form of courteous address (like the French *Madame* or the Italian *Signora*) to someone outside the family; but when a Jew addressed his mother he said '*imma* ('mother'). Jesus was therefore drawing attention away from Mary's blood-relationship with him by addressing her as 'Woman'. And if one objects that on Calvary (Jn 19:25-7) he was certainly regarding her as the mother who gave him birth, is not this begging the question? Perhaps Calvary has a different message too; perhaps Jesus on the cross was thinking of something other than physical ties of blood.

Τί ἐμοὶ καὶ σοί; 'What is that to me and to thee?' It will be convenient to retain this literal englishing of the Greek, precisely because this rendering is so enigmatic. Modern translations, in their attempts to make the phrase comprehensible, offer a rich variety of versions, each of which is *an* interpretation,[4] but not necessarily the one intended by the evangelist. The reasons for this diversity are that the phrase is ambivalent, and that each of its

---

what archaic. However, modern English is deficient in a courteous title of address for a woman who is no longer a "Miss". Both "Lady" and "Madam" have taken on an unpleasant tone when used as an address without an accompanying proper name'. In Britain, 'Lady' might just pass muster in some of the biblical texts, but (for reasons which will become apparent later) in translating John it seems advisable to keep to 'Woman'.

[4] The rendering above is that given in the Douai–Challoner version. Other translations are: 'What have I to do with thee?' (Authorized and Revised Versions); 'What have you to do with me?' (Moffatt and Revised Standard Version); 'Trouble me not' (Torrey); 'Why dost thou trouble me with that?' (Knox); 'Is that your concern, or mine?' (Phillips); 'Your concern is not mine' (New English Bible); 'Why turn to me?' (Jerusalem Bible); 'You must not try to tell me what to do' (Barclay).

Modern translators into languages other than English are equally puzzled, and offer an equal variety of renderings.

two renderings is also affected by the context. In Latin or Greek prose the pronoun of the first person normally precedes that of the second person, and that of the second person precedes the third:[5] thus the more usual order is '*Quid mihi et tibi?*' and not '*Quid tibi et mihi?*' Now the phrase '*Quid mihi et tibi?*' can mean either 'Why should I have anything to do with you?' or 'Why should you have anything to do with me?' The two translations are not synonymous in English, but both would be rendered into Latin or Greek in the same way, and only the context would enable a man to decide which meaning was intended.

Both meanings are found in the Old Testament. In Jdg 11:12 Jephthah asks the king of the Ammonites, 'Why should you have anything to do with me?', meaning 'What have you got against me, that you should invade my land?' In 1 Kgs 17:18 the widow of Zarephath puts the same question to Elijah, meaning again, 'What have you got against me?' But in 2 Kgs 3:13 the meaning is just the opposite. When Jehoram, the son of Ahab and Jezabel, sent in despair to Elijah, the prophet replied: 'Why should I have anything to do with you? Go to the prophets of your father and the prophets of your mother!' In 2 Sam 16:10 and 19:22, the phrase could be taken either way: David could be saying 'Why should I have anything to do with you?' or 'What have you got against me, that you advise me so?' In the five gospel references (Mt 8:29; Mk 1:24; 5:7; Lk 4:34; 8:28) the phrase occurs only in the mouth of the possessed, with the meaning, 'Why should you have anything to do with us? What have you got against us?' Thus the phrase is always a protest, and in certain contexts (2 Sam 16:10; 19:22; 2 Kgs 3:13) a refusal to a request. It may be added that it has the same sense in classical and Hellenistic Greek.[6]

In the Old Testament texts cited, and in the mouth of the possessed, a harsh protest is demanded by the context. But downright rudeness by Jesus to his mother would be unthinkable, most of all in the Fourth Gospel; hence in Jn 2:4 a milder rendering is

---

[5] Some may recall the chagrin of Henry VIII at finding a letter by Wolsey beginning 'Ego et rex meus'. *Se non è vero, è ben trovato!*

[6] E. A. Abbott, *Johannine Grammar* §2230; J. J. Wetstein, *Novum Testamentum Graece*, Amsterdam, 1751, vol. 1, p. 355, on Mt 8:29.

called for, however one interprets the text. With that qualification, it would seem that Jn 2:4 can bear either of the two meanings used in the Old Testament, and that there is no way of deciding which one was intended by the evangelist. It could mean '*Why do you trouble me?*' (the sense used in 1 Kgs 17:18), or '*Why should I listen to you?*' (as in 2 Kgs 3:13). In Jn 2:4 (as in 2 Sam 16:10 and 19:22) either sense suits the context, and the ultimate meaning is the same. In either case there is a protest and an implicit refusal to intervene. St Augustine expressly states that Jesus here refused to perform a miracle at his mother's request,[7] and St John Chrysostom even saw in these words a reprimand to Mary for wanting to parade herself as the mother of a son who could work miracles.[8] (One could argue that Jesus tempered this refusal by addressing Mary very courteously as 'Woman'; or that by calling her 'Woman' and not 'Mother', the firmness of his refusal is stressed. This word does not help either way.)[9]

The reason for this refusal is given in the next clause: 'My hour is not yet come'. The first problem here is that the Greek can be translated either as a statement ('My hour has not yet come') or as a question ('Has my hour not yet come?'). It is evident that if these words are a rhetorical question, the meaning is completely reversed, and the sense is 'Has not my hour now come?' A small number of modern Roman Catholic exegetes have argued vigorously that here we have such a rhetorical question.[10] There is no

---

[7] *Tract. in Ioannem* VIII (*CC* 36.87 = ML 35.1455): see p. 369.

[8] 'She wanted to place them under an obligation to her, and also to make herself more conspicuous because of her child. For she was doubtless subject to the same human failing as his brothers, who said "Show yourself to the world!", wishing to enjoy the reflected glory of his miracles. That is why he replied rather sharply . . .' (*Hom. in Ioannem* 21 = MG 59.130).

[9] The last three paragraphs are a rather free adaptation of the argument in *La mère des fidèles*, pp. 51–3, for the French idioms there used have to be transposed into English. But the ideas are all to be found in Braun's work.

[10] Principally M.-E. Boismard in *Du baptême à Cana*, Paris, 1956, pp. 156–7; and J. Michl, 'Bemerkungen zu Jo. 2:4', *Biblica* 36 (1955), pp. 492–509, who on pp. 506–7 cites a couple of patristic texts in favour of the view, and also lists those modern commentators who adopt it. Braun does not treat this view in *La mère des fidèles*.

way of proving them wrong by an appeal to grammar or syntax, but it is very much a minority view which demands that 'the hour' (now come) be taken either as 'the hour of miracles' or as 'the hour of Jesus' manifestation' in some other way.

This brings us to another (and obviously correlated) problem: what, in this context, is the meaning of 'my hour'? Many suggestions have been advanced, and there are no less than five main interpretations of the word. It is said that in St John's gospel the hour of Jesus is (1) the hour of his Crucifixion; (2) the hour of his exaltation, *i.e.* of his Crucifixion and Resurrection, considered as one event by which he passed from this world to the Father; (3) the hour of his manifestation by signs and wonders, *i.e.* the hour of miracles; (4) the hour of his manifestation as Messiah, but without reference to signs and wonders; (5) the moment for any new and significant move by Jesus, considered as an action determined and ordained not by his own human choice but by his Father's decree. Without entering into detail, it is sufficient to state that Braun follows the most commonly accepted interpretation of 'the hour of Jesus', namely, that it is the hour of his exaltation on the cross, considered as the event which achieves his work on earth and leads directly to his triumphant Resurrection and reign.[11]

There are then three exegetical premises on which Braun bases his interpretation of the teaching about Mary in the story of Cana. First, in addressing her not as 'Mother' but as 'Woman', Jesus was turning attention *away* from the blood-relationship which united them. Secondly, Mary asked Jesus to intervene at Cana and to help in some way (Braun rejects the idea that she was asking for a miracle, judging it 'far more probable' that she left the manner of any intervention to her son's discretion);[12] but Jesus refused to act at her request. Thirdly, the reason for this refusal was that his hour (*i.e.* the hour of Calvary) was not yet come. It is easy to divine where the logic of these three premises will

[11] For further detail on the hour of Jesus see F.-M. Braun, *Jean le Théologien III: Sa théologie, 1e Partie; Le mystère de Jésus-Christ* (Etudes Bibliques), Paris, 1966, pp. 146–50; R. E. Brown, *The Gospel according to John I*, pp. 517–18; and especially R. Schnackenburg, *The Gospel according to St John I*, pp. 328–31.

[12] *La mère des fidèles*, pp. 55–6.

lead, namely, to the conclusion that when the hour of Jesus does come, and his work on earth is achieved, he will accede to his mother's request.

Braun's interpretation is this. When the wine ran short, Mary mentioned it to Jesus in the hope that he would do something to save the situation. Jesus' answer must have come as a shock: 'I cannot now have anything to do with you, woman, for I must begin the work of my heavenly Father, and can no longer listen to your requests. But' (he adds, by way of softening the reply) 'my hour is not yet come.' This last statement implies that when his hour does come, when he has finished the mission on earth ordained by his Father, he will once again be united with his mother, and listen to her requests. The text is therefore parallel to Lk 2:49, which Braun takes as 'I must be about my Father's business'.

The immediate objection to this interpretation is that Mary straightway (Jn 2:5) tells the waiters to do whatever Jesus may ask, as if she had not understood his words to be a refusal; and another equally obvious objection is that Jesus at once acts as if he had agreed to fulfil her request. All commentators on St John are embarrassed by this *non sequitur* from v. 4. Some argue that Mary's confident order to the waiters and Jesus' subsequent action supply clear proof that the words of v. 4 ('What is that to me and to thee?') cannot possibly mark a protest, much less a refusal, no matter what the evidence of the Old Testament, the gospels and classical Greek may say about this phrase. Others (notably Loisy[13] and Bultmann[14]) admit the contradiction and attribute it to the author, whose taste for allegory was not to be restricted by the rules of logic: since the whole episode is an allegory of the substitution of the new wine for the old purification water of Judaism, there is no need to look for coherent logic. Braun admits very honestly that 'we are here faced with a problem for the solution of which one is reduced to conjectures. John was content to summarize the scene very briefly. It was not his intention to forestall the questions which would arise in the mind

[13] *Le quatrième évangile*, p. 270.
[14] *The Gospel of John*, Oxford, 1971, pp. 116–20.

of his readers'.[15] Braun himself thinks the words of refusal must have been followed by an explicit or secret acquiescence (unrecorded in the gospel), perhaps from the way Jesus looked at his mother. Others point to the example of the Syro-Phoenician woman (Mt 15:21–8 = Mk 7:24–30): Jesus at first met her request with a blank refusal, but later acquiesced. There is also the case of Jn 7:1–10, where Jesus first said he would not go to Jerusalem for the feast of Tabernacles, and later went, in secret. This last example is particularly interesting, since Jesus gives as the reason for his refusal to his brothers' invitation the fact that 'his time was not yet come' (Jn 7:5, 8). Braun concludes, on the evidence of Jn 7:1–10, that Jesus refused to act at the behest of his *relatives* (this would make an excellent parallel with Jn 2:3–4); he did act, but only because it was his Father's will. This would account both for his refusal to act at Mary's plea, and for his subsequent working of a miracle (particularly if Mary had asked for something other than a miracle).

The burden of Braun's interpretation is therefore this. At Cana, Jesus told Mary that he must now leave her, to begin the work of his Father, but that when this work was achieved, they would be together again. The physical separation that ensued brought mother and son closer together than ever in charity, in that both were daily placing their human affections lower than the will of the Father. This is the theme of those Synoptic texts where Jesus speaks of those who do the will of God as 'his true brothers',[16] and of Lk 11:27–8, where he subordinates the physical motherhood of Mary to the deeper reason that she is blessed.[17] Mary's final sacrifice came on Calvary, but by accepting the crucifixion of her son and standing by his side, she was there more closely united with him than ever. There, in bitter anguish, she was one with Jesus, and so she remains eternally.

This interpretation of Jesus' words to Mary at Cana is that given by St Augustine, who is followed in almost identical words by St Thomas Aquinas.[18] Augustine writes:

[15] *La mère des fidèles*, p. 63.
[16] See above, pp. 236–8.
[17] See above, p. 347.
[18] *In Ioannem, in loco.*

'His mother was therefore asking for a miracle. But he, as it were, did not acknowledge her blood-relationship now that he was about to do divine things. It is as if he said, "You did not give birth to my power of working miracles, it was not you who gave birth to my divinity. But you are the mother of all that is weak in me, and therefore I shall give you recognition when this weak humanity shall hang on the cross." For that is the meaning of "My hour is not yet come".'[19]

(Braun differs from Augustine and Aquinas only in that he does not postulate that Mary requested a miracle. But even so, the main element in Augustine's comment, that Jesus must be about the work of his Father, harmonizes well with Braun's interpretation.) Rupert of Deutz (d. 1135) is also worth citing:

'It was in no way against the law which commands "Honour thy father and thy mother". . . . It was rather to fulfil the law perfectly that, without in any way dishonouring her, he did not acknowledge his mother. For it is no disrespect to a father or mother when a man prefers more than them not any kind of business, but the honouring or the work of God alone. Jesus was now intent on this great and necessary work of salvation, and that is why he says he will have no more to do with his mother until, when this task is finished, he says, "Woman, behold thy son!" That he would say at the hour of his death. Hence when he had said "What is that to me and to thee, woman?" he at once added "My hour is not yet come".'[20]

Augustine returns to this theme in his commentary on the scene at the foot of the cross (Jn 19:25):

'This indeed is that hour of which Jesus had spoken when he was about to turn water into wine. Then he had said to his

---

[19] *Tract. in Ioannem* VIII, 9 (*CC* 36.87 = ML 35.1455).
[20] *Commentaria in Evangelium Ioannis* (on 2:4): *CC Continuatio Medievalis* 6.105 = ML 169.281.

mother: "What is that to me and to thee, woman? My hour is not yet come". So he had spoken beforehand about this hour (which had not then come), in which he was to acknowledge at the point of death the woman from whom he had been born in mortal flesh. On that first occasion, when he was about to do divine things, he set aside the mother not of his godhead, but of his weakness, as if he did not know her. But now, suffering the lot of humanity, his human affection went out in love to her of whom he was made man. On that earlier occasion, he who had created Mary was about to make himself known in power; now, he to whom Mary had given birth was hanging on the cross.'[21]

This handful of witnesses may be concluded with a citation from Newman:

'If on one occasion, He seems to repel His Mother, when she told Him that wine was wanting for the guests at the marriage feast, it is obvious to remark on it, by saying that she was then separated from Him (*What have I to do with thee?*) because His hour was not yet come; He implied, that when that hour was come, such separation would be at an end.'[22]

Consequently, for a full understanding of the words spoken at Cana, one must turn to the scene at the foot of the cross.

In the Fourth Gospel, the mother of Jesus is never mentioned after the postscript to Cana (Jn 2:12) until she reappears at the foot of the cross, at the very end of the scene, when Jesus is about to die. To understand this passage (Jn 19:25–7), it is essential to see it in its context. The whole section, from 19:17 to 19:42, is composed of details which show the fulfilment of prophecy. In the following list, only the verses directly under consideration (25–7) are passed over without comment.

(i) 17–18: Jesus is crucified between two robbers. Compare Is 53:12, 'He was counted among sinners'.

---

[21] *Tract. in Ioannem* CXIX, 1 (*CC* 36.658 = ML 35.1950).

[22] *Difficulties of Anglicans*, vol. 2 (in the standard edition by Longman), pp. 72–3.

(ii) 19–22: Pilate wrote 'Jesus of Nazareth, King of the Jews'. The irony of this reference to all the prophecies about the royal Messiah is evident. Braun suggests that the evangelist may have had in mind particularly Zech 10:9 ('Behold thy king cometh unto thee, lowly and riding on an ass'), which was cited at Jn 12:15. On the cross, the message is 'Behold thy king cometh unto thee!'

(iii) 23–4: The soldiers divide Jesus' clothes, and draw lots for his cloak. This is presented explicitly as a fulfilment of Ps 22:19, cited *ad litteram* from the Septuagint (Ps 21:19).

(iv) 25–7: these are the verses under discussion.

(v) 28–30: Jesus asks for a drink. This again is explicitly called a fulfilment of Scripture. The reference may be to Ps 22:16 (in some versions, 15), or (more likely) to Ps 69:22 (21): 'In my thirst they gave me vinegar to drink'.

(vi) 31–7: The soldiers did not break Jesus' legs, as they did with the two robbers, but one of them pierced his side. This again is explicitly termed a fulfilment of Scripture. 'Not one of his bones shall be broken' may be either from Ex 12:36 or Num 9:12 (a rubric about the Passover Lamb), or from Ps 34:21 (20), which is about the sufferings of the righteous man. 'They shall look upon him whom they pierced' is a direct citation of Zech 12:10. The quotation from Zech 12:10 is incontestable, and therefore it is by no means fanciful to see in the flowing of blood and water from Jesus' side the fulfilment of another text of Zechariah in the same context, and only four verses later. Nearly all commentators see the blood and water as symbols of baptism and the Eucharist, the sacramental sources from which the stream of life flows to the Church. Zechariah says (13:1): 'On that day a spring shall begin to flow for the house of David and for the inhabitants of Jerusalem, to cleanse them from sin and uncleanness.'

(vii) 38–42: Jesus is buried by Joseph of Arimathaea and Nicodemus. This again may well be a fulfilment of Is 53:9: 'They prepared a tomb for him with the wicked [*alternative reading*: with the rich], and his grave was among criminals.' In the details of the burial, John stresses the way the corpse was anointed with one hundred pounds of aloes, and firmly wrapped up in linen, and placed in a new tomb (Jn 19:39–41) because, he says later (20:9) *'they had not yet understood the Scripture*, that Jesus was divinely destined to rise from the dead'.

If every other incident described between v. 17 and v. 42 is a fulfilment of prophecy, then there is good ground for suspecting that the incident related in vv. 25–7 is also a fulfilment of prophecy. The fact that no text is there mentioned need cause no difficulty, for in the first two examples cited and in the last, the reference is only implied, and implicit allusion is wholly in John's manner.[23] One could add (a point not made by Braun) that the whole gospel is permeated structurally with the idea of seven (though the word itself never occurs)—an indication of its connection with the Apocalypse.[24] The fulfilment of seven prophecies at the death of Jesus would be wholly in line with this careful hidden structure of the Fourth Gospel.

Another argument for the view that Jn 19:25–7 embody the fulfilment of prophecy is that the following verse, 28, begins with μετὰ τοῦτο. *'After this*, Jesus, knowing that now everything was accomplished, that the Scripture might be fulfilled, said, I thirst.' John's more normal phrase for 'after this' or 'next' is μετὰ ταῦτα, (in the plural: so Jn 3:22; 5:1, 14; 6:1; 7:1; 13:7; 19:38; 21:1). He uses the singular (μετὰ τοῦτο) only four times, and always after some significant decision by Jesus. Thus it occurs in 2:12: after 'the beginning of his signs' at Cana, Jesus went to Capernaum

---

[23] See the whole of the splendid volume by Braun, *Jean le Théologien II: Les grandes traditions d'Israel et l'accord des Ecritures selon le quatrième Evangile (Etudes Bibliques)*, Paris, 1964.

[24] See E. A. Abbott, *Johannine Grammar*, §§2624–7. John records seven signs (but see below, pp. 396–7), a small number compared with the Synoptists. Many see the opening events as taking place over seven days, with the manifestation of Jesus' glory at Cana on the seventh. The Passion narrative opens with 'Six days before the Passover' (12:1). The Johannine 'I am' certainly occurs seven times in the sevenfold representation of Jesus' relationship to mankind: (i) 'I am the Bread of Life' (6:35); (ii) 'I am the Light of the World' (8:12); (iii) 'I am the Door for the Sheep' (10:7); (iv) 'I am the Good Shepherd' (10:11); (v) 'I am the Resurrection and the Life' (11:25); (vi) 'I am the Way, the Truth, and the Life' (14:6); (vii) 'I am the True Vine' (15:1).

with his mother and family, but stayed there only a few days before beginning his active ministry. It occurs in 11:7, after Jesus' decision not to visit Lazarus on his death-bed, and in 11:11, when he tells the Twelve that he is going to awake Lazarus. The only other occurrence is in 19:28. If this distinction between the two Greek phrases is valid, then the sense of 19:28 is '*After this significant action . . .*' This is Braun's argument. But perhaps μετὰ τοῦτο (as distinct from μετὰ ταῦτα) means 'after a *short* interval', or calls attention to what follows, not what precedes. (It is used only *before* a significant word or decision, too.) The view that it denotes only a short interval seems much more likely, in view of 11:7 and 11, and if so, this argument for Braun's theory should be discounted.[25]

If, then, the incident in Jn 19:25-7 is the fulfilment of a prophecy, to what Old Testament text does it refer? There are only three texts which refer to the mother of a saviour: Is 7:14, Mic 5:2 ('Until the time when she who is to give birth does give birth'), and Gen 3:15. The first two concern the birth of the Messiah, and may therefore be set aside. This leaves only Gen 3:15.

Habitually, John cites the Old Testament according to the Septuagint,[26] and if he is thinking of Gen 3:15, it will very probably be in the form in which it occurs in the Septuagint. There we read: 'I will place enmity between thee and the woman, and between thy seed and her seed. *He* will lie in wait for thy

---

[25] See E. A. Abbott, *Johannine Grammar*, §2394.

A further argument which could be adduced to support Braun's thesis is that Jn 19:28 is ambiguous. The punctuation is of modern origin, and grammatically there is no reason why one should not translate the verse as: 'After this, Jesus, knowing that now everything was accomplished to fulfil the Scripture, said, I thirst.' By omitting the comma after 'accomplished' and retaining it after 'Scripture', the 'fulfilment of Scripture' would be referred *back* to vv. 25-7. But Braun does not suggest this, and rightly. John always places the words 'that the Scripture might be fulfilled' *before* the quotation, not after the fact (Jn 12:14, 38; 13:18; 15:25; 19:24, 36; *cf.* 18:9, 32). And the allusion afterwards to Ps 69:22 is exceptionally clear, because of the mention of vinegar.

[26] This statement is sometimes contested, but for the evidence see Braun, *Jean le Théologien II*, pp, 20-1.

head, and thou shalt lie in wait for his heel.' This translation is markedly more precise than the Hebrew. In the Hebrew, it is the woman's offspring (literally, her seed) which will 'crush the serpent's head'; but (as in English) the word 'offspring' or 'posterity' may be taken to denote either a single individual or her descendants as a whole (the collective meaning). In the Septuagint there is no such ambiguity: the word for 'seed' in Greek is neuter, and the pronoun which follows is in Greek masculine. Hence in the Septuagint it cannot be the woman's offspring as a whole which wins the victory over the serpent; it must be an individual.[27]

Could John have had in mind Gen 3:15? In the Fourth Gospel, it is the devil who is the great adversary of Jesus (Jn 12:31; 16:11; cf. Apoc 12:4–6), who puts it into the mind of Judas Iscariot to betray him (Jn 13:2; cf. 6:70); and in Apoc 12:9 the devil, or Satan, is openly identified with 'that serpent of old'. If the author of the Apocalypse and the evangelist were one and the same man, then it is clear that in the gospel we may legitimately look for references to Gen 3. If they were not the same, the close relationship of their thought makes the quest of allusions still legitimate, but it should be pursued with more caution. Yet the evangelist would seem to have been conscious of the importance of Gen 3:15, for the curious expression about 'the seed of the serpent' is taken up in Jn 8:41–4, where we read of 'the children of the devil', and in 1 Jn 3:8–10, where the children of God are contrasted with the children of the devil. Then there is the important statement of Jesus to Pilate: 'For this I was born, for this I came into the world, to bear witness to truth' (Jn 18:37). Jesus' whole life was therefore a war against 'the father of lies' (Jn 8:44), a title clearly echoing Gen 3:4 and 13 ('The serpent lied to me'); and his Passion in particular was the supreme battle of this war, in which the prince of this world was stripped of his empire (Jn 12:27–36; 14:30). By comparing 12:23 with 12:31–2 it is evident that the

[27] Perhaps it is worth mentioning that the Vulgate assigns the victory over the serpent to the woman herself ('*Ipsa* conteret caput tuum . . .'). This rendering has had an enormous influence on the development of Marian doctrine within the Roman Catholic Church, but it is an indefensible mistranslation.

victory over the prince of this world takes place at the same hour as the glorification of the son of man. It was on the cross that Jesus 'crushed the head' of that 'serpent of old' (Gen 3:15 with Apoc 12:9) and 'cast him down' (or: out) for all future time (Jn 12:31).

In the texts cited in the last paragraph, there has been mention of the devil and his offspring (explicit in Jn 8:41-4; 1 Jn 3:8-10; implicit in Jn 6:70 and 13:2), and of their enemy, Jesus. Therefore of the four figures named in Gen 3:15, the only one not so far mentioned is the woman, the mother of 'him who crushed the serpent's head'. Yet according to Genesis, she too is at war with the serpent, and one would expect her to share somehow in the victory of her offspring. In Genesis, of course, the woman is undoubtedly the mother of the human race, Eve. But if John, reading the text in the Septuagint, thought of the 'offspring' as an individual, *i.e.* Jesus the Christ, is it not likely that he would have perceived that Mary was the mother of this individual? Having found a place in his work for three of the four figures in Genesis, why should he not also include the mother of him who by the cross crushed the serpent to death? Jesus was descended from Eve by the fact that she was the mother of all the living (Gen 3:20), but he was more immediately the son of Mary. Hence her physical presence 'beside the Cross' (or even: 'beside the Crucified')[28] associates her for ever with the *triumph* of Jesus: for in John the cross is never a gibbet, but always a royal throne ('*Regnavit a ligno Deus*'). Eve, to whom the text from Genesis primarily refers, had been dead for thousands of years, but her enemy, the serpent, lived on. Eve survived only in her children, and so the place assigned to the woman was filled by 'the mother of Jesus'. It is not so much that Mary is presented by John as a New Eve; Eve has long faded into the background, and Mary

---

[28] This is the only instance in the entire New Testament where παρά with the dative is used in reference not to a person, but to a thing. The meaning is therefore essentially 'beside the Crucified'. Perhaps it can best be rendered into English as 'beside the Cross' (with a capital C) to call attention to the special nature of *this* Cross because of him who hung on it. See E. A. Abbott, *Johannine Grammar*, §2355.

as mother of Jesus has become 'the Woman'. Her place in the story blots out all thought of Eve, the first woman. This is one of the most striking examples of what Cerfaux calls 'apostolic exegesis',[29] in which the evangelist, inspired by the Holy Ghost, gives a new and deeper sense (a 'sensus plenior') to the words of the Old Testament.[30]

What, then, is the meaning of 'Woman, behold thy son'? It is usually taken as an act of filial piety, as if Jesus were anxious to provide for his mother after his death. This idea is certainly not absent, but it is hard to accept it as the primary meaning of the gospel for three reasons. First, the rest of the context is concerned with the fulfilment of prophecy. Secondly, on every other occasion when Jesus speaks during his Passion, his words are concerned with his divinely ordained mission; it would be truly astounding if these words, to his mother, constituted a solitary exception. Thirdly, if Jn 19:25-7 is primarily an act of solicitude for Mary, why is the disciple first entrusted to Mary, and not *vice versa*?

Perhaps the best way to approach the problem is to look first at the words 'the disciple whom Jesus loved'. More than once John presents an individual as representative of a group. For example, Nicodemus is a type of the learned Jew seeking after truth (Jn 3:1-15); his attitude is counterbalanced in the next chapter by the story of the Samaritan woman, a simple soul who typifies the poor and unsophisticated looking only for the water of life (4:1-42). So the disciple beside the Crucified is a figure of all who love Jesus. Jesus had promised that all who loved him and kept his commandments would in turn be loved by the Father 'and I too will love him' (14:21, 23; *cf.* 1 Jn 2:5). These men would be his friends (Jn 15:13-15), and the disciple who followed

---

[29] L. Cerfaux, 'Simples réflexions à propos de l'exégèse apostolique', *ETL* 25 (1949) pp. 565-76 (= *Receuil Lucien Cerfaux*, vol. 2, Gembloux, 1954, pp. 189-203).

[30] Braun, in *La mère des fidèles*, p. 89, cites E. Hoskyns, who writes: 'When the Fathers say that Mary is the New Eve, they have caught the meaning of the passage far better than modern commentators' ('Genesis 1-3 and St John's Gospel', *JTS* 21 [1920], p. 221).

him to Calvary seems to have been the closest friend of all (18: 15 ff. and especially 13:25). Probably nearly all modern exegetes would agree that in 19:26-7 this disciple should be taken as a type of all who love Jesus.[31]

'Woman, behold thy son!' In the Fourth Gospel, the words of Jesus are not merely declarative, but also causative (what modern English philosophers term 'performative', as in 'I name this ship . . .'). Jesus is 'the Word by whom all things were made' (Jn 1:3). Hence his utterance changes water into wine (2:7-8), heals the ruler's son (4:51) and the paralysed man (5:8), multiplies loaves (6:11) and gives sight to the man born blind (9:7); his word alone raises Lazarus from the tomb (11:41-3). And just as Peter was placed in a new relationship to the disciples by the charge 'Feed my lambs, feed my sheep' (21:16-18), so Mary was placed in a new relationship to 'the disciple(s) whom Jesus loved' by the words spoken from the cross.

What is Mary's new function to be, as mother of the disciples? It must be in some way bound up with the work of Jesus himself, and the best clue is in Jn 17. Jesus there prays that his disciples may be one (vv. 11-14) and that they may be defended from the Evil One (v. 15; cf. I Jn 2:13, 14; 3:12; 5:18, 19). For this purpose Jesus sacrificed himself (v. 19), and from Cana to the cross Mary shared by spiritual communion in this suffering and sacrifice. The fruit of this sacrifice is that the disciples are to be brought to their home in heaven: 'Father, I desire that those whom thou hast given me may be where I am, together with me, that they may gaze upon my glory, which thou hast given me, because thou hast loved me, before the foundation of the world' (v. 24). If Mary is the mother of all who love Jesus, then her one desire will be that all her children may never be separated from Jesus or from her, that they may all be in the end united with Jesus, to gaze upon his glory. She is charged to pray the same prayer as Jesus at the Supper, on behalf of 'all his brothers', the disciples whom Jesus loves. And correspondingly, the disciples are charged to

---

[31] *E.g.* M. Dibelius, 'Joh. 15:13. Eine Studie zum Traditionsproblem des Johannes-Evangelium', in *Botschaft und Geschichte I*, pp. 204-20, on p. 214 (cited by Braun, *La mère des fidèles*, p. 112).

look upon this woman who stood faithful beside the Crucified as *their* mother, if they would be truly one with their dying saviour.

Jn 19:27 is usually translated 'And from that hour the disciple took her to his own home' (Revised Standard Version, etc.). But if we take careful notice of John's vocabulary, a more meaningfull rendering emerges. In the Fourth Gospel, the verb λαμβάνω has two senses. When applied to material things, it means simply 'to take hold of', 'to pick up', 'to grasp', etc. (*e.g.* 6:11; 12:13; 13:12; 19:23, 40); when applied to immaterial things, it means 'to accept' or 'to welcome', usually as a gift from God (*e.g.* his witness, 3:11; his word, 17:18; his Spirit, 14:17; 1 Jn 2:27). Secondly, the words εἰς τὰ ἴδια, which certainly can mean 'to one's own home' (in a purely physical sense), can also mean 'among one's own spiritual possessions' (compare Jn 8:44 and 15:19, in the Greek). The phrase is found in the prologue with this double meaning of 'physical home' and 'spiritual possession', and in close conjunction with the verb 'to accept or welcome'. 'He came to *what was his own* . . . and to all who *accepted* him, he gave the power to become children of God' (Jn 1:12–13). Jn 19:27 seems to demand a translation which includes both the purely physical and the deeper, spiritual sense. 'And from that hour the disciple took her into his own home, and accepted her as his own mother, as part of the spiritual legacy bequeathed to him by his Lord.'

Chapter Three

THE MOTHER OF JESUS IN THE FOURTH GOSPEL (II): A CRITIQUE OF THIS INTERPRETATION

IT is easy to see why Père Braun's interpretation has been so warmly received in the Roman Catholic Church. It rests on an attentive study of Scripture, it is faithful to tradition, and it contains a religious message of importance. Further, the author's insight into the theology of the Fourth Gospel has been abundantly confirmed by the four volumes published since, under the title *ean le Théologien*. Yet outside the Roman Catholic Church, the impact of *La mère des fidèles* has been negligible; and even within it, many exegetes have voiced a number of reservations about the book's argument. A critique of Braun's thesis is therefore unavoidable.

In its favour, one may say that the interpretation of 'mother of Jesus' as 'mother of the Word Incarnate' (which implies and entails the legitimacy of the term *Theotokos*) is beyond questioning; those who object to this are quarrelling not with Braun but with St John. Secondly, the exegesis of the words spoken by Jesus at Cana ('What is that to me and to thee, woman? My hour is not yet come') is by far the most commonly accepted explanation of these difficult words. Braun's *exegesis* (*i.e.* his exposition of what the words actually mean)[1] will be taken for granted in this chapter (but partially queried in the next). Thirdly, his contention that

---

[1] *I.e.* the explanation set out on pp. 362–7, as distinct from the *interpretation* which he then puts on these words. See the next paragraph. For the interpretation adopted in the next chapter, see pp. 392–4.

the disciple whom Jesus loved is not merely an historical figure, but also a figure symbolic of all who love Jesus, will command wide, though not universal, assent.

But Braun's main thesis is that Jesus' words to his mother at Cana contain a further implication. Since he was about to begin his Father's business, he could no longer be with her until his hour was come; then, on Calvary, they would once more be united. Augustine, Aquinas, Rupert of Deutz and Newman, four solid witnesses of Catholic tradition, hold the same view. But this is not what the text actually says; it is only a deduction from the text. Does this *interpretation* of Jesus' words at Cana follow inexorably from the *exegesis* of Jn 2:4? Personally, I think not, and a different proposal will be put forward in the next chapter.

Secondly, Braun argues that if every other episode on Calvary is a fulfilment of prophecy, it is reasonable to conclude that the scene recorded in Jn 19:25–7 also contains a fulfilment of prophecy. The weakness of this contention is that, of the other six scenes enumerated, only three are expressly mentioned as fulfilments of prophecy. If John had really seen the crucifixion between two criminals as the fulfilment of Is 53:12, why did he not add, 'that the Scripture might be fulfilled: *He was numbered with transgressors*'? Pilate's inscription, 'King of the Jews', can more easily be accepted as an implicit accomplishment of prophecy, for here the irony of the evangelist is evident. But the burial 'with the wicked' or 'with the rich' is not so easily discerned as a fulfilment of Is 53:9; and if it was intended as such, a citation would have been expected (as in 'Not a bone of him shall be broken', where again the allusion is not self-evident). Braun would have had a stronger case if he had drawn attention to the *sevenfold* arrangement of the events on Calvary, and backed it up by other references in the gospel (and in the Apocalypse); but this he does not do, and therefore a question-mark must be placed (temporarily) against the suggestion that the presence of the mother of Jesus beside the Cross must be seen as the accomplishment of some prophecy.

The argument that μετὰ τοῦτο in Jn 19:28 calls attention to the significance of the preceding verses has already been rejected.

It seems far more probable that the phrase means simply 'after a short interval', 'a little later'.[2]

Finally, Braun adduces three considerations to support the idea that the words of Jesus in vv. 26-7 include something more than the providing of a home and a guardian for Mary. First, the rest of the context is concerned with the fulfilment of prophecy: this, as we have just seen, is debatable. Secondly, on every other occasion when Jesus speaks during his Passion, his words are pregnant with meaning, and are concerned with his divinely ordained mission. This is a valid argument, and sufficient on its own to justify the exegete in looking for a spiritual meaning in 19:26-7; indeed, the whole of the Fourth Gospel demands that we treat all Jesus' words this way. Thirdly, Braun asks, if Jn 19: 26-7 is primarily an act of solicitude for Mary, why is the disciple first entrusted to Mary, and not *vice versa*?[3] This third consideration seems very feeble, for it *assumes* that the disciple is 'entrusted' (*confié*) to Mary. This may be so, but it is what the author is trying to prove, and he seems to have been inadvertently guilty of a *petitio principii*. It is just as reasonable to say that when Mary is told to look upon the disciple as her son, it is she who is entrusted to him (not *vice versa*). Nevertheless, the second argument is by itself a strong, and even compelling, suasion in favour of the view that there is some deep spiritual meaning in the words of the evangelist. Probably the majority of Johannine specialists would today assent to this view,[4] and it is somewhat surprising to find

[2] See above, p. 373.

[3] 'En ramenant la scene décrite en 19:25-7 à un acte de sollicitude envers Marie, on insiste trop sur la protection dont le Disciple semble invité à couvrir la mere de Jésus, et pas assez sur le fait que c'est le Disciple qui tout d'abord est confié à Marie' (*La mère des fidèles*, p. 100).

[4] It was not always so. Not one of the three great patristic commentators on John 19:25-7 saw in the scene anything more than a gesture of filial piety: see Chrysostom, *Hom. in Ioannem* 85 (MG 59.462), Cyril of Alexandria, *In Ioannem XII, in loco* (MG 74.664) and *De adoratione in spiritu et veritate* (MG 68.508-13), and Augustine, *Tract. in Ioannem* CXIX, 2-3 (CC 36.658-9 = ML 35.1950-1). For further detail see Th. Koehler, 'Les principales interprétations traditionelles de Jn 19:25-7 pendant les douze premiers siècles', in *La maternité spirituelle de Marie*, BSFEM 16 (1959), pp. 119-55.

Dodd writing that the scene 'whatever its motive, does not seem to be dictated by the Johannine theology'.[5]

Two major points therefore remain open to question. (1) Taking Cana and Calvary together, can one legitimately say that their message about Mary is that she was separated from Jesus for the duration of his public ministry (in which she was to play no part at all), but reunited with him on Calvary (from which hour she does have a role to play, as mother of the disciples)? (2) Is it legitimate to interpret the presence of the mother of Jesus beside the Crucified as a fulfilment of prophecy, and in particular of Gen 3:15? Did the evangelist mean the reader to understand that Mary was here represented as 'the mother of him who crushed the serpent's head'?

M. André Feuillet agrees with Braun's interpretation on the first point (separation at Cana, reunion on Calvary),[6] but half dissents on the second. He does not believe that the evidence adduced by Braun will support the weight placed on it, and there-

---

[5] *The Interpretation of the Fourth Gospel*, p. 428.

[6] From the same starting-point, he reaches the same conclusion, but by a rather novel route. In 'L'heure de Jésus et le signe de Cana' (*ETL* 36 [1966], pp. 5-22), he agrees with Braun that Mary did not ask for a miracle, only for some kind of help. Next, however, he interprets Jesus' reply and refusal of her request as a reference to the wine of the New Covenant, promised for a future age by Gen 49:11-12; Is 25:6; Joel 3:18 (= 4:18), and Cant 1:4; see also Mk 2:22. 'The hour for the gift of that wine', says Jesus, 'is not yet come.' He does, however, then supply in abundance an earthly wine which symbolizes that greater wine of the New Covenant (the Eucharist). This Cana-wine Jesus provides at Mary's instance, implying that when his hour does come (the hour of the Church and of the sacraments), he will again listen to her requests. Meantime, he must be about his Father's business.

Though most exegetes would admit that the Cana-wine is a symbol of the New Covenant, it is hard to believe that the evangelist intended to represent Jesus as deliberately misinterpreting Mary's request. Jn 4:7-16 and 6:26-34 are not true parallels, for there the evangelist, aware of the danger of a misunderstanding, carefully explains what is meant by 'living water' and 'bread from heaven'. In the Cana story he gives no such explanation; and without such a clear pointer (or indeed any clue at all), the reader could not be expected to see that Jesus in v.4 was putting a different meaning on Mary's request for wine, and then telling her that her request for the wine of the New Covenant was premature. All in all, the article is very unconvincing.

fore comes to the rescue with a very different approach, in order to justify the idea that Mary by the Cross is an anti-type of Eve.[7]

'When a woman is in labour, she feels sorrow, because her hour has come; but when she gives birth to the child, she no longer remembers the anguish, for joy that a man is born into the world' (Jn 16:21). In the context (Jn 16:16–24) Jesus is speaking of his impending departure, both by his death and by his final departure after the Resurrection; therefore v. 21 must be concerned with his departure and Resurrection. Some see in it merely a parable, but Feuillet thinks there is here a subtle reference to Eve, for the following reasons. First, Jn 16:21 does not read (as one would expect) 'for joy that a *child* is born into the world', but 'for joy that a *man* is born into the world'. The same curious usage is found in Gen 4:1, where Eve exclaims upon the birth of her firstborn: 'I have got a *man* with the help of the Lord' ('I have got a *child*' would be perfectly normal usage). Secondly, in Jn 16:21, we read 'When a woman is in labour, she feels *sorrow*'. In Greek as in English, the word 'sorrow' is not a natural choice to denote physical pain, least of all that of childbirth: 'sorrow' refers more to mental anguish. Yet it is the word used in Gen 3:16 (Septuagint), where God tells Eve that she will bring forth her children in *sorrow*. (The noun used in the Hebrew text also denotes mental suffering as much as physical pain.) Feuillet concludes from the use of 'man' rather than 'child', and of 'sorrow' rather than 'pain', that Jn 16:21 contains an allusion to Eve, the mother of all the living and of the first-born of the human race (Gen 3:20),[8]

---

[7] He has expounded his view in two articles, the first of which is of a more popular nature: 'Les adieux du Christ à sa mère (Jn 19:25–7) et la maternité spirituelle de Marie', in the *NRT* 86 (1964), pp. 469–89, and 'L'heure de la femme (Jn 16:21) et l'heure de la mère de Jésus (Jn 19:25–7)', in *Biblica* 47 (1966), pp. 169–84, 361–80 and 557–73.

[8] Feuillet also has a third argument, that Philo, in *De Cherubim* xiv = 53–4 (Loeb ed., vol. 2, pp. 40–1) explains the curious phrase 'I have begotten a *man*' (Gen 4:1) from the fact that Cain was 'the first-begotten of men, the first-born, the beginning of human generation'. If this were so, the parallel with the Risen Lord would be obvious. Feuillet takes this text from the article by W. Michaelis in the *TWNT* 6, p. 876, but neither Philo nor Michaelis says or implies that 'la formule exceptionelle de Gen 4:1 vient de ce que Cain est *le premier-né des hommes*'

and this in the context of Jesus' departure and Resurrection.

It is a commonplace of New Testament teaching that the Resurrection is like a new birth into a new world. Paul applies to it the text 'Today I have begotten thee' (Ps 2:7, cited in Ac 13:33), and calls Jesus 'the first-born of the dead' (Col 1:18), a title which recurs in Apoc 1:5. As the first inhabitant of this new world, Jesus is for Paul a Second Adam (1 Cor 15:45). John's perspective is slightly different. Jesus was already a New Adam before the Crucifixion (cf. Pilate's words, 'Behold the Man!' in Jn 19:15), and the hour when he was born into the new world was not Easter morning but Good Friday. This was the hour when he passed from this world to the Father (13:1), the hour when the woman was in labour, as the man was being brought forth in anguish into the new world of the Resurrection (cf. 16:21). So, according to Feuillet, Jn 16:21 clamours for the presence of a New Eve beside the New Adam, and Mary's presence beside the Crucified associates her with Jesus as a second Eve. And it is in order to call attention to Mary's new role as 'mother of all the living' that Jesus addresses her as 'Woman'.[9]

But the full content of Jn 16:21 has not yet been brought to the surface. The prophecy that Zion would in days to come be the mother of countless children is common in the prophets (e.g. Is 26: 17–21 and 66:7–8).[10] Now in Is 26:17–21 we read first of *a woman in travail*, then '*Thy dead shall live, their bones shall rise!*' (v. 19), and finally 'hide yourselves *but a little while*' (cf. Jn 16:16–19). It would seem certain, then, that at 16:21 the evangelist had this text in mind. Further, in Is 66, we read again of *Zion in travail* (v. 7) and of her *bringing forth many sons* (v. 8); and a little later, after a song of joy about the many children of Jerusalem, the prophet says (v. 14): '*You shall see, and your heart shall rejoice*'

(*Biblica* 47 [1966], p. 177: italics by the author). It is a pity that he bases this argument on Philo, for Eve's words are exactly what one would expect if she had never seen a baby before!

[9] The last two paragraphs are a highly condensed and slightly emended version of the argument in *Biblica* 47 (1966), pp. 174–84.

[10] *Biblica, ibid.*, pp. 365–6. (See also above, p. 34.)

(which is very close to Jn 16:22: 'I shall see you, and your heart shall rejoice'). Thus it is fair to see in Jn 16:21 not just an unadorned parable, but an allusion to the prophecies about Zion as the mother of many children. For John, the hour of this birth is indubitably on Calvary. Feuillet concludes:

'The fact that the Virgin Mary on Golgotha is, against all expectation, addressed by her son as "Woman" and not as "Mother", and that she is furthermore proclaimed by him "mother" of the beloved disciple, would seem to indicate that in the eyes of Christ she *represents* Zion, and that he intended to attribute to her the supernatural metaphorical motherhood which the prophets had foretold of Zion.'[11]

How, then, is Mary represented on Calvary—as the New Eve bringing forth the New Adam into the world of the Resurrection, or as a woman symbolizing Zion, the mother of many children? Feuillet thinks the two images are superimposed (as in Apoc 12), and argues that this is characteristic of the Fourth Gospel. Following rabbinical precedents, the evangelist likes to use terms which can refer both to the Pentateuch and to the prophets. Thus, when the Baptist says 'Behold the Lamb of God!' (Jn 1:29, 36), the term recalls both the Passover Lamb and that Servant of the Lord who was led like a lamb to the slaughter (Is 53:7). The mention of 'living water' in Jn 4:10, 14 and 7:37-8 recalls both the water that spelt life in the desert of Sinai (Ex 17:4-7) and the abundance of water from the temple in the New Jerusalem (Ez 47:1-12; Zech 14:8). There is nothing in the least improbable about this superimposing of images. The list could be easily prolonged, particularly as it is a device common in the Apocalypse. See, for example, Apoc 5:5-6 where the Lion of Judah (Gen 49:9) is identified with the Root of David (Is 11:1), after which both are identified, in v. 6, with 'the Lamb that was slain'.

There can be no doubt that M. Feuillet has made out a case for seeing more in Jn 16:21 than a simple parable. The fact that the woman feels *sorrow* and not pain, and gives birth to *a man*, not a

[11] *Ibid.*, p. 370.

child, does make one wonder whether there may not be here an allusion to Gen 3–4. Equally, there is a remarkable coincidence of expressions and ideas that are found in Is 26 and 66. Many may feel that in his endeavour to squeeze the last drop of meaning out of the words in Jn 16:21 he has passed beyond the bounds of sober and convincing exegesis; but others may feel that he has in fact discovered the double allusion, to Eve and Zion.

The real problem, however, is whether Feuillet is justified in using Jn 16:21 as the key to the interpretation of Jn 19:25–7. He has seen, and rightly stressed, that if the disciple is to be taken as a symbolic figure, the mother of Jesus too must be taken as more than a merely historical figure. She too must have a symbolic role, and there is no reason whatever why the evangelist should not have superimposed two symbols, Eve and the Daughter of Zion; both are richly significant symbols, and far from being mutually exclusive, are mutually complementary. But (assuming that this double allusion to Eve and Zion is to be found in Jn 16: 21), Feuillet does not appear to have fully justified the application of it to Mary on Calvary. His arguments for so applying it are that the 'hour' of the woman in 16:21 must inevitably direct the reader to that other hour, the hour of Jesus; and that Jesus then addresses Mary not as 'Mother' but as 'Woman'. Neither reason on its own, nor both together, can be considered wholly persuasive, though they are not without a certain weight *if* there truly is a hidden allusion to Eve in 16:21; for in the story of Gen 3, Eve is normally referred to as 'the woman'. A better argument for seeing Mary by the cross as the New Eve and the Daughter of Zion could be drawn from Apoc 12, but Feuillet seems wary of placing too much stress on this.[12]

---

[12] In the *NRT* 86 (1964), p. 477, he writes: 'En raison du lien évident qui existe entre les deux passages, Apoc 12 autorise donc une exégèse ecclésiologique de Jn 19:25–7, tout autant que Jn 19:25–7, de son côté, justifie une interprétation mariale d'Apoc 12.' But in *Biblica* 47 (1966), p. 566, while admitting 'une étroite relation' and a 'rapprochement' between the woman in the parable of Jn 16:21 and the woman in Apoc 12, he refuses to identify them completely. Hence he cannot invoke Apoc 12 as the link connecting Jn 16:21 with Jn 19:25–7, and enabling one to see Mary by the cross as a second Eve.

The fundamental weakness in Feuillet's essay is that his thesis rests ultimately on the presence of an allusion to Eve in Jn 16:21. The only evidence for such an allusion is the use of the word 'sorrow' where one would expect 'birth-pains' (*cf.* Gen 3:16), and the choice of the word 'man' instead of 'child' (*cf.* Gen 4:1). But the word 'sorrow' is dictated by the context. Both in the preceding verse (Jn 16:20) and in the verse following (16:22), Jesus speaks of the *sorrow* of the Eleven at his departure; and though John could have used 'birth-pains' in 16:21, his preference for 'sorrow' enables him to anchor the parable more firmly in its context. Similarly, the choice of the term 'man' instead of 'child' may be simply due to the evangelist's wish for an elegant variation (he has already used 'child' once in v. 21); or it may be that the woman's joy comes from the knowledge that her baby will one day become a fully grown man. Either of these explanations seems more likely than the idea that Jn 16:21 is making a (very cryptic) reference to Eve's exclamation in Gen 4:1.

The allusion to Eve in Jn 16:21 is therefore so faint as to be scarcely discernible, if indeed it is there at all. Consequently, to connect Jn 16:21 with the scene in Jn 19:25–7 does not provide a very strong argument for affirming that Mary beside the cross is presented as a New Eve, particularly when it is far from proved that the Fourth Gospel presents Jesus as the New Adam. On the evidence so far brought forward, the thesis cannot be accepted.

Feuillet began by accepting Braun's interpretation of the teaching of the Fourth Gospel about Mary, assuming that the message was that Jesus separated himself from his mother after Cana, to be reunited with her when his hour was come. He sought only to justify the reference to Mary as a New Eve, or as the woman of Gen 3:15, by a different argument. But is it really so certain that the main burden of the Fourth Gospel's teaching about Mary is that she was first separated from, and at last reunited with, her son? A different solution will now be proposed.

Chapter Four

THE MOTHER OF JESUS IN THE FOURTH
GOSPEL (III): AN ALTERNATIVE
PROPOSAL

'THERE was a wedding in Cana of Galilee, and the mother of Jesus
was there' (Jn 2:1). In the Fourth Gospel, the mother of Jesus is
mentioned only twice, once at the beginning and once at the end.
Now though it is self-evident that Calvary is the final episode in
Jesus' earthly life, it is not so evident that Cana constitutes the
beginning of his public ministry. The Synoptics do not mention
it, and one might be tempted, in accordance with the Synoptic
tradition (Mt 4:18–22; Mk 1:16–18; Lk 5:1–11), to regard the
call of the first disciples as the beginning of Jesus' public ministry
(Jn 1:38–51). Yet the author of the Fourth Gospel takes great
care to stress that in his judgment it was the miracle at Cana which
marked the start of Jesus' ministry, just as surely as Calvary marked
the end. In Jn 2:11 we read that 'Jesus did this as the beginning of
signs, in Cana of Galilee, and manifested his glory, and his disciples believed in him'; and in Jn 19:28 we read, 'After this,
Jesus, knowing that everything was now completed . . .' The
miracle worked at Cana and the episode concerning the mother of
Jesus and the beloved disciple frame the public ministry of Jesus
as beginning and end.

Bultmann has argued that among the sources used by the
evangelist there was a collection of miracle-stories, a *Semeia-
Quelle*,[1] and Schnackenburg allows that this view has some

---

[1] *The Gospel of John*, passim.

probability.[2] The numbering of the first miracle at Cana as 'the beginning of signs' (Jn 2:11), and of the healing of the ruler's son as the second (4:54), together with the remark at the end of the gospel about 'many other signs' (20:30), certainly favour the theory, and if it is accepted as a working hypothesis, it may facilitate the interpretation of the story about the wedding feast at Cana.

Various attempts have been made to reconstruct the source taken over by the evangelist and edited by him, and perhaps the most remarkable feature of these reconstructions is the degree to which they coincide. Yet significant differences do occur between one author and the next, and anyone who attempts to reconstruct John's source must in the end make up his own mind. The following reconstruction is my own suggestion, based on purely literary criteria. If all the characteristically Johannine words, phrases and constructions are taken to be insertions by the evangelist, and only those verses which do not contain any typically Johannine usage retained, then a perfectly coherent story emerges.[3] It reads as follows.

1   There was a wedding in Cana of Galilee,
     and the mother of Jesus was there.
2   Now Jesus also had been invited,
     with his disciples, to the wedding.
3   So when wine ran short,
     the mother of Jesus told him,
     They have no wine.
6   Now there were six stone water-pots standing there,
     for the Jewish custom of purification,
     each having a capacity of two or three firkins.

---

[2] *The Gospel according to St John I*, p. 67. Though R. E. Brown is very sceptical about a source-theory of the type advocated by Bultmann (see *The Gospel according to John I*, pp. XXXI–II), he admits a source for the Cana stories (p. 195).

[3] For a fuller discussion of this question, and a justification of the reconstruction here proposed, see Detached Note XI: 'A Literary Analysis of John 2:1–11', on pp. 462–6.

7 (So) Jesus said to (the waiters),[4]
Fill the water-pots with water;
and they filled them right up to the top.

8 Then he said to them,
Now draw some out and take it to the head waiter.
So they took it.

9 And as soon as the head waiter had tasted
the water,
he called the bridegroom

10 and said to him,
Every man serves the good wine first,
and when men are half-drunk, that which is inferior;
but thou hast kept the good wine until now.

11 This Jesus did as the beginning of signs,
in Cana of Galilee.

Here is a miracle-story told with graphic economy of words, in which all the stress falls on the wonder performed and the astonishment of the head waiter. It is exactly the type of miracle-story that is found in the Synoptic Gospels.

Let us assume that the writer of the Fourth Gospel had before him this simple but vivid narrative. In this account, there was no dialogue between Jesus and his mother, no word of advice from Mary to the waiters telling them to do whatever Jesus might suggest. But the evangelist was writing a gospel about the manifestation of God's glory in the life of Jesus; he wanted, therefore, to remind his readers that each miracle was not merely a 'wonder', an astounding fact, but also a 'sign'. That is, he wanted his readers to understand that the miracles done by Jesus were not merely astounding events taking place within this world of sense-experience, but first and foremost symbols of great religious truths about Jesus. 'The very works which I do bear witness about me, that the Father has sent me' (Jn 5:36). The story of Cana as given above in its (hypothetical) source would certainly impress

[4] For an explanation of the brackets round 'so' and 'the waiters' see the Detached Note, p. 464. ('The waiters' must be introduced here, instead of 'them', because v. 5 has been omitted.)

as a 'wonder', a 'miracle', an 'astounding happening'; but would it be evident to the reader that here was a sign or symbol of something veiled from human observation and visible only to the eyes of faith? I suggest that the evangelist thought not, and decided to make the sign-value of Cana evident by inserting a short dialogue between Jesus and his mother.[5]

To measure accurately the import of the evangelist's insertion, one must pay very careful attention to the context. We may take up the story at v. 3, where 'the mother of Jesus said to him, They have no wine'. The Greek here is rather unusual. Normally John uses the verb λέγω ('to say') with the dative, as when Mary says to the waiters 'Do whatever he tells you': there are over 150 examples of this construction, with the dative, in the gospel, and no less than six in the eleven verses of the Cana story. By contrast, there are only seven instances where John uses λέγω πρός followed by the accusative, usually in a context which contains a request to give considered thought to some matter, or to do some great favour. So Nicodemus respectfully asks Jesus how a man can be born again (λέγει πρὸς αὐτόν 3:4): this is his main question, and everywhere else in this passage we find the normal construction, with the dative. Similarly the Samaritan woman, once she is over her initial hostility, says to him (πρὸς αὐτόν): 'Lord, give me this water, that I may not thirst' (4:15); elsewhere in this dialogue, we always find the dative. Other examples of λέγειν πρός with the accusative are found in 4:49 (where the ruler pleads for his son), 7:50 (where Nicodemus pleads with the Jews) and 8:31 (where Jesus addresses those Jews who had come to believe in him).[6] We may compare also 11:21, where Martha εἶπεν πρὸς τὸν Ἰησοῦν, 'Lord, if thou hadst been here, my brother would not have died'; in this passage too, all the other verbs of speaking

[5] Perhaps it should be emphasized at this point that this dialogue, and the other words ascribed to the evangelist and not to his source, have not been chosen arbitrarily, or simply in order to make better sense of the passage. The insertions attributed to the evangelist are those phrases which are firmly stamped with the literary hall-marks of Johannine style; the reconstructed source given above is totally devoid of Johannine characteristics.

[6] The other two instances of λέγειν πρός are in 4:33 ('the disciples said *to one another*'—a regular Greek phrase in the New Testament), and 6:5 (Jesus to Philip).

are followed by a dative.[7] In short, λέγειν πρός with the accusative is so unusual and so emphatic that when we find it in Jn 2:3 we cannot simply ignore it. When Mary said to Jesus, 'They have no wine', the sense is not that she was merely passing on information, but that she was respectfully asking him to act, as the whole context (both in the source and in the gospel) implies.[8]

'What is that to me and to thee, woman? My hour is not yet come.' The overwhelming majority of commentators, from the Greek Fathers to modern times, see in these words a refusal to act at Mary's request, and many see in these words a rebuke, however mild. But can one be so sure that this answer is in fact a refusal of the request? The primary rule of interpretation is that the text must be so explained that it makes good sense; and if these words of Jesus are a refusal of his mother's request, it is difficult to see how Mary can tell the waiters to do whatever Jesus may suggest (v. 5). The saying of Jesus in v. 4 must spell out a connection between v. 3 ('They have no wine') and v. 5 ('Do whatever he may tell you'), especially if both vv. 4 and 5 are inserted by the evangelist. Can Jesus' words in v. 4 be so interpreted as to provide this logical connection?

Jesus repeatedly criticizes those who look for astounding miracles, or who see in the wonders he performs nothing more than the externally visible 'marvellous' element. When the ruler from Capernaum pleaded for the life of his son, Jesus said to him and to

---

[7] The same distinction between the use of the dative and of πρός with the accusative holds good for εἶπον. It is used with the preposition and the accusative in Jn 4:48; 6:28, 34; 7:3, 35; 8:57; 11:21; 12:19 and 16:17. 7:35; 12:19 and 16:17 are simply 'they said to themselves, to one another': see the preceding note. Elsewhere, it seems best to take πρός with the accusative as emphatic.

[8] It may, of course, be objected that if this phrase stood in John's source, we have no right to appeal to Johannine usage and to conclude from this that it denotes a request. The preposition with the accusative after verbs of speaking is exceedingly common in Luke, for example, and there carries no special emphasis. May it not have been the same in John's source (cf. 4:48, 49)? Though it is impossible to answer this question, it is reasonable to reply that either the prepositional construction stood in the source at v. 3 (and the evangelist kept it because it suited his usage) or that the source contained a dative (which the evangelist altered). This is as reasonable as postulating pure accident with no literary significance.

those who accompanied him (the verbs here are in the plural), 'Unless you see signs and wonders, you will never begin to believe' (4:48).[9] To the crowds who enthused over the multiplication of the loaves, Jesus said: 'Amen, amen I say to you, you seek me not because you saw signs [*i.e. not because you perceived the spiritual truths symbolized in this and my other miracles*] but [*solely*] because you ate of the loaves and had your fill. Labour not for perishable food, but for the food which remains unto life everlasting, which the Son of Man will give you' (6:26–7). Even when he promises Martha that her brother Lazarus will rise to life again, the same warning recurs. Martha thinks she understands the promise: 'I know he will rise again, at the resurrection, on the last day.' (Here Martha voices the faith of the Christian community.) Jesus is about to raise Lazarus to life immediately, but before doing so he instructs Martha (that is, John the evangelist instructs the reader) that there is a spiritual truth which dwarfs both the imminent miracle and even the joyous prospect of the final resurrection. 'I am Resurrection and Life: he who believes in me, even though he should die [*as Lazarus will*], shall live on, and everyone who lives and believes in me shall never die at all' (11:25–6).

First Mary, then the ruler, then Martha, approach Jesus, and on each occasion he responds with a miracle. Yet on each occasion the evangelist stresses, before the miracle takes place, that we should not look upon the external happening, but on the spiritual truth that is there symbolized and revealed. And on each occasion he conveys this message by placing on the lips of Jesus a profoundly significant saying.

We are now in a position to see how Jn 2:4–5 connect v. 3 with v. 6. Verse 4 ('What is that to me and to thee?') is not to be interpreted as a refusal of Mary's request: for then there is a total *non sequitur* in v. 5, where she says, 'Do whatever he may tell you'. The enigmatic phrase 'What is that to me and to thee?' is not to be

---

[9] Note that here the word 'signs' (in the cliché 'signs and wonders') does not bear its characteristically Johannine sense of 'a miracle symbolizing a spiritual truth' (as in 2:11 or 20:30). It means no more than an externally visible miracle. By contrast, it does carry its typically Johannine reference in the next text cited, 6:26.

explained in the light of Old Testament parallels, or of other gospel texts stemming from a Semitic background (see above, p. 364); rather, it is an insertion by the evangelist, and a thoroughly Greek idiom, meaning 'Of what concern is it to me and to thee?' Consequently, v. 4 should be interpreted as follows. When Mary asks for earthly wine to avert an awkward situation at a village wedding, Jesus first calls her attention (that is, the evangelist addresses us, and calls *our* attention) to the inner significance of the miracle that is about to follow. 'They have no wine.' Jesus answers: 'What is that to me and to thee, woman? Why should I, why should you, be concerned at such a trivial mishap? For I am not come (as you well know) to give men earthly wine, but a far more precious, heavenly gift, of which the richest and most abundant wine is but a symbol, though the hour for that richest gift is not yet come.' The mother of Jesus is here represented as standing with him, over against all others: Jesus addresses her as one who already understands that his mission is to supply not material but spiritual nourishment. And she is so addressed not because of her blood-relationship to Jesus (he does not call her 'Mother', but 'Woman'), but because of her faith. And then Mary the believer says to the waiters (that is, the Church which knows the nature of Jesus' mission says to the world which is hungering for material blessings), 'Do whatever he may tell you' (and you will be astonished at the result). These statements made, the story can proceed. The reader is alerted, warned not to view the stupendous miracle which follows as the real purpose of Jesus' life, or as the best gift he can bestow, but to see it merely as a symbol and a guarantee of something immeasurably greater that will be given later, when his hour is come.

'As soon as the head waiter had tasted the water . . .': so ran the text in the reconstructed source (p. 390). At this point we meet another insertion by the evangelist. First he tells us in two words what had taken place: 'as soon as the head waiter had tasted the water *become wine*'. The reader is thus let into the secret, but he is also warned that the head waiter is not in the secret: 'he knew not whence it came' (only the waiters who had drawn the water knew that). Now it should be noted that these two pieces of information given to the reader by the evangelist are in no way necessary to follow the story. If one checks the version given as the hypothetical source (p. 390), what happened becomes clear from the words of the head waiter: no reader of that version could fail to perceive that the water had been turned into wine. Why, then, does the evangelist, in v. 9, let the reader into the secret so early, and warn him that the head waiter is in ignorance of it? At first consideration, it seems to spoil the dramatic effect of the head waiter's pronouncement.

It is well-known that in the Fourth Gospel Jesus makes a number of statements which are not understood until after his Resurrection (*e.g.* the saying about the temple of his body, in 2:19–22). But other men too utter statements pregnant with spiritual truth, without realizing the import of their words. An obvious example is Caiaphas' prophecy, 'It is expedient that one man should die for the people', and the evangelist calls attention to it (11:50–2). An equally obvious example is the complaint that Jesus cannot be the Messiah because he did not come from Bethlehem (7:41–2). But there are more recondite instances too. Nicodemus, when he says 'We know that you are come from God as a teacher' (3:2), voices the feeling of men sympathetic to Jesus' teaching; but do they realize the sense in which he proceeds from the Father? When the paralysed man healed at Bethzatha 'did not know who he was' (5:13), the straightforward meaning in the narrative is that he could not give the name of the passer-by who had cured him; but the deeper meaning in the Fourth Gospel is that he truly 'did not know who Jesus was'. And there is a subtle rebuke to those who shut their eyes to the truth when the man born blind says (with a double meaning), 'He opened *my* eyes' (9:30). All through the Fourth Gospel there rings this theme, that the Word by whom all things were made came to what was his own, and was not recognized for what he was. His heavenly origin and his creative power were totally unsuspected by the guests at Cana. That is why, when the water was changed into wine, the reader is at once let into the secret by the evangelist, and warned that the head waiter does not know it. The reader is here gently reminded to remember the full truth about the Word Incarnate, and to listen carefully to the words about to be uttered by the head waiter. They will contain far more than appears on the surface.

'As soon as the head waiter had tasted the water (*become wine*) . . . he called the bridegroom and said to him, Every man serves the good wine first, and when men are half-drunk, that which is inferior; but thou hast kept the good wine until now' (Jn 2:9–10). This verse is the key to the primary message of Cana. This changing of six huge jars of water, each holding twenty to thirty gallons, into the choicest wine—this was but the *beginning* of the signs which Jesus did. Later, he healed the ruler's son from twenty miles away (4:46–54), though we are expressly told that the boy was at the point of death (v. 47). And if it be said that youth is resilient, and this could have been a coincidence, what of the next cure, of the poor cripple who had been immobile for thirty-eight years (5:2–9)? And so the different signs in the Fourth Gospel proceed *sempre crescendo* to *fortissimo*. Five thousand men are fed from five loaves and two fishes, yet twelve huge hampers of bread are left over (6:1–15); a man blind from birth is given sight (9), and Lazarus, four days buried, is summoned live from the tomb (11). As we read the Fourth Gospel, looking for the moment only at the externally observable wonders and abstracting for the moment from any spiritual symbolism contained in them, each miracle seems more impossible than the preceding ones; and when we come to the raising of Lazarus, we can only exclaim in astonishment, 'Thou hast kept the best wine till the last'. And even so we should be wrong, for later we discover that even the raising of Lazarus is but a sign, and a pointer to the future, not the greatest of Jesus' works, since it too is a blessing bestowed within the confines of man's earthly life: Lazarus will return to the grave (*cf.* v. 25: 'even though he should die . . .'). Throughout the gospel, our gaze is directed by the evangelist beyond all signs to the victory of the Crucified: from the miracles we must pass *ex umbris et imaginibus in veritatem*.

Six signs are here enumerated: nearly everyone adds the episode of Jesus' walking on the sea (6:16–21), to reach a pattern of seven signs. But there are good reasons for not considering this episode as a 'sign' in the Johannine sense. First, it is by no means certain that the passage does recount a miraculous happening: v. 19 may well mean that the disciples saw Jesus walking beside the sea, on the shore. Secondly, in contrast with the six miracles just mentioned, this episode is nowhere called a sign. Thirdly, it has neither dialogue nor discourse attached, to explain its significance.[10] It seems wisest, therefore, to exclude this episode from the list of Johannine signs, and to posit that in the 'Book of Signs' (that is, Jn 2–12), there are only six signs, not seven. The seventh event in the series will then be not a sign, but the event which fulfils all the preceding signs—the Resurrection.

By this event the six signs in the Fourth Gospel are both explained and transcended. They are explained, in that when we look at them afresh in the light of the Resurrection, we perceive that these astounding miracles are but faint shadows and earthly symbols of the far more wonderful, heavenly gifts bestowed by the Risen Lord. For example, the abundance and the quality of the Cana-wine, the lavish and even prodigal provision of bread for the five thousand, are symbols which point forward to the gift of Jesus' flesh and blood supplying spiritual sustenance and everlasting life to all future generations, in all the nations of the world. By the same token, these six signs are transcended, that is, replaced by a gift so much greater that the blessings bestowed in the earthly life of Jesus become by comparison irrelevant. To give a young boy in Capernaum, or Lazarus in Bethany, a few more years of life on this earth is nothing by comparison with the gift of everlasting life 'in the bosom of the Father' to all the children of God that ever will be (cf. Jn 1:18; 11:51–2; 14:2–3; 17:24). To enable a cripple to walk again after thirty-eight years is very wonderful in itself, but it is not to be compared with enabling the whole race of men to walk upright before God in light (cf. 7:21 with 8:13), and grace, and truth (1:17). The Resurrection reminds us, too, that there is a fate worse than being born without physical sight: the most pitiable of all men are those who, by their own fault, have become spiritually blind (9:40–1), for they have

[10] For further detail see the Detached Note (XII): Did Jesus Walk upon the Surface of the Sea?, pp. 467–9.

deprived themselves of the ability to 'see the glory' of Jesus which he shares with the Father (17:5, 24).

The Resurrection is the key which unlocks all the mysteries contained in the six signs; it is the answer to all the riddles these signs pose to the reader. Many wonder why the God who multiplied the loaves should yearly allow millions to perish from starvation, and why he who cured a handful of the sick should allow suffering and death, when they could be prevented. The answer to these riddles is found in the fact of the Cross and Resurrection; and in the Fourth Gospel, the very signs which raise these problems are used to draw out the answers. It will assist our understanding of Cana if we now review these six signs, to see what kind of story the evangelist has chosen from among the 'many signs' at his disposal (20:30), to see how he has treated the six signs in his editorial presentation, and to see how they all point forward to, and prepare the way for, the full revelation of the mystery of God's love in the Cross and Resurrection.

The first fact to be observed is that all the signs recorded in the Fourth Gospel are manifestations of quite extraordinary power: the miracles are staggering miracles, and defeat every attempt at explanation by rational means. They are either miracles of creation, or miracles concerned with the quickening of life where life is dead. Secondly, the evangelist calls our attention to this fact. On each occasion, *before* the miracle is worked, he takes pains to make clear to the reader that the situation is, humanly speaking, quite beyond hope: 200 denarii would not be sufficient to give everyone even a bite (6:7), Lazarus must be rotting after four days in the tomb (11:39). The point here is to show that all human calculations are proved wrong, and that only when all we possess is lost, more than we ever dreamed of possessing is gained. Thirdly, after each miracle, we are told very clearly whether it resulted in belief or unbelief. Fourthly, in each of the stories there is an interlocutor who makes statements which draw attention to the hopelessness of the situation and thereby underline the magnitude of the wonder: but these statements also serve to clarify the symbolism of the miracle (*e.g.* 6:7: no amount of money—let alone 200 denarii—can buy bread from heaven). These statements therefore summon the reader to look beyond the *signum* to the *significatum*, to discern in the wonders worked by the earthly Jesus symbols and pointers to the far greater spiritual wonders worked by Christ triumphant in his Church. These interlocutors perform the same function as modern interviewers or expert commentators: they elicit by their questions, or indicate by their statements, the spiritual truths contained in the events reported.

This may be easily seen from the following table, in which the second column lists the facts which show how hopeless the situation is, the third column names the interlocutor, and the fourth shows the resultant belief or unbelief. (The numbers in the last three columns refer to the verses of the sign under consideration.)

The last sign, which leads 'many of the Jews' to believe in Jesus, is also, in the Fourth Gospel, the direct cause of the plan to secure his death. 'If we leave him alone, everybody will believe in him, and the Romans will come and take away both our place and our nation' (11:48).

We are at last in a position to understand the place of Mary the mother of Jesus in the Fourth Gospel. Cana saw 'the beginning of the signs' through which Jesus unveiled his glory, and it is only after the narrative of this first miracle that we are told 'his disciples believed in him' (Jn 2:11). Yet it was Mary who occasioned that sign at Cana by her intervention: as a result of her request to Jesus, a village wedding became the *occasion when* the disciples began to believe. John does not tell us how or when Mary herself first came to believe, but he certainly gives us to understand that she truly believed before Cana. For the words addressed to Mary by Jesus ('What is that to me and to thee, woman?') imply that neither Jesus *nor his mother* should be disturbed by so trivial an event as the lack of wine at a wedding. As we have seen,[11] the only satisfactory interpretation of these words is that Mary (like Jesus) knew that his mission was not of this world. Secondly, the evangelist places on her lips words which only one who believed in Jesus totally could utter: 'Do whatever he may tell you'. Thus the mother of the Lord is represented as believing in her son *before* the first miracle.

[11] P. 394.

	The situation cannot be remedied by any merely human means	Dialogue with Jesus	Resultant belief or unbelief
THE WEDDING AT CANA 2:1–11	The wine was exhausted (2, 3)	The mother of Jesus (3, 4)	'His disciples believed in him' (11)
THE RULER'S SON 4:46–54	The boy was at the point of death (47); there was no time to waste (49), for they were twenty miles away (he was sick in Capernaum, 46)	The ruler (47, 49)	The ruler 'himself believed, and all his household' (53)
THE CRIPPLE AT BETHZATHA 5:1–18	He had been thirty-eight years a cripple (5), and could not even crawl to the pool (7)	The cripple (7)	'He proclaimed to the Jews that it was Jesus who had made him well' (15), i.e. he believed, but the Jews did not: see vv. 16–18 and 36–40.
THE FEEDING OF THE FIVE THOUSAND 6:1–15	'200 denarii would not be sufficient to give everyone even a little piece' (7); they had only five loaves and two little fishes (9)	Philip (7) Andrew (8, 9)	The men who saw the sign said he was the prophet (14), but after the discourse many of his disciples withdrew and walked no more with him (66). See also vv. 68–71: Peter believes, and the Eleven (Ten?)
THE MAN BLIND FROM BIRTH 9:1–41	He was quite certainly blind from birth (1, 20, 32)	The blind man (36–8) cf. 7	The blind man believes: 'he is a prophet' (17), 'I want to be his disciple' (27), 'he is from God' (31–3), he is the son of Man (35–7), to be adored (38). The Pharisees do not believe (passim but especially 40–1)

	The situation cannot be remedied by any merely human means	Dialogue with Jesus	Resultant belief or unbelief
THE RAISING OF LAZARUS 11:1–54	Jesus does not go to cure the sick Lazarus (6, 21); Lazarus is dead (11, 13), four days buried (17) and therefore rotting (39)	Martha (21–7): Mary (32): the disciples (7–15)	Many of the Jews believed (45), but some of them went to inform the Pharisees (46).

The wedding at Cana saw the beginning of signs. We turn now to Calvary, where 'all is achieved'. 'There stood beside the Cross of Jesus his mother and his mother's sister-in-law, Mary of Klopas and Mary Magdalen. Jesus, therefore, seeing his mother and standing beside her the disciple whom he loved, said to his mother, Woman, behold thy son!' (Jn 19:25–6).

The pattern of seeing one thing (physically) and seeing in it another thing (spiritually) is native to John, and is sometimes expressed by the combination 'he saw X and said, Behold Y'. Thus the Baptist saw Jesus, and said 'Behold the Lamb of God' (1:29, 36).[12] Andrew saw where Jesus was living, and said to his brother 'We have found the Messiah' (1:39, 41). Jesus looked at Simon, and said 'Thou shalt be called Peter' (1:42); he saw Nathanael, and said 'Behold an Israelite in whom there is no guile' (1:47). This device is used with dramatic effect in the Apocalypse, where it is always worth pausing to examine the connection between what the author hears and what he sees. Thus, when he hears of the victory of the Lion of Judah, he looks, and sees not a Lion but a Lamb, bearing not the laurels of victory but the marks of its slaughter (Apoc 5:5–6).[13]

So on Calvary Jesus first *saw* his mother, and standing beside

---

[12] *Cf.* M. de Goedt, 'Un schème de révélation dans le quatrième évangile', *NTS* 8 (1961–2), pp. 142–50. See also E. A. Abbott, *Johannine Vocabulary*, §§1597–611 ('Seeing').

[13] See especially G. B. Caird, *The Revelation of St John the Divine* (*Black's New Testament Commentaries*), London, 1966, pp. 73–5.

her the disciple whom he loved. We expect, then, some reference to his mother, and to the disciple ('Mother, behold my disciple'). But what we *hear* is 'Woman, behold thy son!' In these words a new truth is revealed. By addressing Mary not as 'Mother' but as 'Woman', Jesus draws attention away from his own blood-relationship with Mary to focus attention on the fact that henceforward she is to be the mother of the disciple, and he is to be her son. That is, Mary is henceforth to find her children not in those closest to her by blood, but in those who share her boundless faith and remain steadfast by Jesus to the very end. For the disciple who stood beside the Cross is a type of all the disciples whom Jesus loves: all these in turn are summoned to look upon Mary as their mother, because her faith, completely independent of signs and wonders, is to be the pattern for their own.

It is sad that Origen's commentary on this passage is now lost, for he certainly regarded it as one of the key texts for the interpretation of St John. At the beginning of his commentary he writes:

'I do not hesitate to affirm that among all the Scriptures, the gospels have pride of place; and among the gospels, pride of place belongs to that according to John. Yet no one can grasp its meaning unless he has leaned upon the breast of Jesus, and also accepted from Jesus Mary, to be his own mother. And this other future "John" must become the kind of person that (like John) may be pointed out by Jesus as being Jesus. For all who think in orthodox fashion about Mary know she had no other son but Jesus, and yet Jesus says to his mother, Behold thy son. Note that he does not say, He too is your son. His words, then, are tantamount to saying, Behold, this is Jesus to whom you gave birth. For everyone that is perfect lives no longer, it is Christ who lives in him; and it is because Christ lives in him that the words addressed to Mary about him run, Behold, Christ thy son'.[14]

Perhaps, if Origen's commentary on Jn 19:25–6 were discovered, we should find him equally eloquent on the text 'Behold thy

[14] *In Ioannem* I, 6 (MG 14.32).

mother'. For, in the mind of the Fourth Evangelist, these words were not uttered simply to the man who stood at Mary's side on Golgotha: rather, they are words addressed by Jesus to all future generations of disciples, at the very moment when he is about to pass over from this world to the Father. He says to each one of us today, 'Behold thy mother'.

Beata quae credidisti. Mary is the prototype and exemplar of faith, and that is why she stands at the beginning and at the end of the earthly manifestation of Jesus, according to St John. She is there at Cana, fully believing, before Jesus has worked a single sign; and she is present beside the Crucified, when all the signs and wonders of the past appear to have been but a snare and a delusion. Where were those who had come to believe in Jesus because he had raised Lazarus from the tomb? Had they perhaps ceased to believe, convinced that there was one thing he could not do—bring himself to life when dead—never suspecting that even at that fateful hour he was still keeping the best wine till the last? But Mary's faith in her son had never been founded on the evidence of astounding miracles, only on complete trust in the mysterious ways of God. That is why it survived even on Calvary, neither looking for nor expecting any visible wonder, but quietly content to 'do whatever he might tell her'. That is why Mary, as she stood beside the Crucified, was there commended by the Word Incarnate to all his disciples, that she might be from that time forward their model and their mother. The portrait of the mother of Jesus in St John is meant to show all future ages what faith really involves, so that whenever all hope is lost, and evil triumphant, we may still be found beside the Crucified, still enduring, still believing that nothing is impossible to God (Lk 1: 37). For to Mary above all others applies the beatitude with which the Fourth Gospel closes: 'Blessed are those who have not seen, and yet have learned to believe' (Jn 20:29).

Chapter Five

THE WOMAN CLOTHED WITH THE SUN (Apoc 12) (I): A SHORT SURVEY OF INTERPRETATIONS

ANYONE who had the rare good fortune to be present at a sung Latin Mass on 15 August might hear, as the priest was entering, a splendid piece of plainsong:

> *Signum magnum apparuit in caelo:*
> *mulier amicta sole,*
> *et luna sub pedibus eius,*
> *et in capite eius corona stellarum duodecim.*

> 'A great sign appeared in heaven:
> a woman clothed with the sun,
> and the moon under her feet,
> and on her head a crown of twelve stars.'

In the Roman rite, this text of Apoc 12:1 has, since 1951, opened the Mass for the feast of Mary's Assumption, and the first stanza of the hymn at Lauds paraphrases it. Since 1969, when the new Lectionary was published, this passage has provided the first reading for the Mass (11:19a; 12:1, 3–6 and 10ab).

In the decree by which Pope Pius XII, in 1950, promulgated the definition of the Assumption, there occurs the sentence:

'Scholastic Doctors recognized the Assumption of the Virgin Mother of God as something signified, not only in the various figures of the Old Testament, but also in that woman clothed with the sun whom St John the Apostle contemplated on the island of Patmos.'[1]

---

[1] *AAS* 42 (1950), p. 763.

Here, of course, the Pope is not in any way claiming th doctrine of Mary's Assumption is attested in Apoc 12:1 merely recording the fact that during the Middle Ages this verse was (like certain Old Testament texts)[2] cited as biblical evidence for the Assumption. Nevertheless, even in our own day there have been Roman Catholic theologians who have claimed to find in these words a biblical justification for the doctrine of Mary's Assumption.[3] What are we to make of this text?

We may begin with a brief survey of the opinions held on the identity of the woman clothed with the sun.[4] To the best of my knowledge, all those who stand outside the Roman or Anglo-Catholic tradition take the woman to be a symbol of the people of God: that is, either as a symbol of Old Testament Israel (or its faithful remnant), or as a figure representing the Church of the New Testament, or as a symbol of both—but certainly not as representing in any way the Blessed Virgin Mary. Max Thurian is, I think, the only exception to this rule in the Reformed Churches: he thinks the figure stands at first for Israel, then takes on the appearance of the Blessed Virgin, the Daughter of Zion, and finally becomes a symbol of the Christian Church.[5]

---

[2] Principally Ps 132:8. For example, Albert the Great writes, in his *Quaestiones super evangelium 'Missus est'*, qu. 132: 'Sine omni putrefactione surrexit. Hoc idem etiam et clara voce praevidens Psalmista clamat cum audacia: *Surge, Domine, in requiem tuam*. Et statim subinfert: *Tu et arca sanctificationis tuae*; quae manifeste creduntur, ut in figura, de Maria, cuius corpus fuit arca corporis Christi' (*Opera omnia*, Paris, 1898, vol. 37, p. 186).

[3] Notably M. Jugie, *La mort et l'Assomption de la sainte Vierge: Etude historico-doctrinale* (Studi e Testi 114), Vatican City, 1944, pp. 33–40; 'Assomption de la sainte Vierge', in *Maria: Etudes sur la sainte Vierge* (ed. H. du Manoir), vol. 1, Paris, 1949, pp. 627–30; 'Le dogme de l'Assomption et le chapitre XII de l'Apocalypse' (*In Constitutionem Apostolicam 'Munificentissimus Deus' Commentarii 5*), *Marianum* 14 (1952), pp. 74–80.

[4] The main monographs are B. Le Frois, *The Woman Clothed with the Sun (Apoc. 12): Individual or Collective?*, Rome, 1954; A. Th. Kassing, *Die Kirche und Maria: Ihr Verhältnis im 12. Kapitel der Apokalypse*, Düsseldorf, 1958; P. Prigent, *Apocalypse 12: Histoire de l'exégèse* (Beiträge zur Geschichte der biblischen Exegese 2), Tübingen, 1959; and (the best of all) H. Gollinger, *Das 'grosse Zeichen' von Apokalypse 12* (Stuttgarter Biblische Monographien 11), Würzburg and Stuttgart, 1971.

[5] *Mary: Mother of the Lord, Figure of the Church*, London, 1963, pp. 179–80.

Within the Roman Catholic Church, two writers have argued that the woman can only be the Virgin Mary, and that there is no reference to the Church at all.[6] Their arguments are that since the woman gives birth to the Messiah (Apoc 12:5), she cannot be a figure of the Church of the New Testament, which originates from Christ; and since she is also the mother of all Christian believers (12:17), she cannot be a symbol of the Jewish synagogue, for in the Apocalypse the synagogue is always portrayed as hostile to the Christian Church (2:9; 3:9). Only Mary can be called both mother of Christ and mother of Christians.

More commonly, however, within the Roman Catholic Church and the Anglo-Catholic tradition, a middle position is held. Those who have treated the text explicitly are broadly speaking divided into three classes: (1) those who say that the writer is there describing primarily the Church, but describing it with the traits of Mary; (2) those who say that he is describing Mary in the first place, but as the archetype or exemplar of the believing Church; (3) those who think he is describing both Mary and the Church at one and the same time, without committing himself to place more emphasis on one than on the other. Needless to say, within each of these classes there are those who think the author is referring to the people of God before the coming of Christ, those who think he is speaking of the Christian Church, and those who prefer to think of both.

The modern scene only reflects the diversity of opinion in the ancient Church. The majority of the Fathers who discussed this text saw in the woman clothed with the sun a figure of the Christian Church, though three (Victorinus, Jerome and Augustine) were careful to stress that by the Christian Church they meant the people of God under the Old Covenant, as well as the New. Here and there a voice was heard referring the text to Mary, but more often than not these writers explained that they were thinking of Mary as the prototype or exemplar of the Church. Indeed, it is fair to say that in the first eight centuries no one identified the

[6] J. Dillersberger, 'Das Weib und der Drache', in *Wort und Wahrheit* (Vienna) 2 (1947), pp. 257–68; and especially J. F. Bonnefoy, *Le mystère de Marie selon le Protévangile et l'Apocalypse*, Paris, 1949.

woman in the Apocalypse as Mary to the positive exclusion of the Church.[7]

Yet it seems quite certain that the woman cannot stand simply for the Church of the New Testament, for in Apoc 12:5 she is the mother of Jesus. How can the Christian Church of the New Testament be called the mother of its Lord? This verse must refer either to Mary or to the people of Israel or to its faithful remnant before the birth of Christ. Secondly, in what sense could it be said that the Christian Church was in torment (12:2) until it brought forth the Messiah? Before the birth of Jesus, it did not exist. To identify the woman with the Christian Church, while excluding both Mary and the people of Israel before the birth of the Messiah, is to do violence to the plain meaning of the text.

Hence many exegetes take the woman to be a symbol of the people of God both in Old and in New Testament times. But here again there is the difficulty of explaining what exactly is meant by the torments the woman endures as she struggles to give birth (v. 2); and secondly, although *we* may find it easy *post factum* to think of Israel as the mother of the Messiah, there is not a single Old Testament text in which Israel as a people, Israel as a community, is said to have given birth to the individual known as the Messiah. In the Old Testament, the community gives birth to a community, but only an individual woman gives birth to the person of the Messiah.

The force of this last argument has, however, been considerably weakened in recent years, for one of the hymns from Qumran speaks of Israel, or of the community, as the mother of a Messiah. Indeed, the text is astonishingly close to Apoc 12 in other ways too, for it speaks of the pains preceding this birth, and portrays all the powers of Hell surrounding the mother before her delivery. The child is snatched out of their reach immediately after his birth, and the enemies of the child are, like Satan and his henchmen in Apoc 12, thrust down into the abyss.

[7] For the evidence to support the statements in this paragraph, see Detached Note XIII: The Identity of the Woman Clothed with the Sun according to the Fathers.

'. . . she labours in her pains who bears the man.
For amid the throes of Death
  she shall bring forth a man-child,
and amid the pains of Hell
    there shall spring from her child-bearing crucible
    a Marvellous Mighty Counsellor;
and the man shall be delivered from out of the throes.'[8]

Some scholars have reservations about the meaning of this text, and question the parallelism with Apoc 12. But the very fact that no one regards this interpretation of the Qumran hymn as *a priori* impossible should dispose of the assertion that the woman in the Apocalypse cannot refer to a community because nowhere in the Old Testament is a community called the mother of the Messiah. Indeed, the Qumran text gives positive encouragement to those who think the woman clothed with the sun stands for the faithful remnant of Zion.

Nevertheless, many Catholic writers continue to hold that the woman is first and foremost a symbol of the Blessed Virgin Mary, for she alone can be called in the fullest sense the mother of the Messiah. But once again there is an obstacle in v. 2. Throughout the centuries, many Christians have held that the birth of Jesus was painless, and many, if not most, of those Catholics who identify the woman with Mary hold this view. They are therefore hard pressed to give a convincing interpretation of Apoc 12:2 ('The woman cried out in pain as she struggled to give birth'). A more serious objection still is that immediately after his birth the child is caught up to God's throne, and the woman thereupon escapes into the desert. What meaning can be assigned to these verses if the passage is taken to refer to Jesus' birth at Bethlehem?

It is clear that, whatever theory be adopted, there are real difficulties to face.

[8] Translation by G. Vermes, *The Dead Sea Scrolls in English*, Harmondsworth, 1965, p. 157 (= 1 QH iii).

Chapter Six

THE WOMAN CLOTHED WITH THE
SUN (Apoc 12)
(II): ARCHETYPE OF THE CHURCH

'A GREAT sign appeared in heaven, a woman clothed with the sun, with the moon under her feet, and on her head a crown of twelve stars. She was with child, and cried out in her birth-pains, in anguish for delivery. And another sign appeared in heaven: behold, a great red dragon, with seven heads and ten horns, and seven diadems upon those heads of his. His tail swept away one-third of the stars of heaven, and cast them on to the earth. And the dragon stood facing the woman who was about to give birth, that he might devour her child when she gave birth. She gave birth to a son, a male child who is to rule the nations with an iron rod, and her child was caught up to God and to his throne. And the woman fled into the desert, where she has a place prepared by God, there to be nourished for one thousand two hundred and sixty days' (Apoc 12:1–6).

It must be admitted that this tableau, strange in itself, is almost incomprehensible if it is taken to refer to the birth of Jesus in Bethlehem. For on that interpretation, what is meant by saying that Jesus was suddenly caught up to God and to his throne? The context gives to understand that this took place immediately after the birth of the child, and one can hardly imagine any Christian writer leaping directly from the birth at Bethlehem to the Resurrection and Ascension, and totally omitting the earthly life of Jesus. And what could be meant by saying that the child's mother (in this case, Mary) fled into the desert, to a place of

refuge reserved for her by God? It is impossible to find a satisfactory explanation of these verses as long as the text is taken to
refer to the birth of Jesus from Mary in Bethlehem, and it is little
wonder that most commentators reject this interpretation. As we
have seen, many of them regard the woman as a symbol of the
people of God, and in that case there is no need to narrow the
reference to the fact of the Nativity in Bethlehem: the text can
be interpreted in a broader sense, as meaning that Israel gave the
world its Messiah. But if this is the true meaning, what is one to
make of the following statement, that the Messiah was caught up
to God and to his throne? It is hard to imagine a Christian author
writing simply, 'Israel gave the world its Messiah, and he was
taken up into heaven'. One would expect at least some reference
to the work of Christ on earth.

This reference to the birth of Christ is the basic problem, and
M. André Feuillet has, I believe, solved it with his suggestion that
the birth of Christ mentioned in v. 5 is not his birth as a child in
Bethlehem, but his birth on Easter morning, by the Resurrection:
the birth-pains of v. 2 will therefore represent the sufferings of
Calvary.[1] Dr Caird offers an almost identical interpretation when
he writes: 'By the birth of the Messiah John means not the Nativity
but the Cross.'[2] There is no need to delay over the very slight
divergence between these two views (Feuillet, birth on Easter
morning; Caird, birth on the Cross), for in the Apocalypse, as in
the Fourth Gospel, the death on Calvary and the Resurrection are
viewed as one event. The Fourth Gospel uses the term 'exaltation'
to denote both the raising up of Jesus on the cross and his being
raised up into the glory of the Father (Jn 3:14; 8:28; 12:32, 34).
The Apocalypse too looks upon Christ's death and Resurrection
as the obverse and reverse of one and the same event (cf. Apoc
1:18, 'I am the first and the last, and the living one: I died, and
behold I am alive for evermore, and I hold the keys of Death and
Hades'; 2:8, 'The words of the first and the last, who died and

[1] 'Le Messie et sa mère d'après le chapître 12 de l'Apocalypse', RB 66 (1959),
on pp. 60–1. Feuillet observes that W. H. Brownlee had previously suggested the
idea en passant, in NTS 3 (1956–7), p. 29, n. 2.

[2] The Revelation of St John the Divine, p. 149.

came to life'). Let us test this hypothesis, then, to see whether it makes good sense to interpret Apoc 12:1-6 of the birth of Christ into the resurrection-world.

It is incontestable that the early Christians used the language of birth to denote the Resurrection of the Lord. The most important text is Ac 13:33: '*God raised up Jesus*, as it is written in the second Psalm,

> Thou art my son,
> *this day I have begotten thee.*'

It will be observed that this is the Psalm cited in Apoc 12:5, and many see an allusion to the Resurrection when the verse just cited is quoted in Heb 1:5; 5:5. Further, in Col 1:18 Christ is termed 'the *first-born* of the dead', a phrase which recurs in Apoc 1:5. Jn 12:24 and 1 Cor 15:36, too, imply that resurrection is a birth into a new life. It is therefore reasonable to say that to talk about Christ's passing over into the world of the resurrection as a *birth* of Christ is entirely in keeping with the customary language of the early Church.

Now if the birth of Christ referred to in Apoc 12:1-6 is his birth into the world of the resurrection, it is an easy, obvious and logical step to identify the sufferings that accompany this birth with the agony on Golgotha. And here 12:2 supplies an important hint which confirms this interpretation. The woman, we read, was 'in anguish for delivery' (Revised Standard Version). The Greek verb here translated 'in anguish' ($\beta \alpha \sigma \alpha \nu \iota \zeta o \mu \acute{\epsilon} \nu \eta$) is never once used in the Septuagint, the New Testament, the apocrypha, the papyri or the Fathers to denote the pains of physical birth;[3] and this is all the more remarkable when one remembers how often the scene of a painful birth is alluded to in these writings. The word can perhaps best be rendered as 'going through torment or torture', and it is therefore a very surprising verb to encounter when one recalls the radiant description of the woman in 12:1. She who is clothed with the sun and has the moon under her feet 'goes through torture' to give birth! This at least is evident, that

[3] B. J. Le Frois, *The Woman Clothed with the Sun*, pp. 141-3.

the verb must signify some extraordinary sufferings, and not merely the natural pains of a normal birth. The choice of this verb finds an excellent explanation if the tableau is taken to refer not to the birth of Jesus in Bethlehem, but to the torments endured on Calvary.

This interpretation finds further confirmation in the fact that the New Testament speaks of the sufferings on Calvary as pains of birth. Thus in Ac 2:24 Peter says that God 'undid the birth-pangs of death' (a phrase taken from Ps 18:4), and Jesus himself, speaking of his coming Passion in St John's Gospel, dwells on the symbolism of birth. 'Amen, amen I say to you: you will weep and lament, while the world will rejoice; you will be filled with sorrow, but your sorrow will be turned into joy. A woman, when she is giving birth, feels sorrow, because her hour has come; but once she gives birth to the child, she is no longer mindful of the affliction because of the joy that a man has been born into the world' (Jn 16:20–1). The allusion to the Passion is evident, and the following verse makes an equally plain reference to the Resurrection: 'And you therefore now feel sorrow, *but I will see you again*, and your heart will rejoice, and no one will take from you the joy that will be yours' (16:22).

In the light of this evidence, it seems very reasonable to understand the birth alluded to in Apoc 12:2 as being not the birth of Jesus in Bethlehem, but his birth into glory; and to interpret the suffering there mentioned not as a reference to the pain attendant on a natural birth, but as a metaphor for the agony on Calvary. Who then is the woman that endured this suffering, and so gave birth to the Risen Christ, bringing him forth amid pain into the world of the resurrection?

To answer that question with as much precision and accuracy as is possible, I think one must turn back to the Johannine parable about the woman in labour (Jn 16:19–22); and to understand that parable fully, one must take into account the two texts of Isaiah from which it is apparently derived. Unfortunately, it is far from easy to decide whether the Fourth Evangelist based his parable on the Hebrew text, the Aramaic Targum, or a Greek version of Isaiah. The question is not unimportant for the interpretation of

the parable, since in one of the texts (Is 26:16–21) the three versions differ considerably in detail, though the basic message is the
same. It is true that as a general rule the evangelist cites according
to the Septuagint,[4] but that is because his final text was written in
Greek for Greek Christians; over against this, there is good
evidence that in the preparation of his work, he made use of the
Hebrew and Aramaic versions as well as the Greek.[5] It would be
very helpful if we could say for certain that in writing the parable
about the woman in labour he had in mind one version of Isaiah
rather than another; but the most that can be said is that it seems
more likely that the writer had the Septuagint text in mind when
writing the parable in question.

The Septuagint text of Is 26:16–21 may be translated as
follows:

16a 'Lord, in affliction I remembered thee;
  b   in a little affliction thy instruction comes to us.
17a And as a woman in birth-pangs draws near to giving
         birth,
  b   and in her birth-pain cried out loud—
  c   so have we been with regard to thy beloved one,
  d   out of fear for thee, O Lord.
18a We conceived, and felt the pains of birth,
  b   and gave birth:
  c   we set the spirit of thy salvation upon the earth,
  d   we shall not fall,[6]
  e   but those who dwell upon the earth shall fall.
19a The dead shall rise,
  b   and those in the tombs shall awake,
  c   and those who are in the earth shall rejoice . . .
20a Come, my people, enter into your secret rooms,
  b   lock thy door,

---

[4] See above, p. 373.

[5] See F.-M. Braun, *Jean le Théologien II*, pp. 20–1. R. E. Brown seems sympathetic to the idea (*The Gospel according to John I*, p. LXI).

[6] The words 'we shall not fall' are found in some texts of the Septuagint, but
not in the majority.

    c   hide thyself away for a little while,
    d   until the wrath of the Lord is past;
21*a*   for behold the Lord from his holy place
    b   is bringing wrath upon those who dwell on the earth . . .'

It is easy to imagine the impact this text of Isaiah would have made on the early Christians, when they searched the Scriptures in the light of the Resurrection. In affliction they had been made to think of God (16*a*), and in the short space of three days, 'in a little affliction', God had taught them a totally new view of life (16*b*). After the Resurrection they could not have failed to see that their grief at Jesus' arrest and crucifixion had been exactly like the pains of a woman in labour (17*ab*): 'so have we been with regard to thy beloved one' (17*c*). When they had followed Jesus, they had in fact been conceiving and bearing in the womb a new world (18*ab*): 'we set the spirit of thy salvation upon the earth' (18*c*). In the light of the Resurrection, they could be confident that their mission would not fail (18*d*), and that all who opposed them would fail (18*e*). For they had a divine assurance that the dead would rise, as Jesus had risen (19*abc*), and that evil would not triumph in the end, as it had not triumphed on that first Good Friday. Verse 20 is closely parallel to certain texts of St John which speak of the Resurrection. When the early Christians read the words

> 'Come, my people, enter into your secret rooms,
>   lock thy door,
> hide thyself away for a little while' (Is 26:20*abc*),

they must surely have recalled the appearance of Jesus to the disciples assembled behind locked doors (Jn 20:19), and the words, 'A little while, and you will no longer see me, and again a little while, and you will see me . . . and no one will take from you the joy that will be yours' (16:16, 19, 22). The Christian application of this text from Isaiah could be summed up by saying that the disciples during the Passion were like a woman in labour, grieving and lamenting at first, and then rejoicing when Jesus was born into the world of the resurrection: the parable in 16:20–1 summarizes it all. Loisy puts it well: 'The woman in the similitude appears to be the same as the woman in the Apocalypse, the believing synagogue, mother of Christ, faithful mankind, mother of the elect'.[7] It was this faithful remnant of Israel which 'set the spirit of God's salvation upon the earth' (Is 26:18c).

By virtue of this loyal remnant gathered round Jesus, Zion became the mother of many nations, and this brings us to the second Isaian text which underlies Jn 16:21–2. Between the first Good Friday and Easter Day, everything had happened so rapidly that it was almost unbelievable at first: certainly it must have been extraordinarily difficult for the disciples to grasp that the whole perspective of world history was now changed, for ever. Yet this was what they believed. The attempt to kill Jesus had failed—he was alive. And in Is 66 it is written (according to the Septuagint):

7a 'Before she that was in labour gave birth,
 b   before the labour of the birth-pangs arrived,
 c   she escaped, and gave birth to a male child.
8a Who has ever heard of such a thing,
 b   and who has ever seen the like?
 c Has earth ever given birth on one day,
 d   or a nation been born in one moment?
 e Because as soon as Zion was in pain
 f   she gave birth to her children . . .
10a Rejoice, Jerusalem,
 b   and join together, all you that love her!
 c Rejoice exceedingly,
 d   all you that grieve over her . . .
14a You will see, and your heart will rejoice . . .'

The Hebrew text of Is 66, and the Aramaic Targum, make the same point about the startling rapidity with which Zion becomes the mother of a great people, and with equal clarity. That the

[7] *Le quatrième évangile*, p. 788.

Fourth Evangelist had this text in mind seems likely partly because of the comparison with a woman in labour, partly because of the theme of Zion's becoming the mother of many children, and partly because 14a ('You will see, and your heart will rejoice') is so close in wording to Jn 16:22 ('I shall see you, and your heart will rejoice').

'A woman, when she is giving birth, feels sorrow . . . and you therefore now feel sorrow' (Jn 16:21–2). John is here suggesting not only that Jesus' Passion may be compared to the pains of birth, but also that the disciples may be compared with the woman who gives birth. Jesus is not merely drawing a parallel, and saying '*Similarly*, you feel sorrow' (οὕτως καὶ ὑμεῖς . . .); he is drawing a conclusion, and saying 'Therefore you feel sorrow' (καὶ ὑμεῖς οὖν . . .), as if it were evident that the faithful disciples occupied in some sense the position of a mother bringing a child into the world. The only satisfactory interpretation is to regard the disciples at the supper as the faithful remnant of Israel. 'You are those who have remained at my side amid my trials' (Lk 22:28), not servants but friends (Jn 15:15), and *therefore* the embodiment on earth of faithful Zion, from whom a new people would be born.

If, according to the Fourth Gospel, the disciples at the supper can be regarded as the embodiment of Zion as mother, at the very moment when the eschatological blessings promised to Zion are about to be realized, it is not hard to accept that the same metaphor of the remnant of Zion as the mother of Jesus, and of many nations, may recur in the Apocalypse. Nor would it be surprising if, in this book so packed with symbols, the 'little flock' of faithful followers were represented as a woman, and as a bride. And this would seem to be the first meaning of Apoc 12:1–6: the woman is there a symbol of faithful Zion, of those disciples who formed the remnant of Israel and the nucleus of the Christian Church. Like a woman in labour, they went through torment, grieving and lamenting as Jesus was being taken from them (v. 2), only to discover that he had been caught up to God and to his throne (v. 5): then they rejoiced that a man was born into the world of the resurrection. If this is the true interpretation of vv. 1–6, it should enable us to interpret the rest of the chapter; and this identification of the woman should in turn be confirmed by the remainder of the chapter.

In apocalyptic writing, it is commonplace to represent life on earth by heavenly symbols. Kingdoms have their guardian angels (Dan 10:13, 21; 12:1); a war between nations on earth is described as a war in heaven; each earthly reality has its heavenly *Doppelgänger*. Apoc 12 supplies a perfect illustration of this manner of writing. The battle between Michael and Satan recorded in vv. 7–13 is the celestial counterpart of the event related in vv. 1–5, *i.e.* of the frustration of the dragon's scheme by the crucifixion and exaltation of Jesus.

Dr Caird has expounded this with his usual clarity:

'. . . *war broke out in heaven*, and a war in which apparently the Messiah was not involved, since the task of overpowering the dragon is assigned to *Michael and his angels*.

It need hardly be said that this is no premundane battle. As we shall see below, the Bible knows nothing of the premundane fall of Satan, familiar to readers of *Paradise Lost*. If John was familiar with a Jewish tradition of a primordial conflict between the angels of light and the angels of darkness . . ., he is certainly using it here, as he uses all his other inherited myths, to draw out the significance of the gospel story. As often happens in the Revelation, what he sees is described largely in traditional imagery, and what he hears gives the Christian interpretation. The theological comment is provided by *a loud voice in heaven. The hour of victory for our God*, the hour which establishes God's *sovereignty* and *the rightful reign of his Christ*, can in the present context be nothing other than the crucifixion. This is why it has to be Michael and not Christ who is God's champion in the heavenly war. Everything that John sees in heaven is the counterpart of some earthly reality. When the victory is being won in heaven, Christ is on earth on the Cross. Because he is part of the earthly reality, he cannot at the same time be part of the heavenly symbolism. The heavenly chorus explains that the real victory has been won *by the life-blood of the Lamb*. Michael's victory is simply the heavenly and symbolic counterpart of the earthly reality of the Cross. Michael, in fact, is not the field officer who does the actual fighting, but the staff officer in the heavenly control room, who is able to remove Satan's flag from the heavenly map because the real victory has been won on Calvary'.[8]

Caird's interpretation of the heavenly battle confirms the view that the woman who gives birth to the child amid agony must be in some way present on earth while Michael fights against Satan in heaven above.

Though the Apocalypse here presents the conflict between Michael and Satan in military terms, only a little beneath the surface there lies another idea, of a lawsuit in heaven. In the book of Job, one of the angels in the heavenly court is called 'the Satan' *i.e.* 'the adversary' (with the definite article): his task is to prosecute men in the lawcourt of God, and when not occupied with his official duties, he spends his time going to and fro on the earth collecting evidence, even to the point of putting temptation in men's way when the necessary evidence is lacking (Job 1:6 ff.). As long as men are guilty of sin, God recognizes the justice of indicting them, and therefore tolerates the presence of their 'accuser' in heaven. In later Judaism, as in the New Testament (Jude 8–9), the counsel for the defence on these occasions is Michael, and so the conflict between Michael and Satan, though represented in Apoc 12 in military terms, is essentially a legal battle. This picture of celestial litigation is yet another reflection of what happens on earth, for in the Fourth Gospel the struggle between Jesus and the devil is often presented as a lawsuit. Though Jesus is condemned to death on earth as a result of the machinations of Satan, this sentence is reversed in the heavenly court of appeal, and his prosecutor is thrown out of the court in disgrace. 'Now is the judgment of this world: now is the ruler of this world cast out' (Jn 12:31). Moreover, since Jesus had taken upon himself the sin of the world, the quashing of his sentence in

---

[8] *The Revelation of St John the Divine*, pp. 153–4.

the court of appeal spelt final failure for Satan in his effort to secure the condemnation of all mankind.

'And Satan, having lost his case, loses also his job. There is no room for him any more in heaven, and it only remains for Michael to drum him out. As Paul puts it, "there is now no condemnation for those who are in Christ Jesus" (Rom 8:1). Or as John puts it, *they were overpowered, and left not a trace to be found in heaven*' (Apoc 12:8).[9]

Satan is from this moment powerless in heaven: all he can do is to vent his spite on men below. Thus the remainder of his activity, *i.e.* his onslaught on the woman and the rest of her children (12:13–17) must take place on earth, as v. 13 expressly notes. Here, then, is further confirmation that the woman symbolizes the disciples of Jesus on earth.

The pursuit of the woman by the dragon in vv. 13–17 is a more detailed account of her flight into the desert, only briefly mentioned in v. 6. It is clear both from v. 6 and from v. 14 that the desert is here a place of refuge and safety, 'a place prepared for her by God', to which she is carried on the wings of a great eagle, as Israel was once carried into the safety of the desert of Sinai (Ex 19:4). There she is secure under the protection of God for three and a half years, *i.e.* during any time of persecution, which never lasts longer than God wills (*cf.* Dan 12:7; Apoc 11:2–3). But the dragon, frustrated, launches two attacks, one on the woman in the desert, and one on the rest of her children. Again, it makes excellent sense to see the woman as a symbol of the Church, and 'the rest of her children' as individual members of the Church.

The great red dragon is by now identified with the serpent of old, the devil and Satan (Apoc 12:9), and in the first attack, on the woman directly, 'the serpent spewed out of his mouth after the woman water like a river, to sweep her away in its flood' (12:15).

[9] *Ibid.*, p. 155. The substance of this paragraph and its verbal felicities are due to Caird, pp. 154–5.

'*Water*, we recall, is his natural weapon, for his home is the primaeval abyss . . .

[But] what was happening in Sardis or Pergamum, Ephesus or Thyatira, when *the serpent spewed out* his *river*, only to see it sink, like the Syrian Abana, into the sands of the desert? What was this rush of great waters, this torrent of destruction, this flood which would have swept God's people away Ps 32:6; 18:4; 124:4), if God had not kept his promise to dry up the rivers through which they must pass (Is 42:15; 43:2; 50:2)? John clearly distinguishes this Satanic weapon from those Satan uses *to wage war on the rest of her children*. It was the failure of the river that sent the dragon off in a storm of temper to summon the monster from the infernal sea. The river then cannot represent either persecutions which had taken place before the time of John's vision or the destruction of Jerusalem by the armies of Titus: for both of these were works of the monster, whose seven heads were the seven hills of Rome. The river must be some more direct activity of Satan and we recall that John has told us in his letters what tricks Satan has been up to in the churches of Asia. In Smyrna and Philadelphia there has been trouble from "Satan's synagogue", "liars who claim to be Jews when they are not". Slanderous attacks from without, false teaching designed to corrupt the church's faith and to destroy it from within—this is the river of lies which the serpent *spewed from his mouth*. To give the lie to the slanders, to hold fast to the true gospel and hate the works of the Nicolaitans, is to escape to the safe *place in the desert*. For the desert is that vantage point outside the great city from which its seductive falsity can be seen in its true colours (17:3)'.[10]

We can see now why at 12:15 the author chooses to speak of 'the serpent' rather than 'the dragon' (though he returns to the word 'dragon' in vv. 16–17): at v. 15, he is calling attention to the nature of the river which the serpent spews out of its mouth. From a serpent, it can only be a river of poison, or (as Caird calls

[10] *Ibid.*, pp. 158–9.

it) a river of lies. This is Satan's first attack on the Church—an endeavour to poison it with lies. But once again he is defeated: 'the earth came to the woman's rescue, opened its mouth and swallowed the river' (12:16). Deadly poison though it was, the river petered out, and the woman was still alive.

For the dragon, there was only one course left:

'Satan is powerless to destroy the church, but he can at least vent his thwarted fury through state persecution on individual Christians—*the rest of her children*',[11]

and so he goes down to the sea-shore to summon up reinforcements, the Roman Empire, the monster with ten horns and seven heads, to wage war on those who keep the commandments of God and hold fast to the testimony of Jesus. The seed of the woman has ground his head, and all the serpent can do is to snap at its heel (*cf.* Gen 3:15), by making war on 'the rest of her seed' (Apoc 12:17).

From this survey, it might seem that everything in Apoc 12 can be satisfactorily explained if the woman is taken to represent the people of God on earth, the Church of the Old and New Testaments. The faithful remnant of Israel grieved and lamented as Jesus was being born into the world of the resurrection; later, it had to face a poisonous stream of lies, and when this failed to destroy it, it was called to withstand persecution by the Roman Empire. Certainly, this interpretation is coherent and, as far as it goes, satisfactory. But it does not appear to do full justice to the description of the woman in v. 1, *i.e.* to the titles by which she is first introduced.

'A great sign appeared in heaven, a woman clothed with the sun, with the moon under her feet, and on her head a crown of twelve stars' (Apoc 12:1). Nearly all commentators take the source of this imagery to be Gen 37:9, where Joseph dreams that the sun, the moon and eleven stars bow down before him: the crown of twelve stars will then symbolize either Israel of the Old Testament (the twelve patriarchs, the twelve tribes), or the Church of the

[11] *Ibid.*, p. 159.

New Testament (the twelve apostles), or both. And so the twelve stars are used to fix the identity of the woman. There is, however, a fatal weakness in this explanation. If the twelve stars symbolize primarily a recognizable earthly reality such as the patriarchs, tribes or apostles, what do the sun and moon symbolize? One cannot seize on part of the description and forget about the other half. In Gen 37:9 there is a perfectly good explanation of the sun and moon (the father and mother of Joseph), as of the eleven stars. It is not so here in Apoc 12:1.[12]

In fact, the immediate Old Testament source would seem to be not Gen 37:9, but the Song of Solomon 6:10:

> 'Who is she gazing down like the dawn,
> fair as the moon, bright as the sun,
> majestic as the marching stars?'[13]

The Song of Solomon here portrays the bride (that is, in allegory, Israel the bride of Yahweh) as adorned with all light, with the beauty of the moon, the brilliance of the sun, and the ordered magnificence of all the constellations as they march across the fields of heaven. And this is what the Apocalypse is saying in 12:1: that all available light—sun, moon and stars: the totality of cosmic light (*cf.* Apoc 6:12–13; 8:12)—surrounds and adorns this heavenly bride.

But in that case, the reader will ask, why only twelve stars? Why does the writer not say 'and upon her head a crown of *all* the stars'? To answer that question, one must say something about the significance of numbers in the Apocalypse.[14]

---

[12] From here on I am much indebted to H. Gollinger, *Das 'grosse Zeichen'*. For the paragraph above see pp. 79–80.

[13] Literally, 'awe-inspiring as a bannered host', *i.e.* 'awe-inspiring as an army marching with its colours flying'. The New English Bible has 'majestic as the starry heavens'.

[14] For the following paragraphs see especially H. Gollinger, *Das 'grosse Zeichen'*, pp. 83–9. For further detail see vol. 2 of the *TWNT*: pp. 628–9 (K. H. Rengstorf on the number 7 in the Apocalypse), 35–6 (Fr. Hauck on the number 10), and

The number 7 is the sum of 3 (the number for God, who was, who is, and who is to come: the thrice-holy) and 4 (the number for the world, with its four points of the compass). Hence 3 + 4 (the number for God plus the number for the world) comes to signify totality. Thus the Seven Churches represent the fullness, the totality, of the Church on earth. The seven stars, the seven candlesticks, the seven angels, the seven seals and the seven trumpets each represent a totality, a complete picture of something either in heaven or on earth. The dragon in Apoc 12:3 has seven heads and seven diadems—complete power on earth.

The second most common number in the Apocalypse is 12 = 3 × 4. And twelve was for the Jews a number pregnant with significance. They counted twelve tribes, though there were in reality thirteen (omitting one when necessary to keep the list right); and the Christian Church has always counted twelve apostles (while setting Paul on a par with them[15]). Now it is interesting to note that in the Apocalypse the number 12 is never used of earthly realities, but only of heavenly things. In this there is a striking contrast with the use of the number 7, which is used both of heavenly and of earthly realities, and with the book's use of the number 10. The number 10 indicates a certain kind of fullness: but it is used only of earthly things, and represents a fullness which will pass away. So the Church of Smyrna will be persecuted for ten days (Apoc 2:10); the dragon (12:3), the monster from the sea (13:1) and the harlot (17:3, 7, 12, 16) each have ten horns—the fullness of power on earth, but a power that is doomed to pass away.

The number 12, however, is reserved for that fullness of perfection which will not pass away. So in Apoc 7:4-8 and 14:1,

---

323-5 (Rengstorf on the number 12 in the Apocalypse). On the combination of 3 and 4 (giving 7 by addition, and 12 by multiplication) see A. Feuillet, *L'Apocalypse: Etat de la question (Studia Neotestamentica Subsidia 3)*, Paris–Bruges, 1963, p. 44.

[15] *E.g.* in the first Eucharistic Prayer of the Roman Mass (the Roman Canon), Matthias is omitted from the first list of the apostles in order to make room for Paul and to leave the number 12 undisturbed. *Cf.* also Ac 1:22, 24-6.

the 144,000 denotes the unimaginably perfect, quite uncountable number of citizens in the heavenly Jerusalem: it is the square of 12 multiplied a thousand times. And curiously, the number 12 is not otherwise mentioned in the book, apart from the text in 12:1, until chapters 21 and 22. There the pages which describe the New Jerusalem are literally bestrewn with it: one could say that it is this number which marks the city as God's New Jerusalem. It is the divine hall-mark (3) stamped on a new creation (4). 'Come, I will show you the bride, the wife of the Lamb . . . and he showed me the holy city Jerusalem coming down from heaven from God . . . The city had a great high wall, with twelve gates, and at the gates twelve angels, and the names inscribed of the twelve tribes of the sons of Israel. On the east there were three gates, on the north three gates, on the south three gates, and on the west three gates' (note the 4 × 3). 'The wall of the city had twelve foundations, and on them the twelve names of the twelve apostles of the Lamb.' The city lay four-square, a cube of 12,000 stadia, with its wall 144 cubits high, adorned with twelve kinds of precious stones, and its twelve gates were twelve pearls. In the middle of the city stood the tree of life, producing twelve kinds of fruit, a different fruit for each month of the year. Apart from Apoc 2:7, this is the first time the tree of life is mentioned in the Bible since access to it was barred to mankind at the end of Gen 3, when man was expelled from the Garden of Eden: John's vision of the New Jerusalem is paradise restored (cf. Apoc 21:9–21 and 22:2).

Now if in the Apocalypse every instance of the number 12 apart from the one under discussion refers to a heavenly reality (the 144,000 elect, and the references to the New Jerusalem), it is highly probable that the woman who wears a crown of *twelve* stars (where one would have expected '*all* the stars') is meant to be in some sense a heavenly figure. This is confirmed by the fact that she appears 'in heaven' (or at least 'in the sky'), is adorned with the sun, and has the moon under her feet: she must be in some sense a heavenly reality. But that does not warrant the conclusion that she represents *only* a heavenly reality. She could represent a heavenly reality which is also in some way present on earth, just as the twenty-four elders in heaven (Apoc 4:4) stand for the twelve patriarchs and the twelve apostles, the old and the new Israel, who certainly once lived on this earth. The twelve stars, then, may well be a reminder that the woman clothed with the sun, though in heaven, is *also* a figure of the ancient and the new Israel here on earth. And the sequel makes it clear that the woman is in some way present on earth, for 'she goes through torment to give birth', a birth which takes place on earth below, on the hill of Calvary, *from which* her child is caught up to God and to his throne.

The woman in Apoc 12 is therefore an ambivalent symbol. She certainly represents the people of God on earth, that is, the Jewish people and its faithful remnant, from whom Christ was born, and the Christian Church which is the mother of all who believe. But she also symbolizes the heavenly Jerusalem which is our mother (Gal 4:26–7), mother of the Messiah and of all the faithful: she is the Church of the Old and New Testaments as existing in the foreordaining mind and will of God.[16] She is not only the Church in history, but the people of God predestined in the city of God.[17]

To make this point with as much clarity as possible, one may perhaps invoke here St Augustine's theory, derived ultimately from Plato, of the ideas in the divine mind,[18] and say that the heavenly Jerusalem is the blue-print of the Church in the mind of God. Every grace and blessing that comes to the Church on earth proceeds from the divine foreknowledge and will, ordaining and disposing all things according to its sovereign good pleasure. This is the theme of the hymn with which Ephesians opens (1:3–14), perhaps the finest text of all to explain what is intended in the present context by speaking of the heavenly Jerusalem:

[16] This idea is well expounded, with copious references to modern authors, in H. Gollinger, *Das 'grosse Zeichen'*, pp. 66–72.

[17] *Cf.* K. H. Rengstorf in the *TWNT* 2, p. 323.

[18] For Plato, see the *Phaedo* 100B–101E; *Timaeus* 28A–29B and 50B–52E; *Parmenides* 132–3. For Augustine, see the *Liber LXXXIII Quaestionum*, qu. 46: ML 40.29. The theory is fully and succinctly presented in St Thomas Aquinas, *Summa theol.*, Ia, qu. 15.

3 'Blessed be that God and Father of our Lord Jesus Christ,
   who has blessed us with every spiritual blessing,
   in the heavenly realms, in Christ!

4 For he chose us out, in him, before the world was made,
   to be holy and sinless in his sight, in charity,

5 when he decreed that we should be adopted sons of his,
   through Jesus Christ.
   Such was the good pleasure of his will . . .

9 He made known to us the secret of his will,
   —the design which it had pleased him to adopt,
   the plan that he had set before himself,

10 to execute when the due time should come—:
   to unite all things in heaven and earth once more,
   by bringing them under one Head, namely, Christ.

11 It was in him too that we were set apart, marked out
   beforehand,
   in accordance with a pre-established plan
   of him who disposes all things
   according to the desire of his will,

12 that we might contribute to the praise of his glory,
   we who had been looking forward to the coming of
   the Christ.

13 It was in him that you also, when you heard the word of
   truth,
   the Good News of your salvation, and believed it,
   were marked with the seal of the promised Holy
   Spirit.

14 And he, the Holy Spirit, is a pledge of our inheritance,
   working to achieve redemption for God's chosen
   people,
   that his glory may be praised.'

Here is the vision of the heavenly Jerusalem in which Jew and Gentile are predestined together, to be one in Christ (vv. 11–14; *cf.* 2:11–22). The divine plan is the exemplar and archetype decreed to be actualized in the Church on earth.

It is not sufficient, therefore, simply to say that the woman clothed with the sun stands for the Church on earth, as realized in history. She is more than a literary symbol of the Church here below, and this is the significance of her celestial adornment—the sun, the moon, the stars. She is also the *causa exemplaris* of the Church. We may add that she is also its archetypal symbol.

Two short quotations from Carl Gustav Jung will explain what is meant here by an archetypal symbol.

> 'The essence of the symbol consists in the fact that it represents in itself something that is not wholly understandable, and that it hints only intuitively at its possible meaning. The creation of a symbol is not a rational process, for a rational process could never produce an image that represents a content which is at bottom incomprehensible.'[19]

When such a symbol takes on a concrete visual form, and is expressed in accordance with a familiar mythological motif, it may be called an *archetypal* symbol.

> 'It then expresses material primarily derived from the *collective* unconscious, and indicates at the same time that the factors influencing the conscious situation of the moment are *collective* rather than personal . . . In this respect it is a precipitate and, therefore, a typical basic form, of certain ever-recurring psychic experiences. As a mythological motif, it is a continually effective and recurrent expression that reawakens certain psychic experiences or else formulates them in an appropriate way.'[20]

In other words, the archetypal symbol is a concrete and visual symbol, in mythological form, which encapsulates both rational ideas and insights that are in strict logic incapable of demonstration. 'The heart has reasons reason does not know', and only an archetypal figure can sum up and give expression to the totality

---

[19] *The Collected Works of C. G. Jung, Vol. 6: Psychological Types*. A revision by R. F. C. Hull of the translation by H. G. Baynes, London, 1971, p. 106, §171.

[20] *Ibid.*, p. 443, §746, and p. 444, §748.

of the deepest experiences, especially when rational and intuitive perceptions are inextricably combined. This is particularly true when there is need to give vivid expression to the *collective* experience of a community of minds and hearts, such as the Christian Church.

The woman clothed with the sun is therefore more than a literary symbol of the Church on earth, more even than its *causa exemplaris*, its blue-print in the mind of God. With the moon (the symbol of all that changes, that waxes and wanes) under her feet, and on her head a crown of *twelve* stars, she is in addition an archetypal symbol of the Church indestructible, the Church perennial; and the writer of the Apocalypse, *before* speaking of persecution, calls the attention of his readers to the fact that the Church *is* indestructible, and will survive all the attacks of its enemies, heavenly or earthly, spiritual or material, whether inside or outside the city of God.

> 'The woman whom the seer beholds in the splendour of heavenly majesty is not, strictly speaking, to be understood as the people of God in its concrete, earthly manifestation, but rather as its exemplar and archetype (*Vorbild und Urbild*): here we see its distinctive nature, and that it is from the very beginning present with God in heaven.'[21]

That is why the woman is described as clothed with the sun, with the moon under her feet, and on her head a crown of twelve stars. That is why it makes so much better sense to trace the origin of this adornment to the Song of Solomon 6:10 than to Gen 37:9[22]: because the point of v. 1 in Apoc 12 is that the woman, as the archetype of God's people, is eternal as the sun, the moon and the stars:

> 'Who is she gazing down like the dawn,
>   fair as the moon, bright as the sun,
>   majestic as the marching stars?'

[21] A. Wikenhauser, *Die Offenbarung des Johannes*, 3rd ed., Regensburg, 1959, pp. 92–3, cited in H. Gollinger, *Das 'grosse Zeichen'*, p. 67.

[22] See above, p. 422.

That is why the woman is, like her son, secure from every attack of the dragon (Apoc 12:14–17): all he can do is to vent his hatred on 'the rest of her children' during their earthly life.

It was said above that the woman is, as a symbol, ambivalent,[23] and we can now perceive that this dual symbolism is essential to the author's purpose, and basic for his argument. For the two aspects are essentially related to each other. The woman is, on one side, a 'great sign' in heaven: she represents the Church as divinely predestined and instituted, and therefore the Church as indestructible. This is the aspect shown forth in vv. 1, 6 and 14–17. She is clothed with the sun, has the moon under her feet, and on her head a crown of twelve stars; she finds security in the desert, in a place prepared for her by God, to which she is carried on an eagle's wings; and the earth itself swallows the river of poisonous lies. At the same time, this woman in heaven is realized, actualized and embodied in the historical reality of the Church on earth: she represents the Church as suffering and exposed to the attacks of the devil. This is the aspect shown in vv. 2–5, 13–17. It is amid suffering that the faithful remnant of Zion sees Jesus born into the world of the resurrection; the serpent seeks to poison the Church with false doctrine, and when this fails, declares war on 'the rest of her children'. The two aspects, heavenly and earthly, eternal and historical, are both essential to the author's concept of the Church, and his thought oscillates at very high frequency between them. This is his vision, in which he is able to find a message of hope and encouragement for the Churches of Asia.

It would seem, therefore, that it is possible to give a wholly satisfactory explanation of Apoc 12 without postulating any allusion to Mary the mother of Jesus. True, Braun and Cerfaux have argued forcibly that there must be an implied reference to Mary because the woman in Apoc 12 is presented as the mother of him who crushed the serpent's head. That the seer had Gen 3 in mind is clear from v. 9 ('the serpent of old'), 15 (the serpent) and 17 ('the rest of her seed'); and only Mary of Nazareth is in the strictest sense the mother of him who crushed this serpent.[24] The

[23] See above, p. 425.
[24] F.-M. Braun, 'La femme vêtue de soleil (Apoc 12)', in the *Revue Thomiste* 55

argument is impressive, but not of itself decisive, for one could say that the faithful remnant of Israel is here presented as the mother of the Messiah.

There is, however, another factor which cannot be overlooked, or set aside as of minor importance. If the author of the Apocalypse was in chapter 12 thinking of Christ's victory on the cross, it is likely that the full meaning of the chapter will not be grasped unless it is read in conjunction with the Fourth Gospel. And in the Fourth Gospel Mary is presented as the mother of all whom Jesus loves.[25]

It has been argued above that the reason Mary is presented in the Fourth Gospel as the mother of all Christians lies in her boundless faith: she who had believed before Jesus had worked a single sign continued to believe, even when she stood beside the Crucified.[26] It is not far-fetched—it is indeed very reasonable—to see in her agony on Calvary those terrible torments which accompanied the birth of Jesus into the new world of the resurrection. After all, if one is going to say that the woman of Apoc 12 stands for the faithful remnant of Israel, *i.e.* for those disciples who recognized Jesus as sent by the Father and who thus formed the nucleus of the Christian Church, then Mary is according to the Fourth Gospel the most outstanding of them. She is openly presented as the model for them all, and for all who later come to believe. In John's theology, Mary standing beside the Crucified is the Daughter of Zion *par excellence* on that great and terrible Day of Yahweh. Just as Luke stresses her role as Daughter of Zion at the moment of the Incarnation, so John stresses that same role at the moment of the Redemption.

It was claimed above that the woman clothed with the sun is an archetypal symbol of the Church as indestructible;[27] but the title of this chapter is 'Archetype of the Church' (not 'Archetypal

---

(1955), pp. 639–69; L. Cerfaux, 'La vision de la femme et du dragon de l'Apocalypse en relation avec le Protévangile', *ETL* 31 (1955), pp. 21–33.

[25] See above, pp. 401–3.

[26] See above, pp. 399 and 403.

[27] See above, p. 428.

Symbol of the Church'). For the woman is not just a vivid mythological symbol, or merely the *causa exemplaris* of the Church. She is also a symbol of the Church as realized in history. But any archetypal symbol, however vivid, is of itself abstract, theoretical and ultimately remote.[28] Yet when we look at the mother of Jesus as portrayed in St John's Gospel we find the archetypal symbol of Apoc 12 made concrete, practical and present in this world. For in the Fourth Gospel the mother of Jesus is the prototype and exemplar of the Christian believer, and may therefore justly be called the archetype of the Church realized on earth. She is above all others the woman who went through torment as she saw Jesus born on Calvary (Apoc 12:2), who saw him taken up to God and to his throne (v. 5), and who was later to witness the sufferings of 'the rest of her children' (v. 17).

St Ambrose saw this clearly, when he identified the mother of Jesus on Calvary with the Church:

'May Christ say to thee also, from the gibbet of the cross, "Behold thy mother!", and may he say to the Church, "Behold thy son!" For then thou wilt begin to be a son of the Church, when thou dost recognize Christ on the cross as a victor.'[29]

When we read chapter 12 of the Apocalypse, and see in the woman clothed with the sun a symbol of that faithful remnant of Zion which became the nucleus of the Christian Church, may we not reverse the identification made by St Ambrose, and say that Mary was in history the living personification of the woman seen on Patmos? For according to St John, Mary is above all others the one person who even in the darkest hour never wavered in her faith. It is because of her faith that the Church from apostolic times has proclaimed that 'all generations shall call her blessed' (Lk 1:48, cf. v. 45). This is the theme of the teaching of the New Testament concerning the mother of Jesus, and in particular of St John. Perhaps, if Origen's commentary on Jn 19:25-7 had

[28] *Cf.* O. Semmelroth, *Mary, Archetype of the Church*, Dublin, 1964, pp. 29-33.
[29] *In Lucam* VII, 5 (on Lk 9:27) = *CC* 14.216 = *ML* 15.1700 or 1787.

survived, we should find that he had glossed the passage, to capture the full depth of the thought of the evangelist, in some such words as these:

'Jesus from the cross still says today, to every disciple whom he loves, "Behold thy mother!" '

DETACHED NOTES

I

AN ARAMAIC OR HEBREW SOURCE
FOR THE LUCAN INFANCY GOSPEL?

René Laurentin has an interesting note entitled 'Le problème du substrat hébreu de Luc 1–2' in *Biblica* 37 (1956), pp. 449–56.

From about 1900, he says, a number of writers have asserted that the theory of a written Aramaic source commands the assent of 'the majority' of scholars, though references are generally not given. He instances E. Klostermann and P. Gaechter. Klostermann, in *Das Lukasevangelium*, 2nd ed., Tübingen, 1929, p. 4, makes this assertion and mentions, in brackets and without references, Bousset and Gressmann. Laurentin could find only one relevant remark by W. Bousset, in his revision of J. Weiss, *Die Schriften des Neuen Testaments. I. Die drei älteren Evangelien*, Göttingen, 1917, where he speaks of an original document 'in Aramaic or Hebrew' (p. 397), while H. Gressmann, *Das Weihnachtsevangelium*, Göttingen, 1914, p. 3, speaks only of a 'semitischen Grundtext' without further specification. Similarly, P. Gaechter, *Maria im Erdenleben*, 2nd ed., Innsbruck, 1954, p. 28, seems to imply that M.-J. Lagrange, P. Joüon and M. Black advocate an Aramaic original (Gaechter himself being a strenuous upholder of an original Hebrew source). Yet both Lagrange and Joüon are hesitant, and note that the Semitisms in Lk 1–2 are not distinctively Aramaic (Lagrange, *Evangile selon s. Luc*, 7th ed., Paris, 1948, p. LXXXVII [*not* LXVI, as Laurentin writes]; Joüon, *L'Evangile de Notre Seigneur Jésus-Christ* [*Verbum Salutis* 5], Paris, 1930, pp. 279–306). M. Black, *An Aramaic Approach to the Gospels and Acts*, 2nd ed., Oxford, 1954, does not decide the case of Lk 1–2, and on p. 114 expressly notes that the original of Lk 2:34–5 may be either Hebrew or Aramaic. (Black maintains his neutrality in the third edition, Oxford, 1967, and even for the hymns in Lk 1–2 writes: 'A decision as between Hebrew and Aramaic is difficult to make, though the tendency now appears to be to assume the former' [p. 156].)

Laurentin concludes that one has to go a long way back to find genuine supporters of an Aramaic original, and cites only F. Godet,

Commentaire sur l'Evangile de s. Luc, 2nd ed., Paris, 1872, p. 85; C. A. Briggs, *The Messiah of the Gospels*, Edinburgh, 1895, p. 42; A. Plummer, *A Critical and Exegetical Commentary on the Gospel according to St Luke*, 4th ed., Edinburgh, 1901, pp. xxvi, 7 and 46; and F. Spitta in the *ZNW* 7 (1906), p. 294. To these can be added (following H. Schürmann, *Das Lukasevangelium I*, Freiburg, 1969 p. 144, n. 349): B. Weiss, *Die Quellen der synoptischen Ueberlieferung*, Leipzig, 1908, p. 195; O. Bardenhewer, *Mariae Verkündigung*, Freiburg, 1905, pp. 28, 32; H. Zimmermann, 'Evangelium des Lukas Kap. 1 und 2' in *Theologische Studien und Kritiken* (Gotha) 76 (1903), pp. 268–73; M. Dibelius, 'Jungfrauensohn und Krippenkind', in *Botschaft und Geschichte*, vol. 1, Tübingen, 1953, p. 8 (but Dibelius there states only that the stories about the Baptist were 'wohl ursprünglich aramäisch überliefert worden': he is referring only to the stories about the Baptist, and does not expressly say that there was a *written* document); E. Hirsch, *Frühgeschichte des Evangeliums II: Die Vorlagen des Lukas und das Sondergut des Matthäus*, Tübingen, 1941, p. 176; B. Schwank in *Oberrheinisches Pastoralblatt* 57 (1956), pp. 317–23; K. H. Schelkle in *Handbuch Theologischer Grundbegriffe*, vol. 2, p. 113 (and also in *Wort und Schrift*, Düsseldorf, 1966, pp. 61–2, where he expresses himself in favour of a written Aramaic source, though without stating his reasons); W. Michaelis, *Einleitung in das Neues Testament*, 3rd ed., Bern, 1961, p. 66. We may also mention J. Schmid, *Das Evangelium nach Lukas*, 3rd ed., Regensburg, 1955, p. 85.

If this list is anywhere near complete, hardly more than a dozen names can be found supporting the thesis that an Aramaic document underlies Lk 1–2, and this over a period of one hundred years. Seven of the thirteen names cited wrote before 1914. It is fair comment to say, as does P. Benoit in *NTS* 3 (1956–7), p. 171, n. 4, that the hypothesis of an Aramaic original is today more and more abandoned. The reason for its appeal at the turn of the century seems to have been the assumption that if there was a Semitic document underlying Lk 1–2, it must almost certainly have been written in Aramaic because Hebrew was a dead language at the time. The discoveries at Qumran alone are enough to wreck the edge of this argument.

By contrast, the theory of a Hebrew *Grundschrift* continues to hold its own, so that it is hardly practical to give full bibliographical details for all its supporters. Laurentin mentions several authors who in various ways and with different reservations opt for an original Hebrew text as the basis of Lk 1–2 (or parts of it) (*Biblica* 37 [1956], pp. 451–2, where full bibliographical details are given). In chronological order they are: P. de Lagarde (1889), A. Resch (1897), L. Conrady (1900), H. Gunkel (1902), G. H. Box (1905), F. X. Zorrell (1905 and 1906: only the Magnificat), R. A. Aytoun (1917: the hymns in Lk 1–2, ten in number), C. C. Torrey (1912 and 1924), P. Joüon (1930: the Magnificat and perhaps the Nunc Dimittis). The fullest modern statements of the arguments for a Hebrew *Grundschrift* then emerge in the 1940s and 1950s: E. Burrows, in *The Gospel of the Infancy and other Biblical Essays*, London, 1940, pp. 1–58; H. Sahlin, *Der Messias und das Gottesvolk*, Uppsala, 1945, pp. 70–311 *passim*; P. Gaechter, *Maria im Erdenleben*, 2nd ed., Innsbruck, 1954, pp. 9–77; and the articles of P. Winter listed in the bibliography for Part I, Chapter 1. To these H. Schürmann adds (*Das Lukasevangelium I*, p. 144, n. 351): Ph. Vielhauer, 'Das Benedictus des Zacharias' in the *Zeitschrift für Theologie und Kirche* (N.F.) 49 (1952), pp. 255 ff.; R. McL. Wilson, 'Some Recent Studies in the Lucan Infancy Narratives', in *Studia Evangelica*, Berlin, 1959, pp. 235–53 *passim* (at least for the Baptist narrative); R. Laurentin, *Structure et théologie de Luc I–II*, Paris, 1957, pp. 12–13 and 19–20, and *Biblica* 37 (1956), pp. 449–56; R. A. Martin, 'Syntactical Evidence of Aramaic Sources in Acts I–XV', in *NTS* 11 (1964–5), pp. 38–59, especially pp. 52–9. And once again we may refer to J. Schmid, *Das Evangelium nach Lukas*, p. 85: 'The author must have been a Palestinian, perhaps a Jewish Christian from a priestly family, and the original language of his written account must have been either Aramaic or (more probably) Hebrew.'

THE PHRASE 'DAUGHTER OF ZION'
IN THE OLD TESTAMENT

M. Henri Cazelles has published a detailed study of this phrase under the title 'Fille de Sion et théologie mariale dans la Bible', in the *BSFEM* 21 (1964), pp. 51–71, and this note merely summarizes his article.

The expression 'daughters of . . .', followed by the name of a town, is found in the earliest strata of the Pentateuch: thus Num 21:25 and 32 (both probably Elohistic) speak of 'the daughters of Heshbon and of Jazer', while Num 32:42 (probably Yahwistic) refers to 'Kenath and its daughters'. It is quite certain that the phrase denotes small towns dependent on a larger one such as Heshbon or Kenath, but it is not so easy to determine the significance of the phrase more accurately, since the expression has no known parallel in Mesopotamia, Phoenicia or Egypt.

One probable explanation is that the word 'daughters' (in Hebrew *benôth*) was mistakenly thought to be derived from the root *banah*, meaning 'to build': the *benôth* would then be the 'built-up towns', as distinct from villages (*haṣerim*: Jos 15:45–47) and cities ('*arim*: Num 21:25). But what is meant by 'built-up towns'? One suggestion is that they were small, fortified towns (*i.e.* surrounded by a wall) as distinct from unwalled and indefensible villages (*cf.* L. Delekat, 'Zum hebräischen Wörterbuch', in *Vetus Testamentum* 14 [1964], on pp. 9–11); another is that they were towns with houses built of stone, as distinct from villages of tents. If the reference to this (false) etymology be granted, either of these two suggestions is reasonable, for the phrase seems to have originated in Transjordan. Stone houses, and *a fortiori* walled towns, would have made a deep impression on those who first saw them after a lifetime spent in the desert, in tents. Compare the report of the spies in Num 13:28, and the phrases used in Deut 1:28 (their ramparts 'reached to the skies') and 3:5 ('strongholds enclosed by high walls, protected by gates and bars').

Transjordanian origin is suggested by a number of clues. Heshbon and Jazer lie east of the Jordan, and though Kenath is not explicitly located there, the context of Num 32:42 implies that the capture of Kenath was part of the conquests made in Transjordan in conjunction with Machir and Jair, sons of Manasseh (Num 32:40–1). Further, when the term 'daughters of . . .' occurs in Jos 17:11 (six times) and in Jdg 1:27 (five times), it is with reference to the conquests of Manasseh, which had lands on both sides of the Jordan. Apart from these two texts in Jos 17:11 and Jdg 1:27, the only text to use the expression with reference to places *west* of the Jordan is Jos 15:45–7: but these verses, which enumerate as part of Judah the cities of Ekron, Ashdod and Gaza 'together with their daughters and their villages' are very clearly a later addition to the text, since Ekron, Ashdod and Gaza were for centuries after the conquest Philistine cities. From this survey of usage, it is justifiable to conclude that the expression 'daughters of . . .' was introduced into Palestine from Transjordan, almost certainly by the tribe of Manasseh, whose clans lived on both sides of the Jordan. Later still, when the refugees from the Northern Kingdom streamed south to Jerusalem after 721 B.C., the expression found its way into Judah.

It is in Micah that we first encounter the expression 'Daughter of Zion'. In describing the downfall of Samaria, he writes (1:9):

> 'Her wound is incurable,
>   and it has come to Judah,
> it has reached to the gate of my people,
>   to Jerusalem.'

Three verses later he says (1:12):

> 'Evil has come down from Yahweh,
>   to the gate of Jerusalem',

and in the very next verse (13) there is his first, and extraordinarily obscure, reference to the 'Daughter of Zion'. There is much dispute about the date of this chapter, for vv. 6–7 certainly envisage the destruction of Samaria as lying in the future, and vv. 9, 13, 14, 15 also refer to Israel (and its kings, v. 14) as distinct from Judah. These details imply that the whole chapter was written *before* the fall of Samaria in 721 B.C. Yet one glance at a map shows that the towns mentioned in vv. 10–16 all lie to the south-west of Jerusalem, in the region devastated by Sennacherib in 701. This was the homeland of Micah of Moresheth.

Cazelles therefore suggests that the whole chapter was originally composed at the time of the Syro-Ephraimite War, when Tiglath-Pileser III brought his army into this region in 734 (cf. J. B. Pritchard, *Ancient Near Eastern Texts*, Princeton, 1950, p. 274), and that Micah reissued the prophecy in a slightly revised form when similar circustances returned, *i.e.* when the Assyrians returned under Sennacherib in 701. The reference to the 'Daughter of Zion' would have been first inserted in this 'revised version', in 701. The main thing to remember is that the expression 'Daughter of Zion' here occurs in a context where Israel is distinguished from Judah, and in close relationship with 'the gate of Jerusalem' (see Mic 1:9, 12, 13, 14).

There are three other verses in Micah which mention the Daughter of Zion: 4:8, 10, 13. Several commentators think that much of Mic 4–5 consists of later, and even post-exilic, insertions, of which Mic 4:10 is an example, since it is there said that the Daughter of Zion shall go forth to Babylon, where she will find salvation (see B. Renaud, *Structure et attaches littéraires de Michée IV–V*, Paris, 1964, especially pp. 56–8). Cazelles points out that the enemy envisaged in these chapters is not Babylon, but Assyria (Mic 5:4–5), and that the Daughter of Zion is depicted as supremely victorious (4:13). It would make good sense, therefore, to interpret Mic 4:8–13 as referring to a time when Jerusalem was hopeful of victory in a struggle against Assyria.

The story of the one short period when this hope was justified is recorded in 2 Kgs 20:12–19; cf. Is 39. After the death of Sargon II, king of Assyria, in 705, Merodach-baladan proclaimed himself king of Babylon and organized a vast coalition in the west, from Egypt to the Taurus, in a bold attempt to tear apart the empire of Assyria. In spite of the note of caution voiced by Isaiah (Is 14:29–31; 20), Judah committed itself to the revolt. But the hope was short-lived. The new king of Assyria, Sennacherib, acted swiftly. In his first campaign (spring, 703) he drove Merodach-baladan out of Babylon; a second campaign took him to the Tigris, and in 701 he moved his forces to the west and into Palestine. The year 704–3 was therefore the only year in which a hope of salvation shone from Babylon. Mic 4–5 fit well into that brief spring-time of hope, and it is not necessary to regard 4:8–13 (or any large part of these verses) as a later interpolation.

What, then, is the meaning of the term 'Daughter of Zion' in Mic 4:8, 10, 13? It is tempting to take it without more ado as a synonym for Jerusalem; on the other hand, the pre-history of the phrase would suggest that it might conceivably denote a small fortified town

dependent on, but distinct from, Zion. And this is very near the truth.
Mic 4:8 begins:

> 'And thou, Tower of the Flock (Hebrew: *Migdal-Eder*),
>   Ophel of the Daughter of Zion . . .'

Ophel was the highest part of Solomon's city, the north-eastern hill
on which the Temple stood. The word 'Ophel' means literally a
'mound' or 'rise' or 'swell', and therefore the meaning of the distich
just cited is that Migdal-Eder (literally, the 'Tower of the Flock')
stood in the same relationship to the 'Daughter of Zion' as Ophel did
to the ancient Jebusite city, the city of David. In other words, Migdal-
Eder denoted a rise or high point upon which a tower was built
from which one looked down on the 'Daughter of Zion', just as one
looked down from Ophel, the temple-hill, on to the city of David. If
Migdal-Eder could be located precisely, this might help in identifying
the 'Daughter of Zion'.

Migdal-Eder can be located. Everyone places it close to Jerusalem,
but Cazelles is audaciously precise: what Micah (4:8) calls the 'Tower
of the Flock' is to be connected (note the names) with the 'Sheep Gate'
mentioned in Neh 3:1, 32. The same 'Sheep Gate' is mentioned in
Jn 5:2, near the pool called Bethzatha: the remains of this pool have
recently been excavated and are now to be seen just north of the
Temple area in the grounds of the Church of St Anne. Migdal-Eder,
the 'Tower of the Flock', must therefore have stood somewhat north
of the Temple; and if it could be called 'Ophel', it must have stood on
a rise in the ground. In all probability, then, it stood on the future site
of the Antonia, which is only 150 yards from the pool of Bethzatha.

If Migdal-Eder stood on the site of the Antonia, then it looked down
upon a new quarter of Jerusalem, first inhabited around the time of
Hezekiah. This area of the city was known a hundred years after
Micah as the 'Second Quarter' (*mishneh*: Zeph 1:10), and in the reign
of Manasseh (687–42 B.C.) a wall was built (or rebuilt and raised in
height?) to protect it (see 2 Chr 33:14). Here there lived in 622 the
prophetess Huldah, who was consulted by Josiah's emissaries after the
discovery of Deuteronomy (2 Kgs 22:14). Was she of northern origin,
one wonders, that she could advise the king's officials about a book
which contains so many traditions from the Northern Kingdom?

Cazelles therefore suggests that in Micah the phrase 'Daughter of
Zion' denotes the new quarter of Jerusalem, north of the Temple, and

that the refugees who fled from the kingdom of Samaria after 721 lived in this quarter, close to the old city walls, near Migdal-Eder, at the gate of Jerusalem. This makes good sense of Mic 1:9, where the prophet says of Samaria,

> 'Her wound is incurable,
>   and it has come to Judah,
> it has reached to the gate of my people,
>   to Jerusalem.'

This new quarter (later walled in) was an area distinct from, but totally dependent on, the old city; it was a true 'Daughter of Zion', in northern parlance. There the remnants of Israel, 'driven from home, lame from their journey, sorely afflicted' (see Mic 4:6–7) awaited deliverance. And it was to this group of refugees huddled in a corner of the city that Micah addressed his message of hope.

If one now reads Mic 4–5 with these ideas in mind, both chapters become clear. They are a message of hope written at the time of the 'Grand Coalition' against Assyria in 704, and addressed in the first place to those refugees from the north. Though the Assyrians, from their new frontier only five or six miles away, could watch every movement in the north of the city (Mic 4:11, 14 = 5:1), Micah saw great hope in the alliance with Babylon (4:10) and eagerly awaited that era of peace when Assyria had been totally crushed by the sword (4:3–4, 5, 13; 5:5–9). A prince from the line of David would once again rule over the Northern Kingdom—Judah alone was too small for his domain (5:2 or 5:1). The 'Daughter of Zion', that lost remnant of Israel, would give birth to a new people (4:9–10). So the theme of Zion as mother entered the Old Testament.

Isaiah, at the beginning of his ministry, spoke of the 'daughters of Zion' (in the plural), meaning thereby the rich women who despised the poor (Is 3:16–17; cf. Amos 4:1), but later he adopted the usage of Micah. Thus in 16:1–2 'the daughters of Moab' are the towns in Transjordan near the gorge of the Arnon, through which the ruler of Moab is invited to send tribute, as in the time of Solomon, to 'the mount of the Daughter of Zion', i.e. to the Temple. This oracle should probably be dated in 711, or at the earliest in 715. Is 10:32 refers to Sennacherib's invasion (701), and though 'the mount of the Daughter of Zion' is generally taken as a synonym for Jerusalem, there are no synonyms in the preceding list, from v. 27. Hence it is permissible to draw a distinction between 'the mount of the Daughter of Zion' (to the north of the city) and 'the hill of Jerusalem' (to the south). Finally, in Is 37:22–9 and 1:8, the 'Daughter of Zion', so close to the Temple, becomes a *religious* synonym for the whole city, and (after the miraculous deliverance of 701) a symbolic name recalling the inviolability of Jerusalem.

Zephaniah is the next prophet of importance. He preached probably between 640 and 630 B.C., in the years following the death of Assurbanipal (640), during the minority of Josiah and before the religious reform of 622. Jerusalem was governed by pro-Assyrian officials, who even copied Assyrian dress (1:8; 3:13) and who clung to the protection of what Zephaniah saw as a moribund empire. It was from the 'Second Quarter' (the *mishneh*), near the 'Fish Gate', *i.e.* from that quarter of Jerusalem which has just been identified with the 'Daughter of Zion', that Zephaniah first heard the clamour announcing the Day of Yahweh (1:10). On that day, Jerusalem would be purified (1:12–13), the rich officials, judges and priests would pay the price of their oppression (3:1–5, 11), and God's judgment would extend to all the nations. It would be a *dies irae* for Jerusalem, but 'the humble of the land, who do the Lord's commands, would be preserved on that day' (*cf.* 2:3; 3:12). Hence the prophet can summon the poor of the city to rejoice at the end of their oppression, and it is to those last remnants of the northern tribes, who lived in hastily-built slums where the mortar had not had time to set and who were oppressed by the traders (1:11), that Zephaniah addresses his message of hope:

> 'Sing aloud, O Daughter of Zion!
>   Shout for joy, O Israel! . . .
> The king of Israel, Yahweh, is in thy midst,
>   thou shalt fear evil no more!' (3:14–15).

As in Micah, the message of joy is directed to the poor, to the remnant of Israel, to the 'Daughter of Zion'.

Jeremiah continues this theme of hope and restoration for the Northern Kingdom, even though his message is often full of sorrow (Jer 30–1). But in the Lamentations the phrase 'Daughter of Zion' is virtually a synonym for the entire city, for in those years of disaster the whole population, rich and poor, were one in adversity. Yet in Lam 2:8 there is still an allusion to the quarter identified as the 'Daughter of Zion': the forward wall and the inner rampart have both been dismantled, *i.e.* both the old wall of the city and the new wall enclosing the 'Second Quarter'.

Thus by the time of the exile, the term 'Daughter of Zion' had become a sacral name for Jerusalem, because the phrase evoked that part of Jerusalem which was closest to the Temple (see Lam 2:1). Yet it was not without echoes of its earlier usage as a term connoting the remnant of Israel to which the prophets had promised eventual restoration. Not surprisingly, the expression was taken up by the post-exilic prophets when they wished to speak of the remnant of Zion as a mother giving birth to a new nation. The ancient phrase recurs in Is 62:11, and the idea (but not the term) can be discerned in Is 66:6–10.

In 520 B.C. Zechariah proclaimed his joy at the rebuilding of the Temple in words taken from Zephaniah: 'Sing and rejoice, O Daughter of Zion! For behold, I am coming to dwell in thy midst, says Yahweh' (Zech 2:15 or 10; *cf.* Zeph 3:14–15). He adds immediately that 'many nations shall join themselves to Yahweh on that day, and shall be my people' (Zech 2:16 or 2:11). This theme (that the Temple will be the focal point of many nations) re-echoes Mic 4:1–4, the famous oracle which precedes directly Micah's message of hope to the 'Daughter of Zion'. The same theme dominates Ps 88, which is rightly entitled 'Zion as the mother of the nations'. It is less frequently observed that Ps 22, the psalm used by Jesus on the cross, also ends with the promise of deliverance 'to a people yet unborn' (v. 31). But it is evident that by the end of Old Testament times, the concept of Zion as the mother of many nations was firmly established in Israel (*cf.* the citation of Is 54:1 in Gal 4:26).

III

SHOULD THE MAGNIFICAT BE ASCRIBED TO ELIZABETH?

Was the Magnificat originally, *i.e.* in Luke's own manuscript, spoken by Elizabeth, not Mary? The theory was first advanced by Loisy, who developed the idea under the pseudonym François Jacobé in 'L'origine du Magnificat', in the *Revue d'histoire et de littérature religieuse* 2 (1897), pp. 424–32. It became generally known, however, through a lecture by Harnack entitled 'Das Magnificat Elisabet (Luk 1:46–55) nebst einigen Bemerkungen zu Luk 1 und 2', published in the *Sitzungsberichte der Kgl. Preussischen Akademie der Wissenschaften zu Berlin* 27 (1900), pp. 538–56, and reprinted in *Studien zur Geschichte des Neuen Testaments und der alten Kirche I*, Berlin and Leipzig, 1931, pp. 62–85.

The manuscript evidence is overwhelmingly against this view. For further arguments see P. Ladeuze, 'De l'origine du Magnificat et son attribution dans le troisième Evangile à Marie ou à Elisabeth', in the *Revue d'histoire ecclésiastique* 4 (1903), pp. 623–44, and Th. Zahn, *Das Evangelium des Lukas*, Leipzig, 1913, Exkurs III: 'Die Sängerin des Magnificat', pp. 745–51.

S. Benko, 'The Magnificat—A History of the Controversy', in the *Journal of Biblical Literature* 86 (1967) surveys all the opinions from Tischendorf to Laurentin, and opts for an original attribution to Elizabeth; but he has missed the extremely important article by Ladeuze.

IV

MARY'S VOW OF VIRGINITY

It is perhaps not superfluous to point out that no Roman Catholic is under any obligation to accept the theory that Mary made a vow or resolution of virginity. The Church has never defined, by an infallible decree, that Mary made such a vow, nor do the Fathers of the Church insist, with moral unanimity, that this interpretation of Lk 1:34 is the only orthodox interpretation of Mary's words, so that whoever rejects it must be refused Holy Communion. Indeed, most of the Fathers take Lk 1:34 to mean solely that Mary is here and now a virgin (see Graystone, *Virgin of All Virgins*, pp. 6–13 for the texts).

The suggestion that Mary had made a vow of virginity before the Annunciation originates, in practice, with St Augustine, and Augustine makes it clear that he is giving his own inference from the text when he writes 'Presumably (*profecto*) she would not say that, if she had not previously vowed her virginity to God'. His use of the word *profecto* indicates for certain that he is giving his own opinion, not bearing witness to a dogmatic tradition handed down from apostolic times. Hence even though his explanation has in practice been accepted for almost a thousand years, it has been accepted only as *an* interpretation of an otherwise difficult text. It cannot be said that all the bishops of the world have put it forward, in their day-to-day teaching, that is, by their *magisterium ordinarium*, as a dogma of faith handed down from apostolic times, or as a necessary logical consequence of any such dogma or dogmas.

Modern theologians are equally restrained when assessing the force of this classical interpretation. Even the more conservative state only that it is the common opinion of theologians, and no one says that it would be heretical to reject it. For example, A. Tanquerey, in his *Synopsis Theologiae Dogmaticae*, ed. 29a, vol. 2, Paris, 1959, p. 832, §1270 (*olim* 1271), writes '*Ita communiter*'. J. A. Aldama, in *Sacrae Theologiae Summa*, vol. 3, Madrid, 1953, p. 373, §76, says that a vow as distinct from a resolution is '*certum in theologia ex consensu theologorum iam a saec. XII . . . et iuxta communem interpretationem responsi Virginis*'

(Lk 1:34). He adds in a footnote: '*Nullatenus ergo doctrina haec potest dici liberae disputationis apud theologos*', but is very mild in his censure: '*hinc approbari nequeunt*' D. Haugg and P. Gaechter. Most authors are content to say that the theory of a vow before the Annunciation is the common opinion of theologians, and to leave it at that. Indeed, some who themselves defend the theory of a vow are anxious to stress that there are other interpretations which are equally consistent with the Catholic faith. Thus J. J. Collins in the *CBQ* 5 (1943), p. 372, and G. Graystone, *Virgin of All Virgins*, pp. 44–5; compare also J. Coppens in the *ETL* 16 (1939), p. 513.

SOME TEXTS OF TERTULLIAN INVOKED
BY SUPPORTERS OF THE
HELVIDIAN INTERPRETATION

In *De Monogamia* 8, 2 (*CC* 2.1239, lines 10–14 = ML 2.939 B), Tertullian is arguing that nobody was more fitted to baptize the Lord than was the Baptist, because he, like the mother who conceived and gave birth to Jesus, was a virgin. The text runs:

'Quis enim corpus Domini dignius initiaret quam eiusmodi caro qualis et concepit illud et peperit? Et Christum quidem virgo enixa est, semel nuptura post partum, ut uterque titulus sanctitatis in Christi censu dispungeretur, per matrem et virginem et univiram.'

It may be translated as follows:

'Who was more worthy to initiate the body of the Lord than flesh of the same kind as that flesh which conceived and gave birth to him? Christ was indeed born of a virgin, who would marry once for all after her child-bearing, so that Christ might have on his birth-certificate a double title of holiness, since his mother was both a virgin and married only to one man.'

Here Tertullian is arguing against the remarriage of widows, and is therefore concerned to stress that Mary was married only once. There is, however, no indication that he thought this marriage had been consummated. Indeed, in the sentence preceding the one just cited, he speaks of the Baptist as a man 'of total continence' (*integra continentia*) and of Zechariah his father as 'chaste in one marriage' (*monogamia pudica*) (see 8, 1: *CC* 2.1239, lines 4–5 = ML 2.939 A). In comparing the Baptist with Mary, therefore (he was '*eiusmodi caro qualis et concepit et peperit*'), Tertullian would seem to imply that Mary remained always a virgin, as did the Baptist, though he does not explicitly say so.

Compared with this statement about the Baptist, the mere assertion that Mary was married after the birth of Jesus (*semel nuptura post partum*) is no evidence that Tertullian believed this marriage to have been consummated, particularly since his stress falls not on the fact of the marriage, but on the fact that Mary was married only once.

Two texts are cited from *De carne Christi*, chapters 7 and 23. In the first text (*CC* 2.886–9 = ML 2.766–9), Tertullian is defending the reality of Christ's birth against certain Docetists who apparently maintained that the words in Mt 12:48 ('Who is my mother and who are my brothers?') contained an implicit denial, by Jesus himself, that he had come into the world by birth as an infant. In reply, Tertullian repeatedly insists that Jesus did have a mother and brothers, but he nowhere states, or even hints, that these brothers were sons born of Mary. Now if he had believed that these brothers were in fact Mary's own children, surely this would have been a good argument to use against the Docetists? Modern scholars argue that the existence of such brothers and sisters underlines the reality and the completeness of the Incarnation; and even those who disagree with this thesis (see Part II, Chapter 6, p. 207) would allow that if Mary did have other children, this would underline the reality of Jesus' *humanity*. Tertullian was never a man to overlook a telling argument; he was the born advocate who never missed an opportunity or failed to spot a weakness in his opponent's case. Therefore the only possible reason for his not explicitly citing the 'Helvidian' interpretation at this point is that he did not believe that the brothers were children of Mary.

The second text from *De carne Christi* is found in chapter 23 (*CC* 2.914–15 = ML 2.790). Here Tertullian is merely defending the fact that Mary was both a virgin at the time of Jesus' birth (because she had never known man) and also the true mother of Jesus (because his flesh came not from heaven but from her flesh). There is no reference to the brothers of the Lord, and no statement for or against the virginity of Mary after the birth of her son.

The final text of Tertullian to which writers appeal in support of the Helvidian view occurs in his *Adversus Marcionem* 4, 19 (§§6–12: *CC* 1.592–4 = ML 2.404 B–405 C). The context is the same as that of *De carne Christi* 7: Marcion had argued from the words 'Who are my mother and brothers?' that Jesus there implied that he was not truly born of a human mother. Again, it must be asserted that Tertullian does not say that these brothers were children of Mary; his words certainly affirm that they were blood-relations of Jesus, but this is not sufficient to prove that he believed them to be children of the same mother. And if he had believed that these brothers were born of Mary, why did he not on both occasions (in *De carne Christi* 7 and here) state so explicitly and end the argument against these Gnostic Docetists with one blow?

There is also a text in *De virginibus velandis* 6, 2–3 (*CC* 2.1215–16 = *ML* 2.897–8) which could be invoked, not in favour of the Helvidian view about the brothers of the Lord, but against the virginity of Mary *post partum*; but again all Tertullian is saying is that Mary at the time of Jesus' birth had not known man.

Lastly, it is occasionally said that Jerome believed Tertullian to have held the same view as Helvidius. Helvidius apparently appealed to Tertullian as an ancient authority in favour of his own view, and Jerome curtly dismissed the appeal with the words: 'Et de Tertulliano quidem nihil amplius dico, quam Ecclesiae hominem non fuisse' (*Adversus Helvidium* 17: *ML* 23.201 B). This is not an admission that Tertullian had held the same view as Helvidius, but an assertion that whatever view he held, he cannot be cited as an orthodox authority. And that, presumably, was the main point Helvidius was anxious to maintain.

VI

THE BROTHERS OF JESUS IN APOCRYPHAL WRITINGS AND THE INFLUENCE OF THE PROTEVANGELIUM OF JAMES

J. B. Lightfoot, *Galatians*, p. 275, mentions some of the later apocryphal writings which supply details about the brothers of Jesus. (1) *The Infancy Story of Thomas* is a work dating at the earliest to A.D. 200: cf. *New Testament Apocrypha I*, pp. 388–400. There is a reference to James the son of Joseph in §16 (p. 398). (2) *The History of Joseph the Carpenter* was written in Egypt around A.D. 400; it combines stories from *The Protevangelium of James* and *The Infancy Story of Thomas;* cf. *New Testament Apocrypha I*, p. 430. In Chapter 2, the names of Joseph's four sons and two daughters are given, though the Coptic and the Arabic versions differ somewhat over the names: Jude, Joset, James and Simon in the Coptic, Jude, Justus, James and Simon in the Arabic. The daughters were called Lysia and Lydia (Coptic), or Assia and Lyddia (Arabic). Both the Coptic and the Arabic texts are translated in *Evangiles apocryphes I*, by Ch. Michel and P. Peeters, Paris, 1911, pp. 191–243. (3) *The Gospel of Pseudo-Matthew* is a Latin work of the eighth or ninth century which repeats the details of *The Protevangelium* 8:4. The text is printed and translated in *Evangiles apocryphes I*, pp. 53–159. Later still, a revised version of the early chapters of this work was put around under the title 'The Birth of Mary'. (4) *The Syriac, Arabic and Armenian Infancy Gospels* are all translated and annotated by P. Peeters in *Evangiles apocryphes II*, Paris, 1914. They may go back to a work of the fifth century, based perhaps on *The Infancy Story of Thomas*.

In this stream of pious fiction, the influence of *The Protevangelium of James* is preponderant. In the East, the work circulated in several translations, in Syriac, Coptic, Arabic, Georgian, Armenian, Ethiopic and Old Slavonic: full references to the sources where these versions may be found are given in E. Hennecke and W. Schneemelcher, *New Testament Apocrypha I*, pp. 370–1. In the West, its view of the brothers of Jesus was savagely condemned by Jerome in his comment on Mt 12:49–50: 'Quidam fratres Domini de alia uxore Joseph filios suspicantur, sequentes deliramenta apocryphorum, et quamdam Melcham vel Escham mulierculam configentes' (*In Matt*. II, 12: ML 26.87–8). Perhaps it was partly because of its view of the brothers of the Lord that *The Protevangelium* was explicitly condemned as uncanonical by Pope Innocent I in 405 (see DS 213 = DB 96) and in the *Decretum Gelasianum* (DS 354 = DB 165). The substance of this part of the *Decretum Gelasianum* may well date back to Pope Damasus I (*cf.* the introductory note to DS 350). Note also, in DS 353, the influence of St Jerome.

There is an excellent study of the teaching of the Apocrypha about Mary entitled 'Marie dans les Apocryphes' by E. Cothenet in *Maria: Etudes sur la S. Vierge*, edited by H. du Manoir, vol. 6, Paris, 1961, pp. 71–156. The article on 'The Relatives of Jesus', by A. Jeyer and W. Bauer, in *New Testament Apocrypha I*, pp. 418–32, though a rich mine for references, refuses to take seriously the possibility that the brothers of the Lord were not sons of Mary (see pp. 424–5) and does not attempt to answer all the objections to the Helvidian view.

THE NAME 'JAMES' IN THE NEW TESTAMENT

'At the time St Paul wrote [1 Corinthians], there was but one person eminent enough in the Church to be called James without any distinguishing epithet: the brother of the Lord who was bishop of Jerusalem' (Lightfoot, *Galatians*, p. 265).

An inspection of all the texts in Luke, Acts and the Pauline Epistles shows that this is solidly established usage. If any other James is meant (either the son of Zebedee, or the son of Alphaeus), a qualifying epithet is added to his name, unless the context renders it unnecessary (as in the combination 'James and John'). The fulllist of the Lucan and Pauline texts is as follows:

Lk	5:10	'James and John, sons of Zebedee'
	6:14	'James and John' (in the list of the Twelve)
	6:15	'James of Alphaeus' (in the same list)
	8:51	'only Peter and John and James' (Jairus' daughter)
	9:28	'Peter and John and James' (the Transfiguration)
	24:10	*Mary the mother of James*

Ac	1:13	'Peter and John and James' (in the list of the Eleven)
	1:13	'James of Alphaeus' (in the same list)
	12:2	Herod put to death 'James the brother of John'
	12:17	*Go and tell James and the brothers* (Peter's release)
	15:13	*James answered and said* (the Council of Jerusalem)
	21:18	*Paul went with us to James* (in Jerusalem)

1 Cor	15:7	*Then he appeared to James*

Gal	1:19	*I did not see any other one of the apostles—only James the brother of the Lord*
	2:9	*James and Cephas and John, who are considered to be pillars*.

In the above texts which are *not* italicized, there is never any doubt which James is meant; either the words used or the context make plain that the text does not refer to the brother of the Lord who became bishop in Jerusalem. In six of the seven texts which are italicized (*i.e.* all except Lk 24:10) it is equally clear that the reference is to James the brother of the Lord, bishop of Jerusalem. Yet only one of these six texts (Gal 1:19) explicitly calls him the brother of the Lord; and this is because in the context of Gal 1–2 he might otherwise have been confused with James the son of Zebedee (*cf.* Gal 2:9). Normally, however, his name alone is sufficient to identify him. Therefore for Luke, his name alone is sufficient to identify his mother: 'Mary the mother of James'. (And in that case his mother was most certainly not the mother of Jesus.)

A MUCH-NEEDED REFORM IN THE LITURGICAL
CALENDAR OF THE LATIN CHURCH

St Jerome's theory about the brothers of the Lord as propounded in the *Adversus Helvidium* identifies James the brother of the Lord and bishop of Jerusalem with James the son of Alphaeus. This interpretation has been so generally accepted in the Western Church that the Roman rite celebrates only two saints called James who lived in apostolic times. 25 July is the feast-day of James the son of Zebedee; and 3 May (*olim* 1 May, and from 1956 to 1970, 11 May) that of Sts Philip and James. In the Roman Breviary used up to 1971, the lessons for the first Nocturn were taken from the Catholic Epistle of James, and those of the Second Nocturn related the life of the bishop of Jerusalem. In the new *Liturgia Horarum* (Vatican Press, 1971), the short introductory note for 3 May expressly states that James was 'a cousin of the Lord, son of Alphaeus, ruler of the Church of Jerusalem and author of the epistle'. The hymn for the Office of Readings calls him brother of Christ, pillar of the Church, first bishop of Jerusalem and author of the epistle.

Since there is nowadays wide, if not universal, agreement that the bishop of Jerusalem was not one of the Twelve, and not 'James the son of Alphaeus', it is highly desirable that there should be two separate feasts, one for the brother of the Lord and one for the son of Alphaeus. The most obvious change would be to leave James the son of Alphaeus sharing a feast-day with St Philip, and to delete on that day all references to the bishop of Jerusalem. A new feast-day could then be assigned to St James, the brother of the Lord and bishop of Jerusalem. The obvious choice for this would be 23 October, when the Greek, Syrian and Coptic Churches keep his feast-day.

The fullest account of the life of James is given in the *Acta Sanctorum* (*Maii*) (the Bollandist series, 1 May), Antwerp, 1680, vol. 1, pp. 18–34. The Bollandists proved beyond all doubt, three centuries ago, that the son of Alphaeus was not the bishop of Jerusalem. It is surely time to accept their conclusion and to correct the calendar of the Latin rite.

THE HISTORICITY OF THE VIRGINAL CONCEPTION: A LIST OF OPPONENTS AND DEFENDERS

I am grateful to Dr Heinrich M. Köster, S.A.C., for permission to reproduce here a list of the principal opponents and defenders of the historicity of the virginal conception. The list is given as Appendix II to Dr Köster's article, 'Die Jungfrauengeburt als theologisches Problem seit David Friedrich Strauss', in *Jungfrauengeburt gestern und heute*, Essen, 1969, on pp. 70–1.

Naturally, this list does not include many Protestant exegetes who have written against the historicity of the virginal conception, or many Roman Catholics who have written in defence of it. But it does try to mention all the significant names, *i.e.* all those who have brought forward new arguments one way or the other (though I observe that no British author, and only two Americans, are included). Dr Köster gives a splendid bibliography on pp. 58–69, where the detailed references to these authors' writings may be found. The names are listed in the order of the first publication by an author on this subject.

1. Those who for one reason or another do not accept that the narrative of the virginal conception records a historical (*i.e.* biological) event, but treat it as a mythical, legendary, pictorial or symbolic expression of the supernatural significance of Jesus. Among these we may count:

(*a*) in the Evangelical Churches:

D. Fr. Strauss (1835)
Gfrörer, A. Fr. (1838)
Weisse, Chr. H. (1838)
Baur, F. Chr. (1847)
Bauer, Br. (1874)
Hase, K. Aug. von (1875)
Harnack, A. von (1877)

Loofs, Fr. (1916)
Leisegang, H. (1919)
Bultmann, R. (1921)
Norden, E. (1924)
Seeberg, R. (1925)
Brunner, E. (1927)
Rühle, O. (1929)

Beyschlag, W. (1885)
Usener, H. (1889)
Lobstein, P. (1890)
Hillmann, J. (1891)
Sell, K. (1892)
Achelis, E. Chr. (1892)
Kattenbusch, F. (1892)
Hering, A. (1895)
Holtzmann, H. J. (1897)
Rohrbach, P. (1898)
Pfleiderer, O. (1902)
Schmiedel, P. W. (1902)
Soltau, W. (1902)
Gunkel, H. (1903)
Clemen, C. (1909)
Gressmann, H. (1909)
Völter, D. (1911)
Bousset, W. (1913)

Klostermann, E. (1929)
Schmidt, K. L. (1929)
Krüger, G. (1930)
Dibelius, M. (1932)
Thieme, K. (1932)
Budde, K. (1933)
Stauffer, E. (1941)
Althaus, P. (1948)
Trillhaas, W. (1953)
Conzelmann, H. (1954)
Lohmeyer, E. (1956)
Loewenich, W. von (1956)
Marxsen, W. (1956)
Bornkamm, G. (1956)
Boslooper, T. (1962)
Campenhausen, H. Fr. von (1962)
Hahn, F. (1963)
Pannenberg, W. (1964)

(b) in the Roman Catholic Church:

Renan, E. (1863)
Loisy, A. (1904)
Saintyves, P. (1907)
Turmel (Herzog), J. (1925)

Buonaiuti, E. (1938)
Schierse, Fr. Jos. (1960)
Schoonenberg, P. J. A. M. (1967)
Halbfas, H. (1968)

[Dr Köster lists here the Dutch Catechism; but see the next Detached Note. It is perhaps worth observing that Renan, Loisy, Saintyves, Turmel and Buonaiuti died outside the Roman Communion.]

2. Those who see in the narrative of the virginal conception not merely a religious truth, but also the record of a truly historical event. Among these we may count:

(a) in the Evangelical Churches:

Mendel, D. (1837)*
Olshausen, H. (1840)
Zahn, Th. (1867)
Weiss, B. (1882)
Schlatter, A. (1929)
Büchsel, Fr. (1926)
Machen, J. G. (1930)

Bornhäuser, K. (1930)
Barth, K. (1938)
Lamparter, H. (1949)
Asmussen, H. (1950)
Stählin, W. (1950)
Grundmann, W. (1956)

(b) in the Roman Catholic Church:

Kuhn, J. (1838)	Boismard, M.-E. (1954)
Lagrange, M.-J. (1895)	Schelkle, K. H. (1954)
Bardenhewer, O. (1898)	Geiselmann, J. R. (1954)
Schrörs, H. (1905)	Laurentin, R. (1957)
Steinmetzer, Fr. X. (1910)	Voss, G. (1965)
Steinmann, A. (1910)	Balthasar, H. U. von (1967)
Prümm, K. (1927–8)	Schnackenburg, R. (1967)
Lösch, St. (1933)	Michl, J. (1969)
Vosté, J. M. (1933)	

* Mendel was the first to make a direct attack on D. Fr. Strauss over the question of the virginal conception.

X

THE NEW DUTCH CATECHISM AND
THE VIRGINAL CONCEPTION

In 1966 a book commissioned by the Roman Catholic bishops of the Netherlands and produced by the Higher Catechetical Institute of Nijmegen appeared under the title *De Nieuwe Katechismus*. An English translation was published in 1967, under the title *A New Catechism: Catholic Faith for Adults*, but it is more often referred to as *The (New) Dutch Catechism*. On pp. 74–5 of the English edition it has a section entitled '*Born of God*', the first three paragraphs of which run as follows.

'As well as Jesus' human origin, the gospels also give his divine origin.

'There are several figures in the Old Testament of whom it is said that their birth was an answer to prayer. A human marriage which was at first childless finally bore fruit after much longing, prayer and a divine promise. This was the way with Israel's ancestors Isaac and Jacob, and also Samson, Samuel and the child from the house of Achaz, who was the sign of God's fidelity in a time of deep distress. Such was the birth of John the Baptist. In these stories something that is true of all parenthood is brought out with particular emphasis: that a new human being—every time something unique—is ultimately from God. The child is "a gift" from God, as we often read in the "births" column of the newspapers—much more than something that the parents have "had".

'Jesus is the climax of all the promises of children fulfilled in Israel. When he came into the world, he was being prayed for by a whole people and promised by a whole history. He was a child of promise in a unique sense, and the profoundest desire of the whole of mankind. He was born wholly of grace, wholly of promise—"conceived of the Holy Spirit". He was *the* gift of God to mankind.

'This the evangelists Matthew and Luke express when they proclaim that Jesus' birth was not due to the will of a man.

They proclaim that this birth does not depend on what men can do of themselves—infinitely less so than in other human births. That is the deepest meaning of the article of faith, "born of the virgin Mary". There is nothing in the bosom of mankind, nothing in human fruitfulness that can procreate him, from whom all human fruitfulness, all the begetting of our race depend: for all things were made in him. Mankind has ultimately no one to thank but the Holy Spirit for the coming of this promised one. His origin is not of blood nor of the will of the flesh nor of the will of a man, but from God: from the Most High.'

It is unfair to say (as some have done) that the Catechism here denies, at least implicitly, the historicity of the virginal conception. These paragraphs do not contain a single statement which explicitly or implicitly rejects the idea of a biologically virginal conception: this is evident from the fact that one can accept the virginal conception as an historical fact and assent to every statement in these paragraphs.

On the other hand, it is fair to say that the same paragraphs do not explicitly or implicitly affirm it (unless the final sentence of the third paragraph, based on Jn 1:13, is meant implicitly to affirm it: but this hardly seems to be the case).

Now when one reflects that belief in the virginal conception as an historical fact has been a cornerstone of Catholic faith from the earliest times (see pp. 330–42), and that this belief is today rejected by many non-Roman Christians, it is easy to understand why many Roman Catholics judged that mere silence on the subject was insufficient. They felt (rightly or wrongly) that if no protest were made, silence would be construed as a tacit acceptance of the idea that it was perfectly legitimate for a Roman Catholic to treat the virginal conception as a purely symbolic way of expressing Jesus' origin from God; and that such silence would also be tantamount to an invitation to view the doctrine in this light. This was all the more true in that the Catechism was issued with the authorization of a much respected local Hierarchy; that it had quickly become a best-seller in English, French and German; and that it was, in its presentation of the faith to modern man, by any standards a masterpiece.

After their monthly meeting in August 1966, the bishops of the Netherlands issued a very strongly worded statement affirming among other things their insistence on the doctrine that Jesus was in truth virginally conceived. This was reported in the Dutch Press on the 20–1

August 1966, and the more important parts of the text are reprinted in the *ETL* 42 (1966), p. 720.

In two articles published in *De Tijd* on 10 and 17 December 1966, Dr Piet Schoonenberg, S.J., one of the authors of the catechism and Professor at Nijmegen, affirmed that the authors of the catechism were convinced that the virginity of Mary was an open question (see *Herder Correspondence* 4 [1967], pp. 157–9): 'The new catechism leaves the virgin birth an open question. This does not mean that they have decided in the negative. But the authors were convinced that there was a question which could be legitimately posed' (p. 159). It was by then evident that the bishops of the Netherlands did not take the same view of the matter as the authors of the Catechism.

When the translations of the Catechism began to appear, the debate took on an international dimension, and many protests were made to Rome. The eventual outcome was that a Commission of six Cardinals was asked to examine and to report on the book. This they did in 1968, and the full text of their report is printed in the *AAS* 60 (1968), pp. 685–91. Since then, the Catechism has been printed with a Supplement (leaving the original text unchanged). The Commission of Cardinals reported on the treatment of the virginal conception as follows (*AAS* 60 [1968], p. 688):

> 'It must be openly professed in the Catechism that the holy mother of the Incarnate Word remained always adorned with the honour of virginity. It must teach equally clearly the doctrine of the virginal birth of Jesus [in the Latin: *factum ipsum virginalis conceptionis Iesu*], which is so supremely in accord with the mystery of the Incarnation. No further occasion shall be given of denying this truth—contrary to the tradition of the Church in reliance on Sacred Scripture—retaining only a symbolic meaning, merely indicating for instance the gift inspired by pure grace, which God bestowed on us in his Son' (translation by Kevin Smyth in the *Supplement to the New Catechism*, London, 1970, p. 24).

Finally, instead of the two paragraphs 'Jesus is the climax of all the promises . . . from God; from the Most High' (printed out above), a new text is put forward in which it is clearly stated that 'Jesus was not procreated by the intervention of man'. The full text (too lengthy to reprint here) is given on pp. 24–6 of the *Supplement*.

A LITERARY ANALYSIS OF JOHN 2:1–11

A number of writers have suggested that in Jn 2:1–11 it is possible to discern (and therefore to separate) a source used by the evangelist, and the evangelist's own insertions. A. Smitmans, *Das Weinwunder von Kana*, pp. 6–8, gives a good summary of the main suggestions.

M. Dibelius, *Die Formgeschichte des Evangeliums*, 4th ed., Tübingen, 1961, p. 98, thinks that v. 4*b*, at least part of v. 5, and v. 11 were added by the evangelist. K. L. Schmidt, 'Der johanneische Charakter der Erzählung vom Hochzeitswunder in Kana', in *Harnack-Ehrung*, Leipzig, 1921, pp. 32–43, holds a similar view: vv. 3, 4 and 11 betray the touch of the evangelist (pp. 37–8).

R. Bultmann, in *The Gospel of John*, pp. 113–15 and 118, argues that the whole of v. 11 could not have been inserted by the evangelist, because 11*a* contains the statement that this was the beginning of Jesus' signs (*cf.* Jn 4:54), and must therefore come from the *Semeia-Quelle*. The additions by the evangelist are (*a*) the mention of 'the third day' in v. 1; (*b*) the characteristically Johannine comment in 9*b* ('and he did not know where it came from, but the waiters knew, they who had drawn the water'); (*c*) the main part of v. 11 ('and he manifested his glory . . .'). Bultmann mentions as another possibility that the references to the disciples in vv. 2, 11 and 12 may be due to a later editor (the disciples being mentioned instead of the brothers in vv. 2 and 11, and along with them in v. 12). It is strange that Bultmann does not see any Johannine addition in vv. 4–5.

R. J. Dillon, 'Wisdom Literature and Sacramental Retrospect in the Cana Account', *CBQ* 24 (1962), pp. 268–96, thinks that under Jn 2:1–11 there lies an older source, going back to John the son of Zebedee, which was very similar to the Synoptic miracle-stories; and that the reference to 'the third day' (v. 1), and vv. 4–5, were added by the evangelist.

R. Schnackenburg, *The Gospel according to St John I*, p. 324, thinks that the mention of Jesus' hour in v. 4 and the second half of v. 11 betray the hand of the evangelist, but otherwise does not commit himself to firm statements about editorial insertions, on the ground that evidence is lacking. R. E. Brown, *The Gospel according to John I*, pp. 101–3, does not commit himself at all.

The most interesting point about these various suggestions is the degree to which they coincide in their judgment about what was added by the evangelist. Moreover, *before* looking at these authors, I myself attempted an analysis of the pericope, using as guides only the fifty positive *literary* characteristics given in F.-M. Braun, *Jean le Théologien I*, pp. 401–3, and the references to this passage in E. A. Abbott's *Johannine Vocabulary* and *Johannine Grammar*. Anything which contained a *positive* indication of the evangelist's style was eliminated, and the result (reached on purely literary grounds) was the following passage, which I suggest was the original version of the Cana-story used by the evangelist.

(1)   γάμος ἐγένετο ἐν Κανὰ τῆς Γαλιλαίας,
      καὶ ἦν ἡ μήτηρ τοῦ Ἰησοῦ ἐκεῖ.

(2)   ἐκλήθη δὲ καὶ ὁ Ἰησοῦς
      καὶ οἱ μαθηταὶ αὐτοῦ εἰς τὸν γάμον.

(3)   καὶ ὑστερήσαντος οἴνου
      λέγει ἡ μήτηρ τοῦ Ἰησοῦ πρὸς αὐτόν,
      Οἶνον οὐκ ἔχουσιν.

(6)   ἦσαν δὲ ἐκεῖ λίθιναι ὑδρίαι ἕξ
      κατὰ τὸν καθαρισμὸν τῶν Ἰουδαίων κείμεναι,
      χωροῦσαι ἀνὰ μετρητὰς δύο ἢ τρεῖς.

(7)   [καὶ] λέγει [τοῖς διακόνοις] ὁ Ἰησοῦς,
      Γεμίσατε τὰς ὑδρίας ὕδατος.
      καὶ ἐγέμισαν αὐτὰς ἕως ἄνω.

(8)   καὶ λέγει αὐτοῖς,
      Ἀντλήσατε νῦν καὶ φέρετε τῷ ἀρχιτρικλίνῳ.
      οἱ δὲ ἤνεγκαν.

(9)   ὡς δὲ ἐγεύσατο ὁ ἀρχιτρίκλινος
      τὸ ὕδωρ
      φωνεῖ τὸν νυμφίον

(10) καὶ λέγει αὐτῷ,
      Πᾶς ἄνθρωπος πρῶτον τὸν καλὸν οἶνον τίθησιν,
      καὶ ὅταν μεθυσθῶσιν τὸν ἐλάσσω.
      σὺ [δὲ] τετήρηκας τὸν καλὸν οἶνον ἕως [νῦν].

(11) Ταύτην ἐποίησεν ἀρχὴν τῶν σημείων ὁ Ἰησοῦς
      ἐν Κανὰ τῆς Γαλιλαίας.

In this reconstruction, I have allowed a possible insertion of καί in v. 7, and of δέ in v. 10, because asyndeton is so characteristic of John. I have also substituted τοῖς διακόνοις for αὐτοῖς in v. 7 (this is necessary if one omits vv. 4–5), and allowed a possible substitution of νῦν for ἄρτι in v. 10, because the latter word is relatively frequent in John (seven times in Mt, never in Mk or Lk, twelve times in Jn). If these minimal retouches are allowed, then the story as reconstructed contains not a single word or turn of phrase which can, even remotely, be regarded as typical of the evangelist's Greek style. And even without them, the story is virtually devoid of Johannine characteristics (there are just two instances of asyndeton, and the choice of the word ἄρτι).

Here is, in fact, an unadorned miracle-story of the type found in the Synoptics. It can very easily be translated word for word into Aramaic, and there is no reason why it should not represent a tradition handed down, in Aramaic, by John the son of Zebedee. This, I suggest, was more or less the original story taken by the evangelist from his *Semeia-Quelle*.

If we now consider the phrases which have been eliminated, we find that they are full of distinctively Johannine expressions. (In the following list, JV and JG followed by §—denote a reference to E. A. Abbott's *Johannine Vocabulary* or *Johannine Grammar*, with its section.)

(i) v. 1: τῇ ἡμέρᾳ τῇ τρίτῃ.

(a) The reduplication of the article after the noun and before the adjective is mainly a Johannine usage, employed as a rule to stress the adjective (JG §§1982–6).

(b) This must be an insertion by the evangelist unless the entire section from 1:19 on is held to be taken from an earlier source (see 1:29, 35, 43)—a theory which no one would hold.

(c) The duplication of the article may be intended as a clue to a latent meaning. Such a clue to a latent allusion would be entirely in the manner of the evangelist (JG §1985); and as the argument of Part III, Chapter 4, shows, the story of Cana seems to be devised to direct the reader's attention forward, to that event (the Resurrection) of which Cana is but a 'sign'.

(ii) v. 4: '. . . woman? My hour is not yet come.'

(a) Only here and in 19:26 does Jesus address Mary as 'Woman'.

(b) οὔπω occurs twice in Mt, five times in Mk, once in Lk, and thirteen times in Jn. It is used of Jesus' hour in 7:30 and 8:20, of his 'time' in 7:6, and of his Ascension in 20:17. In all these texts it is said that his hour, etc. has not yet come. Contrast 13:1 and 17:1, where his hour has come. The reference is therefore typically Johannine: see JV §§1719, 1728.

(c) 'my hour': a characteristically Johannine term.

(iii) v. 5: 'His mother said . . . Whatever he may say to you . . .'

(a) This verse begins with asyndeton (JG §§1996 ff.)

(b) (ἐ)άν τις is a characteristically Johannine construction. It occurs twenty-four times in the Fourth Gospel, four times in 1 Jn, nineteen times altogether in the three Synoptics, and only twice in the rest of the New Testament (Braun, *Jean le Théologien I*, p. 401, n. 3).

(iv) v. 9: '. . . that had become wine, and knew not whence it came, but the waiters knew, they who had drawn the water'

(a) γεγενημένον: the use of a perfect participle for a very recent happening is typical of John (JG §2507).

(b) It is also typical of John to let the reader into the secret in two words, while outside this rapid parenthesis the head waiter talks in twenty. Compare 2:21: 'He was speaking of the temple of his body'. See further JG §§2016–18.

(c) '. . . and *knew* not whence it came, but the waiters *knew* . . .' The word-order puts the two verbs in chiasmus, one of the evangelist's favourite structures (JG §§2554–7).

(d) '. . . they who had drawn the water': the phrase stands in apposition, but is probably corrective, meaning 'Well, not exactly *all* the waiters, only those who had drawn the water'. For a similar construction with the participle see Jn 11:45, and for a very forceful corrective, 4:2. See JG §1939.

(e) 'The head waiter' is inserted at the end of v. 9 in the Greek for the sake of clarity.

(v) v. 10: νῦν or ἄρτι?

Νῦν (i.e. 'at the present time') occurs four times in Mt, three times in Mk, fourteen times in Lk and twenty-nine times in Jn, so that it might seem that the evangelist would never have changed it, had it stood in his source.

But ἄρτι (*i.e.* 'at this last moment') is even more characteristic. It occurs seven times in Mt, never in Mk or Lk, but twelve times in Jn. I suggest only that the evangelist *may* have changed the word.

(vi) v. 11*b*: '. . . and manifested his glory, and his disciples believed in him'.

(*a*) The verb φανερόω is never found in Mt or Lk. It occurs once in Mk 4:22, and twice in the longer ending of Mk (16:12, 14). By contrast, it is found nine times in Jn, and nine times in 1 Jn. See JV §1716.

(*b*) 'Glory' occurs seven times in Mt, three times in Mk, thirteen times in Lk and eighteen times in Jn. The verb 'to glorify' occurs respectively four (Mt), one (Mk), nine (Lk) and twenty-three times (Jn). 'To manifest his glory' carries the hall-mark of John.

(*c*) '. . . and his disciples believed in him'. This verb occurs eleven times in Mt, fourteen times in Mk, nine times in Lk and ninety-eight times in Jn (and nine times in 1 Jn). The construction πιστεύω εἰς with the accusative occurs once in Mt (18:6), possibly once in Mk at the parallel (Mk 9:42), never in Lk, three times in Ac, three times in Paul. By contrast, it occurs thirty-four times in Jn, and three times in 1 Jn.

On the basis of the above observations, it seems very reasonable to conclude that the sentences and phrases eliminated from Jn 2:1–11 to give the hypothetical reconstruction set out above were in fact added by the evangelist.

(Some of the statistics used have been taken from R. Morgenthaler, *Statistik des neutestamentlichen Wortschatzes*, Zürich and Stuttgart, 1958, reprint of 1973. Others have been taken from *A Concordance to the Greek Testament* by W. F. Moulton and A. S. Geden, Edinburgh, 3rd ed., 1926.)

DID JESUS WALK UPON THE SURFACE
OF THE SEA?

The episode related in Mt 14:22–33; Mk 6:45–52 and Jn 6:16–21 is usually entitled 'The Walking on the Water'. We may begin by stating (*a*) that the gospels certainly say that Jesus walked ἐπὶ τῆς θαλάσσης, and (*b*) that it does seem highly improbable that he walked without sinking over the surface of the water, because this would have been a totally unnecessary interference with the laws of nature and of no benefit to anyone. There is no need to dwell on the more outdated rationalist theories such as those which suggest that Jesus walked on a reef, or on a hidden raft, or among the shallows, because they are based simply on a determination to explain away the supernatural, and not on a literary analysis of the text.

It is clear that the whole problem lies in the meaning of the phrase ἐπὶ τῆς θαλάσσης. It is usually translated '*on* the sea' and taken to mean 'on the surface of the sea'. But does it really mean this? John's account gives us the clues to start with.

Jn 6:16 says that the disciples went down ἐπὶ τὴν θάλασσαν, that is, *to* the sea (the accusative of motion towards). Jn 6:19 says: 'They see Jesus walking ἐπὶ τῆς θαλάσσης', where the phrase is in the genitive, and is therefore taken to mean 'on the surface of the sea'. But in Jn 21:1 'Jesus manifested himself once more ἐπὶ τῆς θαλάσσης τῆς Τιβεριάδος' (genitive), where the sense is quite certainly '*beside* the sea of Tiberias', for in v. 4 it is stated that Jesus was standing on the shore. Ἐπί with the genitive can therefore mean 'beside' or 'near' (as in Mk 11:4; 13;15, etc.); and therefore the phrase ἐπὶ τῆς θαλάσσης could in certain contexts mean 'beside the sea, near the sea' (but on the shore). English has a similar usage (St Anne's-on-Sea, Weston-super-Mare).

It could be objected that this is a possible meaning after a verb of standing (for example), but that ἐπί with the genitive cannot have this meaning after a verb of motion. Neither Liddell and Scott's *Greek–English Lexicon* nor Bauer's *Greek–English Lexicon of the New Testament and Other Early Christian Literature* supplies any example or parallel which would justify the rendering of περιπατοῦντα ἐπὶ τῆς θαλάσσης as 'walking beside the sea'. The normal phrase for this would be παρὰ τὴν θάλασσαν.

John, however, never uses παρά with the accusative, and his use of ἐπί with the sea could well be influenced by Hebrew or Aramaic, where the preposition 'al is frequently used to designate localities, especially those beside water (thus Brown-Driver-Briggs, *A Hebrew and English Lexicon of the Old Testament*, Oxford, 1906, pp. 755-6). Ἐπὶ τῆς θαλάσσης would be a natural translation of Hebrew or Aramaic. Secondly, the verb περιπατεῖν means as a rule 'to walk about, to walk up and down', and not 'to walk' in the sense of progression (compare E. A. Abbott, *Johannine Grammar*, §2342). Hence the Greek phrase in Jn 6:19 can very well be taken to mean 'they see Jesus walking beside the sea and getting near to the boat'.

Furthermore, the oldest manuscript containing these verses of St John's Gospel, the Papyrus Bodmer XIV = Papyrus 75, first published in 1961, reads at 6:19 ἐπὶ τὴν θάλασσαν, in the accusative, not the genitive. Though it is the only manuscript that does so, it is an excellent text, dating from A.D. 200 or thereabouts, a century older than the Codex Vaticanus or Sinaiticus; and that means twice as near to A.D. 100, and the probable date of the publication of the Fourth Gospel. *If* this is the original reading, then the obvious meaning of Jn 6:19 would be: 'They see Jesus walking *to* the sea', and approaching the boat. But however important the witness of Papyrus 75 may be, it is hardly likely that it alone has preserved the original reading of the verse, and that all the other manuscripts derive from a copy which had altered an original accusative to a genitive. It is far more probable that the scribe who copied these verses in the Bodmer Papyrus changed an original genitive into an accusative. Could it not be because he feared that if he wrote ἐπὶ τῆς θαλάσσης (in the genitive), his readers might think that Jesus walked *over the surface* of the water? The genitive was ambiguous, the accusative less likely to give the impression of walking over the surface of the sea. I would suggest that this scribe altered the text to an accusative in order to avoid this misunderstanding; and if he did, is it not likely that he was moved to make this alteration because he knew that people were beginning to interpret the story as if Jesus had walked on the water, and knew also that this was not the old, traditional interpretation in previous generations?

Other, secondary, arguments in support of this interpretation can be found in *The Clergy Review* 58 (1973), pp. 90-2, and on pp. 92-4 I have endeavoured to show that this is also the true meaning of the passage in Matthew and Mark. The most significant detail is Matthew's story of how Peter tried to walk upon the water. This might seem a devastating objection to the interpretation just proposed, but in fact it confirms it. For Peter's words are: 'Lord, if it is you, command me to come to you *upon the waters* (ἐπὶ τὰ ὕδατα)' (Mt 14:28). Surely it is significant that Matthew does not write ἐπὶ τὴν θάλασσαν or ἐπὶ τῆς θαλάσσης? He deliberately changes his wording from 'the sea' to 'the waters'. Why did he do so? The most reasonable explanation is that Matthew, having already used both ἐπὶ τὴν θάλασσαν and ἐπὶ τῆς θαλάσσης (in vv. 25 and 26) with the meaning 'beside the sea', wanted to make clear beyond all doubt that Peter was asking to walk upon the surface of the lake. In other words, Peter was asking for a stupendous nature-miracle purely for his own benefit, simply to prove that it was Jesus standing on the shore.

John's interest in the 'signs' that Jesus did is undisputed. He expressly terms the two miracles at Cana 'signs' (2:11; 4:54), and the healing of the cripple at Bethzatha is also a sign (6:2; 7:31). The feeding of the five thousand (6:14, 26), the cure of the man born blind (9:16) and the raising of Lazarus (11:47; 12:18) are also 'signs'. Most of these miracles are accompanied by a commentary, in the dialogues and discourses, which serve to unfold the meaning of the sign. Yet the walking on, or beside, the sea is nowhere referred to as a sign, and has no dialogue or discourse attached. It would seem, then, that John did not regard it as a sign, and did not intend it to be read as a miracle-story (unlike the other incidents just listed). It is simply a lesson of confidence in the Father who looks after Jesus and all who serve him.

XIII

THE IDENTITY OF THE WOMAN CLOTHED WITH THE SUN ACCORDING TO THE FATHERS

The texts mentioned below, and some others, are translated and discussed by B. Le Frois in *The Woman Clothed with the Sun*, pp. 11–61. This work, though it deals with the subject more comprehensively than any other, should be used with great caution, for the author forces the meaning of any text which will support a directly Marian interpretation of Apoc 12, and neglects or misinterprets points which tell against it: see the review by M.-E. Boismard in the *RB* 62 (1955), pp. 293–6. Those patristic texts cited by Le Frois and omitted here are texts where any allusion to Apoc 12 seems quite unjustifiable.

The following writers see in the woman clothed with the sun a figure of the Christian Church: Hippolytus, *De Christo et Antichristo* 60–1 (MG 10.780–1); Methodius, *Symposium*, *Orat.* 8, 4–7 (MG 18.144–9); Pesudo-Cyprian, *Ad Novatianum* 14 (*Corpus Scriptorum Ecclesiasticorum Latinorum*: Cyprian III, p. 64, lines 9–11); Tyconius, *Commentarius in Apocalypsim* (*Spicilegium Cassinense* III, 1 [1897], pp. 326–8); Pseudo-Augustine (possibly Gennadius of Marseilles, more probably Caesarius of Arles), *Expositio in b. Ioannis Apocalypsim*, Hom. 9 (ML 35.2434 or 2441); Primasius, *Commentariorum super Apocalypsim b. Ioannis*, *Lib. III*, *in loco* (ML 68.872–8); Andrew of Caesarea, *Commentarius in Apocalypsim*, cap. 33–5 (MG 106.319–32); Bede, *Explanatio Apocalypsis* (ML 93.165–9).

Victorinus of Pettau (*d.* around A.D. 304) was the author of the first Latin commentary on the Apocalypse, which has survived in four different forms, one of which is a version extensively revised and corrected by Jerome. Jerome, however, made only minor alterations to the commentary on Chapter 12 (mostly verbal changes), and must therefore be considered to have shared the views of Victorinus on this passage. There is a critical edition of the work in the *Corpus Scriptorum Ecclesiasticorum Latinorum* 49, where we read on p. 106: 'Mulier autem amicta sole . . . parturiens in doloribus suis: ecclesia est antiqua patrum et prophetarum et sanctorum apostolorum'. Jerome's virtually identical text is given on p. 107, and the passage can be found in ML 5.336 A.

Augustine writes (*Enarrationes in Psalmos: In Ps.* 142, 3): 'Haec autem mulier antiqua est civitas Dei . . . amicta erat sole, et gestabat visceribus masculum paritura. Idem ipse erat condens Sion et nascens in Sion' (*CC* 40.2061 = ML 37.1846). By the 'City of God' Augustine always means the people of God both of the Old and of the New Testaments.

Epiphanius, however (*Haer.* 78,11: MG 42.716 C), and Andrew of Caesarea (*Commentarius in Apocalypsim* 33: MG 106.319) both record that 'some people' identified the woman clothed with the sun as Mary the mother of Jesus; but they do not say who these people were. The most one can say is that the opinion was known in the fourth century. In the sixth century, Oecumenius made the identification openly (*The Complete Commentary of Oecumenius on the Apocalypse*, edited by H. C. Hoskier, Ann Arbor, 1928, pp. 135–7), as did the Pseudo-Epiphanius in the seventh (*Hom. 5 in Laudes B.V.M.*: MG 43.493 CD). It should be noted, however, that these writers do not positively exclude any reference to the Church (though there may have been little room for it in their exegesis).

Le Frois argues (*The Woman Clothed with the Sun*, pp. 49–50) that Hippolytus (*De Christo et Antichristo* 61: MG 10.780–1) must have had Mary in mind as well as the Church because he there speaks of 'the male and perfect Christ, son of God and son of man'. Le Frois further argues that Augustine also must have had Mary in mind in his sermon on Ps 142 (see above), especially as his disciple and close friend, Quodvultdeus, expressly makes the identification: 'mulierem illam virginem Mariam significasse, quae caput nostrum integra integrum peperit, quae etiam ipsa figuram in se sanctae Ecclesiae demonstravit' (*De Symbolo* 3: ML 40.661). Cassiodorus (*Complexiones in Apocalypsim* 7: ML 70.1411) very probably had the double reference in mind: see Le Frois, pp. 53–4.

Two further writers may be mentioned, both of whom held that the woman was a symbol both of Mary and the Church: Ambrosius Autpertus (d. 784), *In Apocalypsim, Lib. 5* (*Maxima Bibliotheca Veterum Patrum*, Lyons, 1577, pp. 530–2) and Alcuin (735–804), *Commentarius in Apocalypsim 5* (ML 100.1152–3).

BIBLIOGRAPHY

BIBLICAL commentaries are not listed, nor is there any attempt to be complete. The list is restricted to important books or articles in which further information may be found.

THE MOTHER OF JESUS IN THE
NEW TESTAMENT
(General works)

P. GAECHTER, *Maria im Erdenleben: Neutestamentliche Marienstudien*, Innsbruck, Vienna and Munich, 2nd ed., 1954.

J. GALOT, *Marie dans l'Evangile* (= Museum Lessianum: Section théologique, n. 53), Paris and Louvain, 1958 = *Mary in the Gospel*, Westminster (Maryland), 1965.

L. DEISS, *Marie, Fille de Sion*, Paris, 1959.

E. E. MAY, 'The Problems of a Biblical Mariology', *Marian Studies* 11 (1960), pp. 21–59.

B. ROUX, 'Bilan de l'Ecriture au point de vue protestant', *BSFEM* 20 (1963), pp. 39–63.

H. A. OBERMAN, 'The Virgin Mary in Evangelical Perspective', *Journal of Ecumenical Studies* 1 (1964), pp. 271–98 = 'Schrift und Gottesdienst. Die Jungfrau Maria in evangelischer Sicht', *Kerygma und Dogma* 10 (1964), pp. 219–45.

Maria in Sacra Scriptura (*Acta Congressus Mariologici–Mariani in Republica Dominicana anno 1965 celebrati*), 6 vols., Rome, 1967. (Contents in *NRT* 91 [1969], pp. 992–4, by J. Galot.)

H. RÄISÄNEN, *Die Mutter Jesu im Neuen Testament* (= Annales Academiae Scientiarum Fennicae, Series B, n. 158), Helsinki, 1969.

INTRODUCTION: ON SCRIPTURE AND
TRADITION

On the relationship between Scripture and Tradition in general:

J. B. FRANZELIN, *Tractatus de divina Traditione et Scriptura*, Rome, 1870; 4th (final) ed., Rome, 1896.

J. RANFT, *Der Ursprung des katholischen Traditionsprinzip*, Würzburg, 1931.

P. LENGSFELD, *Ueberlieferung. Tradition und Schrift in der evangelischen und katholischen Theologie der Gegenwart*, Paderborn, 1960.

J. BETZ and H. FRIES (ed.), *Kirche und Ueberlieferung* (= Festgabe für J. R. Geiselmann), Freiburg-im-Br., 1960.

J. P. MACKEY, *The Modern Theology of Tradition*, London, 1962.

G. MORAN, *Scripture and Tradition: A Survey of the Controversy*, New York, 1963.

C. BALIC (ed.), *De Scriptura et Traditione*, Rome, 1963.

Y. M.-J. CONGAR, *La Tradition et les Traditions: I, Essai historique*, Paris, 1960; *II, Essai théologique*, Paris, 1963 = *Tradition and Traditions: An historical and a theological essay*, London, 1966 (in one volume).

K. RAHNER and J. RATZINGER, *Revelation and Tradition* (= Quaestiones Disputatae, n. 17), London, 1966.

On oral tradition in particular:

J. BEUMER, *Die mündliche Ueberlieferung als Glaubensquelle* (= Handbuch der Dogmengeschichte, ed. by M. Schmaus and others, vol. 1, Fasc. 4), Freiburg-im-Br., Basel and Vienna, 1962.

M. SCHMAUS, *Die mündliche Ueberlieferung. Beiträge zum Begriff der Tradition*, Munich, 1957 (three essays by H. BACHT, H. FRIES and J. R. GEISELMANN: see below under Marian doctrines, Newman and Trent).

On medieval theology:

P. DE VOOGHT, *Les sources de la doctrine chrétienne d'après les théologiens du 14e siècle et du début du 15e avec le texte intégral des douze premières questions de la 'Summa' inédite de Gérard de Bologne* (+ 1317), Paris, 1954.

——, 'Le rapport Ecriture-Tradition d'après s. Thomas d'Aquin et les théologiens du 13e siècle', *Istina* 9 (1961-2), pp. 499–510.

——, 'L'évolution du rapport Eglise-Ecriture du 13e au 14e siècle', *ETL* 38 (1962), pp. 72–85.

A. FRIES, 'Zum theologischen Beweis des Hochscholastik', *Schrift und Tradition* (= Mariologische Studien 1), Essen, 1962, pp. 107–90.

B. DECKER, 'Schriftprinzip und Ergänzungstradition in der Theologie des hl. Thomas von Aquin', *ibid.*, pp. 191–221.

M. D. KÖSTER, 'Das Schriftzeugnis in der Mariologie des Thomas von Aquin', *Heilige Schrift und Maria* (= Mariologische Studien 2), Essen, 1963, pp. 80–94.

A. FRIES, 'Zur Verwertung und Erklärung der Schrift in der "Mariologie" Alberts des Grossen', *ibid.*, pp. 53–79.

On the Fourth Session of the Council of Trent:

J. DRIEDO, *De ecclesiasticis scripturis et dogmatibus libri quattuor*, Louvain, 1533: Lib. IV, cap. 4–5 (= f. CCLXXIX verso to CCCXI verso).

E. ORTIGUES, 'Ecriture et Traditions apostoliques au Concile de Trente', *RSR* 36 (1949), pp. 271–99.

G. H. TAVARD, *Holy Writ or Holy Church: The Crisis of the Protestant Reformation*, London, 1959.

H. HOLSTEIN, 'La Tradition d'après le Concile de Trente', *RSR* 47 (1959), pp. 367–90.

H. LENNERZ, 'Scriptura sola?' (in German), *Gregorianum* 40 (1959), pp. 38–53.

——, 'Sine scripto traditiones' (in Latin), *Gregorianum* 40 (1959), pp. 624–35.

——, Scriptura et traditio in decreto 4ae sessionis Concilii Tridentini', *Gregorianum* 42 (1961), pp. 517–22.

——, (the above three articles reprinted) in *Schrift und Tradition* (Mariologische Studien 1), pp. 39–67.

J. BEUMER, 'Der Begriff "traditiones" auf dem Trienter Konzil im Lichte der mittelalterlichen Kanonistik', *Scholastik* 35 (1960), pp. 342–62.

A. SPINDELER, 'Pari pietatis affectu: Das Tridentinum über die Heilige Schrift und apostolische Ueberlieferungen', *Schrift und Tradition* (Mariologische Studien 1), pp. 68–84.

N. HENS, 'Was sagt der vorliegende Text der IV. Sitzung des Tridentinischen Konzils über das Verhältnis von Schrift und Tradition?— Eine philogische Erklärung', *ibid.*, pp. 85–8.

J. R. GEISELMANN, *Die Heilige Schrift und die Tradition* (= Quaestiones Disputatae, n. 18), Freiburg-im-Br., Basel and Vienna, 1962. This is the most important work of all on the subject, and it is unfortunate that the English edition of the book, entitled *The Meaning of Tradition* (Quaestiones Disputatae, n. 18), London, 1966, omits nearly two-thirds of the original German, including its scholarly discussion of the text of Trent.

——, 'Das Konzil von Trient über das Verhältnis der Heiligen Schrift und der nicht geschriebenen Traditionen. Sein Missverständnis in der nachtridentinischen Theologie und die Ueberwindung dieses Missverständnisses', *Die mündliche Ueberlieferung*, pp. 123–206.

H. HOLSTEIN, 'Les "Deux Sources" de la Révélation', *RSR* 57 (1969), pp. 375–434.

On post-Tridentine theology:

U. HORST, 'Das Verhältnis von Schrift und Tradition nach Melchior Cano', *Trierer Theologische Zeitschrift* 69 (1960), pp. 207–23.

J. BEUMER, 'Die Frage nach Schrift und Tradition bei Robert Bellarmin', *Scholastik* 34 (1959), pp. 1–19.

T. LYNCH, 'The Newman–Perrone Paper on Development', *Gregorianum* 16 (1935), pp. 402–47.

G. BIEMER, *Ueberlieferung und Offenbarung: Die Lehre von der Tradition nach John Henry Newman*, Freiburg-im-Br., 1961.

N. SCHIFFERS, 'Schrift und Tradition bei John Henry Newman', *Schrift und Tradition* (Mariologische Studien 1), pp. 250–66.

H. FRIES, 'J. H. Newmans Beitrag zum Verständnis des Tradition', *Die mündliche Ueberlieferung*, pp. 62–122.

H. J. BROSCH, 'Zum Traditionsbegriff in der Theologie des 19. Jahrhunderts bei nichtdeutschen Theologen', *Schrift und Tradition* (Mariologische Studien 1), pp. 232–49.

W. KASPER, *Die Lehre von der Tradition in der römischen Schule (Giovanni Perrone, Carlo Passaglia, Clemens Schrader)*, Freiburg-im-Br., 1962.

K. WITTKEMPER, 'Scheebens Lehre über das Verhältnist von Schrift und Tradition', *Schrift und Tradition* (Mariologische Studien 1), pp. 267–80.

On the relevance of this question to Marian doctrines:

H. RONDET, 'La définibilité de l'Assomption: Questions de méthode', *BSFEM* 6 (1948), pp. 59–95.

B. ALTANER, 'Zur Frage der Definibilität der Assumptio B.M.V.', *Theologische Revue* 44 (1948), col. 129–40; 45 (1949), col. 129–42; 46 (1950), col. 5–20.

G. FILOGRASSI, 'Traditio divino-apostolica et Assumptio B.V.M.', *Gregorianum* 30 (1949), pp. 443–89.

——, 'Theologia catholica et Assumptio B.V.M.', *Gregorianum* 31 (1950), pp. 323–60.

J. BEUMER, 'Heilige Schrift und kirchliche Lehrautorität', *Scholastik* 25 (1950), pp. 40–72.

H. M. KÖSTER, 'Das theologische Gewissen und die marianische Frage: Beobachtungen und Bemerkungen', *Theologie und Glaube* 40 (1950), pp. 393–422.

J. R. GEISELMANN, 'Am Vorabend des feierlichen Dogmatisierung der leiblichen Aufnahme Mariens in den Himmel', *Geist und Leben* 23 (1950), pp. 321–36.

E. SCHLINK, G. BORNKAMM, P. BRUNNER, H. VON CAMPENHAUSEN and W. JOEST, *Evangelisches Gutachten zur Dogmatisierung der leiblichen*

Himmelfahrt Mariëns, Munich, 1950 (= *Theologische Literaturzeitung* 75 (1950), col. 577–86).

FR. HEILER, *Das neue Mariendogma im Lichte der Geschichte und im Urteil der Oekumene*, Munich and Basel, 1951.

H. E. W. TURNER, 'The Assumption of the Blessed Virgin Mary', *Theology* 54 (1951), pp. 63–70.

O. SEMMELROTH, *Das neue Dogma im Widerstreit*, Würzburg, 1951.

H. M. KÖSTER, 'Grundfragen der theologischen Erkenntnislehre, zur Kontroverse um das neue Dogma', *Theologie und Glaube* 42 (1952), pp. 248–62.

H. BACHT, 'Tradition und Lehramt in der Diskussion um das Assumpta-Dogma', *Die mündliche Ueberlieferung*, pp. 1–62.

G. SOLL, 'Die Anfänge mariologischer Tradition. Beitrag zur Geschichte der Marienlehre', *Kirche und Ueberlieferung* (Festgabe für J. R. Geiselmann), pp. 35–51.

H. M. KÖSTER, 'Der Stand der Frage über das Verhältnis von Schrift und Tradition unter Berücksichtigung der Mariologie', *Schrift und Tradition* (Mariologische Studien 1), pp. 11–36.

K. SCHWERDT, 'Der Schriftbeweis in den marianischen Lehrschreiben des Päpste seit Pius IX', *Heilige Schrift und Maria* (Mariologische Studien 2), pp. 95–141.

——, 'Die Stellung des Schriftargumentes in den mariologischen Lehrschreiben der Päpste', *ibid.*, pp. 142–8.

K. WITTKEMPER, 'Die Verwendung der Heiligen Schrift in der Mariologie bei M. J. Scheeben', *ibid.*, pp. 149–65.

H. M. KÖSTER, 'Die Rolle der Bibel im Marienverständnis des neueren deutschen Protestantismus', *ibid.*, pp. 166–260 (with an excellent bibliography).

G. A. F. KNIGHT, 'The Protestant World and Mariology', *Scottish Journal of Theology* 19 (1966), pp. 55–73.

On the decree of the Second Vatican Council:

O. SEMMELROTH and M. ZERWICK, *Vatikanum II über das Wort Gottes* (= Stuttgarter Bibelstudien, n. 16), Stuttgart, 1966.

E. STAKEMEIER, *Die Konzils-Konstitution über die göttliche Offenbarung*, Paderborn, 1966.

J. RATZINGER, A. GRILLMEIER and B. RIGAUX, 'The Dogmatic Constitution on Divine Revelation', *Commentary on the Documents of Vatican II*, vol. 3, London, 1969, pp. 155–272 (German original published in 1967).

B.-D. DUPUY (ed.), *La Révélation divine* (Collection: Unam Sanctam, n. 70), 2 vols., Paris, 1968.

L. A. SCHÖKEL (ed.), *Comentarios a la constitución Dei Verbum*, Madrid, 1969.

PART I
MOTHER OF THE SAVIOUR
(*Luke* 1–2)

General works covering both chapters:

E. BURROWS, *The Gospel of the Infancy and Other Biblical Essays*, ed. by E. F. SUTCLIFFE (*cf.* pp. 1–58 'The Form of Luke Chapters 1 and 2'), London, 1940.

H. SAHLIN, *Der Messias und das Gottesvolk. Studien zur protolukanischen Theologie*, Uppsala, 1945.

R. LAURENTIN, *Structure et théologie de Luc I–II* (*Etudes bibliques*), Paris, 1957 (with a long bibliography of 500 items).

S. MUNOZ IGLESIAS, 'El Evangelio de la Infancia en San Lucas y las infancias de los héroes biblicos', *Estudios Biblicos* 16 (1957), pp. 329–82.

M. D. GOULDER and M. L. SANDERSON, 'St Luke's Genesis', *JTS* (New Series) 8 (1957), pp. 12–30.

R. J. DILLON, 'St Luke's Infancy Account', *The Dunwoodie Review* 1 (1961), pp. 5–37.

A. GEORGE, 'Le parallèle entre Jean-Baptiste et Jésus en Luc 1–2', *Mélanges Bibliques en hommage au R. P. Béda Rigaux*, Gembloux, 1970, pp. 147–71.

1 THE AUTHOR AND THE SOURCES OF LUKE 1–2

P. WINTER, 'Two Notes on Lk 1–2 with regard to the Theory of "imitation Hebraisms" (1:78; 2:13)', *Studia Theologica* 7 (1953), pp. 158–65.

——, 'Some Observations on the Language in the Birth and Infancy Stories of the Third Gospel', *NTS* 1 [1954–5], pp. 111–21.

——, 'Magnificat and Benedictus, Maccabean Psalms?', *Bulletin of the John Rylands Library* 37 (1954), pp. 328–47 (French translation in the *Revue d'Histoire et de Philosophie Religieuse* 36 [1956], pp. 1–19).

——, 'The Cultural Background of the Narrative in Luke 1 and 2', *Jewish Quarterly Review* 45 (1954–5), pp. 159–67, 230–42.

N. TURNER, 'The Relationship of Luke 1 and 2 to Hebraic Sources and to the Rest of Luke and Acts', *NTS* 2 (1955–6), pp. 100–9 (a reply to P. Winter's article in *NTS* 1 [1954–5], pp. 111–21).

P. WINTER, 'On Luke and Lucan Sources', *ZNW* 47 (1956), pp. 217–42 (a counter-reply to N. Turner).

——, '"Nazareth" and "Jerusalem" in Luke 1 and 2', *NTS* 3 (1956–7), pp. 136–42.

P. BENOIT, 'L'enfance de Jean-Baptiste selon Luc 1', *NTS* 3 (1956–7), pp. 169–94.

P. WINTER, 'The Proto-Source of Luke 1', *Novum Testamentum* 1 (1956), pp. 184–99.

R. LAURENTIN, 'Traces d'allusions étymologiques en Luc 1–2', *Biblica* 37 (1956), pp. 435–56; 38 (1957), pp. 1–23.

P. WINTER, 'Lukanische Miszellen', *ZNW* 49 (1958), pp. 65–77.

——, 'The Main Literary Problem of the Lucan Infancy Story', *Vox Theologica* (Assen) 28 (1957), pp. 117–22 = *Anglican Theological Review* 40 (1958), pp. 257–64.

——, 'On the Margin of Luke 1–2', *Studia Theologica* 12 (1958), pp. 103–7.

A. R. C. LEANEY, 'The Birth Narratives in St Luke and St Matthew', *NTS* 8 (1961–2), pp. 158–66.

H. H. OLIVER, 'The Lucan Birth Stories and the Purpose of Luke-Acts', *NTS* 10 (1964–5), pp. 202–26.

P. S. MINEAR, 'Luke's Use of the Birth Stories', *Studies in Luke-Acts. Essays Presented in honour of Paul Schubert*, ed. by L. E. KECK and J. L. MARTYN, Nashville, New York, 1966, pp. 111–30.

J. SCHNIEWIND, *Die Parallelperikopen bei Lukas und Johannes*, 1914 (reprinted, Hildesheim, 1958).

J. A. BAILEY, *The Traditions Common to the Gospels of Luke and John*, Leiden, 1963.

2   THE LITERARY FORM OF THE LUCAN INFANCY GOSPEL

S. HOROVITZ, 'Midrash', in *The Jewish Encyclopaedia*, vol. 8, New York and London, 1904, pp. 548–50.

J. THEODORE, 'Midrash Haggadah', *ibid.*, pp. 550–69.

J. S. LAUTERBACH, 'Midrash Halakah', *ibid.*, pp. 569–72.

J. W. DOEVE, *Jewish Hermeneutics in the Synoptic Gospels and Acts*, Assen, 1954.

R. BLOCH, 'Midrash', *DBS* 5, cc. 1263–81.

——, 'Ecriture et tradition dans le judaïsme. Aperçus sur l'origine du midrash', *Cahiers Sioniens* 8 (1954), pp. 9–34.

——, 'Ezéchiel 16: exemple parfait du procédé midrashique dans la Bible', *Cahiers Sioniens* 9 (1955), pp. 193–223.

G. VERMES, *Scripture and Tradition in Judaism*, Leiden, 1961, pp. 127–77 (Midrash in the Old Testament).

S. SANDMEL, 'The Haggada within Scripture', *Journal of Biblical Literature* 80 (1961), pp. 105–22.

M. GERTNER, 'Midrashim in the New Testament', *Journal of Semitic Studies* 7 (1962), pp. 267–92.

——, 'Terms of Scriptural Interpretation: A Study in Hebrew Semantics', *Bulletin of the School of Oriental and African Studies* (London) 25 (1962), pp. 1–27 (on *midrash* and *darash*).

A. G. WRIGHT, 'The Literary Genre Midrash', *CBQ* 28 (1966), pp. 105–38 and 417–57 (also published in book form, Staten Island, New York, 1967).

C. PERROT, 'Les recits d'enfance dans la Haggada', *RSR* 55 (1967), pp. 481–518.

R. LE DEAUT, 'A propos d'une définition du midrash', *Biblica* 50 (1969), pp. 395–413 (review of A. G. WRIGHT).

3 OLD TESTAMENT THEMES IN LUKE 1–2

On the Messiah, the ideal king:

M.-J. LAGRANGE, *Le messianisme chez les juifs* (Etudes bibliques), Paris, 1909.

S. MOWINCKEL, 'Die Königsherrschaft (das Reich) Jahwä's', *Psalmenstudien II*, Kristiania [Oslo], 1922, reprinted Amsterdam 1961, 1966, pp. 146–88.

H. GRESSMANN, *Der Messias*, Göttingen, 1929.

I. ENGNELL, *Studies in Divine Kingship in the Ancient Near East*, Uppsala, 1943.

H. GROSS, *Weltherrschaft als religiöse Idee im Alten Testament* (Bonner Biblische Beiträge, n. 6), Bonn, 1953.

L. CERFAUX, J. COPPENS *et al.*, *L'attente du Messie*, Bruges, 1954.

A. BENTZEN, *King and Messiah*, London, 1955.

A. R. JOHNSON, *Sacral Kingship in Ancient Israel*, Cardiff, 1955; 2nd ed., 1967.

J. KLAUSNER, *The Messianic Idea in Israel from its Beginning to the Completion of the Mishnah*, London and New York, 1955.

G. WIDENGREN, *Sakrales Königtum im Alten Testament und im Judentum*, Stuttgart, 1955.

S. MOWINCKEL. *He That Cometh*, Oxford, 1956 (probably the best and clearest presentation of all).

H. RINGGREN, *The Messiah in the Old Testament* (Studies in Biblical Theology, n. 18), London, 1956.

G. FOHRER, *Messiasfrage und Bibelverständnis*, Tübingen, 1957.

S. H. HOOKE (ed.), *Myth, Ritual and Kingship*, Oxford, 1958.

E. O. JAMES, *Myth and Ritual in the Ancient Near East*, London, 1958.

J. LINDBLOM, *A Study on the Immanuel Section in Isaiah: Is 7:1–9: 6* (Scripta Minora Regiae Societatis Humaniorum Litterarum Lundensis 1957–8, n. 4), Lund, 1958.

P. LAMARCHE, *Zacharie 9–14: Structure littéraire et messianisme* (*Etudes bibliques*), Paris, 1961.

E. MASSAUX et al., *La venue du Messie: Messianisme et eschatologie*, Bruges, 1962.

M. REHM, *Der königliche Messias im Lichte der Immanuel-Weissagungen des Buches Jesaja* (Eichstätter Studien, N.F. 1), Kevelaer/Rheinland, 1968.

On the idea of universal and unending peace:

W. EICHRODT, *Die Hoffnung des ewigen Friedens im alten Israel* (Beiträge zur Förderung christlicher Theologie, n. 25, 3), Gütersloh, 1920.

H. GROSS, *Die Idee des ewigen und allgemeinen Weltfriedens im Alten Orient und im Alten Testament* (Trierer Theologische Studien, n. 7), Trier, 1956.

J. J. STAMM and H. BIETENHARD, *Der Weltfriede im Alten und Neuen Testament*, Zürich, 1959.

J. SCHREINER, 'Segen für die Völker in der Verheissung an die Väter', *Biblische Zeitschrift* (N.F.) 6 (1962), pp. 1–31.

H. W. WOLFF, *Frieden ohne Ende: Jesaja 7:1–17 und 9:1–6 ausgelegt* (= Biblische Studien, n. 35), Neukirchen, 1962.

On the coming of the Son of Man:

S. MOWINCKEL, *He That Cometh*, pp. 346–450.

M. D. HOOKER, *The Son of Man in Mark*, London, 1967, pp. 11–74.

C. COLPE, in the *TWNT* 8 (1969), pp. 403–81.

(All three contain extensive bibliographies.)

On the Day of Yahweh:

J. BOURKE, 'Le jour de Yahweh dans Joël', *RB* 66 (1959), pp. 5–31, 191–212 (much wider than Joel).

G. W. BUCHANAN, 'Eschatology and the "End of Days"', *Journal of Near Eastern Studies* 20 (1961), pp. 188–93.

J. SCHREINER, 'Das Ende der Tage: Die Botschaft von der Endzeit in den atl. Schriften', *Bibel und Leben* 5 (1964), pp. 180–94.

On the Remnant of Israel:

R. DE VAUX, 'Le "reste d'Israël" d'après les prophètes', *RB* 42 (1933), pp. 526–39 = *Bible et Orient*, Paris, 1967, pp. 25–39 (English translation in *The Bible and the Ancient Near East*, London, 1971, pp. 15–30).

On the Daughter of Zion:

S. ZIMMER, *Zion als Tochter, Frau und Mutter. Personifikation von Land, Stadt und Volk in weiblicher Gestalt* (Dissertation, Munich, 1959).

J. SCHREINER, *Sion-Jerusalem, Jahwes Königssitz* (= Studien zum Alten und Neuen Testament, n. 7), Munich, 1963.

H. CAZELLES, 'Fille de Sion et théologie mariale dans la Bible', *BSFEM* 21 (1964), pp. 51–71.

G. FOHRER and E. LOHSE, in the *TWNT* 7 (1964), pp. 291–338 (especially 292–9).

4–7 (THE ANNUNCIATION TO MARY: In general)

See R. LAURENTIN, *Structure et théologie de Luc 1–2* for the literature up to 1956 (over 70 titles).

S. LYONNET, *Le recit de l'Annonciation et la maternité divine de la sainte Vierge*, Rome, 1954, re-edited in *L'Ami du clergé* 66 (1956), pp. 33–48.

J.-P. AUDET, 'L'annonce à Marie', *RB* 63 (1956), pp. 346–74.

N. HABEL, 'The Form and Significance of the Call Narratives', *Zeitschrift für alttestamentliche Wissenschaft* 77 (1965), pp. 297–323.

P. GAECHTER, 'Der Verkündigungsbericht Lk 1:26–38', *Zeitschrift für katholische Theologie* 91 (1969), pp. 322–63 and 567–86.

4 'REJOICE, O DAUGHTER OF ZION!'

S. LYONNET, '*Chaire kecharitômené*', *Biblica* 20 (1939), pp. 131–41.

A. G. HEBERT, 'The Virgin Mary as the Daughter of Zion', *Theology* 53 (1950), pp. 403 (French translation in *La Vie Spirituelle* 85 [1951], pp. 127–39).

A. STROBEL, 'Der Gruss an Maria (Lk 1:28). Eine philologische Betrachtung zu seinem Sinngehalt', *ZNW* 53 (1962), pp. 86–110.

M. CAMBE, 'La *charis* chez saint Luc. Remarques sur quelques textes, notamment le *kecharitômené*', *RB* 70 (1963), pp. 193–207.

U. HOLTZMEISTER, 'Dominus tecum (Lc 1:29)', *Verbum Domini* 23 (1943), pp. 232–7 and 257–62.

5 MOTHER OF CHRIST

A. GEORGE, 'Jésus Fils de Dieu dans l'Evangile selon saint Luc', *RB* 72 (1965), pp. 185–209.

6 ARK OF THE COVENANT

L. LEGRAND, 'L'arrière-plan néotestamentaire de Luc 1:35', *RB* 70 (1963), pp. 161–92.

7–8 No special literature

9 THE MAGNIFICAT

See R. LAURENTIN, *Structure et théologie de Luc 1–2* for the literature up to 1956 (over 90 titles).

M. LUTHER, *Mariae Lobgesang (Das Magnificat) verdeutscht und ausgelegt*, Stuttgart, 1950.

F. JACOBÉ (*vere* A. LOISY), 'L'origine du Magnificat', *Revue d'histoire et de littérature religieuse* 2 (1897), pp. 424–32.

A. VON HARNACK, 'Das Magnificat Elisabet (Luk 1:46–55) nebst einigen Bemerkungen zu Luk 1 und 2', *Sitzungsberichte der Kgl. Preussischen Akademie der Wissenschaften zu Berlin* 27 (1900), pp. 538–56, reprinted in *Studien zur Geschichte des Neuen Testaments und der alten Kirche I*, Berlin and Leipzig, 1931, pp. 62–85.

O. BARDENHEWER, 'Ist Elisabeth die Sängerin des Magnificat?', *Biblische Studien* 6 (1901), pp. 187–200.

P. LADEUZE, 'De l'origine du Magnificat et son attribution dans le troisième Evangile à Marie ou à Elisabeth', *Revue d'histoire ecclésiastique* 4 (1903), pp. 623–44.

R. LEUENBERGER, *Das Magnificat. Eine evangelische Betrachtung des Lobgesanges Maria*, Zürich, 1960.

J. T. FORESTELL, 'Old Testament Background of the Magnificat', *Marian Studies* 12 (1961), pp. 205–44.

J. G. DAVIES, 'The Ascription of the Magnificat to Mary', *JTS* (N.S.) 15 (1964), pp. 307–8.

R. SCHNACKENBURG, 'Das Magnificat, seine Spiritualität und Theologie', *Geist und Leben* 38 (1965), pp. 342–57 = *Theologisches Jahrbuch* (Leipzig) 10 (1967), pp. 124–38.

S. BENKO, 'The Magnificat—A History of the Controversy', *Journal of Biblical Literature* 86 (1967), pp. 263–75 (excellent survey of the question 'Mary or Elizabeth', but see Detached Note III).

10 THE SAVIOUR IS BORN

See R. LAURENTIN, *Structure et théologie de Luc 1–2* for the literature up to 1956.

P. WINTER, 'Lk 2:11: *Christos Kyrios* oder *Christos Kyriou?*' *ZNW* 49 (1958), pp. 67–75.

J. A. FITZMYER, 'Peace upon Earth among Men of His Good Will', *Theological Studies* 19 (1958), pp. 225–7.

K. H. RENGSTORF, 'Die Weihnachtserzählung des Evangelisten Lukas', *Stat crux dum volvitur orbis* (Festschrift für H. Lilje), Berlin, 1959, pp. 15–29.

M. B. BAILY, 'The Crib and Exegesis of Lk 2:1–20', *Irish Ecclesiastical Record* 100 (1963), pp. 359–76.

——, 'The Shepherds and the Sign of a Child in a Manger', *Irish Theological Quarterly* 31 (1964), pp. 1–22.

D. FLUSSER, 'Sanctus und Gloria', *Abraham unser Vater* (Festschrift für O. Michel), Leiden, 1963, pp. 129–52.

A. VÖGTLE, 'Die Geburt des Erlösers', *Bibel und Leben* 7 (1966), pp. 235–42.

C. H. GIBLIN, 'Reflections on the Sign of the Manger', *CBQ* 29 (1967), pp. 87–101.

L. LEGRAND, 'L'Evangile aux bergers. Essai sur le genre littéraire de Luc 2:8–20', *RB* 75 (1968), pp. 161–87.

A. VÖGTLE, 'Offene Frage zur lukanischen Geburts- und Kindheitsgeschichte', *Bibel und Leben* 11 (1970), pp. 51–67 (in particular, pp. 64–7).

P. BENOIT, 'Non erat eis locus in diversorio (Lc 2:7)', *Mélanges Bibliques en hommage au R. P. Béda Rigaux*, Gembloux, 1970, pp. 173–86.

C. WESTERMANN, 'Alttestamentliche Elemente in Lukas 2:1–20', *Tradition und Glaube* (Festgabe für K. G. Kuhn), Göttingen, 1972, pp. 317–27.

11 THE LORD COMES TO HIS TEMPLE

See R. LAURENTIN, *Structure et théologie de Luc 1–2* (up to 1956).

K. BALTZER, 'The Meaning of the Temple in the Lukan Writings', *Harvard Theological Review* 58 (1965), pp. 263–77.

12 SIMEON'S PROPHECY ABOUT THE SWORD

T. GALLUS, 'De sensu verborum Lc 2:35 eorumque momento mariologico', *Biblica* 29 (1948), pp. 220–39.

A. DE GROOT, *Die schmerzhafte Mutter und Gefährtin des göttlichen Erlösers in der Weissagung Simeons (Lk 2:35)*, Kaldenkirchen, 1956.

W. MICHAELIS, in the *TWNT* 6 (1959), pp. 995–8.

A. FEUILLET, 'L'épreuve prédite à Marie par le vieillard Siméon (Luc 2:35)', *A la rencontre de Dieu* (Mémorial Albert Gelin), Le Puy, 1961, pp. 243–64.

P. BENOIT, '"Et toi-même, un glaive te transpercera l'âme" (Luc 2:35)', *CBQ* 25 (1963), pp. 251–61.

J. WINANDY, 'La prophétie de Syméon (Lc 2:34–5)', *RB* 72 (1965), pp. 321–51.

A. CUTLER, 'Does the Simeon of Luke 2 refer to Simeon the Son of Hillel?', *Journal of Bible and Religion* 34 (1966), pp. 29–35.

A. GEORGE, 'Israel dans l'œuvre de Luc', *RB* 75 (1968), pp. 481–525.

13 THE BOY JESUS IN THE TEMPLE

P. WINTER, 'Lk 2:49 and Targum Yerushalmi', *ZNW* 45 (1954), pp. 145–79 and 46 (1955), pp. 140–1.

B. VAN IERSEL, 'The Finding of Jesus in the Temple', *Novum Testamentum* 4 (1960), pp. 161–73.

J. DUPONT, 'Luc 2:41–52: Jésus à douze ans', *Assemblées du Seigneur*, Bruges, 1961, pp. 25–43.

B. F. MEYER, 'But Mary kept all these things . . . (Lk 2:19, 51)', *CBQ* 26 (1964), pp. 31–49.

R. LAURENTIN, *Jésus au Temple: Mystère de Pâques et Foi de Marie en Luc 2:48–50 (Etudes bibliques)*, Paris, 1966 (an excellent monograph with a good bibliography).

R. PESCH, '"Kind, warum hast du so an uns getan?" (Lk 2:48)', *Biblische Zeitschrift* (N.F.) 12 (1968), pp. 245–8.

14 TRADITION AND INTERPRETATION IN LUKE 1–2

See the literature mentioned at the beginning of Part I as covering both chapters, and also that listed under Chapter 1 (Author and Sources). Add:

M. DIBELIUS, 'Jungfrauensohn und Krippenkind. Untersuchungen zur Geburtsgeschichte Jesu im Lukas-Evangelium', originally published in the *Sitzungsberichte der Heidelbergischen Akademie der Wissenschaften, Phil.-hist. Klasse 1931–32, n. 4*, reprinted in *Botschaft und Geschichte I*, Tübingen, 1953, pp. 1–78. (Probably the most important and certainly the most influential of all writings on this topic.)

R. MORGENTHALER, *Die lukanische Geschichtsschreibung als Zeugnis. Gestalt und Gehalt der Kunst des Lukas*, 2 vols., Zürich, 1949.

H. SCHÜRMANN, 'Aufbau, Eigenart und Geschichtswert der Vorgeschichte Lk 1–2', *Traditionsgeschichtliche Untersuchungen zu den synoptischen Evangelien*, Düsseldorf, 1968, pp. 198–208.

K. H. SCHELKLE, 'Die Kindheitsgeschichte Jesu', *Wort und Schrift: Beiträge zur Auslegung und Auslegungsgeschichte des Neuen Testaments*, Düsseldorf, 1966, pp. 59–75.

15 MARY THE DAUGHTER OF ZION

Note H. SAHLIN, *Der Messias und das Gottesvolk* (see above under general works covering Lk 1–2).

See also, under Chapters 4–7, and 4, the studies by S. LYONNET, A. G. HEBERT and A. STROBEL.

PART II

VIRGIN AND MOTHER
(*The Virginity of Mary in the New Testament*)

1 THE BETROTHAL OF MARY TO JOSEPH

P. GAECHTER, *Maria im Erdenleben*, pp. 79–89 (The laws and social customs), 89–92 (The age for betrothal).

P. WINTER, 'Jewish Folklore in the Matthaean Birth Story', *The Hibbert Journal* 53 (1954), pp. 34–43.

S. MUNOZ IGLESIAS, 'El génere literario del Evangelio de la Infancia en San Mateo', *Estudios Biblicos* 17 (1958), pp. 243–73.

——, 'El Evangelio de la Infancia en S. Mateo', *Sacra Pagina II* (Bibliotheca Ephemeridum Theologicarum Lovaniensium, n. 13), Paris–Gembloux, 1959, pp. 121–49.

K. STENDAHL, 'Quis et unde? (An Analysis of Mt 1–2)', *Judentum–Christentum–Kirche* (Festschrift für J. Jeremias), Berlin, 1960, pp. 94–105.

M. M. BOURKE, 'The Literary Genus of Matthew 1–2', *CBQ* 22 (1960), pp. 160–75.

C. H. CAVE, 'St Matthew's Infancy Narrative', *NTS* 9 (1962–3), pp. 382–91.

A. VÖGTLE, 'Die Genealogie Mt 1:2–16 und die matthäische Kindheitsgeschichte', *Biblische Zeitschrift* (N.F.) 8 (1964), pp. 45–58 and 239–61; 9 (1965), pp. 32–49.

2 JOSEPH THE FATHER OF JESUS

A. SALMERON, *Commentarii in Evangelicam Historiam et in Acta Apostolorum. Tom. 3: Qui de Infantia et Pueritia D.N.I.C. inscribitur*, Cologne, 1612. See *Tract. 30: Ioseph autem vir eius*, pp. 233–45.

X. LEON-DUFOUR, 'L'annonce à Joseph', *Mélanges Bibliques rédigés en l'honneur de André Robert*, Paris, 1957, pp. 390–7.

——, 'Le juste Joseph (Mt 1:18–25)', *NRT* 81 (1959), pp. 225–31.

—— (the above two articles reworked) 'L'annonce à Joseph', *Etudes d'Evangile*, Paris, 1965, pp. 65–81.

489

K. RAHNER, 'Nimm das Kind und seine Mutter' (on Mt 1:19–20), *Geist und Leben* 30 (1957), pp. 14–22.

M. KRÄMER, 'Die Menschwerdung Jesu Christi nach Matthäus (Mt 1). Sein Anliegen und sein literarisches Verfahren', *Biblica* 45 (1964), pp. 1–50.

C. SPICQ, 'Joseph, son mari, étant juste . . .', *RB* 71 (1964), pp. 206–14 (against Léon-Dufour).

A. PELLETIER, 'L'annonce à Joseph', *RSR* 54 (1966), pp. 67–8.

3–5   LUKE 1:34 (see also Chapters 12–16)

For the older literature, see B. M. METZGER (ed.), *Index to Periodical Literature on Christ and the Gospels*, Leiden, 1962, nn. 5380–94.

For a survey, see G. GRAYSTONE, *Virgin of All Virgins*, Rome, 1968, which is virtually exhaustive in its coverage of material.

J. J. COLLINS, 'Our Lady's Vow of Virginity (Lk 1:34)', *CBQ* 5 (1943), pp. 371–80.

K. RAHNER, 'Le principe fondamentale de la théologie mariale', *RSR* 42 (1954), pp. 517–22.

O. GRABER, *Die Frage Marias an den Verkündigungsengel. Eine exegetische-dogmatische Studie*, Graz, 1956.

C. P. CEROKE, 'Luke 1:34 and Mary's Virginity', *CBQ* 19 (1957), pp. 329–42.

J. GALOT, 'Vierge entre les vierges', *NRT* 79 (1957), pp. 463–77.

J. B. BAUER, '*Monstra te esse matrem, Virgo singularis!* Zur Diskussion um Lk 1:34', *Münchener Theol. Zeitschrift* 9 (1958), pp. 124–35.

M. ZERWICK, 'Quoniam virum non cognosco', *Verbum Domini* 37 (1959), pp. 212–24 and 276–88.

O. GRABER, 'Maria, die immerwährende Jungfrau (Lk 1:31–4)', *Theol.-prakt. Quartalschrift* 107 (1959), pp. 185–99.

J. GEWIESS, 'Die Marienfrage, Lk 1:34', *Biblische Zeitschrift* (N.F.) 5 (1961), pp. 221–54.

H. QUECKE, 'Lk 1:34 in den alten Uebersetzungen und im Protevangelium des Jakobus', *Biblica* 44 (1963), pp. 499–520.

——, 'Lk 1:34 im Diatessaron', *Biblica* 45 (1964), pp. 85–8.

J. B. BAUER, 'Philogische Bemerkungen zu Lk 1:34', *Biblica* 45 (1964), pp. 535–40.

H. QUECKE, 'Zur Auslegungsgeschichte von Lk 1:34', *Biblica* 47 (1966), pp. 113–14.

On the question of Mary's marriage:

J. AUER, 'Maria und das christliche Jungfräulichkeitsideal', *Geist und Leben* 23 (1950), pp. 411–25.

J. C. DIDIER, 'Le mariage de la s. Vierge dans l'histoire de la théologie', *Mélanges de Science Religieuse* (Lille) 9 (1952), pp. 135–8.

O. GRABER, 'Wollte Maria eine normale Ehe eingehen?', *Marianum* 20 (1958), pp. 1–9.

——, 'Marias Jungfräulichkeitswille vor der Engelsbotschaft', *Marianum* 22 (1960), pp. 290–304.

6–9 THE BROTHERS OF JESUS

Almost any encyclopaedia or dictionary of the Bible will contain an article on this topic, but the following five entries will supply all the information:

JEROME, *Adversus Helvidium de perpetua virginitate beatae Mariae* (ML 23.193–216).

EPIPHANIUS, *Haereses*, n. 78 (MG 42.699–740).

J. B. LIGHTFOOT, 'The Brethren of the Lord', *St Paul's Epistle to the Galatians*, 10th ed., London, 1896, pp. 252–91.

TH. ZAHN, 'Brüder und Vettern Jesu', *Forschungen zur Geschichte des ntl. Kanons und der altkirchlichen Literatur* 6, Leipzig, 1900, pp. 224–364.

J. BLINZLER, *Die Brüder und Schwestern Jesu* (Stuttgarter Bibelstudien, n. 21), Stuttgart, 1967.

10 'HE WAS BORN OF GOD

J. GALOT, *Etre né de Dieu* (*Jean 1:13*) (Analecta Biblica, n. 37), Rome, 1969 (with an excellent bibliography).

See also

M.-E. BOISMARD, 'Critique textuelle et citations bibliques', *RB* 57 (1950), pp. 388–408.

F.-M. BRAUN, ' "Qui ex Deo natus est" (Jean 1:13)', *Aux Sources de la Tradition chrétienne* (Mélanges offerts à M. Maurice Goguel), Paris, 1950, pp. 11–31.

A. HOUSSIAU, 'Le milieu théologique de la leçon *egennêthê*', *Sacra Pagina II*, pp. 169–88.

11 'BORN OF THE VIRGIN MARY'

D. EDWARDS, *The Virgin Birth in History and Faith*, London, 1943.

12–16 THE VIRGINAL CONCEPTION

H. M. KÖSTER gives an excellent bibliography comprising both books and articles, from D. Fr. Strauss to 1968, in *Jungfrauengeburt gestern und heute* (Mariologische Studien 4), Essen, 1969, on pp. 58–69 (over 300 titles).

For articles (but not books) up to 1960 or thereabouts, see B. M. METZGER, *Index to Periodical Literature on Christ and the Gospels*, nn. 8414–74.

The following are the more important books or monographs on the subject:

H. USENER, *Religionsgeschichtliche Untersuchungen: Das Weihnachtsfest*, Bonn, 1889; 2nd ed. (by H. LIETZMANN), 1911.

A. RESCH, *Die Kindheitsgeschichte unseres Herrn Jesu Christi nach Matthäus und Lucas unter Herbeiziehung der ausserkanonischen Paralleltexte quellenkritisch untersucht*, Leipzig, 1896.

L. CONRADY, *Die Quelle der kanonischen Kindheitsgeschichte Jesus': ein wissenschaftlicher Versuch*, Göttingen, 1900.

H. PETERSEN, *Die wunderbare Geburt des Heilandes*, Tübingen, 1909.

H. GRESSMANN, *Das Weihnachtsevangelium auf Ursprung und Geschichte untersucht*, Göttingen, 1914.

G. H. BOX, *The Virgin Birth of Jesus*, London, 1916.

V. TAYLOR, *The Historical Evidence for the Virgin Birth*, Oxford, 1920.

H. LEISEGANG, *Pneuma Hagion: der Ursprung des Geistbegriffs der synoptischen Evangelien aus der griechischen Mystik*, Leipzig, 1922 (pp. 14–72).

E. NORDEN, *Die Geburt des Kindes: Geschichte einer religiösen Idee*, Leipzig and Berlin, 1924.

J. G. MACHEN, *The Virgin Birth of Christ*, New York and London, 1930; 2nd ed., 1932 (reprinted, Grand Rapids, 1965, 1967).

F. KATTENBUSCH, 'Die Geburtsgeschichte Jesu als Haggada', *Theologische Studien und Kritiken* 102 (1930), pp. 454–74 (a critical review of J. G. MACHEN, and a significant monograph in its own right).

M. DIBELIUS, 'Jungfrauensohn und Krippenkind' (see above under Part I, Chapter 14).

G. ERDMANN, *Die Vorgeschichte des Lukas- und Matthäeus-Evangeliums und Virgils vierte Ekloge*, Göttingen, 1932.

D. EDWARDS, *The Virgin Birth in History and Faith*, London, 1943.

T. BOSLOOPER, *The Virgin Birth*, Philadelphia, 1962.

Among more recent articles, the following are important:

R. H. FULLER, 'The Virgin Birth: Historical Fact or Kerygmatic Truth?', *Biblical Research* 1 (1957), pp. 1–8.

T. W. O'MEARA, 'Marian Theology and the Contemporary Problem of Myth', *Marian Studies* 15 (1964), pp. 127–56.

R. SCHNACKENBURG, 'Konkrete Fragen an den Dogmatiker aus der heutigen exegetischen Diskussion', *Catholica* 21 (1967), pp. 12–27 (on the virginal conception, pp. 17–20).

A. VÖGTLE, 'Offene Frage zur lukanischen Geburts- und Kindheitsgeschichte', *Bibel und Leben* 11 (1970), pp. 51–67.

G. SCHNEIDER, 'Jesu geistgewirkte Empfängnis (Lk 1:34 f.). Zur interpretation einer christologischen Aussage', *Theol.-prakt. Quartalschrift* 119 (1971), pp. 105–16.

H. GESE, 'Natus ex virgine', *Probleme biblischer Theologie*. (Gerhard von Rad zum 70. Geburtstag), Munich, 1971, pp. 73–89.

R. E. BROWN, 'The Problem of the Virginal Conception of Jesus', *Theological Studies* 33 (1972), pp. 3–34; reprinted with a useful introductory note in *The Virginal Conception and Bodily Resurrection of Jesus*, London, Dublin and New York, 1973.

J. A. FITZMYER, 'The Virginal Conception of Jesus in the New Testament', *Theological Studies* 34 (1973), pp. 541–75.

For the whole question, see especially the two volumes published by the *Deutsche Arbeitsgemeinschaft für Mariologie*:

Jungfrauengeburt gestern und heute, ed. by H. J. BROSCH and J. HASENFUSS (= Mariologische Studien 4), Essen, 1969.

Mythos und Glaube, ed. by H. M. BROSCH and H. M. KÖSTER, (= Mariologische Studien 5), Essen, 1972.

17   THE RELIGIOUS SIGNIFICANCE OF THE VIRGINAL CONCEPTION

D. EDWARDS, *The Virgin Birth in History and Faith*, London, 1943.

K. BARTH, *Church Dogmatics*, Vol. I, Part 2, Edinburgh, 1956, pp. 172–202: 'The Miracle of Christmas.'

P. BENOIT, 'Préexistence et Incarnation', *RB* 77 (1970), pp. 5–29.

K. H. SCHELKLE, 'Die Schöpfung in Christus', *Die Zeit Jesu* (Festschrift für H. Schlier), Freiburg-im-Br., 1970, pp. 208–17.

18   THE RELIGIOUS SIGNIFICANCE OF MARY'S LIFE-LONG VIRGINITY

See the articles by K. RAHNER, J. GALOT and J. B. BAUER listed under Chapters 3–5. Add:

J. H. NICHOLAS, *La virginité de Marie* (Collectanea Friburgensia, n. 34), Fribourg (Switzerland), 1962.

PART III

MOTHER OF THE WORD INCARNATE
(*Mary in the Theology of Saint John*)

General works covering the whole field:

F.-M. BRAUN, 'La mère de Jésus dans l'œuvre de saint Jean', *Revue Thomiste* 50 (1950), pp. 429–79; 51 (1951), pp. 5–68 = *La mère des fidèles*, Tournai and Paris, 1953; 2nd ed., 1954.

A. KERRIGAN, 'Spiritualis Mariae . . . maternitas. Theologiae Ioanneae investigatio exegetica (Joan. 2:1–11; 19:24b–27; Apoc. 12)', *De Mariologia et Oecumenismo* (ed. C. BALIC), Rome, 1962.

J. GALOT, 'Mère de l'Eglise', *NRT* 86 (1964), pp. 1163–85.

I THE UNITY OF JOHANNINE THEOLOGY

E. MALATESTA, *St John's Gospel 1920–1965* (Analecta Biblica, n. 32), Rome, 1967, gives 'a cumulative and classified bibliography of books and periodical literature on the Fourth Gospel'. See pp. 1–16 and 50–1.

See also B. M. METZGER, *Index to Periodical Literature on Christ and the Gospels* (under various headings).

On the Fourth Gospel and the Epistles:

C. H. DODD, 'The First Epistle of John and the Fourth Gospel', *Bulletin of the John Rylands Library* 21 (1937), pp. 129–56.

W. F. HOWARD, 'The Common Authorship of the Johannine Gospel and Epistles', *JTS* 48 (1947), pp. 12–25.

W. G. WILSON, 'An Examination of the Linguistic Evidence Adduced against the Unity of Authorship of the First Epistle of John and the Fourth Gospel', *JTS* 49 (1948), pp. 147–56.

On the Fourth Gospel and the Apocalypse:

E.-B. ALLO, 'Aspects nouveaux du problème johannique. A propos d'un commentaire récent de l'Apocalypse' [Lohmeyer], *RB* 37 (1928), pp. 37–62 and 198–220.

G. BEASLEY-MURRAY, 'The Relation of the Fourth Gospel to the Apocalypse', *The Evangelical Quarterly* 18 (1946), pp. 173–86.

On the whole question:

F.-M. BRAUN, *Jean le Théologien et son Evangile dans l'Eglise ancienne* (*Etudes Bibliques*), Paris, 1959, pp. 3–62.

2-4 THE MOTHER OF JESUS IN THE FOURTH GOSPEL

M. DE GOEDT, 'Bases bibliques de la maternité spirituelle de Notre-Dame', *BSFEM* 16 (1959), pp. 35–53.

J. GALOT, 'Mère de l'Eglise', *NRT* 86 (1964), pp. 1163–85.

On Cana:

For earlier literature see

E. MALATESTA, *St John's Gospel 1920–1965*, nn. 1321–1428.

B. M. METZGER, *Index to Periodical Literature on Christ and the Gospels*, nn. 6181–222.

A. FEUILLET, 'L'heure de Jésus et le signe de Cana', *ETL* 36 (1960), pp. 5–22.

S. HARTDEGEN, 'The Marian Significance of Cana', *Marian Studies* 11 (1960), pp. 85–103.

J. HANIMANN, 'L'heure de Jésus et les noces de Cana', *Revue Thomiste* 64 (1964), pp. 569–83.

A. FEUILLET, 'La signification fondamentale du premier miracle de Cana (Jn: 2:1–11) et le symbolisme johannique', *Revue Thomiste* 65 (1965), pp. 517–35.

A. SMITMANS, *Das Weinwunder von Kana. Die Auslegung von Joh. 2:1–11 bei den Vätern und heute*, Tübingen, 1966 (an excellent dissertation from Tübingen, 1964).

T. WORDEN, 'The Marriage Feast at Cana', *Scripture* 20 (1968), pp. 97–106.

On the scene at the foot of the cross:

For earlier literature see

E. MALATESTA, *St John's Gospel 1920–1965*, nn. 2089–118.

B. M. METZGER, *Index to Periodical Literature on Christ and the Gospels*, nn. 6713–23.

A. FEUILLET, 'Les adieux du Christ à sa mère (Jn 19:25–27) et la maternité spirituelle de Marie', *NRT* 86 (1964), pp. 469–89.

——, 'L'heure de la femme (Jn 16:21) et l'heure de la mère de Jésus', *Biblica* 47 (1966), pp. 169–84; 361–70 and 557–73.

H. SCHÜRMANN, 'Jesu letzte Weisung (Joh. 19:26–27a)', *Sapienter Ordinare* (Festschrift für E. Kleineidam), Leipzig, 1969, pp. 105–23.

I. DE LA POTTERIE, 'Das Wort Jesu "Siehe deine Mutter" und die Annahme der Mutter durch den Junger (Jn 19:27b)', *Neues Testament und Kirche* (Festschrift für R. Schnackenburg), Freiburg-im-Br., Basel and Vienna, 1974, pp. 191–219.

5–6   THE WOMAN CLOTHED WITH THE SUN

The four basic books (each with a good bibliography) are:

B. LE FROIS, *The Woman Clothed with the Sun (Apoc. 12): Individual or Collective?*, Rome, 1954.

A. TH. KASSING, *Die Kirche und Maria: Ihr Verhältnis im 12. Kapitel der Apokalypse*, Düsseldorf, 1958.

P. PRIGENT, *Apocalypse 12: Histoire de l'exégèse*, Tübingen, 1959.

H. GOLLINGER, *Das 'grosse Zeichen' von Apokalypse 12* (Stuttgarter Biblische Monographien, n. 11), Wurzburg and Stuttgart, 1971.

The following articles are important:

J. SCHNEIDER, in the *TWNT* 1, pp. 559–61 (on *basanos*).

K. H. RENGSTORF, in the *TWNT* 2, pp. 321–8 (on the number 12), and on pp. 623–31 (on the number 7).

L. CERFAUX, 'La vision de la femme et du dragon de l'Apocalypse en relation avec le protévangile', *ETL* 31 (1955), pp. 21–33.

A. DUPONT-SOMMER, 'La Mère du Messie et la Mère de l'Aspic dans un hymne de Qoumran', *Revue de l'Histoire des Religions* 147 (1955), pp. 174–88.

F.-M. BRAUN, 'La Femme vêtue de soleil (Apoc. 12). Etat du problème', *Revue Thomiste* 55 (1955), pp. 639–69.

A. DUBARLE, 'La Femme couronnée d'Etoiles, Apoc. 12', *Mélanges Bibliques redigés en l'honneur de André Robert*, Paris, 1957, pp. 512–18.

A. FEUILLET, 'Le Messie et sa Mère d'après le chapître 12 de l'Apocalypse', *RB* 66 (1959), pp. 55–86.

——, 'Le Cantique des Cantiques et l'Apocalypse', *RSR* 49 (1961), pp. 321–53.

TH. LESCOW, 'Das Geburtsmotiv in den messianischen Weissagungen bei Jesaja und Micha', *Zeitschrift für altestamentliche Wissenschaft* 79 (1967), pp. 172–207.

F. MONTAGNINI, 'Le "signe" de l'Apocalypse 12 à la lumière de la christologie du Nouveau Testament', *NRT* 99 (1967), pp. 401–16.

J. ERNST, 'Die "himmlische Frau" im 12. Kapitel der Apokalypse', *Theologie und Glaube* 58 (1968), pp. 39–59.

A. VÖGTLE, 'Mythos und Botschaft in Apokalypse 12', in *Tradition und Glaube* (Festschrift für K. G. Kuhn), Göttingen, 1972, pp. 395–415.

INDEXES

INDEX OF BIBLICAL REFERENCES

This Index is restricted to texts about which some comment is made. Texts cited without comment are not listed here.

INDEX OF AUTHORS

Most of these references are to be found in the footnotes. To save space and to avoid useless repetitions, the numbers of footnotes are not given in this Index of Authors—only the page numbers.

GENERAL INDEX

woman clothed with the sun, 404–32, 470–1

Zechariah (I), Old Testament prophet, 34, 40–5, 444

Zechariah (II), father of the Baptist, saint of

Old Covenant, 10, 35, 48; and birth of Baptist, 6, 26–7, 133–41 *passim*; also 281, 301

Zephaniah, 32–3, 40–2, 45, 443

Zeus, 288, 302

Zion, 29–30; *see also* Daughter of Zion